RAG, TAG AND BOBTAIL

Books by Lynn Montross

☆

RAG, TAG AND BOBTAIL

THE RELUCTANT REBELS

WAR THROUGH THE AGES

EAST OF EDEN

HALF GODS

THE TALK OF THE TOWN[*]

FRATERNITY ROW[*]

TOWN AND GOWN[*]

*With Lois Montross

Rag, Tag and Bobtail

The Story of
The Continental Army

1775-1783

BY

LYNN MONTROSS

Maps and End Papers
By ALICE WESCHE

HARPER & BROTHERS PUBLISHERS

NEW YORK

Library of Congress catalog card number: 51-11939

TO

MY COLLEAGUES OF

THE HISTORICAL DIVISION

U. S. MARINE CORPS

Contents

Part One: 1775-1776—Rebellion   1

  1. 2,000 Guests for Breakfast   3
  2. The Pick and the Spade   18
  3. An Army of Generals   37
  4. War in the Fourteenth Colony   52
  5. The Liberation of Boston   71
  6. Sir Peter Parker's Breeches   88

Part Two: 1776-1778—Civil War   105

  7. The Fight for New York   107
  8. Devil Take the Hindmost   123
  9. Lock, Stock and Barrel   141
 10. The Crossing of the Delaware   158
 11. A Game of Blindman's Buff   176
 12. The Fall of Philadelphia   192
 13. The Surrender at Saratoga   209
 14. Manna in the Wilderness   228

Part Three: 1778-1779—World War   249

 15. Pull Devil, Pull Baker   251
 16. False Dawn of Victory   268
 17. The Crown of Nettles   283
 18. March to the Mississippi   301
 19. Bayonets at Stony Point   316
 20. Who Look for Succor   330

Part Four: 1779-1783—Victory   345

 21. The Siege of Charleston   347
 22. Disaster in the South   363
 23. Treason and Mutiny   382

CONTENTS

24. Figs from Thistles   398
25. Cornwallis Is Taken   417
26. Nor Good Red Herring   435
27. As the Sparks Fly Upward   451

Appendix
Generals of the Continental Army   469

Sources and Acknowledgments   475

Chapter References   493

Index   507

Maps and Panoramas

The Shot Heard Round the World 9

France Loses a Continent 23

Battle of Bunker Hill 31

Invasion of Canada 53

Siege of Boston 82

Defeat on Long Island 119

Retreat Through Manhattan Island 129

Evacuation of New York 148

Stations of Disaster 156

Surprise at Trenton 161

Lost Ground Reclaimed 169

Formula for Conquest 201

Bennington Engagement 207

First Battle of Saratoga 216

Second Battle of Saratoga 222

Battle of Germantown 230

Fort Mifflin—To the Last Ditch 235

Camp at Valley Forge 244

Monmouth—Alarm and Excursion 284

Newport—Victory of the Storm 292

Vincennes—By Force of Arms 303

Stony Point—Bayonets at Midnight   322

Savannah—Storm of Steel   339

Charleston—City in Bondage   355

The War in the South   376

Cowpens—An Army Destroyed   405

Guilford—Pledge of British Defeat   413

Yorktown—The Captive Army   431

Eutaw Springs—The Tarnished Victory   442

These illustrations will be found following page 214

Boston Panorama

Quebec Panorama

New York Panorama

Trenton Panorama

Philadelphia Panorama

Newport Panorama

Savannah Panorama

Charleston Panorama

PART ONE

Rebellion

To share a common lot, and participate [in] the inconveniences wch. the army . . . are oblig'd to undergo, has been with me a fundamental principle.
—GENERAL WASHINGTON

Chapter 1

2,000 Guests for Breakfast

THE 19th of April had come and gone. The exciting, the tingling and wonder-filled day had passed into history. It was now the 20th of April, 1775, and a bald, fat Massachusetts militia general had a problem on his hands.

Fighting, as every soldier knows, is hungry work. There is nothing like a battle to put an edge on the appetite, and hundreds of Yankee militiamen had been tramping distances of from thirty to forty miles the day before, pausing only to aim another shot at a dejected column of red-coated men stumbling back to safety. It is a safe conjecture that each of these militiamen carried in his pocket a few thick slabs of country bread and bacon, thrust upon him at the back door by some anxious-eyed woman twisting her apron. But all such snacks had long since been devoured, and in a few words General William Heath summed up a problem which did not admit of any delay:

"How to *feed* the assembled and assembling militia, was now the great object."

There was nothing at all heroic about General William Heath. Nobody, least of all his Massachusetts neighbors, would ever have dreamed of comparing him to the Duke of Marlborough, Frederick the Great, or mad Charles of Sweden. In his *Memoirs*, which remain one of the most dependable Revolutionary sources, Heath left this candid portrait of himself: "He is of middling stature, light complexion, very corpulent and bald-headed. . . . From his childhood he was remarkably fond of military exercises, which passion grew up with him, and as he arrived at years of maturity, led him to procure, and attentively to study, every military treatise in the English language, which was obtainable."[1]

Only a month past his thirty-eighth birthday, he met his responsibilities with a calm competence which made him seem older. Other warriors in their memoirs have had to choose between two undesirable alternatives when it came to mentioning the hero of the narrative. A reiterated first-person pronoun is hardly calculated to give the proper air of soldierly reticence. Yet there is something cold and remote about the third person, even though the conqueror of Gaul set such a distinguished example. Every author of military reminiscences up to this time had been impaled on one horn or another of the dilemma, but Heath found the solution by simply referring to himself as "our General."

The morning after the 19th of April, 1775, George Washington was still a member of the Continental Congress. All the other great American soldiers of the next eight years were still civilians when Heath announced some of the first decisions of the war. "On the morning of the 20th," he recorded, "our General ordered Capt. John Battle, of Dedham, with his company of militia, to pass over the ground which had been the scene of action the preceding day, and to bury such of the slain as he should find unburied." There was still the question of what to do about the weary survivors of the British column who had been driven across the narrow neck into the security of the peninsula behind Charlestown. But the Roxbury farmer saw nothing strange in the assumption that his military amateurs could cope with equal numbers of the king's trained soldiers. "The grounds around Cambridge were immediately reconnoitred," he added, "and alarmposts assigned to the several corps; and in case the British should come out in superior force, and drive the militia from the town, they were ordered to rally and form on the high grounds around Watertown."

After settling these preliminaries, he applied himself to the problem of providing nourishment for the multitude. It is anybody's guess as to how many militiamen flocked to Cambridge that morning, but two thousand would be a likely estimate. Many participants in the glorious confusion of the 19th had trudged home at dusk to do the chores; but the following two diary entries, written by a sixteen-year-old Andover schoolboy, tell the story of hundreds of others who arrived too late for the fighting:

April 19, Wednesday. This morning at seven o'clock we had alarm that the Regulars were gone to Concord. We gathered at the meeting house. We heard that the Regulars had killed 8 men before we started from the meeting house. We started for Concord and were within 6 miles of that place when we heard that the Regulars had gone back.

We followed that night to Notami [Menotomy, later Arlington] and there encamped.

April 20. Early this morning we marched on to the common in Cambridge and expected the enemy upon us every moment. They did not come. Folks came in very fast. Nothing happened today.[2]

The day may have been uneventful for Private Phineas Ingalls of the Andover militia company. But General William Heath must have had some anxious thoughts until he remembered that Harvard College, which set a plentiful table for students seated according to social status, had acquired during the past century a good many pots, kettles, mugs and pewter spoons. "All the eatables in the town of Cambridge, which could be spared, were collected for breakfast," recorded Heath, "and the college kitchen and utensils procured for cooking. Some carcases of beef and pork, prepared for the Boston market on the 18th, at Little Cambridge, were sent for, and obtained; and a large quantity of ship-bread at Roxbury, said to belong to the British navy, was taken for the militia. These were the first provisions that were obtained."

After a breakfast rich in proteins and calories, the situation was so well in hand that "at 11 o'clock, A.M., our General appointed Mr. Joseph Ward, a gentleman of abilities, his Aide-de-camp and secretary. . . . This was the first appointment of the kind in the American army. Before noon, a letter was received from the Committee of Supplies at Concord, expressing their joy at the event of the preceding day, with assurances that every exertion in their power should be put in exercise, to forward supplies to the militia in arms. In the afternoon, Gen. Artemas Ward arrived at Cambridge, who, being senior in the order of appointment, took the command accordingly."[3]

This was the single day of the war when Heath alone bore the destinies of America on his broad back. But exactly eight years later, when Congress proclaimed a cessation of hostilities, it was he who commanded at West Point, the strategic bastion of the Republic, on April 19, 1783. And just as he had been first to post a guard against the redcoats, "our General" became the last officer of the veteran Continental Army to inspect and dismiss a guard.

Almost as insistent as the shot heard round the world was the scratching of the quill pens racing across the pages of personal records. Beginning on the day of Lexington, it continued without a pause for eight years, so that the American Revolution ranks as one of history's most literate wars. Old muster rolls indicate that few American soldiers were unable to sign their names; and though the day of popular education had not yet dawned, astonishing numbers were articulate enough to leave journals, diaries, memoirs or letter books. Sometimes these chronicles consist of little except the usual entries about the food, the weather and the marches. Then in a flash some artless comment by a simple soldier may light up a corner of history that the official documents have left in darkness.

The eighteenth century, as the "age of man," was the great era of diaries and letters. Even so, it is a matter for everlasting wonder that so many active participants—Britons and Hessians as well as Americans fighting on both sides—managed to keep a record, month after month, year after year. The sheer mechanics are dismaying to the present-day beneficiary. Pencils were so much a novelty in 1776 that Thomas Jefferson noted the purchase of one for a shilling and sixpence at a time when that sum would have bought a fat goose. Quill pens and an ink which faded to rusty brown served as the implements of diarists who wrote by the light of a dim candle or smoky fire, their lips probably moving in fierce concentration as they shut their ears to the noises of camp. Private Ingalls kept a journal from the day of Lexington until the end of the year, when his militia term expired. Then he went back to Andover and attended school for fifteen and a half days that winter. In July he volunteered again and began a second journal of his service at Ticonderoga. The following year Ingalls re-enlisted in the Continental Army for the duration of a war which had become such an old story that he no longer troubled to chronicle its daily events.

Some wonderful effects in syntax and capitalization were left for posterity by diarists who wrote as they talked. In a day of casual spelling, before Noah Webster introduced his reforms, these writings have provided a historical commentator with the material for a study of dialects of 1775.[4] For the Yankee chroniclers, officers as well as privates, were consistent in clinging to usages which often have a familiar ring to anyone accustomed to present-day New England speech:

Arams for arms; *cateridges* for cartridges; *bums* for bombs; *ridgment* for regiment; *warter* for water; *git* for get; *sartin* for certain; *jine* for join; *jest* for just; *afte* for after; *yestoday* for yesterday; *Salletoga* for Saratoga; *Hushing* for Hessians; *Dullerway* for Delaware; and (greatest triumph of all) *Markis Delefit* for Marquis de Lafayette.

Despite the hardships of composition, most of the journals were neatly inscribed by men who had to carry the materials on their backs during the day's march. Private Samuel Haws even had a habit of scolding himself in the margin for making a blot:

"O you nasty Sloven how your Book Looks."[5]

The patriotism of the early years, before the war became a weary grapple of endurance, burns brightly in these pages. Private Aaron Wright, an enthusiastic young Pennsylvania rifleman of 1775, reveals in nearly every line the effects of what would be known today as indoctrination: "The Red Coated Philistines fired 31 cannon and 3 bums at the Sons of Liberty, who were building a parapet to secure themselves against the diabolical rage of the Parliamentary tools on Bunker Hill."[6]

Opinions as fiercely biased in the opposite direction may be found, of course, in the writings of Britons or American loyalists. Captain Alexander McDonald, who helped to organize the Royal Highland Emigrants regiment after being driven from his Staten Island home, confided to a friend in Scotland that the rebels meant "to Give laws not only to Britain but to all Europe however I hope they will be disappointed & that all true Brittains will spend their lives & fortunes Sooner than to Suffer the Offspring of those Transports & Gaolbirds to get the better of them but I shall say no more about Politicks. Send me a hhd. of your very best Claret by the Surest & Speediest Opportunity."[7]

Nearly all the German mercenaries below the rank of officer were silent. Among the British enlisted men, Sergeant Roger Lamb of the Royal Welch Fusiliers was one of the few to tell his story. American privates and commoners, on the contrary, seemed to have been given an urge toward self-expression as well as self-government in 1775. The result is a collection of diaries by soldiers and noncommissioned officers that would make several books the size of this volume.

Few of these personal accounts, preserved in state archives, state historical magazines, or the collections and proceedings of state historical societies, have met the eye of the general reader. Women and noncombatants, for their part, were not content to remain ingloriously mute. Sally Wister, the young Quaker girl whose Pennsylvania home became a brigade headquarters, kept a diary intended to be a gay record of flirtations with American officers during the winter of Valley Forge. But for anyone who cares to read between those lively lines, there are some fresh and original appraisals of the Marylanders who fought for independence, beginning with the day of their arrival:

How new is our situation! I feel in good spirits, though surrounded by an army, the house full of soldiers, the yard alive with soldiers, —very peaceable sort of people, tho'. They eat like other folks, talk like them, and behave themselves with elegance; so I will not be afraid of them, that I won't. Adieu! I am going to my chamber to dream, I suppose, of bayonets and swords, sashes, guns and epaulets.[8]

If anyone in the Continental Army could have been called the bravest of the brave, it was Captain Robert Kirkwood of the Delaware regiment. Educated for the Presbyterian ministry, he left the academy in 1776 at the age of twenty and distinguished himself in thirty-two actions during the next six years. Yet the evening after a battle ending in the destruction of a small British army, he summed up the day's work in a diary entry of two words:

"Defeated Tarleton."[9]

At times the journals and diaries are filled with the very meat of history, and Lexington is one of those occasions. Both the official British and American documents were carefully constructed by experts with an eye to educational values. If the facts did not always adapt themselves to such an end, the authorities of both sides were but following the accepted practice of all nations in all ages in remolding them to the desired shape.

There were as a result no less than three images—the official versions, and a more trustworthy account which may be pieced together from private sources. The redcoats took great pains to gain the advantages of surprise, it is related by Captain Charles Stedman, a British officer who wrote one of the most unbiased contemporary histories of the war. Captain Frederick Mackenzie, adjutant of the Royal Welch Fusiliers, noted in his diary that practice marches had been undertaken all winter as feints, "to enable the General Gage to send Regiments or Detachments to particular parts of the Country without occasioning so much alarm as would otherwise take place."[10]

For months the patriots had been smuggling arms out of Boston so boldly that they lodged a protest at General Thomas Gage's headquarters when 13,425 ball cartridges were seized. The Americans actually demanded that the ammunition be returned to them.

The war came within a spoken word of beginning late in February when Gage sent a detachment to Salem to seize several brass cannon. The rebels dragged the guns into concealment and made a stand at the bridge before the redcoats arrived. The British colonel, according to American accounts, shouted "Fire!" But the word went unheard or misunderstood in the excitement. At that instant one of the townsmen contributed to history by persuading the officer not to repeat the command.

Worcester and Concord, as Gage knew, were the two chief depots for Massachusetts munitions of war. There was also a good prospect of capturing the two ringleaders of sedition, Samuel Adams and John Hancock, on their way to Philadelphia for the second Continental Congress. Up to this time the British general had been careful not to add any more martyrs to those created in 1770 by the so-called Boston Massacre, and

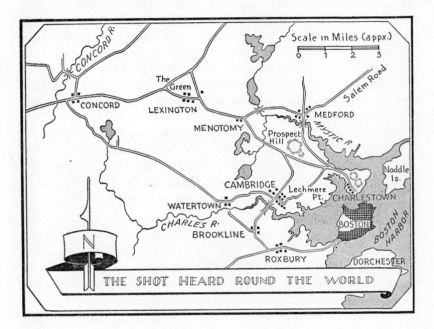

THE SHOT HEARD ROUND THE WORLD

both men had taken part in the fifth commemoration on March 5th in the Old South Church. During the next few weeks, however, Gage received dispatches from London which encouraged him to adopt a firmer tone. And it is possible that if Adams and Hancock had been captured, their heads might eventually have adorned London Bridge or Temple Bar.

As many as five regiments had marched toward Concord in feints, but the patriots were not deceived when Gage set the real expedition in motion early in the evening of April 18th. Neither the lantern in the North Church steeple nor Paul Revere's most famous ride were necessary to alarm the countryside before midnight. That result was accomplished by British officers sent out shortly after dusk with orders to seize messengers on the roads. By the time that Colonel Francis Smith's 800 troops began the march, some of the militiamen were already on their way to the village green where they had a date with destiny. It was a chilly Tuesday night, for there had been snow on the ground as late as the 10th. At two o'clock about 130 rebels lined up with muskets in front of the Congregational church in Lexington. After a long wait in the darkness, with the men grumbling and yawning and stamping their feet, the company was dismissed. Some of them trudged home to bed, others drifted toward the cheery warmth of the tavern for a glass of rum.

The British expedition had already failed in its main objects before the troops were halfway to Lexington. Adams and Hancock were warned with time to spare, and the Committee of Safety had hours in which to remove most of the threatened munitions from Concord and distribute them among nine other towns.

At five o'clock, when the militia company assembled again on the Lexington green, Captain John Parker had only about 70 men left, the others having presumably gone to bed. This time the minutemen were not called out for a false alarm. Shortly after sunrise the advance guard of the redcoats appeared under the command of Major John Pitcairn of the marines. There must have been an awkward as well as tense moment of uncertainty, followed by a bedlam of noise and confusion. Then someone fired a shot which severed the frayed political bonds holding the American colonies in the British Empire.

Major Pitcairn's story, as reported by Gage to London, had it that a band of armed rebels threatened his troops two miles out of Lexington. One of them aimed a shot, it was said, but his musket flashed in the pan. The British then advanced to the village green with strict orders not to fire but only to surround and disarm their opponents. The first four or five shots, wounding a British private and the major's horse, came from behind a stone wall on the right as the Americans dispersed. Not until then, according to Pitcairn, did the redcoats retaliate with a scattered and unauthorized fire which killed and wounded seventeen before it could be silenced by the officers.

Improbable as this account seems, the American version is no more credible. The following description of the critical moment was published in gazettes throughout the colonies:

Just before sunrise the king's troops came in sight, and the militia began to disperse. The troops then set out on the road, hallooing and huzzaing, and coming within a few rods of them, the commanding officer cried out in words to this effect, "Disperse, you damned rebels! damn you, disperse!" upon which the troops again huzzaed, and at the same time one or two of the officers discharged their pistols, which were instantaneously followed by the firing of four or five of the soldiers, and then there seemed to be a general discharge from the whole. It is to be noticed, they fired upon the militia as they were dispersing agreeably to their command, and that they did not even return the fire. Eight of our men were killed, and nine wounded. The troops then laughed, and damned the Yankees, and said they could not bear the smell of gunpowder."[11]

Rebel propagandists were fond of placing oaths in the mouths of British officers, for the good Congregationalists of New England frowned on "prophane swearing." The affidavits of Captain Parker and other American witnesses were unanimous—rather too unanimous—in blaming everything on the enemy. Lieutenant Edward Gould, a British officer wounded and captured later that day, gave a sworn statement which has more of the ring of truth: "Which party fired first, I cannot exactly say, as our Troops rushed on shouting and huzzaing previous to the firing, which was continued as long as any of the Provincials were to be seen."[12]

If the affair had ended on the village green, Lexington would scarcely have surpassed the Boston Massacre as an "incident." The countryside had not yet been aroused to the point of general resistance, and Smith could probably have got back to Boston safely if he had started at sunrise. But he continued six miles farther on his futile mission, tarrying several hours at Concord for an insignificant plunder. This gave the patriots enough time and resolution to assemble 300 militiamen and attack the hundred redcoats guarding the north bridge. Smith had to come to the rescue with his main force, and at noon the action entered its second phase with the militia companies swarming to the attack.

Intelligence of an uprising reached Gage at an early hour. He saved Smith from almost certain destruction by his promptness in sending sixteen companies of foot and enough marines to bring the total up to nearly a thousand. These reinforcements marched out through Roxbury in high spirits at eight o'clock, the fifes squealing "Yankee Doodle" in derision of provincials who would soon be playing that lively tune to taunt the redcoats. The progress of Lord Percy's detachment could hardly be called a forced march, since it was two in the afternoon before he reached Lexington.

Colonel Smith had meanwhile found himself in serious trouble all the way from the Concord bridge back to Lexington. Among the other unknown factors, it is a conjecture as to how many Americans fought that day. Estimates vary all the way from a few thousand up to such preposterous figures as 20,000. An American historian, after offering convincing evidence that only about 4,000 militiamen lived near enough to reach the scene of action, concluded that no more than 250 were engaged at any time.[13]

This assumption is supported by the account of Captain Mackenzie, who observed "a considerable number of the Rebels, but they were much scattered, not above 50 of them to be seen in a body in any place. Many lay concealed behind Stone walls and fences."[14] For there was no central command on the American side, and the companies came and went according to the orders of their captains.

It has long been a tradition for American historians to praise the deadly aim of their forefathers, but a candid analysis is not much to the credit of rebel marksmanship. If it may be supposed that 2,000 militiamen took part throughout the day, firing an average of three shots apiece, total British casualties of 273 out of a compact column of 1,800 men would indicate that about one bullet out of twenty found its target. The fact is that Massachusetts farmers and villagers of 1775 were no better shots than their descendants today. Many of them were doubtless firing from ranges too long for effect, and hasty loading by an excited amateur could render a flintlock quite harmless except for its formidable noise and recoil.

At any rate, enough shots hit the mark so that Colonel Smith's men were hard-pressed. "An incessant though irregular fire commenced," according to Stedman, "which was kept up during the whole of their march back to Lexington, in which they were driven before the Americans like sheep. At that place they were met by the detachment under Lord Percy, with two pieces of cannon. The two detachments rested on their arms, and received some refreshments. Lord Percy now formed his detachment into a square, in which he enclosed Colonel Smith's party, who were so much exhausted by fatigue, that they were obliged to lie down for rest on the ground, their tongues hanging out of their mouths, like those of dogs after a chase."[15]

Before starting the march back to Charlestown, Percy threw out flankers and brought his two brass six-pounders into action. It took cannon balls to drive the rebels away from the Lexington meeting house, where the bright springtime grass was trampled and bloodstained from the encounter at sunrise. Even so, Mackenzie's diary reveals that civilians not accustomed to artillery fire put up a good fight for nearly an hour. "During this time the Rebels endeavoured to gain our flanks, and crept into the covered ground on either side, and as close as they could in front, firing now and then in perfect security."[16]

General Heath conferred all morning with the Committee of Safety at Watertown. From that village he sent a rebel detachment to Cambridge to cut off the British retreat by taking up the planks from the bridge and barricading the approach. "Our General joined the militia just after Lord Percy had joined the British; and having assisted in forming a regiment which had been broken by the shot from the British field-pieces, (for the discharge of these, together with the flames and smoke from several buildings . . . opened up a new and more terrific scene;) and the British having again taken up their retreat, were closely pursued."[17]

Percy prided himself all the rest of his life on saving his column from annihilation. Although he detested Americans in general as "a set of sly, artful, hypocritical rascalls," he paid a soldier's tribute in a letter of April 20th to the courage of farmers and villagers fighting against regulars:

> Whoever looks upon them as an irregular mob, will find himself very much mistaken. . . . Nor are several of their men void of a spirit of enthusiasm as we experienced yesterday, for many of them concealed themselves in houses & advanced within 10 yds. to fire at me & other officers, tho' they were morally certain of being put to death themselves in an instant.[18]

He added a gloomy prediction that the insurrection would not "turn out so despicable as it is perhaps imagined at home. For my part, I never believed, I confess, that they wd. have attacked the King's troops, or have had the perseverence I found in them yesterday."

The British tactics were as good as could have been expected. Percy sent out light troops in advance on either side to clear the way. They drove many of the farm lads back to a respectful distance, which accounts for some of the shots that missed. But there were bolder spirits who compelled the redcoats to halt and fire platoon volleys as well as cannon balls. Dr. Joseph Warren, the idealist of the American cause, stood beside Heath when an enemy bullet came so close as "to strike a pin out of the hair of his earlock."

Other rebels showed a reckless valor, it was reported by the Rev. William Gordon, a Congregational minister who interviewed participants shortly afterwards for his history of the Revolution. "A few Americans, headed by the Rev. Mr. Payson, of Chelsea, who till now had been extremely moderate, attacked a party of twelve soldiers, carrying stores to the retreating troops, killed one, wounded several, made the whole prisoners, and gained possession of their arms and stores. . . . Captain John Ford and Oliver Barron, and Deacon Davis, all of Chelmsford, distinguished themselves in the course of the day. It can be fully proved that Captain Ford killed five regulars."[19]

Percy undoubtedly saved his force from a much worse disaster when he decided to take the route to the heights of Charlestown Neck instead of marching back to Cambridge, where a militia force awaited. There was neither rest nor sanctuary for the redcoats until they crossed the peninsula at dusk, when the flash of the flintlocks could be seen. Mackenzie noted that a Negro, the only one observed that day, was wounded among the last attackers. Other sources disclose that a few civilized Indians also fought with the militia, so that all three races of the New World were represented.

The battle of words began as soon as the last shot was fired. During the next few days the rebel leaders armed themselves with twenty depositions from participants, including two of the British prisoners. Eighteen militiamen agreed under solemn oath that the enemy fired first. The sworn testimony of other American witnesses accused the king's soldiers of a variety of atrocities. The flavor of these indictments may be sampled from the announcement by the Salem Committee of Safety:

> Last Wednesday, the 19th of April, the Troops of His Britannick Majesty commenced hostilities upon the people of this Province, attended with circumstances of cruelty, not less brutal than what our venerable ancestors received from the vilest Savages of the wilderness. . . . It appeared to be their design to burn and destroy all before them; and nothing but our vigorous pursuit prevented their infernal purposes from being put in execution. But the savage barbarity exercised upon the bodies of our unfortunate brethren who fell, is almost incredible: not contented with shooting down the unarmed and infirm, they disregarded the cries of the wounded, killing them without mercy, and mangling their bodies in the most shocking manner.[20]

Gage indignantly denied charges of inhumanity. As a verbal counter-attack, the British declared that the rebels had been guilty of scalping wounded foemen. Lord Percy added an original touch by asserting that the militiamen "cut the ears off some of the wounded men who fell into their hands."

Americans of 1775 could hardly have dreamed that the scalping legend would become a hardy British perennial to be repeated seriously as late as 1902 by the Hon. J. W. Fortesque, historian of the British army. There might have been grounds for suspecting one of the "white Indians" of the frontier, but Massachusetts farmers did not collect enemy forelocks as trophies. Gordon made an investigation soon afterwards which traced the story to the act of a village youth, who dispatched a wounded and helpless British soldier with a hatchet.[21]

The patriots had a better case when they accused the enemy of refusing mercy. Usually, since the human body has only a few vulnerable spots, casualties are to be found in a proportion of at least three or four wounded to every man slain. Thus the 273 British losses included 65 killed, 180 wounded and 28 prisoners. But the 50 killed, 34 wounded and 4 missing out of a total of 88 militia casualties is a ratio to be regarded with suspicion.

Captain Mackenzie and other British writers admitted that little quarter was given to rebels trapped in houses, some of which were pillaged and burned. From the viewpoint of an eighteenth-century regular, trained for an impersonal volley fire, an opponent taking deliberate aim had little claim to mercy. Besides, rebels were held to be traitors who did not deserve the usual humanities of warfare.

Each side realized the importance of being first to tell its side of the story to the public in Great Britain. Time and distance were the curse of propagandists in 1775, when a sailing ship took as long as three months to cross the Atlantic in stormy weather. The rebels let the enemy get a start on them while they were compiling sworn statements. General Gage paused only long enough to draw up a concise and rather dry official report, which he sent to England on a fast sloop. Four days later the Massachusetts authorities sped their message on a ship chartered for the purpose. They enjoined Captain John Darby of Salem to crowd on sail for the race across the ocean, and he not only overtook his rival but made port eleven days sooner. Benjamin Franklin, the representative of Massachusetts in London, was requested to have the American report "immediately printed and dispersed through every town in England."

No better publicist could have been found in the world of that day, and the gazettes devoted columns to the Massachusetts account of "ministerial vengeance against this Colony, for refusing, with her sister Colonies, a submission to Slavery."[22]

Dr. Warren and his associates did not make the mistake of drawing too long a bow. Their version of Lexington for export to England was comparatively moderate in tone, yet the sworn testimony made convincing reading. "On the 29th of May, 1775," according to a British historian, "the leading London newspapers, which then appeared only three time a week, published the story in a special issue; and it was reproduced by the provincial journals as fast as the mail bags could be carried throughout the island."[23]

No mightier journalistic scoop has ever been recorded. Gage's dull official report, when it finally appeared two weeks later, came as an anticlimax. He had lost the battle of words even more decisively than the battle of bullets.

Both factions thought it quite as important to shape opinion in America. And if Captain Darby had come near to equaling the best records for an Atlantic crossing, the express riders who carried the message of Massachusetts to her sister colonies set a pace which must have seemed almost incredible in that day.

The receipts of the village committeemen are dated at all hours of the day and night. Not much imagination is needed to picture these middle-aged patriots being aroused in their nightcaps to sign by the light of a candle or lantern. Then without a wasted moment a new rider on a fresh horse galloped out through the sleeping streets until the hoofbeats were lost in the night. The following is an abridged record of the progress of the news from its arrival in New York to its departure from Philadelphia:

A true copy, received in New York, two o'clock, P.M., Tuesday, April 25, 1775. Isaac Low, Chairman, New York Committee.

Elizabethtown, seven o'clock in the evening, Tuesday, April 25, 1775.

A true copy received at Woodbridge, ten of the clock in the evening, Tuesday, April 25, 1775.

The above received at New-Brunswick, the 25th April, 1775, twelve o'clock at night.

A true copy received at Princetown, April 26, 1775, half past three in the morning.

The above received at Trenton on Wednesday morning, about half after six o'clock and forwarded at seven o'clock.

Philadelphia, twelve o'clock, Wednesday, received, and forwarded at the same time. April 26, 1775.[24]

Fast as such a pace seemed in that day, speed was not reckoned as essential as reaching all centers of a sparse population, so that the news could be spread to smaller communities. Hence the express riders did not always take the shortest route to arrive at Baltimore on Thursday morning, April 27th. After crossing the Potomac next day, the roads through the southern colonies were so poor and the settlements so far apart that it was considered good time to gallop into Savannah as early as May 10th.

The first report to Americans was followed by the lurid details of new depositions by witnesses. Benjamin and Rachel Cooper swore that the British on April 19th "entered the house where we and two aged gentlemen were, all unarmed. We escaped for our lives into the cellar; the two aged gentlemen were immediately most barbarously and inhumanly murdered by them, being stabbed through in many places, their heads mauled, sculls broke, and their brains beat out on the floor and walls of the house."[25]

Such charges, of course, were as highly colored as British tales of scalping. While the propaganda mill ground away briskly, the rebels did not lag in military respects. After the delay in providing breakfast on April 20th, the commissary problem seems to have been satisfactorily solved for a force which grew daily. General Artemas Ward, the senior militia officer, soon had enough troops to extend his lines from Cambridge to Roxbury. Theoretically he had the enemy blockaded in Boston, if allowances are made for the American lack of artillery and warships.

Intercepted letters show that some of the British were impressed.[26] A soldier recovering from a wound wrote on April 28th that "an incredible number of the people of the country are in arms against us." Another wounded man informed his "honoured mother" that the "rebels were monstrous numerous." And a woman camp follower wrote to her family in England on May 2nd: "My husband was wounded and taken prisoner, but they use him well, and I am striving to get to him, as he is very dangerous; but it is almost impossible to get out or in, or to get any thing, for we are forced to live on salt provisions entirely, and they are building Batteries around the Town, and so are we, for we are expecting more troops every day. . . . It is very troublesome times, and I believe we are sold; and I hear my husband's leg is broke, and my heart is broke."

Chapter 2

The Pick and the Spade

IF AN American fired the shot heard round the world, it was in violation of a standing injunction not to pull a trigger save in defense. This makes it the more remarkable that only three weeks later the colonies should have swung all the way to the aggressive. Never in the annals of war was an officer more completely surprised than the British commandant summoned from his dawn slumber on May 10th to surrender Ticonderoga to a backwoods strategist acting "in the name of the Great Jehovah and the Continental Congress." It did not matter that neither of these authorities had sanctioned the attempt. Captain Delaplace, aroused from a warm bed, needed only the persuasion of the muskets pointed at his head by Ethan Allen's band.

The strategic value of the fort was apparent at a glance. Nature had created a water highway from the St. Lawrence and its tributaries to the Hudson and Atlantic by way of Lake Champlain and Lake George. Only a few short portages offered obstacles to an invader from the north, yet there were but two places along the entire route offering any great advantage to the defenders. One was the sharp bend in the Hudson which would later become the site of West Point. The other had been named the "meeting of waters" by the Indians because Lake Champlain contracted to a funnel just opposite the portage to Lake George. Here the guns of Ticonderoga commanded the channel, and a Massachusetts patriot named John Brown appears to have been first to urge its capture while serving the colony as a secret agent in Montreal.

Several months earlier Captain Alexander McDonald had repeatedly advised that a regiment of American loyalists be raised to hold the thinly garrisoned lake forts. "Had it been in General Gage's power to agree to these Proposals," he wrote mournfully after the posts were lost, "I am certain we would have had 5 or 600 men before the Country took the alarm. . . . Ticonderoga and Crown Point would still have been ours. . . ."[1]

The revolting colonists, however, took the initiative. Ticonderoga led the list of those audacious seizures which helped them to survive their inferiority in nearly all material respects. The fort remained in American hands, barring a brief interlude of enemy occupation, throughout the war. Quite as important, it supplied the ill-equipped rebels of 1775 with their only artillery worth mentioning until the colonies were able to import or manufacture cannon. An inventory reveals the following total of munitions captured from the enemy in these early months, largely from Ticonderoga and the other lake forts:

183 cannon; 19 mortars; 3 howitzers; 51 swivels; 52 tons of cannon balls; 40,000 musket cartridges.[2]

The two most stormy and controversial American soldiers of the war were introduced to history in this first rebel offensive operation. The result was a personal quarrel generating more sparks than the seizure of the fort.

Revolutions bring to the front not only heroes but also opportunists and glory hunters. Two men with these potentialities met at Ticonderoga when Ethan Allen and Benedict Arnold entered the fort side by side at the head of 83 volunteers. The musket snapped by a British sentry missed fire, so that not a shot was heard in an attack which needed only the moral weapon of surprise.

The Massachusetts Committee of Safety had commissioned Arnold a colonel on May 3rd and directed him to raise troops on the frontier of that colony for the expedition. Four members of the Connecticut legislature, having already proposed the attempt to Allen without any official authorization, signed personal receipts to obtain funds from the treasury.

Benedict Arnold, the fourth of his family to bear the name, had descended from Rhode Island forebears who could boast a colonial governor as early as 1663. During his restless thirty-four years he had been smuggler, West Indies trader and New Haven merchant after running away from home in adolescence and deserting from the army during the last war. Any further attempt to describe him must take into wary account the prejudices of his biographers. One of them has pictured a monster who found delight during his boyhood in robbing birds' nests and mangling the fledglings. Others have gone to equally absurd lengths by awarding him a martyr's crown as the bravest and best American soldier of the war, forced into treason because he was neglected and misunderstood. Between these extremes it is possible to glimpse a man of action whose abilities were corroded by an almost insane self-love and avarice.

In 1775 this short and swarthy adventurer with the wayward past soon created a reputation for truculence if he did not already possess one. His cold gray eyes conveyed a threat of violence which intimidated some men, but Ethan Allen was not one of them. Arnold caught a Tartar when he tried to snatch the leadership from the forthright Vermont border captain, who asserted himself with more emphasis than tact, though he relented enough to allow his rival to enter the fort beside him. The next day, Arnold slandered the victor in a letter to the Massachusetts Committee of Safety:

> Colonel Allen, finding that he had the ascendancy over his people, positively insisted that I should have no command, as I had forbid the soldiers plundering and destroying private property. This power is now taken out of my hands, and I am not consulted, nor have I a voice in affairs. . . . Colonel Allen is a proper man to head his own wild people, but entirely unacquainted with military service. But as I have, in consequence of my orders from you, gentlemen, been the first person who entered and took possession of the Fort, I shall keep it, at every hazard, until I have further advice and orders from you and the general assembly of Connecticut.[3]

This letter was the forerunner of others in which Arnold took credit for the accomplishments of colleagues or subordinates. Nevertheless, a second letter to the Committee, dated three days later, indicates that he played a plaintive second fiddle at Ticonderoga: "Mr. Allen's party is decreasing, and the dispute between us subsiding. I am extremely sorry matters have not been transacted with more prudence and judgment. I have done everything in my power and put up with many insults to preserve peace and serve the public."

Ethan Allen was a man of words as well as deeds who wrote several books after the war. But he did not mention the squabble in reports giving generous credit to his associates, including Arnold, for their part in capturing the garrison of two officers and forty-two men. Before the end of the month the two rebel leaders penetrated as far as St. Johns in bateaux, destroying the remnants of British power on Lake Champlain by seizing a sloop and other armed vessels.

These exploits were in the tradition of New World colonists who had taken an active part in every British war of the past century. The mother country never found it necessary to put pressure on Americans. The colonists supplied men and money and ships on a voluntary basis— sometimes in larger measure than England herself in proportion to population and other resources.

It would have been enough of a contribution at the early date of 1690 if the thinly settled colonies had offered to raise troops and funds for home defense. But the spirit of Drake and Hawkins was abroad in the New World when Sir William Phips led an American armada against France's two strongest fortresses in Canada. Port Royal fell to the Maine shipwright who had been knighted for his exploits as a plunderer and treasure hunter. Described by Cotton Mather as being "of an inclination cutting rather like a hatchet than a razor," the hard-fisted Phips then pushed up the St. Lawrence against Quebec; but a smallpox epidemic decimated his forces before he could storm the town.

Americans of the next two generations showed a like gusto at smiting the Gaul or Iberian in such operations as the defense of Jamaica in 1703, the attempted expeditions against Canada in 1709 and 1711, the second capture of Port Royal in 1710, and the Cartagena expedition of 1740. Americans died in bloody combat on the quarterdeck, and Americans died of fever in the "graveyard of the British army," as the West Indies were known. It might also be adduced that while Americans were fighting side by side with Britons, they never quite lost their enthusiasm for smuggling at the expense of Britons. Often enough the colonists seemed to be fighting the foe with one hand and carrying on an illicit trade with the other.

In 1745 the colonists won the outstanding victory of a long war in which British forces were twice humbled in European battles by the prodigious Marshal Saxe of France. The expedition of 4,000 New England volunteers which sailed from Boston to Louisburg in a crazy flotilla of fishing boats "had something of the character of a broad farce," it is related in the fascinating account by the historian Francis Parkman.[4] Perhaps the most astonishing feature was the assurance with which an army of farmers and fishermen counted on capturing the necessary siege artillery from professional French soldiers defending the strongest man-made fortress of North America. Yet this is what happened soon after the landing, thanks to a startling combination of luck and audacity. Yankee novices had to ask the officers of British warships to instruct them in firing the 30 captured guns, dragged through a marsh by teams of several hundred men harnessed to each. But the ensuing bombardment, which went on day and night with the amateur gunners scrambling for turns, made such a wreck of the casemates that Louisburg was battered into capitulation.

The next war had much to do with shaping causes as well as results of the American Revolution fifteen years later. A provincial officer named George Washington drew first blood in a new struggle destined to be the decisive clash between France and Great Britain in the New World. Known in Europe as the Seven Years' War, it was called the French and Indian War by colonists making the supreme effort to gain the upper hand over the hereditary foe in North America.

Great Britain, starting with her historical procedure of muddling through, soon incurred more than the usual number of preliminary defeats. General Edward Braddock had an army destroyed in the Pennsylvania forest by inferior French and Indian forces. Admiral John Byng was executed as a scapegoat after retreating from a weaker French squadron in the Mediterranean and abandoning Minorca to a capitulation. In Germany the Duke of Cumberland surrendered Hanover and a British army to the French, though the ministers in London managed to squirm out of the Convention of Kloster Seven by trickery which did no credit to the national honor.

The situation became so maddening that Britain went to the extreme of replacing her traditional brave blunderers with a genius. Even so, William Pitt was hobbled during his first seven months as prime minister and not given a free hand until June, 1757. From that date it took him less than thirty months to transform a half-beaten nation into a victorious power smiting the enemy by land and sea on four continents.

It suited Pitt's purposes that Frederick the Great should claim the spotlight by fighting great battles with Austrian, French and Russian armies. The magnitude of the operations in Germany tended to conceal their futility, since at one period they occupied more than half a million troops in the contending forces. Yet Frederick and his generals won just half of their sixteen principal battles, and after seven years of bloody fighting not a single village changed hands in the treaty of peace.

This was the theater of war which Pitt made the fulcrum for his conquest of the continent of North America and the subcontinent of India. Pitt kept France occupied in Europe by subsidizing Frederick with sums which seemed fantastic in that age. The ministers of Louis XV rose to the bait, so that Montcalm in North America and Dupleix in India were abandoned as strategic orphans.

A born "king of men," scornful of dolts as well as difficulties, Pitt read the human heart with an insight never surpassed in British military annals. Only the vision of genius could have enabled him to select four soldiers for the winning of America who had never given anyone else a glimpse of their potentialities—an obscure colonel, Jeffrey Amherst; another unknown officer, Colonel James Wolfe; an invalid and former Scottish physician, John Forbes; a pleasure-loving young peer, George

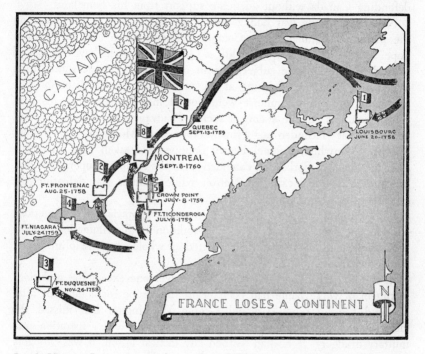

Lord Howe. In an age of patronage Pitt promoted these men over the heads of soldiers who had better claims by right of seniority or political preference.

The British campaign by land and sea might be compared to a great scythe mowing down everything that had grown out of the seeds planted by France in the New World. All distances were appalling from the viewpoint of a European. The shank of the strategic blade struck at Cape Breton while the point aimed at Fort Duquesne (soon to be renamed in honor of Pitt) nearly 1,500 miles away on the Pennsylvania frontier.

Bays, gulfs, marshes, rivers, mountains, forests—all these had to be overcome as well as French and Indians, and Pitt's operations met with some reverses. Most serious of all was the bloody repulse of the Anglo-American army of 7,000 regulars and 9,000 provincials which attempted to storm the outer works of Ticonderoga on July 7, 1758. Lord Howe fell before the action began, and Britons and Americans died together in futile attacks, leaving their bodies draped over an abatis they never penetrated. It was the greatest victory of the brave Marquis de Montcalm, defending Canada without adequate support from his homeland.

No action of the war had as much popular appeal as the battle on the plains of Abraham after Colonel William Howe and his "forlorn hope" led the redcoats up the cliff at Quebec. It would have been hard to find a more suitable subject for an oleograph or heroic stanza than Wolfe and Montcalm expiring at the moment of British triumph. The operations of Jeffrey Amherst were not as melodramatic, but his concentric columns put the enemy at such a disadvantage in their northward advance that Ticonderoga, Crown Point and Montreal fell without a fight. Meanwhile, Colonel Henry Bouquet had taken Fort Duquesne after the death of Forbes. So extended were the combined operations that one provincial force captured Detroit while another was defeating the Cherokees on the Carolina frontier.

Both Pitt and Amherst showed a generous appreciation of American efforts. They put an end to a long tradition of discrimination against provincials, and in return they exacted a wholesome discipline never demanded from Americans before.

In the end there was glory enough for everyone except the ambitious young man whose name had been heard in Europe for a moment after he fired the first shot. Colonel George Washington had missed the victories while plodding through four years of defeat, frustration and military drudgery. If he had learned any tactical lesson, it was probably expressed in a letter written after his participation in the Braddock disaster, while the yells of the savages were still ringing in his ears:

"We have been beaten, shamefully beaten—shamefully beaten by a handful of men, who only intended to molest and disturb our march! Victory was their smallest expectation!"[5]

The panic of the redcoats taught the young Virginian that force in war is not always compounded of mass. Braddock's veterans could have stood up to a hedge of bayonets on a European battlefield; but in the Pennsylvania forest, outside their tactical element, they fled in wild disorder from the moral thrust of surprise.

As commanding officer of the Virginia forces in subsequent operations,

Colonel Washington must have concluded that every moment of action in war is bought with days, weeks and months of dull administration. With only a thousand men, reinforced on occasion by militia, he had the duty of defending a wilderness frontier nearly 400 miles in extent. Plagued by desertions, by lack of troops, by lack of money and supplies, he had to act as intermediary between discontented citizen-soldiers and complaining civil authorities. "My orders," he commented gloomily, "are dark, doubtful, and uncertain; to-day approved, to-morrow condemned; left to act and proceed at hazard; unaccountable for the consequences, and blamed without the benefit of defense."[6]

He stuck it out to the bitter end. Surcease finally came in the spring of 1758, when the capture of Fort Duquesne freed the Virginia frontier from danger. The war had not ended in the north, but it would seldom have occurred to an American of that day to exert himself outside his own colony or section of the country. Colonel Washington, a bit disillusioned with military glory at the age of twenty-six, hung up his sword and took his seat in the general assembly at Williamsburg.

Another young man, the junior of Colonel Washington by six years, was called to the throne of England on the death of George II in the autumn of 1760. The war was to drag on in Europe for two more dreary years, but Britain's empire had already been won. The remnants of Montcalm's forces were being rounded up in America, and Dupleix had lost India to Robert Clive.

Relations between England and her American colonies were never more felicitous. Soldiers from opposite sides of the Atlantic had known a new comradeship instead of the former condescending attitude of regulars toward provincials. Not only had the colonies paid their way; they actually surpassed the mother country, in proportion to population, with their voluntary contributions of troops and funds.

The prime minister had become the beneficiary of an American hero worship expressed in statues, busts and portraits. A visitor to the colonies, surveying the results, might have been forgiven for concluding that Mr. Pitt, wearing a toga and wreath of laurel, had just written the Magna Carta. This iconography would scarcely have pleased the young man who became the new monarch of the world empire created by conquest. One of his first acts was the curt dismissal of the conqueror. And before the signing of the peace treaty George III had seized enough patronage to make himself master as well as monarch, though his subjects still supposed that the issue of personal rule had been settled by two revolutions ousting Stuart incumbents who did not know their places.

Britons were tired of the responsibilities of war. They were tired even of victory and the eccentricities of Mr. Pitt, later known as Lord Chatham after accepting the title for political purposes. The postwar reaction had set in, giving the new "Patriot King" his opening to put an end to the state of semi-independence enjoyed by the American colonies.

It cannot often be said that a young man's virtues do more harm than his faults. But the history of the English-speaking peoples might have taken a different course if George III had possessed a few redeeming vices. Unhappily, he proved to be a model in his private as well as public life. He was honest and upright. He was sober and persevering. He was, above all, plodding and industrious—so industrious that he lost the American colonies a good deal sooner than would otherwise have been possible.

It is a curious circumstance, as if the patience of both sides had fixed limits, that relations between the colonies and mother country approached the boiling point at intervals of about five years. In 1760 the controversy over the revived Navigation Acts and Writs of Assistance had its inception. In 1765 America was united in opposition to the Stamp Act, though more noise than actual sedition ensued. In 1770 the clamor against the Townshend Acts led to the bloodshed of the so-called Boston Massacre. But it was not until 1775 that the struggle reached the stage of avowed hostilities at Lexington and Ticonderoga.

Between the explosions came lulls in which both the colonies and mother country seemed to have forgotten and forgiven. Taxes, as the leaders of both sides realized, were not the main issue. They were but the means of asserting the right of Britain to rule in America. The great question was whether the colonies were to be left in the state of semi-independence that had existed more by circumstance than design for a century and a half.

Americans were very well satisfied with the situation, as they had good reason to be. Barring a few radicals, the colonists were willing to have the name of British subjects if they could have the game of self-government. Chatham, who understood Americans, would have settled the dispute amicably as late as 1775. He would have allowed the colonies a dominion status with their own parliament in return for an acknowledgment of Britain as the head of empire in deciding broad questions of trade and defense. This was also the solution of Benjamin Franklin, the elder statesman of America, who advised the former prime minister in drawing up the proposed bill.[7]

George III was more right than both according to the thought of his own day. He believed that the time had come for a consolidation of the new world empire which would bring the American colonies under the control of the mother country. This was by no means an unreasonable or tyrannical aim at the time. The measures passed for the purpose were far from despotic, and they were repealed in the face of opposition with a haste bordering on timidity. Not until the Boston Tea Party were any steps taken toward chastisement. Then the measures of 1774 which the colonists called the Intolerable Acts were intended to suspend both commerce and self-government in Massachusetts until the colonists should pay for the destroyed tea. Not only did the Port Bill close Boston to trade, but the little seaport of 17,000 inhabitants was placed under military authority by a provision legalizing the quartering of troops on the inhabitants.

George III was not only right in his own day but even patient and indulgent. A German or Russian ruler would have cured such political ills by prescribing a copious bleeding. On the other hand, a few contemporary thinkers had caught a glimpse of the future. Adam Smith, then composing his *Wealth of Nations*, did not agree with the eighteenth-century doctrine that colonies were held in ownership as economic milch cows. Turgot, the great French economist, went so far as to declare, "Wise and happy will be that nation which shall first know how to bend to the new circumstances, and consent to see in its colonies allies and not subjects."[8]

Americans had already proved on a dozen battlefields that they could be allies rather than dependents. They also demonstrated, after the Intolerable Acts went into effect, a dismaying capacity for organizing and combining their resources against the mother country. The causes of the Revolution might be listed in lengthy detail, but it would be hard to improve upon the few lines written by a Maryland clergyman to a friend in England:

> That so vast an Empire as this, at such a distance from the Mother Country, must, one day or another, tear itself off by its own weight, is as plain as a mathematical demonstration, and it would be the wisdom and interest of Britain to protract that period to its utmost distance; but this cannot be done by anything but friendship, lenity, and kindness. Force will neither intimidate nor avail; it will only exasperate and render us desperate.[9]

The members of Parliament who passed the Intolerable Acts did not reckon with the political genius of self-governing colonies. When General Gage landed in Boston to enforce the measures, the framework had already been built for a concerted American resistance. That tireless equestrian Paul Revere, whose rides might have exhausted a latter-day Wyoming cowboy, galloped from Boston to Philadelphia with copies of resolutions passed at a defiant mass meting. The response of the other colonies was so energetic that money and provisions were soon pouring into the beleaguered seaport. Generous aid also came from across the Atlantic, since the American Revolution was the cause of a stouthearted minority in England.

The chronology of ensuing events can only be appraised with allowances for the communications of 1774. A Savannah patriot writing to Boston could not expect a reply in less than two months; and a sailing vessel sometimes took longer for a crossing of the Atlantic. Yet the colonial committees of correspondence agreed in June to summon a general congress. In July and August twelve of the colonies elected delegates. And on September 5th, three months after the Port Bill went into effect, the representatives of an aroused America were meeting in Philadelphia.

The brave word "Continental" came into use at this time to express the first aspirations toward American unity. But the most hopeful patriots could not have imagined that the Continental Congress, as the only visible head of a nation which did not yet exist, would continue to function for fifteen years as a substitute for central government until it won a long war and founded a new republic.

The Continental Army had to wait for its inception until further steps were taken in political organization. But Congress paved the way before adjourning in the autumn of 1774 by passing the Articles of Association.

Ostensibly a nonimportation, nonexportation and nonconsumption agreement, the measure actually set up the machinery of insurrection by recommending "that a committee be chosen in every county, city, and town . . . whose business it shall be attentatively to observe the conduct of all persons touching this association."[10] These few words sowed the dragon's teeth, and there sprang from the American soil hundreds of little revolutionary governing bodies. Generally known as the committees of safety, they were also called committees of inspection or observation in some localities. Every village, every town, every county soon had its own committee or came within the orbit of one; and over all was an elected council for the entire colony, usually dignified with the name of a convention or even legislature.

The nonimportation and nonexportation provisions, from which so much had been expected, proved to be a disappointment. Great Britain was not so easily mastered in economic warfare as the signers of the agreement had supposed. But the Association created the committees which soon had militia companies drilling on every New England village green. These committees took charge of the limited supplies of arms and gunpowder, and they enforced the measures of a Continental Congress which possessed neither legislative nor executive powers.

The committees of safety, in short, provided the local machinery of military administration which enabled the colonies to take the initiative after Lexington. And with the capture of Ticonderoga, the trouble which Parliament hoped to confine to Massachusetts became overnight a rebellion involving all America. For if the Continental Congress had not officially ordered the attack, that council did not balk at accepting the responsibility shortly afterwards.

There ensued a moment of embarrassment, it is true, when the news reached Philadelphia on May 17th, only a week after the second Continental Congress convened. But there is evidence that the assembly had a pretty good idea of what was going on behind its back. At least two of the delegates, John Hancock and Samuel Adams, had been consulted during the planning stage, and some of the others were not entirely innocent.

After accepting the captured British colors, Congress was in a receptive mood when Ethan Allen suggested that "advancing an army into Canada will be agreeable to our friends; and it is bad policy to fear the resentment of an enemy."[11] Plans for invading British territory had to wait, however, until the assembly decided a more urgent question. The New England delegates were clamoring for the adoption of the militia host at Cambridge as the nucleus of a Continental Army representing all the colonies. This issue could not be long postponed, for the burden was too much for the New England colonies alone. Already Massachusetts had been compelled to borrow £75,000 on interest-bearing notes, and a committee appointed to estimate reserves of gunpowder reported "that in thirty-nine towns . . . there were only 67¾ barrels. The rest of the towns in the colony had none worth mentioning."[12]

Nobody could accuse Dr. Warren and his colleagues of timidity, but they knew that the game would soon be up unless Congress came to the rescue. There could be no doubt at all after May 25th, when a great fleet of British warships and transports reached Boston with reinforcements bringing Gage's strength up to about 10,000 effectives.

Although it was a little late in the day, the British general issued another proclamation of pardon on June 12th to insurgents who would lay down their arms, excepting only those hardened wretches John Hancock and Samuel Adams. If he had but known, both of them were plotting more mischief at the moment. For the question of creating a Continental Army was just then being decided by Congress in the affirmative. Before the news could be sent to Cambridge, however, the first pitched battle of the war was fought by the New England militia forces.

All accounts make it plain that Lexington had inspired military amateurs with an exaggerated confidence. "There is an amazing difference in the looks and behaviour of the enemy since the battle," a Philadelphia gazette bragged. "From the general down to the common soldier, they seem to be in a great panic, and are afraid to go to bed for fear the Yankees will kill them before morning."[13]

Americans could not forget the boast of Lord Sandwich before the House of Lords that the cowardly provincial rabble would never dare to look British soldiers in the face. The reply came in a derisive ballad recalling every historical occasion when redcoats had taken to their heels. The sixteenth and final stanza quoted them as commenting on their American pursuers at Lexington:

> As they could not get before us, how could they look us in the face?
> We took care they shouldn't, by scampering away apace.
> They had not much to brag of, is a very plain case;
> For if they beat us in the fight, we beat them in the race.[14]

Yet the lesson of Lexington, if it had been read correctly, was British endurance as much as American aggressive spirit. The men of Colonel Smith's detachment marched all night and fought most of the next day, completing a distance of about 40 miles without much food or rest. At the end of their long travail they were neither demoralized nor incapable of further resistance.

These soldiers, recruited from city slums or rural hovels, were the forerunners of others who would show as much hardihood throughout the eight years as American farmers and frontiersmen accustomed to an outdoor life. Contemporary descriptions agree that the invaders were generally smaller in stature. But neither forests nor swamps nor hills kept those amazingly tough little men from carrying out long marches on poor and monotonous rations.

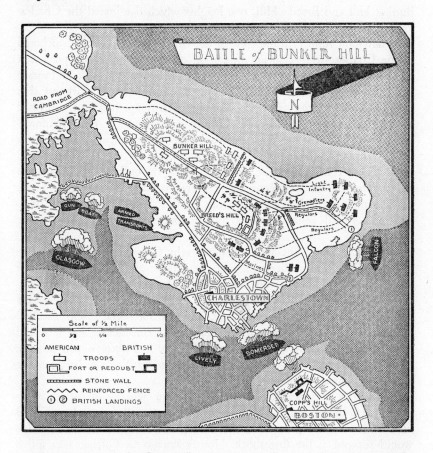

The "nation of shopkeepers" was compared to ancient Carthage by European foemen who implied that their country had inherited the valor of Rome. But on a basis of actual results, no nation of that day had as good a claim to Roman traits as the empire created by Chatham. The Britons of 1775, like the Romans of old, were never balked by heat or cold, by jungle or desert, by climate or geography. The Britons, too, were small and resolute men who conquered as often by an arrogant spirit of invincibility as by force of arms.

After Lexington this spirit upheld redcoats at Boston who never doubted their ability to break through the militia lines extending in a semicircle from Roxbury past Cambridge. The test came when the rebels seized Bunker Hill and Breed's Hill, two heights which dominated the Charlestown peninsula.

At dawn on June 17th the crew of the British warship *Lively*, anchored in the Charles River, had an intimation of two American weapons that would save the cause during the early months. For the pick and spade had been plied so industriously during the few hours of darkness that Colonel William Prescott's 1,000 Massachusetts troops had nearly finished a square redoubt on Breed's Hill. At daybreak about 500 rebel reinforcements straggled in by detachments—some Connecticut troops under Israel Putnam, and a New Hampshire contingent led by John Stark. Prescott took command of the redoubt, leaving the outlying breastworks to be occupied by the Connecticut and New Hampshire companies. These hastily improvised defenses, reaching to the Mystic River, were constructed of rail fences, loosely piled stones and windrows of new mown hay.

Even a civilian might have wondered why Gage had not been first to occupy hills within artillery range of the overcrowded city. After Prescott seized those positions, it was obvious that British warships needed only to command the narrow base of the peninsula to cut the Americans off entirely. This possibility could not have escaped Gage and General William Howe. But British prestige had to be considered, and it would have been humiliating to land troops cautiously in Prescott's rear. Besides, Gage objected on tactical grounds to placing a British force between the rebel detachment on Breed's Hill and the reserves near Cambridge.

The British commanders, like so many other generals of history, were not as wise before the event as afterwards. But battles must be planned on a basis of probabilities, and everything indicated that a frontal attack would succeed at the first shock. Howe's bravery at Quebec was still a legend, and he assured his troops, "I shall not desire any of you to advance a single step beyond where I am at the head of your line."[15]

The American leaders set a like example. Dr. Warren, a militia general carrying a musket instead of a sword, took his stand as usual in the thick of the fire. Prescott walked back and forth on the parapet of the redoubt to show his contempt for the British cannonade while the 2,500 redcoats scrambled out of the boats early in the afternoon and formed for the attack. Few of the embattled farmers were armed with bayonets, and their six small cannon were soon silenced. Thus the military amateurs of Bunker Hill relied almost entirely on their muskets—relics of such varying bores that the bullets had to be hammered or cut to fit. The standard load was "buck and ball"—a round bullet and two buckshot—and the inadequate supply of powder had been measured into paper cartridges.

The flintlocks of 1775 were a great improvement over the matchlocks of the past century, fired by applying a length of smoldering cord to the touchhole. Even so, the effect depended on precision in reloading. Behind the dense cloud of black powder smoke hiding the oncoming foe, the soldier had to bite off the end of a paper cartridge and expose himself in a standing position while pushing it down the bore with a long ramrod. Then the ball and paper wad had to be rammed home tightly, or gas leakage would result in a harmless discharge. Next, the firing pan must be primed by shaking in loose powder, taking care that the breeze did not whisk it away. Last of all, the prudent marksman made sure that the flint was in position to strike a good spark when a pull of the trigger brought it in contact with the steel jaws of the pan.

It took good nerves to go through these motions when the enemy might burst through the smoke with bayonets at any instant, and so slow was the process that the best-drilled soldiers could fire only two or three times a minute. About a hundred yards could be reckoned the extreme range for effectiveness, though the chances of hitting a target the size of a man were speculative at three-fourths of that distance.

All these things had to be remembered by elected militia officers while the scarlet lines were pushing up the hill. Their injunction to aim at the handsome waistcoats had a double purpose: not only was it desirable to pick off enemy leaders, but the tendency of excited men to aim too high had to be corrected.

The redcoats, like other regulars of the day, had been trained to fire platoon volleys at the word of command. Endless drills taught precision in loading, but the soldier's curriculum did not include accurate aim. He simply pointed his piece in the general direction of the foe and pulled the trigger. British tacticians counted on the proved ability of their men to take an enemy volley unflinchingly, then close up the thinned ranks and advance in perfect parade step to a distance where their own fire could not miss. Dettingen, Quebec and a score of other battles had been won by this formula—the redcoats fired at a range suited to dueling pistols and charged with the bayonet to collect their victory.

On this hot June afternoon in 1775 there was no reason to doubt that such tactics would succeed again. General Robert Pigot commanded the British battalions attacking the redoubt, and Howe led his troops against the breastworks. The cannonade ceased as the scarlet lines neared the target area, and there ensued a moment of comparative silence. Then at a distance of fifty yards the rebels opened a ragged fire too murderous to be endured. The attackers stood it only long enough to return an ineffective volley before breaking ranks and falling back down the slope in disorder.

Every age looks with condescension on the weapons of the past. Nevertheless, a flintlock could kill as irrevocably as a machine gun; and the bone-smashing wounds inflicted by large musket balls were ghastly in a day of primitive surgery. Fragments of exploding shells mangled as horribly in 1775 as today, while cannonballs could be even more unnerving to green troops. They ricocheted with an almost personal fury through the ranks, leaving behind them several legless or decapitated victims whose fate turned the knees of onlookers to jelly.

The experience of history proves that the size of casualty lists has varied little throughout the ages in proportion to numbers engaged. The test is the moral endurance of human nature rather than the destructiveness of weapons. Judged by this timeless standard, both sides acquitted themselves well in the misnamed Battle of Bunker Hill. Prescott's men, after toiling all night, finished their redoubt under the fire of British warships and floating batteries as well as the guns of Copp's Hill. The lack of rebel reinforcements owed to the fact that 1,500 men were as many as could be posted to advantage along a line 700 paces in length. But there was little excuse for not sending rations and water to the men on Breed's Hill, and the rebel cannon were so poorly served as to justify an inquiry.

The redcoats had their troubles, too. Their cannonade had not been well directed, and the infantry carried full packs which might better have been sent across in boats after the expected victory. British surgeons were appalled by the terrible abdominal wounds inflicted by militiamen obeying the command to aim low. The volleys of the regulars, on the contrary, overshot to such an extent that the branches of a tree behind Prescott's redoubt were later found to be scarred by bullets.

About three o'clock the attackers plodded back up a hill where fallen comrades lay with the sun beating on them. Dr. Warren, suffering from a headache, took his stand again at the parapet. Seth Pomeroy also served on foot after concluding that a militia general's dignity did not warrant the risk of having a borrowed horse killed. This time the rebel fire at forty paces was more deadly than before. A second time the redcoats straggled down the slope, disordered but not routed. American bullets took such a toll of the officers that all of Howe's subordinates were slain or wounded. Captain Harris, of the 5th, who would live to win renown as Lord Harris of India, was carried off the field to be trepanned. Major Pitcairn of Lexington fame survived two wounds only to be cut down by four more balls. But the day held no more appealing act of gallantry than the request of the mortally wounded Colonel Abercrombie that his old comrade Israel Putnam be spared if any rebels were to be hanged. Not all the friendships of the last war had been forgotten at Bunker Hill.

Howe, whose white breeches were stained with the blood of his officers, never showed more physical and moral courage than in deciding on a third attempt. He also showed tactical sense by insisting that several cannon be placed where they could enfilade the American lines. Previously he had directed that the village of Charlestown be set afire so that it could offer the rebels no refuge. Then, after resting his men, he ordered them to discard their packs before returning to the assault.

Thousands of noncombatants were clustered on the housetops of Boston and surrounding hills where they could witness the spectacle without risk. The five hundred buildings of Charlestown went up in one great bonfire as the guns of the batteries and warships swelled to a new crescendo. But all eyes were probably drawn to the scarlet lines toiling back up the slope toward the redoubt and breastworks.

The outcome can only be imagined if American powder had held out as well as American courage. After one more destructive round, the militiamen had just enough ammunition left for scattered shots. The British met some resistance in taking the redoubt, but lack of bayonets caused most of the defenders to beat a sensible retreat. They had suffered their heaviest losses during those last few minutes from enemy fire at close quarters followed by bayonet attacks.

Although history records few vigorous pursuits after a hard action, Howe has undergone the usual criticism for not pressing the retiring foe. But at the end of such a day his men were doubtless too exhausted for further efforts. At any rate, the American survivors were allowed to make their way to safety across Charlestown Neck, leaving behind them 139 killed and 36 missing in addition to their 278 wounded—a total of 453 casualties which included Dr. Warren, slain among the last stubborn defenders of the redoubt.

The enemy losses have generally been given as 1,054—19 officers and 207 men killed, 70 officers and 758 men wounded. But the British historian Fortesque discovered that nearly a hundred wounded had accidentally been omitted from returns.[16] This brings the total up to about 1,150, or 45 per cent of the troops actively engaged, as compared to 30 per cent for Americans experiencing their baptism of fire. Few battles of history have ever shown such a large proportion of losses endured with so much fortitude.

Chapter 3

An Army of Generals

L ONG after the battles of 1775 had become history, Napoleon asked Lafayette to describe the American Revolution. In his reply that veteran summed up the most striking feature. "The greatest interests of the universe," he said, "were there decided by the skirmishes of picket guards."[1]

The forces engaged at Bunker Hill can only seem insignificant when compared to twentieth-century military establishments numbered in the millions. Yet that fight proved to be one of the largest engagements of a struggle in which every man counted at a worth seldom attained by the private in the ranks. For the soldier of 1775 was not a mere unit, identified by a serial number, of an enormous mass of cannon fodder. He was an individual whose personal behavior might have an influence on some decisive action waged by a few hundred troops on a side.

The Revolutionary soldier was also an individualist who despised both discipline and routine. As he interpreted the dialectics of 1775, an officer was a sort of military foreman elected by his men and governing by consent of the governed. This attitude is reflected in the very first entry, dated June 29, 1775, of the journal kept by Private Aaron Wright of a Pennsylvania rifle company:

> We were sworn to be true and faithful soldiers in the Continental Army, under direction of the Right Honorable Congress. After that we chose our officers. . . . When on parade our 1st Lieutenant came and told us he would be glad if we could excuse him from going, which we refused; and, on consideration, we concluded it was better to consent; after which he said he would go; but we said, "you shall not command us, for he whose mind can change in an hour, is not fit to

37

command in a field where liberty is contended for." In the evening we chose a private in his place.[2]

It was indeed "an army of generals," as Richard Montgomery wryly commented, which the Continental Congress created on June 15th by authorizing a military establishment representing all of the rebelling colonies. The New England delegates themselves took the lead in abolishing sectionalism by nominating a Virginian aristocrat as commander in chief of a militia host composed largely of Yankee "levellers."

There were other veterans of the last war who had taken part in more battles and campaigns. But there was nobody with the experience of George Washington as administrator of a poorly provided force of citizen-soldiers. It had been a severe test for an ambitious young man to serve a long apprenticeship as scene shifter while others were appearing on the stage. But as training for the leadership of an even larger and more poorly provided force of citizen-soldiers, that tedious task was worth more than victories in the field.

It does not appear that the Continental Congress took much account of this qualification. Nor did the delegates hold it against Washington at the age of forty-three that he had only a fair education for his day and no travel outside the country except a brief visit to a West Indies island. More than a third of the other members of Congress had studied at some American or British college, and nearly as many had taken a voyage to England. But the new commander in chief owed his election first of all to a political motive, and secondarily to the impression made by his personality and the blue uniform he wore while serving as a Virginia delegate.

Most of the other generals were chosen for similar reasons. It seemed expedient to elect a Massachusetts man as second in command, but Artemas Ward was neither of an age nor physical condition for an active part. Congress intended Washington's actual assistant to be Charles Lee, a recent British officer of high reputation who had adopted the American cause. Horatio Gates, another convert who had served in the British army with distinction, became adjutant general. The two remaining commissions as major general went to Israel Putnam of Connecticut and a wealthy New York landed proprietor, Philip Schuyler.

Richard Montgomery of New York, a third officer of British experience, was the only brigadier general to be selected outside the New England colonies. The other seven were William Heath, Seth Pomeroy and John Thomas of Massachusetts; David Wooster and Joseph Spencer of

Connecticut; John Sullivan of New Hampshire; and Nathanael Greene of Rhode Island.*

Washington showed a promptness befitting a soldier in taking his leave of Philadelphia at the earliest possible moment. Most of the later descriptions of him were colored by his renown, but Silas Deane of Connecticut had already commented on the imposing stature and "hard countenance" of his fellow delegate. He added, however, that the gentleman from Virginia had "a very young look, and an easy soldierlike air and gesture."[3]

In the last war it had been Washington's lot, through no fault of his own, to participate in none of the decisive battles. The same malign fate seemed to be pursuing him in 1775. For he had not yet reached New York on his way to Cambridge when an express brought the news that the first great test of military strength had occurred at Bunker Hill on the day following his appointment.

On July 3rd, the day after his arrival, the new commander in chief began the task which was to occupy him for the next eight years. Anyone acquainted both with Washington and the New England character could have foreseen that some painful adjustments must be made in coming months. A disciplined man himself, the Virginian aristocrat believed frankly that it was impossible if not undesirable to lessen the gap separating an eighteenth-century gentleman from fellow countrymen of a lower station in life. He abhorred from the beginning the "levelling" doctrines which seemed to him only to drag down the leader without adding anything to the stature of the follower. The New Englanders in their turn accepted Washington with a remarkable lack of enthusiasm at first. They did not learn to esteem him until it dawned upon them that his kind of aristocracy consisted more of responsibility than privilege.

On his very first day the commander in chief must have remarked a great many things about the new Continental Army that were not to his liking. Certainly the encampments, as described by the Rev. William Emerson, did not give much promise of military virtues:

> They are as different in their form as the owners are in their dress; and every tent is a portraiture of the temperament and taste of the persons who encamp in it. Some are made of boards, and some of sail cloth. Again, others are made of stone and turf, brick or brush.

* A list of all Continental generals of the war, with the dates of their appointments, is presented in the Appendix.

Some are thrown up in a hurry; others curiously wrought with doors and windows, done with wreaths and withes, in the manner of a basket. Some are your proper tents and marquees, looking like the regular camp of the enemy. In these are the Rhode Islanders, who are furnished with tent-equippage, and everything in the most exact English style.[4]

There was a reason for this exception. The Rhode Island men owed their regularity to that soldierly young brigadier, Nathanael Greene, who had been read out of the Quaker faith because of his passion for the theory of war. Many of the other New England officers could not have met with Washington's full approval. Such veterans of the last war as Putnam, Stark, Wooster and Pomeroy were generals in shirtsleeves, esteemed as much for their rough and ready informality as any military virtues. The regimental and company officers, chosen for the most part by election, were seldom gentlemen in the Virginia sense of being the superiors of their men in family, education and social station. They included artisans and small farmers, tradesmen and fishermen, mechanics and innkeepers; and Washington was to be shocked by such manifestations as a Yankee captain shaving one of his privates.

Neither the commander nor the army beginning their great adventure together could have had much idea of the odds and hardships they were to encounter. The mother country had four times the white population and an even larger advantage in finances, sea power and the other resources of war. But American writings of 1775 indicate that few leaders expected a long struggle. They counted too heavily on the political influence of Chatham and other friends in England. They expected too much from the commercial pressure of the Association with its non-importation and nonexportation provisions. And they did not reckon sufficiently with the personal rule of a monarch whose obstinacy so often overcame his judgment.

It would be laboring the obvious to cite in detail the military resources that the colonists lacked in 1775—the money, ships, manufactures and other essentials for the building of a war machine. The thing can be put more succinctly by saying that the Americans had no assets at all except unarmed and untrained man power. Time would be fighting on their side a few more months until Britain could send a great expeditionary force. But it is not likely that Washington tried to gaze that far ahead—he had trials enough with the problem of instilling a few rudiments of discipline into his recruits at Cambridge.

Only civilians could find any comfort in geography. They visioned the difficulties of British regulars plodding through the forests and swamps of America after a long crossing of the Atlantic. But Washington foresaw that his men would have to do most of the plodding while the regulars and their supplies were wafted on wings of canvas. All six of the principal American cities were seaports of a coastline shared by all thirteen colonies, and the lesser towns were usually located not far up a river navigable at least for longboats. Even in New York, with its extensive hinterland, nine-tenths of the people lived on the seacoast or along the Hudson and its tributaries.

America seemed to have been created for the convenience of invaders with an overwhelming superiority in ships. The bays, inlets and rivers which were barriers for rebel armies served the enemy as the highways of swift water-borne transportation. Only Pennsylvania and North Carolina, though each had its seaport, offered a few difficulties. Virginia, on the other hand, was so vulnerable along its tidal rivers that a respectable army and chain of forts would have been needed to defend that colony alone.

As if these disadvantages were not enough, there was also the chain of lakes and rivers inviting an army to swoop down from Canada and detach New York and the New England provinces from the rest of the country. Altogether, it is safe to say that the numbers of the invaders were at least doubled in effectiveness by water transport. A British soldier could not actually be in two places at once, but he gave that illusion to rebels marching over miserable roads and waiting for oxen to bring supplies.

If it came to the worst, of course, colonial geography offered a retreat to the forests and mountains of the frontier. This prospect was as comforting to Americans of 1775, most of them townsmen used to civilized comforts, as a flight to the interior of Alaska would be to their descendants today.

As the visible head of government, the Continental Congress reached the point shortly after Bunker Hill of drawing up articles of war and issuing paper money to be redeemed by the colonies. The lack of specified legislative and executive powers did deter the assembly at Philadelphia from acting with authority. Although its decisions were offered as requests or recommendations, they were enforced with all the authority of law by the revolutionary committees set up by the Association.

From the beginning Congress made it plain that the civil power was to be at all times in control of the military, even at the risk of strategic inefficiency. An army of 20,000 men had already been authorized when the assembly appointed a committee of three members in the autumn of 1775 to make the long journey to Cambridge. This was the first of many conferences in which the civil and military heads shared the direction of the war effort on a basis of mutual decision.

The leaves were just beginning to turn red and gold when Dr. Franklin arrived at Washington's headquarters. Although he would soon celebrate his seventieth birthday, he had returned from England in May to serve in Congress. His colleagues were Thomas Lynch, Sr., a wealthy South Carolina planter, and Benjamin Harrison of Virginia, whose broad girth and broader jokes gave him a reputation as the Falstaff of the assembly.

The shortage of American arms had already received the attention of the philosopher who summoned the lightning from the heavens. In the lack of gunpowder, Dr. Franklin suggested a revival of the bow and arrow. That proposal met with no favor, but another of Franklin's ideas was adopted in a resolution passed by the Pennsylvania Committee of Safety:

> At this time, therefore, when the spirit of our People supplies more men than we can furnish with Fire Arms, a Deficiency which all the Industry of our Ingenious Gunsmiths cannot suddenly remedy . . . the use of Pikes in one or two Rear Ranks is recommended to the Attention & Consideration of our Battalions. Every Smith can make these, and, therefore, the Country may soon be supplied with Plenty of them.[5]

Pikes and spears were not only manufactured in quantity but actually used with good effect on several occasions, including an action at the late date of 1781. The problem of weapons, however, was no more urgent than the other difficulties of creating an army out of an armed mob. Americans were beginning to realize painfully how much they had owed in past wars to British administration. The militia host at Cambridge still consisted chiefly of New England short-term volunteers ranging in age from fifteen to sixty. A few Negroes as well as civilized Indians were represented, though the Massachusetts recruiting officers had been enjoined "not to enlist any deserter from the ministerial army, nor any stroller, negro, or vagabond, or person suspected of being an enemy to the liberty of America, nor any under eighteen years of age. . . . You are not to enlist any person who is not an American born, unless such person

has a wife and family, and is a settled resident in this country. The persons
you enlist must be provided with good and complete arms."[6]

The barring of Negroes does not indicate racial antipathy so much as
an aim to prevent the army from harboring runaway servants. Britons,
though profiting from slavery in their own colonial possessions, did not
fail to point out the inconsistency of Americans clinging to that institution
after proclaiming liberty to the world. But there appears to have been no
prejudice against Negro comrades who took a minor but honorable part
in the rebel ranks on several battlefields. Before the war ended, South
Carolina as well as Rhode Island approved plans for raising Negro troops,
with freedom to be held out as the reward of good service.

Dr. Franklin and his colleagues must have observed with keen interest
the Yankee farmers and villagers who had shown so much spunk in opposing the king's troops. Although these military amateurs had done a
great deal of bragging after Lexington, they revealed a capacity for self-
criticism by accepting Bunker Hill as a reverse due in some instances
to incompetence and cowardice. The time would come when June 17th
vied with July 4th as a New England patriotic holiday, but the strategic
blessings were still disguised in the autumn of 1775.

If the committee of Congress had wished to study one of the stoutest
specimens of Massachusetts yeomanry, no better example could have been
found than Corporal Amos Farnsworth of Groton. Two wounds did
not keep him from sticking it out among the last men to leave the redoubt
at Bunker Hill. Yet after eight weeks at the home of his "honoured
father," he returned to the army before his shattered right arm mended.

Farnsworth's diary is filled with lines indicating how much the spirit
of Puritanism supported the rebel cause in New England: "About ten
went to the Chapel and herd the Reverend Doctor Langdon from the
Hebrews 2, 10. He encorridged us to Enlist under the Great General of
our Salvation." The military situation Farnsworth often dismissed in a few
words, "The Enemy has Bin a Cannonading of us: But do little Hurt."
It seemed more important to him to have met "a young Gentleman that
I could Freely convers with on Spiritual things. I find God has a Remnant
in this Depraved, and Degenerated, and gloomy time."[7]

Not all the Yankee lads had such strong religious convictions. Private
David How, a seventeen-year-old leather worker of Methuen who enlisted toward the end of 1775, makes it evident in his diary that Farnsworth often had reason to deplore the godless conduct of his comrades.

The following entries, selected from those of a single midwinter week, hint at some lively moments in the American lines around Boston:

Feb. 7—This Day two men in Cambridge got a bantering Who wodd Drink the most and they Drinkd So much That one of them Died in About one hour or two after.

Feb. 10—There was two women Drumd out of Camp this fore noon. That man was Buried that killed himself Drinking.

Feb. 12—There was a man found Dead in a room with A Woman this morning. It is not known what killed him.[8]

Further evidence of misconduct is supplied by the frequent descriptions of floggings. Although the Massachusetts yeomen had jeered at British "bloodybacks," their diaries and letters show no opposition to corporal punishment on the grounds that it degraded men fighting for freedom. On the contrary, there is a matter-of-fact acceptance of the occasions when soldiers watched a comrade writhing under the lash. Corporal Farnsworth sometimes finds a new proof of the iniquity of human nature: "Paraded with the battalion, and saw two men whipt for Stealing, and Another drommed out of ye Camps. O what a pernitious thing it is for A man to steal and cheat his feller nabors, and how Provocking it is to God!" But the unruffled attitude of David How is much more typical: "There was four of Capt Willey men Whept the first fifteen Stripes for deniing his Deuty the 2nd 39 Stripes for Stealing & Deserting, 3rd 10 Lashes Deniing his Duty & getting Drunk."

Flogging had been the chief disciplinary measure of the New England militia companies before they were incorporated into the Continental Army. A religious note may be found in the early adoption of a limit of the 39 lashes prescribed by Mosaic law. But Washington's secretary, Colonel Joseph Reed, asserted in a letter of 1776 to the president of Congress that culprits were not being sufficiently chastised: "This Army is composed of a greater mixture than any which had yet been collected, and I am sorry to say that we have too many who would equal, if not exceed, the Kings troops in all kinds of disorder and irregularity. To men of this stamp thirty-nine lashes is so contemptible a punishment that it is very frequent for them, in the hearing of their comrades, to offer to take as many more for a pint of rum."[9]

The limit was increased to a hundred lashes in 1776 and double that number later in the war. There are a few instances of fines, running the gauntlet and riding the wooden horse, but flogging remained the standard

American punishment for offenses not serious enough to justify hanging. The drummers and fifers had the duty of applying the whip to the naked back of a man tied to a post or tree. His comrades were paraded to witness the spectacle, though the object lesson seems to have been lost on many of them. Biting a bullet helped the victim to endure the pain, and old offenders took pride in their stoicism.

Such exhibitions struck few eighteenth-century minds as being brutal, and even the hideous practice of tarring and feathering did not shock as it would today. Civil punishments of an earlier America—the pillory, the stocks, the ducking stool—had usually been intended to improve the character by humiliating the body. Few people of 1775 experienced or even desired what would now be considered decent privacy, and young men were conditioned for army life by parents who did not believe in sparing the rod.

Drunkenness was an everlasting problem in spite of all efforts to control the sale of cheap and potent rum to the troops by sutlers. Gambling and profanity were often interdicted in daily orders. And such injunctions as the following are sometimes found in orderly books of 1775: "That all possible care be taken that no lewd women come into the camp; and all persons are ordered to give information of such persons, if there be, that proper measures be taken to bring them to condign punishment, and rid the camp of all such nuisances."[10]

The Yankee passion for swapping kept many of the men out of mischief. There are no more exultant entries in David How's diary than those recording some bargain in which he pocketed a shilling. Although the Methuen youth took his turn at cooking and "makeing cateridges," he never let his camp duties interfere with business: "I bought a pare of trouses of Sergt. Gamble 9/. I sold a pare of Trouses to Nathan Peabody price 10/."[11]

Not only did every Yankee pride himself on being a shrewd trader; he also felt qualified to prescribe home remedies which must have been more dreadful than the disease. Elijah Fisher noted in his journal that he suffered from pains diagnosed as "gravels in the kitteney." He dosed himself with a concoction made from this formula: "A Quart of ginn and a Tea dish of muster seed and a hand full of horseradish roots . . . steep them togather and take a glass of that Every morning."[12] The hardy patient not only survived this medicine but testified with gratitude that he "found Benefit by it."

The practice of having inexperienced men take turns at cooking could only have resulted in some unappetizing messes which added to the sick list. For it is not likely that these novices scrupled too much about cleanliness or sanitation. A daily issue of half a gill of rum was held to be essential for a soldier's health, though the tonic effects of vinegar, molasses and spruce beer were also esteemed. Military surgeons burned tar to fumigate a hospital, and they recommended the daily burning of a pinch of gunpowder to purify the air of a crowded hut or tent.

Only in story and legend did many of the Continentals wear blue and buff uniforms at any time of the war. A few regiments managed as early as 1776 to indulge their own tastes in military dress, but red was a color favored more often than blue. Washington, arriving in Cambridge to find an army clad in every drab shade of homespun, suggested in a letter of July 10th to President John Hancock of the Continental Congress "that a Number of hunting Shirts not less than 10,000, would in a great Degree remove this Difficulty in the cheapest and quickest manner."[13] The first official decision came in a resolution of Congress on November 4, 1775:

> That cloathing be provided for the new army by the Continent, and paid for, by stoppages out of the soldier's wages, at 1 2/3 dollars per month, that as much as possible of the cloth for this purpose be dyed brown, and the distinctions of the Regiments be made in the facings.[14]

Congress had already fixed the soldier's pay at 6 2/3 dollars or 40 shillings a month as compared to the three pence a day received by a British private.[15] The monthly rate for officers was set at amounts ranging from $13⅔ for a lieutenant and $20 for a captain to $125 for a brigadier and $166 for a major general.

The committee at Cambridge and the commander also decided the problem of rations. Before long it would often be a question whether the men could be fed at all, and even in 1775 the following standard was attained more often in theory than fact:

> One pound of beef or three-quarters of a pound of pork, or one pound of salt fish, per day; one pound of bread or flour per day; three pints of peas or beans per week, or vegetables equivalent, at six Shillings per bushel for peas or beans; one pint of milk per day, or at the rate of one Penny per pint; one half pint of rice, or one pint of Indian meal, per man per week; one quart of spruce beer or cider per

man, per day, or nine gallons of molasses per Company of one hundred men, per week; three pounds of candles to one hundred men, per week, for squads; twenty-four pounds of soft, or eight pounds of hard soap, for one hundred men, per week.[16]

The disciplinary lapses brought to the attention of the committee were aggravated by idleness and boredom. Even danger came as a welcome relief, but the aim of the British gunners showed no improvement over the low standard set at Bunker Hill. American diaries abound in such comments as Private Simeon Lyman's entry of October 6th, "In the morning our men fired 2 cannon from Roxbury at the regulars, and they fired 80, and one of the balls struck one of our men and took his arm off, and killed 3 cows besides."[17] Lack of American gunpowder made it a one-sided artillery duel, but the rebels did as much damage with a fraction of the ammunition. So poor was the British marksmanship that a Philadelphia newspaper summed up the results of the first six months on January 13, 1776: "From Bunker's Hill fight to the present day, the regulars have fired, on the Cambridge side, about a thousand balls, bombs, and carcases; and on the Roxbury side, better than two thousand; and they have killed, including those who have died of their wounds, on the Cambridge side, seven, and in Roxbury, five."[18]

The want of artillery in Washington's army led to expedients reminiscent of the Middle Ages, before cannon were mounted on wheels. Dr. Thacher's journal relates that old pieces, relegated to the junk pile because the trunnions had been broken off, "were ingeniously bedded in timbers in the same manner as that of stocking a musket. These machines were extremely unwieldy and inconvenient, requiring much skill and labor to depress and elevate them. Had the enemy been acquainted with our situation, the consequences might have been exceedingly painful."[19]

But the enemy continued to accept a passive role varied by raids or harmless bombardments. As early as September 10th the commander of the rebel army expressed his bewilderment in a letter to his half-brother, John Augustine Washington: "Unless the Ministerial Troops in Boston are waiting for re-inforcements, I cannot devise what they are staying there for, nor why, as they affect to despise the Americans, they do not come forth, and put an end to the contest at once. They suffer greatly for want of fresh provisions, notwithstanding that they have pillaged from several islands a good many sheep and cattle."[20]

Howe, who had replaced Gage as British commander, did not display an energy equal to his bravery in the field. The rebels took the initiative for the most part in the exchange of raids. On one occasion the enemy officers were interrupted at the performance of a farce written by General John Burgoyne, who was a playwright and member of Parliament as well as soldier. A figure representing Washington had just come out on the stage with a rusty sword, followed by an orderly carrying a preposterous wooden musket seven feet long. At that instant a sergeant appeared from the wings and shouted, "The Yankees are attacking Bunker's Hill!"[21] The officers applauded what they supposed to be a line of the farce, and more warnings were needed to arouse them. Meanwhile, a body of rebels had penetrated into the British lines and bagged a few prisoners after burning several buildings left standing in Charlestown.

Either New York or Newport seemed to Howe a better British base than Boston. On October 5th he advised the Earl of Dartmouth "that by the entire evacuation of this Town, and taking hold of Rhode-Island with the force proposed for this place, the Army would be better connected, and the corps would act with better effect on that side, from whence it might possibly penetrate into the country; whereas, in this station, it could only defend the post, and perhaps make some few incursions for fresh provisions, without the power of reducing the inhabitants."[22] .

Impatience got the better of Washington's prudence so far that he called a council of war on October 18th, intimating that "an attack upon Boston, if practicable, was much desired."[23] The generals present were Gates, Lee, Putnam, Greene, Heath, Sullivan, Ward and Thomas. After a brief deliberation they showed good judgment by returning a unanimous negative.

The committee at Cambridge finished its work by recommending to Congress that the regulations governing the army be stiffened with more severe penalties. As a result that assembly approved sixteen amendments for the purpose on November 4th.[24] Among them, as an echo of Bunker Hill recriminations, was a provision that officers convicted of cowardice be disgraced by having their shame "published in the newspapers, in and about the camp, and of that colony from which the offender came."

But if Franklin and his colleagues had seen much to deplore, they might also have found some encouragement. Already the army at Cambridge included troops representing two groups of natural warriors, indigenous to the American soil—the rifleman of the frontier, and the fishermen of the New England seacoast. Both had been trained by their daily life for a skill and hardihood which could never have been taught by European drillmasters.

The fame of the frontiersmen as scouts and rangers in the last war had given them a reputation in England. For two centuries gunsmiths had known that the range and accuracy of firearms could be doubled by spiral grooves in the bore which imparted a spinning motion to the bullet. The rifle did not find adoption in armies because of the several minutes it took to reload by such methods as using a wooden mallet and ramrod to force the ball into the grooves. American woodsmen, depending on the weapon for food as well as defense, overcame this difficulty by seating the ball in a greased patch of leather or linen before driving it home with a few strokes of the ramrod. And though it still took longer to reload a rifle than a smoothbore, this simple invention created the world's first firearm of precision.

Some of the descriptions of marksmanship hint at another frontier accomplishment, the spinning of tall tales. A Virginia newspaper related that the surplus of volunteers in a border county made necessary a shooting test. The judges chalked a drawing of a human nose on a board, and sixty men were said to have riddled the mark from 150 yards away.[25] However this may be, it is at least certain that a good shot with a smoothbore could not have been confident of hitting the board itself at half the distance.

Marksmanship was not the only warlike quality of the men from America's first "wild West." They were also trained to the physical peak of athletes, for the long frontier knew few intervals of relief from the threat of Indian raids. Survival depended on the ability to cope with the savages themselves in woodcraft and endurance, and with the wild beasts in keenness of instinct. There were only the hunters and the hunted in the wilderness, and frontiersmen of the last war had been paid a bounty for Indian scalps.

The first important military decision of the Continental Congress, even before appointing Washington to command, had been the resolution "that six companies of expert rifflemen, be immediately raised in Pennsylvania, two in Maryland, and two in Virginia."[26] The vanguard of these picked troops reached Cambridge when Captain Daniel Morgan's company of 96 Virginia riflemen completed a march of 600 miles in 21 days without a man dropping out from fatigue or illness.[27] The newcomers were aliens to the gaping New England villagers as well as to the redcoats who would soon revise their ideas of the range of firearms. For the riflemen not only had their own weapon but also their own distinctive dress—the frontier hunting shirt, which was actually a loose jacket of leaf-brown linen worn with leather or cloth breeches, buckskin leggings, moccasins and a round hat bearing the legend "Liberty or Death."

"Each man . . . bore a rifle-barreled gun, a tomahawk, or small axe, and a long knife, usually called a scalping knife, which served for all purposes, in the woods," wrote John Joseph Henry in his memoirs. "It was the silly fashion of those times, for riflemen to ape the manners of savages."[28]

The last comment represented the mature view of a Pennsylvania judge recalling his service as a youth in a rifle company of that colony. For the transgressions of the border men were on as lusty a scale as their military virtues. They had no insignificant idea of their own worth, and it was not to be expected that fierce individualists hardened in such a school should have been noted for discipline. The Pennsylvania companies had been in camp but a few days when Aaron Wright noted in his journal: "Great commotion on Prospect Hill amongst the Riflemen, occasioned by the unreasonable confinement of a Sergeant by the Adjutant of Thompson's regiment; and before it was over, 34 men were confined and two of them put in irons at headquarters in Cambridge."[29]

Harvard was already a venerable institution, but traditions meant so little to the frontiersmen that this same diarist could report his march "to Cambridge where a College was kept, called Stoughton's Hall." Yet it would not do to dismiss young Wright too hastily as a barbarian. In a later entry his journal quotes an extract from Monsieur Voltaire's writings which he admired. But instead of adding the conventional "How true!" the Pennsylvania rifleman commented, "Which is d—— near the case, I think."

All frontiersmen were the natural foes of England because of the threat of subsidized Indian raids along the border. The immediate effect of their participation in the siege of Boston was described in the journal of Major Ennion Williams. The redcoats, he observed, "are so amazingly terrified by our riflemen that they will not stir beyond their lines."[30] But he noticed that "our people let their horses and cattle feed and make up their hay without any fear of the balls which the British have often thrown from the cannon and musquets."

Parliament had created another group of Americans into enemies by passing the Fisheries Act which reduced the seamen of New England ports to destitution. The consequences came to the attention of Major Williams on a visit to Marblehead: "Many of the men are in the army and the rest are out of employ, and almost every house swarms with children of these hardy temperate men. Their situation is miserable; the streets and roads are filled with poor little boys and girls who are forced to beg of all they see."

The heads of these families were bound to be implacable foes of the mother country. Life had been no more gentle with them than the frontiersmen, for every Marblehead and Gloucester fisherman was hardened by the stormy seas and freezing weather of the Newfoundland Banks. Their occupation accustomed them to danger and taught a variety of skills that could be made useful in time of war. The fishermen also had their own distinctive dress, consisting of a short pea jacket, woolen trousers and greased boots.

Relentless hatred is the mood of a contemporary account describing the attempt made in the late summer of 1775 by Captain Lindsey of the British sloop of war *Falcon* to seize two American schooners in Gloucester harbor. The fishermen fired from the shore, killing three of the enemy crew. "Upon this Lindzee . . . immediately fired a broadside upon the thickest settlements, and stood with diabolical pleasure to see what havoc his cannon might make. 'Now,' says he, 'my boys, we will aim at the damned Presbyterian church. Well! my brave fellows, one shot more and the house of God will fall before you.' While he was thus venting his hellish rage, and setting himself as it were against heaven, the Almighty was on our side. Not a ball struck or wounded an individual person, although they went through our houses in almost every direction when filled with women and children."[31]

The fishermen gave such a good account of themselves as to recapture the schooners along with 35 of the *Falcon's* crew at a cost of only one man killed and three wounded. This was not the only hard-fought triumph won in 1775 by New England seamen deprived of a livelihood by the acts of Parliament. With the addition of a few small cannon and swivels a fishing vessel could readily be transformed into an armed raider. These craft preyed upon enemy shipping with amazing boldness, taking prizes under the very bowsprits of British warships.

Chapter 4

War in the Fourteenth Colony

PICKED troops were needed for the two-headed invasion of Canada set in motion by Congress in the early autumn of 1775. The project was planned on a scale that might have dismayed the war minister of a nation possessing all the resources the Americans lacked. A left wing under General Richard Montgomery had the task of advancing from Ticonderoga to capture Montreal and outlying forts. Meanwhile the right wing led by Colonel Benedict Arnold would be pushing through the forests of Maine toward Quebec, where the two forces expected to unite if an assault or siege should prove necessary.

The fact that the rebels at Cambridge could not be sure of defending their own lines did not dampen their zeal for the offensive. Volunteers for Arnold's detachment offered themselves with enthusiasm, and a selection was made of riflemen and hardy New England troops. Ships took the 1,100 men from Newburyport to the head of navigation on the Kennebec River. There they assembled at Fort Western on September 23rd, and a fleet of two hundred bateaux provided the means of advancing farther up the stream.

Word had reached Cambridge, as a result of intercepted letters, that Governor General Guy Carleton was left with fewer than a thousand regulars for the defense of Canada. This was one of the reasons for the confidence of invaders who also counted on the disaffection of the *habitants* for sympathy and supplies if not reinforcements.

Never in the course of an articulate war was history written more vividly by the men who created it. Sergeant Ephraim Squier and Major Return Jonathan Meigs of Connecticut, Private John Joseph Henry and Captain William Hendricks of the Pennsylvania riflemen, Captain Henry Dearborn of New Hampshire, Dr. Isaac Senter and Captain Simeon

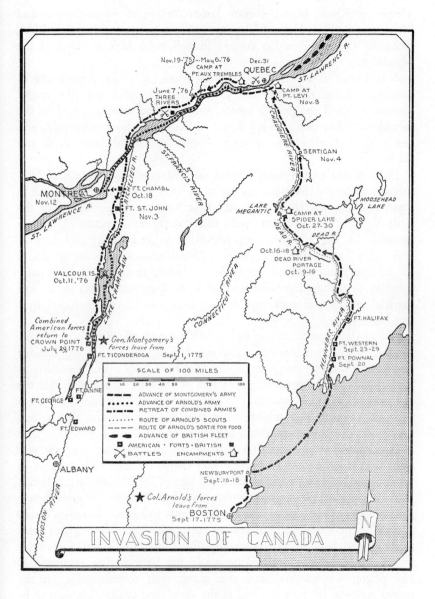

INVASION OF CANADA

Thayer of Rhode Island, Private James Melvin of Massachusetts and Lieutenant William Heth of Virginia—these were some of the chroniclers, including Colonel Benedict Arnold himself, who kept a record of the expedition.

A half-mile of rapids above Fort Western, near the present site of Augusta, offered the first test. Dr. Senter estimated that the empty bateaux weighed 400 pounds apiece, and each had to be portaged on the shoulders of four men. Every barrel of flour was slung from poles and borne by four other men through swamps and woods, over rocks and ridges.

The last day of the month found the little army at the falls of Norridgewock. Arnold described the rapids as "very dangerous and difficult to pass," and Captain Dearborn paid his respects to other stretches of the swift Kennebec. "Any man would think at its first appearance," he recorded in his journal, "that it was impossible to get Boats up it."[1]

A halt of a few days was called at Norridgewock Falls for repairs to the bateaux while waiting for the four divisions to reassemble. No hardships worth mentioning had been met to compare with those ahead, but the trials of the first week were enough to prove that the force contained few weaklings.

One of the most prominent figures was a stocky officer in a scarlet coat —a man who found it more natural to act than reflect. This was Colonel Arnold, supervising every detail with his hard gray eyes. Historians as well as novelists have romanticized him as the idol of his men, but the many journals of the expedition do not give any such picture. They mention him less often than might be expected, but it is apparent that he had the respect of diarists who could be pitiless critics.

The Ticonderoga expedition had already brought out the best and worst in that stormy character. He had shown boldness and decision in his sweep to St. Johns which cleared the lake of British defenders. He had also shown a snarling egotism, plus what would today be known as a persecution complex, when the Massachusetts Provincial Congress found it needful for sound political reasons to replace him. Most officers must at some time bow to such necessities, but the Massachusetts committee reported that Arnold "declared he would not be second in command to any person whomsoever, and after some time contemplating on the matter resigned his post . . . and at the same time ordered his men to be disbanded."[2] Not only was he willing to undo his own work and leave Crown Point undefended, but the report added that he ordered his men to fire on the civilians of the committee.

Another side of his nature was shown by a plausibility in advancing his own interests which soon caused everyone to overlook the black mark against him. For he made such a favorable impression at Cambridge that Washington as well as Silas Deane and a strong faction in Congress agreed that Arnold was the man to head the expedition to Quebec.

If there was any natural leader, dominating by force of personality rather than military rank, the distinction belonged to Captain Daniel Morgan of the riflemen. No officer is mentioned more often by the diarists than this self-educated Virginia frontiersman. Not all the comments are favorable. Henry described him as "a large, strong-bodied personage, whose appearance gave the idea history has left us of Belisarius." But he added in a later passage that Morgan's "severity, at times, has made me shudder, though it was necessary, yet it would have been a pleasing trait in his character if it had been less rigid."[3]

It was inevitable that legends should surround a captain able to enforce discipline with his own fists in a company made up of turbulent six-footers. But the scar on Dan Morgan's cheek testified as to the reality of a wound from a musket ball in the last war. The scars on his broad back were evidence of 500 lashes inflicted as punishment for knocking down one of Braddock's officers. At the age of thirty-nine the border Belisarius could still chuckle with hearty humor because the British count had fallen one short of the prescribed number.

Neither rank nor seniority entitled Morgan to the authority he assumed in leading the vanguard. On September 25th Arnold wrote uneasily to Washington: "I intended Colonel Greene should have gone on with the first division. . . . This was objected to by the Captains of the rifle companies, who insist on being commanded by no other persons than Captain Morgan and myself."[4] Humility was not a virtue of riflemen who claimed prerogatives on the ground that the companies were created by a special act of Congress. But the commander in chief wrote directly to Morgan on October 5th: "My intention is, and ever was, that every officer should command according to his rank. To do otherwise would subvert all military order and authority, which, I am sure, you would not wish or expect."[5]

It came to be tacitly recognized, nevertheless, that Morgan had command of the vanguard breaking a path through the wilderness. His part was scarcely inferior to Arnold's in an expedition which paid more respect to natural leadership than rank.

Some of the other officers would also make their mark in history. Captain Dearborn at the age of twenty-four gave proof of abilities he would use as Secretary of War under Jefferson. Colonel Christopher Greene, a kinsman of the Rhode Island brigadier, would become the national hero of an action in 1777. Aaron Burr, a nineteen-year-old volunteer who found a young Indian woman to share his blanket, would hold the second highest office of the new Republic.

The expedition could even boast the first of those foreign volunteers who adopted the cause of America. Christian Febiger, one of the two adjutants, had been in the country several years as a young Danish trader. Nine days after Lexington he joined a Massachusetts militia company to begin a period of service lasting until 1783. Henry commented on his "open-heartedness" and declared that he "acquired our esteem and entire confidence, as a friend and a real soldier."

Altogether, it was a stout band of men which began an adventure memorable as an epic of American military history. The first severe test awaited in the portages of the Great Carrying Place between the Kennebec and Dead rivers. Private Melvin noted in his journal on October 4th, "We were now to take our leave of houses and settlements, of which we saw no more, except one Indian wigwam, till we came among the French in Canada."[6]

Before the force covered half of the distance, the threat of starvation had been added to the hardships of the march. The bateaux had capsized so often that the dried fish spoiled as the salt washed out, and only a part of the biscuit, dried peas and salt pork could be salvaged. By the middle of October the daily ration had been reduced to twelve ounces of bread and pork, and soon there would be but a remnant of flour to divide.

It might appear that the forest could provide fish and game, but even the smaller beasts fled before the approach of so many men. Henry wrote lyrically of the feast on October 12th when two moose were shot, relating that the men devoured the fat of the entrails and the marrow of the bones. Later a trout or partridge came to be esteemed as a prize.

The Great Carrying Place offered a few easy portages, but there were also some forbidding stretches of swamp, forest and ponds dyed yellow by rotting vegetation. Dan Morgan led the way with the rifle companies to cut a path. Stripped to the waist, his great body a mass of scratches, the Virginian drove his men as hard as himself. "It would have made your heart ache," wrote Henry, "to view the intolerable labors his fine fellows underwent. Some of them, it is said, had the flesh worn from their shoulders, even to the bone." The seventeen-year-old Pennsylvania rifle-man noted that the troops felt "by this time an antipathy against Morgan, as too strict a disciplinarian had arisen."

Before events reached this stage it had been hoped that the worst would be over when the column reached the Dead River. But torrents of rain fell, multiplying the miseries of men without shelter. "A windier nor a rainier day I never see," noted Ephraim Squier on the 21st. At dusk the men "went ashore to camp, and at length with the utmost difficulty kindled us a fire, but could not take much comfort, the wind blowed so high and rained so hard . . . that it obliged us to retreat from our fire, the water next morning [being] 4 feet deep where we made our fire."[7]

The Dead River "had now become live enough," the Rhode Island surgeon wryly commented. Swollen by flood waters, it resembled a broad lake with a fierce current surging though the middle to increase the peril of the bateaux capsizing. Dr. Senter found no adjectives strong enough to picture "a direful howling wilderness not describable." On October 24th some of the troops were "almost destitute of any eatable whatever, except a few *candles*, which were used for supper, and breakfast the next morning, by boiling them in water gruel, &c. Every prospect of distress now came thundering on with a two fold rapidity. A storm of snow had covered the ground of nigh six inches deep, attended with very severe weather."[8]

On the 25th, with barely enough provisions left for five days, there remained 150 miles to cover. The officers of the two rear divisions led by Colonel Greene and Colonel Roger Enos held a council of war as to the advisability of proceeding. Among those deciding, reported Dr. Senter, were "a number of grimacers—melancholy aspects who had been preach-ing to their men the doctrine of impenetrability and non-perseverence." Enough of these defeatists appeared so that the council decided by the margin of a single vote in favor of continuing. Enos voted in the affirma-tive but yielded a few hours later to subordinates who urged that his own division turn back. Worse yet, he consented to leave only two and a half barrels of flour with Greene's detachment. A subsequent court martial cleared him, but Enos stood convicted of cowardice in the hearts of all who had made the harder choice.

The news of his defection reached the forward divisions on the 27th, when the troops were reduced "to taking up some rawhides . . . and chopping them to pieces, cinging first the hair and afterwards boiling them and living on the juice or liquid that they soak'd from it for a considerable time."[9] Captain Thayer described the terrain as "a frightful wilderness . . . without the least sign of human trace."

Few impediments were left when the force came to the twenty-third and longest portage—the four and a half miles to the Height of Land, from which the streams flowed to the St. Lawrence. Nearly all the bateaux had been stove in and abandoned, and it was necessary to throw away most of the damaged gunpowder. On the 28th the men staggered through the snow to finish a portage which they named the "terrible carrying place."

Only the will of Morgan and such officers as Greene and Dearborn kept the companies together as a disciplined force. These leaders supplied a driving energy which freed Arnold and a small party to hasten ahead on the 25th for the purpose of sending back provisions from the first Canadian settlements. For it had become a question of whether the little army could finish the journey without perishing from famine. Each day of hunger counted as a week for exhausted men living on a daily handful of flour while burning up energy at a frightful rate.

The unusual Christian names of Return Jonathan Meigs have inspired a romantic legend about the courtship of his parents. But he was the blunt realist of all the diarists, confining himself to terse factual comments. Hence his entry for November 1st may be taken as a sober account of privations:

> This day I passed a number of soldiers who had no provisions and some that were sick, and not in my power to help or relieve them, except to encourage them. One or two dogs were killed which the distressed soldiers ate with good appetite, even the feet and skins. . . . The travelling this day and yesterday very bad, over mountains and morasses."[10]

The last trials brought out some astonishing contrasts. Nobody stood the march better than young Burr, whose slight frame held a tremendous endurance as well as gusto for life. Nor was there any weakening on the part of two white women who shared the hardships. Every eighteenth-century operation of war had such camp followers, and Henry paid tribute to "the wife of serjeant Grier, a large, virtuous and respectable woman."[11] After breaking ice to cross a shallow pond, the diarist noted that "with her clothes more than waist high, she waded before me to the firm ground. No one as long as she was known to us, dared to intimate a disrespectful idea of her." Yet the ordeal broke the spirit of Rifleman James Warner, described as "young, handsome in appearance, not more than twenty-five years of age; he was athletic and seemed to surpass in bodily strength." His wife Jemima, "beautiful though coarse in manner," found him "sitting at the foot of a tree, where he said he was determined to die. The tender-hearted woman, attending her ill-fated husband several days, urged his march forward; he again sat down. Finding all her solicitations could not induce him to rise, she left him, having placed all the bread in her possession, between his legs with a canteen of water. She bore his arms and ammunition to Quebec, where she recounted the story. . . . Thus perished this unfortunate man."

From the Height of Land the route led past Spider Lake and Lake Megantic to the upper waters of the River Chaudiere, flowing into Canada. This stream proved to be another obstacle rather than highway, for its boiling current had been well named. The men stumbled on, sometimes wading, sometimes picking their way through a wasteland of thickets and frozen bogs along the shore. Henry's account sums up these last few critical days by simply saying that everything "was left to the energy of Morgan's mind, and he conquered."

The day of deliverance would never be forgotten. "This morning, when we arose," recorded Captain William Hendricks on November 2nd, "many of us were so weak that we could scarce stand; I myself staggered like a drunken man. . . . A small stick, lying across the way, was sufficient to bring the stoutest of us to the ground. In the evening we saw some cattle coming up the river, the most joyful sight that we ever had seen."[12]

Dr. Senter intimates that at first the spectacle seemed a delusion of men made lightheaded by starvation. "Upon a nigher approach our vision proved real! . . . A heifer was chosen as a victim to our wants; slain and divided accordingly. Each man was restricted to one pound of beef."[13]

Salvation had come in the nick of time, demonstrating the wisdom of Arnold's decision to leave the expedition and send back provisions. Nobody bothered much about statistics; but after the rescue of snowbound stragglers, the actual losses on the march were fewer than might have been expected. Of the original 1,100 troops, minus 350 who returned to Massachusetts with Enos, about 675 men survived the wilderness to reach the shore of the St. Lawrence.

No time was lost, despite fatigue, in completing the last lap of the journey. American confidence soared in response to the friendly spirit shown by the *habitants* as well as the news brought by Arnold. For he had received dispatches confirming the surrender of St. Johns and Montreal to Montgomery's army.

These victories gave Arnold and his men an added incentive to capture Quebec with their own resources. On November 8th the advance guard sighted the fortress from the bluff on the opposite bank at Point Levi. The British frigate *Lizard* and sloop-of-war *Hunter* commanded the river, but the invaders managed to collect about 35 canoes and dugouts. A few scaling ladders were constructed, and some spear points forged to take the place of bayonets. These preparations used up several days, then a storm made the water too rough for the attempt. Not until the dark night of the 13th did about 500 Americans essay the precarious crossing under the guns of British warships which could have blown their tiny craft out of the water.

If ever a force deserved victory, it was the scarecrow army which in the words of Hendricks "got all safe over in the morning to a place called Wolf's cove." Even Wolfe's daring was tame as compared to the audacity of Americans with no ships, no cannon, and barely enough gunpowder for five rounds.

These men had been fortunate to escape starvation by a few days. As if in payment, it was their fate to miss victory by a narrower margin. An American reconnaissance found no signs of alarm, but the invaders could not have dreamed that the St. Johns gate stood open for a handful of men to surprise the sleeping town. Naturally, it seemed a grave risk to attack at dawn after the climb to the Plains of Abraham. Instead, the weary troops found a refuge in an outlying mansion and flung themselves on the floor to slumber as deeply as the unsuspecting garrison.

Shots had been exchanged that night with a patrol boat from the *Hunter*. But at daybreak it took the capture of an American sentry, George Merchant of the riflemen, to arouse the town. Colonel Allen Maclean had not expected an attempt so soon, though the interception of a letter from Arnold to Montgomery had brought him hurrying down the river with 200 troops to defend Quebec. He arrived just thirty hours before the crossing of the river by Americans who were too late for the capitulation favored by the townspeople. The hard-bitten Scottish officer soon stiffened backbones in Quebec, and Arnold was answered by cannon-balls when he summoned the garrison to surrender. Henry condemned him for the "folly" of drawing up his little army "in a line, in front and opposite to the walls of the city. The parapet was lined by hundreds of gaping citizens and soldiers, whom our guns could not harm, because of the distance. They gave us a huzza! We returned it, and remained a considerable time huzzaing, and spending our powder against the walls, for we harmed nobody."[14] The performance, added Henry, drew criticism from some of the Americans:

It must be confessed that this ridiculous affair, gave me a contemptible opinion of Arnold. This notion was by no means singular. Morgan, Febiger, and other officers, who had seen service, did not hesitate to speak of it in that point of view. However, Arnold had a vain desire to gratify, of which we were then ignorant. He was well known at Quebec. Formerly, he had traded from this port to the West Indies, most particularly in the article of horses. Hence, he was despised by the principal people. The epithet 'Horsejockey' was freely and universally bestowed upon him, by the British. Having now obtained power, he became anxious to display it in the faces of those, who had formerly despised and contemned him.

Other recriminations were exchanged by invaders who saw that the jig was up after Maclean showed a determination to resist. A few days later they prudently withdrew to Point aux Trembles, some twenty miles up the river, and waited for Montgomery to come to the rescue with cannon, gunpowder and warm clothing.

Only a wilderness had been lacking among the troubles encountered by that general, even though he had a few victories to show for his pains. For his green troops had been obstinately opposed by Carleton and nearly all the regulars defending Canada.

Both Montgomery and his adversary were born in Ireland as sons of English Protestant families which had taken root in that island. Both made the army a career and won distinction in the last war—Montgomery with Amherst at Montreal, and Carleton under his friend Wolfe at Quebec. Both found a spiritual home in the New World, but their interests diverged when Carleton became governor general of Canada and Montgomery retired from the army to marry the daughter of Robert R. Livingston and settle in New York.

In a day of impressive noses, Carleton's portrait shows a promontory of unusual size as well as a jutting jaw and the eyes of a fighter. Wounded at Quebec and promoted to brigadier, he returned to Canada in 1766 to govern a conquered people with wise and kindly paternalism.

It proved a hard decision for Montgomery, but the thirty-nine-year-old veteran adopted the American cause when the dispute came to blows. Not the least of his difficulties was the unruly army that he led down Lake Champlain to begin the siege of St. Johns. Discipline could hardly have been expected of the troops after some of the examples set by American leaders. For the campaign had barely begun when Ethan Allen tried to duplicate his performance at Ticonderoga. Again the border captain had little authorization except his acknowledged partnership with the Great Jehovah, but he failed in his attempt to capture Montreal. The *habitants* did not rise in arms to aid him as he expected, and after a brief and farcical fight he had to surrender with 40 followers.

This fiasco added to Montgomery's problems by puncturing the illusion that the Canadian peasants were waiting to welcome the invaders. From the beginning the leaders of revolt had set their hearts on making Canada the fourteenth colony. The Continental Congress appealed to the people with addresses translated into French, and that assembly sent a committee to Ticonderoga to supervise both the political and military efforts.[15] The fifty-one-year-old governor had meanwhile got in the first blow by returning to England early in 1774 as the advocate of legislation to keep Canada loyal to the crown. In spite of his foresight Carleton might have been balked except for the timely boon of the Boston Tea Party. The news of this affront put George III and Parliament in a mood to approve the Quebec Act while passing the so-called Intolerable Acts to punish Massachusetts.

The most important provision was the one granting the French inhabitants the right to profess the Catholic faith. Carleton knew that this single clause had potentialities of turning Canada against invaders who had nothing to offer save political liberties. He did not include any such unwanted gifts in the Quebec Act, which gave full authority to the governor and a crown-appointed council. The measure also enlarged the province by extending it westward and southward to take in the country between the Ohio and Mississippi.

The geographical and religious features enraged the Americans so much that they were cited as grievances in the Declaration of Rights passed by Congress. On the other hand, Carleton soon found that he had overshot the mark in his efforts to conciliate the Canadian clergy and noblesse. The tightfisted *habitants,* loyal as they were to their faith, resented the clause which gave the clergy the legal power of collecting tithes. Nor did they approve the new policy of restoring to the noblesse some of the feudal prerogatives lost since the conquest.

The Quebec Act would in time be hailed by Canadians as the charter of their rights. But these two grievances were enough in 1775 to frustrate British hopes of raising large forces of soldiers. Both Britons and Americans were viewed as aliens by peasants who did not regard the quarrel as their concern.

Montgomery's force brought together such elements as sober, devout New England villagers and the waterfront toughs of the 1st New York regiment. Benjamin Trumbull, a Connecticut chaplain, remarked sadly in his journal that "there never was a more ill governed Profane and Wicked army among a people of such Advantages on Earth." As a Congregational minister who served a single community for sixty years, he set an example which would have won him renown as a "fighting parson" if that term had been current in 1775. For he carried a musket in the ranks when the Americans landed near St. Johns on September 6th to stumble into "an ambuscade, consisting of Indians and Canadians, who began a heavy fire on that Wing. The Army immediately wheeled to the Left in order to Face the Fire of the Enemy, and charged it with great spirit & Firmness. After a fire of about half an hour the Enemy gave way and retreated fast, keeping up a Scattering fire as they ran off."[16]

This encounter was only one sign of enemy preparations for a resolute defense of the fort 30 miles south of Montreal. The American brigadier had little choice but to retire to the Isle aux Noix and wait for reinforcements and ordnance. On September 17th he made a second effort with 1,400 troops and some of the guns captured at Ticonderoga. The rebels devoted a week to the construction of earthworks and emplacements, then a daily artillery duel began without many losses on either side. Sickness thinned the ranks more effectively, for Colonel Henry Livingston observed that "the soil is much too wet & low to render Dwellings on it agreeable. It being one entire swamp almost." At least the American bombardment caused an epidemic of desertions among the unwilling Canadian recruits raised by Carleton after he proclaimed martial law. Livingston commented in his journal that "very few came indeed; in the large district of Laprairie not one man would appear. At Longueuil but 7 or 8 came & so more or less in the rest of the parishes."[17] Nor did the rebels have much better luck at enlisting peasants who preferred to till their fields and sell the produce to both armies.

The two connected redoubts of St. Johns were too strong to storm, and the American guns made little impression on walls described by Livingston as being "composed altogether of Earth, and neatly sodded without, looking as green as the fields around it." Early in October it became necessary to transport more cannon down the lake, including a 13-inch mortar which the men named the Old Sow. But her heavy shells had no more effect than the shot from the batteries or the guns of the sloop *Enterprise* and schooner *Liberty*, anchored in the Richelieu river.

Montgomery complained that his troops "carry the spirit of freedom into the field and think for themselves." This did not prove to be a bad trait on the night of October 12th when a party of volunteers finished the dangerous task of erecting a new battery nearer to the fort. With immense toil the men dragged two 12-pounders over ground "excessively wet and rooty." This gave the besiegers a perceptible advantage, but the turning point came on the 18th with the surrender of a lesser British fort at Chambly.

This post, six miles down the river from St. Johns, fell after a feeble resistance to 50 Americans and a party of Canadian allies led by Major John Brown, the spirited Massachusetts lawyer who had helped to capture Ticonderoga. Once more audacity won for Americans with only a few iron 9-pounders. Major Stopford, the British commander, could plead that the works were weak; but he capitulated before a single man of the small garrison had suffered a scratch. Moreover, he did the victors a greater favor by neglecting to destroy munitions which included 150 stand of arms, 6,564 cartridges, 124 barrels of powder, and 138 barrels of flour and salted meat.

This little triumph gave a moral as well as material impetus to the siege of St. Johns. Montgomery's men were further heartened by the report that Governor Carleton had been repulsed on the 30th when setting out to the relief with a few regulars and 800 halfhearted Canadians and Indians. About 350 New York troops and Green Mountain Boys awaited the British boats crossing the St. Lawrence to Longueuil. Seth Warner ordered the men to hold their fire until they could not miss, and the musket balls were accompanied by a blast of canister from a 4-pounder. Carleton's flotilla turned back without touching shore, having lost a hundred killed and wounded according to the estimate of victors who had no casualties.

The news of this reverse, two weeks after the loss of Chambly, extinguished the last hope of stubborn defenders of St. Johns who had been enduring a daily artillery pounding since the middle of September. On November 2nd Major Charles Preston marched out with the honors of war at the head of 28 officers, 425 regulars, 75 sailors and a few

Canadian auxiliaries. There were no British forces left to bar the way to Montreal, and General David Wooster led the advance on the 6th with his Connecticut regiments.

The sixty-two-year-old veteran had seen service not only in the last war but also at Louisburg in 1745. Never had he found worse roads, however, than those leading to Montreal. Trumbull described the terrain as consisting of "mud and mire and Scarce a Spot of dry Ground for miles together. The Land is all flat in this Country and a great part of it drowned Lands for 50 and an 100 miles on End. Our People have lived in mud and mire most of the time since they began the Siege." Snow drifted down from leaden skies, and the Connecticut chaplain recorded that "some of the Regulars' Wives and Children came up from Montreal in a miserable Plight. Women badly clothed, Children bare foot and almost naked & covered with Mud and Water, and have in these circumstances to go on 400 miles to New England. My Heart pities them, and I wished to be able to do something to help them."[18]

The march that might have been completed in two easy days on dry roads lasted a week for drenched Americans wading "in Mud and Water sometimes midleg high and in general over the shoes." It was no triumphal entry that Montgomery and Wooster made on the 13th, but at least a freeze that day gave better footing. The invaders quietly took possession of a town evacuated on the night of the 11th by Carleton and his last 80 regulars.

The eleven small British ships got as far as Sorel, only to be challenged by the ubiquitous Major John Brown. That bold and energetic officer had mounted cannon in two row-galleys and placed a battery of 12-pounders to command the channel. Still, he prevailed more by bluff than force in convincing the enemy that he had larger cannon farther down the river. These guns, which existed only in Brown's imagination, were so threatening that General Richard Prescott surrendered the flotilla to a detachment that it outnumbered. Montgomery, who had worn a scarlet uniform with more honor, declared upon hearing the news, "I blush for His Majesty's troops!"[19]

In all Canada there could have been no more lonely figure that night than Guy Carleton, who had been so badly supported by his subordinates. But his resolution did not waver at a moment when only five or six men were left to him. The Americans were searching everywhere as he changed to a peasant's garb and slipped past the rebel battery in the darkness of

November 16th. The governor took his turn at the muffled oars of the whaleboat, and a secret passage through the islands near Sorel aided his escape.

As a rule the contempt of regulars for militia or provincials is upheld by results. But during his flight down the river Carleton must have reflected bitterly that the redcoats had not covered themselves with glory in Canada. After they had failed at Montreal and Sorel, it remained for a small force of provincials to save Quebec.

Major Brown reached Sorel too late to trap Maclean, who sent part of his detachment to aid Carleton at Montreal and embarked down the river early in November with 200 men of his own regiment, the Royal Highland Emigrants. These provincials had been recruited in America as well as Canada by retired Scottish officers. Many were kilted veterans of the last war, and the British had no better regiment in 1775, though it was broken up into detachments and scattered to all points of the map.

Maclean paused at Three Rivers long enough to strip the magazines of arms and powder. Any doubts about Quebec being in peril were dispelled by the interception of Arnold's message, and on the evening of November 12th the grim old Scot arrived just in time to silence a meeting at which the townspeople advocated capitulation. The rebels surprised him by crossing the river the following night, but Maclean soon made the best of his few resources. He impressed civilians and merchant sailors into duty—anyone capable of pulling a trigger or carrying a round shot. And if the garrison remained woefully weak, the Americans were still weaker when they decided to retreat to Point aux Trembles.

Carleton at last found some reason for encouragement when he reached Quebec on the 19th to praise Maclean's endeavors. The governor warned the inhabitants that those who would not bear arms must "quit the Town in four days . . . under pain of being treated as rebels or spies." He also tried to detach some of Montgomery's fair-weather friends in Canada by publishing reports of the depredations of the American "banditti."

The duel between the two adversaries was renewed after Montgomery set sail from Montreal on the 28th. He had not built false hopes on reports that hundreds of Canadians were rising in arms under such American sympathizers as Moses Hazen and James Livingston. Nor did he have any illusions about the spirit of his own men, for a majority of them could not be persuaded to serve another moment after the expiration of their enlistment terms. They were miserably clothed for a winter campaign, and fighting on foreign soil did not appeal·to patriots who would have made sacrifices to defend their homes. Only about 800 troops were left to Montgomery late in November for the double purpose of holding Montreal and leading a detachment down the river to capture Quebec.

A foot of snow covered the ground when the flotilla reached Point aux Trembles after gaining the bloodless capitulation of Canada's third city, Three Rivers. Montgomery's numbers added to Arnold's hardly amounted to a thousand, but he had brought powder, clothing and a few cannon. Most of the rebel munitions of war up to this time had been captured from the enemy, so it is not surprising that the men should have replaced their rags with warm British uniforms. Burly Lieutenant William Heth of Morgan's company described himself with a grin as "having on a Tiny Short red Coat, turned up with yellow reach'g at the utmost not above an Inch below the wasteband of a pr. of corded Breeches, that was once white—but had seen their best days—a pair of mixd raw Silk Hose of the same date—a pair of gingerly Shoes."[20]

When Montgomery sent a summons to Carleton, proposing terms of capitulation, the governor showed his dramatic sense by ordering a drummer to pick up the message with tongs and throw it into the fire unopened. A total of 1,168 men had been organized for the defense—200 British militia, 300 French militia, 37 marines, 271 armed seamen from the *Hunter* and *Lizard*, and a few artillerymen in addition to Maclean's 200 provincials. About 3,000 good troops could be reckoned the minimum garrison for safety, but Carleton had the consolation that his opponent must deal with even greater shortcomings. Captain John Lamb, the New York optician commanding the rebel artillery, constructed a battery from the only available materials, snow and ice. Aaron Burr helped to serve the guns, and Return Jonathan Meigs complained of frostbitten feet in the bleak redoubt. Unfortunately, the rebel 12-pounders had no more effect than the 5-inch mortar shells called *bombettes* by the derisive townspeople. The ice battery lasted only until the garrison found the range with 32-pounders, and meanwhile the American riflemen did the enemy more harm by picking off sentries from distances which seemed incredible.

Even if Montgomery's resources had been enough for a formal siege, the approaches and parallels could not have been dug in the frozen ground. He perceived by the middle of December that his only desperate chance lay in a night surprise. The attempt must be made before the end of the month, moreover, because several hundred more enlistments would expire at that time. The American brigadier wrote to Wooster on the 16th that he had decided to wait for a snowstorm: "I propose [during] the first strong northwester to make two attacks by night. . . . We are exceedingly weak, it is true, but the enemy are so too, in proportion to the extent of their works; and as they know not where they will be attacked, all must be guarded."[21]

Montgomery hoped that if he could get possession of the Lower Town, containing Quebec's shipping and commerce, the enemy would eventually have to give up the part of the city built on the bluff. He planned to lead an escalade from the Cape Diamond side while Arnold attacked at the opposite end with most of his men and Lamb's artillery. The garrison would be confused by two pretended attempts on the Upper Town—a noisy feint by Major Brown at the Cape Diamond bastion, and a false alarm created by James Livingston and his Canadians at the St. John's gate.

Luck is likely to be decisive in any such operation, and the last night of 1775 provided as blinding a snowstorm as Montgomery could have asked. It may even be wondered if the weather did not favor the garrison rather than attackers trying to keep their flintlocks dry while dragging a cannon and heavy scaling ladders through the drifts. Between four and five in the morning Montgomery gave the signal by sending up two rockets from the foot of Cape Diamond. Malcolm Fraser, captain of the guard in Quebec, aroused St. Louis Street with his shouts, "Turn out! Turn out!" The bells of the cathedral and the Jesuit college began a wild clanging as shots were heard from the ramparts.

Both of the American feints came too soon to accomplish their full purpose. For a few minutes the defenders were firing excitedly into the storm from all quarters of the Upper Town. But Livingston's pretended attack at the St. Johns' gate was not convincing, and Brown's men did not give a much better demonstration.

Montgomery plodded at the head of his 300 troops from Wolfe's Cove about two miles to the defenses of the Lower Town on the Cape Diamond side. Blocks of ice tossed up by the tide left only a single-file path at the foot of the cliff. Not a shot came from the first barricade as the men tore the palisades apart and plunged ahead into the swirling gusts of snow. The next strong point was a cottage made over into a blockhouse with four small cannon. The occupants, according to Lieutenant Francis Nichols' diary, "deserted their posts and threw down their arms, believing that all was over. . . . A drunken sailor swore he would fire one shot before he would retreat, went to a gun loaded with grapeshot, and with a match fired it off, and unfortunately for us killed the brave Montgomery, Capt. Cheesman and Capt. Macpherson his aid de camps."[22] Quartermaster Donald Campbell, next in rank, ordered a retreat in such haste that the corpses were left to freeze into grotesque positions in the snow. "If Col. Campbell had advanced and joined Col. Arnold's troops," added Nichols, "he would have met little opposition, as the citizens had thrown down their arms. . . ."

As late as the 26th Montgomery had communicated to Schuyler his "great mortification" because of the lack of harmony in Arnold's force.[23] Three of the New England captains went so far as refusing to serve under him, but for the sake of discipline Montgomery would not form their companies into a separate corps, as they requested. All were taking part, however, as the column approached the Lower Town from the side of the River St. Charles. Snowdrifts and ice floes from the St. Lawrence made the narrow path so difficult that the brass 6-pounder had to be left behind. The defenders in this quarter lacked neither alertness nor resolution, and Arnold was among the first Americans wounded by "an incessant fire of musketry from the walls, and from the pickets of the garrison."

John Marshall left an account based on a lost fragment of Heth's diary which modern historians have never seen.[24] There were several majors and a lieutenant colonel in the force, but the men called on Morgan to lead them against the first battery. Two enemy cannon held up the advance until he rushed them at the head of his company. Both were captured along with the gun crews at a cost of one American killed. The final blast of grapeshot which blackened the faces of the attackers would doubtless have been more deadly at longer range.

The rifle captain had lost his way in the darkness when Lieutenant Colonel Greene and Majors Meigs and Bigelow joined him with about 200 troops. At daybreak Morgan led the assault against the second battery in a narrow street of the Lower Town. His men attempted without success to mount ladders and storm the barricade. Exposed not only to grapeshot but also musket fire from upstairs windows, they discovered that the snow had rendered most of the rebel firelocks useless. The stone houses offered a refuge for riflemen who took cover to reload and answer with a few shots of their own.

Captain William Hendricks, whose "mild and beautiful countenance"

Henry admired, had kept a record of marches totaling 979 miles from Carlisle to Quebec. But the Pennsylvania frontiersman came to the end of the road when an enemy ball shattered his heart just as he fired from a window. His journal was found on the body and published for the first time in England.

Lieutenants Humphreys and Cooper were killed and Captain Hubbard mortally wounded in the fight for the second battery. Captain Lamb had one side of his face shot off by canister, and Nichols made a bandage of the black silk stock around his neck. It is credit to the surgery of the day that the victim survived his ghastly wound to fight at Yorktown and become a public figure in New York after the war.

While the way lay open to retreat, Morgan hesitated in the hope that Montgomery might have been successful on the other side of the Lower Town. Carleton and Maclean had not been idle meanwhile, and the Americans soon found themselves surrounded in the narrow, crooked streets. It was a bitter pill for the captain who had taken a brigadier's part, but about ten o'clock Morgan had to surrender after most of his men had already fallen into the enemy's hands.

Seldom have military novices ever shown so much fortitude in their first battle. But they paid a stiff price in losses amounting to 48 killed, 34 wounded and 372 prisoners—a total of 454, or more than half the effectives of the entire American force at Quebec. The death of Montgomery left a gap which could never be filled at this early period of the war. His successor Arnold, carried off the field with a ball through the leg, was left with the wreck of an army ravaged by a smallpox epidemic at the height of a Canadian winter.

Chapter 5

The Liberation of Boston

IN 1775, at the high tide of patriotism, the rebels could doubtless have raised an army of 150,000 long-term troops if man power had been the only question. The rub was how to pay, feed, arm and clothe a tenth of that number during the first winter.

The king's ministers had the problem of finding enough soldiers in the first place, then of transporting them across an ocean which seemed a great deal broader in that day. On a basis of population it would appear that enough recruits could be found among nine million Britons. But the age was impregnated with the tradition of compact professional armies of "volunteers" enlisted by semilegal means of compulsion. The poacher, the tosspot and petty rogue were fair game for recruiting sergeants who preyed upon the unfortunate and vicious elements of the kingdom. It occurred to few decent young workmen or farmers that they owed military service save in such an emergency as defending their own soil.

A strenuous effort was made in 1775 to appeal to patriotism. Major Boyle Roche, a member of Commons, drew "a Prodigious concourse of spectators" when he arrived in Cork with a large purse of gold to reward volunteers and "an elegant Band of Musick, consisting of French Hautboys, Clarionets and Bassoons."[1] An added inducement was "a large Brewer's Dray, with five barrels of Beer, the Horse richly caparisoned and ornamented with Ribands." Roche himself made a rousing speech, declaring that "a more critical period never presented itself, nor had we ever a fairer opportunity of showing our attachment to the illustrious House of Hanover, than the present; as His Majesty's deluded subjects in America are in open rebellion, and, like unnatural children, would destroy their ever indulgent parent."

In his need for troops George III put aside his old prejudice against

Catholics in the ranks, but the results were disappointing in southern Ireland. Although most of the people vaguely favored the royal cause, the high wartime prices paid for farm products proved to be a greater temptation than the king's shilling. And in the northern counties that fierce breed of Protestants known as the Scotch-Irish upheld the principles of the rebellion.

By a process of elimination the north of Scotland became the only fertile recruiting ground in the British Isles. There the Gaelic-speaking crofters, kept in hopeless poverty by a feudal clan system, were willing in large numbers to sell themselves into military bondage for the sake of a farm in America. Hundreds of Highlanders had emigrated within the last few years to form settlements in New York and North Carolina, and in 1775 recruiting agents held forth the prospect of land to be confiscated from the rebels.

The total of British recruits still fell far short of enough to bring the army up to war strength. George III and his ministers had to face the necessity of hiring European mercenaries, and meanwhile they did not shrink from employing American Indians, who needed no transportation across the Atlantic.

The experience of past colonial wars had made it clear that redskins on the warpath could not be restrained from burning homes and warring on women and children. But there was never any doubt about a British policy endorsed by George III. The British historian Lecky has declared it "certain that in the beginning of June, 1775, Colonel Guy Johnson, who had succeeded Sir William Johnson in the direction of one great department of Indian affairs, had, in obedience to secret instructions from General Gage, induced a large body of Indians to undertake 'to assist his Majesty's troops in their operations in Canada,' and in July this policy was openly avowed by Lord Dartmouth. It was defended on the grounds that the Americans had themselves adopted it."[2]

Not much later the Cherokees of the southern frontier were supplied with ammunition by John Stuart, agent of Indian affairs. The same defense was offered by Lord North, who assured Parliament that "there was never any idea of employing the negroes or the Indians until the Americans themselves had first applied to them."

Such excuses are weakened by evidence that the British leaders had not waited for the Americans to decide. As it happened, the Continental Congress agreed in the summer of 1775 on a policy of keeping the Indians at peace. Commissioners for the northern, middle and southern departments of Indian affairs were appointed on July 12th and the sum of $16,666 appropriated for the purpose of bribing the Six Nations, the Cherokees and other tribes into accepting treaties of neutrality.[3] Some of the chiefs foresaw that the Indians themselves would be the victims if they took part on either side. A group of Oneida sachems, including such formidable names as Viklasha Watshaleogh, Quedellis Agwerondongwas and Handerchiko Tegahpreahdyen, went so far as to deliver a stern lecture in a communication of June 12th addressed to the executives of the New England provinces:

> Brothers! Possess your minds in peace respecting us Indians. We cannot intermeddle in this dispute between two brothers. The quarrel seems to us unnatural. . . . Should the great King of England apply to us for our aid, we shall deny him. If the Colonies apply, we will refuse. The present situation of you two brothers is new and strange to us. We Indians cannot find or recollect in the traditions of our ancestors the like case of a similar instance.[4]

Such principles could not long prevail against British inducements. The Oneidas came nearest of all the northern tribes to preserving their neutrality, but the assistance given the British by their kinsmen led within a few years to the destruction of the Six Nations.

The *Journals of Congress*, it is true, contain several explicit recommendations that Indians be taken into the Continental Army, though no serious effort was ever made to recruit them. A few were to be found in the rebel forces, usually serving as scouts, throughout the war. There could be no ethical objections to using Indians as disciplined soldiers, but the British ministers knew the consequences of debauching savages with rum and employing them as confederates under loose military control. The weakness of the redskin for strong drink was confessed in a memorial sent by the Stockbridge Indians to Joseph Warren while they were serving with the Massachusetts militia in June, 1775:

> We, in our own serious hours, reflect with shame upon our aptness to drink spiritous liquors to excess when we are under temptation; by which foolish conduct, when we are guilty of it, we render ourselves unfit for usefulness and service to our fellow-men, and also disagreeable to those who have anything to do with us. We are sensible that we injure ourselves more than anyone else. When we get a taste, we must some of us with shame say, that sometimes no interest of our own will prevent us from procuring more, till we get too much. We therefore desire you would, in your wisdom, do something, during our residence here, that we may get as much as will be good for us, and no more.[5]

In the interests of temperance the Massachusetts authorities withheld the pay of the petitioners until they were dismissed. But it had long been the practice of Americans as well as Britons to ply the redskins with rum before soliciting favors, and the royal agents knew how to overcome reluctance. Thus were planted the seeds of such hideous fruit as the Wyoming Valley and Cherry Valley massacres a few years later.

Even if the Canadian response to the Quebec Act had not been disappointing, it would still have been necessary to hire European mercenaries to bring the British army up to war strength. George III tried first at the court of his royal sister Catherine. The Empress of Russia, though she urged "for God's sake" that the revolt be put down speedily, had nothing to offer save sympathy. A letter in the king's own hand could not persuade her to send 20,000 troops from the armies which had lately defeated the Turks after some hideous massacres.

The petty princess of the German states took advantage of British necessity to drive hard bargains.[6] At a time when the pound sterling had a buying power which seems incredible today, the following sums were voted by Parliament during the war for the hiring and paying of about 30,000 mercenaries:

Hesse-Cassel (8 years)	£2,959,800
Brunswick (8 years)	750,000
Hesse-Hanau (8 years)	343,130
Waldeck (8 years)	140,000
Anbach-Bayreuth (7 years)	282,400
Anhalt-Zerbst (7 years)	109,000
	£4,584,330

This total, while only a small fraction of the amount spent by Great Britain to put down the revolt, is enough to give an idea of the financial odds against the colonies. For the entire debt of the United States, both war and domestic, including all foreign loans, was reported as $42,000,375 down to April 26, 1783.[7]

The use of mercenaries was not a novelty in eighteenth-century warfare. Most of the small professional armies of the day found it necessary to employ auxiliaries in a foreign war of long duration. But the opposition leaders in Parliament thought it degrading to call upon aliens to scourge English flesh and blood in a civil conflict. The bitterness of American reactions is understandable, for German troops trained according to the methods of Frederick the Great had a reputation as the world's best soldiers. "The conduct of England in hiring German mercenaries to subdue the essentially English population beyond the Atlantic made reconciliation hopeless, and the Declaration of Independence inevitable," declared the British historian Lecky. "It was idle for the Americans to have any further scruple about calling in foreigners to assist them when England herself set the example."[8]

Before the first reports reached America, the colonists had been worked up to an emotional pitch by the destruction of Falmouth. This Massachusetts seaport, later renamed Portland when it became a part of Maine, aroused the wrath of Captain Henry Mowat of the British frigate *Canceau* by its zeal in enforcing provisions of the Association. His indignation was as much personal as official when he anchored in the harbor with the *Canceau* and two smaller warships on October 17, 1775. Nevertheless, some responsibility on the part of Admiral Thomas Graves is indicated by Mowat's announcement that he had it "in orders to execute a just punishment on the Town of Falmouth. In the name of which authority, I previously warn you to remove, without delay, the human species out of the said town, for which purpose I give you the time of two hours."[9]

A committee persuaded him to postpone the bombardment until the following morning. Then the warships pounded the wooden village with "a horrible shower of balls, from three to nine pounds weight, bombs, carcasses, live shells, grape shot and musket balls. . . . As nearly as we can judge," the report of the selectmen continued, "about three-quarters of the buildings . . . are consumed, consisting of about 130 dwelling houses, most of which held two or three families apiece, besides barns, and almost every store and warehouse in town. St. Paul's Church, a large house, not quite finished; a fire engine, almost new; the old Town house, and the publick library, were all consumed."

This outrage could not be defended even by the Tories. It was cited throughout the colonies as proof that the British ministers had ordered the destruction of all seacoast towns—an unfounded rumor which even the judicious Franklin believed. Only recently he had written to his friend David Hartley in London that "a little time given for cooling on both sides would have excellent effects. But you will goad and provoke us. You despise us too much; and you are insensible of the Italian adage, that 'there is no little enemy.' "[10]

It is not often that a victorious enemy becomes a hero to his captives, but the journals of the prisoners at Quebec are unanimous in their praises of Carleton. On February 1, 1776, after a month of confinement in the Seminary of Laval, Lieutenant Heth wrote in his diary:

> His Excellency [Governor Carleton] made us a Compliment of a Hogshead of exceeding good Porter—& his Aid de camp—Mr. Lanadier (a Can'n. Gent.) assur'd us his cellar was full of the same—that we were very welcom to what we wanted & beg'd we would send for any Quantity. . . . The Right Revd. Father John Oliver Brian[d] Bishop of the Diocese of Quebec presented us with 2 Hhds. [of] wine called Black Snap—6 Loav's Sugar—& 12 lb. Tea—the Latter of which we returned with a polite note—thanking him for his marks of Generosity, & Humanity—But that in Justice to our *much injured Country*—we had solemnly avow'd the disuse of Tea.[11]

The invaders had no more redoubtable opponent than Bishop Briand, who used his influence to keep the Canadian clergy on the British side. But his enmity was not personal, and the journals of the prisoners testify to kindnesses which rose above political or religious differences. "I was removed to the Hôtel Dieu, sick of the Scarlet Fever," recorded Lieutenant Nichols on March 10th, "and placed under the care of the Mother Abbess, where I had fresh provisions and good attendance. For several days the nuns sat up with me, four at a time every two hours. . . . When I think of my captivity, I shall never forget the time spent among the nuns, who treated me with so much humanity."[12]

Courtesies extended to enemy officers were not uncommon in this age, but Carleton and his staff did not neglect the enlisted men confined in the Jesuits' College. Charles Porterfield, a sergeant in Morgan's company, noted in his diary that "Major Carleton (brother of his Excellency), from his familiar, open and engaging behavior has prejudiced us in his favor. He appeared to feel for and sympathize with us. Every sentence he uttered . . . displayed the polite gentleman and scholar. As a proof of his delicacy and feeling, he replied in a low voice to Col. Caldwell, officer of the day, who was repeating something to us disagreeable and irritating: 'O, Sir, you should not say anything to them that is disagreeable—they are all our brethren.' "[13]

The beneficiaries of the governor's kindness were not naïve. They shrewdly suspected that political motives were mixed with his generosity, making him a dangerous adversary as well as a sincere humanitarian. Rumors soon reached the little American army outside the walls that Carleton had promised to outfit his prisoners with warm clothing and send them home at the earliest opportunity. These reports did not improve the morale of Arnold's disheartened men, who could do little until reinforcements arrived. Commanding from a hospital bed, after being carried back with a ball through his leg, that officer took charge of the situation with spirit and resolution. Nor did he neglect his own interests in reports which won him advancement to the rank of brigadier. "My detachment had carried the first battery," he wrote to Washington on January 14th. "My being wounded, and the loss of their guides, retarded them much."[14] But there is no mention of the part taken by Morgan, who had to wait a year for promotion.

Congress responded with energy after news of the defeat reached Philadelphia. On January 19th it was resolved "that the American army in Canada be reinforced with all possible dispatch."[15] The following day President Hancock informed Washington that "the battalion from Pennsylvania, and that from New Jersey, will set forward the beginning of next week. . . . I am directed to request you to dispatch, from the camp at Cambridge, one battalion, if the service there will permit you to spare one, with orders to march, with the greatest expedition possible, to Canada."[16]

The commander in chief was also asked to call upon the executives of Massachusetts, Connecticut and New Hampshire to send a regiment from each of those colonies. General Wooster, as the ranking officer in Canada, could spare no men from his force at Montreal. The members of Congress hoped that two regiments of Canadians could be raised; but in one of his last letters Montgomery warned Schuyler that the invaders could not expect much help from the *habitants* until they had "a force in the country sufficient to insure it against any attempts."[17]

The coldest winter in years and a smallpox epidemic added to the hardships of Arnold's few hundred men trying to blockade Quebec. Rifleman Henry suspected germ warfare, for he had no doubt that the disease was introduced by "the indecorous yet fascinating arts of the enemy. . . . A number of women loaded with the infection of the small-pox, came into our cantonments."[18]

Nearly a hundred men were in the hospital on February 27th, and within the next three weeks the sick list increased fourfold. The first reinforcements did not appear until March 8th after a long midwinter march by way of Albany and Montreal. At the end of the month the total amounted to about 1,400—a figure subject to daily reduction as the new soldiers caught the disease. By this time it had become a question as to which side could first be brought up to decisive strength. Governor Carleton had sent dispatches on November 22nd, three days after he reached Quebec, appealing for British aid. The *Nancy* made a remarkably fast crossing, for Lieutenant Pringle had an interview with Lord George Germain in London only three days after Christmas. The war minister not only promised to send relief but kept his word handsomely by winning the race of reinforcements.

This outcome could not be charged to neglect on the part of Congress. General John Thomas was appointed to the command of the army in Canada and assured that its numbers would be increased to 9,000 troops. When he arrived at Quebec on May 1st, however, the force consisted of 1,900 men. "Only one thousand were fit for duty, officers included," he wrote to Washington; "the remainder were invalids, chiefly confined with the small pox. Three hundred of the effective were soldiers whose enlistments expired on the 15th ultimo, many of whom peremtorily refused duty, and all were very importunate to return home. . . . In all our magazines there were but one hundred and fifty pounds of powder, no more than six days' provisions."[19]

Every effort had been made to send troops and supplies, but the difficulties may be imagined from the fact that several feet of snow still covered the ground late in April. Wooster and Schuyler had quarreled with such heat that each appealed to Congress for vindication. And when Wooster reached Quebec on April 1st as temporary commander, Arnold discovered the very next day that the condition of his wound made it necessary to take a leave of absence in Montreal.

Some progress had been achieved in spite of dissensions and difficulties. Again the rebels found the enemy their best source of supply when cannon captured at St. Johns provided the means of bombarding Quebec from the other side of the river. Red-hot shot from the 24-pounders damaged the *Hunter* and *Lizard* and set fire to most of the houses of the Lower Town. The American blockade, loose as it was, had at least kept the garrison from receiving supplies of fresh food in any quantity. Thomas arrived in time to inherit the troubles of his predecessors, but he could console himself that the failures of winter transport had been largely to blame. Within the next few weeks both reinforcements and powder could be expected by the middle-aged Massachusetts general, who had been a physician after serving under Amherst in the last war.

No soldier of 1776 was more deserving or unfortunate. For London proved to be nearer than Philadelphia when it came to a test of ocean transport as compared to the long overland route through a frozen wilderness. On May 2nd, the day after his arrival, Thomas learned that fifteen British ships were beating their way up the river at the risk of being sunk by huge cakes of ice. On the 5th he had the moral courage to advocate an immediate retirement even though it was not a decision calculated to make him popular at home. Wooster and the other officers agreed at a council of war on the advisability of withdrawing to Three Rivers, "where there would be a prospect of resisting with success." Preparations began that same evening, though it could hardly be anticipated that the British ships would appear for several days. At dawn the invalids and cannon were being loaded into the bateaux when Thomas had the dismaying news that his scouts had sighted the British frigate *Surprise* behind Orleans Island. The *Isis* and *Martin* were not far behind, and early in the morning the warships began landing troops from their anchorage at the mouth of the St. Charles.

A favorable change in the wind during the night had made possible one of the most daring exploits of the British navy. Carleton himself had not supposed that the fleet could get through the ice before the 10th, and he responded with boldness and energy worthy of the occasion. At noon, before the Americans recovered from their disorder, he led a sally with the first grenadiers and marines landed from the frigates, plus a few hundred garrison troops and four fieldpieces. The attackers, as Carleton reported to Germain, "marched out of the ports of St. Louis and St. Johns to see what those mighty boasters were about. They were found very busy in their preparations for a retreat. A few shots being exchanged, the line marched forward, and the plains were soon cleared of those plunderers; all their artillery, military stores, scaling ladders, petards, &c., &c., were abandoned."[20]

Thomas could not have been caught at a more awkward moment. His Canadian teamsters had fled at the first sight of the ships, leaving him without wheeled transport in the midst of chaos. A few hours of grace might have allowed him to make an orderly even if hasty retreat, but Carleton took full advantage of the fortunes of war. The few hundred Americans drawn up on the Plains of Abraham hardly paused to pull a trigger before taking to their heels. "The whole of our Army fled that were able to travel," reported Lieutenant Eleazer Cleghorn without offering excuses. "The sick we left behind to share the fate of being killed or taken prisoners."[21]

So sudden was the disaster that the victors found General Thomas' dinner still warm on the table at headquarters. If Carleton had realized the extent of the panic, he might perhaps have destroyed the routed army. But he remained in battle formation long enough to offer an escape to fugitives streaming westward on both sides of the St. Lawrence. It was to the credit of the exhausted rebels that Thomas rallied enough of them at noon the next day to beat off British marines landed from the warships pushing up the river to cut off the retreat.

At a council of war on the 7th the American officers decided to fall back as far as Sorel. At least the bulk of the army had been saved, and order was restored as the retreat continued. The losses, in addition to the several hundred invalids left behind, consisted chiefly of sick men who had died of exposure.

As a humanitarian, Carleton addressed "his Majesty's deluded subjects of the neighboring Provinces, labouring under wounds and divers disorders, [who] are dispersed in the adjacent woods and Parishes, and in great danger of perishing for want of proper assistance." Hospital care was offered to all such fugitives in the governor's proclamation of May 10th. "And lest a consciousness of past offenses should deter these miserable wretches from receiving that assistance which their distressed condition may require, I hereby make known to them that as soon as their health is restored, they shall have free liberty to return to their respective Provinces."[22]

Some measure of Carleton's humanity and energy might have profited the British generals at Boston. Although they would have been horrified at the thought of civilized foes desecrating St. Mary-le-Bow, the invaders made firewood out of the Old North Chapel, a Boston landmark for a century. The fate of South Church was recorded in Deacon Newell's diary: "The pulpit, pews, and seats, all cut to pieces, and carried off in the most savage manner as can be expressed. . . . The beautiful carved pew, with the silk furniture, of Deacon Hubbard's, was taken down . . . and made a hog-stye. The above was effected by the solicitation of General Burgoyne."[23]

The gutted building served as a stable and riding school after the floors were covered with earth, and the gallery became a refreshment booth for the sale of liquors. Faneuil Hall was turned into a theater, while the churches on Brattle and Hollis streets were occupied by the soldiers as barracks.

If the redcoats at Boston had been trying to incite the maximum of resentment, they could hardly have improved upon their conduct during the siege. For the British army of this age included a great many undesirable officers who owed their rank to political influence or money. The practice of buying and selling commissions resulted in such farcical situations as the one mentioned by the commander at Dublin in a report to his superiors, "I am extremely concerned that no purchaser can be found for Lieutenant Colonel B——'s commission; for, besides his infirmities, I have his own word, added to the testimony of other people, that he is mad."[24] The Guards officers were younger sons of wealthy and titled families who could afford not only the original price but also the ensuing social expenses of the best commissions. Yet this same system also gave the army some of its most able leaders—those hard-working line officers, sons of rural squires or village parsons, who lacked the means to buy their way into the higher ranks.

There was no place in the army of a conquering empire for a coward or weakling. The death of a Guards officer on some distant battlefield often became the most splendid moment of a stupid life dedicated to unimaginative vices. Of all these dissipations the one most destructive of military merit was the gambling which obsessed all ranks from subaltern to general. The stakes were high enough so that a night's losses could ruin a line officer of moderate family wealth; and though a cheat risked disgrace, there can be no doubt that card sharpers plucked some of the victims.

Months of corroding idleness during the siege of Boston brought out some of the worst qualities of the gentlemen in the handsome waistcoats. An untrained rebel army lacking even gunpowder showed more aggressiveness. Although the Americans had no trained military engineers, they seized Lechmere Point in December and strongly fortified that advanced position as a springboard for an attack on the redcoats penned up in Boston. Colonel Jeduthan Baldwin of Brookfield could not have passed a test in theory but he knew how to get the most in practice from country lads working with pick and spade under fire. A few of the entries in his journal are enough to show the daily routine of troops who built redoubts and batteries on the peninsula within easy artillery range of the enemy lines both on the Boston and Charlestown sides:

Dec. 17. Went to work on Leachmor point . . . & when the Fog cleared away we had a Very havey fire from the Ships, & from Boston but thro' Divine goodness we Recd but little damage. . . . Workt all night, got our men covered.

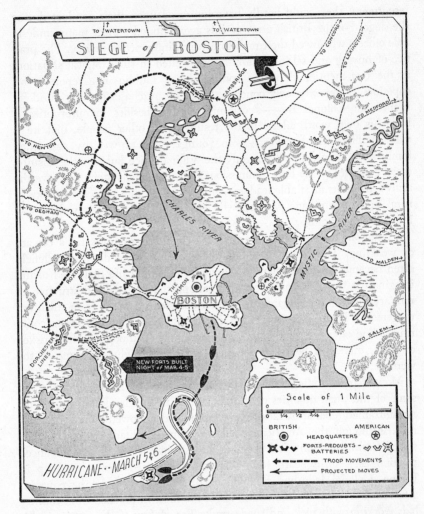

Dec. 19. A No. of Shot & Shells were thrown from Bunker Hill and from Boston at us. . . . Many of the Shot lodged in our Brest work, & some of the Bumbs Brok high in the are & 2 near our works, but no Mischief done this day.

Dec. 20. We recd a No. of 24 lb. shot from Boston into our breast-work & others Just went over all in a direct line hit the wall. Several Bumbs birst in the air. . . .[25]

A detachment of a hundred riflemen guarded against British raids, but Baldwin found the weather his worst enemy by the middle of January: "At Leachmore pint the ground was frozen 22 inches Deep as hard as a rock, & in one night it frose in the trench 8 inches deep so that we pryed up cakes of frosen Earth 9 feet Long & 3 feet broad."

The Brookfield farmer persisted until two redoubts were completed as the spearhead of a system of fortifications extending from Roxbury nearly to the British lines at Charlestown. So strong was this chain that the enemy's passive defense cannot be charged to lethargy alone. General Howe had good reason to believe that the rebel works could not be stormed without frightful losses, though his officers found the situation humiliating. "If something is not speedily done," grumbled a British captain in an intercepted letter, "his Brittanick Majesty's American dominions will probably be confined within a very narrow compass. The Rebel Army is not brave, I believe, but it is agreed on all hands that their artillery officers are at least equal to our own. In the number of shells they threw last night, not above three failed. This morning we threw four, and three of them burst in the air."[26]

Some of Washington's most anxious moments were caused by his own men rather than the enemy. On December 10th the enlistments of several Connecticut regiments expired, and they considered it their right to go home. The sturdy spirit of the Yankees had its drawbacks, as General Charles Lee learned when he tried to bully the men into changing their minds. "We was ordered to form a hollow square," recorded Private Simeon Lyman of Sharon, "and General Lee came in and the first words was, 'Men, I do not know what to call you, [you] are the worst of all creatures,' and flung and curst and swore at us, and said if we would not stay he would order us to go on Bunker Hill [held by the enemy] and if we would not go he would order the riflemen to fire at us."[27]

Anyone familiar with the New England character might have informed Lee that he had taken the wrong approach. On December 2nd he posted an abusive notice intended to shame the men into remaining four more weeks. "Some was mad and said they would not stay 4 days," Lyman's journal continues, "and the paper was took down as soon as it was dark, and another put up that General Lee was a fool."

Washington as well as Lee found it hard to realize that the truculent independence of the Yankees extended to their private lives. A majority were laborers or small farmers who could not serve more than a few months in the army without working a hardship on their families. They were not men who could enjoy the bread of charity, and when an enlistment expired they believed that it was the turn of some other volunteer. Thus it was that the Connecticut troops left Cambridge in a defiant mood after Lee branded them as "deserters now sneaking homeward to infate [infect] their relations and neighbors with cowardice."

Private Lyman made no apologies in his journal. Upon his arrival at Sharon he "ointed for the itch and had a fine wrastle ov it." Then he went to work as a farmhand without worrying about the gap left in the rebel lines.

General Washington had to do the worrying. During the next few weeks, as he put it, "the same desire of retiring into a chimney corner seized the troops of New Hampshire, Rhode Island and Massachusetts, so soon as their time expired, as had wrought upon those of Connecticut." All four New England colonies stirred themselves to keep the ranks filled with fresh troops, so that the commander in chief could report to President Hancock on January 4, 1776: "It is not in the pages of history, perhaps, to furnish a case like ours. To maintain a post within musket shot of the enemy, for six months together, without powder, and at the same time to disband one army, and recruit another, within that distance of twenty-odd British regiments, is more, probably, than ever was attempted."[28]

Washington's sense of duty sometimes operated more strongly than his sense of humor. On January 14th he expressed his disgust in a letter to Colonel Joseph Reed: "I have often thought how much happier I should have been, if, instead of accepting the command under such circumstances, I had taken my musket on my shoulder and entered the ranks; or, if I could have justified the measure to posterity and my own conscience, had retired to the back country and lived in a wigwam."

At any rate the army weathered the crisis with little shrinkage. Returns of January 24th showed a total of 17,633 troops as compared to a British strength (including marines and armed seamen) of slightly less than 11,000.[29] Although the redcoats pretended to hold the pick and spade in disdain, they had strong defensive works on Boston Neck and the Charlestown peninsula. Congress hinted at the desirability of attacking the town, and Washington himself favored the idea after the ice provided a bridge. But time would prove that his subordinates were justified in voting against it at another council of war.

The tall, genial British commander was a better tactician than disciplinarian. When too much leniency led to unsoldierly conduct on the part of officers as well as men, he flew to the opposite extreme. Punishments of five hundred lashes were imposed for pillaging which sometimes had the connivance of officers. Not even the female camp followers, as procurers of liquor or receivers of stolen goods, were spared from public floggings. Throughout the winter Howe's orderly book was filled with such entries as the injunction of January 13, 1776:

> The commanding officer is surprised to find the necessity of repeating orders that long since ought to have been complied with, as the men on all duties appear in the following manner, viz: hair not smooth and badly powdered, several without slings to their firelocks, hats not bound, pouches in a shameful and dirty condition, no frills to their shirts, and their linen very dirty, leggings hanging in a slovely manner about their knees, some men without uniform stocks, and their arms and accoutrements by no means as clean as they ought to be. These unsoldierly neglects must be immediately remedied.[30]

As usual, the Americans seized most of their arms and munitions from the enemy. Washington had not been authorized by Congress to plan sea operations, nor had he been forbidden. In the summer of 1775 he went ahead on his own responsibility to encourage the arming of schooners in Marblehead, Gloucester and other seaports blighted by the Fisheries Act. By the end of October six small privateers were preying upon enemy shipping with astonishing boldness. The *Lee*, commanded by Captain John Manly, brought in a single prize the following month which may almost be said to have saved the army. Washington sent four companies of infantry to Cape Ann to guard the captured British storeship *Nancy* and transport munitions which included 2,000 muskets, 30,000 round-shot, 100,000 flints, 30 tons of musket balls and a 13-inch brass mortar soon to be christened with rum as the *Congress*.

Not all the American efforts were so fortunate, and Captain Martingale was taken as a prisoner to England after he surrendered the *Washington*. But in February a squadron of four armed schooners flew the pine-tree flag with its green emblem on a white background over the motto "Appeal to Heaven." Captain Manly, as the commander, "in the course of four months intercepted stores sufficient to have victualed his squadron many times over, and almost enough liquor to float his little flagship."[31] Among his prizes were "a vessel laden with a hundred butts of porter: a brigantine whose cargo included a hundred and thirty-nine hogsheads of rum, and a hundred cases of right Geneva; a sloop with Indian corn, potatoes and oats; two Whitehaven ships with coal and potatoes; two large merchantmen carrying provisions for the British garrison."

Congress passed resolutions in November which are commemorated as the beginnings of the United States Navy and Marine Corps.[32] But the Continental Army and its commander deserve the credit for having set in motion the first active operations against the enemy at sea.

The British naval activities were so feeble that Howe and Burgoyne cannot be blamed for complaining. It is taking no glory away from the American privateers to attribute their success in part to the bad feeling between two branches of the British service. Vice-Admiral Augustus Keppel, like Amherst, had declined to serve against America. His colleague Graves contributed little during the war's first year except the bombarding of civilians and raiding of the coast for sheep and cattle. "How is the glory of Britain departed!" a Philadelphia newspaper jeered. "Her navy which not long since was the terror of many nations, is now employed in cutting the throats of his Majesty's loyal subjects, and SHEEP STEALING! Felons, indeed!"[33]

The prizes taken by rebel vessels were supplemented by captured guns of Ticonderoga brought over the mountains by Colonel Henry Knox in ox-drawn sleds—8 brass mortars, 6 iron mortars, 2 iron howitzers, 13 brass cannon, 26 iron cannon, a ton of lead and a barrel of flints.[34] Corpulence only seemed to increase the energy of a born cannoneer with the basso profundo voice of a 32-pounder. In his enthusiasm the recent Boston bookseller promised Washington "a noble train of artillery," and it proved indeed to be the key to the long deadlock at Boston.

The commander in chief hastened to make use of his new guns. On February 26th secret preparations were begun for a great combined offensive and defensive operation. The rebel bombardment opened on March 2nd from Cobble Hill, Roxbury and Lechmere Point. Although two 13-inch mortars burst, Knox continued for 48 hours to pound the British on both the Charlestown and Boston sides. During the moonlight night of the 4th a total of 144 shot and 13 shells were fired to mask the movements of 2,000 Americans who seized Dorchester Heights. The frozen ground offered so much resistance that fascines and twisted bundles of hay were used to finish two forts providing a defense against small arms. Howe, upon viewing the spectacle, is said to have exclaimed, "The rebels have done more in one night, than my whole army would have done in months."[35]

Washington did not err in supposing that his opponent would feel compelled to attack a position commanding both the harbor and the town.

The very date had been chosen because it was believed that the anniversary of the Boston Massacre would inspire the defenders. "Perhaps there never was so much work done in so short a time," wrote Heath in his *Memoirs*. "The adjoining orchards were cut down to make the abattis; and a very curious and novel mode of defence was added to these works. The hills on which they were erected were steep, and clear of trees and bushes. Rows of barrels filled with earth were placed round the works. They presented only the appearance of strengthening the works; but the real design was, in case the enemy made an attack, to have rolled them down the hill. They would have descended with such increasing velocity, as must have thrown the assailants into the utmost confusion, and have killed and wounded great numbers."[36]

Washington did not propose to content himself with a defense of Dorchester Heights. While the British were attacking, he planned to embark 4,000 troops from the mouth of the Charles in barges for an assault on Boston under cover of a cannonade from Lechmere Point and the floating batteries.

British preparations went so far that Howe ordered 2,400 men to embark in transports to Fort William for the attempt on the new rebel works. The ensuing double battle, with each side taking both the offensive and defensive, might conceivably have been the bloodiest of the war. But the weather intervened on the afternoon of March 5th with a gale of almost hurricane force. Heavy winds and rains made the water too rough for small boats all the next day. This gave the rebels an additional 36 hours for the strengthening of their Dorchester Heights fortifications. So impressive were the results that Howe feared the consequences of an attack. On the 7th he called a council of officers and made an address explaining his painful decision to save the army at the cost of evacuating the town. The long siege of Boston had ended in an anticlimax instead of a dramatic clash, but it was nonetheless a great victory for Washington and his army.

Chapter 6

Sir Peter Parker's Breeches

THE British generals excused the evacuation on the grounds that they had long wished to withdraw from Boston. But this fact could not dim the importance of the outcome. For the rag, tag and bobtail which Congress created into the Continental Army had not disintegrated as a penalty of inexperience and material poverty. On the contrary, it had shown at least as good discipline as the British regulars, and more aggressiveness. At the finish the invaders had been forced to choose between evacuation or fighting at a disadvantage, and Washington's victory gleams the more brightly because it was won without bloodshed.

Five days after their fortification of Dorchester Heights the rebels put more pressure on Howe. In another night surprise a detachment occupied Nook's Hill, still nearer to Boston, where a battery might make the town and harbor untenable. The artillery fire that night was the heaviest of the war up to this time, with more than 800 shot and shell being exchanged before the rebels suspended the operation. Abigail Adams, destined to be the wife of one President and mother of another, lay awake at her Braintree home and listened to the guns. "A most terrible and incessant cannonade from half-after eight till six this morning," she wrote on March 10th to her husband, attending the Continental Congress at Philadelphia.[1] The night after the seizure of Dorchester Heights she "went to bed about twelve, and rose again a little after one. I could no more sleep than if I had been in the engagement; the rattle of the windows, the jar of the house, the continual roar of twenty-four-pounders, and the bursting of shells, give us such ideas, and realize a scene to us of which we could scarcely form any conception."

Invalidism was the fashion among folk of quality in that day, and both John Adams and his wife took pride in their ailments. But she did

88

not react to the cannonade with a fragility becoming an eighteenth-century lady whose home and four small children might soon fall to the invaders. "The sound, I think, is one of the grandest in nature," she confessed, "and is of the true species of the sublime." And the next day, while the issue was still in doubt, she added, "I hope to give you joy of Boston, even if it is in ruins, before I send this away."

No official negotiation took place between the opposing commanders, though a perfect understanding existed on both sides. Howe tacitly consented to spare the town on condition that Washington allow his army to depart in peace, and both kept the gentleman's agreement as faithfully as if it had been signed and sealed. Not a single rebel cannonball disturbed the redcoats in the confusion of leavetaking, but on the night of the 16th the Americans returned to Nook's Hill. Without replying to the enemy fire, they threw up earthworks and a battery emplacement. These preparations proved needless when reports reached Washington the next day that the British regiments had begun their embarkation.

American scouts discovered wooden sentries guarding Bunker Hill after a cautious approach on the morning of March 17th. The following day a detachment found Boston itself evacuated, and before nightfall Washington started the riflemen and several New England regiments on the march toward New York, where he anticipated that the next blow would fall. General Howe contemplated nothing more warlike, however, than a withdrawal by sea to the British base at Halifax. In the haste of embarkation his men left great piles of shot, shells and other munitions. Even the cannon had been so imperfectly spiked that Yankee blacksmiths restored many of them to usefulness.

For these gifts the victors could thank the preoccupation of the British with pillage. Howe threatened in his orders of March 14th "that the first soldier who is caught plundering will be hanged on the spot." But too often the officers who should have enforced discipline had reason to wink at the violations. Boston was virtually sacked by bands of soldiers, sailors and Tories who prowled the streets, breaking into shops and carrying off the spoils without much interference. Stolen property worth thousands of pounds added to the dangerous overcrowding of the ships taking into exile a thousand Massachusetts loyalists as well as the soldiers. A contemporary account mentions that in a single small cabin thirty-seven men, women and children "were obliged to pig together on the floor, there being no berths."[2]

One of the most terrible maritime disasters of history might have resulted if the fleet on its way to Halifax had been scattered by a storm such as the gale which prevented the attack on Dorchester Heights. A brigantine did run aground on Cape Cod and the Americans recaptured plunder worth £100,000. But the fleet as a whole reached Halifax safely, leaving behind a few British warships in Nantasket road to protect incoming vessels which had not been warned of Howe's departure. They were outwitted before the end of March by Captain James Mugford, of the *Franklin*, who took a storeship loaded with 1,500 barrels of gunpowder.

Earlier in the month the privateer *Yankee Hero* made Newburyport with an enemy brig of 200 tons burden. Captain Manly added two more vessels to his list of captures, both of them loaded with munitions and provisions for Howe's army at Boston. Soon the Continental armed schooners became so bold that Mugford sailed past the enemy warships in broad daylight to bring the British transport *Hope* into Boston harbor. When his prize grounded, the British attempted to recapture her by sending 200 marines and sailors in longboats armed with swivels. The Marblehead captain fired grapeshot at close range while his men lined the decks of the *Franklin* with muskets and pikes to repel boarders. They sank two longboats and claimed with the usual exaggeration to have slain 70 foemen. "Great execution was done with the spears," a Philadelphia newspaper reported. "One man, with that weapon, is positive of having killed nine of the enemy."[3] But the victory was bought at the price of a mortal wound received by Mugford, who continued to encourage his men until they beat off the enemy's boats.

News of this little triumph came just at a time when Americans were being shocked out of their overconfidence by the first reports of the rout at Quebec. General John Sullivan, on his way northward with reinforcements, sent Washington a report from Albany on May 18th which goes far toward explaining reverses in Canada. He had searched diligently for two New York regiments which "are said to be in this Quarter, but upon the strictest Enquiry, can be found no where."[4] Sullivan supposed that "they have been employed on their Farms all the Year. . . . I found in Some Companies not a man fit for Duty or Sick present, in Some there was Eleven others Less."

At a strategic base where two regiments could disappear, it is not astonishing that the New Hampshire brigadier should have discovered "a Number of Barrells of Pork that the Waggoners had Taped & Drawn off the Pickle to Lighten their Teams. This Pork must Enevitably be Ruin'd before it can reach Canada."

Philip Schuyler, as the ranking general, had command of the invasion of Canada, though his continual state of invalidism kept him at the Albany base. The war produced no more contradictory character; for he combined some of the best and worst traits of leadership, just as his ailments were both real and imaginary. Schuyler and Arnold were the most quarrelsome officers of a disputatious army, which makes it odd that they remained on such good terms with each other. At the age of forty-three the New York landed proprietor was more of a grand seignior than many of the barons of the Old World. By inheritance from Dutch patroon ancestors as well as marriage ties with the Van Rensselaers, Van Cortlandts and other lordly clans, Schuyler held a domain along the upper Hudson which included villages. He had a mansion at Albany and a country place at Saratoga, and hundreds of tenants looked up to him as patron and lawgiver.

Other rebels of great wealth—Washington, Hancock, Charles Carroll of Carrollton—managed to keep the respect of the man in the ranks. But they never lost a sympathy which the New York aristocrat never gained. His harsh and overbearing ways offended the Yankees who composed the bulk of the reinforcements bound for Canada, and their dislike soon became so bitter as to impair his usefulness. Yet as a delegate to the first Continental Congress, he had shared with the Livingstons the leadership of the radical party in New York. Schuyler deserved well of his country, but his letters are filled with grumbling and self-pity never matched in a war notable for both qualities.

"If Job had been a General in my situation, his memory had not been so famous for patience. . . ." "There never was a man so infamously scandalized and ill treated as I am. . . ."[5] These are samples of the complaints written by an officer utterly lacking in humor, and both Congress and Washington had to beg him at intervals not to resign. As early as December 24, 1775, the patience of the commander in chief seems to have worn a little thin:

> Let me ask you, sir, when is the time for brave men to exert themselves in the cause of liberty and their country, if this is not? . . . God knows there is not a difficulty that you very justly complain of, that I have not, in an eminent degree, experienced—that I am not every day experiencing. But we must bear up against them, and make the best of mankind as they are, since we cannot have them as we wish.[6]

This appeal, plus the supplications of John Hancock, persuaded Schuyler to remain in the service. But he continued to be an emotional bleeder, and his letters convey a dislike of the common soldier which makes it no wonder that he was repaid in kind.

Sullivan also had a thin skin to protect a sensitive ego, and as he journeyed into Canada he could have found the trail of a greater solipsist by the spore of his quarrels. Self-love in the case of Benedict Arnold was a passion too overwhelming to allow a rival. During his first few months in Canada he managed to make enemies of most of his colleagues. Rifleman Henry hinted that after emerging from the Maine wilderness Arnold profited even at the expense of his famished men by withholding provisions. "Morgan, Hendricks and Smith, waited upon the commander in chief, to represent the grievance and obtain redress. Altercation and warm language took place. Smith, with his usual loquacity, told us, that Morgan seemed, at one time, upon the point of striking Arnold. We fared the better for the interview."[7]

Two Yale graduates of 1771 who knew Arnold in New Haven were both violently outspoken against him. In the spring of 1776 Dr. Lewis Beebe wrote prophetically in his journal, "Let execrations be multiplied and accumulated upon that infamous, villainous traitor, by all future generations."[8] He added that "had we a W——n, or a Lee, to take the command from a Sett of Haughty, ambitious aspiring miscreants, who only pride in promotion & honour, we might have hopes of regaining Quebeck." Beebe's classmate John Brown accused Arnold of having treasonable intentions as early as the Ticonderoga expedition. The hero of Chambly and Sorel had been promised a well-earned promotion, but Montgomery died before he could recommend it. His successor not only withheld advancement but justified himself by accusing Brown of plundering the British officers' baggage at Sorel.

Arnold's own financial accounts were never settled. Later it developed that Congress had advanced him $66,671 for expenses in Canada, but he had no explanation for about $55,000 of this amount except his word that he had turned large sums over to subordinates for public use.[9]

Not only Brown but also Major James Easton and Colonel Moses Hazen had reasons for disliking Arnold. It was the misfortune of General Wooster to be caught between two such fires as Arnold and Schuyler, and their hostility ruined the Connecticut veteran. These were some of the feuds that the committee of Congress encountered upon arriving in Montreal on April 29, 1776. Even distance and inclement weather could not prevent the assembly from having observers on the scene of action. Dr. Franklin had been chosen for his diplomatic ability, Samuel Chase for his zeal, and Charles and John Carroll because of their adherence to the Catholic religion. They had not been in Canada two weeks before news came of the rout at Quebec, the retreat to Sorel and the increase in smallpox cases.

"We cannot find words to describe our miserable situation," Chase and Charles Carroll reported to Philadelphia. Yet the commissioners did find blunt and forceful words to convey that the sympathies of the Canadians had been alienated by American indiscipline, pillaging and disrespect for the Catholic faith. Not more than about 450 *habitants* had joined the regiments of Hazen and James Livingston, and in some localities the people armed themselves against the invaders.

The confusion at Chambly was deplored by Dr. Beebe as a military surgeon in a journal entry of May 28th: "Parts of different Regts. arrived from Sorrell, all being ignorant of their destination, but very few general orders, and they usually countermanded within a few hours after given. . . . If ever I had a compassionate feeling for my fellow creatures, who were objects in distress, I think it is this day, to see Large barns filled with men in the very heighth of the small pox and not the least thing, to make them Comfortable, was almost Sufficient to excite the pity of Brutes."[10]

The disillusionment of the commissioners must have been completed by news of the surrender of the Cedars. This was the name of a small American fort about thirty miles west of Montreal, where a sharp bend of the St. Lawrence impeded navigation. Colonel Timothy Bedel was stationed with 390 men and two cannon to hold the strategic gateway to the upper country. The British were so thoroughly beaten in the region that Captain Forster had only 40 regulars, a hundred Canadians and several hundred Indians when he summoned the Cedars to capitulate on May 18th. Bedel had returned to Montreal as a smallpox victim, leaving Major Butterfield in charge with provisions and ammunition for a stout defense. A few rounds of musketry and a brisk sally took all the fighting spirit out of the Indians and Canadians, and Forster had not a single cannon. His force was at the point of disintegrating when he made up for his weakness by a bloodcurdling bluff. His savage allies were determined to massacre the whole garrison, he informed Butterfield, but the "lives and cloathes" of the Americans would be spared if they should "surrender at discretion in half an hour." Incredible as it may seem, the rebel commander agreed over the protests of men who had suffered no casualties.

No excuse could be found for him except the fact that he lay ill with smallpox. His decision was only the beginning of a preposterous series of events which Britons as well as Americans would recall without pride. Bedel had sent a few rebel reinforcements to the Cedars under Major Sherburne, but after a brief skirmish Forster succeeded again with hints that he could not prevent a massacre if the detachment resisted. About a hundred more Americans were added to his bag of captives.

Forster made a daring attempt to capture Montreal after learning that the town had so few defenders. Arnold hastened to the rescue from Sorel with about 600 troops, and the ferocity of the redskins was demonstrated when all but 80 out of some 500 melted away at the threat of a real fight. The British captain had scarcely enough dependable men left to guard his prisoners, but he saved himself by swearing that all would be slaughtered if Arnold enraged the Indians. Several captives actually were tortured and killed, according to American claims, and others were sent to plead with Arnold for the lives of comrades held as hostages rather than prisoners. The British threats were convincing enough so that he agreed to an exchange of the 500 men on equal terms. During the truce agreed upon for their delivery, Forster and his few regulars made their escape.

The Continental Congress, after hearing the evidence on July 10th, was justified in condemning a cartel obtained by such methods.[11] Carleton, who opposed the employment of undisciplined Indians, did not conceal his disgust; but the British ministers refused to give up their gains. In the end Congress had little choice but to consent to the exchange of redcoats taken in fair fight for the victims of the Cedars.

Panic gripped the entire army in Canada as the smallpox prostrated reinforcements a few days after their arrival. Sullivan had proceeded only as far as St. Johns when he wrote to Hancock on May 28th that "no one thing is right. Every thing is in the utmost confusion & almost Every one Frightened at they know not what."[12]

In their fear the soldiers insisted on inoculating themselves, since those who took the disease naturally were in more danger. General Thomas felt it necessary to authorize the process, though it meant the crippling of his army. At the height of the epidemic he caught the infection himself; and on June 2nd, barely a month after taking active command, the unfortunate general died. That same day 3,300 men were reported unfit for duty at Sorel, or about three-fourths of the force in the path of Carleton's advance to sweep the invaders out of Canada. The American commissioners, just starting their homeward journey, had already seen enough to convince them that nothing was left save an orderly retirement. The minimum needs of the army were estimated at a daily 12,000 pounds of both pork and flour, and toward the end of May only half of these provisions reached the front. "Our soldiers," the commissioners reported to Congress before their departure, "will soon be reduced to the dreadful alternative of starving or of plundering the inhabitants."[13]

Since the first of the year the dismal reports from Canada had been offset by good news from every other quarter. Not only had Massachusetts been freed of invaders but the advocates of the royal cause were also cleared out of all four southern colonies.

The progress of the revolt owed as much to the passivity of the loyalists as the energy of the rebels. For the colonists who cast their lot with the mother country were in a peculiar position. Americans by birth and British by sympathy, they could never be fully accepted by either side. They were caught between the upper and nether millstones, and it was a woeful grist ground out by the war.

Americans trusting in the might of Britain were naturally inclined to underrate the momentum of the insurrection. They failed or rather refused to see in the Continental Congress a council doing an excellent job of governing without authorized executive, legislative or tax-levying powers. The Tories predicted that the assembly would soon die a natural death, and they expressed their contempt in doggerel:

> When insects vile emerge to light,
> They take their short inglorious flight,
> Then sink again to native night;
> An emblem of the Congress.

No more clearly did these British sympathizers perceive that the Continental Army, uncouth as its beginnings were, might some day be driving European regulars from the field. This attitude could be charged in some degree to a snobbish conviction of superiority on the part of Americans supporting the king. The candid evidence of history is against them, for a list of the refugees who left Boston with Howe shows a fairly typical cross section of the population. Those who gave their occupations included 102 commissioners, customs officers and other crown officials; 18 clergymen; 213 merchants and tradesmen of Boston; 382 farmers, traders and mechanics; and 105 described vaguely as "persons from the country."[14] Later lists do not justify any assumption that the loyalists were the superiors of the rebels in wealth, education or social position. The chief difference was that nearly all the former royal officeholders—men described as parasites by the rebels—opposed a revolution which cost them their prerogatives.

Another reason for Tory complacency was the moderation of an uprising which succeeded in its aims without executing a single opponent for his political beliefs—a result which sets the American Revolution apart from every other great insurrection of history. Such minor persecutions as tarring and feathering do not make pleasant reading seven generations later. But these episodes, for lack of the mass slaughters found in other revolts, have been much exaggerated both in numbers and consequences. Nor were the rebels responsible for every incident of this sort. British regulars, with the approval of their officers, tarred and feathered a Massachusetts rebel; and the Tories did not handle their opponents with gloves in communities where they could work their will.

Never did moderation pay greater dividends, for both the British and loyalists were lulled into the comfortable delusion that the rebels were lukewarm. A year after Bunker Hill the opponents of the revolt, judging by their writings, had not the faintest idea that it would create a new nation after involving half of Europe in the struggle for independence. So constrained were the rebel leaders that the Continental Congress made no attempt to disarm loyalists until the late date of January 2, 1776. An accompanying resolution urged that the committees "treat all such persons with kindness and attention; to consider them as the inhabitants of a country determined to be free, and to view their errors as proceeding from want of information rather than want of virtue or public spirit."[15]

If most of the Tories were too slow to realize their danger, Lord Dunmore might have been criticized for erring in the opposite direction. The governor of Virginia showed more energy than judgment when he proclaimed martial law in the autumn of 1775 and tried to arm the Negroes against masters upholding the revolt. This was enough to turn all Virginia against him, including slaveowners who might otherwise have fought for the king.

In the early summer, after repeatedly dissolving the House of Burgesses, he was driven out of Williamsburg by Patrick Henry at the head of the Virginia militia. Dunmore took refuge on board a British warship and tried without much success to rally the loyalists and slaves to his standard. In December the patriots won a victory in fifteen minutes, at a cost of one man wounded, that had more influence on history than some of the battles of Frederick the Great. Colonel William Woodford posted his Continentals and Virginia militia behind earthworks at the end of a causeway from the bridge over the south branch of the Elizabeth River. Dunmore had a small fort on the other bank which commanded the road to Norfolk, twelve miles away. As an apostle of vigorous action, he ordered Captain Fordyce to storm the rebel works with 60 grenadiers and about 230 loyalists and armed slaves. John Marshall, the future chief justice, was present as a twenty-year-old lieutenant. He praised Woodford's plan of posting a detachment behind a ridge to fire on the flank of the enemy column. Marshy ground made it necessary for the attackers to drag their two fieldpieces over the causeway, and American muskets took a heavy toll. "As is the practice with raw troops," wrote Marshall, "the bravest rushed to the works, where, regardless of order, they kept up a heavy fire on the front of the British column."[16] Fordyce fell at the head of his men, whereupon the loyalists and Negroes fled in wild confusion. They were pursued to the gates of their own fort by counterattacking rebels who inflicted severe losses.

The "battle" of Great Bridge, insignificant as it was from a viewpoint of numbers, forced Dunmore to take refuge again on the warships in Norfolk harbor. Woodford advanced into a town ranking as the metropolis of Virginia with its 6,000 population, and the royal governor struck back by ordering a bombardment.

The British, according to intercepted letters, went about their work with enthusiasm. "The detested town of Norfolk is no more!" exulted a midshipman serving on the *Otter*. "Its destruction happened on New-Year's day! About four in the afternoon the signal was given on the *Liverpool*, when a dreadful cannonading began from the three ships, which lasted until it was too hot for the Rebels to stand on their wharves. Our boats now landed and set fire to the town in several places. It burnt fiercely all night, and the next day. . . . No more of Norfolk remains than about twelve houses, which have escaped the flames."[17]

The civilians fled without loss of life, but Colonel Robert Howe of the Continentals reported: "I cannot enter into the melancholy consideration of the women and children running through a crowd of shot to get out of the town; some of them with children at their breasts. . . . Does it not call for vengeance, both from God and man?"[18]

Dunmore could hardly have made a greater contribution to the revolt. So few friends remained to him that he soon returned in disgust to

England. After his departure the wealthiest and most vulnerable of the thirteen colonies was to be left in peace, barring a few raids, during the next five years.

The rebels gained control of North Carolina in an action strikingly similar to Great Bridge. This colony had a large share of the recent immigrants who were more likely than native Americans to side with the British. A civil war atmosphere had prevailed since 1771, when citizens calling themselves the Regulators tried to put an end to embezzlements by crown officials amounting to half the public funds. They were beaten in the battle of the Alamance and their leaders hanged, but many of the old antagonisms added to the new quarrel between loyalists and patriots.

Governor Josiah Martin assured the king that he could crush the "infatuated rebels" with some aid from the mother country.[19] He promised to raise a force of the Scottish Highlanders who had formed colonies in several counties. As heirs of the cause of Prince Charles Edward, they had little reason to love the House of Hanover; but the royal governor needed only to remind them that they held their lands direct from the crown. He planned to march his small army to Cape Fear, where troops were to be landed from the fleet commanded by Sir Peter Parker.

The British ministers specified January as the time, but the 1,200 Highlanders under Donald McDonald did not approach Wilmington until the following month. Even so, they were too early by weeks for a junction with redcoats who arrived in April, after three storm-tossed months at sea. The kilted warriors had meanwhile been routed at Moore's Creek on February 27, 1776.

This is another of the Revolutionary actions with results out of all proportion to the small casualty list. The Scots were wearing the plaids and carrying the claymores of 1745, when their fathers swept across England and terrified London. But the outcome in 1776 would indicate that in spite of the pressure put upon them by Martin, they had not forgotten that George III was the nephew of "Butcher" Cumberland, their foeman of the Jacobite rebellion. At any rate, they had no heart for a fight which ended with 30 Highlanders killed or wounded and 850 captured by rebels who lost two men wounded.

Only overconfidence or imbecility can explain the dawn attack ordered by McDonald's officers over a bridge from which the planks had been removed. Colonel Richard Caswell, until lately a member of the Continental Congress, waited on the other bank with about 1,000 militia behind earthworks. When the first Scots came within thirty paces, making their way precariously over the stringers, the rebel fire stopped them cold. "The insurgents retreated with the greatest precipitation," a New York newspaper asserted, "leaving behind them some of their wagons, &c. They cut their horses out of the wagons, and mounted three upon a horse. Many of them fell into the creek and were drowned. . . . The battle lasted three minutes."[20]

Colonel Caswell reported that his men captured "fifteen hundred Rifle-Guns, all of them excellent pieces; two Medicine Chests, immediately from England, one of them valued at three hundred pounds Sterling; one box, containing half Johanneses and English Guineas; thirteen wagons, with complete sets of Horses; 850 common Soldiers, taken prisoners, disarmed and discharged."[21] In a proclamation translated into Gaelic, the North Carolina Provincial Congress apologized for sending the leaders of the Highlanders to other colonies for safekeeping:

> Justice demanded it at our hands; and in the anguish of our hearts we lament the sad necessity which the frailties of our fellow-beings have allotted to our share; still, we wish the reformation of those who, in this unhappy contest, are severed from us. . . . To these we administer this consolation, that they may rest assured that no wanton acts of cruelty, no severity, shall be exercised to the prisoners; no restraints shall be imposed upon them, but what shall be necessary to prevent their using their liberty to the injury of the friends of America.[22]

It must often have enraged the loyalists to be addressed sorrowfully as sinners whose conversion to the true political faith was desired. But the "sanctimonious rebels" were not hypocrites. Their strength lay in the firm conviction of a righteous cause, and it is noteworthy that the victors of Moore's Creek provided for the destitute families of prisoners. Such treatment, plus a thorough exposure to rebel propaganda, won many of the Highlanders to the American side and kept others neutral. Not until 1781 would the patriots again find it needful to fight on their own soil.

The evangelists of the revolt in South Carolina harangued audiences in frontier meeting houses. A bristling Old Testament text often served to add force to speeches warning that the Tories "have practiced every art, fraud, and misrepresentation, to raise in this province an opposition to the voice of America."[23] Patriots armed by the Lord of Hosts saw no inconsistency in calling their opponents "traitors" as well as "tools of an abandoned Administration." The backwoods people were exhorted to oppose a "hellish plan" to enslave the freemen of the colony.

Loyalists of South Carolina and Georgia were known as scopholites—usually shortened to scophs or scofes—after a leader named Colonel Scophil, described with obvious prejudice as "an illiterate, stupid, noisy blockhead." The Committee of Safety did not make the mistake of underrating this faction, and its missionary work came in the nick of time. For the armada of Sir Peter Parker, after missing its rendezvous in North Carolina, swooped down upon Charleston in the late spring of 1776 with overwhelming land and sea forces.

Three deposed governors stood on the quarterdeck of the *Bristol* as the warships and transports anchored within sight of the metropolis of the South. Sir James Wright of Georgia found it depressing to have been overthrown by "a parcel of the lowest People, chiefly Carpenters, Shoemakers, Blacksmiths."[24] Governor Martin of North Carolina had not yet recovered from the shock of Moore's Creek. But the most resolute of all was Sir William Campbell of South Carolina, who had a vision. He saw the expedition as the opening wedge of a campaign for the winning of the South. The capture of Charleston—which he already counted as accomplished—would be the signal for a general uprising of the loyalists all the way from the Savannah to the Potomac. While they helped to conquer the seacoast, the Cherokees armed by royal agents would be terrorizing the frontier with torch and tomahawk. Germain had been impressed by the plan, and the zeal of Sir Henry Clinton led him to keep his 2,000 troops in the campaign after they were ordered to reinforce General Howe at New York.

Congress, warned long in advance, showed its anxiety by sending as many Continental troops as could be spared. The defense of the seaport was entrusted to General Charles Lee, believed by many patriots to be the foremost American soldier from a viewpoint of professional attainments. But the rank and file placed their trust in a forty-six-year-old local leader, William Moultrie. Over the fort soon to be named in his honor, he flew a blue flag designed by him with a crescent in the upper left corner and the word "Liberty." This has been called the first American battle flag, though there are good arguments for the pine-tree flag or the rattlesnake flag with its motto "Don't Tread on Me."

The war produced no more bizarre figure than the recent British colonel. Seldom seen without a few dogs of dubious manners, Lee also offended with his slovenly dress and sharp tongue. Stooped and gangling, homely to the point of being grotesque, the man was undoubtedly a little mad. Yet the blunt Moultrie paid him generous tribute: "His presence gave us great spirits. . . . It was thought by many that his coming among us was equal to a reinforcement of 1,000 men, and I believe it was, because he taught us to think lightly of the enemy and gave a spur to all our actions."[25]

Military amateurs are all too likely to waste powder, and the defenders of Charleston had but a fraction of the amount needed. Lee made it his mission to pound in a lesson such as that taught in his orders of July 21st to Colonel Thompson of the riflemen:

> The enemy entertain a most fortunate apprehension of American riflemen. . . . It is with some concern, therefore, that I have been informed that your men have been suffered to fire at a most preposterous distance. Upon this principle, I must entreat and insist, that you consider it as a standing order, that not a man under your command is to fire at a greater distance than 150 yards, at the utmost; in short, they must never fire without almost a moral certainty of hitting their object. . . . I extend this rule to those who have the care of the field-pieces: four hundred yards is the greatest distance they should be allowed to fire at.[26]

Such instructions, reiterated day after day, resulted in rebel gunnery at Charleston that was never surpassed by either side during the war. The nine British ships which attacked at noon on June 28th were targets for the 32-pounders of the fort on Sullivan's Island at the entrance to the harbor. "The Provincials reserved their fire until the shipping advanced within point blank shot," an enemy officer reported in an English newspaper.[27] "Their artillery was surprisingly well served. . . . It was slow, but decisive indeed. They were very cool and took great care not to fire except when their guns were exceedingly well directed. . . . I can scarcely believe what I saw on that day; a day to me one of the most distressing of my life."

The two warships leading the British column were hit time after time. Round shot riddled the mainmast of the flagship *Bristol* and weakened the mizzen so that it had to be cut down. Captain Morris was mortally hurt and more than a hundred of the crew killed or wounded. "Twice the quarter deck was cleared of every person except Sir Peter, and he was slightly wounded," added the chronicler. "Captain Scott, of the *Experiment*, lost his right arm, and the ship sustained much the same number killed as the *Bristol*."

The British officer was too respectful to go into details about Parker's wound, which inspired many a ribald quip. For the admiral literally had his breeches shot off, though he escaped with scratches which made it inconvenient to sit down for several weeks. Fate was not in a jesting mood with Campbell, however, and a mortal wound ended his bright dream of conquest.

The rebels in the fort were short on powder, but they did not stint themselves on grog and tobacco. Moultrie recorded in his *Memoirs* that "several of the officers, as well as myself, were smoking our pipes. . . . It being a very hot day, we were served along the plat-form with grog in fire-buckets, which we partook of very heartily; I never had a more agreeable draught. . . . It may be very easily conceived what heat and thirst a man must feel in this climate, to be upon a plat-form on the 28th June, amidst 20 or 30 pieces of cannon, in one continual blaze and roar; and clouds of smoke curling over his head for hours together; it was a very honorable situation, but a very unpleasant one."[28]

Three or four broadsides from the warships shook the fort simultaneously without making much impression on merlons built of palmetto logs filled with earth to a thickness of 16 feet. The British cannonballs buried themselves in the spongy wood without sending off the vicious splinters which ordinarily caused some of the worst casualties. Of the 12 Americans killed and 24 wounded, nearly all were hit through the embrasures.

Thousands of Charleston people watched the action from roofs and steeples. At moments during the sultry afternoon both the fort and squadron were hidden by clouds of their own black-powder smoke. One British shot cut the staff of the rebel flag, but Sergeant William Jasper risked his life to fix it on a sponge-staff planted on the rampart.

An even more anxious period for the spectators came when the American guns remained silent for a full hour. This interval, Moultrie recalled, "was owing to the scarcity of powder which we had in the fort, and to a report that was brought me that the British troops were landed. . . . I ordered the guns to cease firing, that we should reserve our powder for the musketry to defend ourselves against the land forces."

As it happened, Clinton's troops did not advance. This failure led to a furious squabble between the two branches of the service. British soldiers declared they had been misinformed and the shoals could not be forded from their camp on Long Island to the American works on Sullivan's Island. Parker's battered seamen, on the contrary, swore that the water was but thigh-deep. Long after the participants were dead and gone, the controversy was taken up by historians.

The rebels resumed their methodical and accurate firing when Moultrie received 500 pounds of powder from the small store of John Rutledge, the former member of Congress who replaced Campbell as South Carolina governor. "Do not make too free with your cannon," he cautioned in a penciled note. "Cool and do mischief!"

Moultrie carried out these instructions so faithfully that at one time he had five warships helpless. The *Bristol* and *Experiment* were badly riddled when three frigates ran foul of each other in the confusion and grounded. The *Syren* warped off, and the *Sphynx* disengaged herself by cutting away her bowsprit; but the *Actaeon* had to be burned to prevent her falling into the hands of the Americans. At sunset the British officers admitted defeat and took their crippled ships out of range.

The defenders remained on the alert for a week, but the attack was not renewed. Charleston had been saved in one of the war's most decisive actions, and Lee did not flatter Moultrie's 435 Continentals when he declared that "no men ever did, and it is impossible that any can behave better."

The Declaration of Independence was approved by the Continental Congress six days later, and the news of both events rejoiced the land. After June 28th and July 4th the most skeptical loyalist could only admit that the American cause had weathered the first precarious stages. But the most optimistic patriot must have perceived that the real contest was yet to come. For the British Empire had scarcely been scratched by any blows received so far. The British Empire, like Sir Peter Parker, had been wounded in the vanity rather than the flesh. The hurt was not deep, and at the height of rebel jubilation a British expeditionary force reached these shores with twice as many ships and troops as those of the Spanish Armada.

PART TWO

Civil War

Perhaps the Enemy may give us two Months, before they come again. . . . Let us regard these two Months as the most precious Time we have to Live; they may be worth an Age of Droning peace, and, well employ'd, may give happiness and peace to Millions.

—GENERAL GATES

Chapter 7

The Fight for New York

ON A sultry August night in 1776 a miracle was vouchsafed as a warning to the British and German troops on Staten Island. Hundreds of them had gathered about a great campfire to witness the burning of effigies representing rebel leaders. John Witherspoon, president of Princeton College, was the only civilian honored along with three soldiers, Washington, Putnam and Charles Lee. All four figures were hastily set afire as the soldiers ran for shelter when a thunderstorm interrupted the ceremony. Afterwards, according to a British deserter, three were entirely consumed, while Washington's effigy rose triumphant from the drenched embers:

"The figure was found as good as it ever was: a fact which caused a great deal of fear among the Hessian troops, most of whom are very superstitious."[1]

The mercenaries remained doubtful even after their officers explained that there had not been time to give Washington's effigy a coat of tar before the storm broke. Soaked with rain, it resisted the flames while the other three figures burned to ashes.

Certainly the American commander had need of a good omen. For if the coming campaign was to be decided by natural causes, it might have been foreseen that he stood in danger not only of losing New York but also a large part of his army. Manhattan Island could not be defended by an outnumbered force lacking in sea power; and it could not be abandoned without political consequences at a time when Americans were still rejoicing over the Declaration of Independence.

By day the sails of 52 warships and 427 transports testified to British command of the waters, and at night the campfires of 34,000 troops twinkled on Staten Island. There were enough British soldiers and sailors to set a record as the largest expeditionary force of the eighteenth century. Two generations later England would not be able to send as many redcoats across the Channel to Waterloo as the troops which crossed the Atlantic to attack New York in 1776.

The 20,000 men under Washington made up the largest American army of the war, but it was far from being the most effective. The majority had never smelled gunpowder, for the untried forces of the middle colonies were taking part in this campaign. Even the New England regiments included many new recruits, and it would be a conservative statement that sea power doubled the value of Howe's numbers. Ships could land British troops to attack either Manhattan or Long Island, so that Washington felt compelled to divide his army.

The odds against him were increased when the warships gained control of the Hudson River in spite of the American batteries and sunken obstructions. Washington's apprehensions may be read between the lines of his message to the New York Convention on August 17th:

> When I consider that the city of New York will in all human probability be the scene of a bloody conflict, I cannot but view the great numbers of women, children and infirm persons remaining in it, with the most melancholy concern. When the men-of-war passed up the river, the shrieks and cries of these poor creatures running every way with their children were truly distressing, and I fear they will have an unhappy effect on the ears and minds of our young and inexperienced soldiery. Can no method be devised for their removal?[2]

In spite of the persuasions of the New York authorities, most of the inhabitants preferred to take their chances. It had been only a few weeks since they celebrated Independence by toppling over the leaden statue of George III in Bowling Green, and it did not occur to them that his invading troops might soon be revenging themselves on the statue of Pitt.

Down to the eve of the Declaration the leaders of the revolt had protested—too much at moments—their loyalty and devotion to George III. Their petitions and declarations blamed everything on his "artful ministers," and anyone might have supposed the royal victim of such deceptions to be noble of purpose but handicapped by a feeble will and intellect.

Thomas Paine had broken the ice in the first month of 1776 with his attacks on "the Royal Brute of Great Britain" in the pages of *Common*

Sense. But it remained for Thomas Jefferson in the Declaration of Independence to charge all American grievances to the king without once mentioning Parliament.

Before his death in 1820, sixty years after coming to the throne, George III was to gain the affection of Englishmen as the living symbol of resistance to Napoleon and the French Revolution. He was to be forgiven his costly decade of personal rule; he was to be pitied for his unhappy family life and his two plunges into the darkness of insanity. His narrow obstinacy was to be forgotten by Englishmen who remembered his courage, but Americans were not given the opportunity to forget. They remembered only the foeman of 1776 who hired foreign mercenaries to plunder their towns and savages to terrorize their frontiers.

The personal responsibility of the king is established by documentary evidence.[3] "Every means of distressing America must meet with my concurrence," he assured Lord North in 1775. When Howe's methods seemed too mild, the monarch urged that he "turn his thoughts to the mode of war best calculated to end this contest, as most distressing to the Americans." Approval of the bombardments of civilians is indicated by a dispatch "directing the total destruction of any place, large or small, in which the people assembled in arms, or held meetings of committees or congresses."

George III supervised every detail of the war with as much attention and authority as a modern chief of staff. His personal virtues contributed as usual to his public errors, for he was always ready at an hour's notice to sacrifice his comfort and apply himself to a strategic problem.

His foes revenged themselves by uprooting the very idea of monarchy from the American mind. They did it more effectively than the French revolutionists of 1793 who believed that they could destroy the kingship by destroying the king. The Americans used printed words instead of a guillotine; but they made such a monster out of George III that after 1776 any hint of American royalty was viewed by the radical faction as a particularly odious form of treason.

The leaders of the revolt had served a long apprenticeship at shaping public opinion. During the early years John Adams spent many an evening with the Warrens, James Otis and Sam Adams "in preparing for the next day's newspaper—a curious employment, cooking up paragraphs, articles, and occurrences, &c., working the political engine."[4] This experience was helpful after July 4, 1776, when the Revolution entered a new and more serious phase. For the practical politicians who approved the Declaration knew that it meant civil war—not merely a contest in which one section of the country opposed another, but a strife pitting one neighbor against another in the same community.

From the scopholites of Georgia to the loyalists of upper New York, there were Americans in every colony who took the king's side. Some of them esteemed security above liberty; others had their doubts of a liberty gained at the cost of separation from the Empire. They had been slow to make up their minds, these rebels against rebellion; they had hesitated to risk their lives and fortunes while a hope of peaceful settlement remained. But the Declaration of Independence was an ultimatum that could not be ignored, and the vast British armada at New York heartened the timid and wavering.

Contemporary estimates of loyalist numbers vary widely. John Adams believed that they amounted to a third of the population, while another third might be considered neutral or indifferent.[5] The patriots, as the dynamic faction, realized that the outcome might depend on disarming countrymen who could not be converted. Shortly after Congress passed its first resolution urging that course, General Schuyler marched from Albany with 700 militia troops against the Tories of the New York frontier. Before he reached Johnstown, his force had been swelled to 3,000 by recruits who hastened to support what appeared to be the winning side.

Sir John Johnson had inherited on his father's death in 1774 the baronial estate of 100,000 acres along the Mohawk. These lands were the reward of Sir William Johnson for using his influence to keep the Iroquois loyal to Britain in the last war. Schuyler had been a friend and ally in that contest, but he compelled the new lord of Johnson Hall to surrender the muskets and cannon of 300 retainers.[6] Militia detachments were given the task of disarming several hundred other scattered Tories.

This stroke ranks as one of the decisive events of 1776. Johnson eventually raised a loyalist regiment, but Schuyler's display of force impressed the loyalists and Indians of the New York frontier so much that they offered no serious opposition until the following year.

Altogether, at least 5,000 incipient foemen were disarmed by the patriots of the thirteen colonies during the spring and summer of the Declaration. The county and village committees took charge of this work, though they sometimes found it necessary to call upon the militia or Continentals. In a war of attrition the value of this result would be better appreciated a few years later, when the rebels found it hard to put as many as 5,000 troops in the field.

The poor showing of the invaders throughout the first year had given the opening for some merciless comments in Parliament. Fox declared that neither Pitt nor Alexander nor Caesar had ever conquered as much territory as Lord North lost in a single campaign. Some of these charges were inspired by political motives; but the sincere opinion of many liberals was expressed by a modern British historian:

> The acts of aggressive warfare sanctioned or condoned by the ministers . . . had consequences most disastrous to the national interests. They had not occupied a single square furlong of soil, fortified or open, in any of the colonies; but they had shelled three towns . . . and had rendered a few hundred families homeless. They had alienated all the neutral opinion in America, and had lighted a flame of resentment against Great Britain which they continued to feed with fresh fuel until it grew so hot that it did not burn itself out for a couple of lifetimes. England had never reaped so little glory or advantage from so great an expenditure of money.[7]

The rebels of 1776 were sometimes led by wishful thinking to attach too much importance to the speeches of their friends in Parliament. Generally speaking, Britons of all classes approved the efforts of the administration to chastise America. The island contained few tinkers or cobblers so humble that they did not regard the former colonies as national property; and the effects have been estimated by another British historian:

> The undoubted popularity of the war in its first stages had for some time continued to increase, and in the latter part of 1776 and 1777 it had probably attained its maximum. At the close of 1776 the greater part of the Rockingham connection, finding themselves beaten by overwhelming majorities, abstained from attending Parliament except in the mornings, when private business was being transacted. A great part of the majorities against them consisted, no doubt, of courtiers and placemen . . . but the Whigs at this time very fully admitted that the genuine opinion of the country was with the Government and King.[8]

The illusion that Englishmen viewed the war as a mere colonial conflict, worth only a minor effort, is also exploded by contemporary testimony. The struggle lost importance a decade later, it is true, when British land and sea forces began a long participation in the French Revolutionary and Napoleonic wars. But the struggle which ended in 1783 was the first in modern history to cost any nation as much as half a billion dollars, most of it devoted to the unsuccessful effort to put down the rebellion in

America. "So vast a force as was exerted by Great Britain had never been sent to so great a distance, nor resisted by a power apparently so unequal to the contest," commented a third British historian a few years after the peace. At the time his countrymen would have agreed with him that it was "the most extensive, difficult and burdensome war in which Great Britain was ever engaged."[9]

Overconfidence and the distance across the Atlantic account for many of the British failures of the first year. It could hardly have been imagined, moreover, that the rebels would capture most of their weapons from the invaders themselves. Still less could it have been supposed that a people who had been forbidden manufactures would learn how to manufacture their own gunpowder, small arms and iron cannon as early as 1776. Even bayonets offered difficulties at the beginning, and the Maryland Committee of Safety confessed that 400 delivered in that colony were unfit for use. Subsidies were offered by most of the committees, and there is a triumphant note in the report of March 28th from New York that a powder mill "made, before the 12th of this instant, only two hundred weight. The first week after that time we made two hundred weight; the second week we made eleven hundred weight; and I believe this week we shall make twelve hundred weight."[10]

Such quantities fell far short of requirements even when added to the munitions seized from the enemy. But if the Americans lacked skill in manufacturing, they had long known all the tricks of smuggling. The most dependable source of their first year's supplies was revealed in a letter from Charleston of May 29th, only a few weeks before the Sullivan's Island action:

> Last Saturday a sloop arrived here from St. Eustatius with ten thousand pounds of gunpowder, the master of which says that a large vessel had arrived from Holland, deeply laden with arms and ammunition, and that some Philadelphia vessels were loading out of her. He also said that the French ports in the West Indies are open to us, and that the French men-of-war have orders to protect our vessels in and out of their harbors.[11]

The little Dutch island of St. Eustatius had long been a headquarters of American smugglers in the West Indies. Profit was not the only motive of French and Dutch traders bringing munitions, for both of those European nations scented an opportunity to weaken a rival maritime power. In the spring of 1776 the Continental Congress invited secret diplomatic relations by sending Silas Deane as commissioner to France. Meanwhile the Comte de Vergennes, foreign minister of that kingdom, laid before Louis XVI a memorial urging that France aid the rebels with money and supplies. In May, before the arrival of Deane, Vergennes had reached the point of conferring with the playwright Caron de Beaumarchais. In the role of conspirator the French minister agreed with this adventurer that it would be advisable to set up a sham trading firm to mask the sending of munitions to the rebelling colonies of a supposedly friendly nation.

Vergennes might have been more cautious if he had known at this time the extent of the American losses in Canada. Yet Congress still felt confident that the campaign might be saved by adequate supplies and reinforcements. There were about 8,000 men in the army of invasion, half of them victims of the smallpox epidemic. In their report of May 28th, Chase and Carroll asserted that "your Army is badly paid; and so exhausted is your credit that even a cart cannot be procured without ready money or force. . . . The Army is in a distressing condition and is in want of the most necessary articles—meat, bread, tents, shoes, stockings, shirts, &c."[12]

In a previous letter the commissioners had gloomily predicted that "if further reinforcements are sent without pork to victual the whole Army, our soldiers must perish or feed on each other. Even plunder, the last resource of strong necessity, will not relieve their wants." General Sullivan sent back hopeful messages, however, when he took command after the death of Thomas and departure of Wooster. His express of June 5th to Washington was the first optimistic note to come out of Canada in weeks:

> I have no Doubt of the General Attachment of the Canadians, though I Suppose some unprincipled Wretches among them will always appear against us, but a vast Majority will be for us. . . . I may Venture to Assure you & the Congress that I can in a few days Reduce the Army to order & with the Assistance of a Kind providence put a new face to our Affairs here, which a few days since Seem'd almost impossible.[13]

The Continental Congress has been blamed for military shortcomings by nineteenth-century historians in such passages as this indictment: "While Congress was discussing by a warm fire the most eligible method of providing the army with tents and blankets, half the army was sleeping in the snow without either tents or blankets. While Congress was framing elaborate resolutions, and drawing out and equipping regiments upon paper, officers in the field were standing disheartened before their thinned and disheartened ranks."[14]

Such opinions do not appear to have been held by the soldiers of 1776, whose letters and diaries show few outbursts of resentment. There is even less evidence to justify insinuations that the delegates were taking their comfort while neglecting the wants of the army. Washington, Schuyler, Sullivan, Mifflin—these officers were the forerunners of many others who would serve in Congress before putting on a uniform. Of the 342 delegates from 1774 to 1789, indeed, more than a third fought in the armed forces. John Dickinson, who led the opposition to the Declaration of Independence, took the field immediately after July 4th as a militia colonel. Most of the other volunteers were middle-aged men who felt the strain of active service as much as William Livingston of New Jersey, writing to a friend in Congress on August 29th: "My ancient corporeal fabrick is almost tottering under the fatigue I have lately undergone; constantly rising at two o'clock in the morning to examine our lines, which are very extensive . . . till daybreak, and from that time perpetually till eleven in giving orders, sending dispatches, and doing the proper business of Quartermasters, Colonels, Commissaries, and I know not what."[15]

The Canadian campaign may be considered as largely the pet project of Congress, though it had the full concurrence of the commander in chief. Inexperience as well as material poverty had contributed to past failures, but the assembly believed that it still had a trump to play. If the army at Sorel could recover part of its lost ground and seize the village of Deschambault, 40 miles above Quebec, the men in the State House hoped that the enemy could be stopped at this point. On the northern shore a bluff overlooked the rapids of Richelieu, so that a fortification could command the river. British warships would be compelled to proceed upstream in single file, exposed to the fire of American batteries, and an enemy land attack could be launched only with difficulty.

As a first step, General Sullivan decided to send a detachment from Sorel across Lake St. Pierre to surprise Three Rivers, held by 800 regulars and Canadians under the redoubtable Maclean. On June 6th about 1,500 Americans embarked in bateaux, landing in the darkness a league above the British post. General William Thompson, in immediate command, divided his force for a dawn attack at three points. In order to avoid the enemy artillery, the rebels took a route leading through a swamp which held up the advance long enough to rouse Maclean as to his peril.

The thudding of the guns carried across Lake St. Pierre to Sullivan as he began a dispatch to Washington announcing a success, "I am almost Certain that Victory has Declared in our favour, as ye Irregular firing of the Cannon for such a length of time after the Small arms Ceased, Showns that our Men are in possession of the Ground." From Three Rivers it was only a step to the occupation of Deschambault, but the former New Hampshire lawyer's hopes were to be blasted. Before sending the express, he had reports from Thompson which caused him to add a doleful postscript. Maclean, he informed the commander in chief, had given the attackers "so Warm a reception that the Troops Soon Broke & quitted the Ground; the Cannonading & all the firing after that was a Meer random firing, which answered very Little purpose."[16]

The "most horrid Swamp that ever man set foot in," as Colonel Anthony Wayne described it, cheated the Continentals of a victory half won by audacity. The daring young Pennsylvanian and Colonel Arthur St. Clair were delayed so long that they found the enemy prepared. As a further rebel misfortune, enough British reinforcements arrived from Quebec that very morning to give Maclean a numerical superiority. After a hot but brief fight, the attackers were repulsed with losses of about 25 killed and wounded in addition to 236 prisoners.

Strenuous work at the oars brought the bateaux safely back to Sorel just ahead of a British pursuit across Lake St. Pierre. Sullivan and Thompson could feel fortunate that their whole detachment had not been taken, for General John Burgoyne had just arrived at Quebec with a great expeditionary force. The largest artillery train ever seen in the New World and a sum equal to a million dollars in gold crossed the Atlantic for the campaign to drive the rebels out of Canada and invade the colonies from the north. The vanguard reached Three Rivers in time to aid Maclean, and it could be assumed that Sorel would be attacked within a few days.

Even the optimistic Sullivan knew that the game was up, and on June 14th he began a hurried retirement up the Richelieu River from Sorel. The Americans were hard pressed, but adverse winds delayed the British warships long enough for the escape of a disheartened army burdened with sick. Chambly and St. Johns could offer only a temporary refuge, and in a letter of the 10th Benedict Arnold spoke for fellow officers who realized that the struggle for the fourteenth colony had gone against the invaders. "The junction of the Canadians with the Colonies— an object which brought us into this country—is now at an end," he wrote to Schuyler. "Let us quit them, and secure our own country before it is too late. There will be much more honour in making a safe retreat than hazarding a battle against such superiority."[17]

The bad news from Canada was offset by American successes in other quarters. Washington's victory at Boston bore belated fruit in June when American ships captured enemy transports with most of the strength of the 71st Highlanders. These reinforcements had not been warned of Howe's evacuation, and after a long voyage the troopships afforded the rebels an easy harvest of prisoners.

The total amounted to 647 officers and men under Colonel Archibald Campbell. A majority of the kilted warriors had enlisted in the hope of being rewarded with American lands, but it was the Americans themselves who provided the opportunity. For reasons of indoctrination as well as security, the captives were divided among several southern colonies and allowed to hire out as farmhands or laborers. This sort of treatment proved so persuasive that the canny Scots ended in many instances by marrying an American woman and acquiring an American farm on the frontier. Some of them were even converted to the extent of fighting on the American side in later campaigns.

A second rebel success in the summer of 1776 was reported from South Carolina. By July the depredations of the Cherokees had become so serious that James Creswell sent an express to the Committee of Safety from the fort known as Ninety-six: "The savages have spread great desolation all along the frontiers, and killed a great number. . . . Ninety-six is now a frontier. Plantations lie desolate, and hopeful crops are going to ruin."[18]

It had been the original British plan to arm the redskins as confederates in a widespread campaign aiming at the reduction of all four southern colonies. But the unexpected defeat of Parker's squadron at Sullivan's Island left the Cherokees and allied tribes to carry on alone. Once the seacoast had been freed of danger, the southern colonies were able to raise large forces to deal with the Indians.

The first clash took place on July 20th in the wilderness region which later became eastern Tennessee. The Cherokees led by Chief Dragging Canoe tried to ambush a few companies of border militia and were themselves ambushed and defeated with heavy losses. Deckard rifles were the weapons of Scotch-Irish frontiersmen who fought under such natural leaders as the Rev. Charles Cummings, a Presbyterian parson noted for sermons delivered with a shot pouch hanging from his shoulder. The members of his militant flock bragged that he went into action "praying like heaven, and then fighting like hell." From Georgia to Virginia the half-savage "shirtmen" of the border country were victorious everywhere. Early in August a force of 1,150 South Carolinans cut to pieces a band of Tories and Cherokees at Oconoree, and the Georgia patriots wiped out the Creek towns on the Tugaloo River. General Rutherford of North Carolina crossed the mountains to lay waste the territory of the Erati Cherokees, burning thirty or forty towns and destroying crops nearly ready for the harvest. James Robertson and John Sevier guided the Virginians into the fertile valley of the upper Tennessee River, where all the towns and fields were left in ruins. It was a merciless strife of extermination, and the report of several actions ended with the words, "No males were taken prisoners."[19]

About 5,000 rebels and nearly as many Tories and Indians participated in a three-month campaign which might have been described as a war within a war. From what is now northern Alabama to eastern West Virginia the Indians were dispersed and reduced to famine. Oconostata, the chief of the largest body of Cherokees, gave up the hopeless fight in October and ceded a large part of his territory as the hard condition of a peace allowing the remnants of his people their existence.

Thus did one of the most advanced Indian nations pay the price of having heeded British agents instead of accepting the offers of neutrality held forth by the Continental Congress. The campaign was to have a lasting effect on the Revolution, for many of the militiamen needed only this glimpse of the wilderness paradise on the other side of the Alleghenies. Before the end of 1776 the first wave of the great westward migration was pouring into a region where a settler with a rifle, an ax and a stout heart could make himself the master of his own lands. A few years later, at a critical stage of the war, these "over-mountain men" would be returning to wipe out an entire British army as ruthlessly as they had defeated the Cherokees.

The redcoats on Staten Island, judging from their letters, were not enchanted by the land they had crossed the ocean to conquer. One of the Scottish soldiers, James Falconer, wrote to his brother on July 24th: "We sleep upon the sea-shore, nothing to shelter us from the violent rains but our coats and the miserable paltry blankets. There is nothing that grows upon this Island, it being a mere sand-bank, and a few bushes that harbour millions of moschitoes—a greater plague than there can be in Hell itself."[20]

Long Island impressed the invaders more favorably after the landing of 14,000 troops on August 22nd about eight miles from the rebel lines. The apples and corn were ripening, and the Hessians found other booty more to their taste in the homes of Tories as well as patriots. Evidences of bad feeling between Britons and Germans had cropped up already, but nothing had happened as yet to dull the reputation of mercenaries trained according to the principles of Frederick the Great, foremost soldier of the age. These methods were described at a later date in a letter written to Washington by Arthur Lee about exercises he saw at Potsdam:

When the king reviews an army of 40,000 men, not a man or horse, though the former in full march and the latter in full gallop, is discernibly out of the line. The regiments here are in the field every day, where, besides the general exercise, every man is filed off singly, and passes in review before different officers, who beat his limbs into the position they think proper, so that the man appears to be purely a machine in the hand of a workman.[21]

British soldiers did not feel degraded by floggings administered as the punishment of a man convicted at a court-martial. Yet they were shocked at the casual beatings of Germans by noncommissioned officers who carried canes for the purpose. Although the floggings were actually more severe, the redcoats felt that striking a soldier as if he were a dog—often by way of injunction rather than chastisement—robbed him of the last tatters of human dignity. Some of them showed their contempt so vigorously as to be sentenced to their own form of punishment by British officers with strict orders to enforce respect for mercenaries hired at such a drain on the royal treasury.

Neither the rebel batteries nor the 2,100-foot chain stretched across the Hudson could stop the warships from penetrating up the river. With the enemy in his rear, Washington divided his 20,000 men into three groups —a force of 9,000 on Long Island, about 7,000 on Manhattan Island, and the balance scattered in detachments along the New Jersey shore. Sanitary regulations had been observed so carelessly by the undisciplined host that hundreds of men were already unfit for duty. On August 8th General Heath noted that "in almost every barn, stable, shed, and even under the fences and bushes, were the sick to be seen, whose countenances were but an index of the dejection of spirit, and of the distress they endured."[22]

Sir William Howe, rewarded in advance of his expected victory by being knighted at long distance, held a line reaching from the Narrows

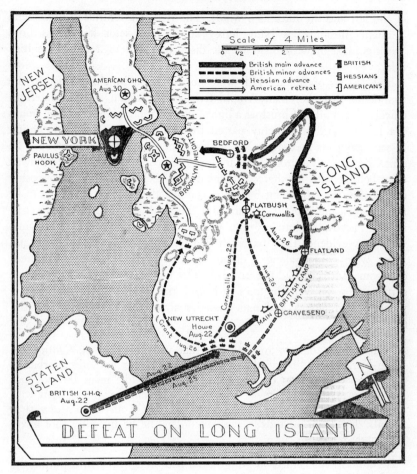

Scale of 4 Miles

British main advance
British minor advances
Hessian advance
American retreat

BRITISH
HESSIANS
AMERICANS

NEW JERSEY

AMERICAN G.H.Q.
Aug. 30

NEW YORK

PAULUS HOOK

BEDFORD

BROOKLYN HEIGHTS

LONG ISLAND

FLATBUSH
Cornwallis

Aug. 26

FLATLAND

Cornwallis Aug. 22

Aug. 26

BRITISH CAMP
Aug. 22-26

NEW UTRECHT
Howe
Aug. 22

Grant Aug. 26

MAIN GRAVESEND

STATEN ISLAND

BRITISH G.H.Q.
Aug. 22

Aug. 22
Aug. 26

N

DEFEAT ON LONG ISLAND

to Flatland. Three roads led through the wooded heights barring the way to Brooklyn. Along this ridge the Americans were entrenched with their right wing defending the coastal route, their center athwart the Flatbush road, and their left drawn up across the Jamaica approach. The reserves occupied a strong system of field fortifications at Brooklyn Heights.

Washington had relied on Greene to direct the strategy of the Long Island forces, but this lifelong sufferer from asthma was prostrated by illness. Sullivan, after distinguishing himself in the retreat from Canada, had returned in time to command the center, while Putnam took charge of the left and the force as a whole. The right was entrusted to General William Alexander, a New Jersey landed proprietor known as Lord Stirling in acknowledgment of his disputed claim to a lapsed Scottish title.

The lessons of Bunker Hill were not forgotten by either side. In the confidence that the enemy would try another frontal assault, American officers placed piles of brush as a line of demarcation and warned the troops not to fire until the enemy passed them. But Howe had no intention of sacrificing his men again. At nine on the evening of August 26th he sent Clinton with a strong force to turn the rebel left. Lord Percy followed close behind with another detachment to wheel in behind the opposing center after the movement had been completed. These attacks were to be masked by a preliminary advance of a third British group along the coast for the purpose of drawing reinforcements to the threatened right wing.

As new evidence that the revolt had become a civil war, Clinton and Percy were guided along a detour by Long Island loyalists, hundreds of whom had welcomed the invaders. The rebels were taken by complete surprise, though Washington's orders of the 23rd indicate that he apprehended an attack and had anxieties about the behavior of his untried troops:

Remember, officers and soldiers, that you are freemen, fighting for the blessings of liberty; that slavery will be your portion and that of your posterity if you do not acquit yourselves like men. Be cool, but determined. Do not fire at a distance, but wait for orders from your officers. It is the General's express orders, that if any man attempts to skulk, lay down, or retreat, without orders, he be instantly shot as an example.[23]

Reinforcements landed on Long Island had brought the British numbers up to double those of the defenders. But Howe did not need this advantage to gain a victory won by skill. Many of the Americans of the left and center had their first intimation of the foe when they were assailed from the rear.

The three British attacks could not have been better timed. An hour before dawn Clinton and Percy were already around the American left and waiting for the diversion on the right. At daybreak General Grant opened the battle in this quarter, then all three detachments fell to their work with swift and deadly efficiency. The only hitch came as a result of the stout resistance of the rebel right under Lord Stirling. There a regiment of Marylanders, wearing new red uniforms, stood like veterans alongside an equally gallant Delaware regiment and repulsed the first assault. If these troops had but known, the day was being lost at this moment on the other side of the line. The American left and center, taken by surprise from front and rear, were speedily put to flight. Sullivan and several hundred of his men had to surrender after being cut off, and the survivors were lucky to escape.

This debacle left Stirling's men to face crushing odds as Lord Cornwallis thrust westward from the Flatbush area to close in behind them. Their retreat was further imperiled by a tidal creek in the rear, yet Stirling stood firm on open ground with more valor than discretion. The Maryland and Delaware brigade not only hurled the enemy back three times but took a respectable number of prisoners, most of whom they were compelled to relinquish later. Colonel Samuel Atlee, whose Pennsylvania riflemen supported the brigade, left an account of the last stand behind a fence to cover the withdrawal of the remnants after the capture of Stirling and his staff:

> Here we kept up a Close and constant Fire for upwards of a Quarter of an Hour, untill the Brigade had retreated out of our Sight. Our ammunition now being entirely spent, and our Retreat after the Brigade cut off, I was obliged to file off to the right with what men I cou'd collect and endeavour to find a way out of that Quarter. After various Struggles, running thro' the Fire of many of the Enemy's detachments, and nearly fatigued to death, not having eat or drank since the day before about 4 O'Clock in the afternoon, no alternative presenting, I was obliged to surrender to the 71st Highlanders, having with me about 40, officers included.[24]

Washington went through the agony of watching the ordeal at the finish. Some of the Maryland and Delaware men were drowned while crossing Gowanus Creek, yet they fought off their pursuers and actually hung on to a few prisoners. Toward noon the last of them straggled back to Brooklyn Heights, having left more than half the brigade behind as captives, dead or wounded.

The British losses were officially listed as 377, though the Americans claimed 500 or more. In turn they acknowledged less than half of the 2,000 casualties the enemy boasted of inflicting. The actual number was never established, but it may have been as many as 1,500, most of them prisoners. It would doubtless have been a much worse disaster if unfavorable winds had not prevented the warships from landing troops on the coast in Stirling's rear.

Howe had taught a severe lesson in tactics, and the journals of American participants tell a tale of wild confusion. Some of the men of the left and center had thrown away their muskets without firing a shot; others had cowered in the underbrush until they were flushed out like fugitives. There had been skulking; there had been panic and disobedience of orders. But the green troops who fled might have found comfort in the fight put up by Joseph Callender of a Massachusetts artillery battalion. After his officers fell, he took command and resisted until an enemy officer paid tribute to his courage by saving him from being bayoneted. This was the Joseph Callender who had been convicted of "abject cowardice" as a captain at Bunker Hill and dismissed from the army. It was as a volunteer that he fought at Long Island, and after his exchange from captivity he served with distinction as an officer throughout the rest of the war.

Chapter 8

Devil Take the Hindmost

THE beaten army found itself in a perilous situation after the battle of August 27th. Its three divisions were separated by rivers commanded by enemy warships as Howe closed in on the rebel works at Brooklyn Heights. This move left Washington with the problem of reuniting his forces before they incurred another and more costly defeat.

Neither general escaped censure. Howe was blamed for not following up his victory by storming the rebel fortifications before the losers recovered from their confusion. In his report of September 3rd to Lord Germain he explained that "the 33rd and Grenadiers . . . approached within musket shot of the enemy's lines at Brooklyn . . . and with such eagerness to attack it by storm, that it required repeated orders to prevail on them to desist from the attempt. Had they been permitted to go on, it is my opinion that they would have carried the redoubt; but as it was apparent that the lines would have been ours at a very cheap rate by regular approaches, I would not risk the loss that might have been sustained in the attempt."[1]

Most of Howe's critics were voicing their opinions from the other side of the Atlantic. Two British officers on the scene, Mackenzie and Stedman, differed by paying tribute to the strength of the American fortifications. Bunker Hill and Dorchester Heights had demonstrated what the rebels could do in a single night with the pick and spade, and months of toil had gone into works at Brooklyn Heights defended by cannon as well as muskets.

Washington in his turn was blamed for being caught by surprise as well as entrusting the Long Island forces to a general so lacking in strategic ability as Putnam. In both instances he had been a beggar rather than chooser. After Greene's illness the choice of the rough and ready

Connecticut farmer was dictated by political reasons, since New England had supplied a majority of the troops. As for the surprise, it may be noted that a year and a half after Lexington the rebels still had no cavalry, though that arm served as the eyes of strategy.

In July a few hundred Connecticut troops actually had appeared on horseback—sober heads of families mounted on family plugs and bearing ancient muskets instead of carbines and sabers. Most of them were clad in the usual homespun, though a few wore a faded uniform coat or tarnished hat from the last war. They made rather a pathetic sight, reminding the army of its deficiencies instead of providing inspiration. Washington had no funds to purchase the nags from their owners or provide forage. The disgruntled dragoons pastured the mounts at their own expense for a few weeks, then rode home in a huff. Before their departure one of them was captured by the redcoats, who were more overcome by laughter than they would have been by any thundering charge of this first American "cavalry."

Howe had few dragoons of his own at the time, but he could depend for intelligence on native Americans of a region overwhelmingly loyalist in sentiment. A letter of September 28th from a Tory refugee on Long Island to his mother in Connecticut offers proof of the devotion of these people to the British cause. The exaggerated figures also hint at disillusionments to follow:

> It has been my Misfortune to leave my Native Shoar to Seek on this Island a place of Refuge from wicked and ungodly men. . . . But our army Consists now of Eighty Thousand besides Rangers and 200 Transports expected every day Loden with men and unless they lay Down their arms and Except of Mercy they will all be Destroyed and cut off, they have lost since August 27, 6000 men in y Rebel Army.[2]

If Washington could have been blamed for anything at all in his first defeat, it was that he expected too much of untried recruits. Bunker Hill left a permanent mark on Howe's psychology, and it might as truthfully have been said that Washington never forgot a confused and dreadful hour in the Pennsylvania woods. Even his official report, written as a young militia officer in 1755, lashed out with shame and rage at the soldiers who failed him: "They broke, and ran as sheep before the hounds; leaving the artillery, ammunition, provisions, baggage, and in short every thing, a prey to the enemy; and when we endeavoured to rally them, in hopes of regaining the ground, it was with as little success as if we had attempted to have stopped the wild bears of the mountains, or the rivulets with our feet; for they would break by, in spite of every effort to prevent it."[3]

On that occasion it was the British regulars of Braddock's defeat who ran and took to cover. Washington had only praise for the American militia troops who "behaved like men, and died like soldiers; for, I believe, out of three companies on the ground that day, scarce thirty men were left alive."

It did not occur to him that the regulars of 1755 found themselves outside their tactical element, while the militiamen were hardened to forest fighting. This myopia might have been charged to youthful intolerance, but as a middle-aged general he could find no excuses in 1776 for fugitives on Long Island who were neither trained nor armed to cope with European soldiers in pitched battle. For in Washington's report to Congress a similar note of condemnation is evident: "Till of late, I had no doubt in my own mind of defending this place [New York]; nor should I have yet, if the men would do their duty, but this I despair of."[4] The beaten forces, he added with more bitterness than accuracy, were going home "by whole regiments, by half ones, and by companies at a time."

Green troops throughout history, whatever their nationality, have always given an uneven performance. Fortesque saw little to approve in the American efforts, yet the historian of the British army commented on the fight put up by some of Sullivan's routed battalions. Their resistance, he chronicled, stopped several light infantry companies until the Guards could be summoned as reinforcements.[5] As further evidence, the casualty lists show that the two armies had about equal numbers of killed and wounded. At least two-thirds of the rebel losses consisted of prisoners, most of whom had been surprised and cut off before they could strike a blow.

Washington's stubborn faith that New York could be defended in the first place, as affirmed in several letters, is enough to indicate that he too had a great deal to learn. Both the general and his army were beginners, and any shortcomings of August 27th were redeemed by them two days later.

Heavy showers came to the rescue of the rebels after their defeat, for it was said in this age that rain converted a good musketeer into a poor spearman. Still, it may be doubted if Howe would have attacked on a sunny day. He had already ordered a formal investment with parallels and approaches when Washington saved his Brooklyn forces in a night operation.

On the 28th he reacted boldly to adversity by strengthening these troops with Pennsylvania riflemen sent across the river from New York. Again the weather fought on his side when fog blinded the enemy on the night of the 29th. In the morning the British sentries discovered that 8,000 men and most of their supplies had vanished as if by magic from the works on Brooklyn Heights. Under cover of the fog and darkness they had been taken across to the Manhattan shore in longboats.

The haggard commander in chief reported to Congress on the 31st that "scarce any of us have been out of the lines until our passage across the East River was effected yesterday morning; and for forty-eight hours preceding that, I had hardly been off my horse, and never closed my eyes. . . . Our retreat was made without any loss of men or ammunition, and in better order than I expected from troops in the situation ours were."[6]

No evacuation can ever shine as brightly as a victory, but this night's work took as much daring and resolution. Washington found the ideal troops to man the boats in a regiment of Massachusetts fishermen led by Colonel John Glover. The men from Marblehead and Gloucester had already earned a reputation as stout fellows. Shortly after Bunker Hill they put a stop to the swaggering of Morgan's riflemen in a tremendous battle of fists that Washington himself had to pacify. Officially the Marine Corps had been created by act of Congress, but Glover's "amphibious regiment" was composed of tactical Jacks-of-all-trades who set traditions for American marines of later wars. Before the Revolution ended, they were to give a good account of themselves as infantry, gunners and engineers. If the need had arisen, they could doubtless have qualified as dragoons.

Intelligence of the withdrawal from Brooklyn Heights was given by one of the Long Island loyalists who reported every American move. Apparently Howe did not trust the information, or he may have thought that the rebels were but leaping from the frying pan into the fire. For Washington had hardly improved his situation by bottling up his army in an island at the mercy of British sea power. Nathanael Greene, in a letter of September 5th, warned the commander that "the city and island of New York are no objects for us: we are not to bring them into competition with the general interests of America. Part of the army already has met with a defeat; the country is struck with a panic; any capital loss at this time may ruin the cause. . . . I give it as my opinion, that a general and speedy retreat is absolutely necessary, and that the honor and interest of America require it. I would burn the city and suburbs."[7]

Washington realized his danger but felt it expedient for political reasons to ask the advice of Congress. Before his express reached Philadelphia, the assembly resolved on September 3rd that "in case he should find it necessary to quit New York, that no damage be done to the said city by his troops."[8]

Neither army made a decisive move for more than two weeks after the American withdrawal to New York. The lethargy of the British commander owed to persistent hopes that some solution of compromise might be reached. Both Sir William Howe and his brother Lord Howe, admiral of the fleet at New York, belonged to the liberal Whig faction in England which made no secret of its sympathy for the rebels. Yet it was not a mystery why two such men had been selected to lead the expeditionary force. George III, though he found their principles distasteful, hoped that their personal influence might sway American leaders overawed by a display of force. Even the king was not so stubborn as to prefer war if the revolting colonists could be induced by peaceful means to return to their allegiance.

Congress went so far on September 7th as to appoint a committee made up of Dr. Franklin, John Adams and Edward Rutledge to hear Lord Howe's proposals at his headquarters on Staten Island. Franklin esteemed the admiral as an old friend, having spent many pleasant evenings playing chess with him and his sister at their London home. But the peace conference was blighted in advance, for the seventy-year-old philosopher had already stated the American position in a letter to Howe of July 20th.

Directing pardons to be offered the Colonies, who are the very parties injured, expresses indeed that opinion of our ignorance, baseness, and insensibility which your uninformed and proud nation has long been pleased to entertain of us; but it can have no other effect than that of increasing our resentment. It is impossible that we should think of submission to a government that has with the most wanton barbarity burnt our defenseless towns in the midst of winter, excited the savages to massacre our farmers and our slaves to murder their masters, and is even now bringing foreign mercenaries to deluge our settlements with blood. These atrocious injuries have extinguished every remaining spark of affection for that parent country we once held so dear; but were it possible for *us* to forget and forgive them, it is not possible for *you* (I mean the British nation) to forgive the people you have so heavily injured.[9]

These blunt words to an old friend are added evidence that Americans had taken an irrevocable step on July 4th. Franklin himself had been foremost of the leaders who hoped to the last that the colonies could gain autonomy within the Empire. And it was the unhappy lot of "Black Dick" Howe, one of Britain's naval heroes of the last war, to be cast in the role of enemy after failing in his ambition as peacemaker. His powers, as the committee interpreted them, allowed him only to offer pardon as the reward of submission, and the conference left the belligerents no nearer to terms than before.

Both of the Howes showed their preference for rebel leaders so openly as to offend prominent American loyalists. But after the failure of the peace conference, the lull in military operations came to an abrupt end on September 15th when the British admiral and general landed troops on Manhattan Island.

This test found American morale at its lowest point. During the last few weeks the discipline of the rebel host had also declined, judging by Washington's general orders.[10] On August 3rd he had nothing more serious to denounce than "the foolish and wicked practice of profane cursing and swearing." On the 21st he condemned "marauding . . . by certain villains." And on September 3rd he thundered against "some instances of infamous cowardice, and some of scandalous plunder and riot."

The disorders he mentioned grew out of sectional rivalries at a time when every American still thought of his colony as a separate homeland, despite the pretensions to unity of the Continental Congress. The New Englanders were the chief victims. If they had been praised too much in 1775 for leading the way, they now had cause to complain of jealousies. Washington himself cannot be wholly absolved, for the New England members of Congress learned of several indiscreet letters in which he deplored Yankee "levelling" tendencies. It was not in a day that the commander in chief developed the tact and impartiality which became two of the pillars of his leadership.

The prejudices of the troops from the middle and southern colonies were not softened by the departure of New England companies the moment their brief enlistment terms expired. Some of the men took a more informal leave, so that a plague of desertions was added to Washington's other troubles. American orators doted on the expression "an army of husbandmen," and it was only too true that a majority of the New England soldiers depended on their crops for a living. They found an advocate

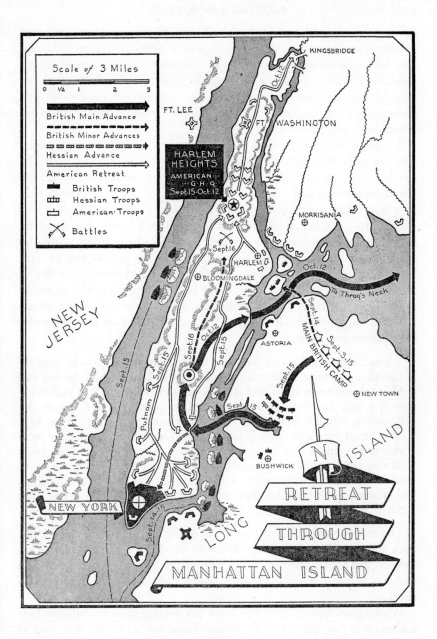

Scale of 3 Miles

0   ½   1   2   3

British Main Advance

British Minor Advances

Hessian Advance

American Retreat

British Troops

Hessian Troops

American Troops

Battles

KINGSBRIDGE

FT. LEE

FT. WASHINGTON

HARLEM HEIGHTS
AMERICAN
G. H. Q.
Sept 15-Oct.12

MORRISANIA

NEW JERSEY

Sept.16

HARLEM

BLOOMINGDALE

Oct.12

To Throg's Neck

Sept.14

MAIN BRITISH CAMP

Sept.3-15

ASTORIA

NEW TOWN

Putnam

Sept.15

Sept.16

Oct.12

Sept.15

Sept.15

Sept.15

Sept.15

Sept. 15

BUSHWICK

N

NEW YORK

Sept.14-15

ISLAND

RETREAT

THROUGH

MANHATTAN ISLAND

LONG

in sixty-six-year-old Jonathan Trumbull, the sturdy patriot who governed Connecticut throughout the war. "The season, indeed, was most unfavourable for so many of our farmers and labourers to leave home," he explained to Washington in a letter of September 10th. "Many had not even secured their harvest; the greater part had secured but a small part even of their hay, and the preparations for the crop of winter's grain for the ensuing year totally omitted."[11]

It was the misfortune of the Connecticut men, already smarting under criticism, to be directly in the path of a perfectly executed British amphibious operation on the 15th. At a council of war three days before, the American generals had belatedly voted to evacuate a city that could only be a trap. The appearance of British warships and transports in the East River during the next two days hastened the withdrawal, but the rebel forces were still dangerously extended on the Sunday morning when the enemy landed from barges at Kipp's Bay, near the present foot of 34th Street. As usual, General Howe had thought of everything. The fire of the warships was so directed as to create a screen of dust as well as smoke to cover the movement. An eyewitness account of the davastating effects is found in the diary of Benjamin Trumbull, chaplain of one of the Connecticut regiments:

> The Ships about 10 o'Clock . . . began from the mouths of near an 100 Canon a most furious Canonade on the Lines, which buried our Men who were in the Lines with Sand and Sods of Earth and made such a dust and Smoke that there was no possibility of firing on the Enemy to any advantage. . . . The Ships from their round Tops kept up a Smart Fire with Swivels loaded with Grape Shot which they were able to fire almost into the entrenchments they were so near. The boats all this time kept out of the reach of the Musquetry and finally turning off to the Left a little north of the Lines in the Smoke of the Ships they made good their Landing without receiving any annoyance from our troops.[12]

The redcoats and Hessians poured out of the barges, then swung around with the precision of trained soldiers to cut off the rebel escape. This menace sent the Connecticut troops into a panic. They scrambled from the trenches and ran in wild confusion which their officers were helpless to check.

Washington himself rode out from his headquarters on Murray Hill and made a vain effort to rally broken battalions which he described as "flying in every direction." His indignation at their "disgraceful and dastardly conduct" exposed him to grave danger of capture. Nineteenth-century historians saved their most passionate rhetoric for this scene, even intimating that the commander courted death. A less emotional view might suggest that the behavior of his troops had been no worse than the generalship which placed them in such a hopeless position. The city should obviously have been evacuated a week before, and Chaplain Trumbull showed his good sense by commenting, "The men were blamed for retreating and even flying in these Circumstances, but the Fault was principally in the General Officers in not disposing of things so as to give the men a rational prospect of Defence and a Safe retreat should they engage the Enemy."

A butchery of prisoners by the Hessians added to the horror. This episode does not accord with descriptions of the mercenaries as pitiful victims of the overlords who sold them into military bondage. "It was, indeed, with a heavy heart," wrote the American historian Fiske in a typical passage, "that these honest men took up their arms to go beyond the sea and fight for a cause in which they felt no sort of interest, and great was the mourning over their departure."[13] It is true that the Germans, like the redcoats and other European soldiers of the day, had not often been given any choice when they were impressed into service. But the letters of their officers bristle with a military spirit which was seldom if ever tempered by sympathy for an unoffending people whose homes they were plundering. Even such a gentle soul as Madame Riedesel, wife of a general from Brunswick, felt astonished and grieved by displays of American resentment.

German officers had the name of the world's best soldiers to uphold, and they stimulated zeal with warnings against the atrocities of American "barbarians." As a result some of the rebel prisoners on August 27th had their last glimpse of this world when they were bayoneted at the moment of submitting to an alien in a blue coat. The same fate, according to a British officer's diary, overtook many of the men who surrendered at Kipp's Bay:

> The Hessian Grenadiers who landed on the left met with a few of the Enemy in Mr. Watts's orchard who fired on them, by which 2 Hessians were killed and about 10 Wounded; but they paid dearly for this, as did some others who came forward soon after, with an intention of surrendering themselves, as the Hessians killed about 60 of them, and took a few prisoners.[14]

It was a doleful day for the Americans, and Washington must have felt fortunate to get off with several hundred casualties, chiefly prisoners, out of several thousand men who might have been surrounded. Two artillery officers not yet twenty-one years old showed the coolness of veterans that Sunday afternoon as Aaron Burr and Alexander Hamilton saved their guns from capture. There were many other instances of bravery, but the fight had been lost in the first few minutes. By nightfall the weary and disheartened rebels were back in prepared positions at Harlem Heights, leaving New York to invaders who would make it their headquarters for the next seven years—the longest period of enemy occupation ever suffered by an American city.

The mental confusion of the beaten army found a somber diagnostician in Colonel Jacobus Swartwout. This stout officer of Dutch ancestry informed the New York Convention on September 10th that his lieutenant colonel was incapacitated by disturbances which today would be regarded as psychological: "He had a disorder very often which rendered him unfit for the service of an officer. The complaint of that disorder is that he is spleeny and [had] a dizziness in the head, and that attends him when he has trouble. We can expect nothing but trouble in our present condition, so, consequently he will not be fit for the service of the present campaign."[15]

An equally morbid case history might have been written of many another American officer elected by popular vote. Nathanael Greene, as an earnest student of war, had already concluded that "we want nothing but good officers to constitute as good an army as ever marched into the field. Our men are infinitely better than the officers."[16]

So far in the New York campaign the army and the command had been pulling together like poorly matched horses not yet broken to harness. This makes it the more amazing that the Americans of Kipp's Bay should have turned on their tormenters the next day and given them a trouncing in the open field.

Sir William Howe, so often criticized for caution, can hardly be blamed for taking no chances with an enemy capable of two such contrasting performances in twenty-four hours. The hot action of September 16th started as usual with an American flight. At the outset the British light infantry companies made easy work of driving back a force of rebels on reconnaissance. The pursuers were rubbing in the humiliation by pretending to be fox hunters when the prey turned on them with reinforcements. The redcoats in turn were strengthened with fresh troops as the struggle surged back and forth through the buckwheat fields of an area reaching today from 114th to 118th Streets.

British officers believed that they had proved at the battle of Long Island a recipe for victory based on the American shortage of bayonets. "It was the General's orders," explained Lord Percy a few days later, "that the troops should receive the Rebels' first fire, and then rush on them before they had recovered their arms, with their bayonets, which threw them into the utmost disorder and confusion, they being unacquainted with such a manoeuvre."[17] This tactical formula did not work as well a second time. The Americans on September 16th gave ground when hard-pressed, but rebounded vigorously to put the redcoats themselves to flight several times. It was nip and tuck for two hours in the trampled buckwheat fields, and Washington had the satisfaction of watching his men outfight the foe. The redcoats were again wavering, after being twice dislodged, when he stopped the action. He had no wish to bring on a general engagement, and discretion won over pride when Howe sent a large body of troops to the rescue.

Taunts of Kipp's Bay had been wiped out by Connecticut and Massachusetts forces led by Colonel Thomas Knowlton, a Connecticut hero of Bunker Hill. Their honors were shared by Virginians and Marylanders under Major Andrew Leitch. Both leaders died of wounds and the victors had about 50 other casualties. Howe listed 14 killed and 78 wounded in his official report.

The action at Harlem Heights was a turning point in more ways than one. It did much to disprove the legend, credited by many Americans themselves, that the rebels could only fight behind field fortifications. It dated the beginning of a closer and more sympathetic bond between Washington and the men he praised warmly. But its most important effect could be traced to British headquarters. If Howe had been cautious before, he displayed a new respect for Washington's strongly entrenched army by not making another move for a month.

This respite encouraged Americans who had apprehensions of their rear being menaced by an invasion from the north. After retiring from Canada in June, the demoralized rebel army had fallen back to Isle aux Noix, at the foot of Lake Champlain, where Sullivan and Arnold awaited orders. This low, unwholesome campsite added to the sick list until whole regiments had not a man fit for duty. Dr. Beebe's journal of these days is filled with some appalling descriptions:

Language cannot describe nor imagination paint, the scenes of misery and distress the Soldiery endure. Scarcely a tent upon this Isle but what contains one or more in distress and continually groaning, & calling for relief, but in vain! . . . The most shocking of all Spectacles was to see a large barn Crowded full of men with this disorder [smallpox], many of whom could not See, Speak or walk. . . . No mortal will ever believe what these suffered unless they were eye witnesses.[18]

The Massachusetts surgeon continued to blame Arnold for all the army's ills. "I heartily wish some person would make an experiment on him," he raged, "to make the sun shine thro' his head with an ounce ball." From this historical distance, nevertheless, it would appear that both Arnold and Sullivan deserved credit for extricating the rags of the tattered army. Their burden was transferred to the shoulders of Horatio Gates on June 17th when Congress placed him in command of the forces on Lake Champlain.

This was the first of several occasions when the assembly entrusted a general with what it fancied to be "dictatorial powers." There had never been any deviation from a policy of civil control over the military. But the emergency on the northern front called for drastic remedies, and Congress gave Gates the authority to appoint or suspend subordinates at will, provided that he report his decisions for the approval of that body.

These were not powers likely to create a new Cromwell, and the former British major would doubtless have preferred a new army. The one that awaited him had been described by John Adams in a letter of July 7th as "an object of wretchedness enough to fill a humane mind with horrour; disgraced, defeated, discontented, dispirited, diseased, naked, undisciplined, eaten up with vermin; no clothes, beds, blankets; no medicines; no victuals, but salt pork and flour."[19]

From the Canadian border the survivors had fallen back to Crown Point near the head of Lake Champlain before Gates arrived. Not more than a few hundred men had been killed or wounded in a campaign of ten months, and even counting the capitulation at the Cedars the prisoners hardly exceeded a thousand. The invaders had kept on even terms with the enemy in these respects, but their worst losses did not appear in the casualty lists. Gates could not have been far wrong on July 16th in estimating a deficit of 5,000 troops since May 1st from desertion and death due to illness.[20] He found 3,000 sick at Crown Point and the remaining third of the force with its morale at half-mast.

Most of the delegates at Philadelphia admitted that the campaign had ended in a major disaster when America most needed defenders. William Williams of Connecticut did not excuse the assembly in a letter of August 7th: "Congress seems to be infatuated, are seeking after a thousand reasons of the miscarriages in Canada by a Comt. of that purpose etc. while the fault is in themselves, in neglecting and abandoning That Army to inevitable Destruction, and then severely censure Officers and Soldiers for their ill Conduct, in not making Brick without straw or even Stubble. . . . Many of Us grieve and lament the Fate of that unhappy Army, but as yet see not how nor what to do."[21]

At least the assembly went far toward compensating for any mistakes by appointing Gates to the command. Before the end of the summer the new leader had restored discipline and created a fighting force out of a demoralized mob.

Organization proved to be the specialty of a veteran who had begun his career under a cruel handicap. In the British army of 1750 he might better have been a well-born scoundrel than to acknowledge such a humble family background—a government clerk as father, and a mother remembered as housekeeper to the Duke of Leeds. Yet the hero of this success story rose by merit and bravery over the heads of Guards officers. At a time when juniors gained promotion by buying the commission of a higher rank, he displayed so much courage in a West Indies victory that General Monckton rewarded him with the honor of carrying the news to England. He added to his reputation by gallant conduct in the American campaigns, and George III himself recommended Gates for the rank of major.

After the war, freed from poverty by a fortunate marriage, he sold his commission and retired to an estate in Virginia. This was to be the beginning of a new military career which would take him to the second highest rank of the Continental Army. In 1776, at the age of forty-eight, he opposed his old royal patron with as much conviction as any native American. But Horatio Gates was no longer the dashing young officer of the last war. A grandfatherly figure wearing spectacles, he impressed most observers as being older than his actual years. He preferred to leave active field service to junior officers, and the army profited as a result from a rare ability as a military organizer and disciplinarian.

It did not take him long to discover that his promotion had aroused jealousies. In older armies the politics played by officers are more subtle, but one of Gates's rivals rode all the way to Philadelphia to protest in person. His mutterings caused the author of the Declaration to write with distaste to a fellow Virginia delegate: "Gen. Sullivan . . . came here to resign on Gate's appointment. His letter of resignation was just in on Friday. It was referred to this morning that a proper rap of the knuckles might be prepared, but on the advice of his friends he asked leave to withdraw it and repair to his duty."[22]

Philip Schuyler did not stir from Albany, though he submitted to the will of Congress with no better grace. His long and tedious complaints failed to undermine Gates, but the feud between the two men was to have its effects on strategy in later campaigns.

The new commander of the northern army brought down upon his head the disapproval of other generals when he ordered a retirement twenty miles up the lake to Fort Ticonderoga. At a council of war his subordinates agreed with him that Lake Champlain could be better defended at that post than Crown Point, where the works of the last war had fallen into sad decay. This decision was questioned by Gates's colleagues of the New York army. Instead of showing his resentment with the usual turgid rhetoric of military squabbles, he turned the other cheek in a letter worth quoting for its gentle humor. Israel Putnam had helped to build the Crown Point works, and Gates addressed him with a smile:

> Every fond mother dotes upon her booby, be his imperfections ever so glaring, and his good qualities ever so few. Crown Point was not indeed your own immediate offspring, but you had a capital hand in rearing the baby. You cut all the logs, which are now rotten as dirt, and tumbled in the dust. No matter for that. Why should you not be fond of Crown Point? If I live to be as old as you, I shall be as fond of Tyconderoga. I can assure you, I fancy already that my booby is a great deal handsomer than yours, and has a thousand excellencies that yours never possessed. But don't be uneasy, the absurdities of your booby time will very soon obliterate; but mine will live for some future great engineer, like myself, to laugh at and despise.

Gates did not back down an inch, for all of his amiability, and future events would prove that he had not erred in his decision. The works at Ticonderoga were also in disrepair, but the new commander found a practical engineer in Colonel Baldwin, who had built the fortifications at Boston. On July 25th that officer noted in his diary, "Genl. Gates & several other officers went over to the point with me & highly approved of the works I had laid out there, & ordered that 220 men Should work there daily at least & as many more as could be employed & was in high good humor."[23]

These labors had the added advantage of restoring discipline to men whose morale had suffered as much from idleness as defeat and disease. The next necessity was a lake squadron to oppose the small warships sent across the Atlantic to Carleton in knocked-down condition for reassembling at St. Johns. The British general had already begun that task when Gates sought an "admiral" to take charge of American efforts. As a soldier who had risen by valor, he had a preference for a fighter; and his appointment of Benedict Arnold was also based on that officer's extensive seafaring experience. A happier choice could not have been made, for the Connecticut brigadier hurled himself into the race of ship-building with characteristic fury.

There were also liabilities. Arnold as usual had been quarreling with his associates, so that Colonel Moses Hazen of the Canadian regiment and Colonel John De Haas now hated him as bitterly as his old enemy John Brown. All three protested their right to courts-martial to clear themselves of Arnold's charges. They were entitled to this justice, but Gates made use of his so-called dictatorial powers to quash the proceedings. He held that the emergency called for a postponement, and during the next few months Arnold might have been likened to a cat choked with cream. He had only to ask in order to receive, provided that his demands came within the limited American resources. Carpenters were rushed to Ticonderoga with the promise of extra pay and rum rations, and by August 20th the rebels had launched nine schooners, gondolas and galleys put together with green lumber and armed with swivels and small cannon. Seven more vessels were added to the little squadron during the next few weeks while Arnold vigorously drilled his crews of landlubbers in preparation for the day of battle.

Hard work and summer sunshine did more than hospital care to nurse back to health the army at Ticonderoga. The comments of two diarists also attest that by October the paternal commander had instilled new confidence into troops who had been defeated in their own minds. "Our Men work with life & Spirits this Day which shows a determined resolution to defend the place to the last Extr.," recorded Colonel Baldwin. It was the grumpy opinion of Dr. Beebe that pride had gone too far. "Our officers & soldiers in general, are remarkably expert in the swearing way," he observed. "Nothing comes more handy, or gives such power or force to their words, as a Blasphemous oath. . . . In short, they Laugh at death, mock at Hell and damnation; & even challenge the Diety, to remove them out of this world by Thunder and Lightning."[24]

The test came in October after Carleton appeared at the foot of the lake with his squadron. If it had taken him longer to build, he could boast of a force that outweighed Arnold two to one in metal. Officers of the Royal Navy directed his tactics on the morning of the 11th as the invaders bore down on Americans anchored in the narrow strait between Valcour Island and the western shore. The ensuing fight was described without heroics in the journal of Bayze Wells, a young Connecticut sergeant who had just been commissioned as lieutenant on the *Providence*:

> Friday 11 Octr this Day the wind at North and Clear thare was Snoe to be Seene on the mountains on the West Shore about Eight A. M. the Guard boat came in and fired an alarm and brought news of the Near Aproch of our Enemy. About ten A. M. a twenty-two Gun Ship hove in Sight and two Sixteen Gun Schooners and two Sloops and one floteing Battery which mounted twenty-Six Guns twenty-four Pounders and A Large number of boats. They Soon Gave us Battle we Returned the Same to them they Soon Disabled one of our Scooners and Obliged our men to Leve her and Get on Shore the Battle Lasted Eight hours Very hot they Landed men on Shore on boath Sides of us Which took Some Lives. . . . After Dark orders was Given for our fleet to Retreat to Crown-point accordingly we did and come by them undiscovered.[25]

The long battle against odds was the most valiant fight of Arnold's life. Its outcome could never have been in doubt, yet he blazed away at the enemy as if victory were in sight. When an inexperienced crew ran his little 12-gun "flagship" aground, he boarded the *Congress*. For five hours he pointed and fired the cannon himself while the enemy made a sieve of a galley which sank at dusk. Musket fire from British auxiliaries on Valcour Island swept the rebel decks as well as cannonballs, and half of the officers were killed or wounded.

The failure of the enemy to blow the American squadron out of the water was charged to impetuosity by Joshua Pell, one of the British army officers. "Our arm'd Boats immediately rush'd in amongst them and engag'd them without waiting for orders," he explained in his journal; "the *Carleton* went to their assistance, and kept up a continual firing until dark, during which time we destroyed a schooner . . . and greatly damaged another; unluckily for us, the wind chang'd and hindered the other part of our squadron from giving the *Carleton* any assistance; had it not thus happened, in all probability, the Rebels whole fleet would have been destroyed. Our loss consisted in two Arm'd Boats been sunk; about ten men kill'd and sixteen wounded."[26]

In the darkness Arnold slipped away through a British force which would have made short work of him in the morning when joined by such craft as the 18-gun *Inflexible*. The next day he had to scuttle two more ships and patch up the others. Adverse winds slowed up the pursuers, but they caught up with him on the 13th and a second action took place. This time Arnold sacrificed part of his remaining squadron in order to save the rest. The *Washington* was forced to strike her colors to three British ships, but the *Congress* and four galleys kept up a running fight for several hours. At last they were driven into a creek ten miles north of Crown Point and burned by crews which made their way back through the forest with the wounded.

This was the single American squadron action of a war dominated by enemy sea power. "Of our whole fleet we have saved only two galleys, two small schooners, one gondola and one sloop," Arnold reported.[27] He listed his killed and wounded as "eighty-odd" in addition to 110 prisoners.

The swarthy brigadier put up a heroic fight in these two actions, yet they delayed the British only a few days. It is as a shipbuilder that he deserves equal credit, for the mere presence of the rebel squadron delayed the enemy a few months at the task of assembling a superior force. The value of this result may be appraised from Carleton's own report to Germain on October 14th. "The season is so far advanced," he admitted after announcing his victories, "that I cannot yet pretend to inform your Lordship whether anything further can be done this year."[28]

This statement left the door open either for advance or retreat, and Carleton made his preference clear during the next two weeks. From his headquarters at Crown Point, evacuated by the rebels on the 14th, he profited from his control of the lake to send out reconnaissance parties both by land and water. The approach of winter left little time for a formal siege, and it had to be decided whether the works of Ticonderoga could be stormed.

The rebel strength had been increased to about 6,000 by reinforcements, and Dr. Thacher's journal gives a picture of an alert and confident army. "Each regiment has its alarm post assigned," he recorded on the 18th, "and they are ordered to repair to it, and to man the lines at daylight every morning. Among our defensive weapons are poles, about twelve feet long, armed with sharp iron points, which each soldier is to employ against the assailants when mounting the breast works."[29]

British vessels, he added, had "approached within a few miles of our garrison, and one boat came within cannon shot distance of our lower battery, in order to reconnoitre and sound the channel." An assault seemed so imminent toward the end of the month that Gates counseled his army in orders of the 27th:

> As the enemy's attack will probably be rash and sudden, the General earnestly recommends to every commanding officer . . . to be deliberate and cool in suffering his men to fire, never allowing them to throw away their shot in a random, unsoldierly manner. One close, well directed fire, at the distance of eight or ten rods, will do more toward defeating the enemy than all the scattered, random shot, fired in a whole day.[30]

Organization and discipline can never compete with the glory won in battle, but the main credit for stopping the British invasion belongs to a grandfatherly warrior with spectacles perched on the end of his nose. His opponent Carleton drew his own conclusions from accurate daily reports of American preparations. And on November 4th, after a suspicious calm, rebel scouts discovered that Crown Point had been evacuated by a British army of 9,000 on its way back to the foot of the lake.

Chapter 9

Lock, Stock and Barrel

I N ALL ages of war the story is the same—men on the firing line soon lose any personal hatred for the foe. General Heath, a kindly soul himself, remarked many friendly exchanges where the lines on Manhattan Island brought redcoats and Yankees within speaking distance. At such points the soldiers "were so civil to each other on their posts that one day, at a part of the creek where it was practicable, the British sentinel asked the American, who was nearly opposite to him, if he could give him a chew of tobacco: the latter, having in his pocket a piece of a thick twisted roll, sent it across the creek to the British sentinel, who, after taking off a bite, sent the remainder back again."[1]

Neither redcoats nor Yankees made much pretense of extending the same military courtesies to the third group of participants. English-speaking soldiers on both sides resented the intrusion in a family quarrel of the foreign mercenaries with their blue coats, thick pigtails and clumsy boots. The fierce mustaches worn by some of the Hessians in a day of smooth-shaven men stamped them all the more as aliens. Hostility on the part of Americans is understandable, but even sentences of five hundred lashes could not curb British animosity the moment an officer turned his back.

Americans took satisfaction in reports of these enemy disputes. "The Hessian and British troops disagree and are kept entirely separate," Ebenezer Hazard informed General Gates. "The latter do not like the former's being allowed to plunder while they are prohibited from doing it. Those rascals plunder all indiscriminately; if they see any thing they like, they say, 'Rebel, good for Hesse-mans,' and seize it for their own use. They have no idea of the distinctions of Whig and Tory."[2]

The redcoats soon became apt pupils, according to reputable testimony of American loyalists. Judge Thomas Jones, a recognized spokesman for the Tory faction, noted in his history of wartime New York the depredations of the king's troops as well as Germans. The scholarly Yale graduate was especially grieved by the pillage of books from King's College, the subscription library and the City Hall. About 60,000 volumes, he estimated, were hawked by soldiers and their doxies without interference from officers. In a grogshop he watched book after book being sold for the price of a few glasses of rum. Yet he had to admit to his sorrow that the rebel forces had not plundered even the Tory districts of Long Island. Such few instances as came to his attention resulted in swift punishments.[3]

British and Hessian larcenies, on the contrary, were perpetrated "with impunity, publicly and openly. No punishment was ever inflicted on the plunderers. No attempts were made by the British commanders to obtain restitution of the stolen goods, nor did they ever discountenance such unjustifiable proceedings by issuing orders condemning such unmilitary conduct. . . ."

Americans of 1776 were not stretching it when they complained of ravages that might have been committed by a horde of barbarians. Their opponents came from the lower orders of the population at a time when dwellers in English city slums and rural hovels were not gentle folk. Brutalized by poverty and cheap gin, oppressed by laws of ferocious severity, they remained freemen who asserted themselves with violence when denied political expression. Madame Riedesel, stopping in Bristol on her way to Canada, looked out of her inn window to see two naked sailors pounding each other into a pulp. Whenever this attractive mother of two little girls ventured into the street, she was surrounded by ruffians of both sexes who shouted, "French whore!"[4]

The British soldiers themselves often gave less cause for resentment than the fierce trollops who followed them across the ocean. Supposedly the legal wives of soldiers, as some actually were, these slatterns were tolerated along with their offspring as laundresses or bearers of burdens. Lists of prisoners contain feminine names which might be adopted by modern writers of cloak-and-sword novels. Ann Sutherland, Frances Edwards, Mary Campbell, Isabel Abbott, Jane Oakley, Catherine Rigby and Ann Keating were among the 66 women and 121 children captured in Canada, according to the Pennsylvania Archives, and marched to a rebel prison camp at Lancaster.[5]

The morals of the camp followers, as might be supposed, were not always above reproach. Still, it does not appear that many of them were prostitutes. Diaries and journals more often give a picture of bedraggled creatures, their faces blackened by the smoke of campfires, their backs bent under heavy loads as they straggled along with savage and unkempt brats. General Burgoyne, who confessed to the besetting sin of venery, found a commissary's wife attractive enough to share his tent in 1777. Many of the other British officers had mistresses, if Judge Jones may be credited, but they could have discovered few beauties among the general run of camp followers.

American prisoners had to run the gauntlet of jeering drabs who befouled them with the vocabulary of Billingsgate and snatched their possessions. Colonel Atlee met with civil treatment from the Highlanders to whom he surrendered at the battle of Long Island. But within the precincts of English regiments the captives were pelted with "the most scurrilous and abusive language, both from the officers, soldiers, and camp ladies, every one at that time turning hangman, and demanding of the guard why we were not . . . put to the bayonet, and hanged, &c., &c., &c., &c., Serenaded thus by the musical tongues of Britons, we arrived at Bedford, where, for sixteen beside myself, we were favored with a soldier's tent, in which we had not room to lie down, and nothing allowed us for covering."[6]

The rebel army also had its female camp folowers. The name Molly Pitcher, applied to several different heroines of Revolutionary legend, was long accepted without question. But there is much to support the theory that this generic term was given to various women who carried pitchers of water for thirsty soldiers on duty. The courage and hardihood of these Amazons cannot be doubted, and many appear to have been faithful wives. Their frailer sisters added to the problems of discipline, and diarists frequently mention the drumming out of camp of some painted doxy. Even such a remote spot as Ticonderoga was not neglected by practitioners of the oldest profession, for Schuyler reported to Congress early in 1776: "The men from Pennsylvania are greatly infected with the venereal disease. Captain Dorsey has left no less than fourteen in the Hospital. . . . All the medicines in the hospital are nearly expended."[7]

Women took the lead in the most aggressive and pitiless plundering by the redcoats. They found New York a rich prize when it fell on September 16, 1776, and looters probably started the great fire that destroyed a fourth of the buildings only a few days later. British officers accused the rebels of being incendiaries, but an impartial investigation in modern times by the New York Historical Society could dig up no proofs of American guilt. Enemy indiscipline seems to have been responsible, and the invaders paid a heavy penalty in discomfort during the next seven years. In defiance of all laws of physics, they tried at one period to squeeze as many as 40,000 troops and loyalist refugees into a town that had never held more than 22,000 inhabitants before the fire. The result was an overcrowding that had its effects on British morale.

Early in the war General Washington declared in a letter to his half-brother John Augustine that a reward of £10,000 would not have tempted him to accept the command if he had suspected the tribulations ahead. A few months later he doubled the figure. And on September 22, 1776, the disgruntled leader reached a grand climax: "Fifty thousand pounds would not induce me to undergo what I have done."[8]

This amount appears to have been his limit, though he found other forceful expressions as his trials increased.

Not the least of the general's qualifications was the broad political experience acquired in the Continental Congress and Virginia assembly. Fearless at opposing popular opinion when the time came, he would nevertheless have agreed with the definition of politics as "the art of the possible." As a Virginia militia colonel he had learned that the leader of a citizen army must depend on public support. During the siege of Boston this aspect of his position, rather than any lust for the applause of the crowd, caused him to write a groping letter to Joseph Reed:

> Nothing would give me more real satisfaction, than to know the sentiments, which are entertained of me by the public, whether they be favorable or otherwise; and I urged as a reason, that the man, who wished to steer clear of shelves and rocks, must know where they lie. I know the integrity of my own heart, but to declare it, unless to a friend, may be an argument of vanity; I know the unhappy predicament I stand in! I know that much is expected of me; I know, that without men, without arms, without ammunition, without anything fit for the accommodation of a soldier, little is to be done; and, what is mortifying, I know, that I cannot stand justified to the world without exposing my own weakness, and injuring the cause, by declaring my wants, which I am determined not to do, further than unavoidable necessity brings every man acquainted with them.[9]

The Pennsylvania colonel wrote a reassuring reply, but Washington was not reassured. He was too much of a realist not to foresee that his value to the cause might eventually be destroyed by circumstances due to

America's material poverty rather than any fault of his own. Public toler-ance of defeat had its limits, and in the autumn of 1776 the commander in chief must have realized that his decisions were being questioned if not actually censured.

Even in its new position behind the strong Harlem Heights lines on September 16th, the army had not escaped the danger of envelopment by an enemy controlling both rivers. The key to the American position was Kingsbridge. This post guarded not only the route of retreat but also the line of supplies. Washington's strategy aimed at nothing more than passive defense, leaving the initiative to a stronger enemy. Most of his provisions came from Connecticut, but in case of disaster he planned to retire through New Jersey rather than take the risk of having his army cornered in New England. For that purpose he kept strong garrisons at Fort Washington and Fort Lee, on opposite sides of the Hudson, even after the enemy warships safely passed the batteries and ran up the river to Dobbs Ferry, far in the rear.

Three lines of rebel entrenchments extended northward from the present location of 145th Street and eastward from the Hudson to the Harlem. On the east side of the Harlem, as far as Throg's Neck, detached redoubts defended the front all the way to Long Island Sound. The total of the army "on paper" reached the impressive figure of 25,735 on October 5, 1776. But Adjutant General Reed reported 8,075 men sick or on furlough, and few of the 44 regiments were fully recruited. As nearly as can be guessed from such admittedly incomplete returns, Washington had a strength of not more than 12,000 effectives.

Brief enlistments, added to illness and desertion, kept the force so fluctuating that he could never be sure of his resources from one day to the next. Many pages might be filled with his bitter comments on the recruiting system, and it has been found convenient to make the Con-tinental Congress the scapegoat. Yet the actual evidence, as summed up by a modern historical writer, proves that this legend is without founda-tion.[10] The Journals of Congress attest that the assembly took the lead as early as the autumn of 1775 in advocating enlistments for the duration of the war. A majority of the delegates were in accord with Elbridge Gerry, of Massachusetts, when he wrote to Gates on June 25, 1776:

> I cannot conceive why we may not, by setting out right, soon make soldiers equal to any that the world affords. . . . And in the first place, I put it down as a fixed, settled principle, that they must be enlisted

for the war, let the necessary encouragement be what it may, which I am happy to find the Generals agreed in, and I think most of the members of Congress.[11]

Scores of similar quotations might be adduced, and Congress demonstrated by works as well as opinions its wish to provide Washington with a dependable army. The assembly sent committees both to New York and Ticonderoga in the late summer of 1776. On a basis of their reports, the delegates resolved on September 16th that "eighty-eight battalions be inlisted as soon as possible, *to service during the present war. . . ."*[12] Italics have been added for emphasis, and the measure offered an incentive by prescribing "that twenty dollars be given as a bounty to each non-commissioned officer and private soldier, who shall enlist to service during the present war, unless sooner discharged by Congress." In addition, a hundred acres of land were to be granted to each recruit.

The zeal of the civilians at Philadelphia went so far that one of them suggested a national training school for officers. John Adams already had a good claim to being father of the Navy, and on September 20th he visioned a future West Point in a letter to Colonel Knox: "I wish we had a military academy, and should be obliged to you for a plan of such an institution. The expense would be a trifle—no object at all with me."[13] The next day he included a postscript to the effect that a committee had been named to draw up a proposal. No report was ever made, but the committee with the army at New York endorsed the idea.

On November 12th, unfortunately, Congress had to back down to the extent of soliciting three-year Continental terms instead of enlistments for the war, offering the same bounty minus the land. The retreat may be charged to the higher bounties announced by Massachusetts and other states, as the former colonies were beginning to call themselves. From that time onward, they were usually able to hold forth more tempting inducements to recruits for short terms in the militia forces of home defense.

This may appear a selfish and parochial policy, but there were reasons for the petty armies and navies that the states insisted on retaining. Most of them were exposed to a surprise attack directed at some point of the long coastline by an enemy squadron. Neither the Continental Army nor Navy had the means of providing a central defense against such threats. As a consequence, the states felt it necessary to maintain a few warships of their own and a militia establishment capable of raising enough short-term troops for the emergency.

The events of coming years would prove that much was to be said on their side. Congress had no resources for creating a fleet equal to the British naval strength, and American seamen soon showed a preference for serving in privateers. Before the end of 1776 these raiders captured more than 250 West Indiamen, inflicting an estimated loss in trade of £1,800,000 which was reflected in insurance rates raised 28 per cent. Arthur Lee could boast that "one week's advices of the captures we have made, according to the estimate in London, exceeds £200,000 sterling in British goods."[14] Flattering to American pride as such results may have been, there were penalties. The high rewards of privateering tempted not only seamen but also shipbuilders and owners at the expense of the infant Navy. On October 17, 1776, an ardent young sea captain named John Paul Jones wrote to Robert Morris:

It is to the last degree distressing to contemplate the state and expense of our navy. The common class of mankind are actuated by no nobler principle than that of self-interest; this, and this only, determines all adventurers in privateers, the owners as well as those they employ. And while this is the case, unless the private enrollment of individuals in our navy is made superiour to that in privateers, it never can become respectable, it never will become formidable, and without a respectable navy, alas America![15]

No remedy was ever found. Privateers continued to sap the vitality of the little American fleet until little more is heard of its operations after 1776. Britannia ruled the waves indeed during the Revolution, and Washington paid a large part of the price in the consequences felt by his depleted land forces.

These were some of the wheels within wheels revolving behind the scenes during the four-week lull at Harlem Heights. Howe believed, apparently with good reason, that the rebel works could not be stormed without exorbitant losses. Enthusiasm was not his outstanding trait, and in a gloomy dispatch of September 25th he asked Germain for more warships as well as troops.[16] "Upon the present appearance of things," he explained, "I look upon the further progress of this army for the campaign to be rather precarious. . . . The enemy is too strongly posted to be attacked in front, and innumerable difficulties are in my way of turning him on either side, though his army is much dispirited, from the late success of his Majesty's arms; yet I have not the smallest prospect of finishing the contest this campaign, not until the Rebels see preparations in the Spring, that may preclude all thoughts of further resistance."

During the interlude the rebels got the better of the daily skirmishes.

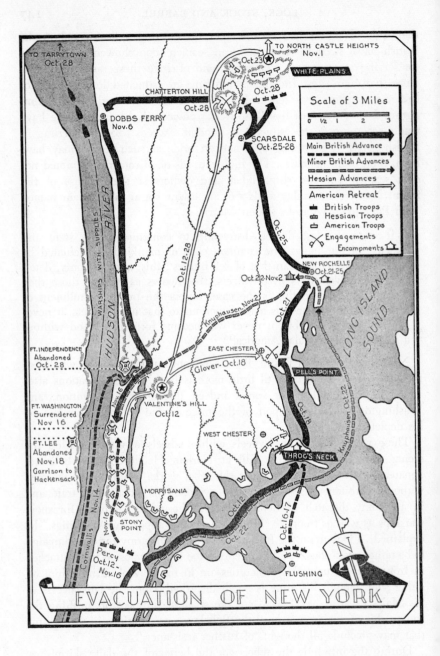

EVACUATION OF NEW YORK

American riflemen found such warfare to their taste, and Howe's forces learned by costly experience to double their ideas of effective small-arms range. The Hessian forces included riflemen called Jägers, distinguished by a green uniform. But their short-barreled weapon proved slower to load and less accurate than the frontier firemen's. Nor did the invaders show as much aptitude at the scouting and raiding which Americans considered a part of rifle tactics.

The British made no move of importance until the middle of October. Then Howe struck with the swiftness and precision of a finished tactician. The result of his attempt to turn the American position was a battle which might without flippancy be described as lost, strayed or stolen from the pages of history.

Rebel strategists had counted too much on their opponents being stopped by the dangerous waters of Hell Gate. But Lord Howe had a reputation for overcoming naval difficulties. With the loss of only a few men drowned, he transferred a large body of troops by water to Throg's Neck.

Washington perceived that the enemy intended to work around to the rear of his entire position, cutting off his main source of food supplies and imperiling his retreat. On the night of the 17th the threat became a crisis when General Howe embarked a picked force of redcoats and Hessians for a landing at Pell's Point. This was the second stage of a great turning movement such as the one which evicted the defenders of Long Island.

The rebel general met the threat by detaching as many troops as possible to the eastward while preparing for a hasty evacuation of the Harlem lines. At dawn on the 18th the future of the cause depended for a few hours on the judgment of a stocky little man, hard as an oaken knot, who stood on a hilltop with his telescope and watched the approach of the enemy transports. For it was up to Colonel John Glover to delay the advance as long as he could with his fishermen and three other Massachusetts regiments—a total of 850 troops and three small fieldpieces.

It is one of the oddities of American history that the ensuing all-day action should have been ignored by chroniclers or dismissed as a skirmish. British historians without exception give it scant attention, and even such a standard American work as Carrington's *Battles of the American Revolution* devotes a single sentence to the contest. Yet the British defeat at Pell's Point involved larger numbers and greater strategic consequences than a dozen other engagements dignified with the name of battles.

The oversight may be explained in part by Colonel Glover's painful reticence. In his own description the red-headed Massachusetts fisherman confessed to trepidation after posting his forces to oppose the landing: "Oh! the anxiety of mind I was then in for the fate of the day. . . . I would have given a thousand worlds to have had General Lee, or some other experienced officer present, to direct, or at least to approve of what I had done."[17]

A professional soldier would probably never have thought of such a simple solution as placing the four regiments at intervals behind stone walls on both sides of the road, thus compelling the enemy column to run the gauntlet of musketry. This narrow lane offered the only practical approach in a countryside of thickets, defiles and boulders which did not invite a flank attack. The British and German officers, moreover, apparently did not look forward to such a determined stand by outnumbered rebels.

Americans estimated the enemy strength as high as 12,000, but any such figure is manifestly absurd. It is not likely that more than 4,000 took part in the fight of the 18th, about three-fourths of them Hessians. This was the conclusion of William Abbatt, an American historical writer of 1901 who made the neglected battle the subject of a monograph based on a study of the ground as well as all available records. He identified four German regiments as having been present, plus such British troops as the light infantry and grenadier companies of the 4th and 14th foot and the dismounted dragoons of the 16th and 17th light horse.[18]

Glover's plan of battle was in effect a calculated Lexington. After posting three of his regiments at intervals behind the stone walls, he ordered each to hold the enemy in check as long as possible, then to make an orderly retirement toward a new position in the rear. It was a game of tactical leapfrog he had in mind, subjecting the attackers to a continual fire without asking too much from Americans who could look forward to recuperation after taking their turn. Behind the three advance units Glover kept his own "amphibious regiment" in reserve with the cannon for a final stand behind a stream with steep banks. Thus the rebels awaited the British advance in the following order:

Colonel Joseph Read	13th Massachusetts	226 privates
Colonel William Shepherd	3rd "	204 "
Colonel Loammi Baldwin	26th "	234 "
Colonel John Glover	14th "	179 "

The action began with an exchange of shots by skirmishers. About eight o'clock Read's regiment awaited the advance of a compact column of red and blue uniforms offering a good target to the rebels crouching behind the stone wall. The men of the 13th held their fire until the foe came within thirty yards, according to Glover's account, "then rose up and gave them the whole charge; the enemy broke, and retreated for the main body to come up. In this situation we remained about an hour and a half, when they appeared about four thousand, with seven pieces of artillery; they now advance, keeping up a constant [fire of] artillery; we kept post under cover of the stone wall till they came within fifty yards of us, rose up and gave them the whole charge of the battalion; they halted and returned the fire with showers of musketry and cannon balls. We exchanged seven rounds at this post, retreated, and formed in the rear of Colonel Shepherd and on his left."

Glover himself remained on the firing line with each regiment in turn, encouraging his men to hold firm and not waste their fire. The redcoats and mercenaries formed again into column, and about ten o'clock the action entered its hottest phase. "They then shouted and pushed on until they came on Shepherd, posted behind a fine double stone wall; he rose up and fired by grand divisions, by which he kept up a constant fire, and maintained his part until he exchanged seventeen rounds with them, and caused them to retreat several times, once in particular so far that a soldier of Colonel Shepherd's leaped over the wall and took a hat and canteen off of a Captain that lay dead on the ground they retreated from. However, their body being so much larger than ours, we were, for the preservation of the men, forced to retreat, and formed in the rear of Baldwin's regiment."

The invaders had made their way by this time to more open country, where they had room for a flank attack. Toward noon, after Baldwin's regiment fired a round or two at the Hessians, Glover decided that "the ground being so much in their favour, and their heavy train of artillery, we could do little before we retreated to the bottom of the hill, and had to pass through a run of water (the bridge I had taken up before) and then marched up a hill the opposite side of the creek, where I had left my artillery. . . . The enemy halted, and played away their artillery at us, and we at them, till night, without any damage on our side, and but very little on theirs. At dark we came off, and marched about three miles, leading to Dobb's Ferry, after fighting all day without victuals or drink, laying as a picket all night, the heavens over us and the earth under us, which was all we had, having left our baggage at the old encampment we left in the morning."

The rebels, fighting behind cover, had only eight men killed and thirteen wounded, and the enemy's losses will always remain one of the war's mysteries. Howe's official report to Germain at the late date of November 30th contains some significant errors and omissions:

> On the march to this ground, a skirmish ensued with a small party of the enemy posted to defend a narrow causeway, who were pursued for a mile, when a considerable body appearing in front behind stone-walls and in woods, some companies of Light Infantry and a part of the Chasseurs were detached to dislodge them, which they did effectually. . . .Three soldiers were killed and twenty wounded. The enemy's loss upon this occasion was a Lieutenant-Colonel killed, a Major wounded, and about ninety men killed and wounded.[19]

Colonel Shepherd actually had been wounded by a ball through the neck, but he lived to fight again on twenty-one other days of battle. Howe's returns of British losses are probably correct, but there is no mention either of the presence or casualties of the Hessians who composed three-fourths of the attacking column. The omission suggests that the British general had reasons for protecting the reputation of the mercenaries in their first real test against the despised provincials.

An American officer mentioned in a letter of October 28th that "two deserters came over to us . . . who say the enemy's loss on Friday was more than eight hundred killed and wounded." This figure is obviously too high, and another American letter of the 19th gives a more trustworthy estimate, "Two deserters from the enemy say they lost one thousand, but I really have the best opinions to believe they lost one hundred and fifty or upwards, as our men fired with great coolness at a good distance."[20]

The retreating Americans had no way of knowing how many enemy dead and wounded had been left behind, and little credence can be placed in Colonel Baldwin's surmise of 200 slain. Abbatt reckoned the total casualties at 800 to 1,000, but this figure also seems too high. It is anybody's guess as to the losses which may have resulted from at least four thousand musket balls poured into a column by men firing from behind cover at ranges of thirty to fifty yards. Allowing for a large percentage of wasted shots, Howe's killed and wounded may have equaled the 377 acknowledged by him at the battle of Long Island.

The strategic effects of the fight on October 18 are best appraised from the dates. Howe made no further move of consequence until the 21st, when he cautiously advanced six miles with two columns brought up to a strength of 13,000 by troops landed from transports. This delay gave Washington added time to extricate his army from the danger of envelopment. Using Kingsbridge as a pivot, he changed front from south to east, occupying a new position reaching from that post eighteen miles northward to White Plains. This maneuver was not so simple in execution, of course, and the three days gained at Pell's Point helped the rebel commander to finish a chain of redoubts along the wooded hills behind the Bronx River. There were some misgivings about leaving 2,500 men behind at Fort Washington, but a council of officers decided that the post should not be abandoned.

The rebels found themselves in the strange situation of holding enemy territory in their own country. Tories outnumbered patriots by far in Westchester County, so that the troops had to be on their guard against such reprisals as spiking unguarded cannon. The officers of one detachment reacted by burning the courthouse at White Plains, but it speaks well for Washington's discipline that he turned the offenders over to civil justice for punishment.

No such restraints curbed enemy soldiers who plundered the Westchester loyalists welcoming them as deliverers. Household goods had a special fascination for the Hessians, who did not neglect even pots and pans when loading their stolen wagons with loot. Such activities go a long way toward explaining Howe's slow progress to White Plains after being further reinforced on the 25th by more Hessians just arrived from Europe.

The redcoats were severely harassed by riflemen in this wooded area. And here for the first time the British made such effective use of their dragoons in skirmishes that Washington found it expedient to deprecate the effects in orders of the 27th:

> The General, observing that the army seems unacquainted with the enemy's horse, and that when any parties meet with them, they do not oppose them with the same alacrity which they show in other cases, thinks it necessary to inform the officers and soldiers, that, in such a broken country full of stone walls, no enemy is more to be despised, as they cannot leave the road; so that any party attacking them may be sure to do it to advantage by taking post in the woods by the

roads, or along the stone walls, where they will not venture to follow them; and, as an encouragement . . . the General offers one hundred dollars for every trooper, with his horse and accoutrements, who shall be brought in.[21]

The rebels still controlled the upper road over which supplies came to them from Connecticut. Howe overtook them on the 27th, and the next day his forces again bought a few acres of ground at an excessive price in blood.

The British commander planned another of his flank attacks, but General Leslie's division delivered the direct blow prematurely while Colonel Rall's Hessians were stealing around the American right. The redcoats had trouble in crossing the river, but their heaviest losses were incurred in the attempt to storm Chatterton's Hill, held by two units which had won renown at Long Island. Haslet's Delaware regiment and Smallwood's Marylanders not only repulsed their assailants but pursued them down the slope in two counterattacks. The rebels appeared to have won the day until the belated German turning movement caught them by surprise and routed some of the defenders of the hill. The others dropped back to prepared positions in the rear, and the battle of White Plains ended without changing the strategic situation.

This time the enemy made no pretense of exulting, and recriminations flew behind the British lines. Most of Howe's officers agreed with Stedman that "the victory, being obtained, was not followed by a single advantage."[22] The official returns listed 214 redcoats and 99 mercenaries killed or wounded—more than double an American loss given all the way from 90 to 130 casualties.

Both armies rested the next day. On the 30th Lord Percy arrived with reinforcements, but heavy rains delayed the assault in force planned by Howe for the last day of the month. Washington retired meanwhile to a position at North Castle Heights which the British general deemed too strong to be stormed.

The stalemate lasted a week, then the rebels were disconcerted to find the enemy retiring not only from the White Plains area but even the temporary New Rochelle base. On November 5th most of the British forces had fallen back to Dobbs' Ferry, where they were supplied by ships. This was evidently one more of Howe's bewildering surprises, and Washington concluded that his opponent "must undertake something on account of his reputation [and] that he would probably go into New Jersey." A council of American generals agreed unanimously that the state must be defended, and Charles Lee was given the assignment. On

November 9th the first division of rebels crossed the Hudson at Peekskill, and by the 14th the bulk of the army was on the New Jersey side, with headquarters at Hackensack.

As early as November 6th the commander in chief had informed Congress that he expected an attack on Fort Washington, but both he and Greene trusted that the post could be safely evacuated in an emergency by a garrison taken across the river in small boats. They did not reckon sufficiently on Howe's tactical ability, and on the 16th he took advantage of divided American forces to strike his heaviest blow of the war.

The five bastions of Fort Washington with their outworks occupied an oblong area about three miles long and half as wide on two ridges parallel to the Hudson. The fort itself did not offer as many obstacles as the surrounding terrain of steep wooded knolls bristling with a system of isolated redoubts, abatis and batteries. Howe reasoned that if these outer defenses could be penetrated, the inner works were so cramped as to become a trap rather than refuge. Deserters had already given the British accurate information of all positions before the four assaulting columns moved forward at dawn while the batteries added their fire to the cannonade from the warship *Pearl* in the river.

Colonel John Magaw's garrison had recently been strengthened, so that about 2,700 Americans (according to Howe's later returns of prisoners) awaited an attack launched from three directions. Knyphausen and his Hessians from the northward, Cornwallis from the eastward, Percy from the southward—these forces were accompanied by a fourth column of Highlanders under General Fraser advancing from the southeast for a feint.

It had been intended that the 5,000 Hessians should strike the decisive blow, but again the reputation of the mercenaries suffered. They were given such a hot reception by rebel riflemen in wooded country that the advance came to a standstill in this quarter. It was the feint which unexpectedly developed into the real attack when the Highlanders broke through the lines and took 200 prisoners. The stubborn resistance collapsed at all points as the remaining 2,500 troops fell back into a fort designed only to hold a thousand. Magaw was justified in concluding that further efforts could only end in a futile sacrifice, and after a brief parley he surrendered. Another butchery of prisoners might have ensued, according to Fortesque, if the British officers had not "checked the Hessians, who, maddened by the resistance of the American riflemen, had begun to ply their bayonets."[23]

Patriots found consolation afterwards in wild rumors, for a Phila-

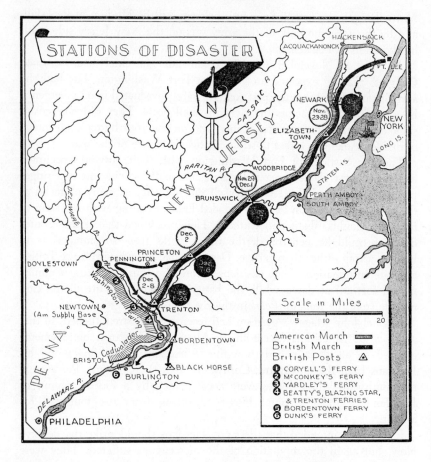

delphia gazette declared that "the enemy lost before the lines of Fort Washington, seventeen hundred killed on the field, and ninety-six wagons of wounded, the most mortally."[24] But Howe's actual losses were not too severe as the price of such a victory—128 British killed and wounded, half of them Highlanders of the Black Watch, and 330 Hessians. The American casualties included 130 killed and wounded.

The British general promptly followed up his success. On the 17th Lord Howe transported a force up the river in flatboats, and Cornwallis crossed at a point near Yonkers. This move forced the rebels to abandon Fort Lee, opposite Fort Washington, and a hundred more prisoners fell to the enemy. The losses of arms and stores at the two posts included 161 cannon, 2,800 muskets and tons of shot, shell and cartridges.

Washington's little army, reduced to 5,410 effectives on the 23rd, had a close squeak near Fort Lee. Greene barely managed to secure the route to the bridge over the Hackensack, holding open an avenue of escape. The hard-pressed rebel forces left Newark just ahead of Cornwallis's flying column of 4,500 troops, reinforced there on the 23rd by nine additional battalions.

It was no longer a question of defending New Jersey. The issue now was whether Washington could keep far enough ahead of the pursuit to save his army from being captured wholesale. His anxiety was increased by the strange behavior of General Lee, whose 7,500 troops could have been useful. But that eccentric warrior went his own way over a northern New Jersey route without paying much heed to Washington's urgent pleas for concerted action.

Cornwallis also felt the strain of forced marches, and the historian of the British army described the redcoats as "half starved and worn out with fatigue" when they halted at Brunswick on the 29th in obedience to orders. The rebel commander stumbled ahead with the few thousand men he had left, reaching Trenton on December 3rd. Here he rested his army while seizing boats up and down the Delaware, and two days later Washington retraced his steps to Princeton. His intention, he reported to Congress, was to make a stand "so soon as there shall be the least prospect of doing it with propriety." But Howe had joined Cornwallis at Brunswick, and their prey had little choice but to beat a hasty retreat to Trenton. The campaign came to an abrupt end on December 8th, when the American forces crossed to the Pennsylvania shore, leaving most of New Jersey to the foe.

Chapter 10

The Crossing of the Delaware

NO BRITISH general of the war ever let himself in for more severe censure than Sir William Howe. Some of his countrymen went so far as to insinuate that his well-known Whig sympathies got the better of his military judgment. Kinder critics attributed his lethargy to nights spent at the gaming table in the company of an American mistress who lost as much as three hundred guineas of his money at a sitting. A good-humored reference to such relaxations is found in contemporary doggerel:

> Awake, awake, Sir Billy,
> There's forage in the plain.
> Ah! leave your little filly,
> And open the campaign.
> Heed not a woman's prattle
> Which tickles in the ear,
> But give the word for battle
> And grasp the warlike spear.

There are times when it would seem that Howe might have pressed his advantage harder against outweighed foes. Yet the testimony of British officers on the spot cannot be ignored, and they paid respectful tribute to the rebel field fortifications of 1776. The pick and spade served military amateurs well as weapons against an adversary too humane to spend the lives of his men recklessly.

Another factor not to be overlooked is the most temperate age of warfare ever known in modern history. The hideous excesses of the Thirty Years' War had led to a reaction toward moderation at the dawn of the eighteenth century. Ethical motives alone would not have been enough to bring about the change, but soldiers themselves found it needful to adopt more conservative tactics after the flintlock and bayonet replaced the pike and matchlock. It took several years to train a recruit for the new linear warfare, so that each infantry private represented an investment worth hoarding. The headlong slaughters and ravages of the past seemed barbarous to generals who prided themselves on the arts of maneuver and siegecraft. Troops depended on magazines instead of picking the bones of the countryside, and noncombatants met with so much consideration that an invading enemy often paid for his supplies. The historian Gibbon and the jurist Vattel both believed that man had risen superior to war, and Marshal Saxe asserted his conviction that a general of parts could wage war successfully all his life without giving battle.

These doctrines had been in vogue for three generations when Howe learned his trade. To judge him on a basis of today's military thought is as ridiculous as expecting a present-day soldier to think in terms of the warfare of the twenty-first century. Sir William Howe was a child of his own age, and after pursuing Washington all the way to the Delaware he naturally concluded that the time had come for going into winter quarters.

As for the effectiveness of his easygoing strategy, Howe might have pointed out that Washington's main army had shrunk from 20,000 to 3,000 troops since August. A reasonable man himself, the British general believed that the rebel cause would shake itself to pieces, like a hastily assembled machine, as soon as Americans had time to recover from their madness. More than half the enlistments were expiring at the end of the year, with little prospect of many of them being renewed. There had been some hope of raising recruits in New Jersey, but Greene is authority for the estimate that fewer than a hundred came forward.

Anyone as genial as Sir William Howe liked to see people enjoying themselves. He would not have begrudged even Washington a pleasant Christmas if such a thing could have been possible for that beaten general. At least the British commander had it within his power to comfort the German officers who had twice been compelled to eat crow along with some of their own words. He had already paid them a compliment, to the disgust of British subordinates, by renaming Fort Washington. That post was now known as Fort Knyphausen after the Hessian general whose troops had been stopped by the rebel riflemen in the action. And Howe further honored the mercenaries in December by assigning them the posts of danger in New Jersey—Colonel Rall with three regiments at Trenton, and Colonel von Donop with about 2,000 men at Bordentown. Other cantonments were located throughout New Jersey to hold that conquered state. Nor did Howe neglect the broader aspects of strategy. Unlike several of his colleagues, he had never underrated the Americans he admired in every respect except their passion for independence. He had long believed it necessary to isolate New England by placing a strong force in Rhode Island until an army could sweep down from Canada and gain control of the Hudson. His plan also contemplated the capture of Philadelphia in the spring to subdue the middle states, and an invasion of the South soon afterwards. Altogether, he estimated that at least 50,000 troops would be required for these combined operations at their peak.

The first step had already been taken when General Clinton sailed from New York to Rhode Island early in December with 6,000 troops transported by Sir Peter Parker's squadron. This force occupied Newport without meeting resistance, and on the 14th Howe was back in New York while Cornwallis prepared to enjoy a leave in England. The British army had gone into winter quarters.

There were times later in the war when the American cause sank lower materially, but this month dates the very ditch of moral poverty. During the flight across New Jersey, with the army in daily peril of capture, Thomas Paine wrote his first *Crisis* pamphlet by the campfire at night after marching all day as a volunteer. But even though he poured out his scorn on every "summer soldier and sunshine patriot" who held back in the emergency, only 3,000 effectives remained when the army reached Princeton. These stalwarts were called together in groups to hear readings of Paine's appeal, and it may be that even Washington was inspired by the words, "America did not, nor does not want force; but she wanted a proper application of that force. . . . A single successful battle next year will settle the whole."

The commander in chief wrote to his half-brother on the 18th that "the game is nearly up."[1] Gordon, who interviewed some of the participants afterwards, asserted that at Newark, with the foe but a few miles behind, Washington told Reed his plans in case of disaster: "My neck does not feel as though it was made for a halter. We must retire to Augusta County in Virginia. Numbers will be obliged to repair to us for safety; and we must try to do what we can in carrying on a predatory war; and if overpowered we must cross the Allegheny mountains."[2]

An enemy advance on Philadelphia was apprehended daily, and on the 13th Congress resolved to leave the panic-stricken city and meet at Baltimore. The decision has been condemned by the heroic school of historians,

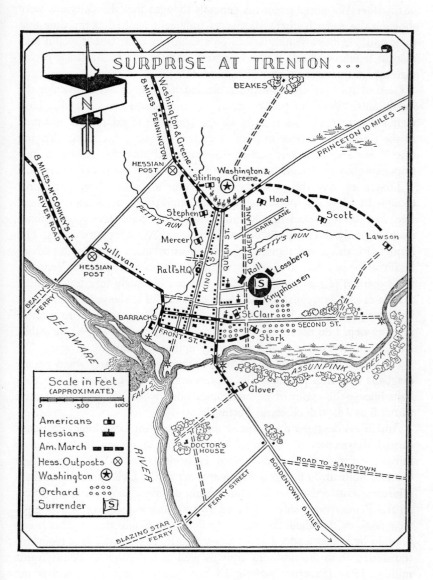

but neither Washington nor his generals thought that the delegates were showing the white feather. All men of judgment realized at the time that the capture of the assembly would be a catastrophe. At best it would take months to elect and seat a new Congress, and the personal courage of the members did not need the proof of bravado.

General Putnam, in command at Philadelphia, endeavored to calm the inhabitants. "Weak or wicked men," he proclaimed on the 13th, "have maliciously reported that it is the design and wish of the officers and men in the Continental Army to burn or destroy the city. . . ." After denying this "false and malicious report," he promised that the American metropolis would be defended to the last "against all invaders and enemies."[3]

That same day the cause benefited from a stroke of good fortune, though its blessings would not be fully appreciated until later. General Lee had been meandering through northern New Jersey, sometimes marching only three miles a day while ignoring Washington's orders. The former British colonel showed signs of an unbalanced mind in the advice he imparted so freely to everyone within reach, including enemy generals. Lee's opinion of his superior's ability was put obliquely in a letter stating that "a certain great man is damnably deficient." He showed his contempt for the civil authority by complaining that "the Congress seem to stumble at every step. I do not mean one or two of the cattle, but the whole stable. I have been very free in delivering my opinion to 'em."[4]

He was in the very act of writing another arrogant letter when enemy dragoons took him prisoner. His captors were thirty troopers of the 16th light horse—the regiment he had commanded when winning his greatest triumph as a British officer in Portugal.

Americans deplored the event at the moment, for Lee's long experience earned the respect of citizen-soldiers. But his army was intact, even if thinned by desertions and expired enlistments; and Washington sent General Sullivan to march the remnants across the Delaware. When these reinforcements arrived on December 22nd during a snowstorm, the forces on the Pennsylvania side numbered 10,106 rank and file, of which 5,398 were sick or detached, leaving a total of 4,708 effectives.[5] The troops brought by Sullivan added about 3,000, and there were also four regiments transferred from the northern army as well as a division of Pennsylvania militia. Thus the army making its headquarters at Newtown was not only stronger in numbers but also morale as compared to the rebel force during the worst of the New Jersey retreat.

All of Washington's tactics make it plain that he never forgot the precept of his first major action. Braddock's disaster taught him that one soldier armed with the moral weapon of surprise is worth a dozen caught mentally unprepared. Never throughout the Revolution did he accept pitched battles he could avoid, and no general ever showed a more marked preference for night attacks despite the risks of confusion.

On the 21st the commander in chief confided to Reed that "some enterprise must be undertaken in our present circumstances, or we must give up the cause." Two days later his plans had matured to such an extent that he informed his adjutant: "Christmas day at night, one hour before day, is the time fixed upon for our attempt at Trenton. For Heaven's sake keep this to yourself, as the discovery of it may prove fatal to us; our numbers, sorry I am to say, being less than I had any conception of; but necessity, dire necessity will, nay must, justify my attack."[6]

Professional soldiers have always distrusted operations calling for concentric columns whose effectiveness depends on precise timing and cooperation. Washington showed no such prejudice when he decided to send three detachments across the river on Christmas night—a right wing under Colonel John Cadwalader to attack Donop's corps at Bordentown; a center consisting of General James Ewing's brigade to cut communications between Trenton and Bordentown; and a left wing led by himself for an attack on Rall at Trenton.

These forces, all told, amounted to about 5,000 men, nearly half of them in Washington's force. He also ordered a few companies of Pennsylvania militia to make a demonstration on the west bank of the river opposite Bordentown, so as to draw Donop's attention away from Cadwalader's attack. The countersign for December 25th, written by the commander himself, was "Victory or Death."

Of all the thirteen states, New Jersey probably came nearest to being neutral in the autumn of 1776. The extreme loyalist and patriotic parties struck a fairly even balance, and the vast majority of the people asked nothing better than to be left in peace. The state had contentedly kept its royal governor until June, yet in July it accepted the Declaration of Independence with composure. In the same bland spirit the citizens renewed their allegiance to the king in December—not from any great love they bore the monarch, but because the presence of his army seemed to promise them the opportunity to go about their daily business undisturbed.

New Jersey soon awakened to a terrible disillusionment. All past ravages by enemy troops were put in the shade by Hessians and Britons who plundered the helpless state from end to end. British and Tory testimony alone is enough to convict the invaders of unrestrained and systematic pillage. "No sooner had the army entered the Jerseys," recorded Stedman in disgust, "than the business (we say business, for it was a perfect trade) of plunder began. The friend and the foe, from the hand of rapine, suffered alike."[7]

All accounts agree that the Hessians were the worst offenders. They not only robbed right and left but left a trail of senseless destruction. These depredations had their effects on strategy when Colonel Johann Rall neglected to build redoubts for the defense of Trenton, as Howe had expressly ordered before returning to New York. The troops at this post, according to Stedman, "were absent on pillaging expeditions, and those who were on the spot were more busily employed in securing their plunder in waggons than in putting the town in a proper state for defense."

The diary of one of Rall's officers, Captain Andreas Wiederhold, relates that "the guns which ought to have been stationed on avenues or places where they might have been put to instant use, were all drawn up in front of his [Rall's] quarters, and every morning two of them had to be dragged to the upper town; only to cause a constant noise and turmoil. He enjoyed himself until the small hours of the night, went quietly to bed, slept until nine, and when we would go to his quarters between 10 and 11 o'clock for the parade, he would sometimes still be in his bath."[8]

This ceremony was the high point of the day for the boozy commandant, who loved display almost as much as brandy. "And since the guardhouse was only six or eight houses distant from his quarters and thus the trumpeteers could not play long enough to satisfy him—he had the officer and picket march first around a church. . . . He would always follow the parade as far as the guardhouse, only to hear the music during the relief." The youngsters of Trenton also enjoyed these daily processions, and the diarist left an amusing picture of "a number of little boys and girls marching in front and singing" while the band of nine pieces played martial airs.

Hessian regiments being named after their commanding officers, the three at Trenton were known as the Rall, the Lossberg, and the Knyphausen. The first two had the usual blue uniforms with tall caps rising to a gleaming brass peak, but the Knyphausen fusiliers wore menacing black.

Washington's plans for the attack had not been kept as secret as he hoped, and loyalists twice warned Rall. Any apprehensions, however, were put to rest by an unauthorized rebel raid on Christmas morning. The Americans had already shown an aggressive spirit by sending a few scouting parties across the river; and during the snowstorm of the 23rd, the gondolas of the Continental marines bombarded the Germans at Bordentown. At dawn on the 25th about thirty men from the 3rd Virginia took it upon themselves, while returning from a reconnaissance, to attack the Hessian picket on the northwest outskirts of Trenton. They wounded six men and drove in the others, creating such an alarm that Rall marched out at the head of his own regiment after Americans who made their escape. This adventure, far from arousing the commandant, seems to have convinced him that the rebels had shot their bolt and nothing more would happen to interrupt the celebration of the holiday.

On the other side of the river Washington devoted the afternoon to collecting the Durham boats hidden away in thickets of the west bank. These craft of river commerce resembled oversized canoes, being pointed at both ends and painted black. Each held thirty to forty troops, and four or five men were needed at the oars. That duty fell to Glover's fishermen. Only skilled boatmen could have kept the heavily loaded transports from capsizing, for the swift current bombarded them with jagged cakes of ice.

At McConkey's Ferry the Delaware was less than a thousand feet wide, and Washington expected to finish by midnight a crossing begun at dusk. But the ice made it a perilous undertaking of fully nine hours. Following a gray and cheerless afternoon, the wind rose in the darkness and whipped up a storm of sleet. "It was as severe a night as I ever saw," wrote Thomas Rodney in his journal. "The frost was sharp, the current difficult to stem, the wind high, and at eleven it began to snow."[9]

Washington never ceased to cherish the subordinates who were with him that Wednesday night. As a southern aristocrat he had not counted innkeepers among his closest friends, yet it was George Weedon who commanded a Virginia regiment crossing the river with a future President of the United States among its junior officers. Stirling and Sullivan had long before been exchanged, and in the dim lantern light the red nose of the self-styled American earl must have gleamed like a friendly beacon. Colleagues solemnly addressed him as "my lord" in letters, but they were more impressed by the hospitality of the fifty-year-old landed proprietor and his charming wife and daughter. "He is accused of liking the table and the bottle," commented Chastellux a few years later, "full as much as becomes a Lord, but more than becomes a general."[10]

John Sullivan could commit every military error in the catalogue, but

Washington never failed to defend the brave blunderer who crossed the
Delaware with him. And if Nathanael Greene wheezed with asthma that
stormy night, no fault could be found with the splendid bellow of Colonel
Henry Knox. Such was the carrying power of his booming bass that he
had the duty of relaying the commander's orders to Glover's men. A
providential war had rescued from frustration a natural gunner who
might otherwise have ended his life as a bookseller, and he further contributed to the victory by inspiring one of Washington's rare jokes. They
crossed in the same boat, and legend has it that the commander told
Knox to shift his weight to save them from capsizing. It was rather a dull
quip at the expense of a fat man, but any spark of humor must have
helped to warm the hearts of shivering troops huddled together with their
backs to the sleet.

Among history's little ironies is the fact that a German hack artist
named Emanuel Leutze, using the Rhine as a background and Germans
as models, should have limned the familiar painting of the crossing. At
the time it is doubtful if Washington's face wore that look of brooding
and heroic calm. For the watches synchronized with his timepiece showed
the hour to be three o'clock when the last of his 2,400 men set foot on the
New Jersey side. A march of nine miles stretched ahead over poor roads,
so that not the faintest hope remained of surprising Trenton before daybreak.

The phrase "bloody footprints," after being long overworked, served
as the flippant byword of a later generation. But it was real enough to
the poor devils plodding through the storm with rags wrapped about their
feet. This military supply problem vexed quartermasters before the dawn
of the Machine Age, and a young American officer noted that the route
to Trenton could be "easily traced, as there was a little snow on the
ground, which was tinged here and there with blood from the feet of the
men who wore broken shoes."[11]

Washington rode alongside the lurching column on a chestnut sorrel.
The slippery road retarded the march, and it was nearly dawn before he
halted the troops at Birmingham, near the halfway mark, to snatch a
hasty breakfast from the cooked provisions they carried in their knapsacks.
A few men fell asleep in the snow and had to be roused when the army
proceeded in two divisions—a right wing under Sullivan and St. Clair
taking the river road, and a left wing led by Washington and Greene over
the upper route.

The new day broke before Trenton had been even sighted. It would have added to Washington's anxiety if he had known that the other two attacks met with failure. Ewing decided that the ice could not be navigated and gave up the attempt to cross opposite the village. Cadwalader did manage to get a few troops over the river at Dunk's Ferry, after trying without success at Bristol, but had to leave his artillery behind. The Pennsylvania colonel soon returned to the west bank after concluding that Washington must also have been balked.

Only his men were left to encounter the first Hessians in broad daylight on the outskirts of Trenton—a picket making an advance post of the home of Richard Howell, the village cooper. *"Der Feind! Heraus!"* the sentries shouted. "The enemy! Turn out!" And at eight o'clock the Virginians began the attack with a ragged volley which dropped several of the mercenaries and sent the others flying to give the alarm.

About a hundred dwellings and public buildings made up the little river port at the falls of the Delaware. The road taken by Washington's detachment led to the convergence of King and Queen Streets, the two chief thoroughfares. Colonel Knox, who earned a brigadier's rank that morning, planted six guns at this point and began a cannonade sweeping both streets as far as Rall's headquarters near the corner of Perry.

Three minutes later Sullivan's men drove in the fifty Jägers on watch at the river road. Glover's amphibians led the pursuit down Second Street as this rebel detachment seized the lower end of the village, placing the enemy between two fires.

The rebel attacks caught Rall sound asleep after a night of drinking and cards. A loyalist sent him a last-minute note of warning, but he did not trouble to have it translated. His first intimation came at eight o'clock, when the alarm brought him groping to a window in his nightshirt. By the time he dressed and joined his troops, the village was being raked from end to end by American grapeshot and musket balls. The befuddled Hessian colonel could only mutter in his own tongue, "Lord! Lord! What is it?"[12]

At last, according to Wiederhold's diary, Rall "shouted to his regiment: 'Forward, March, Advance! Advance!' and he tottered back and forth without knowing what he was doing. Thus we lost the few favorable moments we might still have had in our hands to break through the enemy in one place or another with honor and without losses; as it was we were surrounded before we had time to get out of Trenton."[13]

The attackers soon controlled every street, pouring in a deadly fire from doorways and board fences. Powder smoke mingled with the sleet to lower visibility and add to the confusion. All the German resistance worth mentioning came from the crews of two brass 3-pounders. Their horses being already hitched, the gunners got the pieces into action long enough to fire a dozen shots. By that time eight of the Hessians had been picked off by riflemen or Captain Alexander Hamilton's two guns at the head of King Street.

The only rebel casualties occurred when the Virginians captured the enemy cannon. Burly Captain William Washington, who claimed distant kinship with the commander, was wounded in both hands; and Captain James Monroe had an artery severed in his shoulder.

Afterwards the Hessians found an excuse in the sleet which rendered their muskets useless. Yet they had been under roofs until the moment of attack, while the Americans marched all night with rags tied about their firing pans to keep the powder dry. Nothing prevented the riflemen from keeping up a hot fire, nor did Colonel John Stark's New Hampshire troops let anything interfere with their musketry. Glover's amphibians blazed away from behind a red board fence in the lower town, and it was this regiment that seized the bridge to cut off the escape of Hessian fugitives.

The real story of Trenton is told by the fact that Germans who might have made little forts out of stone buildings did not succeed in killing a single foeman. And though they had boasted of their prowess with the bayonet, there was no proof during the entire forty minutes. After Colonel Rall sagged in the saddle with two mortal wounds, his men suffered themselves to be driven into an orchard east of the Quaker meetinghouse. There under the bare black branches of the apple trees the Hessian officers replied to a summons by raising their hats on swords in token of surrender. Their casualties included 22 killed and 84 wounded in addition to 868 unharmed prisoners. A few score fugitives escaped by fording the creek, but Washington estimated the total of captives at a thousand after rounding up the skulkers hiding in cellars.

The rebel commander added prudence to valor by starting back to McConkey's Ferry that very afternoon with his woeful train of disarmed foes. Some of the Americans had marched forty miles in the last twenty-four hours, and all had gone sleepless. But eighteen-year-old David How, the diarist of the siege of Boston, was not too fatigued to neglect this

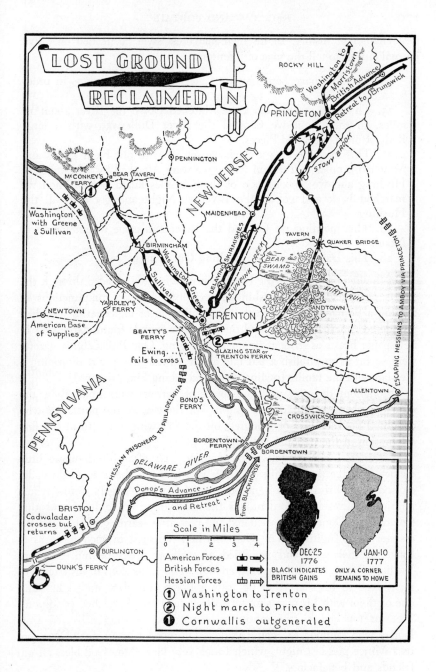

LOST GROUND RECLAIMED

N

ROCKY HILL

Washington to Morristown
British Advance

PRINCETON

Retreat to Brunswick

PENNINGTON

NEW JERSEY

Stony Brook

McCONKEY'S FERRY

BEAR TAVERN

Washington with Greene & Sullivan

MAIDENHEAD

Delaying Skirmishes

Washington & Greene

TAVERN

QUAKER BRIDGE

BIRMINGHAM

Sullivan

ASSUNPINK CREEK

BEAR SWAMP

MIRY RUN

YARDLEY'S FERRY

NEWTOWN

TRENTON

SANDTOWN

American Base of Supplies

BEATTY'S FERRY

Ewing... fails to cross

BLAZING STAR or TRENTON FERRY

ESCAPING HESSIANS TO AMBOY VIA PRINCETON

PENNSYLVANIA

BOND'S FERRY

ALLENTOWN

HESSIAN PRISONERS TO PHILADELPHIA

CROSSWICKS

BORDENTOWN FERRY

DELAWARE RIVER

Donop's Advance... and Retreat

from BLACKHORSE

BORDENTOWN

BRISTOL
Cadwalader crosses but returns

BURLINGTON

DUNK'S FERRY

Scale in Miles

0   1   2   3   4

American Forces
British Forces
Hessian Forces

DEC. 25 1776

BLACK INDICATES BRITISH GAINS

JAN. 10 1777

ONLY A CORNER REMAINS TO HOWE

① Washington to Trenton
② Night march to Princeton
③ Cornwallis outgeneraled

new chapter of history. In his own matchless style he needed only five journal entries to tell the saga of Trenton:

Dec. 24. We have ben drawing Cateridges And provisions in order for a Scout.

25. This Day at 12 a clock we Marched Down the River about 12 miles. In the Night we Crossed the River Dullerway with a large Body of men And Field Pieces.

26. This morning at 4 a clock we set off with our Field pieces and Marched 8 miles to Trenton whare we ware Attacked by a Number of Hushing and we Toock 1000 of them besides killed Some. Then we marched back and got to the River at Night and got over all the Hushing.

27. This morning we Crossed the River and came to our Camp at Noon.

28. This Day we have ben washing Our things.[14]

On the first day of 1777 the Hessian prisoners were paraded through the streets of Philadelphia. Washington evidently felt no compunctions at making a Roman holiday out of the humiliation of mercenaries who had plundered American homes, and the effects on morale found expression in newspaper boasts as strident as enemy bragging. One Philadelphia gazette went so far as to publish a tall tale about a New Jersey girl disarming a Hessian with the family fowling piece and taking him prisoner.[15]

Throughout the new year the spirits of patriots were uplifted by the nine-piece band captured at Trenton. For these were the musicians who delighted the members of Congress on the following July 4th at the first celebration of the national holiday.[16]

Washington himself felt inspired three days after his dramatic little victory to strike again while the iron was hot. On the 27th Cadwalader crossed from Bristol with a motley force of 1,800, largely Pennsylvania militia, and reached Bordentown the next day. There he found that Colonel von Donop had evacuated the post after learning of the Trenton disaster from fugitives. The Germans had retreated in such haste as to leave all their sick and wounded as well as stores behind. Sergeant William Young, a militiaman old enough to have two sons in his company, mentioned in his diary that he "saw a Room full of wounded hessians, one of them with his nose shot off. All of them in a Wretched condition." He was touched by the gratitude of patriots at being delivered from looters who stripped the countryside. "The good woman next Door sent us 2 Mince pies last night, which I took very kind. May God bless all our friends and benefactors."[17]

While Cadwalader boldly pursued the retiring foe, firing at stragglers and taking a few prisoners, Colonel Reed led a detachment to Trenton. He found that village deserted on the morning of the 28th save for a few families terrified at the prospect of another battle. The adjutant immediately sent a message to Washington, suggesting the desirability of further operations.

This proposal found the commander in a receptive mood. His army had needed the rest after a return march against the sleet, for there is a tradition that three men lost their lives from exposure. But victory is an excellent stimulant, and on the 30th he crossed the Delaware again after sending his prisoners to Philadelphia. The river was still choked with ice, though the weather had turned so mild that muddy roads offered the main difficulty.

Any appraisal of Washington's generalship must take into account the fact that he was seldom free to give his full attention to strategy. Even during such an emergency as the New Jersey retreat he ground out a dozen letters a day in decision of questions only indirectly concerned with military operations. There are but few exceptions to this rule, and the Trenton-Princeton campaign is the foremost occasion when Washington shed his other responsibilities. Any estimate of him as a general must rest largely on the events of these ten days.

The strategist who has the good sense not to sacrifice an outnumbered army is sure to be called a new Fabius, but there are few campaigns as bold and daring in all history. On the 30th, back again in Trenton, the commander sent Reed with two officers and ten men of a Philadelphia troop of light horse to reconnoiter as far as Princeton. This operation has a claim to being known as the first American cavalry action of the war, though a few scouts had been mounted as early as White Plains. For the rebel troopers brought back eleven enemy dragoons captured in a surprise, though they failed to penetrate a village strongly held by the foe. This feat, according to Reed's narrative, was accomplished "by 7 horsemen of whom 6 had never before seen an Enemy. . . . Besides these Prisoners a Comisr. was also taken & from the whole a very perfect account was obtained that Ld. Cornwallis with a Body of pickd. Troops and well appointed had the Day before reinforced Grant at Princeton & that this Party was pressing Waggons to begin their March the next Morning in order to dislodge us from Trenton."[18]

Never did a general receive more timely information. Washington estimated that Cornwallis had about 8,000 troops, and he doubtless guessed that his lordship was in no amiable mood after giving up a homeward voyage at the last minute. The rebels at Trenton faced the usual problem of expiring enlistments, for hundreds of the New England men were due to march home on the 31st. Thomas Mifflin, wearing a rose-colored blanket for a cloak, harangued them that afternoon and appealed for further service. His arguments were so persuasive that a majority raised their muskets to indicate compliance. This Philadelphia general of Quaker rearing also managed to recruit nearly 1,600 militia volunteers—farmers and laborers who had never heard a shot fired in anger.

It was a strangely assorted rebel force of about 5,000 that awaited the enemy advance at Trenton on the first day of the new year. Last week's raw militia lads were mingled with such veterans as the remnants of Haslet's and Smallwood's regiments—the Delaware men having been reduced from 800 to 100 effectives at this date, and the Marylanders from 1,000 to 150 fit for duty.

Washington decided that he must somehow gain another day of respite. He gave Colonel Edward Hand and his Pennsylvania riflemen the assignment of marching out to meet the redcoats that night and delaying them for twenty-four hours. Attached to the force were two fieldpieces and several companies of Virginia Continentals. A small contingent of Continental marines, fighting for the first time alongside soldiers, also participated.

The Hessians who evacuated Bordentown were in the advance guard when Hand took a position near Maidenhead on the evening of January 1st. Heavy rains held up the enemy that night, but at dawn he began an all-day action fought stubbornly over muddy roads. This was the first real test of American riflemen against Jägers, and the results left little doubt as to comparative merits. Hand's frontiersmen, hardened in the New York campaign, not only outshot the Germans but showed more adaptability at skirmishing and taking cover in the woods. It was a day of murderous little fights, without much chivalry being shown by rebels who evidently believed that Hessian plunderers were fair game. In a tight spot several riflemen faked a surrender, only to shoot down Lieutenant Friedrich von Grothausen and several of his men. The enemy retaliated later by bayoneting the Rev. John Rosbrugh, a sixty-three-year-old Pennsylvania militia chaplain, after robbing him of his watch and money.

All morning the rebels made use of every shelter to harass the British advance guard. After stopping the enemy on one occasion, they even dared a brief pursuit. About noon Hand deployed his riflemen behind a creek to such good effect that the Hessians formed a line of battle, expecting a large-scale action. This fight lasted for three hours, with both sides using artillery, before the rebels could be dislodged. Hand did not slacken his efforts even after retiring to the northern outskirts of Trenton, where he was reinforced by fresh troops and two more cannon. The Virginians hastily threw up earthworks for a last stand and beat off the enemy until four o'clock while Washington looked on approvingly.

The all-day action was a credit to Americans who brought back "25 or 30 prisoners" and claimed to have killed or wounded a hundred foes. Better yet, they won for the commander the day of grace he asked, for the winter sun had set before the British advance guard poured down King and Queen Streets. The last rebel skirmishers retreated slowly, firing from behind houses and fences until they joined their comrades on both sides of the creek.

At five o'clock the cannon stabbed the dusk with vivid flashes as the redcoats made three unsuccessful attempts to seize the stone bridge before nightfall. The first of these efforts was described by an American militia soldier: "Our People . . . form'd in a line—with 3000 men & 2 field ps in the Main Street [Queen Street]—and 2 field ps secreted behind Mr. Waln's house opposite the Mill—& some Riflemen in the Mill, & artillery all along the Creek—after they were so station'd the Enemy advanced towards the Bridge. While they were advancing a Cannonade on both sides commenced, & the Enemy threw a number of Shells which did no execution, and one Cannon Ball passed through the 3rd Battalion & killed 2 men—the Enemy advanc'd abt half way over the Bridge, when they were repulsed it is supposed with considerable loss."[19]

This conjecture proved to be optimistic, for neither the American nor British cannon did much harm in the early darkness. The enemy gave up hope of taking the bridge after two more efforts, and both armies settled themselves for the night behind hundreds of campfires on opposite sides of the creek.

Not much strategic perception was needed to deduce that Washington had placed his army in a cul-de-sac between two streams. Either to retreat or fight the next morning would be inviting destruction, for Cornwallis had reached Trenton early in the evening with his main force. But the rebel leader's audacity never failed him in this campaign, and at the moment he still hoped for news of a success which might have been one of the most brilliant strokes of the war.

On the night of December 30th he received intelligence that a guard of only 250 men had been left at Brunswick, the enemy advanced base for all New Jersey operations. The next day Washington sent Cadwalader with a body of light troops to raid this post far behind the British lines. Speed being essential both for victory and escape, he ordered the Pennsylvania officer to seize horses and turn his infantry into improvised dragoons. Cadwalader got as far as Cranberry in forced marches, only to learn from spies that the Brunswick guard had just been strengthened by 1,500 men.[20] This gave him no choice but to report to his superior on the night of the 2nd that the attempt had been abandoned.

In the same daring and resourceful spirit, Washington decided before learning of the disappointment to launch an attack of his own on the rear of an enemy waiting to devour him at dawn. Although he called a council of officers, his mind seems to have been fully made up in advance. A change of weather aided his Hannibalic scheme when a sudden freeze that evening hardened the muddy roads. Shortly after midnight, with the campfires burning brightly, the imperiled army began a stealthy march to Princeton over a back road. The wheels of the cannon were muffled with rags, and Washington left 400 men behind for a few hours to keep the fires blazing while pretending to entrench for the next day's battle.

The ruse succeeded to perfection. Cornwallis did not suspect that his prey had escaped until dawn, when he heard the cannon of the rebels attacking his own reinforcements near Princeton, ten miles in the rear. Then he had the horrible thought that an adversary as bold as Washington might push on to Brunswick and seize British stores which included a pay chest of £70,000 in specie.

This was indeed one of the possibilities that the rebel commander visioned. But the all-night march exhausted troops plodding through a dark forest filled with stumps only to enter a wasteland called the Barrens. The sky had turned gray in the east when General Hugh Mercer's advance guard reached cultivated country at Stony Brook, about two miles from Princeton.

At that moment two British regiments, the 17th and part of the 55th, were on their way under Colonel Mawhood to join the main army at Trenton. The opposing forces sighted each other almost simultaneously and began a race for elevated ground. Mercer reached the position first and formed his 350 men in a ragged line.

The fight of the next twenty minutes was one of the most savage of the war. At a range of forty yards the rebel muskets and two cannon drew first blood, then the enemy fired a single poorly aimed volley before charging with cold steel. These tactics routed Americans lacking bayonets, but they rallied when Washington himself spurred forward with reinforcements. The redcoats who had outnumbered Mercer suddenly found themselves contending with the whole rebel army. Regiment after regiment came into action at the double as Colonel Hand's battlewise riflemen threatened the enemy's flank. It was the turn of the British to be put to flight, and after abandoning his guns and baggage Mawhood fell back for a last stand behind a ravine south of the college. Rebel artillery fire soon scattered this force, which lost fifty prisoners to Washington's pursuing troops. Mawhood's remnant found a brief refuge with part of the 40th in Nassau Hall, and 194 were compelled to surrender after Captain Alexander Hamilton fired a warning cannonball.

It was a costly encounter for British regiments, with losses of nearly 400 killed, wounded and prisoners, including a hundred left dead on the field. The small proportion of wounded on both sides is evidence of the furious fighting. Washington had only about 40 casualties, but among them were two subordinates who could be ill spared. Colonel Haslet fell with a musket ball through the head, and General Mercer died of wounds a few days later. That veteran, who emigrated to America after serving as a surgeon with the Highland rebels of 1745, had been stabbed seven times with bayonets.

Washington and his generals enjoyed a breakfast left by British officers at their headquarters. But it was no time for leisure, since rebel scouts had already warned of the rapid advance of Cornwallis from Trenton. The last Americans had barely left Princeton about noon when the British vanguard came in sight, and Washington pressed on to the crossroads at Kingston, three miles eastward.

Here the American generals held a hasty council of war without dismounting from their horses. The prospect of raiding the British advanced base at Brunswick was tempting, and the commander wrote to Congress on the 5th that "six to eight hundred fresh troops upon a forced march would have destroyed all their stores and magazines."[21] But his army consisted only of "poor soldiers quite barefoot and ill clad in other respects . . . many of them having had no rest for two nights and a day." Washington decided not to risk his gains by marching eighteen miles farther with a well-rested and larger British army at his heels. After destroying the bridge over Millstone Creek, he evaded Cornwallis by turning northward to seek a refuge in the wooded plateau country around Morristown.

Chapter 11

A Game of Blindman's Buff

WITHIN ten days Washington had inflicted at least 1,600 casualties on the enemy at a cost of fewer than a hundred to himself. The campaign had freed Philadelphia from danger and made it possible for Congress to return in March.

Cornwallis felt so much concern for his advanced base that he passed Kingston on January 3rd without trying to pursue his weary opponents. He continued to push his own men relentlessly until they reached Brunswick that night, after completing a march of 28 miles since dawn.

The journal kept by Colonel Markham gives an idea of the alarms felt by British officers summoned in the early hours of January 2nd to Brunswick: "It was a very dark night, and we were up to our knees in mire; crossing waters of mill-dams; every now and then walking over sheets of ice; officers and men continually tumbling. I myself had I know not how many falls, every moment expecting to be attacked by the rebels."[1]

At the time, if he had but known, there were no rebel forces within twenty miles. But the British did not trust an opponent who had scored so many surprises in the last few days. It would not be going too far to say that some of their forces in New Jersey were near to panic. No other explanation can be advanced for the rout of 200 redcoats guarding supply wagons. They were assailed on the night of the 3rd by only 30 mounted New Jersey militiamen under Captain John Stryker—mere civilians who rode around the detachment in the darkness, shouting and firing to simulate numbers.[2] Their hullabaloo put the enemy to flight, and the New Jersey men succeeded in reaching Morristown with wagons containing woolen clothing.

It is significant that the heroes of the exploit were militia volunteers from a state which had watched Washington's retreat in December without coming to his aid. New Jersey was neutral no longer. Some of the citizens still had Howe's pardons in their pockets when they armed to strike back at the invaders. British officers were not safe on the road without a guard, and the Hessians dared only to venture forth in strong detachments. As evidence of this change in affairs, Howe informed Germain on the 5th that "Captain Phillips of the 35th Grenadiers . . . was on this day beset by some lurking villains who murdered him in a most barbarous manner, which is a mode of war the enemy seem, from several late instances, to have adopted with a degree of barbarity that savages could not exceed."[3] In the same letter the British commander found it desirable to report his Princeton casualties as "seventeen killed and nearly two hundred wounded and missing"—about half of the actual losses.

Howe's personal kindliness counted for nothing when offset by the indiscipline he tolerated. In his defense several years later before the House of Commons he gave the excuse that his orders did not grant him much control over the Germans committing the worst excesses. But he was absent in New York a great deal of the time, and it does not appear that he made much of an effort. Clinton frankly blamed the loss of New Jersey on the ravages of the invaders, and Gates declared, "Had General Howe seen to it, that the prisoners, and the Jersey inhabitants, when subdued, were treated with as much humanity and kindness as Sir Guy Carleton exercised toward his prisoners, it would have been all up with the Americans."[4]

Both Washington and Congress made political capital of the enemy depredations. The assembly appointed a committee of inquiry which brought in a report on April 18th, based on the affidavits of victims.[5] Even allowing for prejudice, there remained enough proof to establish a guilt that the enemy did not attempt to deny. Nor could the rebel forces be accused of like crimes, for it was no mere gesture when the commander in chief had this proclamation displayed in public places all over New Jersey:

His Excellency General Washington strictly forbids all the officers and soldiers of the Continental army, of the militia and all recruiting parties, plundering any person whatever, whether Tories or others. The effects of such persons will be applied to public uses in a regular manner, and it is expected that humanity and tenderness to women and children will distinguish brave Americans, contending for liberty, from infamous mercenary ravagers, whether British or Hessian.[6]

The invaders had done much to hurt their own cause, but the map attests to the results won by Washington in the brief campaign. Enemy forces overrunning the state and threatening Philadelphia on December 25th had been reduced by the second week in January to the two posts of Brunswick and Amboy. And even this last corner of New Jersey sometimes had no communication with New York except by sea. Washington held a strong position at Morristown, yet the security of his army did not owe to a passive defense behind a chain of redoubts. The British themselves were kept on the defensive all winter by surprise attacks which cost them as much as a lost battle in January alone.

Washington's letters of that month give a picture of New Jersey militia forces swarming like hornets to cut off enemy foraging parties and seize supply trains.[7] As early as the 7th, the day he reached Morristown, the commander reported to Congress several skirmishes "between their parties and some detachments of the militia, in which the latter have been successful and made a few prisoners. The most considerable was on Sunday morning, near Springfield, when eight or ten Waldeckers were killed and wounded, and the remainder of the party, thirty-nine or forty, made prisoners, with two officers, by a force not superior in number and without receiving the least damage." Two weeks later he announced that "General [Philemon] Dickinson, with about four hundred militia, has defeated a foraging party of the enemy of an equal number, and has taken forty wagons, and upwards of a hundred horses." In this combat the Americans waded "through the river middle-deep, and gave the enemy so severe a charge, that, although supported by three field-pieces, they gave way and left their convoy." After a few more such successes of small war, Washington indulged himself in one of his rare moods of complacency when writing to Sullivan on the 28th: "Our affairs at present are in a prosperous way. The country seems to entertain an idea of our superiority. Recruiting goes on well, and a belief prevails, that the enemy are afraid of us."

Only a single failure occurred during the winter months as a discordant note. Bald and corpulent William Heath had long dreamed of martial glory while poring over the treatises of Saxe and Guibert. But when opportunity knocked early in 1777, "our General" could only wait at the door, frozen into helpless irresolution.

In order to draw the enemy's attention away from his New Jersey operations, Washington conceived the plan of threatening Howe's outposts near Kingsbridge. He gave Heath the command of 3,400 New York and Connecticut militia for an attack on Fort Independence, held by about 2,000 redcoats and Hessians. The former Roxbury farmer summoned the garrison by granting it "twenty minutes to surrender or abide the consequences." This was his sole decisive effort. The twenty minutes stretched into ten days as he waited, and at last the enemy took advantage of his indecision to make a sally which created a panic. The fiasco ended in a humiliating retreat of the theorist who failed in practice, and it is to Washington's credit that he did not lose faith in a general who would serve the cause well as an administrator. His private letter of criticism was written "as a friend," and at the first opportunity he appointed Heath to the important but inactive command at Boston.

The victories in New Jersey only heaped fuel on the feuds of military politics which kept the army at the boiling point during the winter. Congress obviously could not please everyone, but the assembly seems to have offended all save the successful candidates when these promotions were announced in February:

Major generals—Stirling, Mifflin, Stephen, St. Clair and Lincoln; brigadier generals—Poor, Glover, Learned, Patterson, Varnum, Huntington, George Clinton, Wayne, De Haas, Hand, Weedon, Reed, Muhlenberg, Woodford, Scott, Conway, Nash and Cadwalader.

Glover at first declined his promotion on the grounds of being unworthy, and Washington had to overcome his sincere hesitations in a personal letter. This unique example of modesty went unnoticed, so loud was the clamor of officers who felt neglected.

The task of soothing disgruntled warriors having fallen to Washington, he counseled one grumbler on March 15th: "Do not . . . torment yourself longer with imaginary slights and involve others with the perplexities you feel on that score. No other officer of rank, in the whole army, has so often conceived himself neglected, slighted, and ill-treated, as you have done, and none I am sure has less cause than yourself to entertain such ideas."[8]

This admonition happened to be addressed to Sullivan, but the commander might have used it as a form letter to be filled in frequently with the names of Schuyler, Arnold and other chronic bleeders. Their plaints may be traced chiefly to the fact that Congress had to award promotions on a political as well as military basis. States contributing a large proportion of troops demanded added recognition, so that mediocre officers really were advanced at times over the heads of better soldiers.

Arnold would perhaps have left the army early in 1777 if fate had not intervened. He was riding through western Connecticut when British forces landed from transports near Fairfield to march inland and destroy rebel stores at Danbury. They were opposed with great energy near Ridgefield by David Wooster, the oldest American general on active duty. On April 25th he marched at the head of 600 militia volunteers and boldly attacked the vanguard of the 2,000 redcoats returning from their mission. Arnold arrived in time to take part along with General Silliman, but the credit for the first phase belongs to a veteran who gave his life. Nathanael Greene paid him a soldier's tribute in a letter which did not mention Arnold: "Had not General Wooster been wounded, ten to one the whole party had been cut off. Before he was wounded, the enemy broke, and ran like fury."[9]

Arnold and Silliman continued to fight bravely until they were overwhelmed by superior numbers. Then the action turned into another Lexington as patriots flocked from all sides to blaze away at the British column from behind stone walls. The retreat, according to Fortesque, cost the enemy 360 men killed and wounded.

On May 2nd Arnold won his coveted rank. Not much glory was left to be buried with Wooster, whose bones had to wait eighty years for an appropriate monument. It was found, upon opening the grave, that a heavy ball from a Brown Bess musket had smashed the spine of an elderly hero whose name is often omitted from accounts of the fight.

The Arnold legend was even then in process of being created at the expense of colleagues whom he slighted in letters or reports. One of them, John Brown, had been slandered as well as neglected. Enraged at being still denied a court martial to clear himself of Arnold's accusations, the Massachusetts lawyer brought thirteen charges of his own against Arnold, some of them equally unfounded. On April 12th he renewed the attack by publishing a handbill that could only have been answered by a duel, according to eighteenth-century codes of honor. Fury got the better of Brown's judgment, but his indictment ended with the prophetic words, "Money is this man's god, and to get enough of it he would sacrifice his country."[10]

It is an ironical note that Arnold profited from the attack. Not yet satisfied with a promotion which left him a junior to major generals appointed in February, he camped on the doorstep of Congress with a copy of Brown's charges as evidence of prejudice. The assembly gave him no satisfaction in seniority but consoled him with the gift of a "properly caparisoned" horse as an added reward for bravery at Ridgefield.

Even the Brown-Arnold dispute was a sideshow as compared to the foremost feud of the Continental Army. For this was no clash of opportunists scrambling for rank. This was the opening gun of of a revolution within a revolution—the ancient struggle between the two oldest political parties on earth.

Philip Schuyler, born to wealth and position, emerged as the protagonist of men who wished to overthrow the old government but not the old codes of property and privilege. Horatio Gates, risen from a modest station, represented the faction of his adopted countrymen who hoped for political changes broadening the base of opportunity. The antagonism of the rivals was no less deep-seated because it found expression in polite phrases instead of the insults bawled by Arnold and Brown. Each had his advocates not only in Congress but also the states and the army.

Congress precipitated the quarrel by failing to define the powers of the two generals clearly enough when appointing Gates to the command of the northern army. Their bickerings were courteous at first, but Schuyler soon came out in the open by attempting to undermine his rival in Congress. Gates was no man to decline such a challenge, for he had a much more nimble pen in a controversy. By October 30, 1776, John Witherspoon was able to assure him "that by far the greatest part of the Congress have a very high sense of your importance and services in a particular Manner for discouraging to the utmost of your power Colonial Jealousies and Distinctions."[11]

What the New Jersey radical meant to convey was that Gates had been accepted as the champion of New England troops who loathed Schuyler. And since the Yankees were the mainstay of the northern army, it meant a great deal to have discovered a general who could call forth their loyal efforts.

The rivals did not content themselves very long with writing letters. Both were soon knocking at the door of Congress. Gates appeared as a lobbyist just before Christmas, giving his critics the opening to accuse him of shirking the battle of Trenton. But neither Schuyler nor Arnold had offered their services, and Gates's plea of illness is upheld by a letter of January 3rd from Elbridge Gerry to Joseph Trumbull. "I am just come from a Visit to our good Friend General Gates who is on the

Recovery, which will doubtless give you pleasure."[12] In the very next sentence the Massachusetts delegate aimed a backhanded slap at the Schuyler faction, "I suspect that a mercenary party in Albany have endeavoured to gravel you in supplying the army."

The feud raged as an issue dividing Congress all winter. The word "intriguing" was usually reserved for Gates's efforts by opponents who quite sincerely believed that Schuyler was merely "presenting his case." Again it is hard to see much difference between the motives of the two men, and it took a good deal of invention to create a picture of an honest Caesar being maligned by a sly and designing Cassius. The principals, as every intelligent man knew, were but the figureheads of a clash involving broader issues than the command of the Northern Department. When Jay, Carroll, Duane, Lynch, Harrison and fellow conservatives of the middle and southern states denounced Gates, they were actually opposing John and Samuel Adams, Jefferson, McKean, Witherspoon, Richard Henry Lee and other radicals of the Revolution.

On a basis of purely military qualifications, Schuyler was at a disadvantage both in experience and native ability. Illnesses, real or imaginary, kept him confined to his bed at Albany so often that he could not be considered fit for field service. His best asset was an influence over the Indians of the Six Nations which kept them comparatively neutral until the summer of 1777—a contribution hard to overestimate in its value to the cause. Gates demonstrated more strategic and administrative capacity, and the issue seemed to be settled when Congress at last placed him at the head of the Northern Department in March. But that decision only incited his opponents to greater efforts. The issue was nip and tuck for two more months, with the factions so evenly divided that the absence of a few delegates could change the verdict. At the next trial of strength, as one historian has put it, Schuyler "was reinstated in May, after fairly presenting his case before Congress."[13] And this was but the first round of a contest that would continue throughout the war until one of the participants had his reputation ruined.

The placating of jealous generals was but one of the problems that kept Washington's nose to the grindstone of "paper work" at his Morristown headquarters. Added to the tremendous bulk of his correspondence were the letters written to Howe in protest of the treatment of American prisoners. On the other side of the ocean, Franklin also did his best to mitigate the sufferings of men rotting away in prison ships or brutally impressed into British naval service.

The rebels themselves had reason to blush for a foul hole in Connecticut—an abandoned mine shaft at Simsbury where Tory political captives crouched in the damp and darkness. But the British, by the admission of their own historians, were guilty of most of the cruelties inflicted on military prisoners. Lecky summed up the evidence fairly when he declared it "but justice to the Americans to add that, except in their dealings with their loyal fellow-countrymen, their conduct during the war appears to have been almost uniformly humane. No charges of neglect of prisoners, such as those which were brought, apparently with too good reason, against the British were substantiated against them."[14]

This does not mean that the invaders wantonly violated the codes of the most temperate age of warfare. Their writings make it plain, nevertheless, that they held rebels to be outlaws not entitled to the usual mercies. Captain Mackenzie was obviously an officer of decent principles, yet in the autumn of 1775 he entered a typical British opinion in his journal:

> An exchange of prisoners is talked of. The measure may be right and politic; but it appears rather extraordinary that under present circumstances we should treat with them as if on an equality. . . . Rebels taken in arms forfeit their lives by the laws of all Countries . . . Not one Rebel has suffered death yet, except in Action. We act thus either from an apprehension that they might retaliate on the prisoners in their hands, or from a desire to bring them back to a sense of their duty by an extraordinary sense of lenity.[15]

Washington believed it to be a deliberate policy on the part of the enemy to treat American prisoners so harshly that the wretches who survived were no longer fit for military service. In a letter of January 13, 1777, he protested to Howe that exchanged rebel captives gave "the most shocking account of their barbarous usage, which their miserable, emaciated countenances confirm. How very different was their appearance from that of your soldiers, who have lately returned to you, after a captivity of twelve months. . . . If you are determined to make captivity as distressing as possible, let me know it, that we may be upon equal terms, for your conduct must and shall mark mine."[16]

There is no proof that Howe had any idea of taking a military advantage. He was undoubtedly sincere in his indignant replies denying the violation of humane codes. Again, as in the case of British plundering, the blame may be traced to the indiscipline tolerated by a man incapable of personal brutality. Unfortunately, the British army at New York was already permeated by a widespread system of graft and peculation. So overwhelming is the evidence on this score that it disgusted British officers devoted to their profession. Howe could inform Washington in good faith that rebel prisoners were given exactly the same food issued to the redcoats. What he did not realize was that little of it ever nourished the captives after dishonest subordinates had profited.

Washington and Congress soon learned that nothing could be accomplished save by retaliations—not on the captured rank and file, but on enemy officers. When Ethan Allen was taken to England in irons, his countrymen promptly clapped General Prescott in a jail for felons. British generals were further disposed to improve the treatment of rebel captives after receiving such plaints as the one addressed to them by Sir Archibald Campbell on February 14, 1777:

> I am lodged in a dungeon of twelve or thirteen feet square, whose sides are black with the grease and litter of successive criminals. . . . Two small windows, strongly grated with iron, introduce a gloomy light into the apartment, and these are at this time without a single pane of glass, although the season of the frost and snow is in the extreme. . . . A loathsome black-hole, decorated with a pair of fixed chains, is granted me for my inner apartment.[17]

Even after the British introduced a few reforms, conditions remained so grievous that they stood to gain from every return of well-fed redcoats for rebels broken in health and spirit. In a war of attrition this factor was of no mean account, and at later critical periods Washington had to harden his heart to American sufferings by deferring such exchanges.

Another problem worried him at Morristown when a new smallpox epidemic threatened the troops quartered in log huts. It is hard for a later generation to imagine the dread of that ailment before the day of vaccination. Fear of disease, as much as disease itself, had defeated the rebel invaders of Canada with heavier losses than any inflicted by the enemy. Inoculation offered the only defense, though several of the American leaders denounced the practice. General Thomas, according to Dr. Beebe's journal, went so far as to assert "that it should be death for any person to inoculate."[18]

Washington did not agree with this view. In the early spring of 1777 he waged a successful campaign against both fear and disease by inoculating a whole army within striking distance of a superior foe. A preliminary test at New York posts had already demonstrated that only four men out of five hundred died of inoculation. These statistics reassured troops at Morristown who filed past the surgeons in endless lines. All the churches of the village were soon transformed into hospitals crowded with patients. It was an army of convalescents which upheld the American cause for several weeks while the New Jersey militia "amused" the enemy, to quote a term of eighteenth-century military jargon.

The Continentals also showed symptoms at times of another malady that the diary of Lieutenant James McMichael blamed on cheap rum: "They have chiefly got a disorder, which at camp is called the Barrel Fever, which differs in its effects from any other fever—its concomitants are black eyes and bloody noses."[19] But Washington prescribed for the spiritual as well as physical health of his troops in such orders as this circular addressed to brigadiers on May 26, 1777:

> Let vice and immorality of every kind be discouraged as much as possible in your brigade; and, as a chaplain is allowed to each regiment, see that the men regularly attend divine worship. Gaming of every kind is expressly forbidden, as being the foundation of evil, and the cause of many a brave and gallant officer's ruin. Games of exercise for amusement may not only be permitted but encouraged.[20]

From year to year Washington repeated his injunction against gambling. He enforced it with such uncompromising severity that no army of history ever had fewer taints of that ancient military vice. His opponents were much annoyed at what they termed "rebel hypocricy," and a loyalist writer jeered that "the American republicans . . . pretend to have the especial favors of God, and none of the devil's on their side, and for that reason we rarely see a proclamation from the rebel camp without a pious sentence bringing up the rear. The late order given by the head rebel at Morristown . . . is a greater illustration of Yankee piety than any yet come out. . . . However easily he may bait old Witherspoon, Billy Livingston, Jacky Jay, and some of the other pious ones, who are hanging in the rear of his *moral* forces; when the time comes, he'll find out he can't 'fool the Lord' with pretended piety or Presbyterian general orders."[21]

It could not be denied, however, that the commander and his official "family" set an example of patriotic virtues. Martha Washington, Lucy Knox and the other wives gathered about the fireplace in the evening, knitting stockings for soldiers. Now and then a dance was given in the commissariat storehouse, attended by Lady Stirling and the daughters of Governor Livingston. But these entertainments were puritanical as compared to the dissipations at Howe's headquarters.

When that indolent general at last bestirred himself in June, every American corporal knew that the invaders were about to launch their

greatest campaign. Washington at Morristown and Schuyler at Ticonderoga stood back to back against larger enemy armies capable of closing
like jaws from the north and south—Burgoyne from Canada and Howe
from New York. Distance kept the forces of both sides from communicating readily with each other, so that the ensuing operations promised to
resemble a game of blindman's buff.

The rebels had recently been heartened by a stirring little victory on
Long Island. On May 21st Colonel Return Jonathan Meigs embarked
from New Haven with 213 men in whaleboats. Crossing the Sound,
he surprised the enemy at Sag Harbor and burned twelve brigs and sloops
as well as valuable stores. The raiders not only got back without a casualty
but brought 90 prisoners after covering nearly a hundred miles by land
and water in twenty-four hours.

American strategists could only guess at Howe's intentions on June
12th, when he marched out from Brunswick to threaten their advanced
position at Middlebrook. But if the British general hoped to find many
friends in New Jersey after last year's plundering, he met with disillusionment. Nearly all the inhabitants had torn up their royal pardons and
sworn allegiance to the patriotic cause. Washington separated the sheep
from the goats by excusing sincere loyalists from the oath and offering
them a safe conduct to the British lines with their personal possessions.
Thus he had cause to congratulate himself in a letter of June 17th on
the "happy circumstance, that such an animation prevails among the
people."[22] Neither civilians nor soldiers were dismayed by the larger
British forces arrayed against them. The reputation of the mercenaries
had fallen so low that this Rabelaisian jibe appeared in a Philadelphia
gazette as a parody on ministerial proclamations:

> His Majesty intends to open this year's campaign with ninety thou-
> sand Hessians, Tories, Negroes, Japanese, Moors, Esquimaux, Persian
> archers, Laplanders, Feejee Islanders, and light horse. . . . For Heaven's
> sake, ye poor, deluded, misguided, bewildered, cajoled and bamboozled
> Whigs! ye dumb-founded, infatuated, back-bestridden, nose-led-about,
> priest-ridden, demagogue-beshackled, and Congress-becrafted independ-
> ents, fly, fly, oh fly, for protection to the royal standard, or ye will
> be swept away from the face of the earth with the besom of destruction
> and cannonaded in a moment into nullities and nonentities, and no
> mortal can tell into what other kinds of quiddities and quoddities.[23]

It was the misfortune of the Hessians to be put to flight in a rear-guard
operation of June 21st. Howe reported later to Germain that he hoped to

bring on a favorable engagement in New Jersey. But the improvement in rebel generalship and discipline must have astonished that expert tactician when his opponents sparred boldly without allowing themselves to be drawn into battle. That result owed largely to the formation of a new American corps adapted to skirmishing. In fact, events of 1777 were to prove that Washington had created the best regiment of the Continental Army when he recommended to Congress that Colonel Daniel Morgan be given the command of 500 picked riflemen. It was this force, combined with General Anthony Wayne's brigade, which struck the Germans of Howe's rear guard after the two armies had been skirmishing near Brunswick. The Hessians, according to Greene, "fled in wild disorder towards the town, hotly pursued by Morgan and his riflemen. In a few minutes the American advance and the British rear stood face to face close to the bridge; and in a few minutes more up came the remainder of the rifle corps, and Wayne with his whole brigade. A brisk charge cleared the town and compelled the enemy to take refuge in their redoubts. . . ."[24]

American estimates of 500 enemy killed and wounded during the two weeks seem too high, but there can be no doubt that Howe had taken the losses of a minor battle before retiring to Amboy the next day, "marking his steps by a long line of smoke and flame from the burning houses and barns." On the 26th the British general made a brief reappearance and Cornwallis got the better of Stirling in a skirmish. Then the strategic mystery deepened when the redcoats suddenly withdrew to Staten Island and embarked in transports during the first days of July.

The game of blindman's buff had now begun in earnest. Washington was not deceived by a supposedly intercepted message to Burgoyne in Howe's own handwriting, announcing too plausibly his departure for an attack on Boston. But it remained a question whether he planned to sail to Philadelphia or meet Burgoyne along the line of the Hudson.

The rebel leader had to be prepared for a swift move either toward the Delaware or the Highlands, and he took a position in New Jersey accordingly. The enigma became still more puzzling when Howe did nothing at all for three weeks. British generals did not concern themselves overmuch with the comfort of their men, and until July 23rd the redcoats sweltered in the foul holds of transports anchored within sight of the shore.

It might have consoled Washington to know that his opponents were also fumbling in strategic darkness. Burgoyne had already written in disgust to General Harvey that he reached Montreal to find a paper "publishing the whole design of the campaign almost as accurately as if it had been copied from the Secretary of State's letter."[25]

On March 3rd Lord Germain had endorsed Howe's plan for an attack on Philadelphia, though he could promise only 3,000 of the requested 8,000 reinforcements. Howe had meanwhile informed Carleton that this campaign would prevent him from giving any aid to the army in Canada. As late as May 18th the British war minister repeated his approval of Howe's plans, adding only his vague "hope" that Philadelphia would be captured in time for the victor to help Burgoyne.

There is a dubious legend, founded on an anecdote by Lord Shelburne, that Germain finally did draw up definite orders for Howe to co-operate with Burgoyne. Then the minister took a holiday over the week end, according to this entertaining tale, and left the dispatch to gather dust in a pigeonhole of his desk. But the actual evidence tells a duller story. Howe had neither been consulted about Burgoyne's campaign, which he disapproved, nor instructed to aid his colleague. As late as July 15th he received a letter from Burgoyne himself, confiding that all was well. With this reassurance in his pocket, Howe and his 17,000 troops set sail a week later in 266 warships and transports, leaving Clinton 9,000 men for the defense of New York.

It would have been a blessing, from the British viewpoint, if the plans for the entire two-headed campaign had been tucked away in some pigeonhole and forgotten. But Washington could not divine this possibility as he waited out the summer, one watchful eye on the Hudson and the other on the Delaware. The great British fleet was sighted now and then, but he knew only that it kept on heading southward. On August 21st his generals concluded unanimously at a council of war "that the enemy has most probably sailed for Charleston." The very next day an express came to Congress with the news that the British ships, delayed by bad weather, were putting into Chesapeake Bay.

Intelligence already received from the northern front indicated that Burgoyne meant business in his campaign, not the feint suspected by Washington at first. Ticonderoga fell without a blow to the invaders early in July, giving them control of the lakes. This left no American posts or forces of enough strength to stop Burgoyne as he began his overland march to the Hudson. Washington did his best for the northern army by sending two New England generals, Arnold and Lincoln, to inspire the militia of the northeastern states. And though the commander needed every asset for the defense of Philadelphia, he also ordered Morgan's riflemen northward in response to a recommendation by Congress.

There were few signs of despondency as Washington's army of about 11,000 men marched to challenge a more numerous foe. Nor did the civilians along the route seem downhearted. "The largest collection of young ladies I almost ever beheld came to camp," Lieutenant McMichael noted in his diary after a halt near Germantown. "They marched in three columns. The field officers paraded the rest of the officers and detached scouting parties to prevent being surrounded by them. . . . They were dismissed after we treated them with a double bowl of Sangaree."[26]

Spectators filled the streets on the Sunday morning when the rebels passed through Philadelphia. Washington strung out the troops to make an impressive array on the march down Front Street and up Chestnut. Homespun or hunting shirts still prevailed after thirty months of war, but in the lack of uniforms the men were ordered to wear a sprig of evergreen on their hats.

The long-suffering redcoats had spent more than seven weeks on board the crowded transports when at last they landed at the Head of Elk on August 25th. Howe took the Chesapeake Bay route on the advice of naval officers, but alternating thunderstorms and calms made it a tedious voyage. Captain John Montrésor, the chief British engineer, filled his journal with such entries as the one for August 19th, "The fleet and army much distressed for the want of fresh water, having been for some time put to an allowance, but not so much as the horse vessels, having been obliged to throw numbers of their horses overboard."[27]

Ambrose Serle, who had long regretted British ravages, felt encouraged by signs that the army was mending its ways. "Two men were hanged, & 5 severely whipped, for plundering," he recorded in his journal on the 25th. "If this had been done a Year ago, we shd. have found its Advantages." Only four days later, however, Lord Howe's secretary admitted that "forty seven Grenadiers, and several other Parties straggling for Plunder, were surprised by the Rebels. The Hessians are more infamous & cruel than any." His next sentence was erased but left legible, "It is a misfortune, we ever had such a dirty, cowardly set of contemptible miscreants."[28]

Lack of cavalry as usual handicapped the American forces, but Captain Henry Lee, soon to be known as Light Horse Harry, reconnoitered with his troop of light horse as the enemy slowly advanced from the Head of Elk. Nathanael Greene wrote to his wife on September 10th that "a dusty bed gave me asthma, and I had very little sleep."[29] During the past two weeks, he added, Washington had chosen to fall back rather than risk a battle at a disadvantage. "Here are some of the most distressing scenes imaginable—the inhabitants generally desert their houses, furniture moving, cattle driving, and women and children travelling off on foot—the country all resounds with the cries of the people—the enemy plunders most amazingly."

Greene himself, as Washington's right-hand man, selected a position of great natural strength on high ground behind the steep, wooded banks of Brandywine Creek. Only a few fords were available for an enemy crossing, while the broken country on either side discouraged flank attacks. But these obstacles did not balk the tactician at the head of the British army, and at dawn on the 11th Howe set his troops in motion.

The rebels accepting their second pitched battle of the war might be compared to a victim who feels confident that he cannot be bilked a second time by the same card trick. In anticipation of a turning movement, they placed strong pickets at every threatened ford and threw out skirmishers on the other side of the stream. Their center, comprising the brigades of Greene, Wayne, Weedon and Muhlenberg, occupied earthworks and a redoubt behind Chadd's Ford. General John Armstrong's Pennsylvania militia forces were thought sufficient for the left wing defending a terrain too rugged to be in much danger. The right wing, also occupying wooded country, consisted of the six brigades commanded by Sullivan, Stephen and Stirling. While these troops were forming, General Maxwell's brigade advanced on the other side of the creek to delay the enemy.

The British plan of battle, simple as it may appear in the telling, depended on precisely timed and synchronized troop movements. About ten o'clock, after driving Maxwell across the creek, Knyphausen appeared opposite Chadd's Ford as if to force the American center. Washington was not beguiled by this conventional opening gambit of a flank attack. About noon his suspicions were confirmed by the warning from a right-wing picket that "a strong body of the enemy, from every account five thousand, marched along this road just now."[30] The commander ordered Sullivan to be on his guard, but that hapless general sent back a message

that the "information must be wrong." Not until two o'clock did he discover that the whole rebel right was imperiled while Knyphausen kept
the center fixed.

Cornwallis, aiming the decisive blow, had been marching since daybreak to make a crossing so far up the creek as to catch the rebels napping.
Only time and distance saved them from a worse disaster, for it was four
o'clock when the redcoats burst out of the woods to rout Sullivan's
brigade during the confusion of changing front. Washington did his
best to relieve the pressure by threatening Knyphausen, but in the crisis
Greene saved the American right wing with one of the most famous
marches of the war. In fifty minutes his Virginia Continentals covered
four miles of broken country to hold off larger British forces until
nightfall. This desperate stand kept open a last route of escape for
hundreds of men who would otherwise have been captured. Greene
managed even to bring off their artillery as the beaten army began its
retreat under cover of darkness toward the Schuylkill.

Chapter 12

The Fall of Philadelphia

MORE than the usual number of recriminations were heard during the next few days. Sullivan was the chief victim, since it had been his misfortune to be surprised a second time by a duplicate of the flank attack that routed him at Long Island. Usually a warrior can disdain armchair strategists who do not venture from their firesides, but the New Hampshire general lacked even this solace. His leading critic happened to be a North Carolina delegate whose opinions had been formed during a singlehanded congressional investigation on the battlefield.

Tact was not Thomas Burke's outstanding quality, but nobody could accuse him of timidity after an afternoon spent at helping to rally broken battalions. Although he did not impugn Sullivan's courage, he declared in a direct communication "that you have not sufficient talents for your rank and office, tho' I believe you have strong inclinations to discharge your duty well."[1]

Many other members of Congress and some of the army officers agreed with Burke. Sullivan's career would doubtless have come to an abrupt end if Washington had not taken a stand against a policy of punishing defeat. The beaten general in this case had not shone as a tactician, but he had never failed his superior in bravery or energy. After giving up a law practice lucrative enough to be envied by John Adams, he had been at his chief's side through thick and thin. And now that such a loyal subordinate faced disgrace, the commander in chief did not hesitate. He informed Congress politely but unmistakably that this was no time to probe a wounded ego, and John Sullivan continued at the head of his brigade.

A later and bloodier revolution would demonstrate the futility of wooing victory by sending unsuccessful candidates to the guillotine. Washington, in contrast, had no more valuable trait of leadership than his protective attitude toward officers serving the cause at a sacrifice.

The rebels had been defeated at the Brandywine, yet the post-mortem findings should have offered a few consolations. As evidence of Greene's stout resistance, losses of 81 killed and 461 wounded were reported by Cornwallis's column in comparison to 40 casualties among the Hessians of the center. Nor could it have been said that Washington suffered too grievously with about equal numbers of killed and wounded in addition to some 400 prisoners. After all the orders and moves had been analyzed in detail, it could only be concluded that the rebels had again been outgeneraled by a tactician who might have beaten a more experienced army.

Howe's forces were too exhausted for a pursuit. At midnight Washington found a refuge at Chester and sent an express to Congress. The assembly called a special meeting at six in the morning and devoted the next twelve hours to coping with problems of supply and reinforcement. Far from breathing a word of reproach, the delegates resolved at the end of the day that thirty hogsheads of rum "be presented to the army . . . in compliment to the soldiers for their gallant behaviour in the late battle of the Brandywine."[2]

This was a timely gesture of good will, for there had been resentment on the part of officers who blamed Congress unjustly for the influx of European officers. Early in the war everyone had granted the desirability of inviting a few instructors in the technical branches. Silas Deane, the American commissioner in Paris, could not resist the importunities of professional soldiers seeking employment in the New World. He precipitated a crisis in 1777 by signing a contract which gave General Philippe DuCoudray the rank of major general and command of both the artillery and engineers. That French officer added to his unpopularity, if possible, by putting on lofty airs when he arrived in June. Congress, as the *Journals* prove, had already passed resolutions to end the indiscriminate employment of European officers. But an assembly is always the most convenient scapegoat, and Greene, Knox and Sullivan threatened to resign. The situation was still hanging fire when DuCoudray met an accidental death by drowning four days after the battle of the Brandywine.

One of the victim's own countrymen, the Marquis de Chastellux, declared it "fortunate . . . that he was drowned in the Schuylkill, rather than to be swallowed up in the intrigues he was engaged in, and which might have been productive of much mischief."[3] But the battle introduced American officers to another type of European volunteer. The Marquis de Lafayette, who was wounded, had paid his own way to America as a sincere convert to the cause. Another ardent young Frenchman, the Marquis de Fleury, fought so valiantly that Congress presented him with a horse.

Washington himself did not escape without censure of his strategy during the ten days following the defeat. Even such a loyal subordinate as Greene joined in the criticism. Certainly the commander did not display the decisiveness of the Trenton-Princeton campaign. After falling back over the Schuylkill, he crossed on the 15th to risk a battle in a weak position with the river to his back. Howe had already begun another of his flank attacks when a terrific rainstorm saved the rebels from almost certain defeat by drenching the powder of both armies. The American retreat through the deluge was described in Captain William Beatty's journal: "All the small Branches that we were obliged to Cross on the march were so rais'd by the Hard rain that they took us to the waist and under the Arms when we waded them. None of our men preserved a single round of Ammunition that did not get thoroughly wet."[4]

Washington left Anthony Wayne near his boyhood home at Paoli to threaten Howe's rear with 1,500 men while the main rebel army crossed the river again to oppose a suspected advance toward Reading. On the 20th the British commander taught a costly new lesson in tactics by detaching General Grey to surprise Wayne in the darkness. That officer won the nickname of "No-Flint" Grey by attacking with the bayonet to inflict more than 300 casualties at a trifling cost to his own force.

The affair was called the "Paoli massacre" by Americans who charged the foe with a butchery of men trying to surrender. This accusation seems to have been advanced as an excuse for a humiliating defeat. Grey was exonerated by the contemporary historian Gordon, who had a low boiling point in regard to British excesses. He concluded that after the rebels had been warned in time for a hasty defense, Wayne erred by forming his men in front of the campfires, so that their silhouettes made targets for an invisible enemy. Night surprises are never famed for tenderness, but Gordon did not find evidences of deliberate British cruelty.

The fall of Philadelphia had already been conceded. Colonel Alexander Hamilton, acting as Washington's aide, sent an urgent warning to the State House two days before the Paoli action: "If Congress have not left

Philadelphia, they ought to do it immediately without fail; for the enemy have the means of throwing a party this night into the city."[5]

Howe showed no haste and his advance units did not enter Philadelphia until the 27th. By that time the members of Congress were well on their way to York, which would become the American "capital" until the following spring.

The reverses of this campaign followed a summer when every express seemed to bring more bad news from the north. No blow of the entire war ever fell with a more sickening impact than the report of the evacuation of Ticonderoga on July 6th without a fight. For Congress had grown to think of that post as the American Gibraltar after it turned back Carleton's invasion of 1776.

The news of Burgoyne's success touched off an explosion of charges and countercharges in the State House. Each faction of the Gates-Schuyler feud blamed the other for the changes in command contributing to the disaster. Gates had hardly more than settled himself, after being appointed late in March, before Schuyler undermined him by methods that might be called "intriguing" if more dignified expressions were not reserved for that general. While he was buttonholing delegates at Philadelphia, his rival did more to make a genuine fortress out of Ticonderoga than had ever been accomplished before. The spirit in which Gates went about his work is evident from a letter to General John Patterson:

> Perhaps the Enemy may give us Two Months, before they come again to *look* at Ticonderoga; let us regard these two Months, as the most precious Time we have to Live; they may be worth an Age of Droning peace, and, well employ'd may give happiness, and peace to Millions.[6]

As it happened, Schuyler supplanted Gates before he had his two months. During the few weeks at his disposal he gave the post the benefit of trained engineering skill for the first time. From Philadelphia he brought with him Colonel Thaddeus Kosciusko, who had studied engineering and tactics in Paris. The tyrannies endured by his own country made this thirty-one-year-old Polish volunteer receptive to the American message. Described as "painfully modest," he could speak no English when Gates earned the worship of the newcomer by taking him into his personal as well as official family. Down to the end of the war their relationship resembled that of Washington and Lafayette.

Colonel Baldwin could always do a good job of practical engineering, and the Polish volunteer supplied the technical theory. As harmonious colleagues, they completed the works on Mount Independence linked by a combination bridge and boom from the Vermont shore to the fort proper. Gates may be credited with the first suspicion that Ticonderoga could be cannonaded from Sugarloaf Hill on the New York side. He ordered Kosciusko to report, and the engineer found that guns large enough to bombard both American positions could be dragged up to the summit if the steep sides were graded by fatigue parties.[7] Before Gates could deal with the problem, he was replaced by Schuyler, who had been given his own terms of "absolute command."

The two men had few enough things in common, but both regarded the Northern Department as a separate branch of the army, subject only to the authority of Congress. Washington shared this view, judging by letters in which he seldom went beyond suggestions. Schuyler put General Arthur St. Clair in charge of Ticonderoga, and Gates warned the new incumbent that Sugarloaf Hill should be occupied. Unhappily, Schuyler despised any opinion voiced by his rival. A conservative and traditionalist, he held that since the hill had never been utilized by an enemy in the past, it never would be in the future. Besides, he pointed out that there were not enough troops available at Ticonderoga to guard such a detached position.

This lack represented one of the prices paid for cramming a New York patroon down the throats of Yankee levellers. Geography dictated that New England should be the recruiting ground of the Northern Department, but the men of that section distrusted a general who seldom ventured forth from Albany. Many a Yankee militiaman, indeed, regarded Schuyler as more of an enemy than Burgoyne. For a decade the settlers of the New Hampshire Grants had been waging a petty civil war with New York. These border people had the sympathy of the New England states at a time when sectionalism was a fact and union only a hope and theory. Any New Yorker would have been under a handicap at the head of the Northern Department, but a worse choice than the pompous Schuyler could scarcely have been made.

The British army had its politics, too. In 1775 Burgoyne spent a few months in Boston and Gage found himself out of a job. In 1776 Burgoyne spent a few months in Canada and Carleton lost favor with the British ministers. It may have been only a coincidence, but in both instances these changes took place shortly after Burgoyne returned to London to sit again in Parliament.

The man who had saved Canada for the crown was allowed to remain as governor-general, though George III had to rescue him from being completely overthrown by Germain. Burgoyne arrived in 1777 to take the command of the northern army which Carleton believed that he himself had earned. He was supposedly consoled for the disappointment by being made a Commander of the Bath. Carleton's wife brought the red ribbon from England along with a special warrant authorizing the new knight to add the title to his name before the monarch's sword touched his shoulder.

These honors probably had less influence on him than an unshakable sense of a soldier's duty. Burgoyne admitted that his own brother could not have been more helpful than a man "who thinks he has some cause of resentment." The army, unlike most expeditionary forces, had been hardened in advance by a year's acclimatization and training. Its winter uniform was long afterwards recalled as a curious but attractive departure —a capote of white wool worn with sky-blue leggings and a fur-trimmed red cap.[8] Carleton had made everything ready to the last gaiter button, so that his new superior could write to Germain two weeks after reaching Quebec on May 7, 1777, "The only delay in putting the troops in motion is occasioned by the impracticability of the roads."[9]

There was just one other hitch. Burgoyne's orders provided for 2,000 Canadian auxiliaries, but only an eighth of that number could be induced to volunteer. The employment of Indians had also been specified, and one of the reasons for Germain's dislike of Carleton was the governor's opposition to that policy. About 400 redskins were recruited, so that the expeditionary force at the end of June consisted of 3,424 British rank and file, 3,016 German mercenaries, 473 artillery troops, 250 Canadians and provincials, and 400 Indians—a total of 7,563 men who embarked at the foot of Lake Champlain in a fleet of canoes, barges and bateaux.

Burgoyne's reputation as one of the most humane soldiers of his age rests on deeds as well as words, but "General Swagger" could never resist the opportunity for a proclamation. He evidently believed in all sincerity that his Indians could be kept in check by an address in which he insisted that "aged men, women, children, and prisoners must be held sacred from the knife or hatchet, even in the time of actual conflict." The redskins, added Burgoyne, would be "allowed to take the scalps of the dead, when killed by your fire, and in fair opposition; but on no account are they to be taken from the wounded or even dying. . . ."[10]

When Edmund Burke learned of this injunction, he treated the House of Commons to a parody in which he imagined London's wild beasts being released from their cages with the admonition, "My gentle lions, my humane bears, my sentimental wolves, my tender-hearted hyenas, go forth: but I exhort ye as ye are Christians and members of a civilised society, to take care not to hurt man, woman or child." This sarcastic thrust, according to Horace Walpole, caused Lord North to chuckle until the tears streamed down his plump cheeks.

In the paper warfare, as an anonymous American pamphleteer put it, "General Burgoyne shone forth in all the tinsel splendour of enlightened absurdity." His proclamation to Americans of June 20th, at the outset of the invasion, laid him open to a satirical flank attack by Francis Hopkinson, a New Jersey member of the Continental Congress and signer of the Declaration of Independence. The two documents had such a wide circulation both in Europe and America that parts are worthy of being quoted side by side—the proclamation on the left and the counterblast in the opposite column:[11]

By John Burgoyne, Esq., Lieutenant General of His Majesty's Armies in America, Col. of the Queen's regiment of Light Dragoons, Governor of Fort William in North Britain, One of the representatives of the Commons of Great Britain in Parliament and Commanding an army and fleet now employed in an expedition from Canada.

The forces entrusted to my command are designed to act in concert and upon a common principle with the numerous armies and fleets which already display in every quarter of America the Power, the Justice and (when properly sought), the Mercy of the King. The cause in which the British armies are exerted, applies to the most affecting interest of the human heart, and the military servants of the crown, at first called forth for the sole purpose of Restoring the rights of the Constitution, now combined with love of their country and duty to their Sovereign, the other extensive incitements which spring

Most high, most mighty, most puissant and sublime General.

When the forces under your command arrived at Quebec in order *to act in concert and upon a common principle with the numerous fleets and armies which already display in every quarter of America the justice and mercy of your king*, we, the reptiles of America, were struck with unusual trepidation and astonishment. But what words can express the plenitude of our horror when the *Colonel of the Queen's regiment of light dragoons* advanced towards Ticonderoga. The mountains shook before thee, and the trees of the forest bowed their lofty heads—the vast lakes of the North were chilled at thy pres-

from a true sense of the general privileges of mankind. To the eyes and ears of the temperate part of the public, and to the breasts of the suffering thousands in the Provinces, be the melancholy appeal, whether the present unnatural Rebellion has not been made a foundation for the compleatest system of tyranny that ever God in his displeasure suffered for a time to be exercised over a froward and stubborn generation. . . . Animated by these considerations, at the head of troops in the full power of health, discipline and valour, determined to strike when necessary, and anxious to spare when possible, I, by these presents, invite and exhort all persons, in all places where the progress of this army may point (and by the blessing of God I will extend it), to maintain such a conduct as may justify in protecting their Lands, Habitations and Families. The intention of this address is to hold forth security, not degradation, to the country. . . . The domestic, the industrious and even the timid inhabitants I am desirous to protect, provided they remain quietly in their houses. . . . The consciousness of Christianity, my Royal Master's Clemency, and the honour of soldiership, I have dwelt upon in this invitation, and wished for more persuasive terms to give it impression; and let not people be led to disregard it by considering their distance from the immediate situation of my camp. I have but to give stretch to the Indian forces under my direction (and they amount to thousands) to overtake the hardened enemies of Great Britain and America. I consider them the same wherever they may lurk.

If notwithstanding these endeavours, and sincere inclinations to effect

ence, and the mighty cataracts stopped their tremendous career and were suspended in awe at thy approach.— Judge, then, *oh ineffable Governor of Fort William in North Britain*, what must have been the terror, dismay and despair that overspread this paltry Continent of America and us its wretched inhabitants. Dark and dreary indeed, was the prospect before us, till, like the sun in the horizon, your most gracious, sublime and irresistible proclamation opened the doors of mercy, and snatch'd us, as it were, from the jaws of annihilation. We foolishly thought, blind as we were, that your gracious master's fleets and armies were come to destroy us and our liberties; but we are happy in hearing from you . . . that they were *called forth for the sole purpose of restoring the rights of the constitution to a froward and stubborn generation.* And is it for this, *Oh sublime Lieutenant General*, that you have given yourself the trouble to cross the wide Atlantic, and with incredible fatigue traverse uncultivated wilds? And we ungratefully refuse the proffer'd blessing?—To restore the rights of the constitution you have called together an amiable host of savages and turned them loose to scalp our women and children. . . . If we go on thus in our obstinacy, what can we expect but that you should in your anger, *give a stretch to the Indian forces under your direction, amounting to thousands, to overtake and destroy us;* or, which is ten times worse, that you should withdraw your fleets and armies and leave us to our own misery, without completing the benevolent task you have begun. . . .

We submit—we submit, most puissant *Colonel of the Queen's regiment of light dragoons, and Governor*

them, the phrensy of hostility should remain, I trust I shall stand acquitted in the eyes of God and men in denouncing and executing the vengeance of the State against the wilful outcasts. The messengers of Justice and wrath await them in the field; and Devastation, famine and every concomitant horror that a reluctant, but indispensable prosecution of military duty must occasion, will bar the way to their return.

of Fort William in North America! We offer our heads to the scalping-knife and our bellies to the bayonet. Who can resist the force of your eloquence? Who can withstand the terror of your arms? . . . Behold our wives and daughters, our flocks and herds, our goods and chattels—are they not at the mercy of our Lord and King, and of his *Lieutenant General, Member of the House of Commons, and Governor of Fort William in North Britain?*

If the victory of ridicule over bombast could have repulsed an invading army, Burgoyne would have been stopped in his tracks. For the Declaration of Independence itself did not achieve a wider circulation on both sides of the ocean than this parody written by a lawyer who already had a reputation for delightful light verses. Horace Walpole thought it was the best piece of humor produced by the war, but the British general soon demonstrated that his high-flown words were backed by an imposing array of disciplined force. Instead of being held up for weeks by the necessity of besieging Ticonderoga, as Congress had anticipated, he took that fort without a fight.

General Phillips, commanding the great British artillery train, either discovered for himself the possibilities of occupying Sugarloaf Hill or learned about Kosciusko's report. He constructed a road to the summit, and on July 5th a British battery was in position for a plunging fire on the American works.

St. Clair held a council of war at which his officers agreed that the garrison of 2,000 must be saved at the cost of evacuating positions that had become a trap. The secret withdrawal under cover of darkness might have been more successful if the premature burning of a house on Mount Independence had not illuminated the scene. Before daybreak on the 6th one British column began a vigorous pursuit while the naval forces found it the work of a few hours to cut through the bridge and boom. By nine o'clock the frigates and gunboats were on their way to Skenesborough at the head of the lake, arriving only two hours after the retreating rebel lake flotilla. The invaders captured or destroyed all the boats, mills and storehouses that the routed Americans could not find time to burn. Three more British regiments were landed to push overland for the capture of Fort George and Fort Ann. The defenders of the last post put up a good

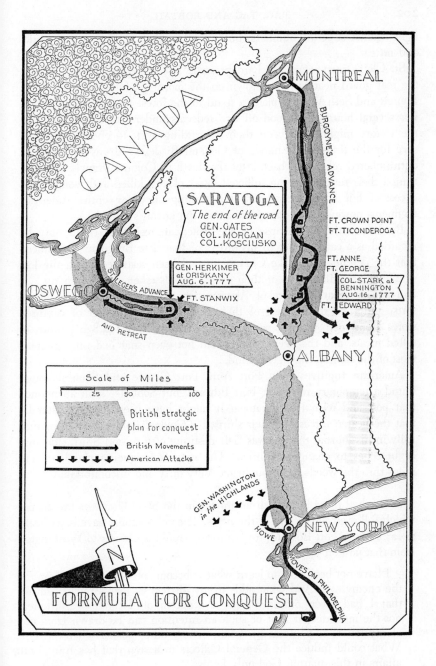

CANADA

MONTREAL

BURGOYNE'S ADVANCE

SARATOGA
The end of the road
GEN. GATES
COL. MORGAN
COL. KOSCIUSKO

FT. CROWN POINT
FT. TICONDEROGA

GEN. HERKIMER
at ORISKANY
AUG. 6 - 1777

FT. ANNE
FT. GEORGE

COL. STARK at
BENNINGTON
AUG. 16 - 1777

OSWEGO

ST. LEGER'S ADVANCE

FT. STANWIX

FT. EDWARD

AND RETREAT

ALBANY

Scale of Miles

25   50   100

British strategic
plan for conquest

British Movements

American Attacks

GEN. WASHINGTON
in the HIGHLANDS

N

HOWE

NEW YORK

MOVES ON PHILADELPHIA

FORMULA FOR CONQUEST

fight against superior numbers, but were forced to set fire to the works and retreat.

St. Clair's men were also hard pressed. The pursuers caught up with the rear guard near Hubbardstown on the morning of the 7th, and John Francis and Seth Warner made a stand in the forest with about 900 men. For several hours they stood off 850 redcoats under General Fraser; and the victory might have been theirs, according even to enemy accounts, save for the timely appearance of General Riedesel's Brunswickers. The outnumbered rebels fell back after the death of Colonel Francis and continued their retreat, having inflicted losses of 203 killed and wounded at a cost of but 40 to themselves. The cutting off of an entire American regiment, however, left 320 prisoners in the enemy's hands.

By July 10th the collapse of the American resistance could only be regarded as a catastrophe. In his orders of that date Burgoyne announced that the defenders of Lake Champlain had been scattered "with the loss of all their Artillery, five of their armed vessels taken and blown up . . . and a very great quantity of Ammunition, Provisions and stores of all sorts, and the greatest part of their baggage."[12] His report of captured stores mentioned 349,760 pounds of flour as well as 143,830 pounds of salted meats, and the fleeing forces had not even snatched time to spike most of the cannon they left behind.

American fugitives from Fort Ann, Fort George and Skenesborough found a temporary refuge at Fort Edward, but Schuyler soon abandoned that post and retired to Saratoga. It might have been recorded literally that the beaten forces lost their shirts, for Colonel Baldwin noted mournfully in his journal that he was "left destitute of a second Shirt, stockings or breeches to change my linen. The long & fatigueing march of 110 miles thro the woods has brought me Very dirty and uncomfortable."[13]

Never had there been such an uproar in the State House as the clamor which followed the receipt of the news. The echoes must have been heard as far away as Fort Edward, for Schuyler wrote his excuses to Washington from that post on July 9th:

> I have not been able to learn what is become of General St. Clair and the enemy. . . . And what adds to my distress is, that a report prevails that I had given orders for the evacuation of Ticonderoga, whereas not the most distant hint of such an intention can be drawn from any of my letters to General St. Clair, or any other person whatever. . . . What could induce the General Officers to a step that has ruined our affairs in this quarter, God only knows.[14]

The inferences conveyed in this report might be forgiven on the grounds of shock and incomplete information. But after St. Clair reached Fort Edward three days later and explained in person, his superior did not offer a word in his defense when writing to Washington again on the 14th. Long later a court-martial gave St. Clair an acquittal with honor, but at the moment he was left to take the blame alone. This he did in a letter of the 17th to Washington, reaffirming his conviction that "a retreat, even with the loss of our cannon and stores, if it could be effected, would be of infinitely greater service to the country and bring less disgrace upon our arms, than an army, although a small one, taken prisoners, with their cannon and stores."[15] It is further to the credit of the scapegoat, a Scottish immigrant who had adopted the American cause, that he did not hide behind the decision of his own subordinates at the council of war. "I was fully in sentiment with them and believe I should have ordered the retreat, if they had been of a contrary way of thinking."

Schuyler's letters of July 7th, 9th and 14th give a picture of confusion on the part of the man most responsible for the debacle.[16] After estimating that his strength in the entire Northern Department did not exceed 4,500 troops scattered in detachments, he did not offer a single idea or even a hope of redeeming the situation. "I am here," he wrote lugubriously from Fort Edward, "at the head of a . . . handful of men, not above fifteen hundred, without provisions, little ammunition, not above five rounds to a man, having neither ball, nor lead to make any; the country in the deepest consternation; no carriages to move the stores from Fort George, which I expect every moment to learn is attacked." In this predicament, the only solution that occurred to Schuyler was to call for help from a commander in chief three hundred miles away who had need of every resource in his coming grapple with Howe's superior army:

> As the Continental troops have lost everything, your Excellency will please to order up to me, the soonest possible, tents for four thousand men, five hundred camp kettles, a quantity of fixed musket ammunition, cartridge-paper, twelve pieces heavy cannon, with travelling carriages, sixteen fieldpieces, and a considerable quantity of ammunition for them; a competent number of artillerymen . . . so as to be sufficient to manage the artillery; all the implements necessary to the artillery, horses, harness, and drivers; about six hundred intrenching tools, sorted, excluding pick-axes, of which we need a considerable number. Please also to send me a good engineer or two.

The extent of Schuyler's confusion is illustrated by the fact that he had with him the best engineer of the Continental Army, for Kosciusko had been busy since the fall of Ticonderoga at destroying bridges in the path of the enemy advance. There were a few passages in the commander's letters of July 13th, 15th and 18th in which his tolerance seemed a bit strained, but as usual he propped up a sagging subordinate with his own resolution.[17] "We should never despair," he counseled. "Our situation before has been unpromising and has changed for the better—so, I trust, it will again—If new difficulties arise, we must only put forth new exertions and proportion our Efforts to the exigency of the times."

Absentee generalship had been the ruin of the northern army, but Schuyler was never lacking in dogged pluck. The same obstinacy that blinded him to his own military lapses now served him in good stead as he got a new grip on himself. Washington sent ten fieldpieces in addition to other arms he could ill spare. Better yet, Washington sent ideas. The ax, he suggested, might be at the moment a better weapon than the cannon; and Schuyler did his part by putting a small army of woodsmen to work at creating a labyrinth of felled trees to impede the progress of Burgoyne's top-heavy artillery and baggage train.

After the first explosion Congress displayed a commendable moderation in discussing the Northern Department. Both factions tacitly agreed that it was no time for a political feud, and the merits of the rival generals were weighed solely on a basis of military qualifications. Even such a prejudiced Yankee as Samuel Adams admitted in a letter of July 15th that due to Schuyler's "large interest and powerful connections in that Part of the Country, no one could so readily avail himself of Supplys for an Army there, than he. A most substantial Reason, I think why he should have been appointed a Quartermaster or Commissary. But it seems to have been the prevailing Motive to appoint him to the Chief Command! . . . It is indeed droll enough to see a General not knowing where to find the main Body of his Army. Gates is the man of my Choice. He is *honest* and *true*, and has the Art of *gaining the Love of his Soldiers* principally because he is *always present* with them in Fatigue and Danger."[18]

Most of the other members agreed with him, and on August 4th Gates was appointed with the concurrence of eleven states.

It was largely due to Schuyler's influence that New York had a fort and militia army to oppose the sweep of a British right wing, co-operating with Burgoyne by making a descent from Lake Ontario. This force of 1,700 loyalists, Canadians and Indians was commanded by Colonel Barry St. Leger, with Sir John Johnson, Colonel John Butler and the Mohawk partisan Joseph Brant as colleagues. On August 3rd the invaders laid siege to Fort Stanwix on the Mohawk River, and the advance of a rebel militia force to the relief brought on the first civil war battle of the Revolution.

Colonel Nicholas Herkimer, the leader of the Tryon County militia, was not unique in the sad reflection that members of his family were armed against him. He marched his 800 men to the aid of Colonel Marinus Willett, who had promised to make a sally from the fort on August 6th with part of the garrison of 950 equally untried troops. Herkimer's column included a few Oneida auxiliaries, but they failed to give warning of the ambuscade prepared by Sir John Johnson two miles west of Oriskany. The rebel army, without scouts or flankers, plunged blindly into a gloomy ravine surrounded by dense woods. Johnson, Butler and Brant did not spring the trap until the whole force, baggage wagons and all, had been surrounded in the defile. Then the Indian war whoop gave the signal for muskets blazing from behind every rock and tree.

The ambuscade might have been more successful if a route of escape had been left open for a militia flight. Herkimer's farmers needed no training to perceive that they were fighting for their lives, and desperation added to an appalling casualty list. The old Dutchman fell severely wounded and had himself propped up against a beech tree, smoking his pipe while giving orders. When a thunderstorm dampened firing pans, the fight continued with hatchets and hunting knives. Brant's Indians, maddened by blood, howled like wild beasts and lost their heads until they could not distinguish friend from foe. After several hours of this horror, Johnson had to march his Royal Greens five miles to Fort Stanwix to deal with Willett's sally. His baggage had already been captured before he arrived, and a panic dispersed the Indians and Tories left behind to continue the battle.

Herkimer had possession of the field, but the victory was bought with heavy losses. Of the original 800 rebel militiamen, 160 were killed and 200 wounded in addition to those borne away as captives. Fewer than half of the column ever survived the slaughter, and the bodies of about 80 Tories and Indians lay among the slain. Two weeks later Herkimer died, calmly reading his Dutch Bible to the last, as the result of an in-fection in his amputated leg.

The siege of Fort Stanwix, if such it could be called, turned into an endurance contest lasting sixteen more days. St. Leger's few fieldpieces were too light to have any effect on the works, and it became a question whether Willett's supplies and nerve would hold out until Arnold marched to his relief. Legend has it that the American flag was first flown from the sod ramparts—a red, white and blue banner sewn by garrison wives from such materials as a petticoat, a soldier's shirt and Colonel Peter Gansevoort's cloak. Another tradition charges St. Leger's retreat to the panic caused among his Indians by an idiot's warning of the approach of Americans "as numerous as the leaves on the trees." It is more probable that the redskins, according to their custom, lost interest in an operation promising no immediate plunder. However this may be, they deserted in such numbers that St. Leger withdrew on August 22nd, bringing to an end the thrust of a British right wing that might have contributed materially to Burgoyne's invasion.

The news of Gates's appointment was reflected at once in the new confidence of Yankee militiamen who had no faith in his rival. As an example of the absurd lengths to which they carried their distrust, Dr. Thacher mentioned in his journal one of those rumors that are never too fantastic to be credited in time of war. After the fall of Ticonderoga, some of the New England troops believed "that Generals Schuyler and St. Clair acted the part of traitors to their country, and that they were paid for their treason in *silver balls*, shot from Burgoyne's guns into our camp, and that they were collected by order of General St. Clair and divided between him and General Schuyler."[19]

Several hundred Massachusetts militiamen, sent to replace troops whose enlistments had expired, turned homeward in a body after reaching Saratoga on July 30th to find Schuyler in charge. Such prejudices were condemned as unpatriotic, but there is something to be said on the side of New England states which had borne the heaviest load of the war. In 1775 they had set a precept worthy of imitation by urging the election of a commander in chief from another section of the country. Two years later they believed it was their turn to be indulged in the appointment of a general to command troops largely raised by New England. Late in July their delegates at Philadelphia sent a memorial to Washington, declaring that "we take the liberty to signify to your Excellency, that, in our opinion, no man will be more likely to restore harmony, order, and discipline, and retrieve our affairs in this quarter, than Major General Gates. He has on experience acquired the confidence, and stands high in the esteem, of the eastern States and troops."[20]

The first reports of Gates's appointment stimulated enlistments in the

New England "village republics." Two weeks later a hastily raised force of Yankee farmers, fighting under their own leaders, won a battle which remains one of the most amazing victories of military amateurs over regulars.

Burgoyne's writings prove that he had hesitated to take the risk of sending out detachments, but an urgent transport problem gave him no option. The mission of seizing rebel horses and cattle suited German mercenaries who looked forward to plundering the fat towns of the Hudson valley. Colonel Baum began his "secret expedition" on August 11th, and the

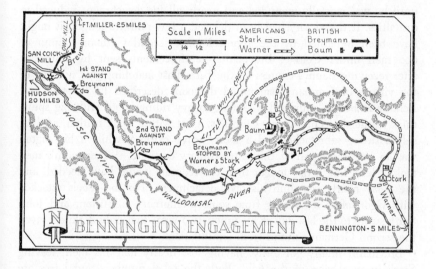

alarm spread with such rapidity that farmers from New Hampshire were awaiting him at the New York border five days later. Seth Warner and a dozen other militia chiefs brought contingents, but the main glory belonged to Colonel John Stark of New Hampshire.

On the night of August 13th Baum informed Burgoyne by express that the "savages," as he called the Americans, were gathering near Bennington. His mission had not been successful so far, he added, due to the fact that the farmers were driving away or even destroying their livestock. Hence he took the risk of proceeding, confident that his 500 Hessians, redcoats and Indians could cope with any number of armed rustics. The next day Baum advanced within four miles of the village, and by the 15th he found it prudent to entrench on a wooded hill.

It had been an old militia custom to rely on earthworks when fighting regulars, but Stark boldly planned to reverse the situation by storming a redoubt held by an enemy with two cannon. A heavy rain compelled him to postpone the attempt until the afternoon of the 16th. Then his little army in shirtsleeves swarmed up the hill, front and rear, to scramble over the ramparts and club down the Hanau artillerymen at their guns. The rebels had the advantage in numbers, but in the end they outfought rather than outweighed the Germans. Stark, who could qualify as an expert, praised the two-hour combat as "the hottest I ever saw in my life."

The Indians fled at the outset, leaving Baum and his regulars to resist until he was mortally wounded and nearly all his detachment reduced to casualties. If the victory had been delayed a few minutes longer, it might have been imperiled by the approach of a second German column of 600 men under Colonel Breymann—reinforcements sent by Burgoyne after receiving Baum's express on the 14th. Fast marching was not one of the virtues of German dismounted dragoons described by Captain von Eelking as being "equipped with long, heavy riding boots, with big spurs, thick leather breeches, heavy gauntlets, a hat with a thick feather; at their side a strong sabretache, and a short, heavy carbine, while a big pigtail was an important part of this extraordinary costume."[21] Breymann's men took at least half a day longer than the redcoats would have needed, and the delay nearly cost him his own detachment. For the rebels attacked with vigor, after recovering from some preliminary confusion, and John Stark swore to the last day of his ninety-two years that only darkness saved the second German column from annihilation.

Breymann finally got away, having lost nearly half his men, leaving Stark in possession of the field. Both the rebel numbers and losses are variously stated, but 40 killed and wounded out of a total of 2,000 is the generally accepted count. Gordon reckoned the enemy killed at 207—a proportion which indicates savage fighting—and the prisoners at about 700, including Tories who had joined the force on the march. But these were minor gains as compared to the moral impetus given to militiamen who went home to mow the hay or harvest the oats. These Yankee farmers would not be content with hunting down enemy detachments next time. A few weeks later they would be encouraged to try their skill at stalking such big game as General Burgoyne's main army.

Chapter 13

The Surrender at Saratoga

THE news of Bennington and Oriskany had not yet raised hopes when Gates was appointed to command. For the second time in a year the northern army was changing horses in midstream after being nearly swept away by the current.

A Hessian officer's letter described the forty-nine-year-old American general as "a man between fifty and sixty years of age; wears his thin gray hair combed around his head; is still lively and friendly, and constantly wears spectacles on account of his weak eyes."[1] The new commander could not be sure that any army would be left by the time he reached the front, but the first reports of the Bennington success awaited him on his arrival.

Gates might also have found encouragement in one of those incidents which upset the calculations of monarchs and ministers. Thomas Paine had already appealed for some Yankee Joan of Arc to arise, but he could hardly have anticipated that the martyr's role would go to a young woman of Tory sympathies. Burgoyne's army was slowly advancing toward the Hudson when Jane McCrea journeyed to the British lines for a meeting —a "tryst," as contemporary writers always phrased it—with the provincial officer to whom she was betrothed. Her murder in the forest by Indian auxiliaries was not the first by Burgoyne's redskins, but it took this tragedy to convict the British ministers of violating civilized codes.

Burgoyne had not been given any option as to the employment of savages in plans drawn up by Germain with the approval of the king. But the responsibility must be shared by British officers whose letters and diaries, far from condemning harsh policies, more often criticize the administration for showing too much forbearance. Captain Mackenzie spoke for many of his colleagues when he held that "the most effectual means of reducing the Country to subjection, is to burn and destroy everything the

Army can get at. . . . Very few parts of America know, as yet, what the horrors of War are, and if their houses, farms, and other property was destroyed and laid waste, their resentment would turn on Congress. . . ."[2]

Ignorance of Indian methods could not excuse invaders who saw their ravages during the last war. For that matter, the redskins of Burgoyne's army were placed under the direction of Colonel La Corne St. Luc, who had been guilty of the worst atrocities of those years. In a few blunt words that need no translation he imparted to his new employers the secret of successful Indian warfare: *"Il faut lâcher les sauvages contre les miserables* rebels, *pour imposer le terreur sur les frontiers.* . . . *Il faut brutalizer les affaires."* Governor Tryon, who reported this advice, added that he was "exactly of opinion with Colonel La Corne St. Luc."[3]

The following year, when Burgoyne had to account before the House of Commons, he blamed the McCrea tragedy on St. Luc. But as usual the handsome British general dug a pit for himself with his own words. For his testimony made it evident that he could have had no illusions when he hired a former enemy "instrumental in scalping several hundred British soldiers upon the very ground where he was this year employed."[4]

Americans whose complaints of past Indian ravages had gone unheard in Europe did not spare their adjectives after the murder of Jane McCrea. Burgoyne's proclamation had laid him open to attack, and his failure to punish the guilty savages left him still more vulnerable. Even after he forbade further scalping and insisted that British officers supervise the conduct of Indians, a Philadelphia newspaper accused him of the worst motives:

> We are credibly informed that Burgoyne, the chief and director of the King of Great Britain's band of thieves, robbers, cut-throats and murderers of every description, now infesting the northern and western frontiers of several of the American United States, has not only discontinued the reward he had offered and given to the savage Tories, Indians, Hessians, Brunswickers, and other profligate scum of the human race, now in his service, for the scalps they brought him, from the murdered and half murdered inhabitants, but has strictly prohibited for the future, the practice of scalping. It must not, however, be supposed, that the chief of the ruffian band was so weak as to be in the least influenced to this prohibition by any motive of compassion or humanity; his inducements were purely political. He had found by experience, that his rewards lessened the number of his emissaries, who not only scalped some of his Tory friends, concealed among the inhabitants, but also scalped one another. . . .[5]

The slain girl's beauty increased with each recital, and it became a frontier tradition of after years that her Tory lover acquired a scalp "with glossy tresses a yard and a quarter long." Each anniversary of the crime, according to legend, he spent in solitude down to "a lonely old age, taciturn and melancholy."

Schuyler offended New England yeomen, who accused him of being too considerate of the feelings of British generals. Elaborate military courtesies did not appeal to farmers who realized that their families might be the next victims of the tomahawk. They found it a welcome contrast when Gates denounced "the polite Macaroni, Burgoyne" for ravages which left "a stain on the honor of British arms." In a letter of August 19th to Washington he declared that "all is now fair with General Burgoyne, even if the bloody hatchet he has so barbarously used should find its way into his own head."[6]

Burgoyne called his adversary "an old midwife" after Gates wrote directly to charge him with hiring "the savages of America to scalp Europeans and the descendants of Europeans" and paying "a price for each scalp so barbarously taken." But the final word on the subject would not be heard until 1782, when the master propagandist of the age dipped his pen in vitriol. The peace negotiations had begun when Benjamin Franklin wrote his hoax purporting to be a letter in a Boston newspaper from one Captain Gerrish of the New England militia. That officer announced the interception of eight bales of American scalps being sent to England by way of Canada. Among the "peltry" listed in the invoice were 88 scalps of women, 193 of boys, 211 of girls and 29 of infants. A Seneca chief making delivery was supposed to have said, "We wish you to send these scalps over the water to the great king, that he may regard them and be refreshed; and that he may see our faithfulness in destroying his enemies and be convinced that his presents have not been made to ungrateful people."[7] The account ended with a description of the trophies being exhibited in Boston, where "thousands of people are flocking to see them."

Dr. Franklin could not have anticipated that his satire would be accepted as gospel truth not only in Europe but even his homeland. Years later the hoax was still being republished in good faith by American newspapers, sending a shudder up and down the spines of a new generation.

The military value of savage auxiliaries, as St. Luc had intimated, was in direct proportion to the terror they could inspire. Burgoyne's redskins did not fail to intimidate Yankees from long-settled communities that had known no Indian ravages for a century. But Washington had already provided the tactical remedy, and Gates wrote in grateful acknowledgment on August 22nd: "I cannot sufficiently thank your Excellency for sending Col. Morgan's corps to this army; they will be of the greatest service to it, for, until the recent success this way, I am told the army were quite panic-struck by the Indians [and] their Tory and Canadian assassins in Indian dress. Horrible indeed have been the cruelties they have wantonly committed on the miserable inhabitants. . . ."[8]

It was soon the turn of the redskins themselves to be terrified by pitiless frontiersmen using their own methods against them. Morgan's men had been in action only a few days when Colonel Henry Dearborn noted in his journal, "An Indian Scalp was Brought in to Day by a Party of our men which is a Rareety with us."[9] The riflemen volunteered with enthusiasm for patrols which had as their object the stalking of savages in the forest. The first effect was to deprive the invaders of intelligence as their scouts grew more cautious. Soon a majority of the auxiliaries had no more stomach for this warfare, and a British officer recorded that "the desertion of the Indians, Canadians, and Provincials, at a time when their services were most required, was exceedingly mortifying."[10]

Gates thought so highly of the riflemen that he created a new temporary corps of 300 light infantry picked from all the regiments of the northern army and placed under the command of Colonel Dearborn to act in conjunction with Morgan's corps. The most convincing tribute to the marksmanship of these two units is to be found in Burgoyne's orders for September 18th, reproaching his army with the fact that "the Service has sustained a loss within ten days that might in Action have cost the lives of some hundreds of the enemy. . . . The life of the Soldier is the property of the King, and since neither friendly admonition, repeated injunctions nor corporal punishments have effect . . . the Army is now to be informed, and it is not doubted the Commanding Officers will do it, solemnly, that the first Soldier caught beyond the advanced Centries of the Army will be instantly hanged."[11]

The musketry of the redcoats themselves had improved so little since Bunker Hill that Americans resorted to hyperbole to express their contempt. An enemy regular, they declared, could not hit a barn from the inside; and it took a platoon volley at ten paces to make sure of killing a steer for food. Now and then some British regiment strove for reform, and Captain Mackenzie relates that soldiers of the 23rd were drilled to fire at life-size targets bobbing up and down in the waves of Boston harbor.

But the effects were never apparent to Americans, who took the most reckless chances. Nor were they much impressed by the shooting or tactics of the Jägers attached to the German regiments.

Two other excerpts from Burgoyne's *Orderly Book* show the change in his tactical ideas after rebel marksmen had taught costly lessons.[12] On June 20th, when the invasion began, he directed his officers "to inculcate in the men's minds a Reliance upon the Bayonet. . . . The onset of Bayonets in the hands of the Valiant is irresistible." This had also been the military philosophy of Howe and Cornwallis, but on September 2nd Burgoyne reached the point of picking from each regiment sixteen "men of good character, sober, active, robust and healthy; they are to be provided with a very good firelock . . . to form a Body of Marksmen."

Schuyler's woodsmen accomplished their task so well that it took Burgoyne twenty days to cover as many miles on the way to Fort Edward. Forty bridges had to be built after the felled trees were cleared away, and British engineers found it necessary to construct a timber causeway two miles long. A baggage train including thirty wagons for Burgoyne's personal effects also accounts for the crawling pace of the advance.

These three weeks were of inestimable worth to the rebels, who evacuated Fort Edward and fell back during the last days of July to Saratoga. The farther Burgoyne proceeded from his base of waterborne supplies on Lake Champlain, the more he became the victim of what Clausewitz has called the "friction of war." The gears of the British military machine were grinding so badly by the second week of August that Burgoyne decided against his better judgment to send out the ill-fated foraging detachment. In his testimony before the House of Commons he justified this risk with the explanation, "I knew that Bennington was the great deposit of corn, flour, and store cattle, that it was only guarded by militia, and every day's account tended to confirm the persuasion of the loyalty of one description of the inhabitants and the panic of the other."[13]

Two days before this detachment met its defeat, Burgoyne took an even more fateful step when he reached the Hudson on August 14th and built a bridge of rafts in preparation for a crossing to the west bank. Schuyler had meanwhile fallen back to Stillwater, where his successor took over the command.

It was a beaten and battered but not yet demoralized army that rejoiced over the change in generals. William Weeks, a twenty-year-old officer who had enlisted as a Harvard student, wrote on August 6th to his twelve brothers and sisters in a New Hampshire village, "After all these trouble-some Scenes I am still the same, in good Health, hoping long to continue so, and live to give our Enemies a severe Flogging yet, and be in possession of my Baggage they took at Skeensborough—I have this to comfort my-self with, that I sav'd myself with what I had on, which happen'd not to be my best."[14]

An army in a mood for puns is not yet crushed, and the Yankees at Stillwater chuckled that Burgoyne had been driven Stark mad at Ben-nington. He might be able to advance through forests, they bragged, but never through Gates.

The new general wriggled uncomfortably on the horns of a strategic dilemma. He wished to restore the aggressive spirit of a retreating army by making at least a nominal advance to challenge an oncoming enemy. On the other hand, he dared not take the risk of exposing a numerically inferior force to a battle against regulars in the field.

At the outset Gates had little choice but to wait until reinforcements increased a strength that had dwindled to about two-thirds of the enemy's numbers. On August 19th, the day he took over the command, Schuyler had written to James Duane that he would "pity" his successor. This sentiment gives an idea of the gloom and defeatism that had handicapped the northern army as much as material weakness. But Gates stood in no need of pity as he demonstrated once more the ability as an organizer and disciplinarian he had shown at Ticonderoga. On September 8th, after new arrivals brought his numbers up to about 5,000, he solved his dilemma by striking a bargain between retreat and a hazardous forward movement.

His plan represented a compromise based as much on psychology as strategy. By contenting himself with a mere four-mile advance beyond Stillwater in the direction of the foe, he put an end to two months of retreat without taking too many risks. And by creating a strong system of field fortifications, he provided an insurance policy in case of disaster.

Gates, in short, intended both to eat and have his cake. In selecting his new position, he relied on the advice of that brilliant but shy engineer whose talents might have gone to waste without a "discoverer." Kosciusko decided upon a narrow meadow where the Hudson on the right and rugged wooded country on the left offered obstacles to protect both flanks. It was a strategic bottleneck which could neither be forced nor avoided without difficulty, and the Polish volunteer added to its

1. Needham
2. Dedham
3. Providence Rd.
4. Dorchester Neck

5. Newton
6. Brookline
7. Roxbury
8. Dorchester Hts.

9. Waltham
10. Watertown
11. Cambridge
12. Charles River

BOSTON
13. Castle Island
14. Governor's Island

15. Concord
16. Menotomy
17. Bunker Hill
18. Charlestown

19. Lexington
20. Medford River
21. Penny Ferry
22. Noddle's Island

23. Mystic Ponds
24. Medford
25. Malden Road
26. Salem Road

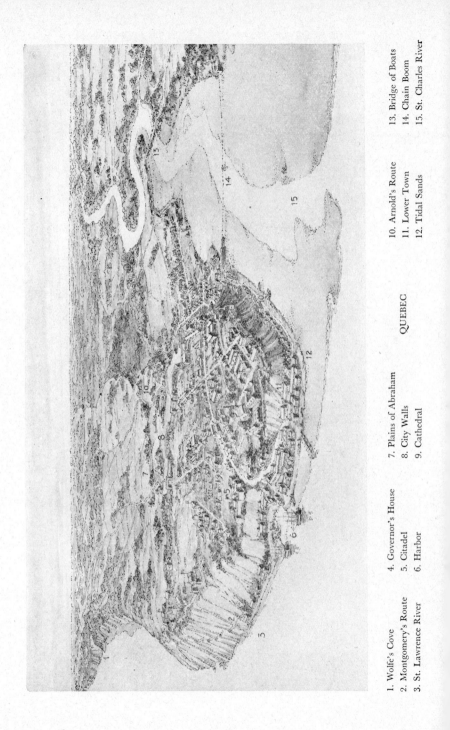

QUEBEC

1. Wolfe's Cove
2. Montgomery's Route
3. St. Lawrence River

4. Governor's House
5. Citadel
6. Harbor

7. Plains of Abraham
8. City Walls
9. Cathedral

10. Arnold's Route
11. Lower Town
12. Tidal Sands

13. Bridge of Boats
14. Chain Boom
15. St. Charles River

1. The Highlands	5. Peekskill	9. Dobbs Ferry	NEW YORK CITY	16. White Plains	20. Pell's Point	24. Connecticut
2. Acquackanonck	6. Hudson River	10. Fort Washington	13. Kingsbridge	17. Hell Gate	21. Throg's Neck	25. Flushing
3. Newark	7. Hackensack	11. Fort Lee	14. Harlem	18. Brookland	22. Long Island	26. Flatbush
4. Elizabethtown	8. Staten Island	12. Paulus Hook	15. Governor's Island	19. The Narrows	23. Bedford	27. New Utrecht

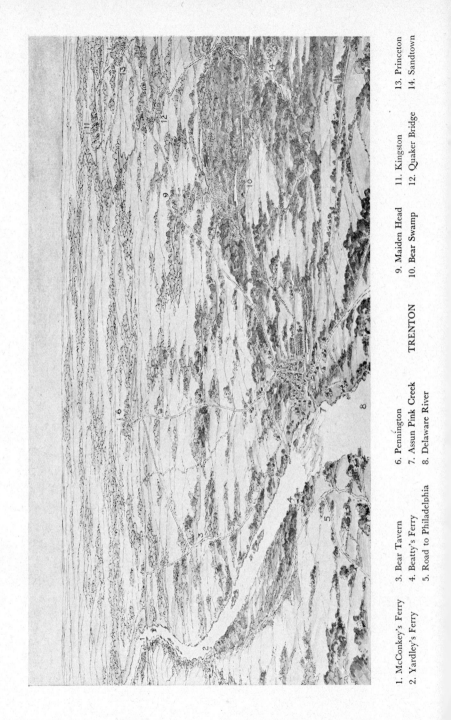

1. McConkey's Ferry   3. Bear Tavern   6. Pennington   9. Maiden Head   11. Kingston   13. Princeton
2. Yardley's Ferry   4. Beatty's Ferry   7. Assun Pink Creek   10. Bear Swamp   12. Quaker Bridge   14. Sandtown
           5. Road to Philadelphia   8. Delaware River   TRENTON

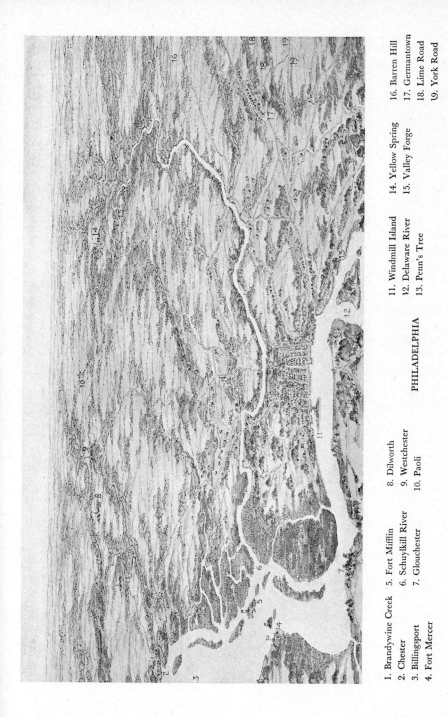

1. Brandywine Creek   5. Fort Mifflin
2. Chester   6. Schuylkill River
3. Billingsport   7. Glouchester
4. Fort Mercer

8. Dilworth
9. Westchester
10. Paoli

11. Windmill Island
12. Delaware River
13. Penn's Tree

PHILADELPHIA

14. Yellow Spring
15. Valley Forge

16. Barren Hill
17. Germantown
18. Lime Road
19. York Road

1. E. Greenwich (Ft. Daniel)
2. Updyke's Harbor
3. Connonicut Island

4. Warwick Neck
5. Brenton's Pt. Ft.
6. Hallidon Hill Ft.
7. Castle Hill Ft.

8. Providence
9. Prospect Hill & Fox Hill Fts.
10. Fts. Sullivan & Independence
11. Kettle Pt. & Hog Pen Fts.

NEWPORT
12. Prudence Island
13. Fort Liberty

14. Miles Bridge
15. Barrington
16. Pappasquash
17. Bristol

18. Honeyman's Hill
19. Barker's Hill
20. Rhode Island
21. Atlantic Ocean

22. Bristol Ferry Ft.
23. Butts Hill Ft.
24. Quaker Hill Ft.
25. Turkey Hill Ft.

1. Governor's Plantation   4. Magazine   SAVANNAH   10. White Bluff Road   13. Little Ogeechee Gate

2. Savannah River   5. Road to the Coast   8. Burying Ground Gate   11. Great Ogeechee Gate   14. Road to Beaufort

3. Hutchinsons Island   6. Bethesda Gate   9. King's Storehouses   12. Yamacraw Gate   15. Marshes

7. Trustee's Gate

1. James Creek
2. James Island
3. Johnson's Fort

4. Ashley River
5. Wappoo Creek
6. South Channel

7. Field of Surrender
8. Schute's Folly
9. Distillery

CHARLESTON
10. Hog Island
11. Hog Island Channel

12. British Hospital
13. Drum Island

14. Cooper River
15. Hobcaw Point
16. Mt. Pleasant

17. Daniel Island
18. Wando River

natural strength with a system of mutually supporting redoubts and entrenchments planned for defense in depth.

A thousand men toiled to complete works which won the praise of one of Europe's foremost soldiers, the Marquis de Chastellux, when he visited the battlefield three years later.[15] On the first of two parallel ridges Kosciusko located "three redoubts placed in parallel directions. In front of the last, on the north side, is a little hollow, beyond which the ground rises again, on which are three more redoubts, placed nearly in the same direction as the former. In front of them is a deep ravine which runs from the west, in which is a small creek. The ravine takes its rise in the woods; and all the ground on the right of it is extremely thick set with woods." The French general observed in this quarter "some pretty steep summits, which were likewise fortified with redoubts." These positions were linked from the river to the forest by a system of connecting entrenchments which "commands the surrounding woods, and resists everything that might turn the left flank of the army."

Burgoyne had made no decisive move since August 14th, when he reached the Hudson and built a bridge of rafts. Exactly a month later he crossed his Rubicon in full knowledge that the reverses at Bennington and Fort Stanwix left him to carry on alone with a depleted army. Critics have argued with the wisdom of hindsight that he should have swallowed his pride and turned back to Fort Edward; and Burgoyne himself did not radiate optimism in his letter of August 20th to Lord Germain:

> The great bulk of the country is undoubtedly with Congress in principle and zeal; and their measures are executed with a secrecy and dispatch that are not to be equalled. Wherever the king's forces point, militia to the amount of three or four thousand assemble in twenty-four hours; they bring with them their subsistance, etc. and the alarm over, they return to their farms. . . . Whatever may be my fate, my lord, I submit my actions to the breast of the king, and to the candid judgement of my profession, when all the motives become public and I rest in the confidence that whatever decision is passed upon my conduct my good intent will not be questioned.[16]

This was hardly the spirit of a conqueror, yet the British general still held an equality in troops and a great superiority in artillery when he encamped on the plain of Saratoga. There was little to choose between the two armies in aggressiveness as the redcoats advanced on the 15th, opposed every step of the way by the bold attacks of rebel skirmishers.

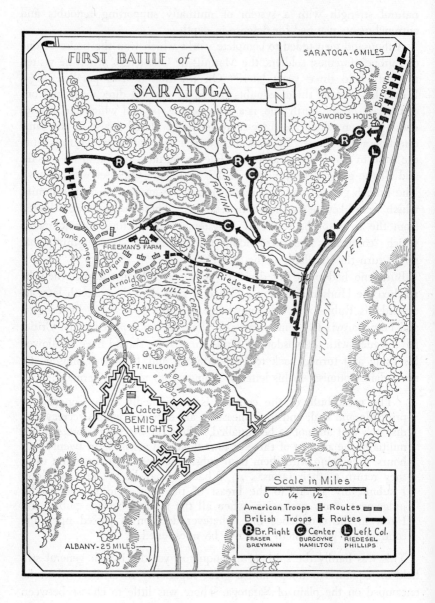

FIRST BATTLE of SARATOGA

SARATOGA-6 MILES

N

SWORD'S HOUSE

Burgoyne

GREAT RAVINE

Morgan's Rangers

FREEMAN'S FARM

Morgan

Arnold

NORTH BRANCH

Riedesel

MILL CREEK

HUDSON RIVER

FT. NEILSON

Gates
BEMIS HEIGHTS

Scale in Miles

0   1/4   1/2   1

American Troops   Routes
British Troops   Routes
R Br.Right   C Center   L Left Col.
FRASER   BURGOYNE   RIEDESEL
BREYMANN   HAMILTON   PHILLIPS

ALBANY-25 MILES

It was during this period, in fact, that Burgoyne had cause to reproach his soldiers for the losses inflicted by American marksmen.

The confidence and fighting spirit inculcated by Gates is reflected in diary entries. "This evening we had orders to lay upon arms and not pull off any of our clothes," Corporal Ebenezer Wild noted on the 15th. The following night his Massachusetts regiment "turned out at 2 o'clk. and stayed under arms expecting the enemy would pay us a morning visit."[17] Colonel Dearborn noted that same day that "we Expected to have been Attacted this morning, But were disappointed—Genrl. Stark joined us to Day with his Brigade from Bennington." By the 18th the British had approached within four miles of the American lines, and Dearborn reported that "we marched with 3000 men to attact the Enimy—we fell in with some small Parties and took about 30 prisoners."[18]

Burgoyne had not counted on the "old midwife" showing so much fight. His intelligence was unsatisfactory, due to the havoc created among his Indians and Canadians by rebel riflemen, when he decided to lead a reconnaissance in force on the 19th to make contact with Gates. But it was the Americans who struck first and kept his troops on the defensive for hours in the decisive battle of the campaign.

In a month from the day he took over the command, Gates had transformed a beaten army into an instrument capable of fighting regulars to a finish in the open field. British officers who had been through the hottest actions of the last war in Europe testified that they never experienced such a contest as this struggle in the woods.

About ten o'clock, after leaving behind a reserve to guard the camp, the 2,000 redcoats advanced in three columns—General Fraser on the right wing with the grenadiers and light infantry, General Phillips on the left with the Germans and artillery, and Burgoyne leading four regiments in the center. Gates was not caught napping. Scouts on the other side of the river sent timely warning, and the American general ordered Morgan's and Dearborn's regiments forward. The riflemen drew first blood at noon by surprising a British picket and driving it back. In the pursuit Morgan's men collided with the main body of the enemy and were themselves compelled to give ground.

At this moment the burly Virginia frontiersman displayed a native genius for tactics. After rallying his shaken troops, he deployed them in a thin firing line, anticipating the warfare of the next century. For it was more than a contest between Britons and Americans when the compact line of redcoats advanced into the clearing, marching in perfect parade step behind their officers. It was a contest of the military future against the past, and the decision went to riflemen whose leaf-brown hunting shirts made them all but invisible in the woods.

Instead of leading his men with uplifted sword, Morgan gave orders to subordinates, who signaled with backwoods turkey calls. The deployed riflemen, taking cover in the woods, offered a poor target to regulars whose aim was uncertain at best. American marksmen, firing at will, considered a shot wasted unless they drew a bead on some opponent, preferably one of the British officers. Burgoyne's description of the scene conveys an impression:

> The enemy had with their army great numbers of marksmen, armed with rifle-barrel pieces; these, during an engagement, hovered upon the flanks in small detachments, and were very expert in securing themselves and in shifting their ground. In this action many placed themselves in high trees in the rear of their own lines, and there was seldom a minute's interval of smoke, in any part of our line, without officers being taken off by a single shot.[19]

The redcoats advancing into the clearing had their ranks thinned by a more destructive fire than they had ever met before. Their own volleys had so little effect that two American corps held off the entire British center until reinforcements arrived. As the new regiments came forward, one or two at a time, they extended the American left.

All afternoon the fight surged back and forth in the clearing. Gates placed his entire faith in Morgan, for there is no convincing evidence that any of the generals took part in the field. This fact goes far toward accounting for the American success. If Arnold had been in the fight, he would doubtless have obliged the foe by leading massed charges of men to a heroic slaughter. Morgan's methods were less theatrical, but the "old wagoner" refused to play at the enemy's own game. The British 62nd regiment, which fought opposite his corps, had only 97 rank and file left unhurt out of nearly 300 who marched out that morning. Of the 48 artillerymen attached to the center column, 36 were killed or wounded. All told, the British casualties appear to have been about 600, two-thirds of them occurring among the 1,100 men of the right and center who received the most punishment from Morgan's and Dearborn's regiments.[20]

As Gates sent fresh troops to the front, the enemy's advantage in numbers vanished. The fight reached a climax about three o'clock, when large British forces tried to turn the American left. Morgan and Dearborn not only changed front successfully but attempted a turning movement of their own which took the 62nd and 20th in flank. "Here the conflict was dreadful," reported Sergeant Lamb; "for four hours a constant blaze of fire was kept up, and both armies seemed determined on death or victory."[21] Another British commentator, Lieutenant Digby of the 53rd, wrote that "such an explosion of fire I never had any idea of before. . . . This crash of cannon and musketry never ceased till darkness parted us."[22]

Neither Burgoyne nor Gates seems to have had any coherent plan of battle. Both simply rushed what reinforcements they could into a combat so confused that the accounts of the participants vary widely. If the American commander can be charged with any grave error, it was his failure to provide artillery support. The most decisive British force of the day was the brave little band of 48 artillerymen which twice lost its fieldpieces in hand-to-hand fighting. Both times the gunners carried away their linstocks and returned to fire again after the infantry recaptured the guns. The rebels would probably have won the field as well as the battle if they had not been stopped at critical moments by this battery discharging grapeshot at ranges suited to musketry.

The turning point came at the end of the afternoon when Phillips arrived on the scene with his slow-marching Germans and another battery of artillery. The rebels put up a good resistance until dusk, then conceded the field after an orderly withdrawal of a few hundred yards. But it was no empty boast when Colonel Dearborn wrote in his journal, "On this Day has been fought one of the Greatest Battles that Ever was fought in America, & I trust we have Convinced the British Butchers that the Cowardly yankees Can, & when there is a Call for it, will, fight."[23]

The British were so thoroughly convinced that most of them agreed with Anbury that "notwithstanding the glory of the day remains on our side, I am fearful that the real advantages resulting from this hard-fought battle, will rest on that of the Americans, our army being so much weakened by the engagement, as not to be of sufficient strength to venture forth."

In proof, Burgoyne put 1,000 men at work the next day on a system of field fortifications as strong as Gates's works. Both armies remained in position on the 20th, each ready to renew the struggle if the other attacked. But the lines remained stationary for nearly three weeks except for skirmishes in which the rebels took the aggressive.

Their losses were given as 64 killed and 248 wounded in an action which has gone by three names—Bemis Heights, Freeman's Farm, and the first battle of Saratoga. The armies remained so close together that Americans could hear the enemy's entrenching tools. On September 21st the redcoats were mystified by a *feu de joie* followed by cheering on the other side. They did not learn until four days later that Gates and Lincoln had sent detachments in a wide sweep around their strategic rear. Colonel John Brown surprised one of the outworks of Ticonderoga, taking 315 prisoners along with several hundred rebel captives they were guarding. He and his associates destroyed 200 British bateaux, 17 armed gondolas and sloops, and an enormous quantity of stores and cannon. This one stroke wiped out all the enemy bases at the south end of Lake Champlain, leaving only a weak garrison at Ticonderoga.

Burgoyne still had an opportunity to retreat, but he had received a message from Clinton which made him hopeful that he could hold out until reinforcements came up the river from New York. Gates, for his part, was content to let time fight for him against an enemy depleted both in troops and supplies. He estimated his opponent's character shrewdly when he addressed this message to the executives and committees of the New England states:

> I have rec'd certain intelligence that Gen'l Burgoyne has caused Skenesborough, Fort Ann, Fort George, Fort Edward, and the post he lately occupied to the southward of Lake George to be evacuated, and the Artillery stores and provisions to be brought to his army. . . . From this it is evident the Gen'l designs to resque all upon one rash stroke, it is therefore the indispensable duty of all concerned to exert themselves in reinforcing this Army without one moment's delay. The militia from every part should be ordered here with all possible expedition.[24]

The response was all that Gates could have hoped. Every day brought new militia contingents which swelled his numbers to about 15,000 by the middle of October. The American general gave his adversary no rest either by day or night in the Saratoga lines. Burgoyne's scouts had nearly all deserted, so that he had little intelligence of rebel movements. "Not a day passes," reported Anbury, "but there is firing, and continued attacks upon the advanced piquets, especially those of the Germans. It seems to be the plan of the enemy to harass us by constant attacks." Even the redoubts, he added, gave no protection from Morgan's marksmen. "The only shelter afforded to the troops was from those angles which faced the enemy as the others were so exposed that we had several men killed and wounded by the riflemen, who were posted in trees. . . ."[25]

Gates had more cause to be worried by a vindictive clique of his own officers than the death struggles of Burgoyne's army. This time he knew better than to grant Arnold the powers which that officer had exerted with the airs of a generalissimo in the lake campaign of 1776. As a protest Arnold remained in camp during the action of September 19th, though he had command of the left wing, including Morgan's and Dearborn's regiments. When the rebels won without his aid, he came out openly against his chief by threatening to leave the army. Gates was not intimidated. On the contrary, he paid tribute to Morgan's tactical ability by making the frontiersman his right-hand man after turning Arnold's command over to Lincoln. Gates then informed the unruly general that he might feel free to depart at any time.

Arnold not only stayed with the army but devoted his energies to open insubordination which could not have been forgiven by any commander. He found eager disciples in two New York officers, Colonel Henry B. Livingston and Colonel Richard Varick, both of whom had served in Schuyler's official family. Personal jealousies were only a minor factor. Again it was the revolution within a revolution that had become a greater issue, with Gates and Schuyler standing for two age-old irreconcilable parties. Down to the last days of their lives they remained in opposite camps, and Gates ended as an ardent Jeffersonian Democrat just as Schuyler died an equally stanch Federalist.

The New York general could hardly be created into a combat hero, but Arnold loomed as the ideal candidate after his quarrel with Gates. The new hagiology is shown in process of evolution by a letter from Schuyler to Varick: "I wonder at Gates' policy. He will probably be indebted to him [Arnold] for the glory he may acquire by a victory; but perhaps he is so very sure of success that he does not wish the other to come in for a share of it."[26]

Thus was fired one of the opening guns in a campaign of character assassination that has few parallels in American history. From that time onward, Gates would be attacked at every opportunity, by fair means or foul, until few rags remained of his military reputation. The story of

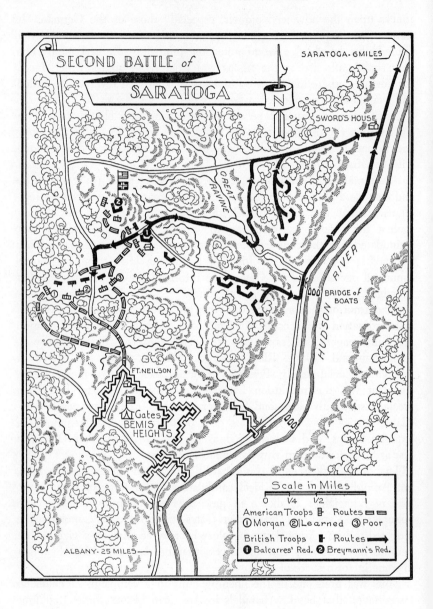

SECOND BATTLE of SARATOGA

SARATOGA · 6 MILES

N

SWORD'S HOUSE

GREAT RAVINE

HUDSON RIVER

BRIDGE of BOATS

FT. NEILSON

Gates
BEMIS HEIGHTS

ALBANY · 25 MILES

Scale in Miles
0   1/4   1/2   1

American Troops ⊟ Routes ▭▭
① Morgan ② Learned ③ Poor

British Troops ⊦ Routes ➡
❶ Balcarres' Red. ❷ Breymann's Red.

Schuyler's silver bullets at Ticonderoga is no more preposterous than some of the slanders about his rival that the New York faction propagated. But if facts rather than legends are to be accepted, Gates's generalship at Saratoga leaves little room for censure. After September 19th he kept the enemy on the defensive at small cost to his own army. Burgoyne's forage problem became so acute that he determined to make a final effort to force a passage around the American left wing. It was a desperate throw of the dice, but the British general gambled on the chances of militiamen being overcome by panic when he advanced on October 7th with 1,500 picked troops.

Gates was ready. Again in the second battle of Saratoga he placed his faith in the ability of a self-educated backwoodsman as a combat tactician. "Order on Morgan to begin the game," he instructed his aide, and the action was fought according to that officer's plan of a double envelopment.[27] While he swept around a wooded hill to burst from concealment on the British right flank, General Learned's brigade was to fix the opposing center as Colonel Poor's 800 Continentals worked around the left flank.

The rebels did not need their great advantage in numbers. Morgan's tactics deserve the main credit for a victory won by skill and furious fighting. The redcoats never had a chance of success after the successive shocks to their wings. On the left Acland's grenadiers had time only for a futile volley before being routed by Poor with heavy losses. A few minutes later Morgan struck General Fraser's light infantry while they were changing front and sent them flying in disorder after their leader's death.

Burgoyne gave the order for a general retirement, but his aide Sir Francis Clark fell mortally wounded before passing on the command. The British army had been beaten when Benedict Arnold made his appearance. After days of inactivity he found it intolerable at the last minute to be ignored by a commander doing very well without his services. The redcoats were streaming back toward their redoubts, after losing all their guns, when he led some of the excited troops of Learned's brigade in a charge on the enemy's fortified camp. Here at the end of the day occurred the worst rebel losses without adding anything to a victory already gained. British cannon, firing grapeshot at point-blank range, repulsed an attempt made without artillery support. A few minutes later Arnold fell wounded while taking a redoubt abandoned by Brunswickers who fled after firing a hasty volley. This contribution was destined to be glorified long after the efforts of Morgan, Poor and Learned were forgotten.

Only a bare hope of survival now remained to Burgoyne as he retreated that night toward Saratoga. After dark on October 9th his army arrived in such a state of fatigue that the men slept on the ground in the rain, too exhausted to build fires. Gates had already blocked the main route of escape by sending forward a detachment to oppose a crossing of the river, and other American forces were swinging around to the rear on the west bank.

On the 10th the victorious army began a systematic bombardment which kept up day and night. Madame Riedesel and her children hovered for six terrible days in a cellar filled with wounded men and even a few skulkers. Her memoirs give some appalling descriptions of the fear and despair of this mass of humanity crowded together in quarters reeking of the stench of sewage and infected wounds. "As the great scarcity of water continued," she recalled, "we at last found a soldier's wife who had the courage to bring water from the river, for no one else would undertake it, as the enemy shot at the head of every man who approached the river. This woman, however, they never molested."[28]

Gentleman Johnny Burgoyne had won many feminine hearts, but the courageous German woman denounced his final "orgies" in General Schuyler's luxurious country home, ending with the dramatic gesture of burning it to the ground—an act that the Marquis de Chastellux condemned as having no military justification when he visited the battlefield. The British general, according to Madame Riedesel, "spent half the nights in singing and drinking, and amusing himself with the wife of a commissary, who was his mistress, and who, as well as he, loved champagne."

It was the last fling of a ruined gambler, for Gates had him surrounded by October 12th beyond hope of escape. The next morning the British officers agreed at a council of war that nothing was left save capitulation. Three days later, after terms had been agreed upon, Burgoyne repented of his bargain for a moment when a deserter brought word that Clinton might yet come to the rescue. That British general actually had pushed up the Hudson with 4,000 men and taken Fort Montgomery on the 6th, but he contented himself with sending a raiding force farther up the river to burn Kingston. Gates had good reason to be anxious about the threat to his rear when he allowed his defeated foe very moderate terms, including a face-saving provision that the surrender should be called a "convention."

The rose had a fragrance by any name for Americans who further spared the feelings of 5,791 captives allowed to march out in comparative privacy on October 17th and lay down their arms. The various diaries, curiously, contain few notes of drama or excitement. Most of them simply record the event in such matter-of-fact terms as Private Elijah Fisher's entry, "Gen. Burgoin and his howl army surrendered themselves Prisoners of Ware and come to Captelate with our army and Gen. Gates."[29] The only noteworthy exception is the journal of Colonel Dearborn, who contributed so much to the result. "This day," he exulted, "the Great Mr. Burgeoyn with his whole army Surrendered themselves as Prisoners of war with all their Publick Stores, & after Grounding their armes march'd of for New England, the greatest Conquest Ever known."[30]

It might have been supposed that Horatio Gates, of all people, would rejoice without stint after mounting to this dizzy peak of renown from a subaltern's rank. Yet the letter he wrote to his wife and son that evening ends with the guarded and sober reflections of a self-made man who had not found it easy to cope all his life with rivals of inherited wealth and position:

> The voice of fame, ere this reaches you, will tell how greatly fortunate we have been in this department. Burgoyne and his whole army have laid down their arms and surrendered themselves to me and my Yankees. Thanks to the Giver of all victory for this triumphant success. . . . If Old England is not by this lesson taught humility, then she is an obstinate old slut, bent upon her own ruin. . . . Tell my dear Bob not to be too elated at this great good fortune of his father. He and I have seen days adverse, as well as prosperous. Let us through this life endeavor to bear both with an equal mind.[31]

Gates would need the consolations of this philosophy during the next few years. For it did not take his political enemies long to rob him of most of the glory.

To say that history was created at Saratoga in 1777 would be an understatement—it has been created ever since, very often out of whole cloth. It has been recorded in imperishable granite as well as mutable ink, and the monument on the battlefield pays tribute to Arnold equally with Schuyler, Gates and Morgan. The only difference is that Arnold's niche has been left empty in recognition of his subsequent treason.

The men who actually fought the two battles could not have rested easily in their graves during the sesquicentennial program on the field. They could never have dreamed that by 1927 the Arnold hagiology would be accepted to the extent of enshrining him as the victor of

Saratoga. That same year such a reputable authority as the Fourteenth Edition of the *Encyclopaedia Britannica* declared that at the second battle "the Americans made a fierce counter-attack, and led by Arnold, inflicted a severe defeat on the British army."[32] This interpretation would have stunned the real victors, but worse was yet to come in the description of the first battle: "Burgoyne advanced to the attack (Sept. 19). But Arnold came out with 3,000 men at Freeman's Farm. After 4 hours' fierce fighting Arnold retired. . . ."

These passages are typical rather than exceptional. Yet the actual firsthand evidence, including Arnold's own words, does not justify any unqualified assertion that he took an active part in the first and decisive battle of Saratoga.

Wilkinson wrote in his memoirs that Arnold did not. But Gates's aide is not reliable enough to be accepted without reservations. Even more dubious as authorities are Colonel Richard Varick and Colonel Henry B. Livingston, the participants whose writings attest that Arnold did take an active part. Two more prejudiced witnesses could not be found than these associates of Schuyler who led the clique of New York officers abetting Arnold in his hostility to Gates throughout the campaign.

American officers with no reason for bias take for granted the absence of the Connecticut Achilles. The single noteworthy exception is Marshall, who was not present himself but accepted the word of Varick and Livingston. Baldwin, who was present, had nothing to say about Arnold in his journal entry.[33] Dearborn, who could hardly have failed to notice his commanding officer, does not allude to him once in an account citing even such minor figures as Cilley, Hale and Scammel.[34] Dr. Thacher, who treated the wounded, is silent about Arnold in journal comments giving the credit to Morgan and Dearborn in both Saratoga battles.[35] Heath, who had charge of the British prisoners, omits Arnold's name after stating that "Colonel Morgan's light corps, and eleven other American regiments were more or less engaged."[36] The contemporary historian Gordon, who made a personal investigation shortly afterwards, is more explicit: "Arnold's division was out in the action, but he himself did not lead them; he remained in camp the whole time."[37]

The testimony of British participants gives very little support to any assumption that Arnold in person, as distinguished from Arnold's division, opposed them on September 19th. Hadden does not refer to him at all; and Burgoyne, in his *State of the Expedition*, mentions Arnold only in connection with the second battle. Nor does Digby go beyond saying that "our advance picquets came up with Colonel Morgan and engaged. . . ."[38]

The diaries of American enlisted men should not be neglected, since it was the contention of Gates's political foes that such humble actors adored Arnold as their champion. And it is significant that his name does not appear in the entries for September 19th of Ephraim Squier, Elijah Fisher or Ebenezer Wild. There is not the least evidence, moreover, that the rank and file made a hero out of Arnold, whose name is scarcely mentioned in the whole campaign.

Arnold could not have asked for a more sympathetic advocate than Robert R. Livingston, who solicited for him the command of West Point in 1780, never dreaming that he was obliging a traitor. Two years earlier, in a letter to Washington, this New York member of Congress included a comment that establishes him as a convincing witness: "General Arnold not being present in the battle of the 19th of September . . . writes only from the reports of those who were."[39]

But it remained for Arnold himself to give the final testimony. In a letter of self-justification written to Gates after the battle of September 19th, he made the revealing statement: "You desired me to *send* Colonel Morgan and the light infantry and support them; I obeyed your orders, and before the action was over I found it necessary to *send* out the whole of my division to support the attack."[40]

Italics have been added to the quotation, but they are hardly needed to emphasize the fact that Arnold would never have used the word "send" if he had *led* his troops in person. Such self-effacement was not in keeping with his character. And his letter further discloses that Gates, far from being the figurehead that his political foes represented, gave orders for the direction of a battle fought by Morgan in the field.

There can be no doubt that after two weeks of open insubordination Arnold took a brave part in the action of October 7th. It is also clear from contemporary accounts that the victory had been gained by Morgan, Poor and Learned before he made his dramatic appearance.

In the long run the war's most decisive campaign was not won by any individual. Gates, Schuyler, Morgan and Kosciusko are entitled to most of the credit, but it would be an injustice to overlook the contributions of such secondary figures as Stark, Lincoln, Dearborn, Poor, Learned and Brown.

Chapter 14

Manna in the Wilderness

WHILE one British army met disaster at Saratoga, the forces which entered Philadelphia at the end of September had troubles of their own. Howe's campaign, far from ending with the occupation, only approached a crisis. If he could not open a line of waterborne communications by clearing the Delaware for navigation, his army faced the prospect of a humiliating withdrawal. The vicinity alone could not provide enough supplies for his 17,000 troops, and the rebels controlled the river below the city.

Dr. Franklin, who was worth an army to his cause, is credited with the invention of a new type of *chevaux de frise* to stop the enemy warships. A foundation of heavy timbers, anchored on the river bottom, bristled with ironshod spikes pointing upward at an angle of forty-five degrees to pierce British hulls. The obstacles could be removed only with difficulty by invaders exposed to the cross fire of cannon from both banks. Fort Mercer on the New Jersey side, and Fort Mifflin on the Pennsylvania shore—these posts commanded the channel where the Schuylkill flows into the Delaware a few miles south of Philadelphia. If they could be held for only two months, Howe would be compelled to evacuate the city.

The Paoli reverse had been a bitter pill for Washington, who often counseled his generals to attack enemy detachments at every favorable opportunity. Howe had given him a dose of his own medicine by surprising Wayne's isolated force, but early in October the rebel general saw an opening for revenge. The British themselves had divided their army into three groups—a garrison at Philadelphia under Cornwallis, another detachment reconnoitering the forts below the city, and a third force commanded by Howe at Germantown. The last was singled out by Washington for a dawn surprise. Four good roads led into the village, and his scouts had brought word that no enemy field fortifications awaited. Early on the evening of October 3rd the four rebel columns were in motion with a view to closing in on Howe from three directions.

There could be little hope for a surprise in a region that the Americans called "enemy territory." Not only were the Quakers unfriendly or neutral at best, but German-speaking farmers whose fathers had been born in America aided the invaders with both intelligence and supplies. Lieutenant McMichael's diary records that in this district he found only a single person who spoke the language. "I was looked upon as a barbarian by the inhabitants, and they appeared to me like so many human beings scarcely endowed with the qualifications equal to that of the brute species. Repeatedly I talked Latin to them, when I found that it was worse than English for them to understand."[1]

Political liberties meant little to these prosperous descendants of immigrants who had left Germany to escape the ravages of war. Yet it could not be forgotten that Frederick Muhlenberg had worn an American uniform under his robes when he appealed from the pulpit for all able-bodied men of his Lutheran congregation to join the force he later commanded as general. Christopher Ludwig, a native of Hesse-Darm-stadt, volunteered in 1776 as a private at the age of fifty-six and worked up to be baker-general of the Continental Army. Nor could any stouter patriot have been found than Jacob Hilzheimer, born in Mannheim, who served as a quartermaster.

These men were some of the exceptions among a Pennsylvania German population that welcomed mercenaries speaking their own tongue. The possibility that this response might have its advantages for the rebel cause could not yet be foreseen by the disgusted troops. Up to that time all efforts to encourage Hessian desertions had met with little success. Franklin suggested the scheme of distributing tobacco wrapped in packets printed with appeals translated into German. Few of the mercenary rank and file were literate, however, and they could not be tempted by offers of free land, much less of political liberties which they neither understood nor desired. Yet the patriots had unwitting allies among the apple-cheeked Pennsylvania farm girls who comforted the Hessians with their kisses as well as apple dumplings. These were propaganda messages that the invaders could comprehend, and the feminine fifth column did more to encourage desertions than any political arguments.

Such benefits had not yet been revealed on October 4th to Americans who could not move without the enemy being informed. Howe had

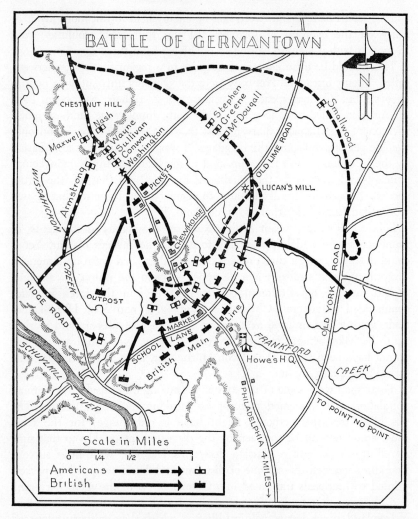

timely warning of the threat to Germantown, and it is strange that an alert tactician did not take a greater advantage. Washington's plan of battle, based on the concentric advance of four columns at night, was one that any European general would have shunned. The most experienced regulars might have found it hard to avoid confusion, not to mention the risk of the forces arriving one at a time to be beaten piecemeal. The miracle is only that rebel regiments which included many late recruits actually did converge with fairly good timing in a morning fog that limited visibility to fifty yards.

Sullivan's division, advancing from the north on the main road, opened the battle by striking the British outpost at Mount Airy. The redcoats were not as prepared as they should have been; and Wayne's men, according to his own account, took their revenge with the bayonet for the rough treatment they received at Paoli. Greene and Stephen were meanwhile closing in from the east, while Armstrong converged from the west with his Pennsylvania militia. A fourth force under Smallwood, following behind Greene, added to the complications.

Victory seemed almost within grasp as Greene turned the British right and advanced on the center after taking 110 prisoners. The first hitch came when Sullivan's division met resistance from six companies of the British 40th regiment, making a fort out of the mansion belonging to Chief Justice Chew. This check called for the attention of General Henry Knox, who had read enough military treatises to know that an enemy force should never be left in the rear. As a good theorist, he moved up his guns and began a bombardment of thick stone walls from which the projectiles rebounded like peas. Infantry attacks had no more effect of dislodging the grim defenders, and the half-hour's delay at this point may have cost Washington the victory. Not only did Sullivan's advance lose its momentum, but the pause ruined the timing of the other assaults, throwing the whole machine out of gear. One of the brigades of Greene's division encountered Wayne's men in the fog, and the two forces exchanged shots. At the height of the confusion Cornwallis and Grey arrived on the double with British reinforcements and drove back Greene's and Sullivan's divisions. Washington prudently ordered a general retirement, and it is to the credit of his baffled forces that they managed to extricate themselves in fairly good order.

Although the British light horse pursued for several miles, the attackers got off with losses of 673 killed and wounded in addition to about 400 missing. Howe reported his casualties as 535 killed and wounded.

No failure of the war ever disappointed Washington more than this repulse. Yet it may be doubted if his army came as near to victory as some of the officers believed. Armstrong's attack made no headway at all on the British left, and there are indications that Greene and Sullivan could not have prevailed even without the delay at the Chew house. Several other rebel generals, it was hinted, had not distinguished themselves. General Adam Stephen, a gallant officer handicapped by age and failing health, was afterwards dismissed after being convicted of partaking too indiscreetly of rum on the morning of battle.

Washington's gloom was increased by apprehensions of the effect that a new defeat on this front—the third in less than a month—would have on the court of Louis XVI. Congress had been making every effort, with Dr. Franklin as its diplomat, to seek an alliance with France. That country had already reached the stage of an undeclared war on Great Britain, for it was no secret that French munitions had made possible all the main American operations of 1777. Congress believed that a single fortunate stroke might be enough to bring Europe's most populous kingdom into the conflict on the American side. The outcome of Germantown did not offer much comfort, and a year passed before Americans learned how impressed French observers had been by Washington's determination. This information was imparted in a letter from Paris by John Adams to a member of Congress on July 26, 1778, several months after the alliance had been consummated:

> General Gates was the ablest negotiator you had in Europe; and next to him, General Washington's attack on the enemy at Germantown. I do not know, indeed, whether this last affair had not more influence upon the European mind than that of Saratoga. Although the attempt was unsuccessful, the military gentlemen in Europe considered it as the most decisive proof that America would finally succeed.[2]

Both armies regarded the battle as a sideshow at the time. A much greater strategic issue was involved in the approaching struggle for control of the river below Philadelphia. Howe had already taken Billingsport on the New Jersey side before the rebels could complete their works, but he realized that Fort Mercer at Red Bank would be a harder nut to crack. The British general saw no alternative to a direct attack, and Count Donop asked the assignment for his Hessian troops.

The first year in America had heaped one humiliation after another on mercenaries who had yet to win a victory of their own. On arrival they had not been polite critics of such British efforts as Bunker Hill; and the redcoats themselves appear to have been a little awed by troops trained in the stern school of Frederick the Great. The Hessian officers were not reticent about boasting to the English what they would do to the rabble when their turn came. This made the results of Pell's Point, Fort Washington, Trenton and Bennington so much the harder to swallow.

Soon another debit would be added to the list when word came of the flight of the Brunswickers from their redoubt at Bemis Heights, followed by the surrender of the whole contingent at Saratoga.

American leaders, though they did not admit it publicly, had been sobered at first by the military reputation of their new foes. Trenton dates the first occasion when they suspected that one tough little redcoat might give them more trouble than two Hessians. The mercenaries were wonderfully drilled, and their stolid bravery could not be doubted; but the rebels found them clumsy, both physically and mentally. Trained for the formal battles of European tactics, they never learned as the redcoats did to adapt themselves to New World conditions.

The Hessians, at the end of their second summer overseas, were no longer the target of so much indignation in rebel diaries and gazettes. Hate being compounded largely of fear, Americans who had beaten the mercenaries began to take a keen interest in their grotesqueries. Some astonishing tales were told of the number of roast fowls that a single plunderer could consume at a sitting. And when a skull with an extra row of teeth turned up in New Jersey, the good folk of the neighborhood concluded that Nature had endowed all Germans with double the usual equipment for masticating their food.

Where once it had been maddening to think of a mercenary sergeant with fiercely upturned moustaches, the spectacle became ludicrous after Trenton and Bennington. It would not appear that the Teutonic reputation for cleanliness had yet been established, for at least two diarists complained that the Hessians smelled. A commentator who witnessed the Saratoga surrender recalled that "their heavy caps were almost equal to the weight of the whole equipment of a light infantry soldier.... The Hessians were extremely dirty in their persons, and had a collection of wild animals in their train—the only thing American they had captured."[3]

It is seldom in the annals of war that invaders have afforded so much amusement to the invaded. When the news of the Trenton victory crossed the ocean, Dr. Franklin responded with another hoax. This time he used the real name (with slight changes in spelling) of one Count Schaumburg who had tried to hire soldiers in Saxe-Weimar as recruiting agent for George III. That courtier was represented as rejoicing at the news that the rebels had killed 1,605 more mercenaries from his petty state, thus adding to his income. In a letter supposed to be written to an imaginary Baron Hohendorf, commanding the troops in America, he included an exhortation in the heroic style:

I am about to send you some new recruits. Don't economize them. Remember glory above all things. Glory is true wealth. There is nothing degrades the soldier like the love of money. He must care only for honor and reputation, but this reputation must be acquired in the midst of dangers. A battle gained without costing the conqueror any blood is an inglorious success, while the conquered cover themselves with glory by perishing with their arms in their hands. Do you remember that of the three hundred Lacedaemonians who defended the defile of Thermopylae, not one returned? How happy should I be could I say the same of my brave Hessians![4]

Even this broad satire hardly seemed too far-fetched to contemporaries. Americans could not understand why the mercenaries did not revolt against the despots who sold them into military bondage. The Germans in their turn found it inconceivable that subjects should rise in arms, whatever their provocation, against a divinely appointed ruler.

Thus it was two peoples at opposite political poles who fought it out at Red Bank on the afternoon of October 22, 1777. Colonel Christopher Greene commanded a garrison of 400 Rhode Island Continentals. The 1,200 picked Hessians had been worked up to a high pitch of resolution by Count Donop, who sought this opportunity to redeem the reputation of the mercenaries. He summoned the rebels to surrender or expect no mercy, and Greene sent back a defiant answer that no quarter would be given to mercenaries who offered such terms. After this exchange of amenities, the Hessian colonel rested his men for several hours before attacking at four in the afternoon.

Greene decided to make the most of his inadequate garrison by sacrificing the outworks and withdrawing to the inner pentagon. As the gunners waited with lighted matches at their fourteen cannon, he walked the parapet and counseled his infantry, "Fire low, men! They have a broad belt just above their hips—fire at that."[5] The Hessians had good artillery support as they advanced on the land side. Their dense columns were thinned by the rebel guns while crossing the open space, but the day appeared to be won when they found the outworks abandoned and the pentagon silent. Donop's men gave a cheer and pressed forward to the abatis of felled trees outside the nine-foot walls, only to be swept back by a last-minute tornado of grapeshot and musket balls that could not be endured.

The second attempt was made with no better success from the river side. This time the Pennsylvania row-galleys added their fire to that of

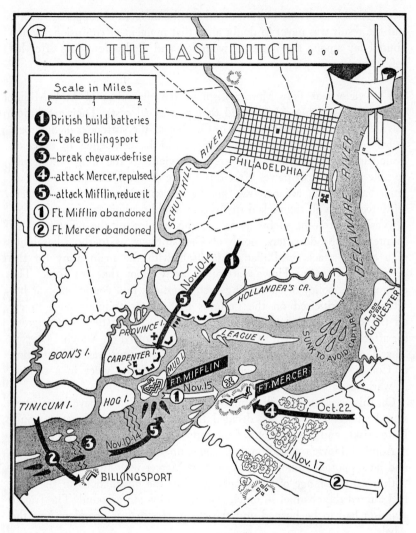

TO THE LAST DITCH...

Scale in Miles
0   1   2

① British build batteries
② ...take Billingsport
③ ...break chevaux-de-frise
④ ...attack Mercer, repulsed
⑤ ...attack Mifflin, reduce it
① Ft. Mifflin abandoned
② Ft. Mercer abandoned

the garrison, and the attackers fled in wild disorder to the woods, leaving more than 400 killed and wounded behind. The Continentals, who had 32 casualties, made prisoners of 20 foemen cowering under the parapet, driven half-mad by fear. Both the prisoners and wounded, in spite of Greene's defiance, were well treated.

The Germans had been beaten in their own minds by the shock of meeting resistance from the inner works at the moment of supposed victory, and the result was never in doubt after that moment of confusion. Donop himself lay among the heaps of wounded and died a few days after his defeat.

The victory at Fort Mercer inspired the defenders of Fort Mifflin on the Pennsylvania side to hold that post at all costs. Their resolution was heightened by the news late in October of the surrender at Saratoga. Rebel leaders believed that if Howe could be compelled to evacuate Philadelphia, the British ministers subservient to the king would not be able to remain in power after the double disaster. The prospect of an immediate French alliance was another incentive and both posts were reinforced with all the picked troops they could contain to advantage.

Washington went so far as to ask the opinion of the officers at his Whitemarsh headquarters, north of Germantown, as to the advisability of a daring attack on Philadelphia itself with the main army for the purpose of drawing Howe's attention away from the two forts. The commander's policy of submitting such questions to a council of war has often been criticized on the grounds that group opinions tend to err on the side of caution. Certainly his hands were not tied by Congress, for after a conference with Greene that body resolved on March 24, 1777, "that General Washington be informed that it never was the intention of Congress that he should be bound by a majority voice in a council of war, contrary to his own judgment."[6]

On this occasion, as well as many others, he appears to have been given sound advice. His generals decided that an advance on the city would be too risky, and the garrisons of the forts were left to their own resources.[7]

Admiral Howe's squadron had come up the river as far as Chester, and he supported Donop's attack on Fort Mercer with an attempt to draw within cannon range of the other post. But the obstructions in the river had altered the channel so much that two ships ran aground. The frigate *Augusta* had to be burned and the sloop *Merlin* was abandoned to the rebels.

The *chevaux de frise* still blocked navigation at two points, and Fort Mifflin on Mud Island could be bombarded only from the land side until the naval forces found a way to co-operate. The British engineers placed a battery on the single dry spot in the marsh near the mouth of the Schuylkill, but this position was flooded at certain ·tides and several redcoats drowned. Necessity kept the working parties toiling night and day to build causeways and platforms which eventually grew into a system of five redoubts mounting guns as large as 32-pounders.

If anyone were to select the most heroic American fight of the entire war, the defense of Fort Mifflin would have to be seriously considered. Attackers have the solace of action, but the sleepless garrison on Mud Island got no rest from an artillery pounding that would be respected by veterans of present-day warfare. At the crisis, it was estimated that a thousand projectiles struck the fort every twenty minutes.[8] This hurricane of shot and shell made rubbish of the blockhouses, shattered the palisades, and ripped the rebel guns from their emplacements. There was little shelter for defenders crouching in an enclosure filled with smoke and flying splinters. Each night the dead and wounded were taken away in boats and their places filled by volunteers who kept the strength up to the maximum of 300 as working parties did their best to repair some of the damage.

Three commanders were used up in rapid succession by wounds or exhaustion before Major Simeon Thayer of Rhode Island took over at the worst of the ordeal. Another hero was the Marquis de Fleury, who served as engineer to the end, declining to be relieved after he was wounded. No native American ever showed more devotion to the cause, and he not only survived but lived to take part with Lafayette at the age of eighty-one in his country's revolution of 1830. Such a prospect could not have seemed likely during those November days on Mud Island when he kept a journal filled with such extracts as the following:

10th. I am interrupted by the bombs and balls, which fall thickly. The fire increases, but not the effect; our barracks alone suffer. *Two o'clock.* The direction of the fire is changed; our palisades suffer; a dozen of them are broken down; one of our cannon is damaged—I am afraid it will not fire straight. *Eleven o'clock at night.* The enemy keep up a firing every half-hour; our garrison diminishes; our soldiers are overwhelmed by fatigue.

11th. The enemy keep up a heavy fire; they have changed the direction of their embrasures, and, instead of battering our palisades in front, they take them obliquely, and do great injury to our north side. *At night.* The enemy fire, and interrupt our works. . . . Colonel Smith, Captain George and myself wounded. Those two gentlemen passed immediately to Red Bank.

12th. Heavy firing; our two eighteen-pounders at the northern battery dismounted. *At night.* The enemy throw shells, and we are alarmed by thirty boats. . . .[9]

By the 14th the British were cannonading from a new floating battery in the river. "The walk of our rounds is destroyed," wrote Fleury, "the block-houses ruined, and garrison is exhausted with fatigue and ill health." But worse was to come that day when Black Dick Howe discovered that the obstructions had turned the current so as to create a new channel between Hog Island and the west bank. On the 15th the British admiral brought six warships within 900 yards to open fire along with the redoubts. Parapets were leveled and embrasures crumpled by a cannonade which killed or wounded sixteen rebel gunners out of twenty. Yet the garrison held out until eleven that night, when two warships drew near enough for the marines to fire muskets and toss grenades from the foretops. This was the end. At midnight the remnants of the garrison were removed; and after spiking their two remaining guns, Thayer and Fleury left the ruins in the last boat.

The survivors insisted that the post might have been held if they had received better support from the "Pennsylvania navy" at the beginning. That flotilla soon paid the penalty of caution when 17 sloops and floating batteries had to be sunk to save them from capture. Three days after the fall of Fort Mifflin, Cornwallis crossed over to Red Bank with 5,000 men, but the rebels abandoned Fort Mercer after destroying the works.

Once the redcoats had made merry over the resort of their opponents to the pick and spade at every opportunity. But before General Howe settled himself in Philadelphia for the winter, he fortified the land approaches with a thoroughness which flattered Washington. From the Delaware to the upper ferry of the Schuylkill a chain of redoubts extended two and a half miles. Even the rebel works at Whitemarsh were not as formidable, though the ubiquitous Chastellux thought it a well-chosen position.

The two armies remained motionless all the rest of November, both of them in the grip of a vast tedium after two months of furious campaigning. Nobody loved an exciting diary entry more than Colonel Dearborn, just arrived from the northern army. But his journal chronicles one of those interludes of heroic boredom that every soldier must endure:

Decemr. 1. We have very Poor Living.
2d. Nothing New.
3d. Do.
4. Do.[10]

There were few dull moments for General Smallwood, Major Benjamin Stoddert and the other Maryland officers making their headquarters at the home of Daniel Wister, a Quaker whose daughter Sally and niece Liddy flirted with the boldness of complete innocence. Such a strict disciplinarian as Colonel Mordecai Gist might have been disconcerted if he had suspected that this description of him was being set down in the diary kept by fifteen-year-old Sally during the winter of Whitemarsh and Valley Forge:

Come, shall we chat about Col. Guest? He's very pretty, a charming person; his eyes are so exceptional; very stern; and he so rolls them about that mine always fall under them. He bears the character of a brave officer: another admirer of Liddy's, and she of him. When will Sally's admirers appear? Ah! that indeed. Why, Sally has not charms sufficient to pierce the heart of a soldier. But still I won't despair. Who knows what mischief I yet may do?

She did a great deal. Several suitors proposed to a Quaker maid who found it so hard to choose that she ended her life as a spinster, noted for good works. One of these admirers, a Lieutenant Tilly, annoyed her as a novice at the flute. "He begins a tune, plays a note or so, then stops. Well, after a while, he begins again; stops again." This young man reported at headquarters after dark to encounter what appeared to be a British grenadier in the candlelit hall. "He darted like lightning out of the front door, through the yard, bolted o'er the fence. Swamps, fences, thorn-hedges and plough'd fields no way impeded his retreat. . . . Figure to thyself this Tilly, of a snowy evening, no hat, shoes down at the heel, hair unty'd, flying across meadows, creeks and holes. Flying from what? Why, a bit of painted wood."

The carved life-size figure of the British grenadier, its colors faded, is still preserved as a relic of the gay nonsense which enlivened Smallwood's headquarters. When Lieutenant Tilly discovered the practical joke, he "broke his silence by the following expression: 'You may all go to the D——l.' I never heard him utter such an indecent expression before. At last . . . he joined heartily in the laugh. I will do the justice to say that he bore it charmingly."

Sally was more than an adorable flirt; she was a good reporter whose diary attests to the consideration shown civilians by the Continental Army, enlisted men as well as officers. The Wisters, as Quakers opposed to war, were appalled in the beginning at the outlook of having their home occupied by the military and the neighborhood overrun by a hungry soldiery. The first appearance of Captain Henry Lee's troopers sent the household into a panic: "Someone came to me in a hurry, screaming, 'Sally, Sally, here are the light horse!' This was by far the greatest fright I had endured; fear tack'd wings to my feet. . . ."

It was a much different scene, only a few weeks later, when Smallwood and his officers rode away to what everyone believed would be a bloody encounter as Howe advanced on the Whitemarsh lines. "About two o'clock the General and Major came to bid us adieu. With daddy and mammy they shook hands very friendly; to us they bow'd politely. Our hearts were full. . . . It seems strange not to see our house as it used to be. We are very still. No rattling of waggons, glittering of musquets. The beating of the distant drum is all we hear."

The expected battle did not develop, and a few days later the officers returned to spend more lighthearted evenings with Sally and Liddy. Then the rebel host marched away again, this time for good; but it had left no harsh or unpleasant memories to be recorded in a young Quaker girl's diary:

> General Washington's army have gone into winter quarters at the Valley Forge. We shall not see many of the military now. We shall be very intimate with solitude. I am afraid stupidity will be a frequent guest. After so much company, I can't relish the idea of sequestration.[11]

Both armies were willing and even eager to fight at Whitemarsh, but neither would accept an engagement save on its own terms. The three-day campaign began on December 5th after Howe marched fifteen miles from Philadelphia with a force estimated at 14,000 men. Like a surgeon gently prodding the patient before operating, he tested the rebel lines here and there to seek an opening for one of his favorite flank attacks. The rebel center felt the deft pressure at dawn on the 5th. "We ware allarm'd at 4 O clock by hearing that the Enemy were advancing," wrote Dearborn, "in consequence of which the whole army Turned out, & formed the Lines of battle."[12] It proved to be a false alarm, and the next morning Howe moved on the American right. "Our Rifle men gave a Party of them a severe Drubing—we hourly Expect a General Ingagement." The rebel left had its threat on the 7th, and again Washington countered with a rapid shift of reserves to meet the new feint.

That was all. On the 8th Lee's light horse reported that Howe was on the way back to Philadelphia, though it could not have been imagined that this would be his last effort until spring. Washington wished to attack with an army numbering little more than half the enemy's strength, but again his officers showed good judgment in counseling prudence. The heroes of the unfought battle were Morgan's riflemen, recently returned from the northern army, and Colonel Gist's Marylanders.

On the 11th the unshod army began its retirement toward Valley Forge. Half of the men, according to Greene, were without stockings, breeches or blankets. The shortage of shoes had been felt as long ago as September, when Washington sent Hamilton to appeal to the people of Philadelphia for offerings. Thus it was no figure of speech when the commander wrote that "you might have tracked the army from Whitemarsh to Valley Forge by the blood of their feet." Hunger made necessary a day's halt mentioned in a letter by Colonel John Laurens, "I could weep tears of blood when I say it—the want of provisions rendered it impossible to march." General James Mitchell Varnum reported the plight of his brigade without mincing words: "Three days successively we have been destitute of bread. Two days we have been entirely without meat. The men must be supplied, or they cannot be commanded."[13]

It is amazing that the famished troops were not driven to widespread desertion, mutiny or pillage. Yet Washington not only held his army together but kept it better regulated than well-fed enemy forces. His orders of November 15th, as passed on to the Delaware regiment, preserved the spirit as well as letter of discipline by striking at the oldest excuse of plunderers:

> No Scouting party on any pretence whatsoever unless Sent for that purpose is to Seize Horses, Cattle or any other property belonging to the Inhabitants on the plea of taking those things within the enemies lines;—Great & erroneous abuses are committed and Infringements, therefore a Disobedience of these Orders in either Officers or Soldiers will be punished with the utmost Rigor. . . .[14]

There continued to be violations, of course, and it is not likely that a barnyard fowl in the path of Washington's march had much chance of reaching old age. But he meant every word of his injunction, and regimental orderly books reveal that the culprits of a starving army actually were flogged for robbing the civilians of a region unfriendly to the American cause.

Never during the war did the commander in chief swerve an inch from his policy that the army should be the instrument of the civil authority, as represented by an elected assembly. As early as March 3, 1776, he expressed this conviction in a letter to Joseph Reed: "I am not fond of stretching my powers; and if the Congress will say, 'This far and no farther you shall go,' I will promise not to offend whilst I continue in their service."[15]

There was no trace of the Cromwell in the character of a man less corrupted by power than any other great soldier of history. But the burden of the army's hardships at Valley Forge told on him, and his relations with Congress were more strained than at any other period of the Revolution.

This situation, curiously, grew out of the reluctance of the general to use the new "dictatorial powers" conferred on him by the assembly on September 17th and November 14th. The object both times was to invest him with the authority "to subsist his army from such parts of the country as are in its vicinity." When Washington hesitated, in spite of his need, the delegates reproved him on December 10th for his "delicacy in exerting military authority."[16] Washington replied tartly on the 23rd to remind Congress that the machinery of supply had broken down: "No man in my opinion ever had his measures more impeded than I have, by every department of the army. Since the month of July we have had no assistance from the quartermaster-general, and to want of assistance from this department the commissary-general charges great part of his deficiency."[17]

Congress took the implied rebuke in good spirit. And if that body had been at fault for not supervising the supply system more efficiently, it made amends by electing five members to make first-hand reports and recommendations. Seldom in history has an elected assembly ever kept in closer touch with an army through all vicissitudes. The commissioners sent to Canada in 1776 took a journey of greater hardships than a trip to Australia would represent today. And the soldiers of Valley Forge could not have asked for more sympathetic or outspoken champions than the delegates who remained in camp all winter as a standing committee.

Americans fond of Biblical precepts might have recalled that David did not get the better of Goliath in a prolonged wrestling match decided by endurance. Washington and Congress alike, as a twenty-two-year-old observer perceived, were the victims of the fact that recent colonies with a rural population and no manufactures did not have the resources to challenge the world's greatest empire. Even when such supplies as food could be had, transport and organization were often lacking to convey them to the army. Young Alexander Hamilton summed up the plight of his country in a letter of 1779 to Robert Morris: "The war, particularly in the first periods, required exertions beyond our strength, to which neither our population nor riches were equal. We have the fullest proof of this, in the constant thinness of our armies . . . the scarcity of hands in husbandry, and other occupations; the decrease of our staple commodities; and the difficulty of every species of supply."[18]

During the winter of Valley Forge, in spite of Washington's reluctance, it became necessary on occasion to requisition supplies from the countryside, giving in payment Continental notes that had depreciated to about a third of their face value. Greene was not as squeamish as his chief, judging from these instructions to one of his officers on February 14, 1778: "Search the country through and through. Mount your pressing parties on horses for expedition's sake. Harden your heart and dispatch business as fast as possible. I have got many parties out collecting wagons, horses, cattle, hogs, and sheep. . . . We are in the midst of a d——d nest of Tories, and as we are in the neighborhood of the enemy, a change of position becomes necessary for security's sake."[19]

Cold and hunger were part of the Valley Forge tradition, but the diaries complain as bitterly about the smoke from green wood fires. Dr. Albigence Waldo wrote in December that he "lay Cold & uncomfortable last Night —my eyes are started out from their Orbits like a Rabbit's eyes, occasion'd by a great Cold & smoke. . . . The Lord send that our Commissary of Purchases may live [on] Fire Cake & Water, 'till their glutted Gutts are turned to Pasteboard." The Connecticut surgeon reported that the soldiers "still show a spirit of Alacrity & Contentment not to be expected from so young Troops." But he left no doubt as to his own reactions:

I am Sick—discontented—and out of humour. Poor Food—hard lodging—Cold Weather—fatigue—Nasty Cloaths—hasty Cookery—Vomit half my time—smoaked out of my senses—the Devil's in't—I can't Endure it—Why are we sent here to starve and Freeze—what sweet Felicities have I left at home; A charming Wife—pretty Children —Good Beds—good food—good Cookery—all agreeable—all harmonious. Here all Confusion—smoke & Cold—hunger & filthyness—a pox on my bad luck.[20]

In spite of this outburst, Dr. Waldo was a fun-loving disciple of his favorite character in the recent book *Tristram Shandy*. The huge daily sick list kept him busy, but he did not take his own remedies too seriously.

"We give them Mutton & Grogg and a Capital Medicine once in a While, to start the Disease from its foundation at once. We avoid Piddling Pills, Powders, Bolus's Linctus's Cordials and all such insignificant matters whose powers are rendered important by causing the Patient to vomit up his money instead of his Disease. But very few of the sick Men Die."

Conditions improved after the first of the year as a military city with regular streets and avenues sprang up on the bank of the Schuylkill in

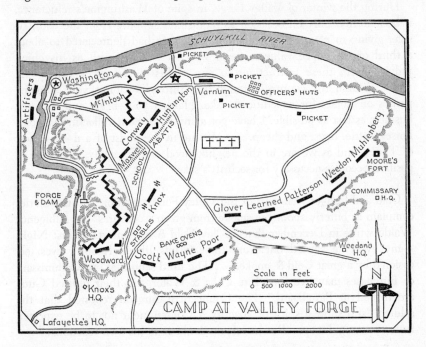

a valley bordered by a creek. Washington offered a cash prize to the working party in each regiment that first completed its log hut, and American mass production of the future was anticipated by orders for exact specifications:

> Plan for the Construction of Hutts dimensions 14 by 16 Foot, Sides Ends & Roof made of Logs, the Roof made light with Split Slabs, the sides made tight with Clay; the fire places made of wood & secured with Clay in the Inside 18 Inches thick, this fire place to be in the rear of the hutt, the door to be in the end next the Street . . . Side Walls 6 1/2 feet high, the Officers Hutts to form a line in rear of the Whole; one hut . . . to every 12 men non Commiss'd Officers & Soldiers.[21]

The camp formed an irregular triangle between the river and creek, with an extensive chain of redoubts guarding every approach. Whether Valley Forge could have been held against a determined enemy attack by an army which dwindled at one time to 4,000 effectives is a disputed question. Many of Washington's officers frankly criticized the location from a viewpoint of supply as well as defense. "I have from the beginning viewed this location with horror!" wrote General Varnum. "It is unparalleled in the history of mankind to establish winter quarters in a country wasted and without a single magazine."[22]

Still, the diaries and letters do not indicate that an atmosphere of unrelieved gloom and despair prevailed at the camp. When food supplies were at their lowest, Lieutenant McMichael mentions that dinners were given "in rotation from the senior to the junior officers. Thus and in many other desirable enjoyments we passed some part of the Winter campaign, making ourselves as happy as circumstances would possibly admit."[23]

The very privations brought about a spirit of cohesion and comradeship that the Continental Army had never known before. Washington had sometimes been a harsh critic of the rank and file in the past, but at Valley Forge he had only the warmest praise. "Naked and starving as they are," he wrote on February 16, 1778, "we cannot enough admire the incomparable patience and fidelity of the soldiery, that they have not been ere this incited by their suffering to a general mutiny and dispersion."[24]

After the worst was over, an atmosphere of hope and optimism became evident in March. The lovable imposter who did most to bring about this change was introduced to America in a joint letter from Franklin and Deane as "the Baron Steuben, Lieut. Gen. in the King of Prussia's Service, whom he attended in all his campaigns, being his Aid de Camp, quartermaster Genl., etc." Both Washington and Congress had long been disgusted at the clamor of foreign volunteers who expected to outrank American officers, but this newcomer could no more be ignored than a brass band when he arrived in a scarlet and gold uniform with a star the size of a dinner plate blazing from his chest. Even such a canny Scot as John Witherspoon was awed by the distinguished stranger bringing his own military secretary, and Congress promptly accepted his offer to serve without rank for the time being.

Another bogus nobleman, born as Johann Kalb, the son of a German peasant, had already attached himself to the army as the Baron de Kalb after adopting that title in the French service. The new "baron" was not only accepted without question at the moment but even by historians.

It remained for a scholarly biography, based on research in the Prussian archives, to expose Steuben admiringly as one of history's most magnificent liars.[25] The son of a poor Lutheran pastor, he had never risen higher than a captain's rank in the Prussian army, and his title was pure invention.

Franklin was probably not much deceived, after an interview in Paris, but he believed that Steuben had great possibilities as a much-needed drillmaster. As a philosopher, however, he realized that it would never do for the portly Prussian to appear in his true colors as a penniless forty-seven-year-old adventurer. Thus it happened that a superb actor, fully worthy of his role, arrived at Valley Forge with just the proper air of becoming modesty. Washington, as a confirmed skeptic, appeared a little dubious at first; but in March he approved Steuben's plan, drawn up with the help of Greene and Hamilton, for a new system of American training.

Up to this time each state had more or less carried out its own ideas, so that thirteen separate and inharmonious systems had evolved, all based to some extent on the British manual of arms. Steuben wrote out each new lesson in French, to be translated and edited by Hamilton and John Laurens. Time was too short for printing, and the various brigades copied the instructions in script before passing them on down to the regiments. Nor did a lack of English frustrate a new drillmaster who took the place of a sergeant in putting an awkward squad through its paces. In time of emotional stress, according to tradition, he called on his French-speaking American assistant, Captain Benjamin Walker, to swear in English for him: *"Viens,* Walker, *mon ami, mon bon ami! sacre!* Goddam de *gaucheries* of dese *badauts. Je ne puis plus.* I can curse them no more."[26]

The daily spectacle was not only educational; it was a good show. It was flattering, moreover, to watch a supposed baron and aide of the great Frederick drilling recruits held spellbound by the enormous decoration gleaming from his chest. A hundred men were picked as a model company for the first six lessons while the others looked on to learn by imitation. Then the American officers, who stood as much in need of instruction as the troops, began drilling their companies in the elements of correct position, marching, halting, and dressing right and left.

Soon the entire army was made up of awkward squads marching up and down the parade ground. Washington withheld his full approval until March 28th, when he announced in general orders that Steuben would act as inspector-general of the Continental Army "until the pleasure of Congress shall be known."

That body gave its sanction by conferring the rank of major general on a showman who had done as much to improve the morale of the troops as their drill. He even made their rags seem a badge of honor, and his French secretary Duponceau credited him with originating the term *sansculottes* to delight young officers who began to brag about their worn-out breeches.

The improvident Steuben eventually cost his adopted country as much as a brigade, but he was worth every cent. On May 6th, the greatest day of jubilation the Continental Army had yet known, his pupils had advanced far enough to celebrate with a military review. The news of the treaty of alliance with France had not come wholly by surprise, but it was no less exciting to the officers and their wives attending the outdoor banquet at long tables shaded by marquees. Mrs. Greene chatted in school-girl French with Steuben, who also paid courtly attention to Lady Stirling and her daughter Kitty. But the feature of the day at Valley Forge was not the band blaring martial airs. It was not even the blinding decoration on the baron's new blue and gold uniform. It was the parade of ragged regiments swinging past with confident precision, wheeling from column into line, halting, grounding arms with a single crash, then going through their recent lessons without a blunder.

An uninvited guest watching the performance was found to be a British spy after being seized and questioned. But he did not suffer the usual fate of informers in time of war.[27] His American captors decided to release him without punishment on condition that he "go back and tell his employers what he has seen. 'Twill pain them more than to hear of his detection and death."

PART THREE

World War

The Huron and Iroquois forests are peopled with my friends: the despots of Europe and their courts, these to me are the savages.

—GENERAL LAFAYETTE

Chapter 15

Pull Devil, Pull Baker

O N THE third anniversary of Lexington the little Continental Army could take pride in a remarkable military achievement. Not only had new troops held their own against European regulars; they had beaten the invaders in a majority of the thirty-four engagements, including the attack and defense of forts as well as battles.

Some of these actions, it is true, were stridently claimed as victories by both sides. But the real story of the three years is told by the casualty lists rather than the assertions of rival generals. So difficult was it to keep armies in the field that every soldier put out of action represented a debit of more than ordinary significance. The British superiority in all the sinews of war was offset by the problems of raising troops and transporting them across the Atlantic. The Americans had a wealth of untrained man power but lacked the material resources to arm and equip recruits. Such a contest could best be appraised from a comparison of casualties, but it is not often that the returns of either side are reliable. Washington waited until the late date of October 8, 1776, before inquiring into the losses of his army at the battle of Long Island on August 27th, and the exact figure never was determined.[1] Howe and Burgoyne also found it useful on occasion to gloss over their own losses while making those of the enemy appear as large as possible.

At least there can be no doubt that Burgoyne's surrender put the rebels ahead in the war of attrition. After three years the greatest expeditionary force of eighteenth-century history had failed, so that the Americans were nearer to an equality in trained troops than ever before. At a council of war held at Valley Forge on May 8, 1778, Washington reckoned his own forces at 15,000, exclusive of horse and artillery—11,500 in the main army, 1,800 at the Hudson River posts, and the rest in smaller detachments or garrisons. He estimated the rank and file of the British infantry at 16,000 effectives on this date—10,000 at Philadelphia, 4,000 at New York, and 2,000 in Rhode Island.[2]

This figure proved to be too low, and it is likely that 20,000 would have been nearer to the mark. Even so, the enemy strength had been nearly double that number only ten months before. The decline from 1777 to 1778 cannot be charged entirely to battle casualties. But allowing for continual troop transfers, it is probable that the losses from all causes, including desertion and disease, could not have been much less than 15,000.

The age of total war had not yet dawned, for eighteenth-century nations did not believe in throwing their entire resources into a struggle until one side or the other was crushed and helpless. Incomplete victories won by small professional armies and navies were the rule; and according to these standards Great Britain had lost the war in America by the end of 1777. This was the opinion of British leaders, who did not hesitate to state it publicly. Even the king was willing to concede everything except independence, and only his obstinacy prolonged the conflict beyond its logical ending.

The most serious American losses up to this time had not been incurred directly on the battlefield. They came as a consequence of overcrowding and malnutrition in British military prisons. Contemporary newspaper accounts must usually be accepted as opinion rather than fact, but such reports as the following required no exaggeration:

> A cartel vessel lately carried about 130 American prisoners from the prison ships in New York to New London in Connecticut. Such was the condition in which these poor creatures were put on board the cartel, that in that short run, sixteen died on board; upwards of sixty, when they were landed, were scarcely able to move, and the remainder greatly emaciated and enfeebled; and many who remain alive, are never likely to recover their former health.[3]

Few of the Americans taken at Fort Washington who survived their captivity were ever able to fight again. Washington's repeated protests had no effect except to bring indignant letters of denial. In the spring of 1777 he flatly refused to send back healthy British soldiers for 2,200 Americans who arrived in such a pitiful state that many died and most of the others were fit only for the hospital.[4] Howe charged his adversary with bad faith, and the dispute had not been settled when Burgoyne's surrender brought the rebels their largest bag of captives so far in the war.

This success would have profited the victors but little if they had not been on their guard. In order to preserve their gains, it became necessary to wage a contest of evasions which might be called the third battle of Saratoga.

Burgoyne did not suspect the anxiety of his victorious opponent at the time when terms were being discussed. For the American general had learned of Clinton's advance up the Hudson which threatened his rear. The capture of Fort Montgomery by storm on October 6th was the decisive blow; and the other rebel posts, inadequately manned by militia, fell in rapid succession. After the redcoats removed an iron chain weighing fifty tons, the river was open to navigation all the way to Albany, only a day's march from the rebel lines at Stillwater. Gates had every reason to dread the prospect of enemy forces capturing this arsenal at the moment when he confronted Burgoyne with the air of an assured victor.

It is to his credit that no suspicion entered the mind of a foeman who boasted of the concessions he had wrung from adversity. This accounts for the legend that the American army numbered 25,000 men. Gates encouraged the delusion for the purpose of soothing British pride and hastening the signing of an agreement euphemistically called the Convention. Actually the rebels did not have an equality until the first battle, and it is doubtful if their numbers exceeded 15,000, including recent militia arrivals, on the day of the surrender.

Such face-saving compromises were not important as compared to Article Three, which stipulated that the Convention troops should not fight again in America after marching to Boston for embarkation to England in British ships. Gates realized that nothing prevented these men from replacing nearly 6,000 garrison troops in various posts of the Empire, thus releasing them for American service. But it was no time to be exacting, for he could not anticipate that Clinton would take so little advantage of his successes. "This delicate situation," Gates explained to Congress, "abridged our conquests and procured General Burgoyne the terms he enjoys."

The men in the State House also perceived that the gains of Saratoga might be wiped out as soon as enemy transports could cross the Atlantic and return. Washington appears to have been first to suspect that the British would not trouble themselves to this extent. The father of his country did not pretend to be a scholar of history, but he was a realist who had few illusions about his opponents. In a letter to Richard Henry Lee, meant for the attention of Congress, he dragged out a skeleton hidden away in a dim corner of the British closet. This was the violation of the Convention of Kloster Seven in the last war, after the Duke of Cumberland surrendered an army threatened with destruction by the French. The terms provided that the troops should not serve again in Germany, but the British ministers of 1757 soon found a way to squirm out of the difficulty. George II, acting as King of Hanover, simply repudiated the agreement which bound him as King of England, though it was no secret that he had the approval if not the instigation of the government.

Empires are not won by playing the game at all times according to rules, and every nation has its incidents which cannot be recalled with pride. This breach of faith was so flagrant, however, that it received decent burial as soon as possible. Fortesque, who devoted a large shelf of books to the annals of the British army, hastened past the Convention of Kloster Seven with a single sentence. Other British historians have shown no more fondness for dwelling upon an episode which left the national honor a little the worse for wear.

Congress has been given no such tender consideration for its efforts to evade the spirit of the Saratoga Convention while respecting the letter. Such expressions as "base and sordid dealing" have found their way into the pages of history, always on the assumption that British intentions were honorable. The American leaders of 1777 were not so gullible. Yet they might have been shocked, dark as their suspicions were, to know that two days before the surrender Burgoyne placed a military advantage above honor. This information appeared in General Riedesel's memoirs, which described the council of war called after a deserter brought news of Clinton's march up the Hudson. "General Burgoyne and several officers were so much elated by this doubtful intelligence, that a great desire arose to break the whole capitulation." Eight affirmatives and fourteen negatives were submitted in reply to the question "whether a treaty which had been definitely settled by fully empowered commissioners—after the promise of the general to ratify all that the commissioners had agreed upon—could be broken with honor."[5] The decision seems to have represented a triumph of expediency rather than virtue. For Riedesel added that "those voting in the negative based their opinion on the ground that the intelligence brought over by the deserter was all of it only hearsay. . . ."

The third battle of Saratoga reached its critical stage after the Convention troops marched to Cambridge to await transportation to England. Burgoyne and the Riedesels had been effusively greeted at General Schuyler's home in Albany, and they expected that wealthy Yankees would compete for the privilege of entertaining a staff which included several peers and six members of Parliament. It was a sad disillusionment to be snubbed by all classes of Bostonians. Not a single home opened its doors to British officers, who had to put up uncomfortably at inns while their troops occupied bleak barracks. New England was not called the hotbed of rebellion for nothing, and people had not forgotten Burgoyne's part in turning Old South Chapel into a riding school and stable. Madame Riedesel found the city "inhabited by violent patriots, and full of wicked people. The women, especially, were so shameless, that they regarded me with repugnance and even spit at me when I passed by them."[6] Someone must have been pulling the good German woman's leg, for she was shocked to learn of a proposal "to chop off the heads of our generals, salt them down in small barrels, and send over to the English one of these barrels for every hamlet or little town burned down; but this barbarous suggestion fortunately was not adopted."

The terms of the Convention gave Burgoyne valid grounds to protest at the poor quarters provided for his officers and men. But the British general could never refrain from painting a rhetorical lily, and in a letter to Gates he complained that "the public faith is broke." This provided Congress with a fulcrum for prizing itself out of an embarrassing situation. John Witherspoon ably headed a committee which found a solution accepted on January 8, 1778, when the assembly decided "that the embarkation of Lieutenant General Burgoyne, and the troops under his command, be suspended till a distinct and explicit ratification of the convention of Saratoga shall be properly notified by the court of Great Britain to Congress."[7]

George III and his ministers, in other words, must come to a virtual recognition of American sovereignty and independence as a condition of fulfillment. Congress justified itself on the grounds that Burgoyne's statement implied a readiness on his part to break faith, so that Americans had a right to demand confirmation before carrying out their part of the bargain.

It was, as historians have sternly charged, a solution of trickery. But it was not, as they have also intimated, a decision taking advantage of an enemy with clean hands. Two months before Congress passed its resolution, the enemy had already schemed to violate the Convention. This skeleton was not only hidden in the closet of Empire but buried deep beneath the floor, never to be exhumed for a century and a half.

The members of Congress could not have known that they would be justified by documentary evidence. It was enough at the time that their sensitive noses smelled a rat. Henry Laurens, president of the assembly, needed only his intuition and good sense to set down in notes of January 8, 1778, some surmises which proved to be prophecy:

> The British Commanders having frequently declared, there is no faith to be kept with Rebels, and having as often acted in conformity, Sir Wm. Howe [or] Sir H. Clinton have directed Burgoyne wherever his troops shall be embarked to order the Transport Ships to go into New York or Delaware as the Winds may permit. . . . That it was not intended to send the Troops across the Atlantic appeared clearly from the inadequate quantity of Tonnage of the Transports which were sent to receive them as well as from the scantiness of Provisions and Water. . . .[8]

Nor was Laurens mistaken in concluding that "General Burgoyne a little staggered by such an Order and feeling for his own reputation devised means for vindicating the intended breach on his part whenever his conduct should be called in question." In almost every detail the president of Congress correctly deduced the enemy's plans, for Sir William Howe had given Burgoyne secret instructions in a letter written eight weeks before. This document came to light among the Sir Henry Clinton papers and was published for the first time in 1932.

Howe found his pretext in Washington's refusal to exchange healthy British soldiers for Americans debilitated in enemy military prisons. On November 16, 1777, he wrote to Burgoyne: "I am to beg that you will be pleased to give your secret Directions to the commanding Officer of the Navy, convoying the Transports, who is instructed to follow your Orders for the Destination of the Troops, that, when they are embarked, he is to proceed with the British Artillery Men and Infantry to New York, my design being to exchange the Officers for those of the Rebels in my possession, and the Soldiers for 2,200 Prisoners of the Enemy, that I sent in last Winter, in full Confidence of receiving an equal Number in Return, which, notwithstanding my repeated Applications, has been pointedly refused under the most frivolous Pretences."[9]

This violation of the Convention terms, if it had succeeded, would have had Burgoyne's redcoats in service at an early date, thus saving the time and expense of sending them home and bringing back an equal number of garrison troops. Howe thought so little of the German mercenaries that he was willing to wait for British soldiers in their place. "The Foreign Troops," he added, "will proceed to Plymouth agreeable to my Letter of the 14th Inst., or to any other Port in England you may direct them to, my views being only to repair an Injury in which Mr. Washington so obstinately persists."

Burgoyne was enjoined "to keep the Destination secret as long as possible, by giving the Masters of Transports the Rendezvous mentioned in my public Letter, and by delivering, when under sail, sealed orders to those, having British Troops on board, to proceed to New York in case of Separation; and I wish some Pretence might be fallen upon by you to conceal from the Captain and Troops the Intention of such Orders, even when they are opened. . . . I conceive it is necessary to use every possible Precaution to keep the Enemy ignorant of my Intentions, as on the least suspicion the Troops wd. be infallibly stopt. . . ."

The suspicions of Congress were not far enough advanced at this date for a decisive step, but during the last weeks of 1777 the assembly interposed delays by quibbling over such minor British violations as failing to give an exact return of troops and neglecting to surrender all bayonets and cartridge boxes. Burgoyne supported Howe at Cambridge meanwhile by goading his captors to the point where their retaliations might provide him with further pretexts when the time came to vindicate his intended breach of faith.

General William Heath, the American commander at Cambridge, soon found himself up against a situation that called for the wisdom of a Solomon and the patience of a Job. With only an inadequate force of militiamen as guards—old men or boys unfit for active service—he had to deal with a concerted attempt on the part of his captives to subvert all authority. American officers were insulted, sentinels taunted and manhandled, passes counterfeited, and civilians robbed in broad daylight. Burgoyne and his generals upheld acts of indiscipline which were intended, as Heath shrewdly perceived, "to enrage the inhabitants of the country, who view such abuses as insufferable."

For weeks the strange contest went on with the intensity of a military campaign—the captives making every effort to incite an "incident" for future self-justification, and the captors trying equally hard to give no satisfaction. Never was there a greater proof of the fierce cohesion which bound together all ranks of the British army. From raffish earls and members of Parliament down to lordly sergeants, the Convention troops were united by insular scorn for their opponents. Paradoxes were the rule rather than exception in this host of latter-day Romans, so that an odd sort of comradeship went hand in hand with caste. British peers of the late eighteenth century included more than a sprinkling of recent weavers, brewers, butchers, carpenters and chambermaids—the newly minted aristocracy of a dynamic nation on the make. Only a step below them on the ladder were the political climbers and possessors of new fortunes who would be the peers of the next decade. Each of these estates had its representatives in the Convention army. Gentleman Johnny himself was the hero of troops who admired his purple prose as much as his taste in champagne and mistresses. Neither the hardihood nor the vulgarity had been bred out of beef-eating barons and gentry who could drink, plunder and fight as heartily as any commoner in the ranks. They could also die if the need arose, and their gallant bones still molder on five continents splashed with the red which nineteenth-century cartographers used to designate British conquests.

These were the artisans who wrought the greatest political fact of the age, the British Empire. They could be killed, wounded or captured, but never defeated. It would have been too much to expect fair play from such men when their aims were endangered. Brick foundations are not built by china painters, and the artisans of the British Empire fought to win. They fought with fair means if possible, with foul means if necessary, but above all they fought to win. So fierce and relentless was the will of the Convention troops that even the women camp followers added to the provocations endured daily by American captors. A British officer described with gusto the discomfiture of an aged rebel sentry who would not permit one of these doxies to pass. "Great altercation ensued, in which the lady displayed much of the Billingsgate oratory, when the old man was so irritated as to present his firelock; the woman immediately ran up, snatched it from him, knocked him down, and striding over the prostrate hero, in the exultation of triumph, profusely besprinkled him. . . . Nor did she quit her post, till a file of sturdy ragamuffins marched valiantly to his relief, dispossessed the Amazon, and enabled the knight of the grisly caxon to look fierce, and reshoulder his musket."[10]

While the soldiers and camp followers made life miserable for the guards, Burgoyne and his officers concentrated on General Heath. It might have been supposed that this phalanx of peers and members of Parliament would make easy work of the Roxbury farmer, but he proved to be a match for them. Neither insults nor flatteries nor sophistries could shake his imperturbable sense of duty, and "our General" remained in full control.

American endurance reached its limits early in January, and Burgoyne had his "incident" when a rebel officer forgot himself so far as to prick an insolent prisoner with his sword. Torrents of swollen rhetoric poured from the British general's pen, but Heath kept his head above the flood without losing either his dignity or authority. He not only called a court-martial but granted Burgoyne the irregular privilege of acting as prosecutor. There may even have been a little guile in Heath's motives, for Gentleman Johnny talked so much that the prisoner owed his acquittal mainly to the tiresome speeches made to convict him. Nobody could listen to Gentleman Johnny very long without a strong desire to choke him, and Heath upheld his tormented troops in a firm letter of January 10th: "The insults and provocations which they have received . . . are unparalleled; and whether you are willing or unwilling, Sir, offenders shall no longer pass with impunity."

It was too late by that time for the pretexts sought by Burgoyne. Congress had decided to hold up the embarkation, and the British plan for violating the Convention receded into the shadows of history. Heath not only kept strict order among his own troops but gave the redcoats a wholesome dose of discipline. When an enemy officer was killed after refusing to obey a sentry's order to halt, a court-martial speedily acquitted the rebel soldier for doing his duty. And when General Phillips defied American authority Heath ordered him confined to quarters. "In military command," he dryly informed his prisoner, "there must be one supreme head: at present, the Honourable Congress have honoured me with the command of this department. . . . You must not expect that I shall allow myself, either by frowns or flatteries, to give up the dignity of command reposed in me."[11]

The British generals, as men who fought to win, ended by respecting a fighter who refused to be bullied or cajoled. Burgoyne and Phillips took their leave of the bald and corpulent patriot with affection, and he bore them no resentment. As the months went by, the Convention army grew to be one of the most profitable and esteemed industries of wartime New England. The terms stipulated that its supplies should be paid for by the British in gold, and this income helped to support the rapidly depreciating Continental paper currency. At last the enemy authorities declined to make such a contribution to the rebel cause, since there seemed to be no prospect of Burgoyne's army ever returning. The rebels had to provide for the captives themselves, and they economized toward the end of 1778 by marching them to Virginia, where food costs were cheaper. There the Convention troops remained until 1781, when they were sent to Pennsylvania to prevent their rescue by an invading army under Cornwallis. Hundreds had already deserted to begin life anew in America, so that only a remnant of the men who surrendered in 1777 ever got back to Europe.

If Howe's secret scheme had succeeded, half of the 6,000 Convention troops would soon have been fighting again while the other half released an equal number of redcoats for American service by the spring of 1778. The effect on the outcome of the war can only be conjectured; but the time would come, two years later, when Washington could not muster as many as 6,000 effectives in his main army.

It is understandable that such liberal British historians as Lecky and Trevelyan, unaware of Howe's letter, should have charged Americans with dishonorable conduct in the third battle of Saratoga. But it is amusing to read the indignant plaints of Burgoyne and the other British generals at Cambridge. For there is no wrath quite so righteous as that of the sharper who finds himself caught in the act by his intended victims.

Victory had its penalties as well as rewards, and the capture of an entire British army did not prove to be an unmixed blessing. Criticism of Washington's generalship had been smoldering for some time, and it needed only the triumph at Saratoga to bring about that imbroglio known to history by the fine alliterative name of the Conway Cabal.

There was more smoke than flame throughout, but the dissension among American officers could not be concealed even from the enemy. On December 19, 1777, the leading Tory newspaper of New York commented that "a junto is formed . . . and said to consist of Generals Mifflin, Thompson, Arnold and Sinclair [St. Clair]; their object is the removal of General Washington from the chief command of the rebel army. The Generals Lee and Gates, with all the Yankees who have resolution enough to declare themselves of a party, wish well to the enterprise."[12]

This account is no more confused than the story which has so often found its way into the pages of history. But it contains some fact as well as legend, so that the Conway Cabal cannot be ignored. About a dozen letters actually do exist, a few of them anonymous, questioning Washington's fitness for the chief command. There is no evidence at all of a plot to supplant him with Gates or any other general. Gates, in fact, was as much the victim of underhanded criticism as his superior.

The supposed conspiracy was named after General Thomas Conway, an Irish adventurer who had served with credit in the French army before coming to America as a volunteer. He was accused of taking part as a ringleader in a clique composed both of officers and members of Congress —Gates, Mifflin, Benjamin Rush, Richard Henry Lee and Samuel Adams being the others usually named. The legend has it that these malcontents not only distrusted Washington's ability as a general but feared that he had the potentialities of becoming dictator. Gates appears in the role of a schemer who took advantage of a victory won by Arnold and Schuyler to intrigue for the chief command.

The piece has its heroes as well as villains. Both Lafayette and Hamilton are praised for standing by their chief in his dark hour. And in the background there is no more noble figure than Schuyler, represented as having been only recently the victim of a similar plot.

So much for the legend. When it comes to examining the facts, it seems incredible that so much could have been made of so little documentary evidence. That there was some unfavorable comment on Washington in Congress is undeniable. But it is not lese majesty when the members of an elected assembly criticize the commander in chief—it is their duty as well as right. Nor can it be said that such officers as Pickering and Greene were guilty of disloyalty when they questioned Washington's generalship during the Brandywine operations.

Even the undercover attacks do not justify any assumption that a conspiracy existed. An anonymous letter traced to Dr. Rush hinted broadly at Washington's ineptitude without mentioning him by name. Another unsigned paper called "Thoughts of a Freeman" declared that "the people of America have been guilty of idolatry by making a man their God, and the God of heaven and earth will convince them by a woful experience, that he is only a man; for no good can be expected from the standing army until Baal and his worshippers are banished from camp."[13]

Washington himself brought this attack to the attention of Congress. "Why should I expect to be exempt from centure; the unfailing lot of an elevated station?" he wrote to President Laurens. "Merit and talents, with which I can have no pretensions of rivalship, have ever been subject to it."[14]

If Congress had a right to criticize the commander, Washington was equally entitled to censure subordinates for the good of the service. One of his greatest assets was an impartiality seldom influenced by his personal likes or dislikes, but he made little effort to hide his prejudice against foreign officers in general and Conway in particular. This bias appears to have been justified by the Irish volunteer's indiscretions as a meddler and babbler. "Heaven," he wrote to Gates, "has been determined to save your country or a weak General and bad counsellers would have ruined it." The letter came to Washington's attention, and he merely sent it to the writer without comment. That was the end of the so-called Conway Cabal. Exposure dampened the zeal of Washington's other critics, and he emerged in the spring of 1778 stronger than before in the esteem of Congress and the Continental Army.

But if there had been no conspiracy, it is certain that two factions carried on a feud during the entire winter of Valley Forge. Gates could hardly help but be implicated, for Washington's critics never failed to cite the victory at Saratoga in contrast to the defeats of the Philadelphia campaign. The former British officer was a self-made man of high ambitions, and he may have hoped that the chief command would be offered to him. If so, he appears to have contented himself with letting matters take their course.

It was the misfortune of Gates to be used as a club by two factions beating each other over the head. His New England supporters in Congress usually wrote to him when they wished to take some sly dig at Washington. And the New York delegates did not neglect a new opportunity to smear the good name of a general who had twice replaced Schuyler with success. The wonder is that Gates and Washington were not made lifelong enemies by partisans who pitted one against the other. The two were not well acquainted, having had little contact save by letter, so that a fertile field existed for sowing seeds of discord. It was inevitable that relations should have been strained, but at the height of the clamor Henry Laurens wrote to his son on February 3, 1778: "In conversation with General Gates without seeking on my side, I discovered an inclination in him to be on friendly terms with our great and good General. It cannot be doubted but that there is the same disposition on the other side."[15]

Both men were as much the victims of friends as enemies. Gates seems to have suspected this possibility when he wrote directly to his chief on February 19th, "I solemnly declare that I am of no faction, and if any of my letters taken aggregately or by paragraphs convey any meaning, which in any construction is offensive to your Excellency, that was by no means the intention of the writer." Washington replied on the 24th, expressing his willingness to bury the whole dispute "in silence, and as far as future events will permit, oblivion. My temper leads me to peace and harmony with all men; and it is particularly my wish to avoid any personal feuds or dissensions with those, who are embarked in the same great national interest as myself, as every difference of this kind must in its consequences be very injurious."[16]

It could not be said that Washington and Gates ever became friends— their temperaments and convictions were too dissimilar for a warm relationship. But they kept the hatchet buried throughout the war, and their respect for each other steadily increased down to the end of a conflict from which they emerged as first and second in command of the Continental Army.

There is more than meets the eye in the Conway Cabal. On closer examination, the dispute may be recognized as the old familiar Gates-Schuyler feud with only a few changes in motives. And even this would be a superficial interpretation. For both of these controversies actually represent the groping beginnings of political parties. Before the victory was won, while the issue remained in doubt, the rebels were divided into two camps holding opposite views as to the new nation they wished to create.

What kind of an America was it that constituted the damp political clay of 1778? A dozen answers might have been given to this question, and all of them would have been correct. It was a pastoral America of hospitable farm and village folk, and it was a mongrel America of immigrants hostile to the ideals of the Revolution. Both of these pictures may be found in the journal of John Charles Philip von Krafft, who reached these shores as a young German officer seeking professional advancement.[17] This stranger, ill-acquainted with the language, found a warmhearted welcome everywhere on a walking trip from Maryland to Valley Forge. As one of several such instances, a poor wagoner named Thomas Anderson gave the wayfarer a ride and put him up for three days. "The honest old man and his wife overwhelmed me with kindnesses, washed my soiled linen, and I was obliged to stay there until the 27 Jan. [1778] Tues. In spite of their protests, [I] bid farewell to this good old man and his wife and seven children. They would not, with all my urging, accept any compensation, but wished me all good luck and the old man accompanied me over half a mile."

At Valley Forge the newcomer met with the same kindly and credulous hospitality. After accepting a first lieutenant's commission and an advance of $30, he repaid his benefactors by deserting to the Hessians in the hope of gaining a higher rank. All the way to Philadelphia he "met hardly any but German people." Among these ill-absorbed immigrants aiding the enemy was a Pennsylvania German serving as "an ensign in the American militia, but an enemy of the so-called Wiecks [Whigs]." Such sympathetic guides escorted Krafft safely to Knyphausen's headquarters, but the Hessians humiliated a former Prussian lieutenant by offering him nothing higher than a sergeant's rank. Two years later he was still weltering in self-pity: "My sighs can no longer move God. I would be glad to die, were it not that I must die a sub-officer."

Another America, a land of opportunists making easy money from war speculations, may be seen as the background to the career of John Carter. This young Englishman, whose real name was John Church Barker, left his own country under mysterious circumstances and wooed fortune rather literally in the New World by eloping with General Schuyler's daughter Angelica. After a reconciliation with her parents, he made himself rich in a few years as a contractor supplying the rebel forces. At Cambridge, according to Madame Riedesel's memoirs, the Carters were the only Americans who entertained the British and German officers. Kosciusko challenged Schuyler's son-in-law to a duel in the autumn of 1778 for a fancied insult to Gates, but Carter declined even after being "published as a coward" in a New York newspaper.[18]

Still another America, a land of outright rogues and scoundrels, is revealed by the new activities of Benedict Arnold after he sought the command at Philadelphia on the plea that his Saratoga wound prevented active service. Four days after his arrival in the summer of 1778, he entered into a secret agreement for using public credit to buy and sell army supplies for private gain.[19] Within a few months a general with a salary of $332 a month in Continental money could afford to move into the luxurious John Penn house, lately occupied by Sir William Howe, and maintain a coach and four along with liveried servants while entertaining wealthy Tories.

These were only a few faces of the wartime America of 1778—an America of heroes and slackers, of patriots and profiteers, of simple farmers and somewhat less simple stockjobbers. It was a yeasty and powerful ferment, and everyone had his own ideas as to how the brave new dough should be kneaded to shape a future nation. This was actually the struggle for power behind the Conway Cabal, as Henry Laurens perceived at the time. For once in his life the hot-headed president of Congress was not a partisan himself, and he made a fatherly attempt to straighten out the confusion in Lafayette's mind. The youthful French volunteer, blinded by the myopia of hero worship, could see no farther than the end of his nose, where a group of malefactors appeared to be lurking to overthrow Washington. Laurens informed him in a letter of January 12th that the supposed conspiracy "amounts to little more than tittle tattle which would be too much honoured by repeating it."

Among the talebearers and troublemakers of the Conway Cabal, the fifty-three-year-old South Carolina merchant stands out as a benevolent neutral. He proceeded to give a lecture in politics to a young stranger who had been running around in frantic circles, emitting cries of anguish and despair. "There is no subject," continued Laurens, "more abstruse than this of party. It is said to be the Sinews of Liberty. I have neither Leisure nor abilities for going deeply into the enquiry, nor is it necessary. I will only say that party animosity between the Eastern States and the Inhabitants of New York is almost coexistent with the *Inhabitants*. These are grand divisions. Each has its own atmosphere. . . . They make the Road rough but not impassible."[20]

Any attempt to define the factions of 1778 would run the risk of the oversimplification that has stultified so much Revolutionary history. The New Englanders, never dreaming that water power would give their section the advantage in future industrialization, visioned a rural America of the future, a pastoral republic of freemen united by Puritan virtues. They were supported by a few southern liberals who believed that men close to the soil could best preserve their political liberties. The New Yorkers, on the other hand, represented the merchants and large landowners of the middle states who favored the development of trade and manufactures.

The New Yorkers were accused of worshiping the golden calf, the New Englanders of attempting by means of demagoguery to make small men the equal of their betters. Both factions were necessary to the America which grew out of compromise after the opposing groups found their protagonists in two men of genius, Alexander Hamilton and Thomas Jefferson. In 1778 they had to content themselves with a Gates and Schuyler, and the issues were still so dim that many of the combatants had only a very vague understanding. When the Yankees maligned Schuyler with unfounded tales of cowardice and double-dealing, they were really striking at the New York patroons and wealthy merchants. And when the New Yorkers slandered Gates by making Arnold the hero of Saratoga on their own prejudiced evidence, they were aiming a lusty blow at such leveling institutions as the town meeting and Congregational church.

If Lafayette had heeded Laurens's advice, he would have saved himself a great deal of needless agonizing about the danger to Washington. Instead, he listened to Schuyler; and it is not a coincidence that the stories of Gates's ambitions reached a climax after the young Frenchman took a journey to Albany.

The occasion arose when the Board of War conceived a new idea of invading Canada. Lafayette and Conway were appointed first and second in command because of their knowledge of the French language, and several French volunteers were to be taken along to organize Canadian regiments for the rebel cause. The plan came to nothing when Lafayette reached Albany in February to discover that not enough troops could be raised. It was a bitter disappointment to the twenty-year-old general, who had already made a trip to York to get de Kalb promoted over Conway. But after a visit at the home of General Schuyler, Lafayette emerged as the most vociferous opponent of Gates in the Continental Army.

Only a few months before, Colonel Alexander Hamilton had also been a guest at the Schuyler home while bearing dispatches. There he met Elizabeth Schuyler, whom he was to marry a few years later. This encounter did not seem so interesting to him at the time as the persuasion that Gates had played a small part at Saratoga in comparison to Schuyler and Arnold. From that moment, Hamilton became one of the leaders of the New York faction along with Duane, Jay, Duer, Robert R. Livingston and Gouverneur Morris.

The excitable young Frenchman returned from Albany with new apprehensions of the peril to Washington. He could no longer believe the assertion in Laurens's letter that "the friends of our brave and virtuous General, may rest assured that he is out of the reach of his Enemies, if he has an Enemy, a fact of which I am in doubt of." The president of Congress added another piece of wise counsel when he informed Lafayette that Americans "are sometimes very troublesome in their disputes, which are carried to such extremes as seem to threaten a dissolution of all friendships. Nevertheless, danger from a common Enemy will reduce them to good order and as it were by a Charm, instantly establish a coalition."

The truth of this prediction had its proof only a few weeks later when authentic news reached America that Lord North had admitted the failure of the British war effort by asking Parliament to pass bills providing for the sending of peace commissioners across the Atlantic. His Conciliatory Acts, hurried through both houses in February, granted practically every aim that the colonists had sought in 1775. There were two omissions, however, which united the Americans of 1778 into a solid front of opposition. The effect, as Laurens had prophesied, was nothing less than magical. Overnight that false alarm known as the Conway Cabal vanished into the thin air from which it had been largely created. Patriots of all classes and sections and factions could not raise their voices at once, though they did their best. It remained for the Continental Congress to speak for them by a unanimous vote on April 22nd in the little courthouse at York:

> Any man, or body of men, who should presume to make any separate or partial convention or agreement with commissioners under the crown of Great Britain . . . ought to be considered and treated as open and avowed enemies of these United States. . . . These United States cannot, with propriety, hold any conference or treaty with any commissioners on the part of Great Britain, unless they shall, as a preliminary thereto, either withdraw their fleets and armies, or else in positive and express terms, acknowledge the independence of the said states.[21]

America had spoken before there was yet any assurance of a French alliance. And with the wounds of the winter's factionalism healed, the soldiers of Valley Forge made ready for the spring campaign. Even Gates and Schuyler could have been considered firm colleagues at the moment, though each might have had a few private doubts about the other.

Chapter 16

False Dawn of Victory

THE spring of 1778 was a turning point of the Revolution in more ways than one. All the former colonies had their own state governments or were in process of drawing up new constitutions and providing for their own elected executives. The new nation itself—for it could almost be called a nation by this time—seemed well on the way to ratifying the Articles of Confederation which had been adopted by the Continental Congress in November.

This first American constitution had not found easy sledding. The debates began shortly after the Declaration of Independence and continued intermittently for sixteen months before the delegates could hit upon provisions which stood a chance of acceptance by states with such diverse interests. Nobody, least of all the creators, considered it a perfect instrument. They realized that many of the compromises could only invite future dissension. Congress finally agreed upon them in a mood of desperation revealed by a letter of November 13, 1777, from Cornelius Harnett to a North Carolina colleague: "The child Congress has been big with, these two years past, is at last brought forth—(Confederation). I fear it will by several Legislatures be thought a little deformed,—you will think it a Monster. I wish, however, some kind of Confederation would take place. Some carry their idea of this matter so far, as to believe that our affairs must be ruined without it."[1]

The victory at Saratoga provided a heaven-sent opportunity to offer the instrument to the states for their ratification, but the response was disappointing. By the following March only Virginia had come forward, and it took the announcement of the French alliance to speed the laggards. After that news eight more state assemblies gave their consent within the next two months, and optimists predicted that the other four would fall in line before the end of the year.

While the thirteen states were becoming a nation, their army had also taken long strides toward unification. For it could not be said that America had a truly national army, with its own discipline suited to its own temper and needs, until the spring of 1778 at Valley Forge.

It is perhaps not surprising that an alien wrought this result, for Steuben was above all a citizen of the world. Fortunately, he had no trace of the martinet in his make-up. And though he had been a Prussian drillmaster, he did not try to adapt that system blindly to the uses of citizen-soldiers of the New World contending for political liberties.

An example of contemporary German discipline is found in Sergeant Krafft's journal. When a Hessian soldier serving as groom incurred his displeasure for some blunder, he naturally thought of beating the fellow. "Having no stick with me, I took my sword with the sheath and struck him several times. But the sheath unexpectedly slipped off and the groom throwing up his left arm, I dealt him a severe cut below the elbow to the bone. I was in anxiety myself, though I had done it unintentionally. I went to Colonel von Gosen, told him the whole story myself and he pardoned me without any reproachful remarks, even in spite of the earnest complaint of the groom."[2]

This sort of thing, however well it may have suited the Hessians, would never have been tolerated by American soldiers. The secret of Steuben's success was his understanding of the temperament of the men at Valley Forge before he learned their language. "In the first place," he wrote to an old Prussian comrade in arms, "the genius of this nation is not in the least to be compared with that of the Prussians, Austrians or French. You say to your soldier, 'Do this,' and he doeth it; but I am obliged to say, 'This is the reason why you ought to do that,' and then he does it."[3]

Steuben did not hesitate to borrow from Prussian as well as British and French sources when they could be shaped to American purposes. But the spirit of his regulations was anything but Prussian, as may be noted from these instructions to company officers:

A captain cannot be too careful of the company the state has committed to his charge. He must pay the greatest attention to the health of his men, their discipline, arms, accoutrements, ammunition, clothes and necessaries. His first object should be to gain the love of his men by treating them with every possible kindness and humanity, inquiring into their complaints and when well founded, seeing them redressed. He should know every man of his company by name and character. He should often visit those who are sick, speak tenderly to them, see that the public provision, whether of medicine or diet, is duly administered, and procure them besides such comforts and medicines as are in his power.[4]

This is only one of Steuben's regulations which is as good today as in 1778. Most of the troubles of the Continental Army during the first three years could be traced to the slackness of inexperienced and poorly qualified company officers. To make matters worse, the rebels had retained the British system, which left the actual drilling to sergeants on the grounds that it lowered the dignity of an officer. This meant that green American officers had little chance to improve. Nor could they depend on those old sergeants, many of them veterans of a lifetime, who were the backbone of British discipline. Steuben changed all that at Valley Forge, setting a precedent followed down to the present day. When a supposed baron and lieutenant general shouldered a musket to show the men how it was done, American captains and lieutenants could not remain aloof. They had to learn the drill themselves in order to become preceptors, and the benefits were apparent at once.

The conflicting systems of American training during the first three years had been deplored in a letter from Washington to Sullivan, "If in all cases ours was *one* army, or *thirteen* armies allied for the common defense, there would be no difficulty . . . but we are occasionally both, and I should not be much out if I were to say, that we are sometimes *neither*, but a compound of both." The consequences of this military bedlam were summed up by Steuben when he first grappled with his problem: "The captains and colonels did not consider their commands and regiments as corps confided to them by the United States for the care of the men as well as the preservation of order and discipline. . . . The idea they had of their duty was, that the officers had only to mount guard and put themselves at the head of their regiment or company when they were going into action."[5]

This attitude had been costing the Continental Army a loss in muskets alone of five to eight thousand a year at a time when the shortage of arms imperiled the cause. Three-month recruits simply took their equipment home with them, having grown to consider it one of the rewards of service. Steuben met the issue by inculcating a sense of responsibility in both commissioned and noncommissioned officers. Franklin had recommended him in the first place because the French ministers complained that arms sent from that country were being squandered, and the new drillmaster soon reduced the leakage to almost nothing.

Better yet, he reduced the appalling waste in the men themselves as represented by large sick lists due to lack of sanitation. His regulations provided for garbage disposal, supervised latrines and other health safeguards that had been neglected by military amateurs. Not only did Steuben adapt his instructions to American needs; he proved that many of the drills existing in old-established armies had no value except for display at reviews. For a century it had been the accepted theory in Europe that a good soldier could not be created for the complex maneuvers of linear tactics in less than two or three years. But the new American inspector-general had only two or three months in which to make recruits the equals of enemy regulars. By necessity as well as choice, he eliminated everything except drills calculated to turn out fighting men instead of parade soldiers. He cut down the motions for loading, introduced a step and cadence suited to rough country, prescribed uniformity of arms and equipment, and taught the men to march in a column of platoons as a preliminary to forming an orderly line.

The results of this system demonstrated beyond a doubt that many of the current European drills had little practical value. Steuben's pupils never learned to dress their ranks in flawless array, but they seldom failed to give a good account of themselves in the field either as enemies or allies of European regulars.

The relationship between tactical theory and practice has been nicely put in the words of an American military historian, "Seeking information at the point of a bayonet is one thing, and looking for it on the shelves of a library is another."[6] After Valley Forge it might have been observed that many young rebel officers, following the example set by Greene, Knox and Wayne, were taking a keen interest in both approaches to knowledge. This trend came to the attention of Captain Johann Ewald of the Jäger corps, who thought so highly of the lessons taught by the Revolution that he incorporated them into a two volume work published in 1785 under the title *Abhandlung über den Kleinen Krieg*—"A Treatise on Guerrilla Warfare." The young Hessian concluded that American officers were far ahead of their British opponents as students of tactics:

I was sometimes astonished when American baggage fell into our hands . . . to see how every wretched knapsack, in which were only a few shirts and a pair of torn breeches, would be filled with such military works as "The Instructions of the King of Prussia to his Generals," Theilke's "Field Engineer," the partisans Jenny and Grand-

maison. . . . This was a true indication that the officers of this army
studied the art of war while in camp, which was not the case with the
opponents of the Americans, whose portmanteaux were rather filled
with bags of hair powder, boxes of sweet-smelling pomatum, cards
(instead of maps), and then often, on top of all, novels or stage plays.[7]

Marshal Saxe's *Rêveries* and Comte de Guibert's *Essai General de
Tactique* appear to have been the treatises which most influenced American
officers, just as those works would later become the hornbooks of French
Revolutionary warfare. Thus it is not surprising that the winter of Valley
Forge should have dated reforms in the command and supply as well
as training of the Continental Army. The privations of the troops, as
everyone realized, had been as much due to lack of an efficient commissary
system as want of provisions. An entry for February 12, 1778, in the
journal of Joseph Joslin, a teamster in the Continental service, is enough
to show the difficulties of transport over miserable roads:

It is Exceeding Stormy Snow North wind and very hard & we heard
they ware a Suffering for hay at Danbury & So we must go we set
out about 10 o'clock and got a littel way and my Cart one wheel Sunk
So far down in a hole that it Over Set the load the Snow was full of
warter & the wheels would Sink into the [mud] and very heavy
Carting indeed and we must waid about knee Deep the Chief of the
way. With 10 Cattel [oxen] we got to Danbury just Dark 7 miles and
then I went to Capt hoyt's & laid in bed it has bin a very tedious day. . . .[8]

When this picture is multiplied to include hundreds of creeping
teams of oxen, some idea may be had of the supply problems confronting
a new army. It is no wonder, considering the lack of system, that the troops
sometimes starved at one post while provisions spoiled in a magazine fifty
miles away. A committee of Congress, appointed to investigate, found
"the property of the Continent dispersed over the whole country; not an
encampment, route of the army, or considerable road but abounds with
wagons, left to the mercy of the weather, and the will of the inhabitants."
The report added that most of the sufferings of Valley Forge might have
been prevented with more efficiency in a branch of the service then without a head. "We find in the course of the campaign, necessary tools and
stores have often been wanting, important and seasonable movements of
the army delayed, in some instances wholly frustrated, and favorable
opportunities lost, through the deficiencies of this department."[9]

Mifflin had done fairly well for a year as quartermaster-general, then

Stephan Moylan took over the thankless job and also resigned. Both Congress and Washington realized that nothing could be accomplished without a complete reorganization, and they prevailed on Nathanael Greene to accept the responsibility. It was a tremendous sacrifice to ask of a soldier with ambitions to distinguish himself on the battlefield. "Who," wrote Greene bitterly to his chief, "ever heard of a quartermaster in history?" In another letter he declared that "there is a great difference between being raised to an office and descending to one, which is my case. . . . I engaged in this business as well out of compassion to your Excellency as from a regard to the public."[10]

Greene consented only on condition that John Cox and Charles Pettit, two Philadelphians with a wide experience in business and administration, be appointed as his assistants. At his request an old Connecticut friend of proved integrity and ability, Colonel Jeremiah Wadsworth, was named commissary-general of purchases. All accepted reluctantly and Congress set a precedent that would have been dangerous with less honest officers by allowing them a commission of 1 per cent on all disbursements in addition to salaries.

For the first time the Continental Army had an efficient supply system, but the miracle was not wrought painlessly. A year later, after the administrative victory had been won, Greene wrote that at the beginning "the line and the staff were at war with each other. The country had been plundered in a way that would now breed a kind of civil war between the staff and the inhabitants."

Another reform in the administration of the Continental Army came from the reorganization of the Board of War. That body, first authorized in the spring of 1776, had been merely a standing committee composed of four or five overworked delegates, all of whom were sitting on a dozen other committees. During the winter of Valley Forge the Board was changed into a council made up of men outside Congress who could devote their full time—three soldiers, Gates, Pickering and Mifflin, serving with a civilian, Richard Peters.

There is some support for accusations that politics entered into the decisions, but warriors have never been averse to that form of strife, despite their protestations. In older armies such activities are less noticeable, though they gain in deadliness from the very lack of noise. Many an officer has found himself robbed of an earned advancement because he made the mistake, twenty years earlier, of marrying the wrong girl or snubbing a fellow subaltern who unexpectedly rose to command. Memories are long and reprisals subtle in long-established armies, while the Continental officers usually came out into the open with their jealousies. Washington himself frankly recognized the necessity for promotions based on qualifications that were not strictly military when he wrote to Heath on March 21, 1781: "But if officers will not see into the political motives by which I am sometimes governed in my appointments, and which the good of the common cause renders indispensably necessary, it is unfortunate; but it cannot, because it ought not, divert me from the practice of a duty, which I think promotive of the interest of the United States, and consistent with the view of that power under which I act."[11]

This is another way of saying that the army of a democracy must always be subject to the prejudices, doubts and enthusiasms of the people as well as purely military considerations. That principle was upheld by the New Yorkers themselves when the shoe pinched their foot. Schuyler's friends clamored for the removal of Putnam, a Connecticut Yankee, as commander of the Hudson River posts, in favor of a New York general, Alexander McDougall. "My reason for making this change," Washington wrote to Putnam on March 16th, "is owing to the prejudice of the people, which, whether well or ill grounded, must be indulged;—and I should think myself wanting in justice to the public and candor towards you, were I to continue you in a command, after I have been almost in direct terms informed, that the people of the State of New York will not render the necessary support and assistance."[12]

McDougall proved to be a much better choice than Putnam, whose career illustrated the dangers of hero worship in a democracy. Americans, as a warlike but not a military people, have exhibited a preference in every conflict of their history for the glory hunter as compared to the tactician. Such a weakness may perhaps be charged to a slight contempt felt by civilians for the scientific side of the profession of arms. But it is chiefly due to a vast impatience to get the job done and return as soon as possible to a state summed up in those nostalgic words "before the war." No better example of this timeless tendency could be found than a letter appearing in the *New Jersey Gazette* in the early spring of 1778, when Washington found it difficult to keep a few thousand men together at Valley Forge:

We have often thought it strange that America, who could bring three or four hundred thousand fighting men into the field, should suffer a paltry banditti to run through her states, and to nestle in her cities. One would be tempted to imagine that we were fond of this destructive war; and yet folly, in her highest delirium, would not wish to protract it. . . . We should change our measures accordingly— bring our thousands into the field—push the enemy with vigor—drive them from our towns—storm them in their strongholds, and never pause until we force them from our shores.[13]

This American spoke for thousands of his countrymen who deplored Washington's "Fabian tactics" at times when the commander in chief dared not risk a decisive battle against superior British numbers. But at least the Continental Army presented a picture of unity and efficiency in the spring of 1778 as compared to a British force corroded by the luxuries of a winter at Philadelphia. Loyalist or British accounts alone are enough to tell a story of unchecked extravagance. "A foreigner held the bank at the game of Pharo," related one of Howe's officers, "by which he made a very considerable fortune; and but too many respectable families in Britain have to lament its baneful effects. Officers who might have rendered honourable service to their country were compelled, by what was termed a bad run of luck, to dispose of their commissions, and return penniless to their friends in Europe. . . . Dissipation had spread through the army, and indolence, and want of subordination, its natural concomitants."[14]

Judge Jones, the loyalist historian of New York, denounced the "harlotry" of British officers who offended strait-laced Tories by flaunting their mistresses in public. At Philadelphia one of these lights of love, wearing a feminine imitation of a British uniform, appeared at a military review in a carriage attended by footmen. While American prisoners ate rats at the Walnut Street jail, enemy commissaries grew rich by robbing them of their rations. In the prison ships of New York Harbor the first words heard every morning were "Rebels, turn out your dead!" The corpses, shallowly buried on the beach, reappeared after every storm to float about the ships within sight of the wretches gasping for air at the portholes.

If Washington could have anticipated the effects on enemy troops of an idle winter in Philadelphia, he might have been seriously tempted to abandon Fort Mifflin without a struggle. On October 22nd, four weeks before the fall of that last obstacle, Sir William Howe had already sent a letter of resignation to Lord Germain. His advice and pleas for reinforcements had so often been ignored, he declared, that he could no longer continue in "this very painful service, wherein I have not the good fortune to enjoy the necessary confidence and support of my superiors."

The war presents no more puzzling enigma than the career of this soldier, whose character seemed to be made up of conflicting traits. The best British tactician of the war, he was likewise the most torpid strategist. A humane man personally, he turned his back on the spectacle of rebel captives dying of starvation and disease. A liberal Whig who liked and admired Americans, he allowed plundering which spared neither Whig nor Tory.

These are only a few of his inconsistencies, but in one respect Howe never changed—he went his own way with a cool indifference to the opinions of his critics. Galloway and the other American loyalists blamed him for most of their troubles, and after his return to England they openly charged that he could have brought the war to an end if he had chosen. His interludes of passivity, they broadly hinted, could be explained by his well-known Whig sympathies rather than his two stock excuses— a lack of adequate reinforcements, and the strength of rebel field fortifications.

Howe, like the other British generals, published a long and dull defense. But his *Narrative*, unlike the other documents, has more the air of a vindication than an apology. He even had the complacency to take credit for saving his army from disaster after the ministers would not send him the reinforcements he asked. Nor did it embarrass him that he should have spent an inactive winter with 20,000 troops in Philadelphia, only a day's march from Washington's ragged and half-starved army, which shrank to as few as 4,000 effectives:

> The entrenched situation of the enemy at Valley Forge, 22 miles from Philadelphia, did not occasion any difficulties so pressing as to justify an attack on that strong post during the severe weather, and though everything was prepared with that intention, I judged it imprudent, until the season should afford a prospect of reaping the advantages that ought to have resulted from that measure; but having good information in the spring that the enemy had strengthened the camp by additional works, and being certain of moving him from thence when the campaign should open, I dropped all thoughts of an attack.[15]

Either Howe had unusually loyal subordinates or they were better qualified to judge the military situation than such angry civilians as Galloway. For the British officers with few exceptions supported their general's assertions that the enemy could seldom be caught at a disadvantage. Thus it may be that Washington's generalship has not been given enough credit in criticisms of Howe which ignore the fact that he had a determined opponent. At any rate the British soldier resumed his seat in Parliament without being much perturbed. He sided with the Whigs who insisted that America could not be conquered—a conviction which he seems to have held all along—and opposed the administration of Lord North. After acquiring new honors, he lived to the age of eighty-five as an interested observer of America's "second war for independence" just before his death in 1814.

When the acceptance of Howe's resignation became known, the devotion of his subordinates found expression in one of the most bizarre spectacles ever seen on American soil—the famous Meschianza of May 18, 1778. This costly extravaganza was more than an entertainment; it was a slap at British army factions which had censured Howe for his supposed lapses in not supporting Burgoyne, Clinton and Cornwallis at various times.[16]

The wealthy young officers at Philadelphia intended the Meschianza, or Medley, to be a Babylonian show that would become the talk of London. Captain John André, as *arbiter elegantiae*, designed invitation cards with General Howe's crest and a view of the sun setting over the western sea. Any unhappy implications were thought to be saved by a Latin motto suggesting that the sun would rise again with even more dazzling effulgence.

The fete began on the river with a grand regatta of barges decorated with banners and pennants. While the bands played martial music and the men-of-war thundered salutes, the galleys proceeded to the Wharton country place south of the city. There a mock tournament took place between the knights of the Blended Rose and Burning Mountain. Hard-bitten sergeants attended as pages or esquires dressed in red and white silk. In the background, surrounded by a forest of lances and mottoes, the pavilions were filled with Tory girls wearing gold, blue and scarlet gowns designed by André.

A lavish Oriental touch was also provided, at the risk of mixing atmospheres, by attiring some of the ladies in rich Turkish costumes. And even the sergeants acting as pages had no worse ordeal than the marines from the warships who appeared in blackface as Nubian slaves with silver collars around their necks. These unfortunates had been drilled to kneel at the approach of General Howe and bend their heads to the ground in token of submission to the conqueror.

After the tournament the knights of the Blended Rose and Burning Mountain escorted their Guineveres and Fatimas to the banquet through a series of triumphal cardboard arches and columns of imitation marble. Mountains of artificial flowers and miles of pale blue and rose pink ribbon decorated a supper room 210 feet long by 40 feet wide and 22 feet high. Fifty-six large mirrors reflected the hundreds of candles, the flaming hearts and the gold and silver shields. At ten o'clock, following the feast, the company filed outdoors again to witness fireworks which André described as a *feu d'artifice* or "magnificent bouquet of rockets."[17] The climax of this exhibition came with an allegorical set piece representing Fame, wearing a halo of stars about her brow, saluting the conquering hero Howe with fiery words blown from a trumpet, "Thy laurels shall never fade."

The amount of thought, effort, money and gunpowder lavished on the extravaganza would have enabled the British army to take the field for a few days. But such reflections did not disturb the officers who returned to the supper room to dance until dawn. These wealthy young men, paradoxically, gave the effect of coming from a country so new that taste and tradition had not yet had time to discipline a society founded on recent and ostentatious riches. Americans might more readily have been mistaken by a foreigner for the older and more settled branch of the English-speaking peoples. This opinion would not have been altogether illusory, for the England of George III actually was a booming new plutocracy as compared to the snug little rural and seafaring England of the past. Already the strident cries of the infant Machine Age could be heard as the treasure of India poured into the seat of Empire. Manufactured goods went out to an eager world in ships which completed the industrial cycle by bringing home the raw products. It was an age for the creating of fortunes rather than traditions, and many officers of Howe's army lived on such a swaggering scale that their army pay hardly sufficed to cover their wine bill.

America was still an agricultural and trading country, like the England of old. Family counted for more than wealth among planters and landed proprietors who often represented the fourth or fifth generation on the same estate, and the merchants of the small cities preferred comfort to display or extravagance. The Meschianza struck such people as a travesty rather than pageant, and the Tories were loudest of all at condemning its excesses.

Their criticisms had less effect on British ears than the demonstration by Captain Allan McLane. This young Philadelphia aristocrat and his colleague John Lacey led troops of rebel dragoons known as market stoppers because of their success at seizing provisions intended for the enemy

During the winter of Valley Forge some large supply trains were captured under the noses of Howe's forces and diverted to the use of Washington's army. On the morning of May 19th, however, McLane's men had other fish to fry. At dawn, just as the Meschianza was breaking up, they feigned an attack in force on the British lines by scattering iron pots filled with gunpowder while galloping past.

The Philadelphia aristocrat had already devoted his entire personal fortune of £115,000 to equipping and paying his troops. And on this occasion McLane's zeal doubtless owed to the fact that girls with whom he had danced before the war were the guests of redcoats. These young ladies soon found themselves without escorts as the knights of the Blended Rose and Burning Mountain hastened to the defense. The lines seemed to be threatened at a dozen points, judging by the explosions of the time bombs, and it added to the confusion when no attackers were to be seen.

This rebel taunt may have goaded the British army at Philadelphia into attempting something more warlike than mock tournaments. For the very next day Howe launched an attack that came near to destroying a large American detachment.

It has always been something of a mystery why Washington sent Lafayette with 2,200 picked troops to put the Schuylkill behind him and advance within twelve miles of the British lines. His orders called for a reconnaissance in force to ascertain whether the redcoats really were preparing to evacuate Philadelphia. But that intelligence could better have been gained from spies, and it appears more likely that the rebel commander wished to indulge a volunteer with important connections in his own country. The ardent Frenchman owed his major general's rank to Washington's personal fondness as well as political reasons, but he gave proof on this occasion of genuine military ability. No fault could have been found with his dispositions as he took a strong position on Barren Hill after sending out pickets and patrols in all directions to keep a careful watch.

Howe had excellent intelligence, as usual, and he struck with a swiftness and secrecy that might have taken the most cautious adversary unawares. The intended victim did not suspect his peril until he found himself nearly surrounded at dawn on the 20th—Howe and Clinton advancing from Philadelphia to envelop both wings, while Grant swept around to the rear with 7,000 troops to cut off all retreat. Lafayette kept his head with a coolness that might have done credit to a veteran of twice his years. His air of confidence reassured soldiers who were showing the first signs of panic. Only a single route of escape remained as he led the way to a ford across the Schuylkill after posting false columns in the woods to deceive Grant. While that British general took time for reconnaissance, the whole rebel force slipped away to safety with only a few casualties.

The Americans at Valley Forge rejoiced as if they had won a victory instead of narrowly avoiding a disaster. It really was a victory of the new drill, for everyone realized that Steuben's lessons deserved a great deal of the credit. In the past the rebels had marched in an "Indian file" so extended that the head of a column ran the risk of being overwhelmed before the tail got into action. This shortcoming alone goes far toward explaining the defeats at Long Island and the Brandywine, when green troops found it a problem to change front against flank attacks. Under the old system, with all its confusion and delays, hundreds of rebels would doubtless have been trapped at Barren Hill. As it proved, they owed their salvation to a swift retreat of compact platoon columns which made their way over the river without the customary disorder and straggling.

The early summer of 1778 dates a peak of American confidence never again attained with quite the same exhilaration. Final victory seemed almost within sight of leaders who did not dream that the longer and harder part of the conflict still awaited. The rumors of British withdrawal from Philadelphia could not be doubted after it became known that the French were sending a fleet powerful enough to hold the balance of sea power in American waters. It was only a question of whether Admiral Howe could withdraw his inferior squadron in time to save it from being bottled up in the Delaware. And even if he made his escape, General Howe's successor Clinton would be left with the unenviable prospect of retreating by land to New York with a burdened column exposed to attack by Washington.

These were not the only possibilities of a major British disaster. The force at New York might be hemmed in by a combined land and sea operation and starved into surrender. Another large enemy detachment in Rhode Island ran a similar risk. Every prospect seemed to favor Americans who had their turn at naval superiority for the first time in the war.

It might have been wished that leisurely drills had not delayed Comte d'Estaing's fleet for nearly three months in its crossing of the Atlantic, but this factor did not seem serious at the time. Certainly the new American allies had done their best to seize an early advantage. France had an investment of 280,000,000 francs in capital and 30,000,000 francs in annual income to protect in her West Indies possessions, not to mention the desirability of aiding the former colonies of her hereditary foe to gain their independence. These were the considerations which influenced the court of Louis XVI, though many of his young nobles shared Lafayette's enthusiasm for republican ideals. Choiseul had built up a navy worthy of British respect, and the rebels also had fond hopes of French loans and land reinforcements at an early date. It would never have occurred to them in the summer of 1778 that they must make the best of their own waning resources for three more years before decisive help of any sort could be expected from abroad.

A few British leaders had been brought by this time to a public admission of defeat. Thomas Pownall spoke for a stubborn Whig minority in Parliament when he declared during the debates of March 21, 1778: "We know that the Americans are and must be independent; and yet we will not treat them as such. If government itself retains the least idea of sovereignty, it has already gone too far for that; if it entertains the least hope of peace, it has not gone far enough; and every step we shall take to put the Americans back from independency, will convince them the more of the necessity of going forward."[18]

Some of America's old friends, on the other hand, had been alienated by the French alliance. These Britons raged that the rebels could now expect to be treated as foreign foes instead of erring brethren, and American loyalists called for the most savage reprisals. The civil war reached a new stage of bitterness when Congress "earnestly recommended to the several states, as soon as may be, to confiscate and make use of all the real and personal property therein, of such of their inhabitants and other persons who have forfeited the same. . . ."[19] This was the final and irrevocable break between Americans of opposing political beliefs. Conversion rather than coercion had been the policy of the rebels up to this time, even though some of the earliest seizures of property had been decreed at their expense in New York during the autumn of 1776. But there could be no retreat from a national confiscation measure which must inevitably drive borderline Tories into one camp or another. Joseph Galloway and scores of other Pennsylvania loyalists chose exile in England after the evacuation of Philadelphia, and those who stayed behind were implacable in their cries for vengeance.

Washington could still write from Valley Forge on March 1st to his old neighbor Bryan Fairfax, "The friendship, which I ever professed and felt for you, met with no diminution from the difference in our political sentiments." But in the same letter he denounced British offers of conciliation as an attempt "to poison and disaffect the minds of those, who wish for peace, and create feuds and dissensions among ourselves. In a word, having less dependence now in their arms than their arts, they are practicing such low and dirty tricks, that men of sentiment and honor must blush at their villainy."[20]

Other patriots, almost without exception, were in perfect agreement with him when the British commissioners finally reached Philadelphia on June 4th with powers to offer the terms of the Conciliatory Acts, subject to the approval of Parliament. The instructions of the three envoys were so liberal as to allow practically every reform the colonists had sought in 1775, plus the prospect of the states electing their own executives and continuing to have a central Congress within the Empire. But it was three years too late for the offer which the colonies would eagerly have accepted at the beginning of hostilities. For Congress had not erred in April when it inferred that Great Britain had no intention of granting either of the two conditions necessary to a peace discussion. So strong were the suspicions of enemy trickery that the assembly hesitated at first to read the papers of the commissioners. Then on June 13th the delegates voted unanimously against any consideration of peace until "the king of Great Britain shall demonstrate a sincere disposition for that purpose. The only solid proof of this disposition will be, an explicit acknowledgment of the independence of these states, or the withdrawing his fleets and armies."[21]

The commissioners had no such powers, and they failed to make any impression on American leaders with hints of bribery. At last, just before leaving the country in October, they dropped the olive branch and issued a proclamation to the effect that the mild chastisement of the past would be replaced by a merciless new warfare of destruction.

The rebels ignored their existence. Having decided to fight instead of bargain for their independence, they went into action as soon as Clinton evacuated Philadelphia. Washington moved out from Valley Forge and took a parallel route through New Jersey. This time he had an equality in numbers, and American hopes of a decisive victory were never more high.

Chapter 17

The Crown of Nettles

THE French declaration of war compelled the British to send troops to the West Indies and other threatened outposts of Empire, so that the forces in America were spread dangerously thin when Clinton evacuated Philadelphia on June 18, 1778. His own numbers did not exceed the 11,000 of the rebel army which marched out from Valley Forge. The British difficulties were increased, moreover, by the necessity of taking most of their supplies; and hundreds of loyalist refugees burdened a column strung out for ten miles along the road.

It would appear that a better opportunity for attack could not have been asked, and yet Washington's generals hesitated. At two councils of war a majority voted against a battle on the grounds that more could be accomplished at less risk by harassing the enemy. The prime mover in urging this policy was Charles Lee, whose recent exchange then appeared to Americans to be one of their greatest blessings. Generals were customarily paroled or held in a comfortable captivity until they could be bartered for a foeman of equal military stature or his equivalent in small fry. Thus a lieutenant general such as Burgoyne, who had been allowed to return to England on a plea of illness, would eventually have the trading value of 1,040 privates, however flattering that estimate might be to his talents. Lee's services had been regained by the exchange of General Richard Prescott, whom the rebels had come to regard as a negotiable security after capturing him a second time. Their elation over the bargain might have been dampened if they had suspected that Lee had offered the enemy a detailed plan for the conquest of America.

This fact, which did not come to light until three generations later, has often been accepted as evidence of treason. Present-day historians, however, are inclined to take the more charitable view that the former

British officer can hardly be considered mentally responsible. Undoubtedly he was an eccentric and egomaniac who had a scheme for every occasion. The invaders, he assured the Howes in the spring of 1777, had it within their power to end the war by capturing Congress wholesale and occupying Maryland and Virginia. There is no indication that the British author-

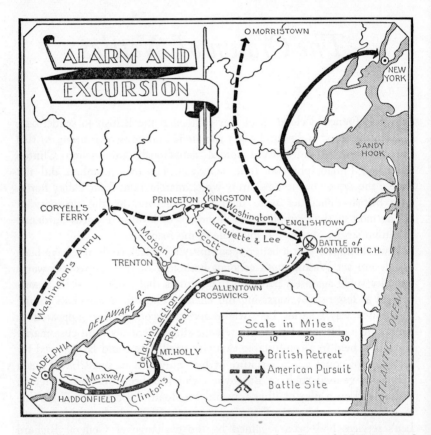

ities paid much attention to this secret letter, for General Howe carried out his own ideas in spite of Lee's warning that "the taking possession of Philadelphia will not have any decisive consequences."[1]

The Americans were more open to conviction after Lee's arrival at Valley Forge in May, 1778. He immediately questioned Steuben's training methods and declared that it would be courting disaster to meet the enemy in the field. Far from advocating an attack on Clinton in New

Jersey, he urged that the rebels themselves ought to build "a bridge of gold" for his safe passage to New York. Lee's professional experience and persuasiveness had their weight with most of the officers at the two councils of war. Hamilton represented a disgusted minority when he grumbled that the decision "would have done honor to the most honorable society of midwives, and to them only."

There might have been no battle if the commander in chief had not used the authority conferred on him by Congress when his army neared Kingston, within striking distance of the foe. First he sent out a detachment of 1,200 men, composed of Morgan's riflemen and General Maxwell's New Jersey militiamen, to prey upon the enemy's right flank. On June 25th Washington committed himself further by ordering an advance corps of about 4,000 picked troops to make a more direct challenge. The command went to Lafayette after Lee declined. Later that eccentric general changed his mind and prevailed on the young Frenchman to accept a secondary position. Washington had meanwhile become more convinced of the desirability of action.

At daybreak on the 28th the British were encamped near Monmouth Courthouse with the rear of their unwieldy column half enveloped. Clinton sent Knyphausen and the Germans ahead with the baggage train and followed with his best troops in readiness for a contest. If his opponents had been equally resolute, the story of the day might have had a different ending. For all the indications were unfavorable to a retreating army overloaded with equipment and exhausted with summer heat which had already caused several deaths on the march. Never did the insolent confidence of the redcoats seem less justified or more admirable, for it was practically the only advantage they had over opponents who held all the strategic trumps.

The American plan, if such it may be called, represented a vague compromise between Washington's attack and Lee's golden bridge. There is no written evidence of any design for a co-ordinated effort aiming at crippling or destroying a vulnerable enemy. Washington was perhaps influenced by the divided opinion of his generals, and he may also have recalled that a third of his troops were recent recruits with only a few days' training. At any rate, he approached the greatest opportunity of his military career with that indecisiveness which has been an occupational disease of other generals. And since half measures in war are often worse than none at all, it is not remarkable that the rebels won only half a victory.

The advance guard was entrusted to the general most opposed to battle in the first place, and Lee's orders gave him the option of declining the attack if "there should be very powerful reasons to the contrary." He compromised in his turn by committing himself only to an attempt to check the redcoats with Wayne's brigade while he worked around their flank with the rest of his force. Then upon becoming convinced that the main British body was not far behind, he sanctioned a retreat which several regiments had already begun as a result of a mistake. A swamp in his rear had to be passed over a single road before he found high ground on the other side which seemed suitable for defense.

Washington arrived on the scene with his main army at this moment. He noticed the stragglers first of all and demanded an explanation of the apparent rout. Lee's reply may not have been tactful, for the commander in chief flew into a rage. "Yes, sir, he swore on that day till the leaves shook on the trees, charming, delightfully," recalled General Scott, who had a reputation of his own for profanity. "Never have I enjoyed such swearing before or since. Sir, on that memorable day he swore like an angel from Heaven."[2]

British descriptions of troop movements make it evident that Lee had not erred in supposing that he was retiring from the enemy's main force. But it was no moment for weighing fine points of justice, and Washington took personal charge of forming a line of battle. Galloping his horse back and forth while giving orders, he made a splendid figure of a soldier on that hot Sunday morning. All doubts had vanished from his mind, and he showed a determination that might have been more effective if it had stiffened his plans a few days earlier.

After this awkward beginning, the battle entered its second phase when the British approached. Although Clinton had every reason to take a cautious defensive, he attacked with a boldness that does more credit to his courage than his tactics. All accounts of the ensuing movements are confused for the simple reason that the action itself was confused. There were, more accurately, several actions fought without much direction on either side. The first charges of the British infantry and light horse met with costly repulses. Then Clinton tried without success to turn both rebel flanks. The redcoats in their heavy woolen uniforms staggered with heat exhaustion and some of them died of sunstroke. But they never quit fighting, and a regiment of the Guards lost half its numbers in an attack on Wayne's brigade.

This was the high point of the day for the Continentals, who proved that they could hold their own with the bayonet as well as musket against the finest regulars of the British army. The Guards did not retire until they were punished beyond endurance, but the victory went to Pennsylvanians with their faces blackened from biting off cartridges. Steuben's pupils also demonstrated at both ends of the line that they could change position and form a new front to meet a flank attack.

Washington wanted to continue the battle after Clinton retreated to a strong position with his wings protected by swamps and woods. But dusk put an end to the day's series of combats, and the rebels remained in line with the expectation of renewing the struggle in the morning. At daybreak, however, they discovered that Clinton had slipped away in the darkness and caught up with his baggage train.

As an American victory, Monmouth is on a par with the British successes at Brandywine and Long Island. The most that can be said for it is that the rebels inflicted far more than their own casualties of 222 killed, wounded and missing. Clinton reported total losses of only 358, but there is good reason to doubt this figure. Washington wrote to Congress that his burial parties found 249 enemy dead on the field in addition to the fresh graves of men buried by the British.[3] This would indicate at least two or three times as many wounded plus about a hundred prisoners after stragglers were rounded up the next day.

Clinton's losses from desertion were also heavier than he cared to admit. On July 4th Arnold made an official return of 576 enemy soldiers who had reached Philadelphia by that date—136 redcoats and 440 Germans. This number had grown to well over 600 within the next four days, and Washington may not have been far from the truth when he estimated that the retreat had cost the enemy 2,000 men from all causes.

Even so, Clinton had good reason to take pride in saving his army from a greater disaster. It would seem a little farfetched to compare his achievement with Xenophon's retreat, but Stedman was justified in commenting that "the British general risked, and even courted an action, while the American suffered the important occasion to pass by, when he might have terminated the war by one great and decisive effort."[4]

If inexperienced rebel troops had sometimes failed their officers in the past, the opposite held true at Monmouth. A few of the units, such as Wayne's brigade, had more than their share of the fighting, while others scarcely got into action at all. No use was made of the best American regiment of the war and the colonel whose tactics shone at Saratoga, for

Morgan's riflemen were left dangling without orders on the British right flank.

Luck came to the rescue of valor when Clinton saved his army by the narrow margin of five days. Avoiding the Raritan River and its marshes, he took the short cut to Sandy Hook, where he had arranged to meet the British squadron escaping from the Delaware. There were many chances for a fatal delay, but Admiral Howe kept the appointment on June 29th and Clinton arrived the following day. It took a week to transport the troops, baggage and artillery by water, and all were safe in New York on July 6th.

On the 9th, ending a voyage of 88 days, the French fleet reached the mouth of Delaware Bay. After learning that Howe had eluded him, Comte d'Estaing made for Sandy Hook. There on the 11th the French admiral discovered that he had just missed an opportunity to attack the enemy army and squadron in the confusion of embarkation.

Among the indirect results of Monmouth, the Americans settled some of the disputes about the status of the foreign officers who had aroused so many jealousies. Lee might better have justified his conduct by letting his tactics plead for themselves, but he wrote Washington a disrespectful letter which made a court-martial necessary. Later he added to the provocation by lobbying for himself at Philadelphia, where his injudicious remarks alienated any friends he had left in Congress. Colonel John Laurens challenged him to a duel for alleged insults to Washington, but Lee got off with a slight wound and more damage to his reputation. Congress suspended him on the strength of the court-martial findings, and an insolent letter of protest left the assembly no choice but to dismiss him from the army altogether. His strange behavior during the remaining few years of his life confirms the theory of insanity; for he continued to write incoherent letters and pamphlets until his death in a shabby Philadelphia waterfront inn in 1782.

Conway, who had been equally annoying as a donor of unwanted advice, made his exit from the stage of Revolutionary history when Congress accepted his petulant resignation. He could no more keep a discreet silence than Lee, and on July 4th he was called to account with pistols at ten paces by the most deadly duelist of the Continental Army, General John Cadwalader. A ball plowed through Conway's neck and jaw, and he believed himself to be on his deathbed when he wrote a pathetic letter of apology to Washington. After his recovery the unfortunate Irishman left the country and ended his career with distinction in the French army.

Both Conway and Lee had been more often guilty of follies than villainies. But their examples served to warn other foreign volunteers, and those who remained in the service gave American officers much less cause for resentment. Two of them, Count Pulaski of Poland and Colonel Armand of France, raised "legions" of their own. These semi-independent forces, composed both of infantry and light horse, attracted a motley assortment of military adventurers, including British and German deserters. Some of the other aliens earned the affection as well as respect of American troops. Steuben and Lafayette were the most popular of all, and after the war many a boy born in a frontier log cabin began life with the splendid given name of Baron or Marquis.

Although Clinton had escaped destruction for the moment, the presence of the French fleet gave Washington a choice between two further opportunities to plan another Saratoga at the expense of a British army. And his letter of July 17th to General Sullivan indicates that he considered both prospects:

> The design of this fleet is to co-operate with the American armies in the execution of any plans, which shall be deemed most advancive of our mutual Interests, against the common Enemy. No particular plan is yet adopted, but two seem to present themselves; either an attack upon New York, or Rhode Island. Should the first be found practicable, our forces are very well disposed for the purpose; but, should the latter be deemed the most eligible, some previous preparations must be made.[5]

Sullivan was directed to strengthen his force in Rhode Island with 5,000 militia to be recruited immediately from the New England states. The commander in chief also ordered him to employ pilots familiar with the waters around Newport and establish a chain of express stations for quick communications with New York.

Comte d'Estaing and Washington had already exchanged letters which found the Virginia planter as fluent in the stately language of diplomacy as the French courtier. John Laurens, Hamilton and Fleury were sent as French-speaking officers to secure pilots for d'Estaing, who expressed enthusiasm for the proposed attack on New York. The rebel army co-operated by beginning its crossing of the Hudson on July 17th.

Three days later Washington encamped at White Plains with 13,000 troops in position to close in from the land side against a British force which he estimated at 14,000.

The situation of the beleaguered army was serious. Not only had most of its supplies from the countryside been cut off; but at a time when stores in the city were low, the annual provision fleet from Ireland would be exposed to capture. Admiral Howe found himself in one of the tightest spots of his career, but he did not intend to let his ships be attacked in the harbor like sitting ducks. Moving boldly out to meet the danger, he stationed the squadron just inside the channel leading past Sandy Hook. His largest vessels mounted 64 guns, while the twelve French ships of the line included one of 90, one of 80 and six of 74 guns. But if Howe was outweighed in ships, guns and crews, he had the advantage of a land battery on Sandy Hook; and his squadron could pour at least two broadsides into the French ships, coming bows on, before the enemy would be able to retaliate.

D'Estaing made inquiries for several days about the depth of the channel, then notified Washington on July 19th that he had given up the attempt. "It was the Count's first wish to enter at Sandy hook," Washington reported to Congress, "in order to possess himself of, or to destroy if possible, the whole of the British fleet lying in the bay of New York. . . ." Unfortunately, added the American general, "the water, from the experiments made, was too shallow at the entrance to admit his large ships; or, if they could be got in, it appeared that it would not be without a great deal of difficulty and risk."[6]

American pilots were said to have warned the French captains that there was only 23 feet of water on the bar at high tide. This excuse has been called a subterfuge by the American naval historian Mahan, who cited a letter written by Admiral Arbuthnot to the effect that the channel had a depth of 30 feet during the high tides each month. Howe's preparations for defense make it evident, however, that he did not count on shoal waters for protection. On July 22nd the combination of a spring tide and northeast wind actually did provide 30 feet, and the French admiral still declined. After working up to windward with apparent resolution, he abandoned the attempt and sailed away in a southerly direction. Mahan concluded that d'Estaing "probably reasoned that the French had nothing to gain by the fall of New York, which might have led to peace between America and England, and left the latter free to turn all her power against his own country. Less than that would have been enough to decide his wavering mind as to risking his fleet over the bar."[7]

Comte d'Estaing protested too much to be convincing in a letter to Congress of August 26th: "The pilots procured by Colonels Laurens and Hamilton destroyed all illusion. . . . I offered in vain a reward of fifty thousand crowns to any one, who would promise success. All refused, and the particular soundings which I caused to be taken myself, too well demonstrated, that they were right."[8]

At the outbreak of the war Louis XVI, speaking through his ministers, had ordered the admirals to "attack with the greatest vigor and defend themselves, on all occasions, to the last extremity." It was in line with French naval policy of the past two centuries, however, that before a single frigate left port these bold words were qualified with secret instructions imposing caution.

D'Estaing cannot be fairly criticized for placing the interests of his own country before those of America at Sandy Hook. There is less to be said in defense of an 88-day, fair-weather crossing of the Atlantic which could have been made in half the time if the French admiral had not stopped so often for drills.

He flew to the opposite extreme after deciding to give up the attempt on New York, and his haste made for wasteful strategy. For his sails were barely out of sight when the crippled ships of Admiral Byron's squadron began limping into port, shattered and dismasted. They had been dispersed by a storm on the way to reinforce Howe, and all would have fallen an easy prey to the French admiral if he had waited. He might also have stood a good chance of capturing the great provision fleet from Ireland, which arrived safely soon afterwards to relieve the supply problems of the anxious garrison.

Washington's reports to Congress make it plain that his ally sailed away to Rhode Island the day before Sullivan received the letter written on the 17th, giving him his first notification. It remained for him to request the New England governors to call out their militia, so that d'Estaing could only arrive too soon to be of any help. The main American army left behind at White Plains was not strong enough to risk an attack on British fortified positions, and Washington commented in a letter of August 20th, "It is not a little pleasing, nor less wonderful to contemplate, that after two years' manoeuvring and undergoing the strangest vicissitudes . . . both armies are now brought back to the very point they set

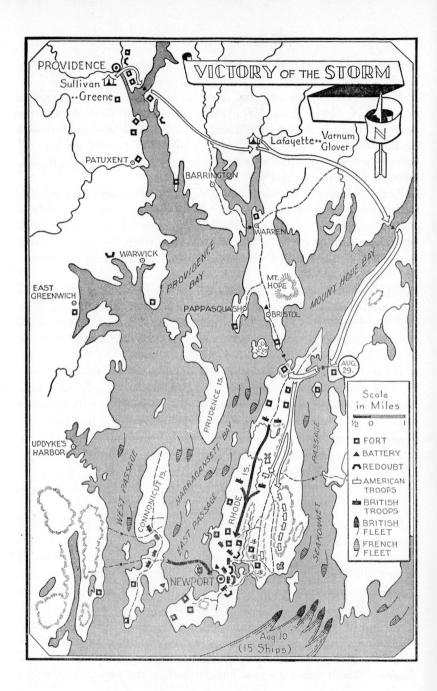

VICTORY of the STORM

N

PROVIDENCE
Sullivan
··Greene

PATUXENT

BARRINGTON

Lafayette·· Varnum
Glover

WARREN

WARWICK

PROVIDENCE
BAY

MT.
HOPE

MOUNT HOPE BAY

EAST
GREENWICH

PAPPASQUASH
○BRISTOL

PRUDENCE IS.

MOUNT
HOPE
IS.

AUG.
29.

UPDYKE'S
HARBOR

WEST PASSAGE

CONNONICUT IS.

NARRAGANSETT BAY

EAST PASSAGE

RHODE IS.

SEAKONNET
PASSAGE

Scale
in Miles
½ 0   1

▢ FORT
▲ BATTERY
⌐ REDOUBT
⌂ AMERICAN
  TROOPS
▰ BRITISH
  TROOPS
◣ BRITISH
  FLEET
◢ FRENCH
  FLEET

NEWPORT

Aug. 10
(15 Ships)

out from, and that which was the offending party in the beginning, is now reduced to the use of the spade and pickaxe for defense."[9]

Never did a general show more enthusiasm than Sullivan after receiving Washington's message of July 17th, which reached him six days later. Without delay he requested the New England governors to call out their militia; and he made such a vigorous search for supplies that Heath complained of the "raiding" of Massachusetts stores.

Fate had been most unkind so far to one of the most ambitious generals of the Continental Army. But this time Washington had given him a command of such exciting possibilities that Greene wrote from White Plains: "You are the most happy man in the world. What a child of fortune! The expedition going against Newport cannot, I think, fail of success."[10]

Washington was never the commander to interfere with his generals at long distance, and Sullivan had a free rein in organizing his campaign. Greene, chafing at the inactivity of his quartermaster's duties, was given a holiday by being ordered to Rhode Island with 2,000 Continentals. His knowledge of local conditions made him a good choice, and Lafayette was sent for political reasons as a liaison officer to aid in conferences between allies.

The commander in chief specified that both officers were to share the command of a division as subordinates to Sullivan. He displayed so much energy during the first four days that he could report to Washington on the 27th: "I have the pleasure to inform you that we have already Collected a magazine amply Sufficient for all possible demands. . . . My numbers I trust will be Sufficient for the purpose. . . . I have now & I trust Shall have as many Boats as I could wish."[11]

The French fleet arrived on the 29th. There was little that d'Estaing could do except to blockade British forces which withdrew all detachments during the following week to the entrenched camp at Newport.

August 10th was set as the date of an American attack to be aided by 4,000 troops attached to the French fleet. Sullivan crossed from Tiverton to occupy the north end of Rhode Island on the 8th, and the French forced the middle and eastern passages in preparation for a landing.

Relations between the allies up to this time had been good—perhaps a little too good. Some fulsome compliments were exchanged, but d'Estaing topped them all when he wrote to Sullivan on the 3rd: "I fear that you left on my table a plan, which I have had the presumption to keep, because anything made by yourself is too precious a keepsake to be allowed to slip through one's fingers. As I do not wish, however, to make myself entirely guilty, and as you may need it, I send you a copy. I beg you, Sir, to be kind enough to accept some pineapples and two barrels of fresh lemons that Colonel Wall kindly offers to have forwarded to you at the earliest possible moment."[12]

Such pleasantries would soon be faded and melancholy memories. For the arrival of Lord Howe's fleet on August 9th upset the plans for a combined Franco-American attack the next day and nearly caused an outright feud between the allies.

The French admiral held that he had little choice but to give up the attempt on Newport and fight at sea in defense of his own fleet. "Our ships," he explained in a letter to Congress, "would shortly have been battered . . . by a deliberate cannonade from the land, and we should in a short time have had to combat a squadron well protected, and provided with ketches, fire-ships, and all the means which ensure the greatest superiority over ships, that are altogether destitute of them, and which are forced to engage at anchor, and between two shores in such an unequal combat."[13]

The Americans argued with equal plausibility that d'Estaing needed only to defend the mouth of the harbor against a weaker adversary exposed to the fire of Allied shore guns. If he would but curb his impatience, they insisted, he had it within his power to defeat Howe's object by helping to wipe out an enemy garrison which could not withstand either a storm or siege.

D'Estaing had the last word. And on the 10th he took his troops on board again and stood out to sea. Although Howe had more ships after repairing the storm-tossed vessels of Byron's squadron, he still had only about two-thirds of his opponent's strength in guns and weight of shot. For twenty-four hours the two fleets maneuvered for an advantage. Then both were dispersed on August 12th by a gale of hurricane fury. The 90-gun French flagship *Languedoc* lost her rudder and all her masts, and the *Tonnant* had only a single mast left standing. They were attacked the next day by two British 50-gun ships which had escaped without much damage, but the combat ended indecisively. D'Estaing limped back to Newport on the 20th with all his ships save one, which put into Boston. Even so, he was in better shape than Howe, who had some of his vessels driven as far south as Virginia. The British admiral returned to New

York to refit, leaving Rhode Island to his adversary. The Americans supposed that d'Estaing would renew the attack; and it came as a crushing blow when he announced that his fleet would sail to Boston for refitting.

The land forces of both sides had been hard hit by the storm. At Butts Hill the rebels lost men and horses by drowning, and their powder was so drenched that an attack would have found them helpless. The enemy could not have been in any better situation, for Mackenzie noted in his diary on the 13th: "Most of the British tents blown down and torn to rags . . . everything belonging to the men being perfectly soaked with the rain." The next day five corpses of French seamen drifted to shore along with wreckage, and the beleaguered army had dreams of being relieved when ships were sighted on the 20th. "At first we had great expectations of their being part of Lord Howe's fleet, and were not without hopes of his having engaged and defeated the French Fleet, but about 2 o'clock it was plainly discovered that they were French, and were a good deal damaged." Even at this moment of disappointment, British faith in Black Dick Howe is shown by the next sentence, "No idea is entertained that our fleet has been beaten, even if there has been an action."[14]

The redcoats could never have believed that it would be their fabulous good fortune within the next few hours to be reprieved from disaster by Comte d'Estaing himself. In spite of American protests, he sustained the decision of his captains that the safety of the fleet depended on sailing immediately to Boston for refitting. This announcement stunned Americans who had so far recovered from the storm as to advance their lines two miles nearer to Newport. It did no good to remind the French admiral that the New England militia had been called out because of his promise to take part with the warships. Nor could d'Estaing be moved by the almost certain prospect of capturing or destroying General Robert Pigot's whole army, amounting to 6,679 officers and men in British returns of August 10th. The reaction of his American allies is evident from a letter written by Greene to Charles Pettit:

> I only have time to tell you the devil has got into the fleet; they are about to desert us, and go round to Boston. The British garrison would be all our own in a few days if the fleet would but only co-operate with us; but alas they will not. They have got a little shattered by the late storm, and are apprehensive a junction of Byron's and Howe's fleets may prove their ruin. They are, therefore, determined

to quit us immediately. I am afraid our expedition is now at an end. . . .
To evacuate the Island is death; to stay may be ruin."[15]

In a last desperate effort to save the campaign, Greene and Lafayette
went by boat to the *Languedoc*, hoping to persuade the French captains
to change their minds. D'Estaing, as a soldier and lieutenant general, was
believed to be thwarted by the prejudice of his sea officers—the victim
of a pernicious French system in which admirals were chosen on a basis
of noble birth rather than naval experience. He listened politely on his
flagship to Lafayette and called a second council which reaffirmed the
decision.

Before the fleet weighed anchor, the American officers drew up a final
protest on August 22nd which Lafayette refused to sign. This statement
presented nine convincing reasons why the French ran no grave danger
if they refitted at Newport while continuing the campaign. Unfortunately,
the petition ended with an outrageous breach of international courtesies:
"We therefore . . . do in the most solemn manner protest against the
measure as derogatory to the honor of France, contrary to the intentions
of His Most Christian Majesty and the interest of his nation, and
destructive in the highest degree to the welfare of the United States
of America, and highly injurious to the alliance formed between the two
nations."[16]

It was hardly the part of American officers to point out d'Estaing's duty
to him, and he declared that "this paper imposed upon the commander
of the king's squadron the painful but necessary law of profound silence."
Sullivan was so heartbroken that he let his grief and rage get the better
of his discretion. On August 24th, as the French sails disappeared over
the horizon, his public orders contained the injudicious sentence, "The
General yet hopes the event will prove America able to procure that by
her own arms, which her allies refuse to assist in obtaining."[17] Lafayette
prevailed on him to correct the unfortunate impression made on French
officers, and Sullivan published an awkward explanation two days later
which only widened the breach.

At this date he had 8,974 troops, most of them inexperienced volunteers,
but the New England militia forces were going home at the rate of
hundreds a day. On the 28th Sullivan's last hope of victory vanished when
a message from Washington informed him that Lord Howe had put to
sea again, probably with British reinforcements for Rhode Island—a
surmise which proved to be correct. That night the Americans retreated

from the Newport vicinity to the north end of the island in preparation for evacuation. The redcoats followed and a two-hour combat took place the next day—the only action of the campaign—when the rebels turned on their pursuers at Quaker Hill to get the better of a hard-fought little engagement. Their losses were 211 killed, wounded and missing as compared to a British total of about 300 casualties.

Sullivan showed good generalship in the retirement. While working parties pretended to throw up defenses in front, the bulk of the army withdrew in the darkness of August 30th to the mainland at Bristol and Howland. General Glover, a veteran of such tight squeezes, took charge of the boats. "Before twelve o'clock," Sullivan reported to Congress, "the main army had crossed with the Stores and Baggage. . . . Not a Man was left behind, nor the smallest Article lost. . . . The Event had prov'd how timely my Retreat took place—as One hundred Sail of the Enemys Ships arrived in the Harbour the Morning after the Retreat. . . ."[18]

Both Washington and Congress made every effort to silence criticisms of their allies. "It would be in a great Degree impolitick at this Juncture to suffer an Odium to be cast on the Count D'Estaing," Samuel Adams wrote to James Warren on September 12th. "If there could be a disposition to do it, I am perswaded Men of Discretion and Influence will check it."[19]

Three days later a French officer was killed while trying to quiet an affray between a Boston mob and sailors from d'Estaing's ships. The very next morning the Massachusetts General Assembly voted that a monument be erected in his memory, while Warren and other leaders paid public tributes. The incident actually brought the allies closer together in sympathy, and the French officers were handsomely entertained before sailing away to the West Indies on November 3rd. Admiral Byron had appeared off the harbor on the first day of the month, but another storm disabled the squadron which had been waging a losing fight against the weather since its departure from England in the spring.

Washington assured Comte d'Estaing in a letter of September 11th that "the whole Continent sympathizes with you."

The well-guarded private sentiments of the commander in chief were conveyed a few days later in a letter to John Augustine: "An unfortunate storm . . . and some measures taken in consequence of it by the French Admiral, perhaps unavoidably, blasted in one moment the fairest hopes that ever were conceived; and from a moral certainty of success, rendered

it a matter of rejoicing to get our own troops safe off the Island. If the
garrison of that place, consisting of nearly six thousand men, had been
captured, as there was, in appearance at least, a hundred to one in favor
of it, it would have given the finishing blow to British pretensions of
sovereignty over this country; and would, I am persuaded, have hastened
the departure of the troops in New York, as fast as their canvas wings
could carry them away."[20]

There could be no question that enemy spirits were raised as much
by Comte d'Estaing's mishaps as if the British had won victories. Even
such a stout warrior as Captain Alexander McDonald had been so discouraged by the news of the French alliance as to despair of beating
the rebels: "Nothing but independence will serve them and that once
granted them and they left to themselves, in five years time they would
have an Army & Navy Superior to Great Britain. . . . I dont see how
its possible to reduce the Americans now to their former obedience &
Allegiance." McDonald undoubtedly spoke for most of the British
officers when he blamed the Whig minority in the homeland, "The honor
and Grandeur of Great Britain were never in a more despicable situation
than the present owing entirely to the Misconduct of the Villainous
Minority and I hope in God if the Army is obliged to leave America that
the first thing they will do when they land in Britain is to Scalp every
son of a Bitch of them."[21]

As if to atone for such fainthearted moments, many of McDonald's
colleagues were in favor of scalping the rebels as punishment for their
presumption in forming an alliance with the hereditary foe. The diarist
Mackenzie did not mince words in expressing his approval of the
Wyoming Valley massacre:

> The expedition of Colonel Butler, and his Indian allies, who are
> now advancing thro' the back parts of Pennsylvania . . . with great
> Success, and spreading Terror, and dismay thro' that country, promises
> much, and if properly assisted, may prove of singular advantage in
> favor of Government. . . . 'Tis surprizing what an effect the burning
> & destroying their property, has had upon the Rebels. 'Tis now become
> evident, that this way of carrying on the war, is the only effectual
> method of bringing them to a sense of their duty. . . . The mistaken
> lenity of Government has prolonged the war, and brought the Nation
> into the present dangerous crisis.[22]

Several other operations of the summer and autumn of 1778 furnished
added evidence that harshness could now be considered a semiofficial

British policy. On September 27th General Grey of Paoli fame was again accused of killing prisoners when he defeated a detachment of Colonel Baylor's light horse at Tappan. And on October 15th, when 3,000 redcoats surprised a troop of Count Pulaski's legion at Little Neck, rebel charges of cruelty were supported by enemy testimony. For the British report candidly announced a rebel "loss of fifty killed, none wounded. . . . It being a night attack, little quarter could of course be given; so that there are only five prisoners."[23]

British advocates of ruthlessness might have been disconcerted to learn that thoughtful rebel leaders feared such policies less than the humanities of an adversary regarded as their most formidable opponent. Light Horse Harry Lee agreed with Greene when he declared "that the kindness of Carleton was more to be dreaded than the bayonet of Howe; and mentioned as an undeniable fact, that in the various districts to which our captured troops returned, not excepting the faithful state of Connecticut, the impressions made by the relation of the treatment experienced from him, produced a lasting and unpropitious effect."[24]

The thousand farms of the Wyoming Valley had supplied at least as many soldiers to the rebel cause in addition to large supplies of grain. Only boys and old men were left to defend the forts on July 3rd when Colonel John Butler's 1,600 Tories and Indians burst out of the mountains. Surrender did not save the victims, for a contemporary newspaper account related that "about seventy of the men . . . they inhumanly butchered, with every circumstance of horrid cruelty; and then shutting up the rest, with the women and children in the houses, they set fire to them, and all perished together in the flames."[25]

The entire valley was laid waste, the cattle driven away, the crops destroyed and the dwellings burned. The same scenes of destruction and cruelty were repeated in New York the following November during the Cherry Valley massacres.

Earlier in the year the American views with regard to using Indians had been defined by Washington himself. "You will perceive, by the enclosed copy of a resolve of Congress," he wrote to Schuyler on March 13th, "that I am empowered to employ a body of four hundred Indians, if they can be procured on proper terms. Divesting them of their savage customs exercised in their wars against each other, I think they might be made of excellent use as scouts and light troops, mixed with our own parties." The distinction between such a policy and the practice of inciting whole tribes to go on the warpath against frontier settlements was explained to Parliament in 1777 by Edmund Burke:

> No proof whatever had been given of the Americans having attempted offensive alliances with any one tribe of savages; whereas the imperfect papers now before that House demonstrated, that the King's ministers had negotiated and obtained such alliances from one end of the continent of America to the other; that the Americans had actually made a treaty on the footing of neutrality with the famous Five Nations, which the King's ministers had bribed them to violate, and act offensively against the colonies; that no attempt had been made in a single instance on the part of the King's ministers to procure a neutrality; that . . . the difference of employing them against armed and trained soldiers, embodied and encamped, and employing them against the unarmed and defenceless men, women and children of a country, dispersed in their houses, was manifest, and left those, who attempted so inhuman and unequal a retaliation, without excuse.[26]

Schuyler had done wonders with his personal influence to keep the New York redskins neutral, but British bribes and promises of plunder frustrated him in the spring of 1778. Washington could only report to Congress on May 3rd that "there is but little prospect of succeeding in the plan for engaging a body of Indians. . . . The advantages which the enemy possess, in having the means of making presents much more liberally than we can, has made a strong impression on their minds. . . ."[27]

This was the last American attempt of the war to raise Indian troops on any large scale. Nor did the British ever profit enough from such raids as the Wyoming massacre to compensate for the odium they incurred both in Europe and America. On the contrary, the war's greatest conquest of territory might never have been achieved at their expense if they had not given the incentive by offering rewards to the savages of the West for scalps. In retaliation, a small band of frontiersmen journeyed 1,200 miles to the Mississippi under George Rogers Clark and captured the forts which the British were using as bases for their Indian operations. Never since Cortez and Clive had so few men made such a tremendous mark on history. For the possession of this vast area served as the claim for securing it permanently to the United States in the peace treaty of 1783—an inland empire comprising the present extent of the five largest midwestern states.

Chapter 18

March to the Mississippi

THERE were a few British officers who agreed with Sir Guy Carleton that the inciting of Indian ravages could no more be justified on practical than humanitarian grounds. Edward Abbott, later the lieutenant governor of Detroit, wrote to Carleton from that post on June 8, 1778:

> Your Excellency will plainly perceive the employing Indians on the Rebel frontiers has been of great hurt to the cause, for many hundreds would have put themselves under His Majesty's protection was there a possibility; that not being the case, these poor unhappy people are forced to take up arms against their Sovereign, or be pillaged & left to starve; cruel alternative. This is too shocking a subject to dwell upon; Your Excellency's known humanity will certainly put a stop if possible to such proceedings, as it is not people in arms that Indians will ever daringly attack, but the poor inoffensive families who fly to the deserts to be out of trouble, & who are inhumanly butchered, sparing neither women or children.[1]

Abbott concluded his letter with a rebuttal of the favorite British argument in defense of hiring savages, "It may be said it is necessary to employ Indians to prevent their serving our enemies, I will be bold to say their keeping a neutrality will be equally (if not more) serviceable to us, as their going to war."

This was a minority opinion, for the British policies had been drawn up by the king's ministers with his full approval. Lord Germain could always find officers who had no qualms about putting these plans into effect; and Henry Hamilton, commander at Detroit, became known throughout the West as "the Hair Buyer."

Officers of his stamp justified themselves with the age-old excuse of terrorists that all warfare is unpleasant to the victims, and the most forthright methods are in the long run the most merciful. There was essentially very little difference, they insisted, between being spitted on the bayonet of a regular and having one's skull cleft by the tomahawk of a savage auxiliary. And though scalping and burning captives alive were admittedly barbarous, it could always be proved that British employers discountenanced such methods, even though they could do nothing to prevent them.

Such sophistries were naturally more convincing to the British officers themselves than the frontier families who lived in dread of being scalped or burned alive. Most of the pioneers were too far removed from the seat of hostilities to take any part in battles which they learned about weeks later. Although a majority of them sympathized with the political causes of the rebellion, they would have been content to stay out of it, given the opportunity. It was Hamilton the Hair Buyer and men like him who made such implacable enemies of the frontiersmen that hatred of Britain and all things British became a border tradition.

The individual fighting qualities of the frontiersmen counted for little, since they were too scattered to meet Indian raids effectively. Leadership was the main need of these political orphans, and they found their champion in a young Virginia surveyor named George Rogers Clark. A veteran Indian fighter of Lord Dunmore's War in 1774, he acquired lands in the forest region later created into Kentucky. At the outbreak of the Revolution nobody foresaw more clearly both the vulnerability of the frontier and the opportunities for conquest at British expense. He perceived that the settlers could never rely for defense on a militia system against a swift and secret enemy—the only defense was a bold offensive against the British posts inflaming the savages against American pioneers.

Six of the thirteen colonies had laid claim to western lands on the strength of old charters, even to the extent of insisting on an indefinite right of expansion to the "South Sea." Virginia had a better case than most of the "three-sided" states, and, as the elected representative of a Kentucky mass meeting, Clark went to Williamsburg to appeal for military aid. He returned to take command of the border militia after convincing the Virginia assembly that its western claims needed the support of gunpowder rather than legal arguments. His plan for an expedition against the British forts on the Mississippi was a proposal of breathtaking boldness, but Governor Patrick Henry and his council gave their approval in 1777. There was little else they could give, so straitened were Virginia's wartime finances, and Clark went ahead to recruit a band of nearly 200 men.

These volunteers started their 1,200-mile journey by floating down the Monongahela to the Ohio. Sixty miles from the junction of that river with the Mississippi, Clark hid his boats and marched northward over the Illinois prairie toward Kaskaskia. The men had been two days without food when they approached the town in the summer darkness, but their

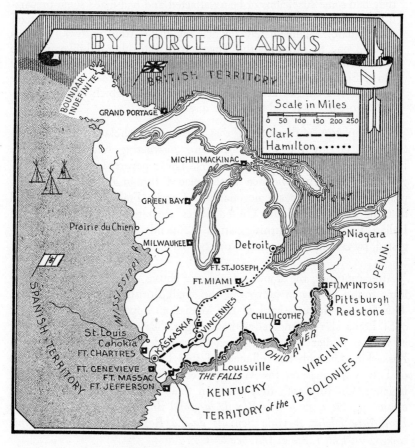

twenty-six-year-old leader did not hesitate. Audacity succeeded where numbers might have failed, for there was never a more devastating surprise in the war. Although Kaskaskia had a strong stockade and citadel, Governor Philip Rochblave's men were disarmed before they could fire a shot. The whole thing was accomplished in fifteen minutes, according to a description in Clark's own words:

On the evening of the 4th of July we got within three miles of the Town Kaskaskias, having a River of the same name to cross to the Town. After making ourselves ready for anything that might happen, we . . . found plenty of Boats to cross in; and in two hours Transported ourselves to the other shore with the Greatest silence. I learned that they had some suspicions of being attacted and had made some preparations, keeping out Spies, but they making no discoveries, had got off their Guard. I immediately divided my little Army in two Divisions ordered one to surround the Town, with the other I broke into the Fort, secured the Governour Mr. Rochblave, in 15 minutes had every Street Secured, sent Runners through the Town ordering the People on pane of Death to keep close to their Houses, which they observed, and before daylight had the whole disarmed.[2]

So complete was the surprise that Governor Rochblave had no opportunity to destroy the secret documents instructing him to incite the Indian tribes against American settlers. These papers, forwarded to Virginia, added to the evidence which placed Britain in an embarrassing position during the peace negotiations of 1782. Franklin boldly asserted that the enemy owed the United States reparations for the ravages of Indian "scalping and burning parties."[3] Amends might be made, he suggested, by ceding Canada and Nova Scotia.

After capturing the stone fort and 250 houses of Kaskaskia, the Americans found it easy to overpower the small British garrison at Cahokia. This fort, on the east bank of the Mississippi opposite the Spanish post of St. Louis, also surrendered without a fight. Clark proved to be a diplomat as well as soldier when he gained the confidence of Father Gibault at Kaskaskia. Through the influence of that French priest, the inhabitants of Fort Vincennes on the Wabash were persuaded to change their allegiance. On July 20th they swore in their archaic French *"de renoncé a toute fidélité a gorge troy Roy de la grand Bretaigne Et Ses Successeurs Et d'Aitre fidelle et vraie Seujaits de La Republique de La Virginie comme un État Libre et Independent. . . ."*[4]

If these recent subjects of George III had known more about American politics, they would have understood why the free and independent "Republic of Virginia" did not ask any aid from the other twelve states. Already the dispute over western lands had grown into an issue which kept the Articles of Confederation from being ratified. Virginia, with the most extensive and best-founded claims, was singled out for the attacks of the "four-sided" states with fixed boundaries. So far was American union from being realized in the summer of 1778 that Maryland held out for thirty more months rather than join a Confederation which might be dominated by the states with large western holdings.

When the news of the defection of Vincennes reached Detroit, Lieutenant Governor Hamilton promptly led an expedition which recovered that important post. Again the French inhabitants changed their allegiance with more amiability than sincerity. Only about 10 per cent of them were literate, the Americans learned when collecting signatures, and even a smaller proportion took any interest in the quarrel between Great Britain and her former colonies.

Hamilton went into winter quarters at Vincennes, depending for security on the inability of his foes to attack from such a distance in severe weather. The "Illinois country," as the whole vast region was called, had been made part of Quebec Province by the Quebec Act of 1774. Detroit seemed the most logical headquarters and Vincennes the best advanced base for the British plan of setting a backfire of Indian warfare along the entire frontier from Canada to Florida. The Hair Buyer had already sent out a few scalping parties in preparation for the spring campaign when 130 Americans surprised him after a terrible midwinter march across the "drowned lands."

Portraits of the tall, blond rebel leader show the bald head and predatory beak of an eagle. Upon learning that Hamilton had recaptured Vincennes, he resolved to attack first. "I cannot account for it but I still had every inward assurance of success," he recalled long afterwards, "and never could when weighing every Circumstance doubt it." Clark needed all his confidence to complete a 16-day march described in his letter to George Mason:

We now had a Rout before us of two hundred and Forty miles in length, through, I suppose, one of the most beautiful Country in the world; but at the same time in many parts flowing with water and exceeding bad marching. . . . Arriving at the two little Wabachces although three miles asunder they now make but one, the flowed water between them being at Least three feet deep, and in many places four: Being near five miles to the opposite Hills, the shallowest place, except about one hundred Yards was three feet. This would have been enough to have stop'd any set of men that was not in the same temper that we was But in three days we contrived to cross, by building a large Canoe, ferried across the two Channels, the rest of the way we waded;

Building scaffolds at each to lodge our Baggage on until the Horses Crossed to take them.[5]

A journal kept by one of the officers, Major Joseph Bowman, indicates that the hardships of the expedition began on the second day and mounted steadily toward a climax at the finish:

> February 8th. Marched early thro' the Water which we now began to meet in those large and level plains where (from the Flatness of the country the Water rests a considerable time before it drains off) notwithstanding our Men were in Great Spirits, tho much fatigued.
> 12th. Marched across bad plain saw and killed numbers of Buffaloe, the roads very bad from the immense Quantity of Rain that had fallen, the Men much fatigued. . . .
> 16th. Marched all day thro' Rain and Water. . . .
> 17th. Travelled till 8 O Clock in mud and water but could find no place to encamp on. Still kept marching. We found the Water fallen from a small spot of Ground staid there the Remainder of the Night drisly and dark weather.
> 21st. We thought to get to town that Night, so plunged into the Water sometimes to the Neck for more than one league when we stop'd . . . there being no dry land near us on one side for many leagues. Rain all this day no Provisions.[6]

On the 23rd, after long hours of wading with rifles held overhead, the scarecrow army reached dry land within sight of Vincennes. Clark found concealment in a grove and allowed his men a few hours for rest and drying their clothing. Exhaustion did not deter him from attacking at dusk, for he had "resolved to appear as Darring as possible, that the enemy might conceive by our behaviour that we were very numerous and probably discourage them."

The official report of Colonel Hamilton bears witness to the impact of the rebel surprise: "About five minutes after candles had been lighted we were alarmed by hearing a Musquet discharged; presently after some more. I concluded that some party of Indians was return'd or that there was some riotous frolic in the Village, going upon the Parade to enquire I heard the Balls whistle, order'd the Men to the Blockhouses, forbidding them to fire till they perceived the shot to be directed against the Fort. We were shortly out of suspence, one of the serjeants receiving a shot in the breast. The fire was now return'd, but the enemy had a great advantage from their Rifles, and the cover of the Church, Houses, Barns, &c."[7]

Clark's boldness had the desired effect and Hamilton estimated his numbers at five hundred or more. The French inhabitants were sufficiently impressed to decide once again that their bread was buttered on the other side, for the rebel leader reported to Governor Patrick Henry that they "surrendered with joy, and assisted in the siege. There was a continual fire on both sides, for eighteen hours. I had no expectation of gaining the fort until the arrival of my artillery. The moon setting about one o'clock, I had an entrenchment thrown up within rifle shot of their strongest battery, and poured such showers of well directed balls into their ports, that we silenced two pieces of cannon in fifteen minutes without getting a man hurt."[8]

The following day the two leaders met at the church for several conferences to settle terms of capitulation. When Hamilton complained that his adversary was harsh, Clark reported that he said, "Could I look on you Sir as a Gentleman I would do to the utmost of my power, but on you Sir who have embrued your hands in the blood of our women and children, honor, my country, everything calls on me alloud for Vengeance."

It was Hamilton's misfortune that one of his scalping parties returned this very day from a bloody raid on Kentucky settlements. Clark's men might have had relations killed, for all they knew, and nobody troubled to inquire. Major Bowman recorded with stark brevity that the riflemen "brought the Indians to the Main Street before the Fort Gates there tomahawked them and threw them into the River. . . ."

The British colonel himself was a horrified witness of this scene, as the Kentuckians intended him to be. Many of the king's officers who incited Indian raids had never seen the effects, and the deadly silence of the riflemen appalled Hamilton as much as the death chant of the Indians. "One of them was tomahawked immediately," he reported. "The rest sitting on the ground in a ring bound—seeing by the fate of their comrade what they had to expect, the next on his left sung his death song, and was in turn tomahawk'd, the rest underwent the same fate. . . ."

This spectacle had its influence on an officer who realized that Clark's men would rather have had him as a victim. It was protection that the Hair Buyer sought when he surrendered on February 24th; and his adversary found it prudent to grant terms to a force stronger than his own. He kept his word by having Hamilton taken safely back to Virginia for captivity. The evidence of British rewards for scalps was so damning that even the liberal Jefferson, just taking office as governor, wrote to ask Washington how severely Hamilton might be treated.[9] The commander in chief replied that since the British colonel had not surrendered at discretion, the terms must be observed in spite of the evidence of past crimes.

Clark had hoped to keep his force free of encumbrances so that he could march against Detroit in June, 1779, when his promised reinforcements arrived from Virginia. But the bankrupt state could give him little help, and he had to postpone his expedition until a tomorrow that never dawned. At least Clark managed to defend his conquests after withdrawing to Fort Nelson, the post he established at the falls of the Ohio. The enemy threatened only twice more in the Illinois country. In 1780 Clark destroyed the towns of the Shawnee Indians, and two years later he led his Kentucky rifleman in another expedition against the same tribe.

His later life has been cited as an example of the ingratitude of republics. Neither he nor his men ever received a cent of pay, and the greatest conqueror of the Revolution found himself responsible even for the debts incurred by his campaigns. Although the Virginia officials did not deny the obligation, poverty kept them from fulfilling their promises. While Clark's creditors were hounding him on the frontier, the state itself was so destitute by 1780 that James Madison had to borrow from a Philadelphia moneylender to meet his personal expenses as a member of Congress.[10]

The hero of Kaskaskia and Vincennes had the further misfortune to run afoul of James Wilkinson. As Gates's aide at Saratoga, that twenty-year-old officer started his lifelong career of double-dealing by slandering his superior. After the war he became a traitor in the pay of Spain, though his perfidy could not be proved until many years later. In 1787, coveting Clark's army command and office as Indian commissioner, Wilkinson forged papers representing him to be a drunkard and incompetent. The false evidence convinced Governor Edmund Randolph of Virginia so thoroughly that he removed Clark and appointed his traducer. As a consequence, the frontier leader's reputation was not vindicated until after his death in 1818.

It took more than Clark's efforts to defeat the British plans for arming the redskins against the United States along the entire border. Several other campaigns were necessary for that purpose, so that the rebel strategy of the year 1779 was devoted largely to operations against the enemy's savage auxiliaries.

From the viewpoint of the British ministers, it was an economical means of making war at a time when the forces of the Empire were perilously stretched. Such was the mobility of the painted raiders, traveling by canoe, that several times their own numbers were required for defense, not to mention the forts and magazines of supplies. After the Wyoming massacre, despite the urgent need for troops in Rhode Island, Congress resolved that an expedition must be sent immediately against "the tories and other banditti" inciting the Six Nations.[11]

Washington did not have enough troops for this purpose in 1778, though he detached several companies of Morgan's riflemen shortly after Monmouth for service on the New York frontier. This duty offered more hardships than glory, and hideous tortures awaited the captives of a defeated force. Even experienced woodsmen sometimes failed to guide a force safely through forests in which every glade might be entered only at the risk of an ambush. One New York militia column of 149 men, pursuing Joseph Brant's redskins after the burning of Minisink, were trapped in this manner and only 30 men escaped to tell the story.

Not until the summer of 1779, after the Cherry Valley massacre had supplied an added incentive, could the commander in chief detach enough troops to strike a crippling blow at the Six Nations. He offered Gates the first chance, but that general declined with regret on the grounds that it was "the only command, to which I am unequal."[12] The campaign, he added, called for someone with more youthful energy. The choice then fell upon John Sullivan, who set out from the desolated Wyoming Valley on the last day of July. No doubt the New Hampshire general would have preferred to raze the homes of the Britons and Tories, but as dupes the Indians had to pay a price amounting to destruction. More than forty of their towns were burned by soldiers whose hearts had been hardened by sights along the way, according to an entry in Colonel Adam Hubley's journal:

> I was struck on this day's march with the ruins of many houses, chiefly built of logs and uninhabited; though poor, yet happy in their situation until that horrid engagement, when the British tyrant let loose upon them his emissaries, the savages of the wood, who not only destroyed and laid waste those cottages, but in cold blood massacred and cut off the inhabitants, not even sparing gray locks or helpless infancy.[13]

Even granting the military necessity, it is enough to make an anthropologist weep to think of the primitive civilization uprooted by Sullivan's

3,000 troops. Benjamin Franklin had long been an admirer of the political institutions of the Six Nations, declaring that the redskins set an example in confederation worthy of emulation by the thirteen colonies. Agriculture had reached a high stage of development, and it took the army a month to devastate the apple and peach orchards and the fields of grain and vegetables. "This morning," Hubley recorded on September 15th, "the whole army, excepting a covering party, were engaged in destroying the corn, beans and other vegetables, which were in quantity immense, and in goodness unequaled by any I ever yet saw. Agreeable to a moderate calculation, there was not less than two hundred acres, the whole of which was pulled and piled up in huge heaps, mixed with dry wood, taken from the houses, and consumed to ashes."

The apple and peach trees were girdled after the ripe fruit had been burned or left on the ground to rot. Some of the houses, according to the diarists, were built of planks and painted, and the Indians had well-kept cemeteries with wooden monuments. "Genessee town, the capital of the Seneca nation," wrote Hubley, "is pleasantly situated on a rich and extensive flat, the soil remarkably rich, and great parts well improved with fields of corn, beans, potatoes, and all kinds of vegetables. It contains one hundred and seven well-finished houses."

The warriors of the Six Nations had the choice of fighting at a disadvantage or seeing their primitive civilization wiped out. Their British employers could spare only twenty regulars to aid them, and at the battle of Newtown on August 29th about 500 Indians and 200 Tories went down to overwhelming defeat. These forces made a stand behind a breastwork half a mile long, "most artfully covered with green boughs and trees" so that it seemed part of the landscape. The position, according to Sullivan's report to Washington, "was in a bend of the [Tioga] river which, by turning northward, formed a semicircle. There was a deep brook in front of this work, over which the road passed. . . ."[14]

Sullivan had a great superiority of numbers but he did not propose to pay too high a price for victory. While the riflemen crept up on front under cover to "amuse" the enemy, Colonel Proctor's artillery opened fire on the breastwork and Poor's and Clinton's brigades swung far around to the rear. It took from early morning until three in the afternoon for these forces to arrive, and after a brief fight the enemy fled to escape encirclement. Their losses in the combat and pursuit were estimated at more than a hundred by Americans who had three men killed and 39 wounded.

No campaign of the Revolution ever inspired more diaries. Sullivan's supplies were so limited that the men lived on the country, but the daily record kept by Colonel Hubley attests that they had few hardships. "After encamping," he noted on August 7th, "[we] had an agreeable repast of corn, potatoes, beans, cucumbers, watermelons, squashes, and other vegetables, which were in great plenty, [produced] from the cornfields already mentioned and in the greatest perfection; distance of march this day, six miles."

During the entire campaign the forces commanded by Brant and Butler were able to strike only one blow. On September 13th they ambushed a party of 26 rebel riflemen and killed all but nine who escaped. The others, according to Hubley, were "massacred in the most cruel and barbarous manner that the human mind can possibly conceive, the savages having put them to the most excruciating torments possible, by first plucking their nails from their hands, then spearing, cutting, and whipping them, and mangling their bodies, then cutting off the flesh from their shoulders by pieces, and severing their heads from their bodies, and then leaving them a prey to their dogs."[15] But even in his indignation at the fate of Lieutenant Boyd and his party, the diarist realized that the redskins were dupes: "May his fate await those who have been the cause of this. Oh! Britain, behold and blush."

On the eastern shore of Lake Erie a similar campaign took place meanwhile as Colonel John Brodhead pushed northward from Fort Pitt with 600 riflemen. A letter from one of his officers reported that the column "penetrated the Indian country, lying on the Allegheny river, one hundred and eighty miles, burnt ten of the Mingo, Munsey and Seneca towns in that quarter, and destroyed all the fields of corn, computed to be five hundred acres, with only the loss on our side of three men slightly wounded."[16] On the return march the force crossed the creek where the nation's first oil well would be drilled eighty years later. The curiosity of the soldiers was aroused by a "black liquid which oozes from the sides and bottom of the channel and the adjacent springs . . . and if applied to woollen cloth burns it in an instant."

Both campaigns came to an end in September. So ruthlessly had the New York lake country been devastated that the homeless redskins had to depend all winter on scanty British doles of food, and hundreds died of starvation and disease. The organization of the Six Nations never recovered from the blow, just as the great Indian civilization of the South, as represented by the Cherokees and Creeks, had already been crippled by the Revolution.

While Virginia conducted her own private little war to defend her western lands, Massachusetts authorized the ill-starred Penobscot expedition for similar reasons. The enemy offered the provocation when Colonel Francis McLean, operating from Halifax, established a British post near the present site of Castine, Maine. The purpose was to kill two birds with one stone by establishing a source of ship timbers and founding a colony of the American loyalist refugees, who had already become a problem.

Massachusetts, as the claimant to the territory later included in Maine, did not wait for the approval of General Washington and Congress. The state raised its own funds, ships and troops for the armada which reached Penobscot Bay on July 25, 1779. At this period of the war the four northeastern states still led other sections of the country when it came to sending soldiers to the Continental Army. And on top of a contribution surpassing that of New York and Virginia combined, Massachusetts managed to arm 20 vessels with 300 guns and equip nearly 3,000 militia in 24 transports for this expedition.

The operation is notable for a landing by Continental marines who had found a mission in amphibious assaults. As early as the spring of 1776 a small force of marines had conducted a successful ship-to-shore attack for the capture of British munitions in the Bahamas. At Penobscot Bay these specialists, in the role of mobile striking force for the fleet, landed under cover of naval gunfire and captured an island providing artillery positions against the enemy frigates. The support of a shore battery enabled the marines to cross to the mainland and fight their way through the woods to seize a ridge from the redcoats which covered the landing of the militia.

In spite of this promising beginning, the expedition came to a dismal end. Each ship and militia company seemed to be going its separate way, for the Massachusetts leaders could not agree while an opportunity remained to storm Colonel McLean's position before his 600 men entrenched. The ensuing siege made such slow progress that the enemy had time to send a relieving squadron from Sandy Hook. The Massachusetts ships, bottled up in the harbor by a superior force, were destroyed by their own crews to prevent them falling into the enemy's hands. Militiamen, sailors and marines alike had to make their way back through the woods to

Boston. Some of them died of hunger or exposure on the 180-mile journey; and the fury of the recriminations, if expended on the enemy, would have won a dozen victories.

The failure became the more humiliating when the enemy treated Maine as a conquered province and renamed it New Ireland. Penobscot was made into a permanent base and fortified so strongly that it remained in British hands until the end of the war, secure from anything except an attack supported by naval superiority.

Hopes of a new Canadian invasion had not yet been abandoned, and the French alliance seemed to offer a brilliant new opportunity for the conquest of the fourteenth colony. As a first step, Franklin had been instructed in the autumn of 1778 to hold forth the lure of the Newfoundland fisheries to the ministers of Louis XVI when proposing a combined operation. Congress had such delusions of grandeur as to envision an army of 12,500, invading from Detroit, Niagara and New Hampshire, while 5,000 French soldiers and a great fleet came up the St. Lawrence to capture Quebec. But the commander in chief, who trusted no motives save those of self-interest, declared against any scheme which might suggest to France the possibility of recovering her former colonies:

> I am heartily disposed to entertain the most favorable sentiments of our new ally, and to cherish them in others to a reasonable degree. But it is a maxim, founded on the universal experience of mankind, that no nation is to be trusted further than it is bound by self-interest; and no prudent statesman or politician will venture to depart from it.[17]

In this instance Washington's suspicions were not justified. Although he would have found it incredible, the French minister was instructed not to encourage any plan for the invasion of Canada. Vergennes had come to the conclusion, as the French archives later revealed, that his country should content itself with the profitable West Indies possessions, which could be more readily defended. He preferred, moreover, that Canada remain in British hands as a future bone of contention which promised to keep the English-speaking peoples divided.

Washington had no means of knowing about these secret decisions when he used his influence against the new plan of invasion. Lack of resources finally decided the issue in the State House, and the dream of conquering Canada came to an end in 1779, never again to be revived. Congress considered it "very problematical whether they could make any solid impression in that quarter, even on the uncertain contingency that the troops of Great Britain should evacuate the posts they now hold."[18] As it happened, Newport was the only position to be abandoned; and many British officers shared Stedman's opinion that the occupation of Rhode Island "had no use except to keep a large body of troops unemployed during three years."[19] Nevertheless, a garrison was retained at that base until late in 1779.

Rebel leaders, glancing back over the first year of the French alliance, could only have concluded that their fondest hopes had been dashed. Even Washington, who seldom let optimism delude him, had thought it quite possible that the enemy might be compelled to use the New York garrison for defense of the West Indies. Several members of Congress went so far as predicting that the invaders would find it necessary to withdraw entirely from America.

The three great theaters of the new world war were America, India and the West Indies. It was a reasonable hypothesis that one of these British outposts might be sacrificed in order to defend the other two, and America seemed the most logical choice. Prospects of such a painless victory were at their brightest in the autumn of 1778, when troop transfers to East Florida and the West Indies reduced the British strength in America from 34,064 men on August 15th to 22,554 on November 1st.[20] But the capture of the French island of St. Lucia gave the enemy an opening victory in the West Indies.

Again it was d'Estaing's fate to arrive a few days too late. An enemy fleet with 5,000 reinforcements preceded him in time to seize St. Lucia and throw up earthworks. The French admiral led an equal number of his own troops to the assault, only to be repulsed with losses of 1,400 killed and wounded.

The British had even more reason to congratulate themselves on winning a foothold in the southern states, left undisturbed since the Declaration of Independence. The weak garrison at St. Augustine had been threatened that summer by a rebel invasion, but the campaign was decided against the Americans by indiscipline, disease and desertion. The account by Colonel William Few of Georgia indicates that these familiar faults of militia operations had serious consequences in the lowlands of the South:

> The hot weather commenced, and the fever raged in their camp and destroyed more than a general action. A retreat became necessary to save the remainder of the troops, of which near one-half had been destroyed or dispersed without seeing the face of an enemy. Thus

terminated an expedition foolishly planned and worse executed. We had neither stores of provisions, munitions of war, nor money in our treasury.[21]

Governor William Houstoun of Georgia quarreled with General Robert Howe, commanding a few companies of Continentals stationed in Georgia. They were still disputing in December when Colonel Archibald Campbell landed on Tybee Island with a motley force of 3,500 redcoats, Highlanders, Hessians and American loyalists.

Howe chose to defend Savannah at a point where troops landing from the river must march along a narrow causeway leading through rice swamps to the town. He had about 1,200 militia and Continentals, few of whom were trained or experienced. His position seemed so safe, however, that he did not doubt his ability to hold the causeway against several times his own numbers.

It was a terrible awakening when the British frontal advance proved to be only a feint while the real attacking column stole around to the rear by way of a little-known path pointed out by loyalists. The raw rebel troops were totally routed. Throwing away their muskets, they surrendered by platoons or drowned while trying to swim across a creek. Campbell claimed to have taken Savannah with 451 prisoners, 48 cannon and large supplies at a cost of only three men killed and nine wounded.

Howe came in for furious censure from southern leaders who declared that he should have known about the path to his rear. He was also blamed for electing to fight with full knowledge that General Benjamin Lincoln would reinforce him a few days later. "Had General Howe retired from Savannah, and gone up the country," declared Moultrie, "we should soon have joined him, and made a body of 2,000 men; besides, such reinforcements were marching to us from Augusta, Ninety-Six and many other parts of Georgia and Carolina, that in a short time we should have had an army of 4 or 5,000 men; with them we could have marched down to Savannah, before the British had time to fortify. . . ."[22]

During the first days of the new year General Prevost advanced from St. Augustine and took charge of operations in Georgia. When Lincoln neared Savannah with 950 troops, he found the remnants of Howe's force in flight and the enemy too strongly entrenched to be attacked. Georgia had been lost beyond any immediate hope of recovery.

Chapter 19

Bayonets at Stony Point

AMONG the British leaders advocating the complete withdrawal of troops from America was Lord Jeffrey Amherst, the Empire's foremost soldier and the one best acquainted with New World conditions. He urged that these forces be used to overwhelm France at her weakest point, the West Indies. If that country could be brought to terms by a concentrated land and naval attack, Amherst believed that an exhausted America, left without allies, might come back into the Empire of her own accord. But he had never from the beginning held forth much hope to the Ministry that the patriots could be conquered by force of arms.

The strategy adopted by Great Britain was exactly the contrary. Instead of concentrating on any one point, the land and naval forces of 1779 were dispersed so that they remained weak everywhere. Clinton lacked the strength for an attack in force, and the plundering raids sent out from New York incited so much hatred that in the long run they benefited the American cause. "Vast numbers of peaceable and inoffensive people who did not make a shadow of resistance were ruined and outraged," asserted the British historian Lecky, "and the expeditions of the British were probably much more efficacious in arousing indignation and alienating loyalists than in intimidating the enemy."[1]

If Sir William Howe had sometimes hurt his cause by lethargy, Clinton erred at the other extreme by mistaking activity for progress. In May, 1779, he sent Admiral Collier and General Mathews with a strong squadron and 2,500 troops to devastate Virginia, which had not been troubled by an enemy since Lord Dunmore's futile efforts of 1775. It was good strategy, of course, to strike a blow at the most populous of the thirteen states. Virginia had been supplying the Continental Army with most of its salted meats, and exports of tobacco from this region supported the credit of Congress with foreign nations. But military objectives were of only secondary importance, and discipline was so poor that much senseless destruction resulted—homes being burned while wharves and warehouses were left standing. Portsmouth was sacked for no good military reason; unarmed civilians were robbed and shot, and violence to noncombatants included instances of rape.

Crimes of personal violence had been rare up to this time. Congress made a detailed investigation of British excesses in New Jersey during the winter of 1776-1777, and not much evidence could be found of anything except indiscriminate plundering. From 1779 to the end of the war, however, there can be no doubt that noncombatants ran the risk of rape and murder as well as pillage by British forces. It is not necessary to cite American accusations; the testimony of British and Tory witnesses is enough to convict the invaders of outrages which did immeasurable harm to their own cause. Many of the officers were not so much interested in winning the war as retiring to the life of a country gentleman, and their activities provided Judge Jones with the material for a bitter chapter entitled "The Base Transactions of Commissaries, Quartermasters, Barrackmasters, and Engineers in America."[2]

The damage done by the expedition sent by Clinton into Virginia was estimated at £2,000,000, but a great deal of the plunder had been carried away with a view to private profit. Valuable war stores were left undisturbed because they could not readily be converted into cash, and it was hardly to be expected that officers lining their own pockets should have supervised the conduct of their men too closely.

Congress had issued a "manifesto" threatening reprisals in October, 1778. The British, it was charged, had "laid waste the open country, burned the defenseless villages, and butchered the citizens of America." A long statement of grievances ended with a resolution passed by a unanimous vote:

> We, therefore, the Congress of the United States of America, do solemnly declare and proclaim, that if our enemies presume to execute their threats, or persist in their present career of barbarity, we will take such exemplary vengeance, as shall deter others from a like conduct.[3]

This is a sample of other such declarations published from time to time until the end of the war. They may be considered as political measures passed to placate enraged Americans, for the enemy paid little attention and Congress lacked the opportunity for reprisals.

Purely military campaigns by the forces at New York were so unusual in 1779 that the expedition sent up the Hudson in May is worthy of notice. Clinton himself led the troops which took Stony Point without opposition and drove out the 70 Americans defending Verplanck on the eastern shore.

These successes represented the first threat since the Saratoga campaign to the rebel strategic lifeline of the Hudson and Lake Champlain. The British had evacuated Ticonderoga shortly after Burgoyne's surrender, and Clinton fell back to New York without attempting to hold Fort Montgomery. For more than a year the rebels commanded both waterways while Kosciusko created West Point into the strongest fortress of America. Clinton's successes gave him control of the lower Hudson after he fortified Stony Point. As a consequence, American troops marching from the middle states to New England had to make a detour of 90 miles through the Catskills to cross the river without enemy interference.

An honest and hard-working even if uninspired professional soldier, Clinton would doubtless have accomplished more if left to his own inclinations. But he was caught between the devil of ministerial interference and the deep blue sea of subordinates intent upon private gain. And after the brief Hudson campaign his forces at New York returned to the more congenial task of plundering Connecticut civilians.

These forays were customarily described in official reports as being made for the purpose of seizing rebel munitions. During the raid of July 5th on New Haven, however, homes were ransacked for money and silver plate while stores of bulky army provisions escaped. The redcoats, according to the *New York Journal*, "plundered the houses of everything they could carry away or convert to their own use, and broke or destroyed every whole article of household goods and furniture, together with the window glass and sashes."[4]

General Garth was prevented from completing his plan of burning New Haven by the disorder of his men, who were showing the effects of pillaged liquor. He got them safely on board the ships before large militia forces gathered, and on July 7th the raiders landed at Fairfield. There was little pretense, according to the *New London Gazette*, of any military purpose: "They entered the houses, attacked the persons of Whig and Tory indiscriminately, breaking open desks, trunks, chests, closets, and taking away everything of value; they robbed women of buckles, rings, bonnets, aprons, and handkerchiefs. . . ."[5]

It is understandable that most contemporary American accounts of such depredations should have been highly colored and overdrawn. This description is one of the few which may be accepted as fairly accurate reporting:

> Another party that came on were the American refugees, who, in revenge for their confiscated estates, carried on the same business. They were not, however, so abusive to the women as the former [Hessians], but appeared very furious against the town and country. The Britons were the least inveterate. Some of the officers appeared to pity the misfortunes of the country, but in excuse said they had no other way to gain their authority over us. . . . Individuals among the British troops were exceedingly abusive, especially to women. They solicited, they attempted their chastity; and though no rape was committed, yet some were forced to submit to the most indelicate and rough treatment.

The Germans were described as "a banditti of the vilest that was ever let loose among men. . . . They may emphatically be called the sons of plunder and devastation." General Garth and Governor Tryon, leading the loyalists, decided that Fairfield must pay for the resistance of militia volunteers who had defended the village green with a fieldpiece, inflicting a score of casualties before they could be dislodged. Several Tories, former residents, directed the soldiers of the rearguard who set fire to the town. After their departure the townsfolk managed to save a few dwellings, but most of Fairfield lay in ashes before morning.

The redcoats, holding the advantage of sea power, crossed the Sound to Long Island and waited until large Connecticut militia forces went home. Four days later Garth and Tryon plundered Norwalk and burned it to the ground before returning to New York.

The fate of the three communities, grievous as it may have been for the residents, had the moral value of as many victories for the rebel cause. Although the patriotism of Connecticut needed little stimulation, these object lessons warned other states as to what they might expect from enemy invaders.

The effects on British morale were correspondingly bad. For the plundering raids were reported in the homeland as military victories. Thus the diaries of American loyalists in England record the jubilation over the news and the confidence that the rebellion would be put down before the end of the year.[6] There was bound to be an unfortunate reaction when Britons began to suspect the truth. General Conway, speaking before the House of Commons in the early summer of 1779, denounced such methods of waging war and blamed the clergymen of the realm for their approval:

> The robe and the mitre animating us in concert to massacre, we plunged ourselves into rivers of blood, spreading terror, devastation, and death over the whole continent of America; exhausting ourselves at home both of men and money, dishonoring forever our annals, we became the objects of horrour in the eyes of indignant Europe! It was our reverend prelates who led on this dance, which may be justly styled the dance of death! . . . Such is the horrid war which we have maintained for five years.[7]

Conway brought his speech to a climax with an eloquent plea that his countrymen "put an end to the war of America, to the end that we may unite more efficaciously all our efforts against the House of Bourbon." This appeal was addressed to a growing group of Englishmen who opposed American independence in principle but felt that it was not too great a price to pay for having both hands free to smite France and Spain.

Some of the worst effects of British plundering were felt by Clinton's army, which soon found itself in the position of having fouled its own nest. For the surrounding countryside, one of the most fertile agricultural areas of America, had been looted so grievously that the inhabitants themselves took to looting as a means of subsistence. Thus the farming regions of Long Island and Westchester County, originally Tory strongholds, were turned into wastelands filled with prowling bands of outlaws. The British troops, who might have been well supplied with fresh food, had to depend on such familiar staples as flinty salt pork and moldy dried peas brought all the way from England. When storms delayed the provision fleet, diaries and letters complained about the monotonous and reduced rations of an army which blighted a quartermaster's paradise.

The loyalist refugees in New York soon clamored for a share in the spoils. With Governor Tryon as their champion, they won permission from the Ministry in 1779 to establish a jurisdiction called the Honorable Board of Associated Loyalists. They were allowed to elect their own officers and keep all plunder in reward for service as raiders by land and sea. The competition between them and the British officers grew so brisk that little booty remained for either in the New York area, and farmers despaired of trying to grow a crop that would inevitably be devoured by others if it came up to maturity. Not much was left for a poor man except to turn robber himself, and the resulting demoralization led to a reign of anarchy in Westchester County and the nearby Connecticut shore. This sinister no man's land became known as the Neutral Ground, for the various bands paid only lip service to political doctrines. Many of these guerrillas were rebel or loyalist by turn as it suited the purposes of pillage, and supposed enemies often combined for a large-scale raid and divided the proceeds. As the rewards grew progressively poorer, it was only a step from robbery to seizing important persons and holding them for ransom. Judge Jones declared that he had seen receipts for such payments which ran as high as a hundred and fifty guineas.

There was no law save force in the Neutral Ground, and the regulars were no safer than civilians if they allowed themselves to be surprised or outnumbered. The German mercenaries, who had set the example, found themselves regarded as prey when the supply of victims began to decrease. Sergeant Krafft recorded in his journal on August 5, 1779: "The English soldiers . . . perpetrate daily the grossest highway robberies and even kill. One night some English soldiers attacked a Hessian Grenadier Sergeant with their bayonets, wounded him in many places, robbed him of everything and left him lying on the spot, where he soon after died. Innumerable like incidents occur, even in the day-time."[8]

Whether the Tories or patriots prevailed in the end, so many crimes had been committed in the New York area by 1779 that men identified with the losing side could expect little pity after the war. British officers admitted that the guerrillas violated humane codes but indignantly denied any guilt on the part of the king's regulars. Candidus, writing in the semiofficial New York Gazette, came forward with a typical rebuttal of American accusations on August 16, 1779:

> The charge of "deflowering defenceless women" is one of those deliberate, malicious falsehoods which are circulated by the rebels, purely to incense the inhabitants against the British troops. As to burning "unguarded towns," this writer should know that the King's troops burn no houses except public magazines, and those from which they are fired at, or otherwise annoyed. This was lately the case at Fairfield and Norwalk.[9]

The members of the Continental Congress, declared Candidus, were "justly chargeable, before God and the world, with all the calamities which America now suffers, and with all the other and greater calamities which it will probably hereafter suffer in the course of this unnatural contest."

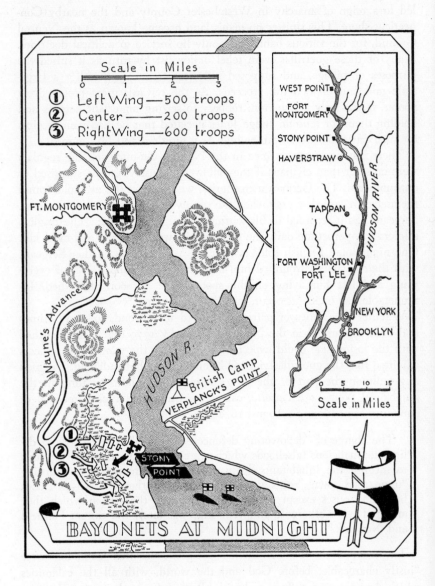

Scale in Miles

0   1   2   3

① Left Wing —— 500 troops
② Center —— 200 troops
③ RightWing —— 600 troops

FT. MONTGOMERY

Wayne's Advance

HUDSON R.

British Camp
VERPLANCK'S POINT

①
②
③

STONY
POINT

WEST POINT
FORT MONTGOMERY
STONY POINT
HAVERSTRAW

TAPPAN

FORT WASHINGTON
FORT LEE

NEW YORK
BROOKLYN

HUDSON RIVER

0   5   10   15
Scale in Miles

N

BAYONETS AT MIDNIGHT

Even when accusations of atrocities could be proved beyond doubt, they did not disturb invaders holding that rough treatment must be expected by rebels who might feel pampered to have escaped the gallows. But the king's regulars had their vulnerable spot. From Clinton down to the last private, they could be shamed by anything hurting their military pride. And it was infuriating to read such gibes as Washington's comment on "the conflagration of Fairfield, Norwalk, and New Haven, by the intrepid and magnanimous Tryon, who, in defiance of all the opposition that could be given by the women and children, inhabitants of those towns, performed this notable exploit with two thousand brave and generous Britons, thereby adding fresh lustre to their arms and dignity to their King."[10]

Taunts of this sort might have been less damaging if Washington's troops had not won a victory at Stony Point in the summer of 1779 which British officers doubtless envied more than any other success of the war so far.

Washington's planning deserved as much credit as the execution, and Anthony Wayne swore that he would storm hell if the commander made the preparations. His force of about 1,200 picked light infantry started after dark on July 15th and marched single file through rugged country to reach the British fort on the Hudson. Complete secrecy was preserved all the way to the abatis, and Wayne ordered that "if any soldier presume to take his musket from his shoulder,—attempt to fire, or begin the battle, until ordered by his proper officer, he shall be instantly put to death by the officer next him."[11]

At midnight the attacking forces crossed the causeway at low tide and passed the abatis so swiftly that only 15 men were killed and 83 wounded as the price of victory. All British resistance within the fort collapsed before the onslaughts of three columns which met according to schedule. Wayne was slightly wounded in the head by a musket ball, and both Fleury and Febiger distinguished themselves. Sixty-three redcoats were killed and 74 wounded by rebel bayonets, but Wayne ordered that the lives of the 543 prisoners be spared. No rebuke could have been better calculated to get under the enemy's skin, for a British staff officer admitted that the rebels "would have been fully justified in putting the garrison to the sword: Not one man of which was put to death but in fair combat."[12] The victors had every reason to be elated, and Colonel Christian Febiger wrote to his American bride the next morning:

My Dear Girl:

I have just borrowed pen, ink and paper to inform you that yesterday we march'd from Fort Montgomery, and at 12 o'clock last night we stormed this confounded place. . . . I can give you no particulars as yet. A musquet ball scraped my nose. No other damage to "Old Denmark." God bless you.

> Farewell—
> Febiger.[13]

There was more than glory to be gained at Stony Point. On the 17th Wayne directed the officers "to get the men shaved, and made as clean as circumstances will admit. . . . The plunder of the fort, (except the Ordnance, Military Stores, Entrenching Tools, Tents, and Marquees, which will be paid for by the publick) [is] to be collected together on the Flag Bastion at three o'clock and there exposed to sale, for ready money, or to be paid in ten days, for the benefit of the brave soldiers who fought for it. . . ."[14]

The proceeds, amounting to a total of $158,640, were divided among the troops in proportion to the pay of officers and men. But the fort itself had to be destroyed and evacuated within a few days, for Washington did not care to expose a detachment of his own to a similar fate. Clinton had come to the rescue in time to save Verplanck's Point on the other side of the river, and it could be assumed that he would soon cut off any garrison left at Stony Point. Several months later the British general in turn abandoned both posts after finding that too many troops were required to hold them securely.

The redcoats were further embarrassed on August 19th by a small-scale duplicate of Stony Point. Major Henry Lee surprised the British fort at Paulus Hook located on an isthmus of sand—an island at high tide—where Jersey City now stands. Four hundred picked troops crossed the Hackensack after dark, made a secret march down the west bank of the Hudson, and stormed the works with the bayonet at two o'clock in the morning. Not a shot was fired by rebels who killed or wounded about 50 foemen and took 158 prisoners.

Light Horse Harry Lee had to hurry to make his escape from superior British forces crossing from New York to the rescue. But he got back to the American lines safely after a night's march of 30 miles through morasses and defiles.

It was obvious that neither American attack had any great strategic purpose. Washington planned them in the hope of raising morale at a time when he lacked the resources for more ambitious operations. Both sides had reached a stalemate in the North, for lack of decisive numbers, which would last until the end of the war. Clinton could not venture too far from his ships and fortifications at New York, or stay away too long. Washington was similarly tied to West Point and the nearby posts in the Highlands.

The ease with which Clinton had taken Fort Montgomery in 1777 led to the choice of West Point as the citadel of the defensive system. Kosciusko's fortifications were supplemented by *chevaux de frise*, fireboats, gunboats, chains, outlying redoubts—every imaginable obstacle to discourage attacks by land or water. After the summer of 1778 a strong garrison always occupied the fort, however urgently troops might be needed elsewhere. Washington usually took a position extending from Morristown in New Jersey to White Plains on the east side of the river with a view to using his main army for the defense of the posts in the Highlands. Clinton could no more dream of attacking this stronghold than Washington could hope to storm the works of New York, and for three years the armies sullenly faced each other without risking an action of any consequence.

The military problems did not worry the rebel commander as much in 1779 as questions of national morale. "I never was, much less reason have I now, to be afraid of the enemy's *arms*," he wrote to General John Armstrong on May 18th; "but I have no scruple in declaring to *you*, that I have never yet seen the time in which our affairs (in my opinion) were at so low an ebb as they are at present; and without a speedy and capital change, we shall not be able to call out the strength and resources of the country."[15]

With the war entering upon its fifth year, the lack of industrial and financial sinews for such a prolonged contest became every day more apparent. As the Continental currency declined in value, the opportunities for stockjobbing increased; and Philadelphia became the headquarters for black-market operations.

Washington had appointed Benedict Arnold to that important command with instructions "to preserve tranquillity and order in the city, and give security to individuals of every class and description." This was equivalent to placing the lambs under the protection of the wolf. Arnold apparently solicited the post for dishonest purposes, since he came to an agreement during his first week for defrauding the army by the private purchase and sale of public supplies. His secret partners were James Mease, clothier-general, and his deputy William West; and the three men boldly signed an agreement drawn up to prevent them from cheating one another.[16] Such were the consequences that Arnold might as well have stolen the shirts from the backs of the soldiers. And though the commander in chief did not suspect peculation, he complained about clothing irregularities in several letters, notably his report to Congress of March 15, 1779:

> When I have such striking proofs of public loss and private discontent, from present management of the clothing department; when accts. inadmissible, if any system existed, frequently remind me of the absolute necessity of introducing one; when I hear, as I often do, of large importations of cloathing, which we never see, of quantities wasting and rotting in different parts of the country, the knowledge of which reaches me by chance; when I have reason to believe that the money, which has been expended for cloathing the army, if judiciously laid out and the cloathes regularly issued, would have effectually answered the purpose . . . I cannot forbear discovering my anxiety to have some plan decided for conducting the business hereafter in a more provident and consistent manner.[17]

Arnold may have relied upon Washington's unfailing trust of his generals, for he made little effort to conceal his luxurious new scale of living. No profiteer of Philadelphia flaunted his recent wealth more ostentatiously than this general with his liveried servants and coach and four. His dinners were soon the talk of the town; and before he had held the command a month, Nathanael Greene commented in a letter of July 25, 1778, "I hear that General Arnold has rendered himself not a little unpopular with the officers of the army in Philadelphia, by not giving them an invitation to a ball he gave the citizens."[18]

Some of the guests at Arnold's receptions were the same wealthy Tories who had been entertained in the John Penn house when Sir William Howe occupied it. Others were profiteers who had made money from both the British and American war needs and had no cause save that of private gain. Although Arnold came from a good old Rhode Island family, his efforts to ingratiate himself would be ascribed today to a social inferiority complex. No doubt he wished to live down the odious name "horse jockey," found in contemporary letters and diaries as an unflattering reference to his activities as trader before the war. For the thirty-eight-year-old widower was wooing Peggy Shippen, daughter of a prosperous

Philadelphia loyalist; and one of his love letters was copied word for word from sentiments written the year before in an unsuccessful suit for the hand of Betsy Deblois, daughter of a prosperous Boston loyalist.[19]

Not all of Arnold's ventures at Philadelphia were dishonest. Few Americans of 1779, either army officers or civilians, were so virtuous that they had never indulged in some sort of war speculation. It was even held to be patriotic to own a share in a privateer, and many of those swift raiders returned profits of several thousand per cent in a year. Arnold had his finger in a dozen such pies, some of them legitimate speculations and others taking advantage of his "inside knowledge."

His success during the first eight months may be measured by the fact that after a winter of extravagant entertaining he was able to buy the beautiful estate on the Schuylkill known as Mount Pleasant and settle it upon his eighteen-year-old bride. He had aspired even higher, for in a letter to Schuyler he suggested the possibility of acquiring the 34,000-acre estate at the head of Lake Champlain which had been confiscated from the loyalist Philip Skene.

Congress probably had Arnold in mind as well as other Philadelphia profiteers when the assembly "earnestly recommended to the several states to take the most effectual measures for . . . the suppressing of theatrical entertainments, horse racing, gaming, and such other diversions as are productive of idleness, dissipation and a general depravity of principles and manners."[20] This resolution was to some extent a sop to the Puritanical codes of the New England delegates, but the most worldly members recognized the political necessity. Foreign volunteers no longer commented admiringly on republican simplicity, and patriots visiting the ctiy were shocked by the parade of luxury and self-indulgence. "If I was to be called upon to draw a picture of the times and of Men, from what I have seen, and heard, and in part know," wrote Washington to a friend late in 1778, "I should say in one word that idleness, dissipation & extravagance seems to have laid fast hold of most of them.—That speculation—peculation—and an insatiable thirst for riches seems to have got the better of every other consideration and almost of every order of Men." Far from changing his mind the following spring, the father of his country wrote to James Warren:

Nothing, I am convinced, but the depreciation of our currency . . . aided by stockjobbing and party dissensions, has fed the hopes of the Enemy and kept the B. arms in America to this day. They do not scruple to declare this themselves, and add, that we shall be our own conquerors. . . . Our cause is noble. It is the cause of mankind, and the danger to it is to be apprehended from ourselves.[21]

Arnold's profiteering went on under the noses of Congress; and Washington himself spent the early weeks of 1779 at Philadelphia. Yet it remained for the Pennsylvania Council to bring charges against a general who was given the benefit of every doubt by the commander and a majority of the members of Congress.

The explanation is to be found in the necessity for indulging Continental officers at a time when many were retiring permanently. Sullivan and Schuyler, both of whom had threatened so often to resign, served no more in the army after the autumn of 1779. Daniel Morgan, crippled by rheumatism and feeling with good cause that he had been neglected, returned to his Virginia home shortly after Monmouth. Even such promising young officers as Aaron Burr and James Monroe were giving up their commissions in alarming numbers. The twenty-year-old Virginia captain, disappointed in his hopes of promotion, wrote to Lord Stirling that he had "retired from society, with almost a resolution never to return to it again."[22]

Some of the most patriotic officers could not afford to continue in the service, so grievous were the hardships imposed by mounting prices and a declining currency. Washington, as ever the champion of his subordinates, did his best to offer such inducements as could be provided by a nation fast approaching bankruptcy. One of his favorite projects had been a measure introduced in Congress during the winter of Valley Forge to reward officers with half pay for life after the war. The suggestion met with so much opposition, particularly from the New England members, that it made no headway. The following May the assembly passed a compromise calling for half pay for seven years if an officer remained in the service throughout the war without holding a position of profit. This plan did not satisfy Washington, who again urged a lifetime basis early in 1779. But in spite of his warnings that the army was threatened with dissolution, Congress defeated the measure twice again before the end of the year.

Arnold had less reason for complaint than most officers on the score of promotion. Nor could he have had as many financial hardships, considering his cavalier attitude toward public funds. Yet as commander at Philadelphia, betraying his trust, he was protected by a general policy of favoring officers who retained their commissions. No proofs of the contract with Mease and West appeared until long afterwards, but eight specific charges of profiteering and misconduct were brought against him in January, 1779. The delegates of every other state voted against the Pennsylvania motion to suspend him from command, and Congress reduced the charges to four. Arnold complained of persecution, and after delays in his court-martial he wrote hysterically to Washington on May 5th, "If your Excellency thinks me criminal, for heaven's sake let me be immediately tried and, if found guilty, executed." There was, as he knew, no possibility of capital punishment being inflicted, but he declared that "a set of artful, unprincipled men in office may misrepresent the most innocent actions. . . . Having made every sacrifice of fortune and blood, and become a cripple in the service of my country, I little expected to meet the ungrateful returns I have received from my countrymen; but as Congress have stamped ingratitude as a current coin, I must take it."

After several more postponements the court-martial was finally held in January, 1780, and the verdict came as near to being an acquittal as was possible in the face of such damning evidence. Arnold was convicted on only two counts, the most serious being an "impudent and improper" request for public wagons to transport private property. As punishment, he was sentenced "to receive a reprimand from his Excellency the commander in chief."

From start to finish, every effort had been made to hush the scandal. The long-drawn affair ended on April 6, 1780, when Washington merely included a mild rebuke in his daily orders. By that time Arnold had been a traitor for at least ten months, since later evidence disclosed that he opened negotiations with the enemy the preceding June.

Chapter 20

Who Look for Succor

THE presence of a few rotten apples in the barrel did not spoil the rest, and it was a studious little American army which spent the winter of 1778-1779 in New Jersey cantonments. In March the correspondent of the *Pennsylvania Packet* was impressed by General Henry Knox's "academy" in the artillery park at Pluckemin. This new building, surrounded by the usual log huts, was "capped with a small cupola, which had a very good effect. The great room was fifty feet by thirty, arched in an agreeable manner, and neatly plastered within. At the lower end of the room was a small enclosure, elevated above the company, where the preceptor to the park gave his military lessons."[1]

The winter's instructions in gunnery ended with the equivalent of graduation exercises—"a very elegant entertainment and display of fireworks given by General Knox and the corps of artillery." General Washington and his wife were guests of honor along with Mrs. Knox, Mrs. Greene and Lady Stirling. "The company was composed of the most respectable gentlemen and ladies for a considerable circuit around the camp, and as many of the officers as could possibly attend. . . . When the fireworks were finished, the company returned to the academy: the same room that had served to dine in served to dance in; the tables were removed, and had left a range for about thirty couples, to foot it to no indifferent measure. As it was a festival given by men who had not enriched *themselves* by the war, the lights were cheap, and of their own manufacture; and for the *knights of different orders*, there were hardy soldiers, happy in the thought of having had some hand in bringing round what they celebrated." Lest his readers should miss this allusion to the Meschianza, the correspondent of the *Packet* added, "Through the whole, there was a remarkable style of looks and behaviour, undebauched by British manners or British entertainments."

Other American writings of 1779 show that the officers of the main army led a Spartan life as compared to the profiteers of Philadelphia. Washington called attention to the plain fare at headquarters in one of his rare humorous passages when inviting a company of ladies and gentlemen to dinner:

Since our arrival at this happy spot, we have had a ham, (sometimes a shoulder) of Bacon, to grace the head of the Table; a piece of roast Beef adorns the foot; and a dish of greens, (almost imperceptible,) decorates the center. When the cook has a mind to cut a figure, (which I presume will be the case to-morrow,) we have two Beef-steak pyes, or dishes of crabs, in addition, on each side the center dish, dividing the space & reducing the distance between dish & dish to about 6 feet, which without them would be near 12 feet apart. Of late he has had the surprising sagacity to discover that apples will make pyes; and its a question, if, in the violence of his efforts, we do not get one of apples, instead of having both of Beef-steaks. If the ladies can put up with such entertainment, and will submit to partake of it on plates, once Tin but now Iron—(not become so by the labor of scouring), I shall be happy to see them. . . .[2]

There were not many reasons for congratulation in the summer of 1779, but at least the Continental Army had safely weathered the overconfidence inspired by the French alliance. Even the difficulties of keeping the main army recruited up to a safe strength could be charged to economic conditions rather than lack of patriotism. In January, after conferences with the commander in chief, Congress offered bounties as high as $200, in addition to existing rewards of clothing and 100 acres of land, to men enlisting for the duration of the war.[3] A recommendation that the states revoke their bounties failed of passage, and they continued to hold forth higher inducements. Congress was at such a disadvantage in this competition that in a letter of March 21st James Duane conceded the "necessity of leaving it to the States to fill up their quotas of the Army in their own way; Virginia having taken her measures without consulting us. . . . She has been so excessively liberal as to grant 400 dollars and 300 acres of land to every volunteer who shall enlist in her battalions during the war. While States thus interfere no general system can be adopted; but each must be left to its own prudence."[4]

Massachusetts, Connecticut and New Jersey also offered bounties which soon reached fantastic figures in terms of the dying Continental currency. Selfish as this policy appears, experience had demonstrated that only local forces offered any hope of defense against plundering raids. Often enough the militia could not gather in time to protect the seaports, but the punishment inflicted on the redcoats retreating from Danbury in 1777 had proved that inland towns could be looted only at a risk. The lesson taught by that reverse saved other communities by discouraging the British from venturing too far into the hinterland.

The necessities of home defense were not the only reason for the seeming perversity of the states. America was primarily an agricultural country, and the farms needed men as urgently as the armed forces. Nearly every military shortage could be traced to the general lack of resources, so that the scythe and hoe contributed as much to the war effort as the musket. State executives believed that militiamen could fight with both types of weapons, since they were producing food while safeguarding their homes from a potential enemy incursion. The Continentals, on the other hand, appeared to represent a drain on the treasury during the intervals between Revolutionary campaigns.

Not only Virginia but the other southern states were facing virtually their first direct experience of the war in its fifth year. Victories in small combats of the early months had won them a comparative immunity up to this time which would soon prove to be a mixed blessing. For lessons in war are seldom learned at second hand, and the southern states were not as well prepared in 1779 as New England had been after Lexington.

The fall of Savannah had little effect on the general spirit of overconfidence. Even such an astute observer as Dr. Franklin was deceived when he wrote to an English friend on March 21, 1779: "You have now got a little army into Georgia and are triumphing in that success. . . . But if they stay through the summer in that climate there is a certain *General Fever* that I apprehend will give a good account of most of them."[5]

General Fever's victims, unfortunately, were to be chiefly native troops without benefit of training, equipment or medical care. Not much resistance could be expected from Georgia, which had a white population of about 17,000. South Carolina, as the first line of defense, depended on militia troops raised by a modified form of conscription which permitted the hiring of substitutes. Such a system, as the experience of history proves, is invariably resented by troops who grumble about "a rich man's war but a poor man's fight." In order not to make the service too burdensome for small farmers, according to a contemporary historian, the battalions were "made up of draughts from the inhabitants of the country, changed every second or third month. . . . Unacquainted with military stratagems, deficient in discipline, and not thoroughly broken to habits of implicit obedience, they were often surprised; and had to learn by repeated misfortunes, the necessity of subordination and the advantages of discipline."[6]

Only a few preliminary successes were needed to bolster an unfounded conviction of superiority, and South Carolina forces defeated the first two British attempts at invasion early in 1779. Colonel William Moultrie, the rugged hero of Sullivan's Island, got the better of a detachment of 200 redcoats sent from Savannah to take possession of Port Royal Island. The rebels, with about equal numbers, drove the invaders back to their ships after inflicting losses which included "almost all their officers."

A second encounter took place in February when a body of about 500 South Carolina loyalists attempted to join the British at Augusta for a new invasion. They were pursued by Colonel Andrew Pickens, whose 300 rebel militia routed them at Kettle Creek with losses of 40 killed and more than a hundred prisoners. The survivors scattered over the countryside, some of them surrendering to the patriots and others never drawing rein until they reached their homes.

There were further penalties to be paid by Tories who had not scrupled to incite the Cherokees of the frontier. This brought up the delicate question of what constitutes treason in a civil war, and the South Carolina authorities took the political risk of trying loyalist leaders on that charge. About 70 were condemned to death; and though only five went to the gallows, another dangerous precedent had been added to the British murders of prisoners at Savannah.

After these two successes the South Carolina authorities no longer discussed the defense of their own soil. They envisioned a campaign to drive the British out of Georgia and pursue them into East Florida for the capture of St. Augustine. General Lincoln sent two militia forces across the Savannah River against the enemy posts on the south bank, and the rebels had everything their own way at first. General Ashe with 1,500 troops forced Campbell to abandon Augusta, the main stronghold. The patriots followed as far as Briar Creek, where they were attacked by General Prevost after a secret march of fifty miles to get in their rear. "Never was an army more completely surprised," Moultrie recorded in his *Memoirs*, "and never were men more panick struck. . . . The poor fellows! most of them threw down their arms, and run through a deep swamp, 2 or 3 miles, to gain the banks of a wide and rapid river [Savannah], and plunged themselves in, to escape from the bayonet; many of them endeavoring to reach the opposite shore, sunk down, and were buried in a watery grave; while those who had more strength, and skill in swimming, gained the other side, but were still so terrified, that they straggled through the woods in every direction. . . ."[7]

Again it had been demonstrated, this time at American expense, that defeat usually meant annihilation in southern militia operations. About 150 rebels were captured and an equal number killed or drowned, but it would be more accurate to say that Ashe's little army had ceased to exist as a military force. "Many of them made no stay anywhere until they got to their homes in North-Carolina," added Moultrie. "The loss of arms was almost total, and it was a very serious consideration to us at the time, as we could not replace them."

This victory strengthened the British hold on Georgia and awakened the South Carolina authorities to their danger. The assembly passed new laws offering higher bounties to encourage militia recruiting and imposed stiff fines for failure to report. By April the patriots had about 7,000 troops, but there was little co-operation between the South Carolina militia under Governor Rutledge and the forces of General Lincoln, composed of a few raw Continentals and militia from all the southern states. Each went his own strategic way without consulting the other, so that Prevost had an advantage with half the numbers. The British general found his opening when Lincoln marched up the Savannah in April to cut the communications of the redcoats with western Georgia and confine them to the coast. Prevost did not wait for any such development. Lincoln's absence gave him an opportunity to cross the river for a bold advance on Charleston, defended by three widely separated forces. The ensuing chaos was summed up in Moultrie's journal entry for May 8th:

> At this time there never was a country in greater confusion and consternation; and it is easily accounted for, when 5 armies were marching through the southern parts of it, at the same time, and all for different purposes; myself retreating as fast as possible to get into town; the British army of 3,000 men commanded by Gen. Prevost in pursuit of me; and Gen. Lincoln with the American army of 4,000, marching with hasty strides to come up with the British; Gov. Rutledge from Orangeburgh, with about 600 militia, hastening to get to town lest he should be shut out, and Col. Harris, with a detachment of 250 continentals pushing on with all possible dispatch to reinforce me. . . . In short, it was nothing but a general confusion and alarm.[8]

There is no doubt that Prevost could have taken Charleston easily if he had kept up his rapid pace. But the lure of plunder had more attraction than an almost certain victory, and the invaders stopped midway. to loot the plantations. The halt of two or three days saved the city, Ramsay concluded, when "Moultrie, Rutledge and Harris, with their respective commands, all reached Charleston on the 9th and 10th of May, the last having marched nearly forty miles a day for four days successively. Their arrival, together with that of the militia from the northern parts of the state, gave hopes of a successful defence."9

On the 11th the plunder-laden British army summoned the city to surrender. That same day the garrison was strengthened by Colonel Pulaski's legion from the North. Two hours after reporting, the gallant Pole led his light horse against the British mounted troops of the advance guards and routed them with heavy losses. In spite of this little success, a council of citizens—wealthy merchants and planters—agreed on a compromise of defeatism. If the British army would withdraw, they replied to Prevost's summons, South Carolina would remain neutral during the rest of the war and give her allegiance afterwards to the winning side. This is a chapter of state history that South Carolinians have always wished to forget, and several native sons wept with shame at the time. Young John Laurens refused to carry the message, and Moultrie did not mince words in expressing his opinion of men who put property above patriotism. Christopher Gadsden, one of the fiery radicals of the first Continental Congress in 1774, also thundered against the proposal. Pulaski, Lachlan McIntosh and the other soldiers insisted that Charleston could be defended, but the civil authorities had their way.

South Carolina retained some tattered remnants of her honor the next day only because Prevost rejected the offer and demanded a military surrender. The citizens had no wish to become captives, and Moultrie reported that "the governor and council looked very grave and stedfastly on each other and on me. . . . I then said, 'I am determined not to deliver you up prisoners of war—WE WILL FIGHT IT OUT.' Upon my saying this, Colonel Laurens who was in the tent, jumped up, and said, 'thank God! we are upon our legs again!' and as I was coming out of the tent, General Gadsden and Mr. Ferguson, two of the council who were against giving up the town, followed me and said, 'act according to your own judgment and we will support you.' "10

Prevost's force, as Moultrie reckoned it, amounted to 3,620 troops in addition to 120 Indians. The defenders had 3,180 men, including 300 Continentals and the 200 veterans of Pulaski's corps. Thus the British were at a disadvantage in numbers as compared to most besieging armies, not to mention their lack of heavy guns.

Once the rebel soldiers got the upper hand in Charleston, preparations for defense went ahead so energetically that Prevost lost his opportunity within a few hours. Where there had been no works on the land side, trenches were dug and cannon mounted. All night hundreds of blazing tar barrels made the scene as bright as day for the militiamen awaiting an attack. And at dawn the chagrin of the fainthearted citizens was complete when scouts discovered that the enemy had retreated under cover of darkness.

A year later it would require one of the largest British armadas of the war to besiege the city, but Prevost's officers seem to have been more interested in pillage than victory. Having already sampled the loot of wealthy plantations, they plundered while retiring to James Island before Lincoln could cut off their escape. Their baggage wagons were soon loaded with silver plate, jewels and money. Houses were stripped by parties which spread out through the countryside, guided by slaves to whom they offered freedom for information as to the hiding places of family possessions.

This might have been a good opportunity for the British to recover lost moral ground from rebels proclaiming liberty to the world while clinging to the ancient evil of slavery. There was no weaker joint in the political armor of Americans who had given the invaders a bad name in Europe for violating codes of humane warfare. But greed again got the better of such judgment as Prevost's officers may have possessed. Far from freeing the Negroes who trusted them as liberators, they added the poor wretches to their plunder. About three thousand were eventually taken to St. Augustine and sold into bondage in the West Indies by officers who divided profits amounting to thousands of guineas.

One of the most shocking episodes of the war resulted when Prevost's army finally left the islands off the South Carolina coast in June. After weeks of plundering which did not spare family tombs, the invaders had too much loot to be crammed into the ships taking them away. Most of the horses had to be shot, and the problem of the surplus slaves might have been solved more mercifully that way. Afraid to return to their old masters after dire British warnings, these Negroes swam out and clung to the gunwales of the longboats so desperately that the crews had to beat them off with oars. Some of them drowned and so many were left to starve that their bones could be seen a generation later. Britons and

Americans alike shared the guilt, since about half of Prevost's troops were northern loyalists belonging to such regiments as the Queen's Rangers.

Lack of boats had prevented Lincoln from threatening the redcoats in their island strongholds, but on June 20th he attempted to surprise them at Stono Ferry in the confusion of departure. The 1,200 rebels attacked so vigorously that they nearly carried three enemy redoubts defended by cannon. Two companies of the 71st Highlanders, making a sally, met with such a warm reception that only a few got back to their lines. Most of the enemy gunners were killed or wounded, and Lincoln's victory seemed assured until Prevost's main army came to the rescue of the 700 threatened troops. The rebels retreated in some disorder after a final charge by Pulaski's horse, and the action ended inconclusively with losses of about 165 on each side.[11]

Two months later the British foothold in the southern states was imperiled by the arrival of a French fleet. As soon as the loss of Savannah became known, Congress chartered a fast ship in January and sent a message to Comte d'Estaing, suggesting the desirability of another combined land and sea operation. Lafayette, who was suspected by his own countrymen of being more American than French in sympathy, appealed directly to Louis XVI and his ministers after a voyage to his homeland in the spring of 1779. France's policy of devoting all her resources to the defence of the West Indies, he warned, was endangering an equally important object of the war, the winning of American independence. Gérard, the French minister at Philadelphia, also urged in his dispatches that more aid be given to the rebels in their hour of need.

These solicitations came at a time when d'Estaing had recovered from his early reverses and inflicted several costly defeats on the British in the West Indies. In June he captured the island of St. Vincent and a small enemy garrison without a fight. Several weeks later the French admiral took Grenada after carrying field fortifications which the defenders believed to be impregnable. Admiral Byron flew to the rescue a few days too late with his squadron and met with a defeat in the first large-scale naval battle of the war. D'Estaing could probably have destroyed the enemy squadron if he had followed up his advantage, but he contented himself with winning the greatest naval success gained by his country over the British in a century.

The triumph gave the French a brief superiority in American waters, and the recent entrance of Spain into the war encouraged the ministers of Louis XVI to attempt an invasion of England. Every conflict between the hereditary foes had seen a revival of that perennial plan, but never were the prospects for success better than in the summer of 1779. A combined French and Spanish fleet commanded by Comte d'Orvilliers eluded Sir Charles Hardy's 40 ships of the line and arrived off Plymouth on August 16th. The docks and naval magazines were so defenseless that England had her worst fright since the Spanish Armada. But the traditional caution of the French ministers robbed D'Orvilliers of his opportunity when his orders were countermanded. He cruised for two weeks off the southern coast and chased Hardy's fleet into port, then abandoned the expedition in obedience to orders from Paris.

John Paul Jones, with less resources but more resolution, actually dealt the enemy a harder blow a few days later in one of the most dramatic sea fights of history—the famous moonlight duel off Flamborough Head on the night of September 23rd. Commanding the *Bonhomme Richard*, an ancient merchantman made over into a man-of-war, he forced the much superior *Serapis* to strike her colors. His battered tub sank a few hours later, and the victor brought his prisoners back to France in the captured enemy warship.

Continental marines, firing their muskets from the foretops, had a prominent part in all of Jones's sea fights. They also participated in his raid on Whitehaven in 1778—the single occasion when Americans carried the war to English soil. The countrymen of the naval hero could only speculate as to what he might have accomplished with a small squadron of warships. For after 1779 a bankrupt nation could never give him another opportunity to fire a broadside; and his shout of defiance to the captain of the *Serapis* might have served as an ironical epitaph to his own career, "I have not yet begun to fight."

National poverty goes far toward explaining the decline of the little navy. Certainly it was the most comforting answer, but Americans also had themselves to blame for trusting too much in the illusory victories won by privateers. Jones foresaw as early as 1776 that these raiders with their lure of prize money would cripple the navy by attracting the best seamen. As a remedy he proposed that the sailors of the warships be allowed more income from captures. "What is the paltry emolument of two-thirds of prizes," he asked in a letter to Robert Morris, "to the finances of this vast Continent?"[12]

The statistics of American privateering vary widely, but some authorities

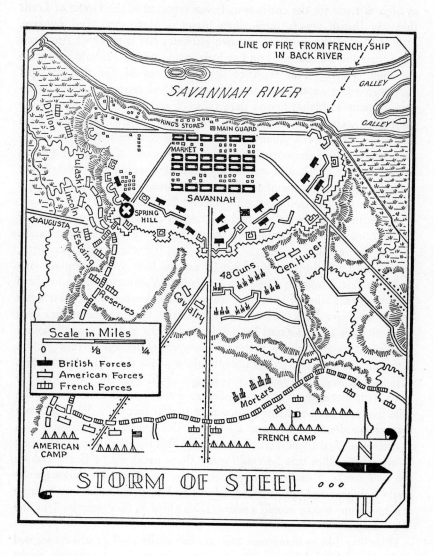

LINE OF FIRE FROM FRENCH SHIP
IN BACK RIVER

GALLEY

SAVANNAH RIVER

GALLEY

KING'S STORES   MAIN GUARD

MARKET

SAVANNAH

⟨AUGUSTA

Pulaski

Lincoln

d'Estaing

Reserves

SPRING
HILL

Cavalry

48 Guns

Gen. Huger

Scale in Miles

0   1/8   1/4

British Forces
American Forces
French Forces

Mortars

AMERICAN
CAMP

FRENCH CAMP

N

STORM OF STEEL ...

have placed the number of captured or destroyed enemy merchant ships as high as 1,500 for the entire war. It was reported to the House of Lords that 733 British vessels were taken between May, 1776, and January, 1778.[13] One of the most conservative estimates has it that 792 American ships, carrying 13,000 guns and swivels, made voyages as raiders during the eight years.[14] This form of aggression was by far the principal American effort on the sea, and it accomplished enough to drive insurance rates up to higher figures than those of any former war. Meanwhile the British were not turning the other cheek. While their merchant ships took some hard knocks, enemy warships and raiders virtually wiped American commerce off the ocean by 1779. This was one of the chief reasons for the decline of Continental money—the new nation could not export enough produce to maintain its credit abroad, though such staples as tobacco, rice and indigo were in demand at high prices.

American entreaties at last had their effect on d'Estaing in 1779 after his victories gave him a temporary naval superiority in American waters. Having discretionary orders to aid the rebels if circumstances permitted, he appeared off the Georgia coast so unexpectedly on September 11th that four British warships fell into his hands. Washington had tried hard to persuade his allies to lend their sea power for combined land and water attacks on New York and Newport after the Georgia operations. In a letter of May 1st to Gérard he promised that the patriots would "collect a sufficient force to give a reasonable prospect of success to an operation decisive in its nature. . . ." It is not often in war that the same opportunities beckon a second time within a year, but again Washington hoped for "important successes, so as to disembarrass these States of the whole or the principal part of the enemy's force now within them. . . ."[15] And again the commander in chief came up against that parsimonious spirit which so often stultified French naval strategy. In this tradition Comte d'Estaing informed his allies that he could grant them naval aid in Georgia alone for two weeks. Between the gracious lines of diplomatic language he made it ungraciously plain that the boon had been extended only because the hurricane season would endanger his ships if they remained in the West Indies.

D'Estaing, like so many men who are habitually too late, always seemed to be in a frightful hurry. The Americans, warned that tardiness might cost them the capture of Savannah, were given short notice to collect the force of South Carolina militia accompanying Lincoln's Continentals. It took the French admiral five days meanwhile to land 3,500 troops and advance a few miles up the Savannah for a junction with the Americans on the 16th.

Even after this delay it is evident from enemy testimony that if d'Estaing had attacked promptly he might easily have taken a city surprised with its forces widely separated and its works half completed. General Prevost could only sink several old ships to obstruct the river while sending messages to his subordinates at Sunbury and Beaufort to hasten to Savannah with their detachments, amounting to half of the total British numbers.

From the beginning the relations between allies were more strained than is usually the case in combined operations. On the 16th, according to Lee, "the comte d'Estaing summoned the British general in the name of his most christian majesty only. This offensive style violated the respect due from one sovereign to another, and could not have been relished by the American general, though policy may have forbid his noticing it at the moment."[16]

Where Sullivan would have blown up in a rage, Lincoln perhaps erred on the side of conciliation. Afterwards, it was asserted, d'Estaing explained that no slight had been intended. At any rate, the French admiral took the responsibility for granting a truce of twenty-four hours to foes who cleverly gave the impression that they needed this time to agree upon terms of surrender.

All contemporary authorities insist that Savannah was saved by the day of grace. Prevost made his request, as one of his officers boasted, "with nothing else in view but to steal time." The garrison used every minute to good advantage by toiling frantically on the unfinished works, and Colonel Maitland barely had time to arrive from Beaufort with 900 reinforcements after a secret march through a swamp.

At the expiration of the truce Prevost returned a defiant answer, though Lee declared that "any four hours before the junction of lieutenant colonel Maitland was sufficient to have taken Savannah." The fortifications had been so strengthened that d'Estaing decided upon a formal siege, and the next two weeks were devoted to bringing up 53 cannon and 14 mortars from the French fleet. A letter from a British officer, Colonel John Harris Cruger, described the beginning of the bombardment:

> On Sunday night ye 4th Octbr at 12 o'Clock the French opened their Bomb Battery, consisting of 7 or 8 Mortars, & continued throwing Shells till revellee next morning, when they opened at once all their

Battering Artillery, wch was immediately returned with equal fury from ours. . . . Carcasses were thrown for 2 nights, wch only burnt 2 Houses—their shells, perpetually flying, did little or no damage, but their shott greatly injured the Town; scarcely a House has escaped, several are irreparable. The whole Rebel Army all this time, Continentals and Militia, about 2500, under Genl Lincoln, laying idle, so much despised by the french as not to be allowed to go into their Camp, no communication together.[17]

Although a good deal of prejudice colored this account of the relations between allies, it is obvious that some foundation existed for the rumors which comforted the British garrison. Yet the rebels had already demonstrated that they were not contemptible associates by winning one of the most astonishing little successes of the war. On the night of September 30th Colonel John White of the Continentals, accompanied only by a captain and four volunteers, had the audacity to demand the surrender of the British regulars and sailors manning five small vessels anchored in the Ogeechee River about 25 miles from Savannah. As a stratagem he had his soldiers build enough fires to give the illusion of a formidable encampment. Then he warned the British captain, according to a contemporary historian, "that nothing but an instant compliance could save his men from being cut in pieces by a superior force. . . . The deception was carried on with such address, that all the prisoners, amounting to 141, were secured, and afterward safely conducted, by three of the captors, for 25 miles through the country, to an American post."[18]

Tedious progress was being made meanwhile by the besieging forces which began their parallels and approaches on September 23rd. While this work went on, the British had an opportunity to complete their redoubts and mount about 80 cannon. There was little question but that they must eventually be bombarded or starved into capitulation, but the French admiral concluded that he could not wait. His naval captains warned that the warships might be attacked in an unfavorable position if an enemy squadron came to the relief, and the crews were suffering from scurvy. D'Estaing finally announced to Lincoln that it had come to a choice between abandoning the siege and attempting a storm. After five days of bombardment the morning of October 9th was fixed for the assault, and 3,450 troops advanced in three columns at dawn.

Prevost could not have asked for anything better, since his only other hope of victory lay in the slender chance of a British squadron coming to the rescue. Throughout the operations of 1779 he had shown a high order of generalship when not diverted by plunder, and he correctly judged that the main allied effort would be pressed against the redoubts of his right wing. In this quarter Comte d'Estaing and Lincoln took personal command of a force composed of 3,100 French regulars and Continentals while a smaller French column attacked the center and 350 rebel militia made a feint on the left.

Ever since 1775 the rebels had hoped for another Bunker Hill, but history was to repeat itself at their expense on this October morning. For the attacking forces were exposed to a deadly enfilade fire from the British ships as well as the batteries of fortifications extending in a semicircle from the river. Legend has it that the British guns were loaded with scrap iron, scissors and even lengths of chain. In any event they worked terrible destruction at point-blank range among troops which d'Estaing had massed to capture the Spring Hill battery. A few of his men forced the abatis and planted their standards on the parapet as Count Pulaski led his horsemen between two redoubts in an attempt to reach the enemy's rear. Then a counterattack of British grenadiers dislodged the allies and sent them reeling back in a complete repulse.

D'Estaing was wounded and Pulaski slain in an action which ranks as one of the bloodiest of the war. Of the 600 Continentals, 234 were killed and wounded during those fifty-five minutes, while the French had 637 casualties among the 2,500 troops engaged on the British right. There were enough additional losses among the French forces of the center and the American militia to bring the total up to nearly a thousand. Prevost's men, fighting from cover, reported only 120 killed and wounded.

"There cannot be a doubt," Moultrie summed up mournfully in his *Memoirs*, "but if the French and Americans had marched into Savannah on the 17th, they would have carried the town very easily. . . . After this repulse we were in a worse condition than before. The Count d'Estaing departed; the unfortunate militia of Georgia . . . were obliged to seek shelter in a strange country or live in the backwoods of their own. It depressed our spirits, we began to be apprehensive about the safety of these two Southern States; it also depreciated our money so low that it was scarcely worth anything."[19]

Lincoln retired into South Carolina with a force reduced by militia desertions as misfortune continued to pursue d'Estaing. For his fleet was scattered by a gale soon after its departure, so that four frigates fell into the hands of the enemy.

The bad news from Savannah added to the disillusionment of patriots

who had expected so much from the French alliance and the entrance
of Spain into the war. The British and loyalists were correspondingly
elated over a triumph which inspired thirteen exultant stanzas in James
Rivington's *Gazette*. Usually such efforts were so filled with abuse as to
be tiresome, but this time the Tory writer had come uncomfortably close
to the secret doubts which disturbed the stoutest rebels at the end
of 1779:

> Joy to great Congress, joy an hundred fold,
> The grand cajolers are themselves cajol'd;
> What now is left of Continental brags?
> Taxes unpaid, though payable in rags.
> What now remains of Continental force?
> Battalions mould'ring, waste without resource.
> What rests there yet of Continental sway?
> A ruined people ripe to disobey;
> Hate now of men, and soon to be the jest,
> Such is your state, ye monsters of the West.
> Yet must on every face a smile be worn,
> Whilst every breast with agony is torn;
> Hopeless yourselves, yet hope you must impart,
> And comfort others with an aching heart.
> Ill-fated they, who lost at home, must boast
> Of help expected from a foreign coast;
> How wretched is their lot to France and Spain,
> Who look for succor, but who look in vain.[20]

PART FOUR

Victory

*Don't you think that we bear beating very well,
and that . . . the more we are beat, the better we
grow?*

—GENERAL GREENE

Chapter 21

The Siege of Charleston

ANY graph of the American war effort would doubtless show that the low point was reached in the first month of 1780. Although Valley Forge has gone down in history as a synonym for privations, it could not compare with the sufferings of the winter at Morristown. "Our prospects are infinitely worse than they have been at any period of the War," the commander in chief reported to Congress on December 15, 1779, "and unless some expedient can instantly be adopted a dissolution of the Army for want of subsistence in unavoidable—A part of it has been again several days without Bread—and for the rest we have not either on the spot or within reach a supply sufficient for four days."[1]

Past shortages had often been due to poor organization or lack of transport, but this crisis was more serious. Ever since 1775 it had been apparent that the inadequate military resources of America must some day approach the vanishing point, and that time seemed to have come as the war neared its sixth year. For Washington emphasized that his deficiencies did not "proceed from accidental obstructions as has been the case on former occasions but from the absolute emptiness of our magazines everywhere and the total want of money or credit to replenish them."

Bitter cold added to the sufferings of soldiers who recalled that the last winter had been the mildest in memory. Not until the middle of January had there been a first light snowfall at West Point, and the apple trees bloomed late in March. In cruel contrast, the winter at Morristown seemed bent on breaking all records for severity. Before the log huts were half finished, the worst blizzard of the century blew down tents and buried the encampment in snow. Dr. Thacher wrote in his journal that "the sufferings of the poor soldiers can scarcely be described; while on duty they are unavoidably exposed to all the inclemency of storms and severe ground; at night they now have a bed of straw on the ground, and a single blanket to each man; they are badly clad, and are destitute of shoes. . . . The snow is now from four to six feet deep, which so obstructs the roads as to prevent our receiving a supply of provisions. . . . The consequence is, the soldiers are so enfeebled from hunger and cold, as to be almost unable to perform their military duty, or to labor constructing their huts."[2]

Even if there had been no lack of supplies, the army was isolated for days by snowbound roads. Relief necessarily had to come from the surrounding countryside, and the New Jersey farm and village folk responded with a patriotism never surpassed by any other section of America during the war. Many of the same people had watched Washington's forlorn retreat in 1776 without contributing even moral support. The devastations of Howe's troops made such confirmed rebels of them that three years later they shared their own food with the soldiers at Morristown.

Washington, according to the contemporary historian Gordon, "was obliged to call upon the magistrates of the Jersey state; to expose his situation to them; and to declare in plain terms that he and his army were reduced to the alternative of disbanding or catering for themselves, unless the inhabitants would afford them aid. He allotted to each county a certain proportion of flour or grain, and a certain number of cattle to be delivered on certain days. To the honor of the magistrates and the good disposition of the people, be it added that his requisitions were punctually complied with, and in many counties exceeded. Nothing but this great and patriotic exertion . . . could have saved the army from dissolution or starving, as the troops were bereft of every hope from the commissary."[3]

The Continental Army made few pretensions to democracy in an age when every officer and gentleman held himself to be a cut above the rank and file. But when it came to dangers and hardships, Washington and his generals could teach a lesson to professional soldiers of the present day. "To share a common lot, and participate in the inconveniences, wch. the army, from the peculiarity of our circumstances, are oblig'd to undergo, has been with me a fundamental principle," the commander in chief wrote to Greene on January 22nd. It did strike him as a little excessive, however, that "I have been at my prest. quarters since the 1st day of Decr., and have not had a Kitchen to cook a Dinner in, altho' the Logs have been put together some considerable time by my own Guard. . . . Eighteen belonging to my family, and all Mrs. Ford's, are crowded together in her

Kitchen, and scarce one of them able to speak for the colds they have caught."[4]

Washington's hardships might have been worse except for the fiercely protective attitude of Elizabeth Thompson, his housekeeper. When "not a farthing" was forthcoming to buy better food for the general, she guilefully persuaded him to grant requisitions for army salt. Then plodding out into the snow, the seventy-six-year-old domestic "traded to the country people for supplies and set a good table for the next few days."[5] In all parts of the country the salt shortage added to war privations, and Americans never forgot the craving induced by months of tasteless food. Prizes were offered by several states for some method of obtaining a supply by evaporation of sea water, but no practical solution seems to have been found.

Mrs. Thompson not only survived the war but was voted a pension at the age of eighty-one by Congress. So many thousands of other women aided the cause in 1780 that the newspapers were filled with praises of their efforts.[6] Although Baltimore was no more than an overgrown village, the women sewed 600 shirts for soldiers. In Annapolis their subscriptions amounted to $16,103, half of it in specie, while Philadelphia women raised a total of about $300,000 in Continental. Unhappily, the rapid depreciation often made the money of less value to the recipients than the donors; and peculators in high places continued to rob the soldiers of more clothing than feminine needles could provide.

Congress decided to stop the printing press after two hundred million dollars had been emitted in Continental paper. The assembly stuck to its resolve upon reaching that limit in November, and the new policy was summed up in a committee report adopted on January 31, 1780:

> That supplies of provisions for the army in its greatest number can certainly be obtained within the United States; and the Congress, with the co-operation of the several states, can take effectual measures for procuring them in such manner as that no operation will be impeded. . . . That Congress rely on the contributions of the states by taxes, and on moneys to be raised by internal loans for the pay of the army. That supplies of clothing, or tents, of arms and warlike stores, must be principally obtained from foreign nations; and the United States must rely chiefly on the assistance of their ally for them. . . .[7]

Theoretically, no fairer plan could have been hit upon, but results depended in the long run on voluntary contributions. Even if the states had the will to meet their quotas, it remained a question whether they had the means, Nathanael Greene, the quartermaster-general, appeared doubtful after conferring at the State House. "The public is insolvent to all intents and purposes," he wrote to Washington on March 28th. "The treasury is without money, and the Congress are without credit. . . . The best people who are in Congress think that the new system of drawing supplies from the States, will be found totally incompetent to the business."[8]

This gloomy prediction proved before the end of the year to be only too well founded. Nor did Congress succeed in soothing the unpaid army at Morristown by promising to make good the deficiencies resulting from the depreciation of the currency. Unpaid American soldiers might have got as bad a name as the enemy for crimes of violence if Washington had not shown more backbone than the opposing generals. He did not content himself with admonitions, and such scenes as the following, reported in a corporal's journal, became all too familiar:

> The two criminals were brought from the Provost under a strong guard. Their coffins were borne just before them. The Dead March was played behind them. . . . Where the Brigade was paraded, the Criminals were brought in front for everyone to see them, after which their sentences was read, which was to be shot. The coffins were set down by the edge of their graves. The men who were to be their executioners had their guns loaded for that purpose, and marched up to within a rod of the coffins. The criminals were made to kneel . . . but at the moment they were to be shot their reprieves were read. The brigade marched back to our camp & was dismissed.[9]

In later years there must have been several hundred Continental veterans whose knees went weak when they recalled a similar experience. For Washington made a practice of combining mercy with severity by pardoning a majority of the men sentenced to capital punishment. He made sure of the moral effect by waiting until the last moment; and enough offenders actually were executed to make it a frightful ordeal for the survivors. Even so, it is related by another diarist that a man forgiven in May had to be hanged in June for repeating his crime. Desertion and looting were the main offenses, and Dr. Thacher witnessed the spectacle when three culprits found no mercy awaiting them: "These unfortunate young men came to the gallows overwhelmed with the horror of death. Their whole frames were thrown into a tremor, and they were tortured at the sight of the gallows and halters. . . . Their mournful cries and lamentations were distressing beyond description."[10]

Several feet of snow remained on the frozen ground until the end of March. Ironically, the cold kept the soldiers from completing the log huts until the greatest need for them had passed. Men undergoing such sufferings were not in a mood to be reasonable, and Washington's orders of January 29th declared that "a night scarcely passed without gangs of soldiers going out of camp and committing every species of robbery, depredation, and the grossest personal insults. These violences are committed on the property and persons of those, who, on a very late alarming occasion for the want of provision, manifested the warmest attachment to the army, by affording it the most generous and plentiful relief."[11]

It was characteristic of Washington that he exaggerated rather than glossed over offenses which his stern discipline kept at a minimum. Fear of the gallows cowed the ruffians in the ranks, and most of the troops were decent young fellows who needed little correction. The phrase "an army of husbandmen" took on a literal meaning when soldiers were permitted to hire out as farmhands in the vicinity, thus earning their keep and a little money while solving an urgent wartime labor problem. Among the men taken into the homes of neighboring farmers was Elijah Fisher, whose struggles with syntax enliven the journal he kept from 1775 to 1784. Working long days for a man named Wallace, the Massachusetts private doggedly continued his fight against illiteracy every night by candlelight: "I stayed there and follows my Riting and sifering the same as I had Dun the Evenings before. For Every Evening from six of the Clock till Nine I used to follow my study and Mr. Wallais was as Desirus of my learning as myself and used to showe me." Fisher made such progress during the winter that he took great pride a few months later in his ability to keep the company records: "Capt. Lunt was at home on furlow and one of the Leut was at home recruting the other on command so I had to take the howl Care of the Comp'y and all the returns to Sine and Clothing to git and State stores and the like."[12]

The little army at Morristown kept the initiative against a much larger and better provided enemy. New York Harbor and the Hudson were frozen solidly for the first time in memory, and British writings reveal that Knyphausen's troops remained on the alert against an attack over the bridge of ice. "We expected it hourly," Sergeant Krafft admitted in his diary, "and therefore the best measures were taken. The sailors on the ships received guns and had to serve on land and with the pickets at night.

All the citizens and country people between 16 and 60 years of age received guns."[13]

Although the rebels had more reason to adopt a passive strategy, they struck first in one of the most curious operations of the war. On January 14th, while the country was still snowbound, 500 sleighs left Morristown with 2,500 picked troops. Lord Stirling, his red nose protruding from a cocoon of blankets, led the strange expedition through four-foot drifts in an attempt to cross over the ice and surprise the British works on Staten Island. The rebels persisted for twenty-four hours in sub-zero weather, but spies warned British troops who withdrew to inner fortifications too strong to be stormed. Stirling brought back captured stores and a few prisoners, but more than 500 of his men were frostbitten. The only American gains were moral, for the enemy continued on the defensive for two months in expectation of another attack from opponents showing so much resolution. Neither side essayed anything more ambitious than minor raids, and the stalemate lasted until after the melting of the ice. Washington had done enough to bring his army safely through the worst winter of the war; and on April 19th he invited the new French minister, the Chevalier de la Luzerne, to a military review at Morristown. His secretary Marbois—in later years the Marquis de Barbé-Marbois who negotiated the Louisiana Purchase treaty for Napoleon—wrote letters which indicate that the visitors had already formed favorable first impressions of America:

> In a journey of 150 leagues I have seen nothing which corresponds to the rough and savage pictures which I had formed of it. There are many uncultivated spots, but that is lack of labor, and most of them are capable of a large population and a high degree of cultivation. Prosperity and abundance reign in all the dwellings. From Boston here [Philadelphia], we have not seen a single pauper, we have not met a peasant who was not well dressed and who did not have a good wagon or at least a good horse. . . . We have not entered a single dwelling in the morning without finding there a kettle in which was cooking a good fowl, or a piece of beef, or mutton with a piece of bacon; and a great abundance of vegetables; bread, cider, things from the dairy, and a profusion of firewood; clean furniture, a good bed and often a newspaper.[14]

Other accounts testify as to the paradox of rural plenty during the winter of the army's worst privations. It might seem that more of this food could have been transferred from the farmer's table to the soldier's mess, but the problems of military supply are not solved quite so easily. Such great financial minds as Hamilton and Robert Morris were unable to find the answer, for even in the eighteenth century a simple rural economy could not meet the industrial needs of a complex war effort. The declining currency rather than the farmer's kitchen was the true index of American resources in 1780, and Washington doubtless felt fortunate to have kept together an army capable of marching past the new French minister while the cannon fired thirteen salutes.

"A large stage was erected in the field," Dr. Thacher noted, "which was crowded with officers, ladies, and gentlemen of distinction, among them were Governor Livingston . . . and his lady." Washington wished also to make a good impression on Don Juan de Miralles, who had been sent by Spain apparently in a private capacity but actually to report on American conditions. Congress at the time was courting an active Spanish alliance by hinting at such inducements as exclusive navigation of the Mississippi and a free hand in conquering the Floridas from the British. But the military review followed by firewords proved too strenuous for Miralles, and he died of "pulmonic fever" a few days later. The whole army turned out again for a magnificent funeral described in awed detail by Dr. Thacher: "The coffin was most splendid and stately, lined throughout with fine cambric and covered on the outside with rich black velvet. . . . The top of the coffin was removed, to display the pomp and grandeur with which the body was decorated. It was in a splendid full dress, consisting of a scarlet suit, embroidered with rich gold lace, a three cornered gold laced hat, and a genteel cued wig, white silk stockings, large diamond shoe and knee buckles, a profusion of diamond rings decorated the fingers, and from a superb gold watch set with diamonds, several rich seals were suspended."[15]

The occasion was symbolic of American hopes for Spanish aid. Such aspirations might as well have been buried with the unfortunate Miralles, for the court at Madrid had no wish to encourage the growth of republican institutions in a continent where it held important possessions. Spain was the enemy of Great Britain and the ally of France; but at no time during the war could that kingdom have been considered the friend of the United States.

Both countries, however conflicting their war aims may have been, had cause for alarm as they observed the new British campaign in the South. Spanish as well as American territory would be in jeopardy if Clinton's forces succeeded in gaining a permanent foothold in South Carolina. North Carolina and Virginia would undoubtedly be next, for it was apparent that the invaders meant to keep the southern states in the Empire even if the others contrived to win their independence.

The plans were made in the early autumn of 1779, when it was expected by the British as well as their opponents that Savannah would be taken by d'Estaing. Admiral Arbuthnot reached New York too late for succor, but his fleet brought reinforcements and supplies which enabled Clinton to take the offensive with more troops than had been at his disposal since the summer of 1778. As a first step he withdrew Pigot's detachment from Newport on October 25th. The Americans paid generous tribute to a departing foeman who had occupied Rhode Island for three years without any of the usual British plundering. Gordon, who questioned the inhabitants shortly afterwards, asserted that the British "were in sufficient force while at Newport, to have made predatory excursions, and to have done much mischief; notwithstanding the troops that Gen. Gates, who was stationed at Providence, had under his command. But Gen. Sir Robert Pigot's humanity might revolt at such barbarous excursions; which is the most probable, from the strict and positive orders he gave for the observance of the most exact regularity and discipline during the evacuation. . . . The men were in no wise chargeable at their quitting the island, with any wanton cruelties, or needless destruction, or with an unjust seizure of property."[16]

The Franco-American reverse at Savannah had little effect of arousing South Carolina to fresh exertions for her own defense, though the authorities had timely warning of the approach of Clinton's armada. After wealthy merchants and planters had set the example of saving their property, men of humble station could hardly be blamed for wanting to save their own skins. They turned out indifferently when Governor John Rutledge ordered the militia to collect, and the manual labor of digging trenches proved to be distasteful to all classes of an aristocratic social order. The Yankees who had long been criticized for their leveling institutions might have pointed out that the fortifications of Bunker Hill went up in a single June night. At Charleston the problem remained unsolved for several weeks until the assembly authorized the governor to put 600 Negro slaves to work.[17]

These conditions distressed such leaders as Moultrie, Ramsay, Gadsden and the Rutledge brothers, who were as ardent and self-sacrificing patriots as could have been found anywhere in the country. John Mathews, the

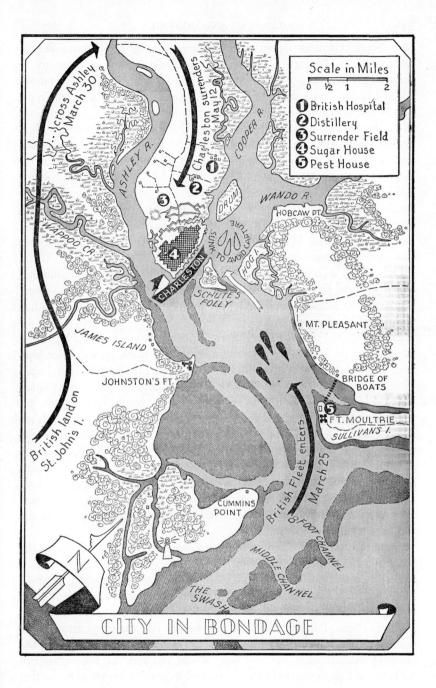

CITY IN BONDAGE

fiery South Carolina delegate in Congress, wrote to Thomas Bee at Charleston on January 3, 1780: "Good God! is there nothing to be done? . . . In passing through No. Carolina and Virginia, whenever I urged the necessity of their sending men to our aid, the constant reply was how can South Carolina expect we will send men to their support, when they will do nothing for themselves. Our men go there, sacrifice their healths, their lives, and the So. Carolina Militia are snug at their own homes. It is too much for them to expect us to fight their battles for them."[18]

The militia of the state came forward in such inadequate numbers that South Carolina officials appealed to Washington to send reinforcements from the North. Difficult as it was for him to spare troops at Morristown, he ordered General Woodford on the long march southward with 700 Continental veterans of the Virginia line.

Only about a third of the defenders of Charleston, chiefly militia and armed citizens, were recruited in South Carolina. Nevertheless, General Lincoln again found himself under the thumb of civil authorities who had questioned his decisions in 1779.

Luckily for the unready garrison, the British fleet was buffeted by winter storms. Several vessels were lost at sea, among them an ordnance ship with most of the heavy cannon; and two transports fell into the hands of rebel privateers. Prisoners brought to Charleston gave information which dispelled any last doubts as to that seaport being the objective, yet American participants agreed that Clinton could have taken the unfinished works easily if he had attacked at once. Instead, the fleet blockaded the harbor while the army made cautious preparations for a formal siege. After establishing a depot on James Island, the invaders took a full month from the time of their landing before crossing the Ashley River on March 29th and appearing before the rebel lines. This interval gave the garrison enough time to finish a system of redoubts and entrenchments all the way across Charleston Neck.

America's fourth city in population consisted of 1,020 buildings on the peninsula between the mouths of the Ashley and Cooper rivers. Broad Street, a hundred feet wide, extended from one river to the other—a thoroughfare of beautiful homes and landscaped gardens. Docks and warehouses testified as to the prosperity of the commercial capital of the South at a time when planters and landed proprietors were the forerunners of the industrialists of a later America. Tobacco, rice, cotton and indigo took the place of manufactures in the New World economy of the eighteenth century, and the great producers occupied a position comparable to that of multimillionaires in a day of larger incomes. The four southern states led all the rest in the proportion of young men sent to Europe for education and travel. This region also had the distinction of being the only part of America that had actually profited from the war during the first few years. At a time when the small farmers of the northern and middle states were producing little more than local subsistence, the crops of the South found an eager market at high prices as long as American ships could run the British blockade. It was this prosperity, more than any other factor, which accounted in 1780 for the lethargy of a section which had been aflame with patriotism in 1776. The war seemed remote to wealthy planters who could not realize that their possessions as well as liberties might be at stake. These men were probably no more selfish or complacent than the general run of humanity, but the time had come when they must pay the fiddler a long-overdue account.

Sir Henry Clinton did not intend that Charleston should get off as easily as in the summer of 1776. His force included about 7,000 troops, and the sailors and marines of Admiral Arbuthnot's fleet brought the total up to nearly 10,000. So thorough were the preparations that great mantelets had been constructed in New York to be used as portable shields for working parties, and the provision ships were filled with enough supplies to maintain the expedition for several months.

There had not been as yet a methodical siege of any duration in the whole war unless the brief investment of Savannah could be counted. The tactics for such operations had long been worked out in precise detail by the experience of European warfare. After isolating the city or fortress from outside aid, the assailants began by establishing a line of entrenchments and batteries known as the first parallel. From this position the troops burrowed forward in a zigzag fashion, always under cover, toward the enemy's works. Upon coming within more effective artillery range, they strengthened their position with a second parallel resembling the first. Then another laborious maze of approaches took the military moles to a point where they could locate their third parallel within musket shot of the defenders. This was the climax of the siege. The attacking army summoned the garrison to surrender; and if a bombardment or storm failed, the outcome depended on whether the post could be starved into submission. No operation called for more technical skill, and Clinton completed his first parallel early in April.

Among his forces were six regiments of Germans—the largest contingent to go on active duty in more than two years. It was no secret that the 30,000 mercenaries brought overseas at such enormous expense had disappointed their employers. General Haldimand, writing to Clinton from Quebec in 1779, went so far as to declare that "the Germans were unfit by nature and education for the American service."[19] Naturally the mercenaries resented this attitude, and it was a typical reaction when an officer wrote home to complain of "the confounded pride and arrogant bearing of the English, who treat everyone that was not born on their ragamuffin Island with contempt."[20]

It added to the chagrin of the Hessians when Frederick the Great, their idol and inspiration, showed his contempt by taxing as cattle the mercenaries who passed through his dominions. This insult could not be attributed, as some Americans fondly supposed, to approval of the rebel cause. It owed rather to Frederick's hatred of his allies in the last year. So fierce was his prejudice that only English profanity could express his opinion of the English minister Hugh Elliot in 1777. Writing in his own hand to the Comte de Malzan, the Prussian monarch exploded: *"Oh! l'homme incomparable que votre goddam Elliot! En vérité, les Anglais devraient rougir de honte d'envoyer tels ministres aux cours étrangères."*[21]

Clinton decided that the slow and methodical Germans had more aptitude for siege warfare than battle. Among the Jäger riflemen at Charleston were two young officers, Captain Johann Ewald and Captain Johann Hinrich (or Heinrichs), whose letters and diaries tell a detailed story of the expedition. The first, like most of his colleagues, viewed the war professionally without concerning himself much with the political causes. Hinrich, on the other hand, wrote an unpublished treatise on "the present state of learning in America." By 1778 he had half finished another work on the origin and progress of the war. It vexed the studious German that so many commentators had published accounts of America based on a brief tour. "All the books that have been written heretofore," he asserted, "are superficial, erroneous, dreams!" After two years in the country he summed up the causes of the Revolution in a letter to his homeland:

It is nothing more nor less than an Irish-Scotch Presbyterian Rebellion. The true Americans who take the greatest part therein, are the famous Quakers. . . . They were the first to institute a light company; they let the Germans go in first, afterwards they extricated themselves, and left their dupes in the muddle; they bought houses and lands with Congress money and afterwards called themselves friends of the King and said their religion forbade them to fight.

The American officers, Hinrich concluded, were "partly infatuated by the heat of their imagination, partly educated in wrong principles . . . and just as Congress consists of scoundrels, so the Army consists of people, warmed up in part by the war party, also their only support is the war, who . . . fear that their former masters, whose serfs they are, would harness them to the yoke, as soon as they surrendered their Captain's and Subaltern's patents."[22]

The young Hessian's observations may be taken more seriously with respect to military operations, and he had the highest praise for the mantelets constructed by the British engineers. They afforded so much protection that the besiegers had scarcely any losses while completing their first parallel. The approaches were being pushed forward during the second week of April when a single hour's work by the British fleet decided the fate of Charleston. Fourteen warships ran past the guns of Fort Moultrie on the afternoon of the 9th and anchored between Sullivan's Island and the city. The *Richmond* lost her masts and the *New Vigilant* had to be burned after grounding on a sandbank; but the other vessels got off with minor damage, and only 27 men were killed and wounded among the crews.

This unexpected blow stunned Americans who had trusted to the 32-pounders of the fort to guard the harbor. The moment that Washington heard the news, he seems to have given up all hope of saving Charleston. "At this distance it is difficult to judge . . . but it really appears to me," he wrote to Colonel Laurens on the 26th, "that the propriety of defending the town depended on the probability of defending the bar, and that, when this ceased, the attempt ought to have been relinquished."[23]

Clinton summoned the garrison to surrender the next day, but the civil authorities were encouraged by the arrival of the 700 Virginia Continentals after a march of 500 miles in 28 days. If it occurred to Lincoln that this force would only add to the disaster in case of surrender, he did not show any signs of misgivings. About the same number of North Carolina militia had just departed when their enlistments expired, so that the garrison remained at the old strength.

The rebels withdrew their nine small warships to the Cooper River and sank hulls across the mouth to keep the British fleet from entering. All crews and guns were removed to reinforce the shore batteries after the enemy began a vigorous bombardment on the 12th from the guns of the first parallel.

Not enough South Carolina militia could be recruited to threaten

Clinton's rear, but Lincoln kept a force of 300 cavalry in the field to cut off supplies. This detachment was surprised at Monck's Corner on the 14th by the horsemen of Colonel Banastre Tarleton, whose name would soon become a frightful legend in the South. Only about 25 rebels were killed or captured, but the others took to their heels in a complete rout.

Four days later Clinton received 3,000 reinforcements from New York. Lincoln still had a hope of escape by land, but the wildest optimist must have perceived that the city would soon be encircled. Under comparable circumstances, St. Clair had the moral fortitude to give up Ticonderoga in 1777 and save his army to fight another day. The decision brought a storm of censure down upon his head, though he was exonerated by public opinion as well as a court-martial when the facts became known. Lincoln delayed until April 18th before suggesting a similar course, then let himself be dissuaded by the civil authorities. On the 21st, after his engineers declared the works untenable, he called a second meeting of officers to vote on the question of evacuating the Continentals. "When the citizens were informed upon what the council was deliberating," wrote Moultrie, "some of them came into council, and expressed themselves very warmly, and declared to General Lincoln, that if he attempted to withdraw the troops, and leave the citizens; that they would cut up his boats, and open the gates to the enemy: this put a stop to all thoughts of evacuation of the troops, and nothing was left to us, but to make the best terms we could."[24]

The town held out for eighteen more days, but the last hope of defense vanished after the British began their third parallel on the 24th at a distance of 80 to 150 yards from the American lines. That morning the rebels made their only sally, and eleven redcoats were captured. But this gesture had no effect on an outcome which had been decided by the British fleet rather than the land forces.

At least it could not be said that the civilians of Charleston lacked courage. They took their part in the lines along with the soldiers, and several women and children lost their lives in the bombardment. The only panic of the siege, curiously, occurred on the night of the 25th among the attacking forces. "Toward twelve o'clock," Captain Ewald noted in his journal, "the enemy commenced a severe small-arms fire . . . which so filled our workmen and their guard with terror that the former ran away and the latter withdrew to the second parallel more or less in disorder. This terror also seized the second parallel. Everywhere they saw rebels. They believed that the enemy had made a sortie and fired musketry for half an hour, though not a single rebel had passed the ditch."[25]

The Hessians behaved well throughout the siege, and their opponents paid tribute to the marksmanship of Jägers firing from cover at ranges of less than a hundred yards. American riflemen were at a disadvantage because of the superiority of enemy artillery which kept them at a respectful distance. Exhaustion also added to the trials of the garrison, and Colonel Moultrie related that a round shot killed one of his officers without waking a comrade sleeping at his side. "The fatigue in that advance redoubt, was so great, for want of sleep, that many faces were so swelled that they could scarcely see out of their eyes."

When the rain of enemy projectiles endangered a powder magazine behind St. Philip's church, the rebels removed 10,000 pounds of explosive and bricked it into the masonry. There it remained undiscovered throughout the long British occupation until the end of the war.

On May 6th the small garrison at Sullivan's Island surrendered to the warships. "The embrazures of the enemy's batteries in the third parallel opened last night," wrote Moultrie in his journal of the siege. "Our meat quite out, rice, sugar and coffee served out." Two nights later the resistance of the garrison reached a gallant even if futile climax. "The mortars from both sides threw out an immense number of shells; it was a glorious sight, to see them like meteors crossing each other, and bursting in the air; it appeared as if the stars were tumbling down. The fire was incessant almost the whole night; cannon-balls whizzing and shells hissing continually amongst us; ammunition chests and temporary magazines blowing up; great guns bursting, and wounded men groaning along the lines: it was a dreadful night! It was our last effort, but it availed us nothing. . . ."[26]

Negotiations for the capitulation began on May 8th. Lincoln agreed on the 12th to enemy terms which stipulated that the Continental troops should remain prisoners until exchanged. His casualties numbered 89 killed and 138 wounded in addition to 11 militia. Clinton reported his losses as 76 killed and 189 wounded.

Only a single untoward event occurred to mar the success for victors who stored 5,000 American muskets in a powder magazine. Rebel incendiaries were blamed for a terrific explosion which destroyed the captured arms and cost the lives of some forty redcoats. All the nearby buildings, including the town brothel and poorhouse, were lost in an ensuing fire which threatened the entire city for a few hours.

Otherwise it was the greatest British triumph of the war so far, and the victors multiplied their glory by claiming to have taken 5,600 prisoners. This figure, according to Moultrie, included all adult males— "the aged, the timid, the disaffected, and the infirm, many of them who had never appeared during the whole siege, which swelled the number of militia prisoners to, at least, three times the number we ever had on duty: I saw the column march out, and was surprised to see it so large; but many of them we had excused, from age and infirmities, however, they would do to enroll on a conqueror's list." Lincoln's official returns show that he surrendered 1,977 Continental privates and 246 officers, of whom 500 were sick or wounded in the hospital.[27] Not more than a thousand militia and armed civilians took part, so that the prisoners probably did not exceed 3,300 in all.

Even so, the only American army in the South, including the entire Virginia line, had been lost in the disaster. Before Clinton returned to New York in June with the bulk of his forces, he sent out detachments which occupied every strategic post in South Carolina. All resistance seemed to be paralyzed, and the inhabitants submitted everywhere without firing a shot.

The German mercenaries, as their letters reveal, were particularly elated at recovering some of their lost prestige. On July 4th Captain Hinrich wrote from New York to his brother: "Clinton's entire army to the very last man has comprehended that it was the Jägers alone who humbled the foe, that their intrepid courage, their indefatigable energy alone was able to silence 80 cannon of from 24 to 32 pounders. . . . God was with us, and preserved us, so that out of a million of bullets few did strike." Two days later, writing to the Hessian court counselor, the hero improved upon the statistics of glory: "The Jägers had to silence the 24 pounders of a fort with their rifles. The English now praise us and every one shouts hurrah! when they see a Jäger. That was a feat. The enemy had 311 cannon at Charleston with 22 mortars. . . . It was terrible and only well disciplined troops, such as ours were, fit for the work. What would have become of America if this nucleus of the Army had been lost? I dare not think of it."[28]

At this rate, considering that Hinrich lived until the year 1834, it may be supposed that he had a fairly tall tale to tell his grandchildren about Hessian exploits at the siege of Charleston.

Chapter 22

Disaster in the South

THE news of the British victory at Charleston reached England at a time when its moral effect was most needed. Never had the American war been less popular or the king's personal rule more resented. So outspoken were the protests that twenty-five English counties passed public resolutions denouncing the corruption of Parliament and the powers seized by the crown.[1] Although the realm had the unprecedented total of 314,000 men in arms, supported at a cost of twelve million pounds, the year 1779 had brought a succession of defeats and alarms. The subjects of George III reacted with a storm of popular disapproval which reached a climax summed up by Lecky:

> Perhaps never since the convulsions of the Commonwealth had political agitation spread so widely through England as in the recess of Parliament of 1779 and 1780. In nearly every county great meetings were held for the purpose of drawing up petitions. Much was said about the necessity of obtaining a thorough reform of Parliament, and much about the necessity of arresting the war in America, but the main object of complaint was the corrupt influence of Parliament.[2]

The British historian declared that "the distress produced by war, added to the commercial restrictions imposed by the English Parliament, had reduced the country to virtual bankruptcy." The resulting unrest might have put an end to the American war and generated some political reforms at home if it had not been for one of the greatest red herrings of history. George III, of course, had nothing to do with instigating the great London riot in the early summer of 1780; but that outbreak of mob violence probably saved his personal rule. For three terrible June days the city was at the mercy of looters whose political grievances had been channeled into religious prejudice by a half-mad Scottish peer, Lord George Gordon. After destroying Catholic chapels, the mob set fire to Newgate, attacked the Bank of England and attempted to storm the House of Commons. Hundreds of buildings were sacked and about 450 persons killed or wounded before the soldiers put down disturbances which threatened the whole city with conflagration.

George III never lacked for courage, and he regained a brief popularity by his firmness in restoring order. It seemed symbolical of a new English unity that John Wilkes, the rebel of 1760, should have been his main supporter. But England was given a fright which chilled a movement promising wholesome reforms in the government. Even tyranny, corruption and a burdensome war were preferable to anarchy, and Englishmen faced the future in a grim spirit of seeing the thing through to the bitter end.

The news of the triumph at Charleston crossed the ocean just at the psychological moment when the realm was recovering from the shock of the Gordon riots. Any minor victory would have been a welcome relief, and Clinton's success was important enough to renew hopes that the former colonies would soon be brought back into the fold.

Accounts of the privations at Morristown added to British optimism. Two Connecticut regiments had threatened to mutiny in May; and though they speedily repented, the grievances of the troops were reported with a good deal of hyperbole to the enemy at New York. On June 6th a British expedition advanced into New Jersey under Knyphausen and Tryon for the purpose of testing resistance. Some of the British leaders, including Germain, believed that rebel disaffection had reached the point of collapse; but the invaders found no grounds for any such premise. The militia assembled promptly and did good work in harassing the flanks of the 5,000 redcoats and Hessians marching from Elizabeth to Connecticut Farms. As punishment for their bold opposition, the enemy plundered the little settlement and burned it to the ground. This outrage provided the American cause with another martyr when Elizabeth Caldwell, the wife of the Presbyterian minister, was killed with a nursing infant in her arms. It is quite probable, as British officers claimed, that her death could be charged to a stray bullet or the impulse of a drunken looter. But armed civilians turned out in such numbers that Knyphausen found it prudent to retreat that night to his ships, and the Americans claimed to have shot down more than a hundred of his troops.

A recent burning and plundering raid on Hackensack had provoked a comment in the *New York Packet* which British generals might have studied with profit: "Though they distress a few, they can subdue the spirits of none, but on the contrary, render them still more determined to oppose their rapacious enemy. The spirits of freemen are not to be depressed by horse-thieves, house-breakers and such ragamuffins. Such are the British measures, and such is the conduct of the tools of despotism, which they have invariably pursued during the present war."[3]

When Clinton returned from the South he made another experiment to test the supposed American collapse. On June 23rd he compelled Washington to divide an army which had shrunk to 3,760 men fit for duty, according to recent official returns.[4] The commander in chief took a position where he could defend West Point if the enemy's threat should prove to be serious. Greene stayed behind with the rest of the Continentals and militia to oppose the advance of two strong British columns into New Jersey. At Springfield his little force put up such a good fight that he had every right to boast a small victory, though forced by superior numbers to retire to the hills behind the village. There is good reason to accept the American claim that Clinton was deterred from proceeding toward Morristown after suffering losses of 150 killed and wounded at a cost of 61 rebel casualties. The British general contented himself with pillaging and burning Springfield, then retreated that afternoon.

The combat added to Greene's reputation for generalship; and in his report to Congress, Washington paid a compliment to a branch of the service he had often criticized: "The militia deserve every thing that can be said on both occasions. They flew to arms universally, and acted with a spirit equal to any thing I had seen in the course of the war."[5]

These experiments appear to have convinced Clinton that the rumors of American disaffection had been exaggerated. His own looters, as usual, had been the best Continental recruiting agents, and the little army doubled its strength during the summer. Again it may be noted that rebel numbers depended on material rather than moral factors, since the patriots raised more troops than they could arm and supply. Even when Washington's force at Morristown could show fewer than 4,000 effectives, the decline had owed less to lethargy than the shortages summed up in a report to Congress of May 25, 1780:

> That the Army was five months pay in arrears, that it has Seldom or ever, since it took this cantonement, had more than Six days provision in advance. That at present it is without meat, and has been on

half, and on quarter allowance for some days past. That the commissaries cannot give any assurances of doing more than bearly subsisting the Troops from day to day. . . . That the Sick in Hospitals have not a sufficiency of *those* articles necessary for their comfort. That carriages in considerable numbers are wanted. . . . That as every department of the Army is without Money, and not even the Shadow of Credit left, consequently no article however necessary can be procured. That the Transportation even of the inadequate supply of flour, forage, and other articles hitherto furnished by the states is at a stand.[6]

These were but a few of the privations mentioned by a committee which Congress appointed on April 6th to reside at Washington's headquarters as a link between the assembly and the army. The three members, John Mathews, Philip Schuyler and Nathanael Peabody, were given extraordinary powers to deal with the emergency, but they failed in their turn to find a practical solution. Already, after only a few months of trial, it had to be admitted that the new system of requisitions was a disappointment. In June the Committee at Headquarters sent circular letters directly to the governors, of which the following is a sample:

> *To Connecticut*—The supplies allotted to be furnished by your state, are 1500 barrels flour per month, 666,035 pounds of beef per month, 100 Hogsheads of Rum per month, and 500 Bushels of Salt per month, to be transported to, and delivered where the commissary general shall direct; 30,000 pounds of Bacon, in three equal parcels monthly to the last of september, transported and delivered as aforesaid, 9142 bushels of grain for forage per month, 100 Ox carts, and 400 Oxen with the requisite numbers of yokes, bows, chains, clevesses and pins, also 1,000 draft horses.[7]

The poor response owed more often to poverty than selfishness or indifference. Nor did Congress, lacking executive powers, have any better success at collecting the monthly sums of money requested from the states to support the war effort. The bleak fact had to be faced that both the states and national government, if such it could be called, were destitute. Some of the funds at the disposal of Congress in recent months had been derived by the dubious expedient of selling bills of exchange, payable at six months' sight, drawn on Franklin and other ministers in Europe. Congress, in other words, was forced to the desperate resort of borrowing indirectly, without asking the consent of the prospective lenders, on the strength of foreign loans which had yet to be consummated. It was up to Franklin to make good on these transactions, and his success is perhaps the greatest achievement of a diplomatic career unmatched in American history.

The men in the State House were scarcely in a position to be choosers. Nor could the assembly be accused of blatant optimism when it assured Luzerne on January 31st "that the United States have expectations on which they can rely with confidence of bringing into the field an army of 25,000 effective men, exclusive of commissioned officers."[8] This astonishing estimate was submitted to the minister in answer to his request for information as to rebel resources if French aid should make possible a combined operation in 1780. It is doubtful if a single delegate seriously believed that the country could raise such a force, but Congress was in a mood to snatch at any straw. Promises which could not be fulfilled seemed better than none, and the assembly solemnly affirmed that provisions for French forces could be secured and stored in magazines.

It is not likely that the minister was much deceived, since he had good sources of information as to what went on behind the closed doors of the State House. Perhaps he gave his allies credit for determination in the lack of more tangible assets. At any rate, he wrote guardedly favorable reports to his country; and Lafayette returned from France in May with the thrilling news that the court had consented to send an army as well as fleet to the United States.

Not only did Franklin's efforts play a part, but Lafayette aided as an unofficial ambassador. It may also be noted that members of Congress and army officers never failed to suppress every hint of friction between allies. The Savannah campaign had given this policy another severe test; but Lincoln and d'Estaing parted with warm assurances of esteem, and Americans found occasion to pay the admiral many graceful compliments.

Washington was second only to Franklin as a pillar of allied amity, though he had no illusions that French aid would be immediately decisive. Writing to Joseph Reed on May 28th, he estimated the prospects for victory with remarkable penetration:

> We ought not to deceive ourselves. The maritime resources of Great Britain are more substantial and real, than those of France and Spain united. Her commerce is more extensive, than that of both her rivals; and it is an axiom, that the nation which has the most extensive commerce will always have the most powerful marine. . . . In modern wars, the longest purse must chiefly determine the event. I fear that of the enemy will be found to be so. Though the government is deeply in debt, and of course poor, the Nation is rich, and their riches afford a

fund, that will not be easily exhausted. Besides, their system of public credit is such, that it is capable of greater exertion than that of any other nation. Speculatists have been a long time foretelling its downfall; but we see no symptoms of the catastrophe being very near.[9]

In these few lines may be read a history of the world war growing out of the American Revolution. For it is taking no glory away from the stout fight put up by Great Britain against three enemy nations to emphasize that most of the advantages were on her side. By the same token, it is not to the discredit of the United States, lacking these resources, that the country could not raise half of the 25,000 troops promised her allies. The French themselves fared no better against their powerful foe. Admiral de Terney reached Newport on July 10th with 6,000 troops under Comte de Rochambeau, but an enemy squadron promptly blockaded both the land and naval forces and kept them locked in Narragansett Bay for months to come. Another British squadron prevented the second French contingent from leaving Brest, thus bringing to an end the allied plans for a decisive American campaign in 1780.

Before these reverses became known, Washington had suggested a combined attack in August on Clinton's army at New York. He accepted the disappointment with his usual composure, and the excellent discipline maintained by Rochambeau's troops in Rhode Island took away any doubts as to their reception. Where it had been feared that differences in language and religion might result in unpleasant incidents, the relations between the soldiers and inhabitants were genuinely friendly throughout the winter.

Washington could do nothing meanwhile with his main army except to take a position near the Hudson for the defense of West Point. That post had a new commander in August after Schuyler and Robert R. Livingston used their influence to get Benedict Arnold appointed.

While the armies of Washington and Clinton sullenly watched each other in the New York area, the only decisive operations of the year took place in the South. In January the French minister warned Congress that "should the enemy be in possession of any part of the United States, at the close of the next campaign, it will be extremely difficult to bring Great Britain to acknowledge their independence. . . ."[10] And in a report to Vergennes six months later, Luzerne wrote that the British plan "was to sever the Carolinas and Georgia, and they seemed at this time to have abandoned the northern states. . . . It is possible that the British will make a proposition to the ten northern States tending to assure their independence; and their scheme will be to form into a new government the two Carolinas, Georgia, East Florida and the Bahama Islands, which together would make a respectable possession."[11]

This prospect seemed all the more dangerous in view of the intelligent policies applied in the pacification of Georgia. Up to that time, every part of America occupied by the British had been placed under army rule. Sometimes, as in the case of Howe's winter at Philadelphia, an effort had been made to protect friendly inhabitants and keep them well disposed to the king's cause. But a military administration at best was onerous, and even the loyalists of New York petitioned in vain down to the end of the war for a restoration of their civil liberties.

Georgia loomed as the single exception. There the British opened courts of justice, brought back the old colonial legislature, restored civil rights, and appointed a royal governor and other officials down to justices of the peace. The results were such that the plan should have recommended itself for further adoption. Even allowing that the small population contained a strong loyalist element, it had to be admitted by the patriots that the state seemed to have forsaken its ideals of independence. Georgia, in fact, was the one scrap of American territory that the invaders could pretend to have actually conquered.

After the fall of Charleston it appeared that they were about to use equally farsighted methods in South Carolina. Moderation was shown at first toward inhabitants who were persuaded that submission opened the way to a blessed neutrality. As a further incentive, British propaganda convinced many of these people that the northern states had abandoned them to their fate. These insinuations were circulated with such good effect by a new British gazette published in Charleston that Congress found it necessary to make public denials.

South Carolina people soon had alarming glimpses of the fist beneath the velvet glove. After Colonel Tarleton's little cavalry victory at Monck's Corner, his troops behaved like a horde of Scythians. Prisoners were "mangled in the most shocking manner," according to British testimony, and women "barbarously treated."[12] Such British officers as Stedman and Colonel Patrick Ferguson were so horrified that the last "was for putting the dragoons to instant death." But the looters went unpunished, and a few weeks later they perpetrated one of the worst butcheries of the war.

Professional soldiers as a rule are no more fond of taking life than members of gentler professions. The most notable exception in the Revolution was a short, thickset Liverpool colonel who found the war a welcome escape after being educated as a lawyer. Only twenty-six in 1780, Banastre Tarleton had shot up from a lieutenancy in recognition of his boldness and energy. But it would have been no injustice to describe him a sadistic little monster who disgraced a uniform worn by such men as Carleton and Pigot. Americans might have felt less bitter if they could have blamed his ravages on the British temperament, but his troopers consisted largely of volunteers recruited in New York from among the sons of old Tory families.

Shortly after the fall of Charleston a force of 380 Virginia militia troops, arriving too late for the defense, retreated to the Waxhaws settlement of western South Carolina. Tarleton's horsemen covered a hundred miles in two days and demanded the surrender of the detachment. While the flags were passing back and forth during the discussion of terms, he took advantage of the parley to send men through the woods to Colonel Abraham Buford's rear. The truce had not ended, according to the Americans, when the British charge took them in utter confusion, not knowing whether to fight or capitulate. A few fired on the foe but the majority were sabered while begging for quarter. Tarleton's official report stated that 113 patriots had been killed on the spot, 150 so badly wounded that they could not be moved, and 53 taken prisoners. The fact that his own men had only 17 casualties makes it further evident, as he coolly admitted, that the troopers "showed a vindictive asperity not easily restrained."[13]

Lord Cornwallis, in charge of British forces after the departure of Clinton, gave his official sanction by warmly praising Tarleton in dispatches to England. This was the beginning of a warfare of frightfulness in the South. The people of the Waxhaws settlement could feel no mercy for any loyalist after seeing the dreadfully hacked men left on the field by Tarleton's troopers without any effort to provide surgical care. And though the women of the neighborhood turned the Presbyterian meetinghouse into a rude hospital, most of the victims died of their wounds.

Among the witnesses of their sufferings was a gangling thirteen-year-old frontier lad who gave little promise of becoming the seventh President of the United States. Young Andrew Jackson and his brother joined one of the rebel companies which sprang up everywhere in reaction to the Waxhaws massacre. Within a few weeks these volunteers numbered 600 men on the South Carolina border. They found a natural leader in

Colonel Thomas Sumter, a farmer who took up arms after the British burned his home and drove his family to the woods. On July 12th a force of 133 rebel riflemen cut to pieces a mixed British and Tory detachment sent out by Tarleton under Captain Christian Huck. The patriots killed or wounded nearly half of their 200 foes in a dawn surprise and pursued the remnants for miles without giving much quarter.

This nameless combat became the forerunner of other fights occurring every few days, sometimes with fewer than fifty men on a side. Soon the whole border country was in arms, and it grew increasingly plain that there had been a misunderstanding about the submission of South Carolina.

At the outset the rebel faction had taken the British at their word when they proclaimed a general pardon implying no obligation except neutrality. Those who wished could take the oath of allegiance and become British subjects again, but the vast majority preferred to give their parole, promising not to bear arms against the king. This decision was influenced to no small extent by general disgust at the leadership which had failed the state. On June 5th, two days before Sir Henry Clinton sailed, 210 of the leading citizens, some of whom had taken part in the defense of Charleston, publicly congratulated the British general on his victory.[14] These were the wealthy merchants and planters who had kept Lincoln from saving his army and had been willing to compromise with Prevost in 1779. The small farmers of South Carolina can hardly be blamed for their resentment, but the British made it impossible for them to remain neutral. A second proclamation abrogated their paroles and left them the choice of taking the oath of allegiance or being considered enemies. This meant that no protection for property or opportunity to earn a living could be enjoyed by anyone who refused. On the other hand, those who accepted must be prepared to shed American blood; for the British insisted that "the young men should be ready to assemble when required, and serve with the King's troops for any six months of the ensuing twelve that might be found requisite, under proper regulations."[15]

British policies of moderation, in short, lasted only three weeks before the invaders instituted a military rule more harsh than any part of America had known before. Plundering had a great deal to do with this abrupt change of face. Prevost's army had been too hurried to do a thorough job, but the redcoats of 1780 were systematic. Among the shiploads of booty sent to the West Indies for sale, more than 2,000 Negro slaves left in a single embarkation.[16] Tobacco, indigo and other bulky stores were collected in such quantities that a major general's share amounted to £4,000, while the private plunder of individuals sometimes exceeded this figure.[17] After the cream had been skimmed, the pillagers continued in a business-like manner to search the state for lesser spoils. Stedman, who served as a commissary officer under Cornwallis, related that an appearance of legality was given to these seizures by issuing certificates.[18] Payment depended on the loyalty of the victim to the British at the end of the war—that question, like the value of the property, to be decided by the British themselves. Receipts given in rare instances had a cash value in Charleston, but the certificates were considered worthless.

An arbitrary military rule enabled the officers to decide whether property was entitled to the protection extended in theory to loyal subjects. Farms and plantations were confiscated wholesale, according to Stedman, at the decree of invaders who shared the profits: "The residue of the annual produce of their estates was to be accounted for to the paymaster general, and to be applied to the public service. . . . Instant death was again denounced against those who, having taken protections from the British government, should afterwards join the enemy."[19]

Hundreds of former rebels subscribed to the oath rather than see their families exposed to starvation or violence. But no pity awaited these apostates in the hearts of patriots who had made the sacrifice. It was a typical rather than unusual case when Andrew Jackson's widowed mother took refuge in the woods three times during the summer of 1780. "The men who were able to bear arms were generally away with their companies," his biographer Parton recorded, "and the women, children and old men passed their days and nights in fear, ready at any moment for flight."[20]

Two months after the first proclamation of military rule, Colonel Sumter had a small army in action. On August 6th he attacked a British fortified camp, winning an action important enough to be called a battle by Revolutionary standards. As a preliminary, 80 dragoons and mounted rifle-men surprised a post held by a hundred North Carolina loyalists at Rocky Mount. Few of the Tories escaped from a disaster in which no prisoners were taken save wounded men. Young Andrew Jackson and his brother fought in this typical border combat, and both took part when Sumter's 800 patriots tried to capture the strong position at Hanging Rock defended by 500 troops, including infantry of Tarleton's legion and regulars of the Prince of Wales regiment.

Although the rebels of these operations were called militia, the term "guerrillas" would have been more accurate. Untrained, unpaid, depending for subsistence on the country, they were good marksmen with a natural aptitude for ruse, ambush and other tactics of Indian warfare. Unlike the militia of the North, these southern irregulars were nearly always mounted, though usually fighting on foot. Sumter's force made a rapid night advance to Hanging Rock, then left the tough little backwoods horses under guard and attacked at dawn. They put the Tories and legion infantry to flight at the first shock, but the regulars formed a square for a desperate stand with two cannon. Before the issue could be decided, the half-starved rebels took to plundering enemy stores of rum and provisions, and Sumter contented himself with an incomplete victory. His men had about a hundred casualties, and the enemy admitted losses of 192 killed and wounded—70 regulars, 52 legion infantry and 70 Tories.

The moral effect of the fight at Hanging Rock was tremendous. Not only had a band of armed rustics beaten trained troops; they had proved to the fainthearted that safety lay in the direction of boldness rather than submission. This lesson was not lost on hundreds of men hiding in the woods, and the patriots won no less than twelve combats between July 12th and the middle of August.[21] About 300 redcoats and Tories were killed or wounded in these little actions and 200 taken prisoners at a cost to the rebels of half as many casualties.

It might have been supposed that Sumter's life would not have been worth a Continental note. Regarded as a traitor and outlaw by his opponents, the burly South Carolina guerrilla leader ran a daily risk of betrayal or assassination. Yet he recovered from several wounds and lived until the year 1832 to become at the age of ninety-eight the last surviving American general of the war.

As the rebel resistance increased, the British tried to put out the fire with still more drastic methods. On a Sunday morning in August the leading citizens of Charleston were roused from their beds by soldiers and taken to a prison ship in the harbor. This was the beginning of a long captivity in St. Augustine shared by Gadsden, Dr. Ramsay and other patriots. The fact that the seizure was in violation of the surrender terms did not trouble enemy officers who could stretch military necessity to cover any contingency.

The victims would have been astonished to learn that other Englishmen were at that moment digging into their pockets to raise a fund for the relief of rebel war prisoners. The response was generous at a time of heavy taxation, and a contemporary American historian acknowledged that his enemies "exhibited a compassion and liberality to the Americans that does credit to human nature."[22]

It was a many-sided England which pillaged with one hand while giving with the other, and the redcoats in South Carolina partook of the national genius for inconsistency. Where it might have been supposed that the oppressors would grow soft on the spoils, they were ready and even eager to exchange the comforts of Charleston for a summer campaign in the steaming swamps. Both Cornwallis and Rawdon were a little pudgy in appearance, their waistlines giving thanks to good food and wine. The portraits of other British officers show a tendency to double chins, pallid complexions and languid, pampered hands. Yet the seeming softness of these men was as deceptive as the pink, velvety muzzle of a bulldog. They were conquerors bred by as relentless a process of selection, and the two leaders in South Carolina devoted the rest of their lives to plundering other peoples for the glory of the Empire. Their careers were strikingly similar. As viceroy of Ireland and governor-general of India, Cornwallis seldom varied his old methods. Lord Rawdon, only twenty-six years old in 1780, won so much renown in the same outposts that he acquired two more titles, Earl of Moira and Marquess of Hastings. Both men were deservedly praised for personal acts of kindness, and neither ever hesitated to send large numbers of rebels to their doom with a curious blend of official ferocity and righteousness.

Their methods would prove in the long run to be better suited to the subjection of Asiatic hordes than the freemen of the New World. Still, it could be said even in 1780 that England, like ancient Rome, usually gave more than she took. England had a stake in the Revolution as well as America, and only the king's gold had bought a temporary victory for tyranny and corruption.

Such philosophical conclusions could not have been expected to comfort the South Carolina farmers who were paying the piper. Terrorism only multiplied the reprisals, and soon the invaders had reason to doubt the loyalty of nominal Tories. "Even the most violent revolutionist," wrote Stedman, "unless he chose to leave the country, was obliged to assume the appearance of loyalty. . . . The loyalists murmured because notorious rebels, by taking the oath of allegiance, and putting on a shew of attachment, became entitled to the same privileges as themselves."[23]

Cornwallis, sitting in the middle of his vicious circle, had only 4,000 troops to hold a supposedly vanquished state. At least half as many rebels were in arms by August. And though the patriot bands were still

scattered and unorganized, an army of Continentals and militia was marching from the North to their relief. The decisive test was at hand, for there
could be no doubt that a rebel victory would put the invaders in a precarious situation.

The nucleus of the new American army was a force of Maryland and
Delaware Continentals which had marched from Morristown in April
to reinforce the garrison at Charleston. News of the surrender reached
the troops in Virginia, where they were left stranded without orders or
supplies. Congress appointed Horatio Gates to the command of the Southern Department, and on July 25th he joined the troops in North Carolina.

Although the Gates-Schuyler feud seemed to have died a natural death,
it had merely found new protagonists. In reality the same forces were
arrayed against each other with even more bitterness. Late in 1778 the
next clash arose from an investigation of the conduct of Silas Deane and
Arthur Lee as commissioners in France. Immediately the conservatives
of the middle and southern states upheld Deane, while the liberals of
New Jersey, Virginia and the four New England states supported Lee.
This time the army officers took little part, but for two years the controversy had been raging with such heat in the State House that physical
encounters marred the dignity of the assembly.

Again it had become evident that separation from England was not
the only issue. The revolution within a revolution was still boiling, for
Americans were no nearer to agreement as to the sort of new nation they
wished to create. In South Carolina this difference of opinion aided the
enemy by opening a gap between the tidewater aristocrats and the small
farmers of the uplands. And on the floor of Congress the apparently
irrelevant Deane-Lee dispute split the delegates into the two same irreconcilable camps. It might even have been said that the Gates-Schuyler
feud only slumbered, for the New York delegates made it plain that they
had never forgiven the victor of Saratoga. John Jay, taking advantage of
his position as president of Congress, tried to revive the quarrel in a
letter to Washington of April 21, 1779: "Gratitude ought to have attached
a certain gentleman to the friend who raised him; a spurious ambition,
however, has, it seems made him your enemy."[24] The New York lawyer
hinted that Gates had been criticizing the commander in chief behind
his back, but he could offer little proof after raking over the cold ashes
of the Conway Cabal. The only new evidence brought to light was a
letter written by Gates to Washington on September 27, 1778: "While
I continue to serve, I shall cheerfully obey all orders from Congress, your

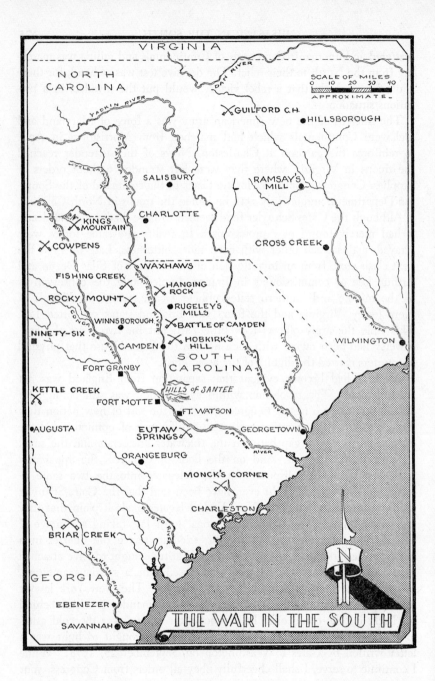

THE WAR IN THE SOUTH

Excellency, or any of my superior officers. Your Excellency has, therefore, only to signify your commands, to have them instantly obeyed."[25]

Jay succeeded in stirring up some resentment, but the matter went no further than an exchange of letters. His attack was not aimed at Gates so much as the group in Congress which had backed that general before supporting Arthur Lee. But the new head of the Southern Department must have realized that he had political enemies who wished him no personal success, however much they may have desired an American victory.

Prospects for either could not have seemed bright when he took over the command. The little army in North Carolina had been so neglected that Sergeant Seymour of Delaware noted in his journal, "Sometimes we draw a half a pound of beef per man, and that so miserably poor that scarce any mortal could make use of it—living chiefly on green apples and peaches, which rendered our situation truly miserable, being in a weak and sickly condition."[26]

Congress was too impoverished to offer much aid, and Gates reached Richmond to find the treasury of Virginia literally bare, the last dollar having been disbursed a few days before his arrival. Nor could Governor Thomas Jefferson promise more than a fraction of the expected tents, arms and provisions. In a letter of July 4th to General Lincoln, the defeated colleague whom he replaced, Gates summed up his difficulties:

> I feel for you most sensibly—I feel for myself who am to succeed, to what? To the command of an Army without Strength—a Military Chest without Money. . . . I wish to recover the Territories we have lost. I wish to restore you to your Command and to reinstate you to that Dignity, to which your Virtues, and your Perseverence, have so justly entitled you:—with me you have experienced that the Battle is not to the strong. Poor Burgoyne in the pride of Victory was overthrown. . . . You will oblige me very much by communicating any Hints or Information, which you think will be useful to me in my Situation. You know I am not above Advice, especially where it comes from a good Head and a sincere Heart.[27]

No general of the war had shown himself better able to make the best of poor resources, and Gates soon wrought some order out of the chaos. Governor Richard Caswell called out the militia of North Carolina to support him, while Jefferson sent the few supplies he could collect. There were no tents, unfortunately, to shelter troops drenched by a three-day downpour at the beginning of the march.

Both armies settled upon Camden as an objective, making it inevitable that a clash would occur near that strategic South Carolina village. In this campaign the British lived for the first time on the country. And though the redcoats never learned to like green corn, they subsisted largely on that staple and lean little backwoods steers. In order to conserve his regulars, Lord Rawdon gave the Tory militia the dangerous duty of foraging in hostile districts "through rivers, creeks, woods, and swamps, to hunt out the cattle. . . . They were frequently opposed, sometimes worsted, and with no inconsiderable loss. In short, so essentially necessary was this unfortunate description of people," Stedman acknowledged, "that it was impossible to have supported his Majesty's army in the field without them."[28]

This is one of the few tributes paid by any British officer to the Americans who made up more than half the force. While Rawdon took a position a few miles beyond Camden, Gates approached by the direct route from Hillsborough. Several of his officers recommended a detour through a friendly country with more supplies, but he depended on assurances that provisions would overtake him. These hopes proved to be false, so that the rebels were reduced to a lean diet of green corn and unripe peaches.

On August 13th they reached Rugeley's Mills as the enemy retired from that point to Camden. Two days later the rebels won an encouraging little success when Gates lent Sumter a hundred Continentals to combine with his guerrillas for the capture of a large convoy of clothing, arms and stores on the way to the British at Camden. The surprise was complete and about a hundred prisoners were taken along with the supplies.

That evening an American council of war decided unanimously to advance. No less than thirteen generals were present, chiefly militia appointees, and the army had an equally disproportionate number of colonels. Recent returns showed a total of 3,052 troops fit for duty, about two-thirds of them militia; but there were no better soldiers in either army than the Continentals of the Maryland and Delaware regiments.

Again, as at Saratoga, the rebel general seemed more of a patriarch than his years would warrant. It could not have been supposed from his energy and optimism that he was undergoing a personal crisis, due to the dangerous illness of his only son. His cheerful assurance, on the contrary, may have added to the general spirit of overconfidence. For there were few doubts troubling the officers who led the march on the night of August 15th in the hope of overwhelming a numerically inferior enemy.

The troops were not as buoyant. Along the route they began to suffer from the effects of the day's rations, consisting of the usual green corn and peaches. Never was there more reason for the ancient belief that the bowels were the seat of courage, for it was a sick little army which stumbled ahead through the summer darkness. "You must observe," explained Sergeant Seymour in his journal, "that instead of rum we had a gill of molasses per man served out to us, which instead of enlivening our spirits, served to purge us as well as if we had taken jallap, for the men, all the way as we went along, were every moment obliged to fall out of the Ranks to evacuate."[29]

Gates had been correctly informed that Rawdon led only about 1,300 troops. What he did not know was that Cornwallis had arrived with enough reinforcements to bring the enemy's strength up to 2,239—three regiments of regulars and as many of provincials equal in training and experience. The British commander had a choice between abandoning Camden and accepting battle, and he did not hesitate to take the bolder course. The two forces advanced at about the same hour, each ignorant of the other's intentions, and collided shortly after midnight in a desolate region of thickets and swamps. There ensued a skirmish of advance guards in the darkness, then the armies formed in line to wait for dawn.

More by accident than design, each general placed his supposedly best troops opposite the enemy's poorest—the regulars of the British right against the Virginia and North Carolina militia, and the provincials of the left facing the Continentals. The battle opened at daybreak with a British advance all along the line. A heavy ground mist, combined with the gunpowder smoke, quickly enveloped the field. This added to the alarms of militiamen unnerved by the ordeal of waiting hours for their first test. At the sight of the regulars charging with bayonets through the haze, two-thirds of the rebel army took to flight, leaving the Continentals to fight it out against crushing odds.

The story of the battle was told in a single sentence in the journal of Captain Robert Kirkwood of the Delaware line, "The British advanced and attacked our Left Flank where the Militia Lay, who gave way which gave the enemy's horse an opportunity to gain our Rear, and their Line advancing in our front which Caused the Action to become very Desparate; which continued for the space of half an hour."[30]

At the end of those thirty minutes the rebel army had ceased to exist as a fighting force. Gates tried vainly to rally fleeing militiamen who threw away loaded guns and scattered through the woods. The Continentals, nearly encircled, were meantime holding off double their own numbers.

It was largely a civil war battle, with American at the throat of American, since the provincials of the left wing did most of the British fighting. At last the Continentals reached the limit of endurance, and the remnants joined in the rout after General de Kalb fell mortally wounded.

British claims were obviously inflated for propaganda purposes, and nobody ever knew the true casualties of a rebel army which seemed to have vanished. Gates reported to Washington that the militia "scattered in so many Directions upon their Retreat, that few have fallen into the Hands of the Enemy." But all the guns and baggage were lost, and the American killed, wounded and prisoners may have reached a thousand. At any rate, only about a fourth of the army reassembled miles in the rear. The enemy, according to Tarleton, had 324 killed and wounded as the price of the most complete British victory won on any battlefield of the war. His dragoons added a postscript, moreover, by surprising Sumter's band at Fishing Creek on the 18th and recovering all the stores and prisoners taken in the capture of the British supply train.

Gates had never been a great tactician, but few generals have ever equaled his resolution after such an appalling disaster. Reaching Charlotte that evening, he rode on to Hillsborough for reasons mentioned in a letter of August 22nd to Governor Caswell: "I therefore resolved to proceed directly thither, to give orders for assembling the Continental Troops on the March from Virginia, to direct the Three Corps of Horse at C[ross] Creek to cover the stores . . . and to urge the Resources of Virginia to be drawn forth for our support. I have also forwarded some Volunteer Horse . . . to succour our People and Waggons retiring from the Enemy."[31]

Hillsborough, far in the rear, was the logical base for nursing the demoralized army back to strategic health, and Gates was at his best as an organizer. Although he realized that "as unfortunate Generals are most commonly recalled, I expect that will be my case," it probably did not occur to him that his political foes would insinuate cowardice. Alexander Hamilton was the leading character assassin, for on September 6th he wrote to James Duane of New York: "Was there ever an instance of a general running away as Gates has done from his whole army? And was there ever so precipitous a flight? One hundred and eighty miles in three days and a half! It does admirable credit to the activity of a man at his time of life. But it disgraces the general and the soldier."[32]

This letter, circulated almost as a tract by the New York faction, did not represent the opinion of fighting men who knew conditions in the South. Both Sumter and Moultrie defended Gates, and Light Horse Harry

Lee praised him in particular for his "flight" to Hillsborough. "It does him honor," he declared in his memoirs, "as it proves his mind capable, amidst confusion and distress, of discerning the point most promising to renew with expedition his strength: at the same time incapable of being withheld from doing his duty, by regarding the calumny with which he was sure to be assailed."[33]

Greene, who replaced Gates, wrote to him months later, "After the action I had an opportunity of viewing the ground where you fought as well as the disposition and order of battle, from all which I was more fully confirmed in my former sentiments that you was unfortunate but not blameable."[34]

Any tactical errors that Gates may have made were redeemed by his courage and dignity during the next three months. Crushed by the death of his son and expecting a court-martial with the possibility of disgrace, he stuck to his job until he restored morale and discipline to the shattered army. A committee of Congress finally exonerated him of misconduct on the evidence of officers present at Camden, and the assembly decided by a unanimous vote of states to drop the inquiry. The Virginia legislature went even further. When the beaten general returned in December, a resolution assured him "that the remembrance of his former glorious services cannot be obliterated by any reverse of fortune, but that this house, ever mindful of his great merit, will omit no opportunity of testifying to the world the gratitude which, as a member of the American Union, this country owes to his military character."

Chapter 23

Treason and Mutiny

CAMDEN, the British supposed, had been the finishing stroke to rebel resistance in South Carolina. Such was their confidence in this premise that only 22 regulars were detached to escort 150 of the Continental prisoners to Charleston. On the way the guards were surprised and their captives freed by a party of 16 patriots.

The hero of this dawn ambuscade was Colonel Francis Marion, a forty-eight-year-old planter who soon rivaled Sumter as a guerrilla leader. Small and wiry, a descendant of Huguenot immigrants, he depended on age-old tactics of stratagem and ambush rather than numbers. "I have never yet had more than 70 men to act with me," he wrote to Gates on October 18th, "and sometimes they leave me to 20 or 30." Often he was reduced to hiding in the swamps with a dozen followers, only to burst out upon his foes the moment they turned their backs. Marion had no illusions about the fact that some of his best fighters were outlaws or border ruffians who changed sides according to the prospects for plunder. Using such grist as came to his mill, he won a sequence of little successes reported in other letters to Gates:

> On September the 4th, marched with 53 to attack a body of 200 tories who intended to surprise me:—surprised a party of 45, killed and wounded all but 15, who escaped:—met and attacked the main body, and put them to flight, though they had 200 men. . . . Marched to Black Mingo, September the 24th, where there was a guard of 60 men of the militia; attacked them on the 28th:—killed three, wounded and took 13 prisoners.[1]

No longer could it have been said that South Carolina was not fighting her own battles. Marion made the eastern part of the state his preserve, leaving the border counties to Sumter and such lesser leaders as James Williams, William Davies and Elijah Clarke. The last three united their bands only a few days after Camden to defeat a detachment of about 500 redcoats and Tories at Musgrove's Mills. Hastily entrenching behind log breastworks, the patriots routed the enemy with losses of 223 killed, wounded and captured. The next morning they scattered to their homes, having covered a hundred miles on their tough little horses in forty-eight hours.

Insignificant as such combats may seem when compared to Camden, they resulted in a continual drain of troops which the invaders could ill afford. From July 12th to August 27th the rebels were the assailants in fifteen actions which cost the enemy a total of 1,105 killed, wounded and prisoners.[2] Nearly half of these casualties were British regulars or trained loyalists of equal military value, while the 638 men lost by the rebels were armed civilians for the most part. Unpaid, living on the country, providing their own rifles and horses, depending on captures for their very ammunition, they made up in hardihood and mobility what they lacked in discipline and cohesion. After a campaign of a few days, the patriot bands simply dispersed, so that it cost nothing to supply and maintain them between operations.

Generally speaking, the thousands of native Americans on the British side could be divided into three groups—militia used as auxiliaries; volunteers serving in the regular army or navy; and the recruits of such regiments as the Volunteers of Ireland, who took their place alongside the regulars and gave as good an account of themselves on the battlefield.

Widely varying estimates have been given as to the number of Americans who fought for the invaders during the eight years. The historian Van Tyne believed that "New York alone furnished about 15,000 men to the British army and navy, and over 8,000 loyalist militia. All the other colonies furnished about as many more, so that we may safely state that about 50,000 soldiers, either regular or militia, were drawn into the service of Great Britain from her American sympathizers."[3]

Able-bodied Tories who flocked to New York from all the states, bringing their families to eat the king's bread, were naturally expected to shoulder a musket. The invaders did not hesitate to impress rebel captives starving on prison ships, and hundreds of them died of fever in the West Indies or wounds received in naval actions. "There is nothing but death or entering into the British service for me," wrote one of the victims in a letter published by a Philadelphia newspaper. "Our ship company is reduced to a small number (by death and entering into the British service) of nineteen."[4]

Enemy officers fostered a legend that Washington's army was made up of recent immigrants who did the fighting for native Americans. "The Rebels," noted Joshua Pell in a typical comment of the sort, "consisted largely of Irish redemptioners and Convicts, the most audacious rascals existing."[5] This belief had some basis in the fact that the so-called Scotch-Irish—Presbyterians of Scottish ancestry from Ulster—backed the cause of rebellion solidly. Allowing for this exception, the loyalist regiments probably had a larger proportion of the newcomers to America. Irish loyalists, celebrating St. Patrick's Day at New York in 1780, expressed their sentiments in verse:

> This day, but the year I can't rightly determine,
> St. Patrick the vipers did chase from the land;
> Let's see, if like him, we can't sweep off the vermin
> Who care 'gainst the sons of the shamrock to stand.[6]

It is quite likely that the Tories, as they claimed, had more long-term troops in service than the rebels from 1778 down to the end of the war. This comparison is no reproach to patriots who so often lacked the resources to pay and supply their soldiers. The British not only provided for the troops of the principal loyalist regiments but also their families. During the eight years no less than 69 of these units sought volunteers in America.[7] And though most of them never got much beyond the stage of adopting an impressive name, 21 regiments, averaging several hundred men each, served in the field.

Behind the scenes the relations between loyalists and regulars were not as cordial as they pretended. British officers made no secret of their conviction that American sympathizers had not exactly flown to arms during the first three years. The regulars showed their impatience none too tactfully; and some of them may have had more respect for rebels fighting against heavy odds. After all, a rebel had a clearly defined position, while a loyalist remained something of an anomaly. American by birth and British in principle, he could never be quite accepted by either, whatever the outcome of the war.

Samuel Curwen's diary gives a touching picture of homesick loyalists in London who came to resent British disdain so much that they felt a perverse glow of pride over the surrender of Burgoyne's army. This reaction would have been understood by Tory soldiers in America who felt that they were being treated shabbily. Neither British contemporaries nor historians gave them much credit for the victories at Savannah and Camden, though the loyalists took part in equal numbers and did their full share of the fighting. In the event of defeat or indiscipline, however, it seemed to them that they were singled out for particular notice. Lord Rawdon, in the summer of 1780, offered "the inhabitants ten guineas for the head of any deserter belonging to the Volunteers of Ireland; and five guineas only if they bring him in alive."[8] This savage proclamation must have been a death sentence for more than one blameless soldier captured in guerrilla warfare. Even so, the established loyalist regiments were shown more consideration than Tory militia assigned to the most dangerous and humiliating tasks. At least one British officer felt ashamed of this discrimination on an occasion when "the horses were taken out of some of the waggons, and the militia, harnessed in their stead, drew the waggons through the creek. We are sorry to say, that, in return for these exertions, the militia were maltreated by abusive language, and even beaten by some of the officers. . . . In consequence of this ill usage, several of them left the army next morning, for ever. . . ."[9]

The invaders might have profited if more of them had followed the example set by Colonel Patrick Ferguson, who displayed none of the usual contempt for provincials. Although his corps included a few regulars, he gave the Tories no cause to complain of favoritism. The inventor of a breech-loading rifle which his superiors declined to adopt, Ferguson had not scorned to learn lessons in tactics from the enemy. It was the ambition of this military scientist to train his men especially for American warfare and it became his fate to meet opponents who knew more about those tactics.

British strategists may have wondered what would happen if enough patriot bands united to form a small army. This was exactly what occurred at King's Mountain on October 7th, and the result was a battle of annihilation at Ferguson's expense. It is ironical that one of the most humane British officers should have paid the penalty for his superior's new severities after Camden. "I have given orders," wrote Cornwallis in a letter intercepted by the rebels, "that all the inhabitants of this province, who have subscribed and taken part in this revolt, should be punished with the greatest rigor, and their whole property taken away from them or destroyed. . . . I have ordered in the most positive manner, that every militia-man, who has borne arms with us, and afterwards joined the enemy, shall be immediately hanged."[10]

These policies were not carried out gently. Americans were executed in effect for their political beliefs on the evidence of their accusers. At Augusta thirty "traitors" went to the gallows, and eleven others at Ninety-Six. The patriot bands, never inhibited, revenged themselves on Tories whom they had come to regard "as wild beasts, that are to be slain on sight, and without warning."

It was Ferguson's misfortune to be within striking distance when the new repressions inflamed the whole border country. All summer he had been campaigning in that region, making an effort to pacify rather than terrorize the inhabitants in preparation for an invasion of North Carolina which Cornwallis planned after the season of hot weather and fevers. The patriots themselves acknowledged that Ferguson called on rebel families in person to point out the error of their ways and promise protection. Slight of figure, his right arm crippled by a wound at Brandywine, this British leader might have become a more dangerous foe than Tarleton. The frontiersmen seemed to have recognized that fact when five bands assembled on September 25th to make up a total of 1,390 mounted riflemen. From Virginia came a contingent of 400 under William Campbell, and North Carolina sent 300 under Benjamin Cleveland and 160 under Charles McDowell. The remaining two forces consisted of pioneers from the region which later became Tennessee—240 led by Isaac Shelby, and an equal number by John Sevier.

These were the "over-mountain men" who had taken little part in the war against the British up to that time. Upon them had fallen the brunt of defending the long frontier against Indian raids throughout the war. They could have done the cause no better service, but in the process they had taken on the cruelty and cunning as well as hardihood of the redskins. "This race of men," wrote a major serving under Cornwallis, "are more savage than Indians, and possess *every* one of their vices, but *not one* of their virtues. I have known one of them to travel two hundred miles through the woods, never keeping any road or path, guided by the sun by day and the stars by night, to kill a particular person belonging to the opposite party."[11]

The over-mountain men, for their part, doubtless had an equally low opinion of British officers who bribed the Cherokees. Some of Ferguson's pursuers had ridden night and day for two weeks to stalk him as if he were an Indian or wild beast. When they cornered him at King's Mountain, a force of 910 picked riflemen attacked on foot while the others guarded the horses. The British leader, with about 950 troops, made a stand on a height along the border between the two Carolinas. Relying on the natural strength of his position, he did not entrench. The sides were so steep that he planned to charge downhill just as the patriots approached the summit after an exhausting climb. These tactics had little effect against opponents who fought in Indian fashion, shooting from behind trees as they advanced, then falling back before counterattacks which only exhausted the enemy. Ferguson's elusive foes soon had him surrounded and helpless, his men exposed to a deadly fire from all sides. He fell with seven bullets through his body, though a rebel rifleman claimed to have brought him down with a pet weapon named "Sweet Lips" in a spirit of playful ferocity. The loyalists raised handkerchiefs on their ramrods, but after the surrender a stray ball mortally wounded a patriot leader, Colonel James Williams. His men revenged themselves horribly by firing into the huddled mass of prisoners until the officers put an end to the slaughter.

The victors, who had only 28 killed, burned the British wagons and retired with their plunder and wounded. On the march the 600 miserable loyalist survivors, loaded with burdens, had several men shot down for disobedience or trying to escape. Their charges of cruelty seem to have been well founded, judging by the astonishing order issued by Colonel Campbell on October 11th, "I must request the officers of all ranks in the army to endeavor to restrain the disorderly manner of slaughtering and disturbing the prisoners."[12]

Both the patriots and their horses were worn out, but the leaders did not pause until they passed out of danger of an attack from Tarleton in the confusion of retreat. Then they held a grim tribunal by torchlight at which the British forces were called to account for a long list of hangings, burnings and floggings. As devout Presbyterians, the over-mountain men had absorbed their ideas of justice from the Old Testament, and they decreed an eye for an eye by condemning some forty of the prisoners to death. Nine had been hanged on the nearest trees when the executioners decided that the object lesson sufficed, and the rest of the trembling wretches were pardoned. Cornwallis protested to Gates against the "savage barbarity" of reprisals which he thought "shocking to humanity." But the patriots could not see much distinction between backwoods justice and the 41 hangings known to have resulted up to this time from the British general's proclamations.

King's Mountain, which had brought together rebels from three states as well as the wilderness, should have warned farsighted British strategists that they could never occupy the South permanently. Their forces would always be exposed to surprise attacks from riflemen riding several hundred miles in a week and dispersing as quickly as they assembled. Already, as news of the battle spread by word of mouth, so many men were joining the forces of Sumter and Marion that Cornwallis had to abandon his plan of invading North Carolina. "There was scarce an inhabitant between the Senate and the Pedee," he confessed, "that was not in arms against us."

The British were reduced to a defensive strategy, and Gates had grounds for reporting to Congress that the campaign of the summer and autumn had gone against the enemy. Decisive as the victory at Camden had appeared, any gains had been offset by subsequent British reverses.

The first reports of King's Mountain reached the northern states when they were recovering from the shock of Benedict Arnold's treason. Inconsistent as it may seem, no success of the war did more to strengthen the rebel cause morally than the discovery of the plot to betray West Point. Americans felt that they had survived treachery as well as defeat, and the new popular sport of hanging the traitor in effigy revived an enthusiasm that had not been known since 1776.

It is not likely that any other general could have had such an opportunity for double-dealing. Few of Arnold's colleagues knew him very well personally, and those who made his acquaintance usually ended by quarreling with him. His brief period of active service had been limited chiefly to the northern front, so that his reputation in 1780 rested for the most part on his own letters plus the praises sung by Schuyler's friends in an effort to discredit Gates. Arnold had also benefited from Washington's policy of upholding his generals, and even his shady career at Philadelphia did not arouse any suspicions when he applied for the command at West Point.

The importance of the fort had recently been brought to public attention by British raids on the northern front which penetrated as far as the Saratoga battlefield. Ticonderoga had been abandoned, and the other small posts at the head of Lake Champlain were held by only a few militia companies. There was little to oppose another invasion from Canada if the enemy tried again, which made it the more essential to hold West Point at all costs.

Washington himself happened to arrive on the very morning when the conspiracy came to light. He had been conferring with Comte de Rochambeau at Hartford, and so low were American finances that he set out from

New Jersey with doubts as to his ability to pay for his staff at inns. Half of his borrowed $8,000 in Continental paper had been spent on the way through New York, but Governor Trumbull saved him embarrassment by ordering that Connecticut defray all expenses in that state. On the return trip the commander reached West Point a few minutes after Arnold made his escape to a British warship in the river. Washington learned that a few slips had led to the capture of Major John André, of the British secret service, with the incriminating papers. So trustful were the captors that one of them sent a report to Arnold, enabling him to save his neck from what would undoubtedly have been the most popular hanging ever held on American soil. As it turned out, André went to the gallows, mourned by friend and foe alike, after confessing to being taken as a spy in disguise. Washington offered to free him in exchange for Arnold, but the British protected the traitor, however much they may have regretted the necessity.

It had only been a few generations since General George Monk made treason respectable by betraying the Parliamentary army, thus ending the Great Rebellion and restoring the House of Stuart to the throne. Arnold in turn might have won a grudging respect for the very magnitude of his crime if he had had any other motives except avarice. But he was a retail scoundrel rather than another Monk, and during his brief command at West Point he had not scrupled to pocket a few dollars by selling rum, pork, salt and other public stores. As a final act of petty rascality, he delivered as prisoners of war the soldiers who saved his life by rowing him to the British warship in the faith that they were carrying out legitimate military orders.

The announcement of the treason was particularly humiliating to the political faction still rejoicing over Gates's defeat at Camden. Not only had that general's enemies made a hero out of Arnold, but Schuyler and Robert R. Livingston could only regret their gullibility in recommending him for the West Point command. It was also ironical that the traitor's admiring aide at the fort had been Colonel Richard Varick, one of the New York officers whose letters glorified Arnold at Saratoga to the prejudice of Gates. Both members of Congress were blameless dupes, and young Varick had no difficulty in clearing his name of suspicion.

Clinton had agreed upon a price of £10,000 sterling for the delivery of the post with its artillery, supplies and garrison of 3,000 men. Eventually Arnold received £6,315 for his unsuccessful attempt, in addition to various pensions and perquisites for himself and family which amounted to a fortune in that day. A few of his old colleagues predicted that he might feel remorse, but Washington was not enough of a sentimentalist to agree. "He wants feeling," wrote the commander in chief. "From some traits of his character which have lately come to my knowledge, he seems to have been so hackneyed in villainy and so lost to all sense of honor and shame, that while his faculties will enable him to continue his sordid pursuits there will be no time for remorse."[13]

The father of his country could scarcely have imagined that seven generations later Arnold would be regarded by many Americans as the fallen Lucifer of the Revolution—a battlefield hero driven by the neglect of Congress to his downfall. This opinion owed very often to a generous impulse to give the devil his due. Yet if Arnold had not dramatized himself by treason, it is unlikely that he would have cut much of a figure in history on the strength of his participation in one battle as commander and three as subordinate. Greene, Wayne, Morgan, Knox, Stirling, Sullivan and a dozen other generals made a greater contribution and risked their lives on more fields. The best explanation of the Arnold legend is probably to be found in the timeless popular preference for the glory hunter as compared to the soldier of cerebral capacity. War is rather a dull business on a basis of the ungilded facts, and every conflict of American history has found some self-seeker creating a dashing reputation at the expense of his betters.

Apparently the traitor was not a hero to his contemporaries. No better evidence could be found than his failure to fill the ranks of his own legion after going over to the enemy. Although desertions were common at the time and Westchester County swarmed with loyalists, Arnold could not attract enough volunteers by offering the bounty of three guineas in gold for troops "who are to be clothed, subsisted, and paid as the other corps are in the British service." In the autumn of 1781, a year after his proclamation, only 212 men had come forward, with 684 "wanting to complete."

Nor did Arnold have any better success at justifying his treason by appealing to religious prejudice. Next to the winning of political liberties, the Revolution had no greater result than establishing freedom of worship and separation of church and state. This was a radical departure from the thought of the last century with its religious wars and persecutions. Several American colonies had been founded by men who held bigotry to be a virtue, and lax Puritans took warning from Thomas Dudley's couplet:

Let men of God in courts and churches watch
O'er such as do a toleration hatch.

So many shades of Protestant doctrine were represented in the first
Continental Congress that tolerance won an initial victory of expediency.
The invasion of Canada and alliance with France made it only politic
to respect Roman Catholic opinion, and by 1780 it might truly have been
said that necessity had grown into a virtue. Arnold tried to undo these
results by creating an issue out of the funeral of Don Juan de Miralles:
"Do you know that the eye which guides this pen lately saw your mean
and profligate Congress at mass for the soul of a Roman Catholic in
purgatory and participating in the rites of a church against whose anti-
Christian corruptions your pious ancestors would have witnessed with
their blood?"[14] But this incitation only added to the prejudice against
Arnold himself, and the Protestant towns of Massachusetts burned more
effigies of him than Catholic districts of Maryland.

It was too late, unfortunately, to repair the harm done to one of the
victims of the Arnold legend. John Brown, first to warn Americans of his
townsman's character, had never been given an opportunity to clear his
own name of unfounded charges. He was still a colonel in the autumn of
1780, after winning three victories early in the war, when he fell at the
head of his men in a bloody combat on the New York frontier.   .

Nobody in the Continental Army could have been more vulnerable
to the emotional shock of treason than the commander in chief. As one
of the greatest spy-masters of military history, he had employed enough
double-dealers to know that many men had their price. Inevitably the
exposure of the West Point plot made him doubtful of other American
officers who had been suspected of such tendencies.

The secrecy of a spy's duties has left this branch of warfare enveloped
in a mist of legend. Several Revolutionary heroes won renown after the
war, when their stories could be told, for risking death and dishonor to
bring back intelligence. John Honeyman of New Jersey, according to
"well established tradition," gave Washington the information which
made possible the attack on Trenton in 1776.[15] A butcher and dealer in
cattle, he posed as a Tory while observing British movements, then allowed
himself to be captured and taken to the rebel general. After reporting, he
"escaped" to the enemy lines to resume his loyalist role. New Jersey
records show that Honeyman was twice arrested for treason; but he

managed to get free, perhaps with the connivance of rebel authorities, and eventually died in bed at the age of ninety-three.

There are other tales, compounded both of myth and fact, about the patriotism of Revolutionary spies. Washington took the bleakly realistic view that most informers were interested primarily in being paid promptly and well. He kept a fund of gold guineas for that purpose, no matter how low Continental finances sank, and his letters on the subject are educational even though they would hardly supply plots for spy novels. "I am really at a loss what opinion to form of this man," he wrote to General Robert Howe about a new spy in the summer of 1779. "We must endeavor to make it his interest to be faithful; for, as it is apparent he means to get something by the business, and will even receive double wages, we must take care, if possible, not to let motives of interest on the other side bear down his integrity and inclination to serve us."[16] The letter ended with a summary of the pessimistic creed which guided Washington in his dealings with spies, "Few men have virtue to withstand the highest bidder."

He was no more disturbed than his opponent Clinton by the fact that some of the most reliable intelligence in the New York area came from double spies, serving both sides for no other motive than profit. These experts had been in the business of treachery long enough to know what sort of information was wanted, and they were often more trustworthy than some well-meaning but blundering amateur. Each army feinted on occasion or propagated false reports, and only a man who knew military values could sift the grain from the chaff. The double spy, moreover, realized that his life as well as income depended on building up a reputation for accuracy, so that certain codes of honor prevailed in a trade based upon dishonor.

Invisible ink was frequently used for writing reports, and spies accepted as faithful old employees had their own code names such as "Culper" and "Culper Junior." Ciphers of the day were often based on words found in a book supposedly known only to the communicating parties. Thus the numbers 114-17-6 might refer to the page, line and word in *Entick's Dictionary*, a contemporary work which each side fondly believed at one time to be its own exclusive preserve. Spies reduced their risks whenever possible by reporting through a third person who might be quite innocent of the part he played. A letter from Washington to Major Benjamin Tallmadge reveals these methods in practice:

I send twenty guineas, and two phials containing the stain and counterpart of the stain for Culper Junior. . . . It is my further most earnest wish, that you would press him to open, if possible, a communication with me by a more direct route than the present. His accounts are intelligent, clear, and satisfactory. They consequently might be valuable, but owing to the circuitous route, through which they are transmitted, I can derive no immediate or important advantages from them. . . . . I am sensible of his situation and the necessity of caution. . . . But if he cannot form the first link of the chain of communication himself, and will let me know it, I believe I can name one or two men to him, who will receive and convey to me, through others, such intelligence as he may think important; but he should avoid making use of the stain on a blank sheet of paper. . . . A much better way is to write a letter a little in the Tory style, with some mixture of family matters, and, between the lines and the remaining part of the sheet, to communicate with stain the intended intelligence.[17]

It was worth a patient effort, as this letter hints, to train as well as protect a promising beginner. A single timely warning of an enemy movement might be worth a brigade, and it is a tribute to Washington's ability as spy-master that his forces in the New York area were never once surprised in a major attack. The best double spies realized that it was to their own interests to save both clients from the fate of the golden goose; and they did not find it practical to divulge information giving either army too much of an advantage. The ideal was to strike a nice balance, and Washington held his own against enemies with more money to pay for information. His account of personal expenses at the close of the war reveals that about one-eighth of the amazingly small total of £16,311 was dispensed for secret intelligence—£1,982 as compared to £1,874 for reconnoitering and traveling.[18]

A spy-master dared not err on the side of credulity, yet his eternal distrust must be varied with interludes of relying on the honesty of double-dealers. Faith was as essential as suspicion, and Washington did not allow these activities to sour his belief in his own officers. Only once was this policy cruelly tested, for Arnold's treason gave him a moment of black despair in which it seemed that honor had perished from the cause. In this hour he turned to a man he could trust implicitly, and General William Heath was summoned to take over the command of West Point.

In an old established European army, permeated by traditions of caste and seniority, the Roxbury farmer might have been able to purchase a lieutenant's commission. It is not likely that he would have gone much higher, nor is it probable that a Boston bookshop proprietor would have risen to be chief of artillery. Revolutionary armies bring out abilities never suspected even by their possessors; and it was the fate of William Heath to become the leading diplomat and administrator of the Continental Army after failing in his ambition to win battles. In the summer of 1780, when victory depended on French aid, "our General" proved to be the man for the delicate assignment of welcoming Rochambeau. Although he could not speak a word of French, his native tact and dignity commanded the respect of Europeans trained in the courtesies of international relations. Rochambeau did not mean it as an empty compliment when he wrote to Washington on August 17th, "I shall keep with me, if you think proper, General Heath, whose ardor, spirit and activity are absolutely necessary to me."[19]

Mutiny had been more dreaded than treason at this crisis of American affairs, and Washington was to experience both within a period of four months. He had no more than gone into winter quarters, after reinforcing the West Point garrison and placing Heath in charge, when 1,300 troops of the Pennsylvania line took matters into their own hands on the first day of 1781.

The patience of the Continentals up to this time had been the marvel of all observers. Some of them had not been paid for a year, and Congress could offer little save promises to men who needed clothing. The Pennsylvanians felt that they had an added grievance in being held beyond their supposed three-year enlistment terms by state authorities who contended that they owed service for the entire war. When the question could not be settled to their satisfaction, they elected sergeants as leaders and started marching from Morristown to Philadelphia.

At the outset a serious riot threatened. The officers, according to Captain Joseph McClellan's diary, were alarmed "by the men parading with their arms, and firing some scattering shots, which soon became general throughout the division. The men at length seized upon the artillery and began to drag them off on the road. During this time Captain Bitting was shot through the head and soon died. Captain Tolbert was badly wounded. Several shots were fired from the artillery as they kept them moving, the men in general being by this time in arms, huzzaing, and firing their pieces in the air."[20]

Most of the troops were hard-bitten Scotch-Irish frontiersmen with a fondness for strong drink. But the sergeants quickly restored order, and there ensued the strange spectacle of the little army marching off quietly with its own cannon and supplies. The mutineers even shared their provisions with the officers left behind at Morristown, and they allowed General Anthony Wayne and two colonels to accompany them.

"They behave well to the people of the country," admitted President Joseph Reed of Pennsylvania in his first report, "and hitherto have committed no excesses. . . . They say they will march against the enemy under the command of Gen'l Wayne, Cols. Butler & Stewart, but will not have their other officers." On January 7th the chief executive of Pennsylvania witnessed an incredible scene when the outlaws paraded at Princeton to receive him with the respect due his position. Any alarms he may have felt were laid to rest by sergeants who gravely assured him that "yr. Excellency need not be in the least afraid or apprehensive of any irregularities or ill treatment—that the whole Line would be gratified in settling this unhappy affair." The guards turned out and saluted smartly. Reed found the main body drawn up before the college, standing at rigid attention. "We passed up the front," he related, "the sergeants having the place of their officers respectively, and saluting. I did not think it prudent to refuse them the usual attention, though much against my inclination."[21]

Unorthodox as it might be for a governing body to treat with mutineers, Congress had very little choice. Neither the New Jersey nor Pennsylvania militia could be trusted to quell the uprising, nor could enough troops be spared from Washington's army. Every minute counted, since it could be assumed that the enemy would lose no time at taking advantage of the opportunity. The assembly promptly appointed a committee of three members, Sullivan, Witherspoon and Mathews, who reached Princeton on January 6th to learn that Clinton had already sent two agents to the mutineers with offers calculated to tempt unpaid men. The Pennsylvania troops were promised "a free pardon for all former offenses, and that pay due to them from Congress faithfully paid to them, without any expectation of military service, except it may be voluntary, upon laying down their arms and returning to their allegiance. . . ." These inducements must have given the members of the Congressional committee a few anxious hours, but on January 7th John Witherspoon reported to the State House that the mutineers showed "so much firmness and Indignation that they not only rejected the Proposals but seized the two Agents and delivered them to General Wayne."[22]

A similar note of pride rings out from the other messages to Congress, and Wayne went so far in his enthusiasm as to promise fifty guineas to each of the two sergeants who handed over the British spies to be hanged. From the beginning the influence of this warmhearted and impulsive general had been a great factor in controlling men to whom he had long been a hero. His faith in the troops was further justified when the board of sergeants expressed thanks for the offer of "a sum of gold as a compensation for our fidelity, but as it has not been for the sake or through any expectation of receiving a reward, but for the zeal and love of our country that we sent them [the enemy agents] immediately to Gen'l Wayne, we therefore do not consider ourselves entitled to any other reward but the love of our country, and do jointly agree that we shall accept of no other."[23]

The mutineers reiterated their willingness to resist an enemy attack. But since there seemed to be no immediate danger, they agreed to Wayne's proposal that they march to Trenton as a more suitable place for conferences to settle their grievances. Strict discipline was enforced on the route, and John Sullivan informed Congress on the 8th that the troops "have in Every Instance Shown a Disposition to return to Duty upon receiving Compensation for their past Services and Justice being done to them respecting the term of the Inlistment and by no means to join the British but upon a Conviction that Justice could not be obtained."[24]

By this time the members of the committee did not conceal their admiration for soldiers who had given proof of so much shrewdness as well as patriotism. Paradoxical as it might seem, American ideals of self-government were being upheld by mutineers conferring with the heads of state. The troops discussed each proposition among themselves and put it to a vote before sending replies which compare very favorably with the messages written by their superiors. It might also have been noticed that the men displayed no mean degree of political ability. Never once did they lose their moral advantage to authorities whom they kept on the anxious seat. They treated officers with respect, but they let Reed wonder if General Wayne were not being held as a captive or hostage. They delivered the British spies, but they took care to allow some hours of suspense to pass. They rejected General Clinton's offers, but again they did not spoil the effect by appearing too eager. A good deal of horse-trading guile, it would appear, entered into the negotiations of sergeants who were bargaining with their heads in a noose after demonstrating their competence to command an army.

The outcome was a victory for the mutineers—a victory so complete that their superiors congratulated themselves on having settled the affair by granting practically every demand. John Sullivan thought it a "happy issue" when writing to Luzerne on January 13th, "Perhaps history does not furnish an instance of so large a body of troops revolting from the command of their officers, marching in such exact order, without doing the least injury to individuals and remaining in this situation for such a length of time without division or confusion to themselves and then returning to their duty as their reasonable demands were complied with."[25]

On second thought, after breathing a sigh of relief, some of the heads of state may have taken less satisfaction. When Congress conceded that the term of service had been for three years, many of the troops could not be tempted to enlist again by promises of redressing other grievances. It was a much shrunken Pennsylvania line that emerged, and there might also have been concern about the example set for the Continentals of other states. The dangerous precedent of creating heroes out of Wayne's men had its effect only a few days later when the soldiers of the New Jersey line repudiated the authority of their officers. But this time Washington was ready for a contingency he had been expecting. General Robert Howe marched out at the head of a few loyal regiments, quickly surrounded the mutineers, and compelled them to lay down their arms. Two ringleaders were condemned to death on the spot, and twelve other offenders compelled to act as their executioners. The New Jersey troops looked on thoughtfully, then returned to their huts to seek some other means of demanding their arrears in pay.

Chapter 24

Figs from Thistles

THERE is no more remarkable phenomenon of the times than the wave of optimism and hopefulness which swept over the country during the first weeks of 1781. On practical grounds it would appear that conditions were worse in every respect than a year before, when popular morale sagged to the depths. But it may be that this is the explanation. After surviving one prolonged crisis of privation, defeat, treason and mutiny, Americans may have concluded that fate had no more outrageous stings than those which had already been endured.

The long-expected collapse of the Continental currency came in the spring, but it did not result in the bloody riots which had been predicted. Some of the victims, judging by an enemy account, seem to have reacted with the ribald cheerfulness of those who have nothing more to lose. "Congress is bankrupt!" exulted the leading Tory newspaper of the country. "Last Saturday a large body of the inhabitants with paper dollars in their hats by way of cockades, paraded the streets of Philadelphia, carrying colors flying, with a DOG TARRED, and instead of the usual appendage and ornament of feathers, his back was covered with the Congress' paper dollars."[1]

The expression "not worth a Continental" has come down from this day when a pound of beef sold for several hundred dollars in paper. Congress had tried to stop the deluge, at the risk of breaking faith with its own pledged word, by proclaiming a basis of one-fortieth of face value. Thus the two hundred million dollars from the printing press were reduced to five millions by an assembly which had promised that they would be redeemed at par. Dire necessity justified this step, but the paper continued to seek its own level until it was being accepted at five hundred to one and lower in the spring of 1781. Profiteering and misery went hand in hand as speculators rode from one state to another to make a killing by taking advantage of fluctuating rates of exchange.

It should have been a melancholy satisfaction that on April 18th a committee of Congress estimated the war debt for six years at $24,057,157 in specie.[2] Such had been the financial resources of rebels defending their independence against a realm able to raise an average of about $70,000,000 for the war expenses of a single year. The loans fondly expected by Congress from European nations had not yet materialized, though France had lent indirectly by agreeing to honor bills drawn on Franklin to the amount of four million livres, or about $800,000. Luzerne sternly warned on March 18th against this "ruinous measure of drawing bills of exchange without the previous knowledge and consent of his majesty's ministers."[3] It was time, he added bluntly, "while Congress are making the necessary arrangements for the ensuing campaign, that they should know for certain that they are to count only on their own resources for defraying the expenses that it will require."

Results of the war at sea had only too well upheld Washington's gloomy prediction that the naval and commercial resources of Great Britain would prove superior to those of France and Spain combined. The French soldiers sent to the aid of America were still being blockaded at Newport and Brest in the spring of 1781. Three inconclusive naval actions had been fought during the past year while the Spanish forces made slow progress in their siege of Gibraltar. Even the entrance of Holland into the war, after months of secretly aiding America with supplies, brought no advantage. Without waiting for a formal declaration, the British seized 200 Dutch merchant ships in European waters with cargoes valued at $5,000,000. This blow was followed by Admiral George Rodney's capture of "Statia"—the little Dutch island of St. Eustatius in the West Indies. About 2,000 American seamen and traders fell into his hands along with 180 merchant ships of all nationalities and 7 Dutch men-of-war. Rodney's officers became rich after dividing a vast plunder snatched from their own countrymen as well as enemies and neutrals. British merchants had not been averse to turning a dishonest penny by supplying Americans, and they saw no inconsistency in bringing suit after the war to recover some of their losses.

The fall of Statia early in 1781 deprived the rebels of a smuggling and privateering base which had been the principal gateway for incoming European munitions and the outlet for such American products as tobacco, rice and indigo. Only six miles long and three in width, this dot on the map of the Caribbean served as the meeting place for illicit traders of all nations. Profit was the god of Statia, and the very streets were crammed with merchandise which overflowed the warehouses. Rodney stripped the rocky isle of everything, then added to his spoils by flying the Dutch flag and lying in wait for ships that had not been warned. About fifty more American vessels were taken in this manner, most of them loaded with the tobacco which had been the chief means of obtaining a little hard money for Congress.

Spain continued to go her own way, so that two victories won in West Florida meant nothing to the United States. Don Bernardo de Galvez, the energetic governor of Louisiana, followed up his capture of Mobile in 1780 by taking Pensacola in the following spring with a British garrison of 900, including contingents of Germans and American loyalists. One of the Tory officers, indignant at his treatment by the redcoats, deserted to the enemy and directed the artillery fire which blew up the powder magazine. This success, far from helping the rebels, added to their worries when the victors allowed the paroled prisoners to be transported to New York on such terms that they were available for service against Washington's army.

France alone of Britain's foes could be considered a direct ally by the rebels, though the enemy blockade frustrated a combined operation in 1780. Washington promised at the conference in Hartford to raise 15,000 men for an Allied land and water campaign against New York the following year. Rochambeau counted on the arrival of the troops from Brest to bring his army up to about equal numbers, and Admiral de Terney had hopes of enough reinforcements for the naval superiority essential to any such attack. The talks went no further than plans to be submitted for the approval of the ministers in Paris, but both Frenchmen were more co-operative than the unfortunate d'Estaing.

The Hartford conference gave Washington's countrymen a faith in the future that subsequent disasters could not shake. The moral turning point began shortly after Arnold's defection, accelerated after the mutiny of the Pennsylvania line, and reached a climax after the death of the Continental currency. This was no passing gust of enthusiasm, for Americans had known too many disappointments since the French alliance to be swept away by their emotions. Nor was it a mood of desperation driving a war-worn people to a last grim effort. It was a new belief in themselves arming Americans who had come safely through so many disasters—a new confidence that 1781 was to be the year of decision.

Faith was supported by works to an extent never known in the last two years. Congress spoke with unwonted authority, and the states responded with more troops and provisions than at any time since the requisition system went into effect. Most encouraging of all, the appointment of Nathanael Greene to command in the South appeared to have restored American fortunes in that imperiled region.

Of all the American generals, none loved war as much as the ex-Quaker from Rhode Island. But it was a passion of the intellect rather than the heart, a devotion not to be compared to Wayne's gusto for the hot reality of combat. Greene was fascinated by the clash of minds and wills, and his approach was that of the cool and reasoning strategist. Second only to Washington in breadth of character, he admired his chief more as a great patriot than a soldier. A frank critic of Washington's indecisiveness at times, he took over his new command with a secret resolve to hold none of the usual councils of war. His professional attitude was such a departure from past American practice that he thought it wise to tread cautiously, and on his arrival in North Carolina he sounded out sentiment among officers and soldiers. That, too, was characteristic of a man who never blundered from excess of haste or want of preparation.

A quarrel with Congress in the summer of 1780, ending in his resignation as quartermaster-general, nearly lost him his long-sought opportunity for an independent command. But after Camden the delegates forgave his tart remarks, and he began his new assignment with their blessing in December. Gates handed over a total of 1,482 effectives, plus the assurance of 700 reinforcements on their way from the North. This gave Greene an army of about 2,200 to oppose the 3,224 regulars under Cornwallis and the Tory militia holding a chain of small forts in South Carolina and Georgia.

The departing general had not only restored discipline and fighting spirit after his disaster at Camden; he also won a little victory near that melancholy field during his final week. On November 28th Gates sent a detachment under Colonel William Washington to attack a fort held by 112 loyalists at Rugeley's Mills. This veteran of Trenton, finding the post too strong to storm without artillery, resorted to one of the oldest stratagems of war. Mounting a supposed fieldpiece, he gained the surrender of foes who did not realize until too late that they had been deceived by a "Quaker gun"—a pine log painted to resemble a cannon.

The importance of this little success was not lost on Greene when he took over the command a few days later. As a strategist, he realized that battlefield victories meant less than reducing the posts holding the timid and wavering in submission. Mobility was the answer to this problem, and he decided that "cavalry and partisan corps were best adapted to the make of the country and the state of the war in that quarter, both for leading and encouraging the militia, as well as protecting the persons and property of the inhabitants."[4] Greene found his ideal dragoon leader in Colonel Henry Lee, who had been a classmate of Aaron Burr and James Madison at Princeton. Colonel William Washington took charge of a smaller force of light cavalry, and such guerrilla leaders as Sumter and Marion were encouraged to fight as well as travel on horseback.

Many other small forts held by a hundred men remained to be taken, and the ancient wiles of ruse and stratagem were not to be despised in this sort of warfare. For the new commander of the Southern Department was not the only American who had made the transition in spirit from citizen-soldier to professional. Six years of war had created a group of young men who accepted as a vocation the only trade they had ever known since reaching an age of maturity. Their diaries are concerned with marches and tactics rather than the fiery sentiments so often found in early journals; for they regarded the British less as political enemies than opponents in a deadly game of skill and endurance. Where such burning patriots as Nathan Hale had been the inspiration of 1776, the officers of Greene's command esteemed military virtues. No amateur could have won the applause of such colleagues, but there is no doubt about their admiration for twenty-five-year-old Captain Robert Kirkwood of the Delaware line. Light Horse Harry Lee, whose standards were high, referred to him as "the brave, meritorious, unrewarded Kirkwood."[5] The young veteran had the further distinction of leaving the most professional diary of the war—an unadorned record filled with such terse entries as the following:

> Nov. 28th. Col. Washington went down to Col. Ridgely's [Rugeley's], and with the Deception of a pine knot took the garrisons. . . .
> Decmbr. 6th. This day Maj. Genl. Green took command of the Southern Army in room of Maj. Genl. Gates.
> 17th. March'd to Charlotte.
> 21st. March'd to Biggon Ferry on Catawba River.
> 22nd. Crossed the Ferry and March'd.
> 23rd. March'd.
> 24th. March'd.[6]

Thus did Captain Robert Kirkwood chronicle the opening of Greene's campaign for the reconquest of the South, and in the margin he kept a record of the weary miles covered each day. The total was already

1,621 for Delaware Continentals who had come all the way from Morristown in April and fought with bravery at Camden. Before the remnants got back to their homes in 1782, they would have marched 5,006 miles in all, most of that distance through southern woods and swamps.

A like spirit of professionalism appears in the letters of such battle-scarred officers as Henry Lee, William Washington, Edward Carrington, Otho Holland Williams and John Eager Howard. It was a hard core of Continental veterans which made up the strength of the army, though more than half of the bulk consisted of Virginia and North Carolina militia. Christmas was only another day of military routine to these American regulars, and Kirkwood noted in his journal, "25th. Marched to Pacolet."

Gates had not possessed so much as a dollar in hard money to turn over to Greene. Such were the other material wants of the army that it would have been more simple to list the few assets—muskets, a limited number of horses and cannon, provisions for three days, and the rags worn by the troops. Although the states were contributing more money and supplies than before, Congress found its resources strained by the necessity of sending a force to Virginia while preparing for the decisive campaign in combination with the French. The army in the South, as the farthest removed, was most neglected of all. Its provisions could be found near at hand, but arms, tools and medicines had to come from Philadelphia. Colonel Febiger, supervised the war's longest line of land communications, and in January it took a month for a wagon train to reach Greene with muskets, ammunition, clothing and blankets. "The publick stores are so Exhausted," wrote Febiger, "that unless Paul Jones arrives soon I fear my Continuance here [Philadelphia] will be of very little service. . . . My prospects, unless a new Scene opens, are gone. But in all events I'll do my best."[7]

If Gates had not been able to leave many supplies, he did his successor a greater favor by attaching Kosciusko and Morgan to the southern army. The former British officer convinced Congress that Morgan had been treated shabbily, and announced his intention of placing him "at the Head of a Select Corps from whose Services I expect the most brilliant Success."[8] At Gates's request the assembly made his old subordinate a brigadier and transferred Kosciusko to the South as chief engineer. Neither arrived until after Camden, so that Greene benefited from the services of two specialists who were outstanding in their fields.

Altogether, the officers of the army which advanced to challenge Cornwallis made up the most able group of subordinates that ever served any American general of the war. Far from resenting Greene's policy of holding no councils, they found it an interesting game to guess his secret intentions. They had no illusions about the burden of responsibility borne by the thirty-eight-year-old commander who paced the camp, deep in his own thoughts, on nights when his asthma kept him sleepless. And they knew enough about strategy to realize that he was violating one of the oldest precepts when he divided his army in the face of a stronger enemy.

This is not an opening gambit for an amateur, but some of the greatest victories of history have been won by generals who refused to be bound by the rules. Greene joined this select list in January when his right wing, led by Morgan, destroyed a small British army in the tactical masterpiece of the Revolution—a battle so brilliantly conceived that it served as a model for future American operations.

The British forces in South Carolina held a strong defensive line based on three posts—Winnsborough in the center, Camden to the right, and on the left an old colonial fort named Ninety-Six, because of its distance in miles from the Cherokee country. On the map the three form a wedge, with Winnsborough as the northern point, commanding the Broad, Wateree and Saluda rivers.

Greene knew his opponent well enough to suspect that Cornwallis did not intend to remain long on the defensive. A sudden invasion of North Carolina was more to be anticipated, for the purpose of cutting the long rebel line of supplies. The American general decided to meet this danger by taking the risk of threatening both enemy flanks. With the larger division he advanced on the British right at Camden, while Morgan's detachment swung around as if to attack Ninety-Six. This unorthodox move soon placed the two forces about 130 miles apart, so that several days were required to send a message.

If Cornwallis had been a better strategist, he might have attempted a campaign on "interior lines" by striking each rebel division in turn with his full strength. But such an operation is more easily planned than executed in rough country, and he detached Tarleton to crush Morgan. With his main body, the British general intended "by rapid marches to get between General Greene and Virginia, and by that means force him to fight . . . or, failing of that, to oblige him to quit North Carolina with precipitation. . . ."[9]

On his march westward Morgan won two minor successes. His dragoons,

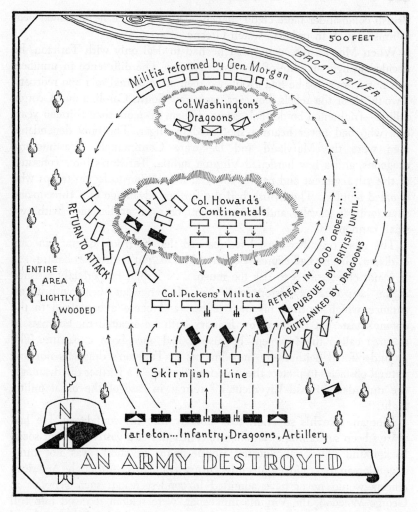

led by Colonel Washington, routed a body of 250 Tories with heavy losses and took 40 prisoners. The next day the horsemen compelled 150 loyalist militia to evacuate a fort which the rebels destroyed after carrying away stores of grain.

Tarleton came on with his usual rapidity and Morgan beat a hasty retreat northward, supposing that Cornwallis planned to get in his rear and place him between two superior forces. This hypothesis gave the

British commander more credit than he deserved, since he remained near Winnsborough in order to watch Greene.

When Morgan discovered that he had to deal only with Tarleton, he decided to fight in spite of his disadvantages. The difference in numbers was not serious, for he had about 900 men as compared to 1,000 redcoats. Two-thirds of the rebels, however, were raw South Carolina and Georgia militia—frightened border lads, some of them no more than thirteen years old, who had never heard a shot fired in anger. The only dependable men were the Maryland and Delaware Continentals, Washington's dragoons, and a few hardened Virginia militia. Tarleton's force consisted of the 7th regiment and part of the 71st in addition to legion troops who equaled regulars. The British had the further advantage of a three-to-one superiority in cavalry and a detachment of royal artillerymen with two small cannon.

The rebel brigadier must have realized that he risked disgrace in case of defeat. Greene had expressly ordered him to "put nothing to hazard. . . . It is not our business to risk too much. . . . I shall be perfectly satisfied if you keep clear of misfortune."[10] Yet Morgan went ahead with an assurance which worried his own officers and chose a battlefield to the enemy's taste. At daybreak on January 17th he awaited the redcoats in an area called the Cowpens because it had once been a pasture. The ground offered neither any impediments to Tarleton's dragoons nor any natural obstacles to protect the American flanks. As a further disadvantage, the unfordable Broad River cut off retreat in case of the usual militia flight.

Morgan, like his superior, took nobody into his confidence. He had always been something of an alien to colleagues of a vastly different social background. The self-educated frontiersman, in short, was not quite a gentleman by rigid eighteenth-century standards. Although American officers would never have admitted to condescension, such generals as George Weedon, the Virginia innkeeper, were seldom received into full comradeship by landed proprietors of the type of Schuyler. Morgan shared the hardships of Valley Forge, but there is no record of his taking part in the councils and frolics. And though the stripling Hamilton had a voice in the consultations before Monmouth, the tactician of Saratoga was ignored and left without orders on the outskirts of the battle. Juniors were promoted over his head a few weeks later, after his famous rifle corps had been broken up for Indian fighting on the New York frontier. American officers found it hard to understand a colleague with the rough-and-ready manners of a man in the ranks. A strict disciplinarian, Morgan regarded flogging as degrading and had been known to enforce order with his own competent fists. Where other officers accepted the British doctrine that flight was disgraceful, the old Indian fighter clung to the more flexible code of the frontier. This attitude was never better expressed than in the instructions given by Colonel Cleveland to his backwoods riflemen just before King's Mountain:

> Every man must consider himself as an officer, and act from his own judgment. Fire as quick as you can and stand your ground as long as you can. When you can do no better, get behind trees or retreat, but I beg of you not to run quite off. If we are repulsed, let us make a point to return and renew the fight. Perhaps we may have better luck in the second attempt than the first.[11]

All of these things had taken place at King's Mountain. Some of the over-mountain men gave ground, but they returned to annihilate the enemy. Morgan in his turn had no illusions about the probability of his militiamen taking to their heels. He made a virtue out of a necessity by putting them in the first line and granting permission for them to retire after firing three shots. Afterwards he explained his strange choice of a battlefield: "I would not have had a swamp in view of my militia on any consideration; they would have made for it, and nothing could have detained them from it. As to covering my wings, I knew my adversary and was perfectly sure I should have nothing but downright fighting. As to retreat, it was the very thing I wished to cut off all hope of. I would have thanked Tarleton had he surrounded me with his cavalry. It would have been better than placing my own men in the rear to cut down those who broke from the ranks. When men are forced to fight, they will sell their lives dearly."[12]

The little American army was drawn up in three lines. In the first the 553 Georgia and Carolina militia were placed on opposite wings, with picked riflemen thrown out in front as skirmishers. The second line, 150 yards to the rear, consisted of all the dependable infantry—the 277 Continentals and Virginia militia. About the same distance farther back, concealed by a low ridge, Washington's 80 horsemen formed the third line.

Tarleton knew no other tactics than the headlong charge that had so often scattered green troops. Never suspecting that he was thrusting his head into a psychological trap, he found the field to his liking. "The ground which General Morgan had chosen . . . was disadvantageous for the Americans," he wrote in his memoirs, "and convenient for the British: an open wood was certainly as proper a place as Lieut. Col. Tarleton could desire."[13]

At the last moment Morgan rode along the militia lines, encouraging the men with bluff paternalism. "Let me see," he said, "which are most entitled to the credit of brave men, the boys of Carolina or those of Georgia." As the redcoats came in sight, he appealed, "Just hold up your heads, boys! Three shots and you are free!"[14]

The militia gave more than the three volleys he asked. Some of the men fired four or five times before the first line broke and filed off to the left toward the rear. Behind the ridge Morgan waited to rally the fugitives while the enemy paused to re-form ranks thinned by enough casualties to halt the advance. At least the militia had not disintegrated, as at Camden, and the outnumbered Continentals awaited the second shock. The fighting of the next fifteen minutes was as hot as had been known on any field of the war. American and British regulars slugged it out first with the musket and then the bayonet at close quarters. Colonel Howard's Virginians recoiled for a moment, but he managed to change front and make a new stand. The Continentals, according to a participant, "behaved with uncommon and undaunted bravery, but more especially the brave Captain Kirkwood and his company, who this day did wonders, rushing on the enemy without either dread or fear. . . ."[15]

Washington's dragoons charged meanwhile to meet the British horsemen pursuing the militia, and a wild melee with pistol and saber resulted. Behind the ridge Morgan was appealing to the pride of Georgia and Carolina rustics for a second effort. Although these military amateurs knew that "Tarleton's quarters" was a synonym for a butchery, they formed ranks again and followed their general back into action. Washington had just thundered down on the right flank of the British infantry, after driving the cavalry off the field, when the militia swung around to strike the left flank. Since their flight these troops had made almost a complete circuit of the field, and the shock of their attack was too much for redcoats who found themselves beset from three sides.

The battle ended with the strange spectacle of British regulars throwing down their muskets and surrendering wholesale to militia. The rebels were already shouting "Tarleton's quarters!" and their officers found it hard to restrain them from inflicting the kind of mercy they would doubtless have received. Morgan reported the enemy's casualties as 300 killed and wounded in addition to 600 prisoners. Fewer than a hundred mounted fugitives, including Tarleton, rejoined Cornwallis during the next few days. The American losses were 12 killed and 60 wounded to gain a victory which seemed within the enemy's grasp only fifteen minutes before the climax. Tarleton never understood just how he had been outgeneraled, and in his memoirs he blamed it all on his troops: "Neither promises nor threats could gain their attention; they surrendered or dispersed, and abandoned the guns. . . . All attempts to restore order, recollection or courage, proved futile."[16]

It had been left to a frontiersman to create the most subtle battle of the war—a cerebral exercise in tactics which depended on reading the enemy's mind as well as the thoughts of scared country lads. Above all, Morgan demonstrated at Cowpens the injustice of condemning militiamen because they could not take the place of regulars. Henry Lee also came to the defense of this despised branch of the army when he wrote that "a government is the murder of its citizens, which sends them into the field uninformed and untaught, where they are to meet men of the same age and strength, mechanized by education and discipline for battle."[17]

The consequences of Cowpens would long be felt by the enemy. Cornwallis had lost his best light troops, infantry as well as horse, at the outset of a campaign in which Tarleton's men were particularly needed. The moral effect of destroying the army of the British Attila, moreover, was bound to stiffen the resistance of the inhabitants he had terrorized.

On the afternoon of January 17th it remained a question whether Morgan could profit from the victory. That very evening he started northward to rejoin Greene before Cornwallis cut off his retreat. Not only were his forces burdened with prisoners and the captured baggage train, but Morgan himself was so crippled by rheumatism that he could hardly sit his horse.

His prisoners were urgently needed to create a more favorable balance for the exchange of Continentals surrendered at Charleston. These unfortunates had been so crowded together on prison ships in the summer of 1780 that they had scarcely more than standing room until their comrades died. About 800, or a third of the total, perished of their sufferings within thirteen months.[18] In June, 1781, when an exchange took place, only 740 were ever restored to Continental service. There is reason to believe the American accusation that these crimes against humanity could be charged to official policy, as shaped by Cornwallis and Rawdon. Their agents visited the famished and diseased wretches, offering a hope of life for those who would volunteer for British service. As an added inducement, the victims were promised that they would be sent to the West Indies and not asked to fight against their own countrymen. Some 530 were coerced into accepting, though Moultrie protested to enemy authorities against "the impressing of American soldiers from on board the prison ships, taking them away by violence, and sending them on board the transports, to be carried from the continent of America, most of them leaving wives and young children."[19]

The 600 foes surrendered at King's Mountain might have been exchanged in time to rescue some of these men who survived the prison ships only to die of fever or French bullets in the West Indies. But the disorganization of the Southern Department was so complete that neither the generals nor the civil authorities had any funds to provide quarters for the captives. Scores of them joined the patriot forces, and others found it easy to desert and make their way homeward, so that only about 160 remained.

Morgan determined that the fruits of Cowpens should not be lost. Fortunately for his hopes, Cornwallis delayed several days to collect the remnants of Tarleton's army and await the arrival of 1,500 reinforcements. The British commander then set a stern example by burning his personal baggage, and the army pushed ahead with a few wagons for hospital stores and ammunition. Morgan had been reduced by expiring militia enlistments to about the numbers of his captives, but he crossed the Catawba safely two days ahead of the pursuit. His superior rejoined him late in January and the united American forces continued to retreat through North Carolina.

On sleepless nights Greene had already evolved the strategy that was to save the South. His main object, as he saw it, was not to win battles but to avoid defeats. Retreat suited his purposes as well as combat if he could draw Cornwallis after him, so that the patriots could harass the British rear. Greene not only gave every encouragement to the forces raised by Sumter, Marion and Pickens, but sent Lee's legion to their aid whenever possible. This made a total of four partisan bands engaged in such small war as cutting communications, pouncing on detachments and capturing minor forts.

Greene's strategy, as a South Carolina contemporary explained, placed Cornwallis between the horns of a dilemma: "While the British kept their forces compact, they could not cover the country, and the American general had the precaution to avoid fighting. When they divided the army, their detachments were separately and successfully attacked. While they were in force in the upper country, light parties of Americans were annoying their small posts in the low country near Charleston. The people soon found that the late conquerors were not able to afford them their promised protection."[20]

At least Cornwallis proved himself to be the most energetic British general of the war. He realized that his invasion of North Carolina was premature, since the Tories of that state had been given no opportunity to rally to the British forces. This object could be attained only by an inspiring victory, and he drove his men forward in pursuit. The campaign turned into a race of the two armies to reach the rivers which might be either an escape or a trap for Greene. He passed the Catawba and the Yadkin only two marches ahead, then pressed on toward the Dan. Here a few hours of delay might have meant disaster, but the rebels crossed the rain-swollen stream safely into Virginia after some of the troops had marched 40 miles in twenty-four hours.

Tarleton attributed the American escape to "a train of fortunate incidents," but this explanation takes no account of Greene's preparations. For he had sent Kosciusko on ahead to plan field fortifications on the Virginia bank and construct boats so ingeniously designed that they could be mounted on wheels and used as baggage wagons during the march.

Cornwallis fell back to Hillsborough and resorted to proclamations to arouse the lukewarm North Carolina loyalists. The results were unsatisfactory, by his own admission, and Greene embarrassed him by crossing back into the state with 600 militia reinforcements just received from Virginia. The American troops were enjoying this military game, according to their diaries and letters, and taking pride in the ability of their leader. Cornwallis could not send out a detachment without exposing it to the danger of being surprised. Lee caught Tarleton napping late in February and inflicted severe losses on new dragoons who could never take the place of the veterans lost at Cowpens. On the night of March 6th Kirkwood led a force of light infantry and riflemen which came even nearer to cutting off that same adversary. Tarleton managed to escape, but in the darkness he attacked a party of his own men by mistake. "There commenced a smart skirmish," noted Sergeant Seymour, "in which great numbers of Tories were sent to the lower regions. We marched for camp which we reached about daybreak, having marched all night through deep swamps, morasses and thickets . . . twenty-six miles."[21]

Cornwallis could not protect even the few parties of loyalists which came forward in response to his proclamations. Lee destroyed the largest of these forces by means of a stratagem when 300 Tories assumed that the green coats of his troopers were British uniforms, since Tarleton's horsemen wore the same color. They were disillusioned when the rebels fired at close range and finished the bloody work with sabers. Both Stedman and Tarleton accused Lee of butchering defenseless men, but he declared that "the fire commenced upon us, and self-preservation commanded the limited destruction which ensued."[22] Tory casualties of 90 killed and upwards of a hundred wounded would indicate, however, that the rebels had not given much quarter.

When Cornwallis left Hillsborough and moved to the Alamance region to encourage the loyalists, he found Greene again at his heels, preying upon foraging parties while avoiding battle. The redcoats, according to one of their officers, had more than fifty deaths during the campaign from exhaustion alone.[23] Lacking magazines, the British general had to scratch for a living in North Carolina, thus running the risk of sending out detachments while angering the very inhabitants he hoped to recruit. Only a battlefield victory could revive his drooping fortunes, and to his surprise Greene offered him the opportunity on March 15th.

The spirits of the rebels must have been high, judging by the lyrical sentiments of St. George Tucker, a young Virginian who had worked up from private to major in the militia. "The lark is up, the morning grey," he wrote to his wife on March 4th, "and I am seated by a smoky fire to let my dearest Fanny know that her soldier is as blithe as the mocking bird which is at this moment tuning his pipe within a dozen yards of me. If the fatigues of the remainder of the campaign sit as well on my limbs as those which I have hitherto experienced, you may be assured that I shall return to Cumberland the most portly, genteel fellow that the country will be able to boast of."[24]

This prediction was fulfilled when the former William and Mary student became a learned as well as portly and genteel judge in later life. As an officer he shared the admiration of his comrades for Greene: "He has an aspect which commands respect—something of the Washington about it." Even the rebel general's secrecy appealed to Tucker, who boasted that "we little folks walk about with a bandage over our eyes, and with wool in our ears."

Recent arrivals of short-term troops from Virginia and North Carolina brought the American strength up to 4,234 foot and 161 cavalry. But

Greene knew that the militia might melt away overnight, and he decided to fight before he lost the advantage in weight. Only about a third of his men, as represented by the 1,490 Continentals, were dependable troops, so that he was in the same situation as Morgan on the eve of Cowpens. That general had been compelled to retire on account of his rheumatism,

GUILFORD COURTHOUSE

RETREAT TO REEDY FORK

Scale in Miles
0   ¼   ½

Continentals

British
4th Position...

W O O D S

Virginia   Militia

British
3rd Position.....

N. Carolina   Militia

Washington

Lee

British
2nd Position...

British
1st Position..

W O O D S

N

PLEDGE OF BRITISH DEFEAT

but his spirit lived on when Greene adopted the same tactical formula. During the retreat he had made a mental note of a position at Guilford Courthouse which seemed to have been created for another Cowpens. A single building stood in a clearing offering no obstacles to an enemy advance, and on the morning of the 15th the American leader drew up his army in three lines with the most unreliable militia in front. Behind them, about 300 yards to the rear, he formed a second line of more dependable Virginia militia, whose officers had orders to shoot any man who ran. The third line, some 400 yards farther back, consisted of Continentals; and the dragoons under Lee and William Washington waited on either side to strike the British flanks.

Cornwallis, who showed a good deal of agility at military arithmetic, claimed afterwards that he brought only 1,560 men to Guilford against "more than 7,000" Americans. If this figure is to be taken seriously, it meant that he had already lost half of the 3,200 troops he led into North Carolina. Much more credible is the American estimate of 2,400 foes on the battlefield, which left the redcoats the glory of attacking double their own numbers.

They came on about noon with no more tactical finesse than Tarleton had shown in his disaster—a brief bombardment, followed by a frontal advance all along the line. Greene, according to his biographer and grandson, clung to the Cowpens formula so faithfully as to ride along the first line, appealing to the North Carolina militia, "Three rounds, my boys, and then you may fall back!"[25] He made a single change, however, that was to frustrate his purpose. At Guilford the divisions were much farther apart, so that the militiamen in front found themselves nearly half a mile ahead of the Continentals of the third line. This gave the raw recruits a sense of being isolated, and the first sight of the gleaming British bayonets threw them into a panic. A few paused long enough for a harmless shot, but the majority threw away loaded muskets and pounded rearward in disorderly flight.

The militia of the second line stood firm for several well-aimed volleys while the two rebel fieldpieces plowed gaps in the scarlet lines and Lee and Washington attacked the flanks. This resistance brought the advance to a standstill, and Greene had hopes of a complete victory until the right wing of the Virginians gave way. The officers tried in vain to stop the retreat, and Major Tucker wrote to his wife, "I received a wound in the small of my leg from a soldier, who, either from design or accident, held his bayonet in such a direction that I could not possibly avoid it as I rode up to stop him from running away."[26]

When the Virginians of the other wing retired, the advantage in numbers passed to the British. Only the Continentals of the third line were left, and the new 2nd Maryland regiment broke under the strain, endangering the others. At this crisis the men of the 1st Maryland, including Kirkwood's Delaware company, saved the day with a burst of blazing courage. These veterans not only held their ground but counterattacked so furiously as to drive back several times their own strength. Washington's horsemen and Howard's Virginians joined a fight which turned into a savage melee at close quarters. In a few minutes the rebels were sweeping everything before them, and Stedman admitted that "at one period of the action the first battalion of the Guards was completely broken."[27]

After routing twice his own numbers, Cornwallis now found himself in the odd situation of being routed by half as many. He put an end to the retirement, according to British testimony, by one of the most desperate expedients ever seen on a battlefield—firing grapeshot at close range to stop the American pursuers at the cost of mowing down his own retreating men. "It is a necessary evil," he declared to one of his officers, "which we must endure to avert impending destruction."[28] His artillery was in good position, and the rebels were finally checked at a terrible cost to the opponents they drove toward the British cannon. Greene might still have kept possession of the field by sending in the Continentals he had in reserve, but with his usual prudence he chose to give up the ground and retain the other advantages.

The Americans withdrew three miles, easily repulsing a British attempt at pursuit, and waited for their stragglers to join the force. Greene reported his losses as 327 killed, wounded and missing, though eight or nine hundred of the militia took an informal leave in their fashion. Cornwallis's official returns listed 532 casualties, but the mournful accounts of his officers seem to verify Greene's estimate, "From undoubted information we learn that the enemy's loss in the battle of Guilford amounted to 633, exclusive of officers, and most of their principal officers were either killed or wounded." Tarleton described the result as "the pledge of ultimate defeat," and Stedman declared that a few days afterwards the army was reduced to only 1,435 effectives.[29]

As a British victory, therefore, Guilford is in a class with Bunker Hill. Understatement had apparently not yet become a national trait, for Cornwallis revised his first high claims of American strength by writing that he was "obliged to fight a battle against seven times my own number."[30] After issuing a proclamation boasting a complete triumph, he left seventy of his wounded to American care and retreated toward Cross Creek. Greene, who had not taken his clothes off for "upwards of six weeks," wrote to Joseph Reed, "The enemy have been so soundly beaten, that they dare not move towards us since the action, notwithstanding we lay ten miles of them for ten days."[31] Late in March he followed his retreating opponents with the intention of forcing another battle on them before the rest of his militia went home. The rebels pursued so hotly that they breakfasted one morning on the newly killed beef left behind by the enemy. But Cornwallis succeeded in crossing the Deep River and taking a position too strong to be attacked.

Although the British general once came within 60 miles of Camden, he continued his retreat down the Cape Fear River toward Wilmington, 90 miles away. American officers found it hard to believe that their adversary intended to abandon the Carolinas, and some were in favor of pursuing him into Virginia. But Greene perceived that his great opportunity lay to the southward. "All these considerations," he wrote to Sumter, "have determined me to change my route, and push directly into South Carolina. This will oblige the enemy to give up their prospects in this State or their posts in South Carolina. . . . I beg, therefore, you will give orders to General Pickens and Marion to collect all the militia they can to co-operate with us."[32]

Coming events were to make it more evident every day that Guilford had been the decisive battle for possession of the three southern states. Cornwallis took a month to recuperate his shattered army at Wilmington, then went his separate way into Virginia. This left Greene free to proceed systematically to the reduction of the posts held by Rawdon with inferior forces.

Chapter 25

Cornwallis Is Taken

EARLY in May, when Cornwallis finally reached Virginia, he must have found the strategic outlook more to his liking. His recent campaign had been the only important operation of the war in which a British general fought on equal terms with rebels lacking naval power and magazines of supplies. North Carolina, in fact, was one of the few states that could not be controlled by invaders in possession of the seaports. Exactly the contrary held true in Virginia, where the waterways took the place of roads. This explains the lack of cities in America's most populous state, for distribution centers were not needed in an area where each large plantation had its own dock on some tidal river.

Not only was the richest of the thirteen states the most vulnerable, but the political situation added to the difficulties of defense. Neither Patrick Henry nor Thomas Jefferson, in spite of their other great qualifications, had been wartime governors to compare with Livingston in New Jersey, Trumbull in Connecticut, Clinton in New York, or Caswell in North Carolina. And though Virginia led all her sisters in establishing political rights, not enough provisions had been made for the temporary sacrifice of liberties which freemen have always found necessary in time of war. The result was chaos. The state was helpless when Cornwallis arrived, an easy prey during the past six months for invaders who enriched themselves with an enormous plunder.

It would have been impossible for Virginia to build enough forts and collect enough small warships to defend her tidal rivers everywhere. But the authorities seemed powerless to call forth so much as a limited effort at a single threatened spot. They might have protected Richmond, for instance, by placing a battery at a point called Hoods. There the River James narrowed to a width of 800 yards, so that a few cannon could easily have stopped enemy warships. Colonel Christian Senff, serving under Gates as an engineer, urged the necessity in the spring of 1780 and promised to have a battery in position if the state would provide the labor of fifty men for two weeks. Months went by in inaction, despite the warning of the British plundering raid of 1779 with its memories of rape and murder. Nothing at all had been accomplished when General Leslie invaded the state the following October, making his headquarters at the mouth of the James and sending out parties of redcoats who looted without meeting any opposition. The British general found Virginia such a helpless prize that he decided to turn his plundering raid into a permanent occupation. He had taken steps to establish a base at Portsmouth when his men were sent to Charleston in December to reinforce Cornwallis.

It might appear that a second painful object lesson should have been enough to arouse a state which boasted a theoretical militia strength of 40,000 for home defense. But even after Leslie's providential departure it proved impossible to call out fifty of these men for a task of two weeks. The treasurer had no funds for paying laborers, nor did Governor Jefferson have the authority to summon the militia for fatigue duty. So well had the rights of freemen been safeguarded that the labor of slaves could not be commandeered without the consent of their owners. Virginia, like South Carolina, had become intoxicated with political liberty before recovering from the effects of social aristocracy, and the combination seemed to drug the nerve of action.

There could be no doubt about the bravery already demonstrated by the Virginians at Quebec, Trenton, Brandywine and a dozen other fields. Virginians had been among the first to volunteer, yet the most populous state let its Continental line fall into decline in the spring of 1779. After that year's new recruits arrived, the thirteen battalions could muster only a third of their allotted strength of 6,786 troops. And the following May the Virginia line came virtually to an end with the surrender of most of its remaining men at Charleston.

Enough volunteers appeared in 1780 so that 700 Continentals could be sent to Greene as well as later contingents of militia. Then recruiting could not be stimulated even by high bounties; and when General Steuben reached Chesterfield the following spring to collect 500 promised soldiers, he found just five awaiting him. Three of this number deserted before he could place muskets in their hands.[1]

On the next occasion the redcoats were led by Benedict Arnold, making his first appearance in an enemy uniform. Washington had been so determined to hang the traitor that he offered a large reward for his capture. One of Henry Lee's troopers, Sergeant John Champe, volunteered for the attempt and enlisted in Arnold's legion at New York after pretending to desert. He was near to success when his intended victim sailed for Virginia; and Champe had to serve for a time with the plunderers of his own state before finding a chance to slip back to the American lines.

The 27 British warships and transports were sighted on the first day of 1781 as they beat their way up the James. Again it could only be regretted that Virginia had not built the small fort which might have stopped the invaders. Arnold landed at Westover, just past Hoods, and burned the public buildings at Richmond. The ordnance repair shop at Westham and the clothing depot at Chesterfield were destroyed next. The state called out the militia, and about 4,000 men finally assembled after the invaders retired to Portsmouth to divide the spoils.

General Phillips conducted a new series of raids in April. Just before his arrival the Virginia authorities had at last found a way to build a fort at Hoods without endangering the rights of freemen. Volunteers were offered credit for six weeks' militia service if they worked twelve days, but the men had only half finished the battery when Phillips appeared. They promptly dropped their tools and absconded, so that once more the redcoats met little resistance. Steuben made a brave futile stand with a few militiamen, but the enemy swept him aside and went on to plunder vast stores of tobacco at Petersburg.

The next chapter of the woeful tale began in June when Cornwallis and Tarleton led a fifth wave of looters through a state that seemed to offer inexhaustible spoils. Although Jefferson became the scapegoat, he did more than the legislature to save Virginia from disgrace and ruin. In response to Steuben's pleas, the governor tried to find a means of impressing horses to solve the transportation problems of landlocked defenders who were outmaneuvered by the mobility of waterborne invaders. The assembly blocked his efforts, and the animals withheld from the rebel forces added to the spoils of Cornwallis. Soon he was able to mount even his light infantry on blooded race horses, and Tarleton's troopers cut the throats of colts too young to be used.

This bit of barbarism infuriated horse-loving Virginians more than the wholesale looting and burning of homes. But they could do nothing except curse the ravagers who came within an hour of seizing Jefferson and the legislature at Charlottesville. Greene's army also had to pay the penalty when Tarleton pounced upon a wagon train taking supplies from Philadelphia to the forces in South Carolina.

After the war it became the standard excuse of defeated British generals to blame Lord Germain for the loss of America. The minister of war, it was charged, invited disaster by trying to manage campaigns by remote control, thus frustrating soldiers who hinted that otherwise they might have succeeded brilliantly.

Such excuses might be taken more seriously if British operations had not been weakened so often by plundering raids. A policy of allowing officers to enrich themselves by dividing the spoils naturally tended to encourage private enterprise at the expense of strategy. Time after time the looters avoided disaster because of their great advantage in sea power, money, troops, supplies and all the other sinews of war. These escapes gave them a fatal sense of immunity from the usual penalties of violating strategic principles. Never does it seem to have occurred to the five men who raided Virginia that they might in their turn be imperiled by the vulnerability of that state to attack from the sea. But this possibility had not been overlooked by Washington, and in the first month of 1781 he planned an operation which foreshadowed Yorktown.

The opportunity was provided when a storm crippled the British blockading squadron off Newport. Washington tried to persuade the French to send a decisive force of ships with enough soldiers to trap Arnold's army in Virginia. He immediately started Lafayette marching southward with 1,200 Continentals to co-operate, but his allies contented themselves with the half measures which so often hurt French naval operations. Instead of granting the fleet and army that Washington requested, Admiral des Touches parted only with three frigates. This force accomplished nothing except the capture of a few small ships taken by surprise, and again Arnold escaped the hangman.

It was further typical of French naval strategy that after the British blockading squadron had been give time to refit, Admiral des Touches set out at last with his whole force. The enemy came on in rapid pursuit, and on March 16th the two fleets met in an indecisive action near the mouth of Chesapeake Bay. Although the British declined a fight to the finish after suffering heavy damage to rigging, the French did nothing to follow up their advantage. They retired to Newport shortly afterwards, while a crippled British squadron remained on the scene to defend Arnold in Virginia.

Washington lost his famous composure long enough to indulge in some understandable even if indiscreet grumbling. His private letter was intercepted by the enemy and published to create ill feeling between allies. He got out of the embarrassing situation by a letter to Rochambeau which was a model of diplomacy, and the French general declared himself satisfied with the apology.[2]

The only American gain from the fiasco had been the sending of a small army to the defense of Virginia. Washington appointed Lafayette as general in the hope that he might be able to persuade his countrymen to give decisive naval aid at some future date. It was also desirable to replace Steuben, whose criticisms had created so much antagonism in Virginia as to impair his usefulness. The drillmaster had long wished to exchange his duties for an active command, but he did not possess the tact required for leading inadequate forces of raw militiamen.

It was no small achievement for the rebels to have armies on three fronts as the war entered its seventh year. Not only were the four southern states unable to contribute much, but they drew heavily upon the resources of the others for their own defense. This was something to be viewed with pride, for American unity seemed a fact rather than a hope, now that the Articles of Confederation had at last been ratified. The event was celebrated on March 1st with as much fervor as Independence Day, even though American leaders realized the imperfections of the first crude constitution adopted in the autumn of 1777.

American finances were still in ruins, but on the wreck of Continental currency Robert Morris laid the foundations of the new national bank approved by a resolution of Congress on May 6th.[3] Hopes of French financial aid were realized, moreover, when Luzerne announced to Congress on May 25th that "the king has resolved to grant the United States a subsidy of six million livres tournois, and to enable Dr. Franklin to borrow four millions more for the service of this year."[4]

Another old dream came true as Connecticut countryfolk lined the stone walls for their first sight of the French soldiers. More than three years had passed since the rejoicing over the treaty of alliance, when Americans fondly anticipated that their new allies would soon have troops in the field. It had been a long wait, but even the undemonstrative Yankees were thrilled by the spectacle of the spotless white uniforms piped with crimson, dark green, rose and violet to distinguish the infantry regiments. The artillerymen wore blue coats lined with white, and a corps of light troops appeared in sky-blue coats and red breeches.[5]

The very names of the regiments had a romantic appeal to Americans who could not have pronounced the words—the Royal Deux-Ponts, the Soissonais, the Saintonge, the Agénois and the Auxerre. Better yet, the discipline of the visitors was as perfect as their alignment and marching, for no incident happened along the route as a discordant note. During the entire past year Rochambeau had kept such strict order that Rhode Island people watched the troops depart with a regret which was not altogether due to losing a cash market for their produce.

The Frenchmen in their turn were fascinated by the most common-place things in America. Baron Cromot du Bourg, soon after arriving, recorded one of these discoveries in his diary: "I was not a little surprised to see the two meadows on the sides of the road . . . covered with sparks of fire. . . . I got down suddenly from my horse to pick up one of these sparks which seemed to me so extraordinary, and I could not have been more astonished by anything than I was at finding in my hand a sort of fly which threw out a great light; this insect is in this country called the *firefly*." Rochambeau's aide thought that Rhode Island "must have been one of the most pleasing spots in the world before the war, since notwithstanding the disasters it has suffered, some of its houses destroyed, and all its woods cut down, the Island is still a charming residence."[6]

The French forces saw very little of the seamy side of the war during their first year—the poverty, the profiteering, the towns ravaged and burned by the enemy. There had been just enough devastation in Rhode Island to glorify Americans fighting for liberty, and the large Quaker population gave the visitors a favorable first impression of a sober, decent, pastoral people, far removed from the vices and follies of the Old World.

Each army had reason to be disappointed in the other when the junction took place on July 6th within striking distance of the British lines north of New York. French military aid had been long delayed, and it amounted to less than half of the promised numbers, since the contingent from Brest never arrived. Washington, on the other hand, had not been able to raise half of the troops he specified. Yet the French officers were generally sympathetic in their comments. Baron du Bourg noted that the American officers "seem to like their profession and study it." Claude Blanchard, the French commissary, declared that the rebel soldiers "marched pretty well, but they handled their guns badly. There were some fine looking men; also many who were small and thin, and some children twelve or thirteen years old. They have no uniforms and in general are badly clad." Even the dinner given by Washington did not displease visitors taking pride in their national cookery, "The table was served in the American style and abundantly: vegetables, roast beef, lamb, chickens, salad dressed with nothing but vinegar, green peas, puddings, and some pie, a kind of tart . . . all this being put on the table at the same time."[7]

In answer to British attempts to divide the allies, the French acknowledged Washington as generalissimo—an honor which has rarely been paid in history by an army with such proud traditions. The fifty-five-year-old French general, educated as a priest before turning soldier, probably had no fears that his colleague would take an undue advantage of a diplomatic courtesy. Rochambeau had seen enough of Washington at their two conferences to acquire an admiration shared by his officers, and they were never disillusioned throughout the campaign.

The New England militia, after six years of war, could still respond to Washington's summons with 5,000 volunteers. These men took the place of Continentals as garrison troops, so that he had an army of about 4,500, largely veterans. Rochambeau brought nearly equal numbers, but the combined force was obviously too small to attempt an attack on New York even with naval superiority. The French general sent a dispatch to Comte de Grasse in July, requesting that the admiral bring "four or five thousand" troops when he set sail from the West Indies in August. In his memoirs Rochambeau declared, "I presented to him, as my private opinion, that an enterprise in the Chesapeake Bay against Lord Cornwallis would be the most practicable, and the least expected by the enemy, who counted on our distance from that quarter."[8] This passage may have been inspired by wisdom after the event, but letters written by Washington and Lafayette also indicate that the alternative of a Virginia campaign had not been overlooked.

Although several lively skirmishes occurred north of Kingsbridge, with the Allies taking the initiative, the prospect of a New York operation grew more remote every day. Clinton's army, including 3,000 recently arrived German mercenaries, enjoyed the superiority in numbers that the attackers needed. The enemy had fortified New York strongly during a long occupation, and the island had been so stripped of trees as to offer no cover. In the end it was Admiral de Grasse's decision that set the Allied forces in motion toward Virginia. He sent dispatches announcing his plans to sail for the Chesapeake on August 3rd, and in a joint reply of the 17th Washington and Rochambeau informed him that their armies would march southward in the hope of trapping Cornwallis. If that opponent escaped, an attack on the British army at Charleston was suggested as an alternative.

The Allies made every effort to deceive Clinton after crossing the Hudson on the first lap of their long march. Bake ovens were built in New Jersey, as if in preparation for a long siege of New York, and spies propagated false reports. Such stratagems did not entirely beguile the British general, but he could not be sure enough of Allied intentions to send reinforcements to Cornwallis. On September 2nd he finally concluded that Virginia was the objective and wrote his colleague a letter of warning. But it was already too late, for Washington's vanguard reached Philadelphia on that date.

Clinton still felt confident, after divining the purpose of his adversaries, that the British fleet could defend the Chesapeake region. He decided meanwhile to create a diversion by threatening New England, defended only by militia. Early in September he sent Arnold with 1,700 regulars and loyalists in 32 ships to attack New London. The traitor found himself on familiar soil, having spent his boyhood only a few miles away. He took a battery on the east bank of the Thames without any difficulty, but on the west side the 130 defenders of Fort Griswold put up a heroic fight against 800 assailants, inflicting 193 casualties before being overwhelmed. As punishment, about 80 of the patriots were massacred after Colonel William Ledyard had been killed with the sword he surrendered to a British officer.[9] Arnold was blamed for this slaughter, though it does not appear that he had any direct responsibility. There can be no doubt, however, that he gave orders for burning 65 homes and other buildings of no military value in New London.

As a diversion, the operation proved to be a failure. That very day de Grasse reached the Chesapeake and the Allied troops approached the Head of Elk. Washington had given his opponents more credit than they deserved when he feared a move against West Point. He left General Heath in charge of that fort with almost as many troops as his own force, but the enemy did not threaten seriously during his absence.

After it was all over, Clinton and Cornwallis engaged in such a heated controversy that the charges and countercharges fill several volumes. Each made out a good case to prove that he was blameless, yet the official returns of September 1st show that the British had 36,445 troops in

America—16,701 at New York, 8,885 in Virginia, 9,775 in the Carolinas, and 1,084 in Georgia, including Germans and trained provincials.[10] It was not men or ships that the two British commanders lacked as much as generalship; for the Allies had only about half the numbers, counting the 4,000 at West Point as well as the forces in Virginia and South Carolina.

Again it can only be concluded that the invaders had come to depend on their advantages in sea power and material resources so much that they had grown careless. As late as July 31st, according to a letter from Lafayette, Cornwallis was less concerned with strategy than disposing of his spoils: "His Lordship has . . . a large quantity of negroes, very valuable indeed, but no vessels it seems to take them off." The French volunteer ended his letter to Washington with a conjecture that might have occurred to his adversary, "Should a French fleet now come into Hampton Road, the British army would, I think, be ours."[11]

Cornwallis, who boasted that he would soon capture "the boy," could not have dreamed that Lafayette's summer campaign in Virginia was comparable to the light left jab which precedes the knockout punch. After beginning operations early in May with 1,200 men, the young Frenchman summed up his prospects in a letter of the 8th: "There is no fighting here, unless you have a naval superiority, or an army mounted on race horses. Now it appears that I have business to transact with two armies, which is rather too much. Each is more than double the superior of me. We have no boats, few militia, and less arms."[12]

Lafayette added that he "was afraid of myself as much as the enemy." Apparently he conquered any tendency to recklessness, for his maneuvers were a model of watchful prudence—dodging, parrying, retreating, keeping on the alert day and night to avoid disaster. The arrival of Wayne in June with 800 Continentals seems to have provided something of a spectacle as well as reinforcements. For the Pennsylvania officers, according to St. George Tucker, had acquired military spirit to such an extent that they wore plumes with their rags: "They put me in mind of the army marching to Dunsinane when mistaken by Macbeth for Birnam Wood; for the feathers appear before you can well discover the shoulders to which the head that supports them is annexed."[13] The happy warrior from Virginia also testified to the confidence felt by the troops in a young commander who had not fully mastered their language, "His extreme popularity renders the idea of his talents indisputable."

Of all the foreign volunteers, none loved America as much as Lafayette and Kosciusko. Both were to find a spiritual home in the New World, and both were to fail a decade later in their efforts to transplant the ideals of the Revolution in their own countries. Both would be captives in the summer of 1794—Lafayette a prisoner of state in Prussia after being declared a traitor by the revolutionists of France who repudiated his moderate principles; Kosciusko a wounded prisoner in St. Petersburg after leading the patriots to defeat against overwhelming forces of Russians, Prussians and Austrians who divided the remnants of Poland in the Third Partition. Lafayette spoke for both of them in a letter written during his long exile, "The Huron and Iroquois forests are peopled with my friends; the despots of Europe and their courts, these are to me the savages."[14]

In the summer of 1783 the young Frenchman could do little except to avoid disaster and keep the enemy occupied. Only once did the enemy catch him off guard. On July 6th he blundered into a trap at Green Spring after Tarleton bribed a dragoon to pretend desertion and give false intelligence. The desperate stand of Wayne's Continentals got the army out of danger, and Cornwallis feared an ambuscade too much to follow up his incomplete victory. This was the last blow he struck at foes with a third of his numbers. Immediately afterwards he fell back to Portsmouth, where the slaves and other loot of the British raids had been accumulating.

Neither Washington nor Rochambeau had any idea as yet that their objective was not New York. Not until August 15th, upon learning that de Grasse was on the way, did the generalissimo give Lafayette the difficult assignment of preventing Cornwallis from taking alarm and making his escape into North Carolina. The little rebel army in Virginia could hardly have stopped him, but Cornwallis had no such prudent course in mind even after he had reason to suspect the danger of French naval intervention. For he left Portsmouth, a weak enough position, and chose a still weaker one at the mouth of a river which could readily be bottled up by a hostile fleet.

It was small wonder that in a letter of September 6th, his twenty-fourth birthday, Lafayette predicted the surrender of the British army six weeks before the event. Major Tucker wrote to his wife the same day that "unless our own ill conduct prevents it, or the immediate hand of providence interposes in behalf of Lord Cornwallis, there is no doubt but that we shall have a *Burgoyneade* in Virginia." Youth sang so joyously in his veins that he felt it necessary to add an apology: "Can you assign a reason, my Fanny, why my style . . . so often breaks out into bombast? I wish I could avoid what I so cordially condemn; but I find that I am imperceptibly led from the exultation of mind, which I have for a fortnight experienced, to burst out into a turgid manner of writing which I condemn no less in myself than in others."

As a final contribution, Lafayette declined a premature operation which might have spoiled the Allied chances. De Grasse and Comte St. Simon urged an immediate advace with his army and 3,000 reinforcements from the fleet. But the young general refused with more wisdom than his elders and influenced them to wait for Washington and Rochambeau. "Having so sure a game to play," he declared, "it would be madness by the risk of an attack to give anything to chance."

There were enough possibilities of failure to keep Washington on the anxious seat. Among his difficulties, the rebel troops had not been paid for months; and he deemed it prudent not to pause at Philadelphia. "The streets being extremely dirty and the weather warm and dry," noted Dr. Thacher in his journal, "we raised a dust like a smothering snow storm, blinding our eyes and covering our bodies with it; this was not a little mortifying, as the ladies were viewing us from the open windows of every house as we passed through this splendid city. . . . Our line of march, including appendages and attendants, extended nearly two miles."[15]

Robert Morris tried to persuade Rochambeau to lend him enough specie for a month's pay. His efforts were unavailing until an express rider brought the good news that de Grasse had reached Chesapeake Bay. Then the French general consented, and Lieutenant Reeves of Pennsylvania exulted that this hard money was "the *first* of the kind that any of our Line ever received."

The rain of American blessings swelled to a downpour when news came to Philadelphia that the *Resolue* had just anchored at Boston with 2,000,000 livres of the money promised by Louis XVI. After a voyage of 62 days, the French frigate was so long overdue that everyone had feared for her safety. Morris gave directions for the casks containing the coins to be packed in oaken chests attached to the wagons by iron bands. Four oxen drew each load on the long journey to Philadelphia with a cavalry escort. Never did a greater or more legitimate opportunity for plunder await the redcoats as the column crept through New England. But the money arrived without incident to be displayed in heaps at the new national bank for the purpose of restoring confidence.

The Philadelphians who cheered the tattered rebel army were treated to another kind of military spectacle two days later when the Soissonais regiment, wearing tall grenadier caps with white and rose plumes, paraded through the streets. The members of Congress stood with bared heads outside the State House to receive the salute reserved for royalty. Most of the American officers would have agreed that these middle-aged civilians deserved a tribute for their conduct of the war. Poverty and lack of powers accounted for the lapses of the Continental Congress more often than neglect; and Washington later paid his respects in no equivocal terms:

> Our assemblies, in politics, are to be compared to the wheels of a clock in mechanics. The whole, for the general purposes of war, should be set in motion by the great wheel, Congress; and, if all will do their parts, the machine will work easily; but a failure in one disorders the whole. Without the large one, which sets the whole in motion, nothing can be done. It is the united wisdom and exertions of the whole in Congress, that we are to depend upon.[16]

Relations between the French and American troops remained genuinely cordial, despite the differences in language and religion. In the New York lines the British had recently made an effort to divide the allies by singling out the French for little courtesies such as the rebels had never known since the departure of the Howes. "The parleys between us and the English were displeasing to the Americans," wrote Blanchard, "and even to General Washington; they were unaccustomed to this way of making war."[17] But the good relations were not impaired, and French officers found the poverty of their allies touching. "These brave fellows make one's heart ache. It is almost unbelievable! For the most part they were almost without clothes. They had only trousers and a little coat, or jacket, of linen. The greater number were without stockings."

As the march continued in summer weather, the rags of the rebels had their advantages. The fine woolen uniforms of the whitecoats were not as well suited to the climate, and scores of them dropped out of the ranks from exhaustion and sunstroke.

A young Pennsylvania officer noted that the war had gone on so long that the scars of the early years were healing. Riding past the old encampment at Valley Forge on a recruiting mission, he commented that "some of the officers' huts are inhabited, but the greater part are decayed, some are split up into rails, and a number of fine fields are to be seen on the level ground that was cleared, but in places where they have let the shoots grow, it is already like a half grown young wood." Lieutenant Reeves also left a record of a dance given by a Pennsylvania community for the troops about to march to Virginia:

> On the evening before the party marched on half an hour's notice, all the young ladies of the place were assembled to a dance that a few of us had at Mrs. Whitehead's. As there were not enough ladies sufficient for partners for all the officers, we invited as many as could be supply'd and had a genteel little Family Hop. . . . We had no supper, but apples, nuts, &c., substituted in the room of it, with wine, punch, &c. The evening was spent with all the mirth and gaiety possible, and always to be found in companies that can be free together, in preference to large and fixed Assemblies. The company broke up about one o'clock in the morning, when each waited on his partner home. . . .[18]

It was a smiling countryside that the troops passed through on the way southward. Apples and peaches bent the limbs of the orchards, and the harvest of grain had been so rich that 1781 brought the most bountiful crops of the war. At the head of Chesapeake Bay it seemed that the Allies had at last been deserted by the fabulous good fortune which accompanied them so far. Then a courier came with assurances that de Grasse was sending transports for the footsore soldiers. Washington had ridden on ahead, and it did not escape his notice that the war in its seventh year had drawn him back to the vicinity of his own home. He paused for a brief visit at Mount Vernon before proceeding to Williamsburg, where he arrived on September 15th to take charge of operations.

The good Earl, as Clinton sometimes referred to Cornwallis, had possessed a comfortable superiority in numbers during the past two weeks over the combined forces of Lafayette and St. Simon. There was nothing to prevent him from making a sally, yet he spent this time at strengthening the field fortifications at Yorktown. The energy he had shown in his Carolina operations was conspicuously absent, and it can only be concluded that a summer of plundering had softened both the general and his army.

Washington's anxieties were not at an end when the allied forces assembled at Williamsburg—8,800 rebels, including Virginia militia, and 7,800 French soldiers supported by 40 ships of the line manned by 20,000 sailors and mounting 2,000 guns. British naval efforts to rescue Cornwallis had failed after a fleet commanded by Admiral Graves reached the mouth of the Chesapeake on September 5th. De Grasse sailed out to meet the enemy with an advantage both in ships and guns, and the British were worsted in the ensuing action. Graves lost 336 killed and wounded as compared to 220 French casualties, and several of his ships were so badly damaged that he returned to New York for repairs. This withdrawal cleared the way for the safe arrival of Comte de Barras from Newport with five ships bringing the French siege artillery, so that de Grasse felt free to bottle up Cornwallis at the mouth of the York River. At that moment, with the victory almost assured, Washington had the dismaying news that the French admiral proposed to leave the scene entirely and put out to sea again in readiness to meet the enemy fleet if it returned.

It must have seemed to the despairing generalissimo that the history of d'Estaing's fiascos was about to repeat itself. Eighteenth-century admirals lent aid grudgingly sometimes to the land forces, preferring the greater glory of combat in their own element. But it was monstrous and inconceivable that the fleet should abandon the siege after all the other difficulties of a complicated operation had been vanquished. The real crisis of the campaign came on September 24th, when Washington begged his fifty-nine-year-old ally to "cruise with your ships within view of the capes, so as effectually to prevent the entrance of any British vessels." The next day, in company with Lafayette, he paid a visit to the flagship *Ville de Paris*, and the sea captains called a council of war. "The result has been," announced de Grasse, "that the plan I suggested was the most brilliant and glorious, but it would not fulfil the views we had proposed. It is consequently decided, that a large part of the fleet shall anchor in the York River. . . ."[19]

If Washington had written a candid history of the campaign, he would doubtless have confessed that de Grasse gave him more anxious moments than Cornwallis. No prejudice against Americans was involved, for Rochambeau shared the rebel general's worries. De Grasse was simply impatient to return to the West Indies, and the passive role of the fleet at Yorktown had small appeal. The traditional French naval policy of avoiding risks also entered into the equation when he refused to station several frigates above the enemy position because of the danger of attack by fireships. Thus the British with their few vessels remained masters of the upper river, so that Cornwallis had a desperate chance of escape if his resolution had been equal to his opportunity.

While the generals had their worries, the young officers were enjoying themselves. Virginia was so impoverished that a moneylender disdained the security of the state: and funds were advanced only when Governor

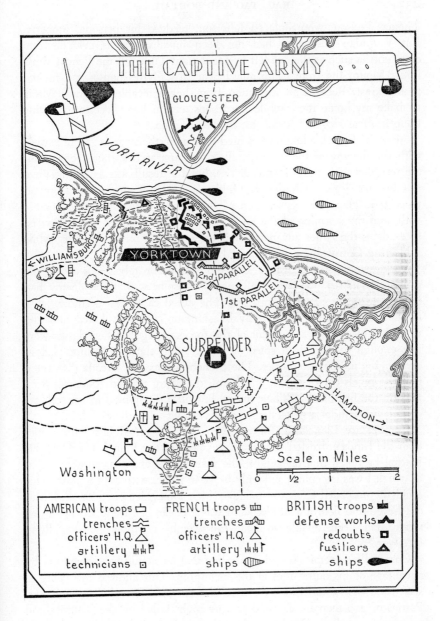

THE CAPTIVE ARMY . . .

GLOUCESTER

YORK RIVER

WILLIAMSBURG

YORKTOWN

2nd PARALLEL

1st PARALLEL

SURRENDER

HAMPTON

Washington

Scale in Miles

0   ½   1   2

AMERICAN troops   FRENCH troops   BRITISH troops
trenches   trenches   defense works
officers' H.Q.   officers' H.Q.   redoubts
artillery   artillery   fusiliers
technicians   ships   ships

Thomas Nelson, who replaced Jefferson, pledged his personal property. But Virginian hospitality had not been impaired, as is evident from diary entries such as the one left by Lieutenant Tilden of the Pennsylvania line: "Mount the front camp guard near Mrs. Byrd's house; and invited to breakfast. Receive an invitation from her agreeable daughter Maria to make my home there while the troops remain here [Westover]. Dine there in great elegance, drink tea in the afternoon."[20]

After the French admiral consented to remain, the siege began in earnest with the digging of the usual parallels and approaches. These operations are recorded with gusto in the diaries, but the result was as foreordained as Clinton's siege of Charleston. Only two events of much tactical importance took place—the evacuation of the British outworks on September 30th, and the storming of the enemy redoubts on October 14th. Between those dates the Allies advanced their lines without much difficulty while subjecting Cornwallis to a continual bombardment.

Yorktown, in short, was a strategic picnic for rebels possessing the superiority in sea power and all material resources that the enemy had held in so many former campaigns. The allied casualties, according to a military diary recently begun by Washington, were 72 killed and 190 wounded—less than 2 per cent of the forces engaged. These losses were just enough to provide a spice of danger, and the two armies vied in exchanging military courtesies. The French officers had already discovered that the rebels could march, and Baron du Bourg praised American firmness on the firing line: "Their troops, but little disciplined in general, are extremely so under arms. There is perfect order and quiet. . . ."[21]

Commissary Blanchard, for his part, was concerned less with tactics than the funds entrusted to him for payment of the French troops. In his journal he noted that one night "the floor of the chamber adjoining that in which I was [sleeping] suddenly broke in pieces with a loud noise. This accident proceeded from the money which I had deposited there; it was on the ground floor and underneath was a cellar . . . the floor, being too weak, had been unable to bear the weight of those 800,000 livres in silver."[22]

Cornwallis's enemies found it puzzling that he should have given up the advantage of his outer lines at the beginning. This allowed the Allies to start their first parallel at a distance of 600 yards from his inner works. Parties of 400 men by day and 900 by night toiled on the batteries and approaches, and on October 10th the second parallel was located about 300 yards away. Only two British redoubts remained as formidable obstacles. These were carried on the night of the 14th, with Colonel Alexander Hamilton leading the rebels and Lafayette the French. News of the Fort Griswold massacre had just arrived to provide the Americans with a new watchword, "Remember New London!" But it is to their credit that no prisoners were slaughtered in revenge.

This success left Cornwallis a choice between submission and being pounded to pieces by Allied shot and shell. The besiegers had thrown a strong detachment across the river at Gloucester, so that few hopes of escape remained. British losses during the campaign were 552 killed, wounded and missing, but a much larger percentage of the original 8,340 men (including 840 sailors) could be considered casualties of illness or exhaustion. On the 17th, the fourth anniversary of Burgoyne's surrender, the British at Yorktown capitulated. They tried to obtain the same favorable conditions that their predecessor had won; but Washington, unlike Gates, was not embarrassed by having another enemy at his back. He granted exactly the same terms which Clinton had given Lincoln at Charleston, and that American general was designated to receive the sword. Cornwallis pleaded indisposition at the last moment, so that General O'Hara took his part in the ceremony of the 19th.

"The British prisoners," according to Lieutenant McDowell's journal, "appeared to be much in liquor."[23] By a coincidence Lieutenant Feltman used these same words in his account: "The British army marched out and grounded their arms, in front of our line. Our whole army drew up for them to march through, the French army on their right, and the American army on their left. The British prisoners appeared to be much in liquor."[24]

Commissary Blanchard reported that "the English displayed much arrogance and ill humour during this melancholy ceremony; they particularly affected great contempt for the Americans. . . . There was a battalion of English grenadiers of great height and good appearance. The remainder of the English were small; there were some Scotch troops, strong and good soldiers. . . . The Germans preserved order and a certain discipline; on the contrary, there was little order among the English, who were proud and arrogant. There was no call for this; they had not even made a handsome defense, and, at this very moment, were beaten and disarmed by peasants who were almost naked, whom they affected to despise and who, nevertheless, were their conquerors."[25]

Most of the rebel diarists confined themselves to brief and matter-of-fact descriptions without a single note of jubilation. Typical of these comments is Captain Davis's journal entry for October 20th, "Lay quiet in Our Camp cleaning Ourselves."[26] The civilians did the rejoicing when Philadelphia had its first news on the night of the 22nd in the thick accents of an old German watchman, "Basht dree o'clock and Gornwallis isht taken!" The celebration began before daybreak and had been going on stridently for forty-eight hours when a staff officer rode into the city with official dispatches from Washington. Then the rejoicing broke out anew with such vigor that Tories who refused to illuminate their windows were reminded of the omission by boisterous crowds. "Scarcely a Friend's House escaped," a Quaker girl recorded in her diary.[27] "We had nearly 70 panes of glass broken; sash lights and two panels of the front Parlor broke in pieces; ye Door cracked and violently burst open."

Chapter 26

Nor Good Red Herring

THERE is no evidence that anyone in the Continental Army, from private to commander in chief, let himself believe for an instant that Yorktown might be the last important operation of the war. Washington did his best to persuade Admiral de Grasse to follow up the success with another combined operation at the expense of the British in Charleston. In a letter of October 20th he predicted that the South Carolina seaport could be "carried with as much certainty as the place which has just surrendered. This capture would destroy the last hope, which induces the enemy to continue the war. . . . It will depend on your Excellency, therefore, to terminate the war, and enable the allies to dictate the law in a treaty. A campaign so glorious and so fertile in consequences could be reserved only for the Count de Grasse."[1]

The French admiral refused on the grounds that he had already overstayed his allotted time. He led Lafayette to hope that limited naval aid might be given to an expedition against the small British garrison at Wilmington, but this prospect came to nothing. The French fleet sailed on November 5th for the West Indies and Rochambeau remained in Virginia for the winter. Washington divided his army, sending a few regiments to Greene as reinforcements while the rest marched northward for the defense of West Point and the Hudson.

The Allies parted company on the same cordial terms they had maintained throughout the campaign, each giving generous credit to the other for the victory. American leaders would have been lacking in honesty as well as gratitude if they had pretended that any progress could have been made without French troops, ships, money and siege artillery. Once these lacks had been supplied, Washington's army held up its end of the actual operations.

As to the conception, it is impossible to fix any date or sponsor for the decision to slip around the enemy at New York and trap Cornwallis in Virginia. The plan grew naturally out of circumstances, and several men seem to have thought of it simultaneously. If Washington deserves more glory than the others, it is because he had been driving steadily toward some such campaign since the early summer of 1778, usually with New York as an objective. More than a score of his letters during the next three years are devoted to this fixed idea of striking a fatal blow at a British army in a combined land and water operation.

As a departure from the usual gilding of a victory, Washington warned his countrymen repeatedly that they might find it necessary to make their greatest military effort in 1782. He had no idea that Lord North would receive the news of Yorktown, according to Germain's account, "as he would have taken a ball in the breast." This shock was due in large part to the absurdly exaggerated reports which Cornwallis had sent of his supposed triumph at Guilford. The British ministers took his word that he had swept on to conquer Virginia after reducing the Carolinas, and the news of the surrender came as a terrible disillusionment. Lord North is said to have cried, "It is all over!" But the king was as determined as ever to subdue the former colonies, and his placemen in Parliament could still muster a majority of 89 votes in favor of continuing the American war.

Cornwallis fared much better than Burgoyne after returning to his homeland. He managed to insinuate that Clinton had been chiefly to blame for the debacle, though that grumpy professional soldier had sailed to his rescue with 7,000 reinforcements, only to arrive several days after the surrender. The controversy was long and bitter, and Clinton tried in vain to bring on a duel after resigning his command at New York in 1782. But his colleague proved to be a much better politician than soldier, so that he emerged as the British hero of the war in America. Such was his reputation that he was rewarded a few years later by being sent to India as governor-general to supersede Warren Hastings. There he found a field more suited to his talents than Virginia, and he reaped further laurels for those curious victories won with ease by a handful of Europeans over vast hordes of Asiatics.

Clinton, with more military ability but less political influence, never again held an important command during following years while Cornwallis and Rawdon were distinguishing themselves as administrators of the Empire. Both of them contrived even to gain a reputation for humanitarian virtues, so that the liberal British historian Trevelyan praised

Cornwallis as "an English aristocrat of the finest type . . . careful and industrious; modest in success and equable in adversity; enlightened, tolerant, and humane; contemptuous of money, and indifferent to the outward badges of honor." The Americans of 1782 had a less flattering opinion, for it was proposed in the Continental Congress that the captured opponent be treated "not in the light of a British general, but a barbarian. In proof of their justice for classing him in so degrading a predicament, they appeal to the impartial history of his conduct during his command in the southern and middle states."[2]

Washington valued the new harvest of prisoners as the greatest gain of Yorktown, though his allies generously allowed him to keep all the arms and stores taken from the enemy. Throughout the war he had observed that the welfare of captured rebels depended on how many red-coats were held as potential hostages. Clinton remained the single notable exception to this rule in 1781, and the American commander acknowledged that "for above two years, we have had no reason to complain of the treatment of Continental land prisoners in New York, neither have we been charged with any improper conduct towards those in our hands."[3] Generally speaking, Washington believed that only the fear of retaliation kept the enemy within bounds. This conviction explains his solicitude for a former foeman when he wrote to Congress that "General Burgoyne is said to be in ill health; his death would deprive us in exchange of the value of 1,040 privates or officers equivalent, according to the tariff which has been settled."

Gentleman Johnny lived to be exchanged, and the surrender of Cornwallis and his army undoubtedly saved many Americans from a lingering death. Liberals of England may also be credited with improving conditions among rebels confined in that country, though the impressment of captives for naval service continued to be a grievance.

The political effects of Yorktown, judging by letters and journals, made a deep impression on the loyalists. Anna Rawle, the Quaker girl who reported the celebration at Philadelphia, commented in her diary, "Those joyful days when all was prosperity and peace are gone, never to return; and perhaps it is as necessary for our Society of Friends to ask for terms as it was for Cornwallis."[4] Most of these people, political conservatives and sectarians opposed to all war on religious grounds, had given so little offense that with few exceptions they were allowed to retain their property and standing in the community.

The great strategic lesson of the victory, as Washington interpreted it, was the confirmation of his belief that "without a decisive naval force we can do nothing. . . . A constant naval force would terminate the war speedily; without it I do not know that it will ever be terminated honorably." In a letter of November 15th to Lafayette, then about to sail for France, he reiterated this doctrine in words meant to be conveyed to that country: "No land force can act decisively, unless it is accompanied by a maritime superiority; nor can more than negative advantages be expected without it. For proof of this, we have only to recur to the instances of the ease and facility with which the British shifted their ground, as advantages were to be obtained at either extremity of the continent, and to their late heavy loss the moment they failed in their naval superiority."[5]

Washington had been able to wring from de Grasse only his tentative and none too enthusiastic consent to another combined operation the following May. This was better than nothing, but the rebel commander must have regretted that the British forces in South Carolina had been allowed to escape the fate of Cornwallis. For Greene had driven them into Charleston, ready to be plucked, after a campaign which distinguished him as the greatest strategist of the war.

The decisiveness of Guilford became every day more apparent as the rebel army hastened southward after Cornwallis went on to Virginia. New British repressions in South Carolina had disgusted even a majority of the supposed Tories. At Ninety-Six, as a typical measure, Colonel Balfour issued a proclamation, according to a contemporary historian, "that every man who was not in his house by a certain day should be subject to a military execution." The state was under the heel of such a harsh military administration that Lord Rawdon "called on the inhabitants in and near Camden to take up arms against their approaching countrymen; and confined to the common jail those who refused. In the midst of summer, upwards of 160 persons were shut up in one prison; and twenty or thirty of them, though citizens of the most respectable characters, were loaded with irons."[6]

Greene realized, as he marched toward Camden to challenge Rawdon, that only a few successes were needed to win most of the loyalists away from a hateful tyranny. Added to their resentments was the fact that British officers had found bribery more profitable than plunder after the state had been despoiled. Nearly every exaction could be softened if influential palms were greased; but it was a safe assumption in the spring of 1781 that the only stanch Tories were those bound to the British cause by ties of guilt or profit.

Lee's legion and other Continentals being on detached duty, Greene had about 1,200 troops and three fieldpieces when he approached Camden. On April 24th he took a position at Hobkirk's Hill, just outside the village, and Rawdon decided to attack by surprise the next morning before his opponent could be reinforced. The rebel general had time only to draw up a line of battle. On this occasion he hoped to envelop the flanks of a British army numbering fewer than 1,000 men. Rawdon extended his line to meet the threat, but the rebels gained ground at first and took scores of prisoners.

The seeming British rout gave fresh hopes to American captives at Camden who expected to be freed in a few hours. Among the knothole spectators was fourteen-year-old Andrew Jackson, suffering not only from smallpox but also a saber cut dealt by a British officer when the youth refused to black his boots. He and his brother were among 250 prisoners, most of them ill or dying of the disease, crowded together in a stockade without medical care. Andrew described the battle for men too weak to stand, but after the first excited comments his voice began to falter. Soon the sounds of musketry receded, and new captives were brought to the stockade to confirm fears of a rebel reverse.

The victory had been snatched away from Greene when the two Maryland regiments mistook a command to form a new line as an order to retire. Once begun, the withdrawal could not be checked; other regiments gave way, and Greene could only retreat to save his artillery. The rebels managed to bring off a few of their prisoners while Colonel Washington's dragoons beat back the pursuers, but the enemy had clearly gained a tactical victory in spite of equal losses of about 250 on a side.

British reports did not stress the fact that Hobkirk's Hill was actually a loyalist success, since only the regulars of the 63rd took part alongside such veteran regiments as the King's Americans, the New York Volunteers and the Volunteers of Ireland. Stedman declared that the victory, "like that at Guilford Court-house . . . produced no consequences beneficial to the British interest" and incurred losses "which in the present perilous state of the province could not well be spared."[7] And though the result disappointed Greene, he could console himself that his forces had made a more worth-while gain, only two days before, with the capture of Fort Watson.

This log stockade on the bank of the River Santee, held by 80 regulars and 40 loyalists, was another link in the chain of small forts which bound South Carolina. Lee's legion and a band of Marion's irregulars lacked artillery, and the defenders had the provisions and water supply to withstand a long siege. They also held an advantage in the exchange of musketry, since the fort was built on a mound overlooking the surrounding clearing.

Lee and Marion found an ingenious solution which threatened the security of every other little post in the South. All night on April 22nd the garrison heard axes ringing in the nearby woods. In the morning they found themselves at the mercy of a log tower, filled with sand and reared to such a height that rebel riflemen could fire through the loopholes and pick off troops in the stockade. Light Horse Harry Lee was familiar enough with the classics to know that the Romans had often captured walled towns by building such towers as a shelter for their archers. Twenty centuries later the ancient device proved so effective that the garrison surrendered at discretion. This seemingly minor success had more strategic importance than Rawdon's victory, for Fort Watson commanded his main supply route to Charleston. Two weeks later he found it necessary to evacuate Camden, after destroying vast stores, and retire to the seacoast.

Official British returns had already testified to the effect of Greene's strategy on Cornwallis during a three-month period when that general was sending glowing reports of victories to England. On January 15th he had 3,224 men fit for duty. This total had shrunk to 2,440 on February 1st, 2,213 on March 1st, 1,723 on April 1st, and 1,435 on April 15th when he withdrew to Wilmington.[8]

It was now Rawdon's turn to be placed between the upper and nether millstones of strategy—Greene's small army keeping the enemy's main body occupied while the forces of Marion, Sumter, Lee and Pickens preyed on the detachments. The rapidity of the British collapse is shown by the operations of a single week. Camden was evacuated on May 9th, Fort Motte surrendered to Lee and Marion on the 12th, and Lee took Fort Granby on the 15th.

The rebels bagged more than 800 prisoners in these operations. Ninety-Six, Augusta and Orangeburg were the only British posts left in the interior by June 1st, and the Georgia fort surrendered four days later. Greene's successes had given new hope to the patriots of that state, most of whom had been exiles or fugitives while the British governed with an able and moderate civil administration. Georgia militia forces began the siege late in April but lacked the resources to make it effective. Lee and Pickens marched to their aid, and another log tower placed the loyalist garrison at such a disadvantage that Augusta capitulated on June 5th after a brave resistance.

Greene had meanwhile begun the siege of Ninety-Six with his main body. The works consisted of a stockade connected to a strong star redoubt by a covered way and defended by 550 loyalist troops under Colonel John Cruger. Several log towers were not enough to compel a surrender, and Colonel Kosciusko took charge of working parties digging a regular system of parallels, approaches and batteries. The Polish engineer left a journal of the siege which indicates that the language still offered difficulties after six years in the country. "Her [here] the Workmen began to be exposed to the Continuel of the Enemy's fire all night and the suckiding [succeeding] but, more danger foreseen, was immediatly conteracted by more Exertions of the Troops," he recorded on completing the first parallel. "As the Nature of the Ground was very hard and aproched very much to Soft Stone the Approches Could not be so fast advanced."[9]

Although Kosciusko had the misfortune to be wounded slightly in the buttocks, neither the pain nor the customary ribald jests kept him from duty. The rebel lines and batteries were pushed forward vigorously, but even the regulars at Guilford had never given Greene as much trouble as these Americans under Cruger. When Lee joined the besiegers on June 8th and paraded the Augusta prisoners as a warning, the garrison replied with a sally and a desperate fight took place in the trenches of the third parallel. The rebels had long been spoiled by the comforts of British marksmanship, but at Ninety-Six they learned to their cost not to take the usual reckless chances. For the loyalist riflemen, according to Kosciusko, "were so industrious and great marksmen that no finger could be held up half second without been Cut of." As a trained European soldier, he paid his respects to the defenders "for their Vigilance, frequent judicious Sallies and proper means to counteract the assaliant measures."

In spite of such a valiant resistance, Ninety-Six was near to the end after a siege of 28 days. A new rebel battery commanded the redoubt from a distance of 140 yards when a messenger slipped into the fort with the news that relief was on the way. Greene learned that large reinforcements from England had just reached Charleston, enabling Lord Rawdon to march to the rescue with 2,000 men. The American general dared not risk a battle with half the numbers, and on June 18th he tried to storm the works. Some of the rebels penetrated the abatis, but the attack on the redoubt failed after an hour of desperate fighting. Greene abandoned the siege two days later, after total losses of 185, and retreated beyond reach of Rawdon's force.

The American reverse had little effect on the strategic situation, for Rawdon perceived that Ninety-Six could not be held after the loss of

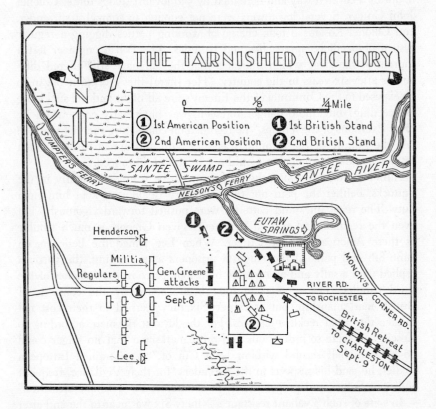

the other forts. A few weeks later he destroyed the works and retired to Charleston, followed by a train of Tory refugees whose lives depended on British protection. The young commander was so depressed by the outlook that he took his first opportunity to return to England.

In July the invaders held just two posts in South Carolina of any importance, Charleston and Orangeburg. Greene had gone so far toward gaining his objectives that he left the small war to Marion and Sumter after retiring with his army to a comparatively healthy region known as the high hills of Santee. There he rested troops who had been on the march for seven months, though they were not allowed to neglect their drill or discipline. At the end of August the rebel general made a 70-mile circuit and crossed the Santee to attack Orangeburg with 2,600 troops, including about 1,600 Continental veterans. A British army of 2,300 opposed him at Eutaw Springs, where the last pitched battle of the war took place on September 8th.

Colonel Archibald Stuart had encamped in a clearing with his tents surrounding a planter's brick house. He advanced with the only tactics that British officers in the South seem to have known—a simple frontal shock all along the line. Greene depended again on the Cowpens formation, and this time the militia of his first line did not disappoint him. They stood as firm as the redcoats, firing not three but seventeen volleys without wavering. When at last they were forced back, Greene threw in his Continentals against a battered enemy while Lee and Washington charged the flanks.

The redcoats could not stand up to the Continental bayonets, and in a few minutes Stuart's army was routed. Some of the troops scattered to the woods; others never paused in their flight until they reached Charleston. At last it appeared that Greene had won a complete victory, and his famished men celebrated by plundering the enemy stores of rum and provisions. This lapse gave Stuart an opportunity to make a fort out of the brick house and draw up his remnants in a new line behind a thicket. Only a part of the Continentals could be brought back into action, and they found it impossible either to storm the house or batter down the walls with fieldpieces. The redcoats in the thicket also held firm, though Colonel Washington was wounded and captured in an attempt to dislodge them with cavalry.

Most of the rebels were still pillaging the British tents when the counterattack caught them in disorder and drove them from the camp with the loss of their artillery. Even so, Greene could claim one of those technical victories such as the enemy so often boasted. His army had inflicted the highest proportion of losses ever suffered by any force in the war—693 killed, wounded and missing, according to official British returns. But only 232 of this number were listed as missing, and Greene's capture of more than 500 prisoners indicates heavier casualties than the enemy admitted.[10] Nor did his own army get off lightly, for he reported 114 killed, 252 wounded and 42 missing.

Stuart had scarcely half of his force left, allowing for the men who took to flight. The next day he destroyed 1,000 stand of arms and left 70 wounded redcoats to American care before retiring to the seacoast. Neither side could pretend to have accomplished anything except attrition at Eutaw Springs; and in that respect Greene had the advantage, however much he regretted his failure to destroy the enemy in another Cowpens. Orangeburg was evacuated shortly afterwards by weakened British forces which withdrew to Charleston, leaving the interior to Greene as his undisputed territory.

All accounts agree that the patriots took a terrible vengeance for their sufferings of the past year, when the Tories had the upper hand. American officers could control the Continentals and even the organized militia, but they were helpless to check the ravages of local bands settling private grudges. "Such scenes of desolation, bloodshed and deliberate murder I never was a witness to before!" lamented Major William Pierce, one of Greene's officers. "The two opposite principles of whiggism and toryism have set the people of this country to cutting each other's throats, and scarce a day passes but some poor deluded tory is put to death at his door. For the want of civil government the bands of society are disunited, and the people, by copying the manners of the British, have become perfectly savage."[11]

A British officer has left a description of one of these Tory refugees which might have been multiplied by hundreds in the last months of 1781: "He had scarcely the appearance of being human; he wore the skin of a raccoon for a hat, his beard was some inches long, and he was so thin, that he looked as if he had made his escape from Surgeon's hall. He wore no shirt, his whole dress being skins of various animals. . . . He said, that he had lived for three years in the woods, under ground; that he had been frequently sought after by the Americans, and was certain of instant death whenever he should be taken."[12]

Most of the rebel leaders condemned the atrocities of both sides equally. "The conduct of these two parties was a disgrace to human nature," declared Moultrie, "and it may with safety be said that they destroyed more property, and shed more American blood than the whole British army."[13]

It was the misfortune of the Tories that they had no leaders of enough character and ability to save them from becoming the dupes of a British policy of dividing and conquering. For it was not a coincidence that native Americans figured prominently in some of the most resented atrocities of the war—the butcheries of prisoners by Tarleton and Simcoe, the plundering of Connecticut towns by Tryon, the Indian massacres on the frontier, the persecutions of the Carolina patriots in 1780. If the Americans upholding the king's cause had been led by a Washington or Franklin, their brave efforts in the field might have profited them more. But Galloway chose to seek an early refuge in England, and Judge Jones preferred the role of critic and historian. Not a single Moses emerged to guide Americans who were hated by their fellow countrymen and despised by the British. And in the end only hardship and exile awaited the thousands who had given so much offense that they could not hope for forgiveness.

The loyalists who followed Rawdon to Charleston found such a grudging charity that they had to subsist in a miserable settlement of huts on the outskirts. This community they resentfully named Rawdontown while awaiting the ships to take them to Canada or the West Indies. Great Britain did not shirk the financial responsibility, and huge sums were appropriated by a war-weary realm to recompense Tories for property losses and establish them in new homes. But it was inevitable that they should have been regarded as a burden and often treated with scant courtesy.

More actual sympathy was shown by Governor John Rutledge and the South Carolina legislature after establishing anew the civil government in a temporary village capital. Although they had every incentive for a legal revenge, the authorities offered a pardon to citizens who had joined the British if they would serve six months in the patriot militia. The worst offenders had a hearing before a commission and an opportunity to submit evidence in their own defense. General Moultrie, who acted as chairman, asserted that "a great part of those names which were upon the confiscation, banishment and amercement lists, were struck off; and after a few years, on their presenting their petitions year after year, almost the whole of them had their estates restored to them, and themselves received as fellow citizens."[14]

The flight of loyalists from the British lines began shortly after Yorktown and reached its height in 1782. One of the Continental officers serving under Greene was amused by the spectacle of "the D——t quantity of Scofes I ever saw in my life. . . . This day I mounted guard and was much troubled with Scofes coming from Town [Charleston] to lay hold of the Govr's proclamation."[15] Even a counterproclamation by General Leslie, threatening dire penalties, had no effect of stopping the scramble for a rebel pardon.

The numbers of loyalists who left the United States have been estimated all the way from 40,000 to 100,000, and the total probably came nearer to the last figure. In some respects the conflict was more deadly than the struggle three generations later; for neighbor fought neighbor in 1781, while the sectional lines were sharply drawn in 1861. The effects of this first civil war were described at their worst by Moultrie after a visit to the South Carolina headquarters of Greene's army:

> It was the most dull, melancholy, dreary ride that any one could possibly take, of about one hundred miles through the woods of the country, which I had been accustomed to see abound with live-stock and wild fowl of every kind, and now destitute of all. It had been so completely chequered by the different parties, that not one part of it had been left unexplored; consequently, not the vestiges of horses, cattle, hogs, or deer, &c. was to be found. The squirrels and birds of every kind were totally destroyed.[16]

Before the end of 1781 the British evacuated Wilmington, and only Charleston and Savannah were left to them in the South. "Don't you think," wrote Greene to Dan Morgan, "that we bear beating very well, and that we are something in the nature of stock-fish, the more we are beat, the better we grow?"[17]

He considered his main purpose already accomplished, since the enemy could no longer lay claim to the southern states in the peace negotiations on the grounds of possession. American government was established again in Georgia, where Wayne controlled the interior with a small force of Continentals and militia. He had been instructed by Greene to "try with every means in your power, to soften the malignity and dreadful resentment subsisting between Whig and Tory; and put a stop, as much as possible, to the cruel custom of putting men to death, after they surrendered themselves prisoners."[18]

The presence of the Continentals, keeping the enemy at bay in the two southern states, gave the inhabitants some assurance of harvesting the crops if they planted their weed-grown fields. And by the second month of the new year Major Pierce could report that "the people throughout the whole country appear to be our friends. They seem disposed to adopt any measures that may be thought well calculated for the public good."

The campaign was in some respects more difficult than the operations of the past year, when constant action kept the morale of the troops at a fine edge. In 1782 the country was neither at war nor yet certain of peace; the enemy was obviously preparing to withdraw from the South,

and yet a sudden change in the international situation might bring about
a renewal of fighting. Late in February the Whigs gained enough strength
in Parliament to pass a measure authorizing the king to conclude a peace
or truce with America. The news reached Greene in April, only to add
to the contradictions of his problem.

Americans of 1782, after six years of hard fighting, now found themselves in the strange position of being bystanders—spectators of a world
war they had instigated in their efforts to win a new national existence.
During a year when a few nameless skirmishes took place in the New
World, the operations in Europe, India and the West Indies reached their
climax. Every incoming ship brought accounts of battles by land and sea,
most of them resulting in British reverses.

Only a few weeks after the news of Yorktown reached England, the
realm learned that the Marquis de Bouille had surprised the garrison
at St. Eustatius so completely that the redcoats were overwhelmed while
drilling on the parade ground. The victors not only recovered the former
Dutch island but also a sum estimated at two million francs, representing
a part of the plunder originally taken by Rodney the year before.

Another British disaster occurred in February when French and Spanish
forces captured Minorca. This island was a possession which had been
regarded as second only to Gibraltar in its importance to Mediterrean
operations, and the loss further weakened the position of the Tories upholding the administration.

The news of this defeat was hardly cold before reports came of the most
staggering blow ever dealt so far by the French in the West Indies—a
defeat which the British put in a class with the surrender of Cornwallis.
From St. Eustatius the energetic Marquis de Bouille had gone on to
capture the island of St. Christopher, usually known as St. Kitts. While
de Grasse held off the smaller fleet of Sir Samuel Hood, the French land
forces drew their parallels and approaches around the supposedly impregnable position of Brimstone Hill. On February 12th, after a siege of a
month, the garrison laid down its arms; and Nevis and Montserrat fell
shortly afterwards, leaving the British only three islands in the West
Indies.

Lord North's tottering ministry could not survive the announcement,
and on March 20th he handed in his resignation. The new administration,
headed by Lord Rockingham, found its leaders among the very men who
had been the warmest friends of America and harshest critics of the king
—Fox, Burke, Barré, Conway, Cavendish, Lord Camden and the Duke of

Richmond. Immediately Rockingham came to an understanding with the monarch that peace must be made with America even at the cost of granting independence. The personal rule of George III was at an end.

It was doubtless fortunate for the United States that the test of strength in Parliament did not develop a few weeks later, for on April 12th the British won their greatest naval victory of the war. Admiral de Grasse, far from keeping his tentative date with Washington in May, became a prisoner on his flagship *Ville de Paris* after four other vessels fell into the enemy's hands. His defeat, ironically, resulted from the French policy of saving ships. After a first unwelcome brush with Rodney, he had made his escape when a damaged warship fell behind. De Grasse returned with his whole fleet to rescue her and was caught in disorder between the islands of Guadeloupe and Dominica. All but five of his 35 ships of the line survived the disaster; and the allies soon added the Bahamas to the other former British islands they retained until the end of the war.

A few months later the British were heartened by a decisive success in the memorable siege of Gibraltar, which lasted from the late summer of 1779 until the second month of 1783. After failing to starve into submission a garrison supplied by ships, the Spanish forces attempted a grand assault on September 13, 1782. The defenders replied with red-hot shot and destroyed every ship of the battering fleet. This was the climax of a long-drawn struggle which fascinated professional soldiers, and the garrison held out until the signing of the preliminary peace articles.

On the other fronts it could hardly have been said that England remained true to her tradition of losing the first battle and winning the last. No war of the past three centuries had found the island kingdom so badly battered at the finish. The pride of a maritime nation took further blows in 1782 when an unknown French admiral, Pierre de Suffren, emerged as the greatest sea fighter of the war. After being accustomed to cautious foemen, the British caught a Tartar when this fifty-three-year-old adversary, described as "prodigiously obese," fought five furious actions against Sir Edward Hughes for the control of India. And though the "French Nelson" lacked the ships to strike a decisive blow, he had both the British land and sea forces at a disadvantage when the news of the preliminary peace treaty put a stop to hostilities.

The patriots of America, as bystanders, could only await the arrival of ships bringing news of French and Spanish operations long after the event. In spite of Washington's warnings, his countrymen relaxed their efforts in 1782. Public opinion no longer upheld the methods of impressment which enabled the states to meet part of their quotas before York-town, and the soldiers were worse supplied than ever. "For more than two months," Greene wrote in August, "more than one third of our men were entirely naked, with nothing but a breech cloth about them, and never came out of their tents; and the rest were ragged as wolves. Our beef was perfect carrion; and even bad as it was, we were often without any."[19]

Until he learned whether the outcome was to be war or peace, Greene kept his troops constantly in motion. It was necessary to make an impression both on the enemy and the inhabitants, and even more essential not to allow the army to rust in idleness. Sergeant Seymour's journal, like all the others, is filled with an endless chronicle of the expeditions of small war: "May 18th, marched and crossed Broad River and encamped on the other side, fifteen miles. On the 19th marched twenty-five miles. This day were executed three more of our deserters. . . . Next day, being the 20th, we marched seventeen miles. On the 21st of May we took and killed twelve Tories. Marched sixteen miles."[20]

At this rate the veterans of Camden had completed 5,000 miles when they returned to their homes, and even the Continentals who joined the force after Yorktown could boast of nearly half as many. Several times Greene gave the enemy an alarm by advancing to the outskirts of Charles-ton. "This is meant as a challenge," commented Major Pierce on one of these occasions, "and if I am not mistaken will shortly produce a fight. We have the best troops in the world to fight them with, and the whole army put such implicit confidence in General Greene that we shall struggle with great obstinacy to obtain a victory should the enemy see fit to hazard a battle."[21]

But the pretense of aggressive warfare could not be kept up after the British evacuated Savannah in July and withdrew the garrison to Charles-ton. Wayne joined Greene shortly afterwards and the combined forces attempted nothing more ambitious than skirmishes during the rest of the war. Colonel John Laurens was killed during a clash of advance guards in August; and on November 14th the last bloodshed of the Continental Army occurred on James Island. Kosciusko led a rebel detachment which dispersed a British foraging party after two officers and three men of the Maryland line paid with their lives for a petty tactical success.

In general, there was more trading than fighting with the enemy during these months of anticlimax. The British garrison needed fresh provisions, and American officers renewed their acquaintance with brandy, coffee, tea and other unwonted luxuries. Even such a stern disciplinarian as

Greene found it wise in the interests of morale to wink at the traffic which went on daily between the lines.

On December 14th the British evacuated the seaport. Wayne marched in at the head of the Continentals while the hundreds of enemy sails were still to be seen in the harbor. Only one more thing remained to be accomplished, for Mrs. Greene had "set her heart" on a grand ball of celebration. Kosciusko decorated the hall "with magnolia leaves hung up in festoons, and pieces of paper curiously cut in imitation of the flowers."[22] Thus the war in the South, the most deadly of all the Revolutionary campaigns, came at last to an end with music and dancing.

Chapter 27

As the Sparks Fly Upward

BOTH Washington and Rochambeau had anticipated another campaign in 1782. But in May they had the news of de Grasse's defeat instead of assurances that he would lend naval aid to a combined operation of the two armies. And that same month Sir Guy Carleton replaced Clinton at New York as the commander chosen to carry out the policies of the new Rockingham ministry.

This change did not have the intended effect of soothing American leaders. They would never have believed that Carleton actually did have secret instructions to withdraw all British garrisons. Still less would they have credited that he was ordered to use his influence to reconcile "the minds and affections of his Majesty's American subjects by such open and generous conduct as may serve to captivate their hearts and remove every suspicion of insincerity."[1]

The Rockingham ministry could not have sent anyone more calculated to arouse American doubts and alarms. Although the new commander had not been appreciated in his own country, his opponents of 1782 would have agreed with General Heath's estimate: "Sir Guy Carleton was probably the greatest general which the British had in America during the war; and it was fortunate for the Americans that he was kept so long within the limits of Canada."[2]

Carleton, who genuinely liked and admired Americans, had the misfortune to arrive at a moment when their animosities were at white heat. The British had just added the last straw to their excesses of the war by hanging a New Jersey militia hero, Captain Josiah Huddy, on charges of shooting down an escaping Tory prisoner. Later evidence proved even to the satisfaction of the enemy that he had been a captive himself at the time, but his vindication came too late to save him from the gallows.

The news reached Philadelphia before the cooling of the fury aroused by the execution of Colonel Isaac Hayne, who had been unjustly hanged by the enemy in Charleston. Congress had reacted so violently that hotheaded John Mathews of South Carolina proposed a resolution:

> That should any further acts of inhumanity be perpetrated by the British armies, within these United States . . . orders will be immediately given to the officers commanding our troops to put to death all persons found in arms against these United States without discrimination. And we do further declare, that we shall conceive ourselves to be fully justified by the laws of self defence and sound policy, to employ persons to reduce to ashes the towns of Great Britain, as a just retaliation for the wanton acts of cruelty committed by the enemy, and as a duty we owe our constituents.[3]

This emotional measure was never passed or even published. It was merely one of many outbursts of helpless rage at a time when an unfavorable balance of prisoners left the Americans in no position to retaliate. The Huddy case found them in a better situation as a result of Yorktown, and Carleton inherited the debacle at a time when he wished to restore good will. His opponents acknowledged that he denounced the crime and brought to trial Captain Richard Lippincott, whom the rebels accused. But a court-martial acquitted that officer, and Carleton naturally declined to give him up afterwards, disgusted as he had been at the verdict.

Washington had meanwhile put the question up to twenty-five of his subordinates at West Point. "It was found," recorded Heath in his memoirs, "that the officers were unanimous in their opinion that a retaliation ought to take place; that it should be inflicted on an officer of equal rank. . . ."[4]

One of the most gruesome lotteries of history resulted when a group of British captains drew numbers in a Pennsylvania prison stockade with the knowledge that a blameless man must go to the gallows. The unlucky lot fell to Charles Asgill, whose youth as well as innocence moved his captors to pity. But neither Washington nor Congress relented, and Carleton found it necessary to carry out his policies of pacification in this hostile atmosphere.

As the months dragged on, Americans shrank more and more from the prospect of hanging the nineteen-year-old British captain. They realized that retaliation had been delayed until it could no longer serve any good purpose. Carleton's many acts of kindness proved so embarrassing meanwhile that Congress took every opportunity of reprieving Asgill. At last the decision could no longer be postponed, and everyone felt relieved when the intervention of Vergennes on behalf of the young officer's mother provided a good excuse for setting him free.

Carleton's opponents respected him, but they did not err in assuming that he served the interests of his country ably and faithfully. Thus their admiration was tempered by distrust, so that his most generous overtures were viewed with dark suspicion. One of his first moves, in obedience to instructions, was an attempt to open negotiations with Congress. Although the British pretended to hold the rebel parliament in contempt, their private writings often went to the opposite extreme of crediting the delegates with the most sinister powers and Machiavellian motives. "No one was permitted to be present at their deliberations," commented an enemy officer, "and all of their proceedings, except those which they thought fit to publish, were kept profoundly secret. Assembled in the cause of freedom, they nevertheless thought fit to observe a form practiced only in the most despotic governments. . . . Their decrees, when promulgated, were received like the oracles of ancient times, as the dictates of profound wisdom."[5]

This opinion would doubtless have flattered delegates who were not accustomed to so much respect from their own constituents. At any rate, they refused to communicate with Carleton; and he had no better fortune when he offered to negotiate with the governors. As a final resort, the British general tried to appeal directly to the people through the medium of the New York newspapers. Again he failed flatly in what his opponents took to be an effort to divide the states. They suspected his purposes even when he freed 700 rebel prisoners in England, some of whom had been confined since 1776, and allowed the well-treated captives at New York to be visited by their wives.

Every prospect seemed to point to peace throughout 1782, yet the rebels had to be prepared for war. In August they dared not put any faith in Carleton's assurances when he informed them, quite truthfully, that negotiations were already under way in Europe. The British commander, like young Asgill, had to pay for the sins of his predecessors, so that his most friendly acts were interpreted as sly attempts to gain a military advantage.

Such suspicions appeared to be confirmed by several Indian raids on the New York frontier during the summer, though Carleton denied any complicity in a form of warfare he had always detested. He wrote to

Washington on August 26th that "these proceedings not only have my disapprobation, but I shall very willingly assist in restoring tranquillity to that frontier also." Future events were to prove his sincerity when he promised Washington that "if war must prevail I shall endeavour to render its miseries as light to the people of this continent, as the circumstances of such a condition will possibly permit. . . . How much soever, Sir, we may differ in other respects, upon this one point we must perfectly concur, being alike interested to preserve the name of Englishmen from reproach, and individuals from experiencing such unnecessary evils, as can have no effect on a general decision."[6]

Americans blew hot and cold during the long months of waiting as every ship brought conflicting reports. Hopes of a favorable settlement were dealt a blow by the news that Fox, Burke and other friends had left the ministry after the death of Lord Rockingham on July 1st. Lord Shelburne, the new prime minister, was a much less liberal Whig and a friend of the king. More weeks of suspense ensued until official dispatches reached Philadelphia on December 23rd to the effect that Great Britain had obliquely recognized independence by authorizing peace commissioners to treat with "the Thirteen United States of America." But not until the following March did it become known that the provisional treaty had been signed on November 30, 1782.

It is not the least of Washington's achievements that he kept the unpaid army together during a period of idleness and discontent. Rochambeau marched northward to join him in the Hudson Highlands in September, and there were half-formed plans of threatening the British at New York to prevent the sending of troops to the West Indies. These prospects came to nothing, and the final operation of the Continental Army took place nearly three months after the provisional peace when a force on the New York frontier lost its way one night in the snow and darkness. Washington reported this bloodless action in a letter to the president of Congress on February 25, 1783: "I am sorry to acquaint your Excellency . . . that a project, which I had formed for attacking the enemy's post at Oswego, as soon as the sledding should be good and the ice of the Oneida Lake should have acquired sufficient thickness to admit the passage of the detachment, has miscarried."[7]

In the lack of other occupation, the bored young officers at West Point fought one another on the field of honor. At an earlier date Dr. Thacher reported two duels in as many days, resulting in two deaths and a serious wound. "Is there no remedy," he inquired rhetorically, "for this fashionable folly, this awful blindness and perversion of mind, this barbarous and infernal practice, this foul stain on the history of man!"[8]

State and sectional rivalries also brought about some heated barrack-room discussions which were settled by fists as well as argument. On a basis of statistics, however, there can be no doubt that the New England states led all the rest in enlistments. The following figures are probably as reliable a record as has ever been compiled of the relative contributions of troops:

New Hampshire	12,497	Delaware	2,386
Massachusetts	69,907	Maryland	13,912
Rhode Island	5,908	Virginia	26,689
Connecticut	31,939	North Carolina	7,262
New York	17,781	South Carolina	6,417
New Jersey	10,726	Georgia	2,679
Pennsylvania	26,679		
		Total	234,782[9]

These statistics do not distinguish between Continental and militia service, nor do they take any account of the fact that the same man often served several enlistments during the war. Some of the irregulars of the three southern states appear to be left out of the reckoning, though they played a vital part in defeating the British in that region. Finally, the comparative figures do not indicate the variations in the quality of the troops. New Jersey did not have a large militia establishment, but it was perhaps the most effective of all. By the same token, Maryland and little Delaware surpassed most of the larger states at keeping their Continental regiments recruited up to strength.

Washington, needless to add, never had more than an inadequate fraction of these 234,782 men in his army at any period of the war. After 1778 he could feel fortunate if his total amounted to as many as 10,000 long-term troops on all fronts. It would be a safe estimate that he was out-numbered at least two to one in trained soldiers throughout the conflict, and his handicap was much greater in the material resources which are the sinews of war.

The numbers of rebel soldiers were limited at all times by the new nation's ability to provide for them, so that the odds may be summed up more accurately in terms of dollars and pounds rather than men. In the spring of 1783 the entire national debt of the United States amounted to $42,000,075, while a contemporary British historian estimated that the war "cost Great Britain 115,654,914 pounds, and the additional annual burden, in consequence of that war, 4,557,574 pounds, from January 1775 to the peace in 1783."[10]

The rebels could never have weathered the storm without French financial aid, yet the single item of the British outlay for German mercenaries was four times the total of the $4,500,000 representing all the war loans from France to the United States.[11]

A survey of the battles and sieges indicates that the two branches of the English-speaking peoples were evenly matched in the field. The following are the sixty principal actions of the war, with the British victories being listed in italics:

1775—Lexington, Ticonderoga, Bunker Hill, Chambly, St. Johns, Great Bridge, *Quebec*

1776—Moore's Creek, Siege of Boston, *Three Rivers*, Sullivan's Island, *Long Island, Kipp's Bay*, Harlem Heights, Pell's Point, *White Plains, Valcour Island, Fort Washington*, Trenton

1777—Princeton, Ridgefield, *Ticonderoga, Hubbardstown, Fort Ann*, Oriskany, Bennington, Fort Stanwix, First and Second Saratoga, *Brandywine, Germantown, Fort Montgomery*, Fort Mercer, *Fort Mifflin*

1778—Monmouth, Kaskaskia, *Newport, Savannah*

1779—Vincennes, Newtown, Stony Point, Paulus Hook, *Penobscot, Briar Creek, Stono Ferry, Siege of Savannah*

1780—*Siege of Charleston, Camden, Fishing Creek*, Springfield, Hanging Rock, Musgrove's Mills, King's Mountain

1781—Cowpens, Guilford, *Green Spring, Hobkirk's Hill, Siege of Ninety-Six*, Eutaw Springs, Yorktown

The rebels, it would appear, got the better of the invaders in thirty-three of the sixty engagements. But any such summary must take into account the difference of opinion as to what constituted a victory. American soldiers claimed a success at Oriskany on the grounds of occupying the field afterwards, just as the British boasted a triumph at Bunker Hill, Guilford and the first battle of Saratoga for the same reason. But a war of attrition was not decided by such fine points of military prestige, and the real victory belonged in each instance to the side which gained everything except that empty honor.

The comparison is further complicated by the fact that a tactical decision did not always lead to strategic gains. Thus the rebels repulsed Carleton's invasion of 1776, though they lost the only action at Valcour Island. By the same token the redcoats saved themselves from disaster at

Newport in 1778, though the Americans won the single fight of the campaign.

It is also noteworthy that the largest battles often had the least importance in a war waged by small armies. From a viewpoint of numbers, Monmouth was the most impressive American victory next to Saratoga and Yorktown, yet it could only be called a barren tactical success. The British in their turn did not profit as much from Long Island and Brandywine as the triumph won at Camden by a few regiments.

Without splitting hairs, it might conservatively be said that Washington's forces prevailed in half of the principal clashes of the Revolution. No account need be made of such slaughters of prisoners as Tarleton's massacre at the Waxhaws. Nor could plundering raids on undefended towns be included, since they did more harm to the British cause than the ravaged communities. The skirmishes of the eight years are too numerous for mention, yet it was probably in this department that the rebels got in their best blows. For the great majority of the petty fights ended in favor of Americans who usually had the advantage in mobility and marksmanship. It would not be going too far to conclude that the war in the South was decided by scores of little combats in which the invaders lost a total amounting to a Revolutionary army.

When the quality rather than quantity of the victories on each side is considered, there can be no mystery as to why the Americans won a long-drawn war of attrition. Fourteen actions occurred in which the losing army was captured wholesale or destroyed as a fighting force, and the invaders were the victims on nine of these occasions—Moore's Creek, Trenton, Bennington, Saratoga, Vincennes, Stony Point, King's Mountain, Cowpens and Yorktown. The total British losses, exceeding 20,000, were serious enough to be decisive in a war waged on such a small scale, not to mention the moral effects. The redcoats, for their part, were able to annihilate five opposing forces, totaling about 8,000 men, at Fort Washington, Camden, Briar Creek, the battle of Savannah and the siege of Charleston.

One of the most overlooked factors in the contest is the great and often unacknowledged debt owed by British generals to the loyalists in the later campaigns. Lord Germain boasted in an intercepted letter of 1781 that "the American levies in the King's service are more in number, than the whole of the troops in the service of the Congress."[12] Yet it was seldom enough that these auxiliaries received much official credit.

In spite of such omissions, there was hardly an important action after 1778 in which the redcoats were not aided by at least one regiment of loyalists who gave as good an account of themselves in the field. Six actions were fought almost entirely by provincials on the British side— Oriskany, Hanging Rock, Musgrove's Mills, King's Mountain, Hobkirk's Hill and the siege of Ninety-Six. Five others—Camden, Briar Creek, Cowpens, Savannah and the siege of Savannah—found Tories represented in about equal numbers with the regulars, though it could not be said that they won equal glory in the dispatches.

Certain it is that the Americans fighting for the king gave the rebels more trouble during the final four years than had been experienced from the Hessians in the early part of the war. Only about 60 per cent of the German mercenaries ever returned to their homeland with such shreds of military reputation as they had left. Of the 29,867 who reached these shores, some 5,000 deserted and 7,754 found a grave in America, including deaths from disease as well as battle.[13] A large proportion of the 17,313 survivors had been wounded or captured without the consolation of winning a single fight in which Hessians exclusively were pitted against Americans. Far from learning any tactical lessons in the New World, the mercenaries departed with an unshaken faith in the outworn methods of Frederick the Great. These delusions of grandeur lasted until an October day in 1806, when two great Prussian armies were crushed in a few hours by the forces of Napoleon at Jena and Auerstedt.

The Hessians remaining in this country were quickly absorbed into the population. Their lot could not always have been easy, for the mishaps of one simple fellow fill several pages in the Pennsylvania Archives. A deserter in 1778, he began a curious bondage of four years, working for Americans who took advantage of his status to pay him nothing. In 1782, when the victim balked at further servitude, his employer beat him and had him clapped into jail. At last Secretary of War Benjamin Lincoln intervened in his behalf, and the odyssey of Isaac Clinkerfoose came to an end when he married a Pennsylvania woman and settled down as a farm laborer.[14]

After the first few years, judging by diaries, the Hessians were not hated as bitterly as the loyalists and redcoats. Yet the excesses of the Revolution could not be called typical of British military operations. Amherst's army had been well disciplined in the last conflict, and the forces of Moore and Wellington would behave with moderation in the next one. For that matter, the redcoats of the Revolution upheld the amenities in their contacts with other enemies. The most exquisite courtesies were exchanged between adversaries in the West Indies; and the British officers at Gibraltar repaid as best they could the gifts of fruit sent by their Spanish besiegers. Dr. David Ramsay, who was a captive at St. Augustine, charged the ravages in America to a decline in the quality of British personnel:

> The officers, privates, and followers of the royal army, were generally more intent on amassing fortunes by plunder and rapine than on promoting a re-union of the dissevered members of the empire. The general complexion of the officers . . . was very different from what had been usual in better times. In former wars, dignity, honor, and generosity, were invariably annexed to the military character. Though the old officers of the British regiments in America were for the most part gentlemen . . . vacancies both on the commencement and in the progress of the American war had been filled up by a new set, greatly inferior in education and good breeding.[15]

American combatants were not as tolerant as this member of Congress, and Major Pierce concluded that "there is a certain triflingness in the composition of a British officer that can only be accounted for by their extreme ignorance and uncommon share of foppery."[16]

Among the French participants were two of Napoleon's future marshals, Jourdan and Berthier, and several of his generals. Most of Rochambeau's officers were impressed by American rifle tactics, and a few brigades of light infantry used the weapon during the early years of the French Revolutionary Wars. When Napoleon gained control of the army, however, he had all rifles withdrawn on the grounds that they took too long to reload.[17]

It remained for a British ensign who reached America in 1778 at the age of seventeen to perceive that the small operations of the Revolution held the key to great future decisions. Ten years afterwards this scholar of war had risen no higher than a major's rank, but in 1803 the threat of an imminent invasion of England gave Sir John Moore his opportunity. At Shorncliffe he took charge of a training camp which became one of the most famous military laboratories of history. At a time when other armies were copying the heavy columns of Napoleon's victories, Moore went back to the American war for his inspiration. Mobility and fire power were the gospel he preached at Shorncliffe; and he revived rifle tactics by creating his celebrated Light Division out of three regiments armed with that weapon.

The test came after Napoleon's invasion of Spain, when a British army went to the rescue. Moore was killed in the first campaign, but Wellington used his tactics to beat a succession of French marshals. The "thin red line," drawn up in two ranks instead of the usual three, and preceded by riflemen as skirmishers, cut the opposing columns to pieces in the Peninsular operations. French soldiers, who had come to regard the musket as merely a handle for a bayonet, were defeated but not instructed. And in the end Napoleon himself met disaster at Waterloo against the methods adapted in large part from a colonial war of the last generation.

Moore's pupils were not so fortunate when they tried their rifle tactics against the sons of the original preceptors. In the "second war of independence" American militiamen ran as usual from enemy regulars until the final engagement. On that January day in 1815, watching the redcoats advance at New Orleans, General Andrew Jackson may have recalled the morning when he stared at another British force through the knothole at Camden. This time the thin red line of Peninsular veterans and the riflemen of the Light Division did not fare as well against Kentucky marksmen as they had against Napoleon's columns. When the smoke cleared, the attackers had suffered one of the worst repulses incurred by British arms since Bannockburn. But the fight had a brighter historical significance. For it is remembered as the last time that Britons and Americans have ever met on a battlefield save as allies.

In the spring of 1783 there could be no doubt as to who had won the Revolutionary War when the terms of the provisional peace treaty were announced. The American rebels had gained more than their independence; they had wrested from the enemy an inland empire representing one of the greatest permanent conquests of history—that broad domain, formerly a part of Quebec Province, which includes the present area of Michigan, Illinois, Ohio, Indiana and Wisconsin.

Great Britain had paid dearly at the peace table for such violations of accepted military codes as the employment of savages and the plundering raids conducted for private profit. When the king's commissioners demanded the return of confiscated loyalists estates, Dr. Franklin reminded them of the burned American towns and looted homes. He hinted that the British were so deeply in debt to the United States for these excesses that only the cession of Canadian territory would balance accounts. The British envoys had to accept a face-saving compromise, though it meant an added cost to their country of several million pounds as compensation for loyalists. For the issue was settled by a promise that Congress would "recommend" to the states that they restore loyalist property, an assurance which both sides recognized as an empty diplomatic gesture.

An official British policy of inciting Indian massacres had led to George Rogers Clark's expeditions, giving the Americans a claim of possession to the territory now occupied by such great industrial cities as Chicago, Detroit and Cleveland. This was by far the most impressive gain made by any of the victors. Spain kept Minorca and both Floridas as her reward, and France contented herself with the island of Tobago in addition to the restoration of possessions in India and the West Indies lost in the last war. The great French object had been the establishment of American independence as a means of dividing the English-speaking peoples and securing a share in the trade which had been made a British monopoly by acts of Parliament.

The rebels were conceded their claim to a northern boundary including the present area of Maine, and they won the right of sharing in the Newfoundland fisheries. Practically every one of their demands was granted in a treaty representing such a triumph that it resulted in the downfall of the Shelburne ministry. Even such old friends of America as Fox and Burke joined in the outcry at the loss of a territory several times as large as the British Isles.

Some of the rebel leaders confidently believed that they had wrecked the British Empire. "Were I to turn prophet," wrote Arthur Middleton in a typical comment of 1782, "I should not think much of hazarding a Prediction of the National Bankruptcy, the absolute separation of Ireland, probably that of Scotland, and to crown the whole the Expulsion of the present evil race of Geese Drivers [the House of Hanover] and all the curses attendant upon those wars called civil which lead to and are consequent of an entire Revolution in Governments. . . ."[18]

Such gloomy predictions reckoned without the British people, who had been as much the victims of the king's ambitions as the Americans. Thus the overthrow of the monarch's personal rule in 1782 might have been considered one of England's greatest compensations. Further boons had to wait until after the long struggle of the Napoleonic Wars, but in the Reform Bill of 1832 Englishmen gained most of the political benefits of the American Revolution—benefits upheld in 1776 by Burke, Fox and Chatham as well as Washington, Franklin and Jefferson.

It had not been a popular war in England after its purposes were fully comprehended. Throughout the last years the subjects of George III showed their coolness by the most accurate of all barometers. "In August, 1774, before the Revolution began," commented a British historian, "the Three per Cent. Consuls stood at 89. A month before the news of Long Island arrived in London they were at 84; a fortnight after that news they were at 82; and that was all the effect produced by a complete rout of the Americans. . . . By October 1777 Consuls had fallen to 78. The tidings of the capture of Burgoyne brought them down to 70. They fell and fell, until the capitulation of Lord Cornwallis reduced them to 54; and they could hardly have gone lower if they were to retain any value at all. . . . And yet Consuls, when the situation came to be understood, rose six points on the mere prospect of a peaceful settlement with our former colonies; although England was still at war, all the world over, with France, Spain and Holland."[19]

The British Empire was compensated for its territorial losses of 1783 when India proved to be a much more valuable asset than America had ever been. While a Jeffersonian democrat might have questioned the right of the conquerors to rule this subcontinent with its two hundred million souls, he could only have admitted that British government was a vast improvement over the tyrannies of the native despots. Annual revenues of £15,000,000, in addition to equal profits from the commerce of the East, soon gave the nine million people of Great Britain a larger income than any nation had ever known in modern history. India had been for centuries the depository of such hoardings that the treasure of the princes included coins minted in the time of Alexander the Great. This gold helped to frustrate the ambitions of another renowned warrior when Britain subsidized the armies which defeated Napoleon. As a more sweeping result, the frozen capital representing the wealth of India fertilized the new Machine Age by rewarding inventions and financing the development of English manufactures.

Few conquering hosts of history have ever wrought so many changes in the world's map as those shaped directly or indirectly by the little Continental Army. But such distinctions were not exciting in the spring of 1783 to Washington's forces quartered at West Point and Newburgh. Like American soldiers of other wars, they were impatient to disband at the earliest possible moment and return to their farm and village homes.

The troubles of the United States did not end with the assurance of a victorious peace. It had been hard enough to raise troops for the war, and now the exhausted nation had the problem of discharging them without any money in the treasury for their long-overdue pay.

Although Bonaparte was only fourteen at the time, the student officer would have perceived at a glance that the time had come for Washington to plan a *coup d'état*. Another country gentleman of another British revolution had shown the way; for Oliver Cromwell was about Washington's age when he made himself Lord Protector with a victorious but discontented army as his instrument. Dictators thrive by offering security in fair trade for liberty, and the America of 1783 seemed to be ready for such an exchange. Two years of trial and error had demonstrated that the Articles of Confederation did not provide the Continental Congress with enough powers. Anarchy appeared to be just ahead, and a good many sober, decent Americans were willing to sacrifice some of the ideals of 1776 for stability. One of them, a middle-aged colonel named Lewis Nicola, hinted to Washington a possibility that had already entered the secret thoughts of other republicans: "Some people have so connected the ideas of tyranny and monarchy, as to find it difficult to separate them. . . . But if all other things were at once adjusted, I believe strong arguments might be produced for admitting the title of KING, which I conceive would be attended with some material advantages."

Washington must have realized that he could count on hundreds of aggrieved young officers who had never known any other trade but war. He must have realized that thousands of Continental veterans, unpaid and discouraged, would follow him without question. But there was to be no monarch in the place of George III, for the Virginia planter replied in disgust: "Be assured, Sir, no occurrence of the war has given me more painful sensations, than your information of there being such ideas existing in the army, as you have expressed, and I must view with abhorrence and reprehend with severity. . . . If I am not deceived in the knowledge of myself, you could not have found a person to whom your schemes are more disagreeable."[20]

This incident was trivial as compared to the crisis that has gone down in history under the name of the Newburgh Addresses. For months the officers had been represented in the State House by a deputation headed by General Alexander McDougall. Their chief grievance was the old issue of half pay, which still had not been settled satisfactorily after coming up in Congress at various times since 1777. The sufferings of both the officers and soldiers, McDougall warned, had reached a dangerous stage. But neither Congress nor Robert Morris, the superintendent of finance, had the means of redress. In the spring of 1783 an anonymous pamphleteer, later identified as Major John Armstrong, Jr., hurled a rhetorical bomb filled with enough explosive to blow up the country. "If your determination be in any proportion to your wrongs," he exhorted the officers, "carry your appeal from the justice to the fears of government. Change the milk-and-water style of your last memorial. Assume a bolder tone, decent, but lively, spirited, and determined; and suspect the man, who would advise to more moderation and longer forbearance."

Again Washington's personal leadership came to the rescue. On March 11th he called a meeting of officers at Newburgh, with General Gates presiding. And after listening to an address by the commander in chief, the officers passed five unanimous resolutions which left no doubt that they had rejected the invitation to take matters in their own hands. "Had this day been wanting," declared Washington, "the world had never seen the last stages of perfection, to which human nature is capable of attaining."[21]

Congress settled the issue as best it could by passing a measure, with only two dissenting votes, to commute half pay for life into full pay for five years. But this solution gave the officers no immediate relief, since they must wait for the bankrupt states to make the final payments. The soldiers were also offered the shadow instead of the substance of their arrears. At Washington's suggestion Congress decided to furlough the troops. They were to be allowed to keep their muskets as a gratuity, but the nation could not raise so much as $750,000 for three months' pay. Until the settlement of their accounts, the men were to be given notes with the promise of a discharge when the definitive peace treaty should be concluded.

There were several occasions which might be called the last day of the Continental Army; for Washington did not write his farewell address until November, and the following month he resigned his commission. More by design than accident, April 19th was selected for the modest ceremonies which symbolized the end of the long road for the officers and men at Newburgh. "At noon the proclamation of Congress for a cessation of hostilities . . . was followed by three huzzas," wrote General Heath; "after which a prayer was made by the Reverend Mr. Ganno, and an anthem (*Independence*, from Billings) was performed by vocal and instrumental music."[22]

In his general orders on this eighth anniversary of Lexington, the commander in chief declared that "happy, thrice happy, shall they be pronounced hereafter, who have contributed any thing, who have performed the meanest office, in erecting this stupendous *fabric of freedom and empire* on the broad basis of independency; who have assisted in protecting the rights of human nature, and establishing an asylum for the poor and oppressed of all nations and religions."[23]

There had been more stimulating food for the morale of other armies—uniforms, medals, parades and the applause of the crowd. Congress, it is true, did confer twelve medals during the war; but they were awarded so impulsively that two battles received half of the honors. Wayne, Fleury and Colonel Walter Stewart were singled out for distinction at Stony Point, and Morgan, Howard and William Washington at Cowpens. Five of the remaining medals went to Washington for the siege of Boston, to Gates for Saratoga, to Henry Lee for Paulus Hook, to Greene for Eutaw Springs, and to John Paul Jones for the capture of the *Serapis*.[24] The only men below the rank of major to be honored were Paulding, Williams and Van Wart, the captors of André who disclosed the plot to betray West Point. It remained a question whether these New York guerrillas were actuated by motives of patriotism or profit, but Congress gave them the benefit of a grave doubt.

The Continental veterans had no assurance of pay or transportation to their homes, yet the only disorders of 1783 occurred among troops at Philadelphia whom they would never have owned as comrades. Congress was threatened on June 21st by a riot of recently enlisted men described by Washington as "Recruits and Soldiers of a day" who had "very few hardships to complain of." The disturbance was settled without bloodshed while the real heroes of the war were departing for their homes "with perfect good order," as Washington reported on June 24th, but "without the settlement of their Accounts or a farthing of money in their pockets."

Even the notes promised in lieu of pay did not reach Newburgh until most of the men were on the way. But it made no difference, since a majority of the needy veterans would sooner or later find it necessary to sell these notes to speculators for a fraction of their value in cash.

Never in history has a victorious army come so humbly to the end. There was no such crescendo as Waterloo, no such twilight as Appomattox. There was not so much as a last review with blaring bands and saluting generals. The Continental Army simply melted away in little groups which straggled along the country roads, making their way homeward on foot, sleeping under the stars, begging for food at inns or farmhouses. These tattered vagabonds were not conscious of being historical figures, and it is likely that they did a good deal of grumbling. It is also probable that they enjoyed a larcenous chicken dinner now and then in the dark of the moon, and some may have bartered their muskets for a few quarts of rum.

Few of them troubled to chronicle their emotions, but Private Elijah Fisher did not neglect the journal he had been keeping since 1776. Not quite seventeen when he fought at Bunker Hill, the Massachusetts farm-hand had enlisted three times and served a total of six years. In April, 1783, he was released from the "old Jarsey prison ship" at New York, and a few days later he recorded a despair which must have been shared by hundreds of comrades: "I Com Down by the markett and sits Down all alone allmost Discouraged and begun to think over how that I had ben in the army, what ill success I had met with there, and all so how I was ronged by them I worked for at home, and lost all last winter, and how that I could not get into any besness, and no home, which you may well think how I felt."[25]

Gloomy as the situation was, Fisher still had reserves of courage which eventually brought him through to a secure middle age as a Maine farmer and progenitor of a large family. "But then Come into my mind," he continued on that spring day in 1783, "that there were thousands in worse circumstances than I was, and having food and rament be with these Content, and that I had nothing to reflect on myself, and I [resolved] to do my endevor and leave the advent to Provedance, and after that I felt as contented as need to be."

The commander in chief was undoubtedly thinking of men like Elijah Fisher when he wrote a letter which remains the greatest tribute ever paid to the Continental Army.[26] For it was not intended as a public acknowledgment or eulogy, but simply a private opinion from one soldier to another.

"If historiographers," wrote General Washington to General Greene, "should be hardy enough to fill the pages of history with the advantages that have been gained with unequal numbers, on the part of America, in the course of this contest, and attempt to relate the distressing circum-stances under which they have been obtained, it is more than probable that posterity will bestow on their labors the epithet and marks of fiction; for it will not be believed, that such a force as Great Britain has employed for eight years in this country could be baffled in their plan of subjugating it, by numbers infinitely less, composed of men oftentimes half starved, always in rags, without pay, and experiencing every species of distress, which human nature is capable of undergoing."

Appendix

Appendix

Generals of the Continental Army

GENERAL AND COMMANDER IN CHIEF

George Washington.   June 15, 1775, to December 23, 1783

MAJOR GENERALS

Artemas Ward.   June 17, 1775, to April 23, 1776 (resigned)

Charles Lee. June 17, 1775, to January 18, 1780 (dismissed)

Philip Schuyler.   June 19, 1775, to April 19, 1779 (resigned)

Israel Putnam.   June 19, 1775, to June 3, 1783 (retired)

Richard Montgomery.   December 9, 1775, to December 31, 1775 (killed in action)

John Thomas.   March 6, 1776, to June 2, 1776 (died of illness)

Horatio Gates.   May 16, 1776, to November 3, 1873

William Heath.   August 9, 1776, to November 3, 1783

Joseph Spencer.   August 9, 1776, to January 13, 1778 (resigned)

John Sullivan.   August 9, 1776, to November 30, 1779 (resigned)

Nathanael Greene.   August 9, 1776, to November 3, 1783

Benedict Arnold.   February 17, 1777, to September 25, 1780 (deserted to the enemy)*

William Alexander, Lord Stirling.   February 19, 1777, to January 15, 1783 (died of illness)

Thomas Mifflin.   February 19, 1777, to February 25, 1779 (resigned)

Arthur St. Clair.   February 19, 1777, to November 3, 1783

Adam Stephen.   February 19, 1777, to November 20, 1777 (dismissed)

Benjamin Lincoln.   February 19, 1777, to October 29, 1783

Marquis de Lafayette.   July 31, 1777, to November 3, 1783

Philippe DuCoudray.   August 11, 1777, to September 15, 1777 (drowned)

Baron de Kalb.   September 15, 1777, to August 19, 1780 (died of wounds)

* Although Arnold was not promoted until May, his appointment was later set at February 17th in order to give him seniority rights.

469

Robert Howe.   October 20, 1777, to November 3, 1783
Alexander McDougall.   October 20, 1777, to November 3, 1783.
Thomas Conway.   December 13, 1777, to April 28, 1778 (resigned)
Friedrich Wilhelm von Steuben.   May 5, 1778, to April 15, 1784
William Smallwood.   September 15, 1780, to November 3, 1783
Samuel Holden Parsons.   October 23, 1780, to July 22, 1782 (retired)
Henry Knox.   November 15, 1781, to June 20, 1784
Chevalier Louis Duportail.   November 16, 1781, to October 10, 1783
William Moultrie.   October 15, 1782, to November 3, 1783

Major Generals by Brevet
Under Resolution of Continental Congress, September 30, 1783

James Clinton	George Weedon
Lachlan McIntosh	George Clinton
John Glover	Edward Hand
John Paterson	Charles Scott
Anthony Wayne	Jedediah Huntington
John Philip DeHaas	John Stark
Peter Muhlenberg	

Brigadier Generals

Horatio Gates.   June 17, 1775, to May 16, 1776 (promoted)
John Thomas.   June 22, 1775, to March 6, 1776 (promoted)
Richard Montgomery.   June 22, 1775, to December 9, 1775 (promoted)
David Wooster.   June 22, 1775, to May 2, 1777 (died of wounds)
William Heath.   June 22, 1775, to August 9, 1776 (promoted)
Joseph Spencer.   June 22, 1775, to August 9, 1776 (promoted)
John Sullivan.   June 22, 1775, to August 9, 1776 (promoted)
Nathanael Greene.   June 22, 1775, to August 9, 1776 (promoted)
Seth Pomeroy.   June 22, 1775 (declined the appointment and was superseded
    on July 19, 1775)
Joseph Frye.   January 10, 1776, to April 23, 1776 (resigned)
Benedict Arnold.   January 10, 1776, to February 17, 1777 (promoted)
John Armstrong.   March 1, 1776, to April 4, 1777 (resigned)
William Thompson.   March 1, 1776, to September 3, 1781 (died of illness)
Andrew Lewis.   March 1, 1776, to April 15, 1777 (resigned)
James Moore.   March 1, 1776, to April 9, 1777 (died of illness)
William Alexander, Lord Stirling.   March 1, 1776, to February 19, 1777
    (promoted)
Robert Howe.   March 1, 1776, to October 20, 1777 (promoted)
Baron de Woedtke.   March 16, 1776, to July 28, 1776 (died of illness)
Thomas Mifflin.   May 16, 1776, to February 19, 1777 (promoted)
John Whetcomb.   June 5, 1776 (declined the appointment)
Hugh Mercer.   June 5, 1776, to January 11, 1777 (died of wounds)
James Reed.   August 9, 1776, to September, 1776 (resigned)
John Nixon.   August 9, 1776, to September 12, 1780 (resigned)

Arthur St. Clair.   August 9, 1776, to February 19, 1777 (promoted)

Alexander McDougall.   August 9, 1776, to October 20, 1777 (promoted)

Samuel Holden Parsons.   August 9, 1776, to October 23, 1780 (promoted)

James Clinton.   August 9, 1776, to November 3, 1783

Adam Stephen.   September 4, 1776, to February 19, 1777 (promoted)

Christopher Gadsden.   September 19, 1776, to October 2, 1777 (resigned)

William Moultrie.   September 16, 1776, to October 15, 1782 (promoted)

Lachlan McIntosh.   September 16, 1776, to November 3, 1783

William Maxwell.   October 23, 1776, to July 25, 1780 (resigned)

William Smallwood.   October 23, 1776, to September 15, 1780 (promoted)

Chevalier de Roche Fermoy.   November 5, 1776, to January 31, 1778 (resigned)

Chevalier De Borre.   December 1, 1776, to September 14, 1777 (resigned)

Henry Knox.   December 27, 1776, to November 15, 1781 (promoted)

Francis Nash.   February 5, 1777, to October 17, 1777 (died of wounds)

John Cadwalader.   February 21, 1777 (declined the appointment to serve in Pennsylvania militia)

Enoch Poor.   February 21, 1777, to September 8, 1780 (died of illness)

John Glover.   February 21, 1777, to July 22, 1782 (retired)

John Paterson.   February 21, 1777, to November 3, 1783

Anthony Wayne.   February 21, 1777, to November 3, 1783

James M. Varnum.   February 21, 1777, to March 5, 1779 (resigned)

John Philip DeHaas.   February 21, 1777, to ———, 1783 (retired)

William Woodford.   February 21, 1777, to November 13, 1780 (died of illness)

Peter Muhlenberg.   February 21, 1777, to November 3, 1783

George Weedon.   February 21, 1777, to June, 1783 (retired)

George Clinton.   March 25, 1777, to November 3, 1783

Edward Hand   April 1, 1777, to November 3, 1783

Charles Scott.   April 1, 1777, to November 3, 1783

Ebenezer Learned.   April 2, 1777, to March 24, 1778 (resigned)

Jedediah Huntington.   May 12, 1777, to November 3, 1783

Joseph Reed.   May 12, 1777, to June 9, 1777 (declined)

Thomas Conway.   May 13, 1777, to December 13, 1777 (promoted)

Count Pulaski.   September 15, 1777, to October 11, 1779 (died of wounds)

John Stark.   October 4, 1777, to November 3, 1783

Chevalier Louis Duportail.   November 17, 1777, to November 16, 1781 (promoted)

Jethro Sumner.   January 9, 1779, to November 3, 1783

James Hogun.   January 9, 1779, to January 4, 1781 (died of illness)

Isaac Huger.   January 9, 1779, to November 3, 1783

Mordecai Gist.   January 9, 1779, to November 3, 1783

William Irvine.   May 12, 1779, to November 3, 1783

Daniel Morgan.   October 13, 1780, to November 3, 1783

Otho Holland Williams.   May 9, 1782, to January 16, 1783 (retired)

John Greaton.   January 7, 1783, to November 3, 1783

Rufus Putnam.   January 7, 1783, to November 3, 1783

Elias Dayton.   January 7, 1783, to November 3, 1783

Charles Tufin Armand, Marquis de la Rouarie.   March 26, 1783, to November 3, 1783

BRIGADIER GENERALS BY BREVET

UNDER VARIOUS RESOLUTIONS OF CONGRESS

James Wilkinson.   November 6, 1777, to March 6, 1778 (resigned)

Chevalier de la Neuville.   August 14, 1778, to December 4, 1778 (resigned)

Moses Hazen.   June 29, 1781, to January 1, 1783 (retired)

Thaddeus Kosciusko.   October 13, 1783, to November 3, 1783

Stephen Moylan.   November 3, 1783

Samuel Elbert.   November 3, 1783

Charles Cotesworth Pinckney.   November 3, 1783

William Russell.   November 3, 1783

BRIGADIER GENERALS BY BREVET

UNDER RESOLUTION OF CONGRESS OF SEPTEMBER 30, 1783

George Baylor

Daniel Brodhead

Richard Butler

Thomas Clark

John Crane

Christian Febiger

John Gibson

John Gunby

Richard Humpton

Henry Jackson

Michael Jackson

John Lamb

Chevalier de Laumoy

George Mathews

John Nevill

Lewis Nicola

Mathias Ogden

Elisha Sheldon

William Shepard

Walter Stewart

Heman Swift

Benjamin Tupper

Philip Van Cortlandt

Gozen Van Schaick

Joseph Vose

Samuel B. Webb

Sources and Acknowledgments

Sources and Acknowledgments

The story of 1776 is not a new one. Still, no apologies are in order for an attempt to bring out new values from old as well as new sources. A well-known librarian and historical writer has put it very neatly:

"Each generation has to rewrite history for itself—and sometimes from the same sources used by previous generations."*

The Continental Army of these pages is offered to a generation that has experienced the actuality of two World Wars and the imminent peril of a third. It is, of all generations since 1776, the one best equipped to understand the alarms of Americans whose soil was invaded, whose homes were pillaged, and whose six largest cities were occupied for long periods by the foe. They were a writing as well as fighting people, and the most instructive sources of this book have been the diaries, journals and letters of the participants—privates as well as generals, redcoats as well as rebels, women and civilians as well as soldiers.

Few historical books are singlehanded efforts, and this one is no exception to the rule. Although the author is accountable for infelicities of style and interpretation, it is no perfunctory acknowledgment to point out that every page has benefited from generous and expert assistance.

Dr. Malcolm G. Wyer, Miss Olive Broughton, Miss Sylva Tanberg and the librarians of the Denver Public Library have been of unfailing help throughout the research.

Mrs. Eulalia Chapman and the staff of the Denver Bibliographical Center have aided immeasurably in supplying sources.

Mrs. Dorothy Bauer and Mrs. V. A. Grodsky of the Carnegie Institution of Washington are entitled to thanks for adding to the convenience and accuracy of research.

Miss Constance Nelson, of Cambridge, Mass., has found sources at the Harvard College Library and the Library of Congress which otherwise might not have been available.

The editors and production staff of Harper & Brothers have as usual given the benefit of their advice and experience during the preparation of the manuscript.

* Randolph G. Adams in Foreword to *Guide to the Manuscript Collections in the Clements Library*, Howard H. Peckham, editor, University of Michigan Press, Ann Arbor, 1942.

Finally, the book is indebted for permission to use quotations to Mr. Howard C. Myers, Jr.; Appleton-Century-Crofts, Inc.; the Bobbs-Merrill Co.; Duffield and Co.; Encyclopaedia Britannica; the Charles E. Goodspeed Co.; Garden City Publishing Co.; Longmans, Green and Co.; Harvard University Press; University of Michigan Press; Yale University Press; the Library of Congress; the Clements Library; the De Burians; the Huntington Library; the Carnegie Institution of Washington; the Polish Institute of Arts and Sciences in America; the Connecticut Historical Society; the Historical Society of Delaware; the Illinois Historical Society; the Massachusetts Historical Society; the New Hampshire Historical Society; the New Jersey Historical Society; the New York Historical Society; the Winchester (Virginia) Historical Society; *Maryland Historical Magazine, Pennsylvania Magazine of History and Biography*; and the *American Historical Review*.

CONTEMPORARY SOURCES

ADAMS, ABIGAIL. *Letters.* 2 vols., Little, Brown, Boston, 1840.

ADAMS, JOHN. *Works.* Charles Francis Adams, editor. 10 vols., Little, Brown, Boston, 1850-1856.

ADAMS, SAMUEL. *Writings.* Henry A. Cushing, editor. 4 vols., Houghton, Boston, 1907.

BOUCHER, JONATHAN. *Reminiscences of an American Loyalist.* Houghton, Boston, 1925.

BURGOYNE, JOHN. *Orderly Book,* 1777. E. B. O'Callaghan, editor. Munsell, Albany, 1860.

——. *State of the Expedition from Canada.* Almon, London, 1780.

BURKE, EDMUND. *Miscellaneous Works.* 2 vols., Greenleaf, Boston, 1813.

CLINTON, SIR HENRY. *Narrative and Correspondence.* Debrett, London, 1873.

Connecticut Historical Society Collections. *Orderly Books of Connecticut Officers, 1775-1778.* Vol. VII, Hartford, 1899.

CORNWALLIS, EARL OF. *Correspondence.* Charles Ross, editor. 3 vols., Murray, London, 1859.

CURWEN, SAMUEL. *Journal and Letters.* George A. Ward, editor. Little, Brown, Boston, 1864.

DEANE, SILAS. *Correspondence.* Connecticut Historical Society Collections, II, Hartford, 1870.

ESTAING, COMTE D'. "General Orders at the Siege of Savannah." *Magazine of American History,* I, 548-551. New York, 1877.

FORCE, PETER (editor). American Archives. 9 vols., Force, New York, 1885.

FORD, WORTHINGTON C. (editor). *Journals of the Continental Congress.* 34 vols., Library of Congress, Washington, 1904-1937.

FRANKLIN, BENJAMIN. *Writings.* Albert Henry Smyth, editor. 10 vols., Macmillan, New York, 1905-1907.

GALLOWAY, JOSEPH. *Letters to a Nobleman on the Conduct of the War in the Middle Colonies.* Wilkie, London, 1780.

GEORGE III. *Correspondence with Lord North from 1768 to 1783.* 2 vols. Murray, London, 1867.

GIBBES, R. W. *Documentary History of the American Revolution.* 2 vols., Appleton, New York, 1855.

GORDON, WILLIAM. *History of the Rise, Progress and Establishment of the Independence of the United States.* 3 vols., Campbell, New York, 1794.

GRAYDON, ALEXANDER. *Memoirs.* Wyeth, Harrisburg, Pa., 1811.

HAMILTON, ALEXANDER. *Writings.* John C. Hamilton, editor. 7 vols., Joint Library Committee of Congress, New York, 1850.

HEATH, WILLIAM. *Memoirs.* Rufus Rockwell Wilson, editor. Wessels, New York, 1904.

HENSHAW, WILLIAM. *Orderly Book.* Wilson, Boston, 1877.

HOWE, SIR WILLIAM. *Narrative.* Baldwin, London, 1781.

HUGHES, J. M. (editor). *Notes Relative to the Campaign against Burgoyne.* Massachusetts Historical Society Proceedings, III, Boston, 1858.

HUTCHINSON, THOMAS. *Diary and Letters.* Peter O. Hutchinson, editor. 2 vols., Low, London, 1883-1886.

JAY, JOHN. *Correspondence and Papers.* Henry P. Johnston, editor. 4 vols., Putnam, New York, 1890.

JEFFERSON, THOMAS. *Writings.* H. W. Washington, editor. 10 vols., Derby, New York, 1861.

JOHNSON, SIR JOHN. "Orderly Book, 1777." William L. Stone, editor. *Magazine of American History,* VI, 204-216, New York, 1880.

JONES, THOMAS. *History of New York During the Revolutionary War.* Floyd DeLancey, editor. 2 vols., New York Historical Society, New York, 1879.

LEE, HENRY. *Memoirs of the War in the Southern Department.* Force, Washington, 1827.

LEE, RICHARD HENRY. *Letters.* James Curtis Ballagh, editor. 2 vols., Macmillan, New York, 1911.

MADISON, JAMES. *Writings.* Gaillard Hunt, editor. 9 vols., Putnam, New York, 1920.

MARSHALL, JOHN. *Life of George Washington.* 2 vols., Crissey, Philadelphia, 1850.

MONROE, JAMES. *Writings.* S. M. Hamilton, editor. 7 vols., Putnam, New York, 1898.

MOORE, FRANK (editor). *The Diary of the Revolution.* Documents, letters and extracts from newspapers, 1775-1783. Burr, Hartford, 1875.

MORRIS, GOUVERNEUR. *Diary and Letters.* Anne Carey Morris, editor. 2 vols., Scribner, New York, 1888.

MOULTRIE, WILLIAM. *Memoirs of the American Revolution.* 2 vols., Longworth, New York, 1802.

New Jersey Archives. *Extracts from American Newspapers, 1775-1782.* 2nd Ser., I, II, III, IV, V. Trenton, 1901-1917.

New York Historical Society Collections. *Material on Battles of Bennington and Saratoga.* V and XII, New York, 1905 and 1912.

Northern Army Orderly Book. Gates at Ticonderoga and Mount Independence from October, 1776, to January, 1777. Munsell, Albany, 1859.

Pennsylvania Archives. *Material on Mutiny of the Pennsylvania Line in 1781.* 2nd Ser., XI, 657-706. Harrisburg, 1895.

RAMSAY, DAVID. *History of South Carolina.* 2 vols, Duffle, Newberry, S. C., 1858.

ROCHAMBEAU, COMTE DE. *Operations of the French Army During the American Revolution.* Dobson, Philadelphia, 1817.

ST. CLAIR, ARTHUR. *Papers.* William H. Smith, editor. 2 vols., Clark, Cincinnati, 1882.

SPARKS, JARED (editor). *Correspondence of the American Revolution.* 4 vols., Little, Brown, Boston, 1853.

STARK, JOHN. *Memoirs and Official Correspondence.* Caleb Stark, editor. Lyon, Concord, N. H., 1860.

STEDMAN, CHARLES. *History of the Origin, Progress and Termination of the American War.* 2 vols., Byrne, Moore and Jones, Dublin, 1794.

STEUBEN, FRIEDRICH VON. *Manual of Arms.* U. S. Army, Hartford, 1787.

STEVENS, BENJAMIN F. (editor). *The Campaigns in Virginia, 1781—the Clinton-Cornwallis Controversy.* 2 vols., Malby, London, 1888.

SULLIVAN, JOHN. *Sullivan Papers.* Otis G. Hammond, editor. 3 vols., New Hampshire Historical Society, Concord, 1930.

TARLETON, BANASTRE. *History of the Campaigns of 1780 and 1781 in the Southern Provinces of North America.* Cadell, London, 1787.

WALPOLE, HORACE. *Letters on the War of American Independence.* Blackie, London, 1908.

WASHINGTON, GEORGE. *Writings.* Worthington C. Ford, editor. 14 vols., Putnam, New York, 1889-1893.

———. *Writings.* Jared Sparks, editor. 12 vols., Hilliard, Gray, Boston, 1834-1837.

WHARTON, FRANCIS (editor). *Revolutionary Diplomatic Correspondence of the United States.* 6 vols., Library of Congress, Washington, 1889.

WILKINSON, JAMES. *Memoirs of My Own Times.* 3 vols., Small, Philadelphia, 1816.

DIARIES, JOURNALS AND LETTER BOOKS

ANBURY, THOMAS. *Travels Through the Interior Parts of America.* A British officer's journal of the Saratoga campaign and Burgoyne's army. 2 vols., Lane, London, 1789.

ANDRÉ, JOHN. *Journal.* Comments by a famous British officer on operations of 1777-1778. Henry Cabot Lodge, editor. 2 vols., Bibliophile Society, Boston, 1903.

ANGELL, ISRAEL. *Journal.* An American officer's account of campaigns of 1778-1781. Edward Field, editor. Privately published, Providence, 1899.

ANONYMOUS (soldier of Pennsylvania line). "Journal." Campaigns of 1781-1782. *Pennsylvania Magazine of History,* XXXVI, 237-292.

ARNOLD, BENEDICT. "Memorandum Book." Ticonderoga campaign, 1775. *Pennsylvania Magazine of History,* VIII, 365-376.

ATLEE, SAMUEL. *Journal.* An American colonel at the battle of Long Island. Pennsylvania Archives, 2nd Ser., I, 509-515.

BALDWIN, JEDUTHAN. *Revolutionary Journal*. Trials of the army's first engineer, 1775-1778. Thomas J. Baldwin, editor. De Burians, Bangor, Maine, 1906.

BANGS, ISAAC. "Journal." An American military surgeon's observations, 1775-1776. *New Jersey Historical Society Proceedings*, VIII, 120-125.

BARBÉ-MARBOIS, MARQUIS DE. *Our Revolutionary Forefathers*. A French ally's letters of travels in America, 1779-1782. Eugene Parker Chase, translator and editor. Duffield, New York, 1929.

BARLOW, SETH. "Journal." An American sergeant in the Canadian campaign of 1775. *American Historical Register*, II, 641-649.

BEATTY, WILLIAM. "Journal." A Maryland captain's comments, 1776-1781. *Maryland Historical Magazine*, III, 104-119.

BEEBE, LEWIS. "Military Surgeon's Journal." A Yankee physician in the retreat from Canada, 1776. *Pennsylvania Magazine of History*, LIX, 321-361.

BELKNAP, JEREMY. "Journal." An American chaplain at the siege of Boston. Massachusetts Historical Society Proceedings, 1st Ser., IV, 77-86.

BELL, ANDREW. "Journal." A British officer's account, 1778. *New Jersey Historical Society Proceedings*, VI, 15-19.

BIXBY, SAMUEL. "Journal." Siege of Boston from American viewpoint. Massachusetts Historical Society Proceedings, 1st. Ser., XIV, 285-298.

BLANCHARD, CLAUDE. *Journal*. An officer of Rochambeau's army in America, 1780-1782. Thomas Balch, editor. Munsell, Albany, 1876.

BOARDMAN, OLIVER. "Journal." An American officer's record of Saratoga and later campaigns. Connecticut Historical Society Collections (1899), 221-237.

BOUDINOT, ELIAS. *Journal*. The war as seen by a member of the Continental Congress. Bourquin, Philadelphia, 1894.

BOWMAN, JOSEPH. "Journal." An American major at the capture of Vincennes. *Illinois Historical Society Collections*, VIII, 155-162.

CHASTELLUX, MARQUIS DE. *Travels in North America in the Years 1780, 1781 and 1782*. Descriptions of Revolutionary soldiers and battlefields by a French general. Republished from original edition, New York, 1828.

CHEEVER, WILLIAM. "Journal." American account of Bunker Hill and siege of Boston. Massachusetts Historical Society Proceedings, LX, 91-97.

CLARK, GEORGE ROGERS. "Diary, Letters and Memoirs." Kaskaskia and Vincennes campaigns, 1778-1779. *Illinois Historical Society Collections*, VIII, 1-19, 114-154, 155-174, 208-302.

CRAFT, BENJAMIN. "Journal." An American lieutenant at the siege of Boston. Essex Institute Historical Collections (1861), 51-57, 133-140, 219-220.

CRESSWELL, NICHOLAS. *Journal*. American travels of a British civilian. Dial Press, New York, 1924.

CROSS, RALPH. "Journal." Burgoyne's surrender witnessed by a Massachusetts captain. *Historical Magazine*, XVII, 8-11.

CRUGER, JOHN. "Letters." A British colonel at the siege of Savannah. *Magazine of American History*, II, 489-491.

DAVIS, JOHN. "Journal." An American captain at Yorktown. *Pennsylvania Magazine of History*, V, 290-305.

DEARBORN, HENRY. "Journal." The Saratoga campaign described by one of the leading American participants. Massachusetts Historical Society Proceedings, 2nd Ser., III, 102-133.

DE GALVEZ, DON BERNARDO. "Journal." Spanish military journal, 1780 1781, by the governor of Louisiana. *Louisiana Historical Quarterly*, I, 44-84.

DEUX PONTS, COMTE WILLIAM. *My Campaigns in America*. A French officer's reminiscences. Samuel A. Green, editor. Wiggin, Boston, 1868.

DIGBY, WILLIAM. *The British Invasion from the North*. The Saratoga campaign as seen by a lieutenant under Burgoyne. Munsell, Albany, 1887.

DU BOURG, BARON CROMAT. "Journal." A French officer in America, 1780-1782. *Magazine of American History*, IV, 205-441.

DUDLEY, DOROTHY. *The Cambrige of 1776*. A feminine view of the Continental Army. Centennial Committee, Cambridge, 1876.

DUNCAN, JAMES. *Journal*. An American captain at Yorktown. Pennsylvania Archives, 2nd Ser., XV, 743-752.

ELD, GEORGE. "Journal." A British colonel's comments, 1779-1780. Massachusetts Historical Society Proceedings, Ist Ser., XVIII, 73-79.

EMERSON, WILLIAM. *Literature of the Nineteenth of April*. An American chaplain at Lexington. James L. Whitney, editor. Privately published, Concord, Mass., 1876.

EWALD, JOHANN. *The Siege of Charleston*. A Hessian captain's military journal. Bernhard A. Uhlendorf, editor. University of Michigan Press, Ann Arbor, 1938.

FARMAR, ROBERT. "Journal." An American loyalist's observations, 1781. *Historical Magazine*, IV, 166-171.

FARNSWORTH, AMOS. "Journal." A Massachusetts corporal's experiences, 1775-1779. Massachusetts Historical Society Proceedings, 2nd. Ser., XII, 74-107.

FEBIGER, CHRISTIAN. "Letters." A Danish volunteer in the Continental Army, 1779-1781. *Magazine of American History*, VI, 188-203.

FELTMAN, WILLIAM. *Journal*. A Pennsylvania lieutenant at Yorktown. Pennsylvania Archives, 2nd Ser., XI, 712-737.

FISHER, ELIJAH. *Journal*. Glimpses of the entire war from the viewpoint of a simple soldier. Privately published, Augusta, Maine, 1880.

FISHER, JOHN. "Journal." A Connecticut private in the early campaigns. *Magazine of History*, XIII, 184-186.

FRENCH, CHRISTOPHER. "Diary." Prison journal kept by a British major, 1776. Connecticut Historical Society Collections (1860), 189-225.

GALLOWAY, GRACE GROWDEN. "Diary." Wartime Philadelphia from a loyalist viewpoint. *Pennsylvania Magazine of History*, LV, 32-94.

GRIMKE, JOHN F. "Journal." An American major's account of southern campaigns, 1778-1781. *South Carolina Historical Magazine*, VII, 60-69, 118-134, 190-206.

HADDEN, JAMES MURRAY. *Journal and Orderly Books*. A British lieutenant's notes on the Saratoga campaign. Horatio Rogers, editor. Munsell, Albany, 1884.

HASLEWOOD, WILLIAM. "Journal." A British captain's comments on campaigns from 1775 to 1778. *Mississippi Valley Historical Review*, VII, 51-58.

HAWS, SAMUEL. *Military Journal of Two Private Soldiers.* Campaigns of 1775-1776 as seen by an American volunteer. Privately published, Poughkeepsie, N. Y., 1855.

HENDRICKS, WILLIAM. *Journal.* An American captain on the march to Quebec. Pennsylvania Archives, 2nd Ser., XV, 22-50.

HENRY, JOHN JOSEPH. *Journal.* A Pennsylvania rifleman in the Quebec campaign. Pennsylvania Archives, 2nd Ser., XV, 61-191.

HERBERT, CHARLES. *The Prisoners of 1776.* Journal of an American held captive in England. R. Livesey, editor. Rand, Boston, 1854.

HETH, WILLIAM. *Journal.* A Virginia rifle lieutenant as a prisoner at Quebec. B. Floyd Flickinger, editor. Annual Papers of Winchester (Virginia) Historical Society, I, 27-117.

HINRICH (HEINRICHS), JOHANN. *The Siege of Charleston.* A Hessian captain's journal. Bernhard A. Uhlendorf, editor. University of Michigan Press, Ann Arbor, 1938.

———. "Letters." The same Hessian officer's comments on Revolutionary America. *Pennsylvania Magazine of History*, XXII, 137-170.

HOW, DAVID. *Diary.* An American private at Boston, Trenton and Saratoga. Morrisania, New York, 1865.

HUBLEY, ADAM. *Journal.* Sullivan's expedition of 1779 as recorded by a Pennsylvania colonel. Pennsylvania Archives, 2nd. Ser., XI, 12-48.

INGALLS, PHINEAS. "Journal." An American private in the early campaigns, 1775-1776. Essex Institute Historical Collections, LIII, 81-92.

IRVINE, WILLIAM. "Extracts from Papers." Comments of a Pennsylvania officer. *Pennsylvania Magazine of History*, V, 259-275.

JENNIFER, WILLIAM. "Journal." An American seaman at the siege of Charleston. *Pennsylvania Magazine of History*, XV, 101-108.

JOSLIN, JOSEPH. "Journal." Adventures of a Connecticut teamster transporting military supplies, 1777-1778. Connecticut Historical Society Collections, VII, 297-369.

KEMBLE, STEPHEN. *Journal.* Diary of a New Jersey loyalist officer, 1773-1779. New York Historical Society Collections (1883), 1-247.

KIRKWOOD, ROBERT. *Journal and Orderly Book.* Daily record kept by a Delaware captain, 1776-1778, 1780-1782. Delaware Historical Society Publications, LVI, 1-277.

KRAFFT, JOHN CHARLES VON. *Journal.* A Hessian sergeant's chronicle of the war, 1776-1784. New York Historical Society Collections (1882), 1-200.

LAMB, ROGER. *An Original and Authentic Journal of Occurrences During the Late American War.* A British sergeant as the historian of campaigns from 1777 to 1781. Wilkinson, Dublin, 1809.

LINCOLN, RUFUS. *Papers.* An American officer's journal, 1776-1780. Houghton, Boston, 1904.

LIVINGSTON, HENRY. "Journal." Montgomery's campaign of 1775 as seen by a New York major. *Pennsylvania Magazine of History*, XXII, 9-33.

LYMAN, SIMEON. "Journal." An American private at the siege of Boston. Connecticut Historical Society Collections, II, 113-154.

MACKENZIE, FREDERICK. Diary. Detailed record kept by a British adjutant, 1775-1781. Allen French, editor. 2 vols., Harvard University Press, Cambridge, 1930.

McCLELLAN, JOSEPH. Diary. Brief account by a Pennsylvania captain of campaigns in 1781. Pennsylvania Archives, 2nd. Ser., XI, 709-711.

McDONALD, ALEXANDER. Letter-Book. Comments of a loyalist officer stationed in Canada, 1775-1779. New York Historical Society Collections (1882), 205-498.

McDOWELL, WILLIAM. Journal. A Pennsylvania lieutenant in the campaigns of 1781-1782. Pennsylvania Archives, 2nd. Ser., XV, 296-340.

McMICHAEL, JAMES. "Diary." Record kept by a Pennsylvania lieutenant of campaigns from 1776 to 1778. Pennsylvania Magazine of History, XVI, 129-156.

MEIGS, RETURN JONATHAN. "Journal." A Yankee major's account of the Quebec march. Massachusetts Historical Society Collections, 2nd. Ser., II, 227-247.

MELVIN, JAMES. Journal. The march to Ouebec as seen by an American private. Andrew A. Melvin, editor. Bryant, Portland, Maine, 1902.

MENONVILLE, M. DE. "Journal." The Yorktown campaign reported by one of Rochambeau's generals. Magazine of American History, VII, 296-301.

MILES, SAMUEL. Journal. Account of the battle of Long Island by a Pennsylvania officer. Pennsylvania Archives, 2nd. Ser., I, 559-562.

MONTRÉSOR, JOHN. "Journal." Howe's Philadelphia campaign described by a British captain of engineers. Pennsylvania Magazine of History, V, 393-417.

MORGAN, NATHANAEL. "Diary." An American ensign at the the siege of Boston. Connecticut Historical Society Collections, II, 101-110.

MUNCHAUSEN, FREDERICK VON. "Journal." A Hessian captain's story of the battle of Germantown. Pennsylvania Magazine of History, XVI, 197-201.

NASH, SOLOMON. Journal. Campaigns of 1775-1776 recorded by an American private. Charles I. Bushnell, editor. Privately published, New York, 1861.

NICE, JOHN. "Journal." A Pennsylvania captain at the battle of Long Island. Pennsylvania Magazine of History, XVI, 399-411.

NICHOLAS, FRANCIS. "Journal." The march to Quebec and ensuing captivity as related by an American lieutenant. Pennsylvania Magazine of History, XX, 504-511.

OGDEN, MATTHIAS. "Journal." An American major's diary of the early campaigns, 1775-1776. New Jersey Historical Society Proceedings, XIII, 17-30.

OSWALD, ELEAZER. "Journal." Brief diary of 1775 by an American captain. American Archives, 4th Ser., III, 1058-1062.

PARKER, ROBERT. "Journal." An American artillery officer's record of campaigns, 1779-1781. Pennsylvania Magazine of History, XXVII, 404-420.

PAUSCH, GEORG. Journal. Notes by a Hessian captain on operations of 1776-1777. William L. Stone, editor. Munsell, Albany, 1886.

PEALE, CHARLES WILLSON. "Journal." The portrait painter as an American captain, 1776-1777. *Pennsylvania Magazine of History*, XXXVIII, 271-286.

PELL, JOSHUA. "Journal." A British officer's account of Carleton's invasion of 1776. *Magazine of American History*, II, 43-47, 107-112.

PERCY, EARL. *Letters.* Comments on battles from Lexington to Long Island by a British leader. Charles Knowlton Bolton, editor. Goodspeed, Boston, 1902.

PIERCE, WILLIAM. "Letters." A Virginia major in Greene's campaigns. *Magazine of American History*, VII, 431-444.

PORTERFIELD, CHARLES. "Diary." Journal of captivity at Quebec kept by a Virginia sergeant of riflemen. *Virginia Magazine of History*, IX, 144-152.

RAWLE, ANNA. "Diary." Philadelphia in 1781 from the viewpoint of a loyalist girl. *Pennsylvania Magazine of History*, XVI, 103-107.

REED, JOSEPH. "Narrative." The Trenton-Princeton campaign reported by an American colonel. *Pennsylvania Magazine of History*, VIII, 391-402.

REEVES, ENOS. "Letters." Operations of 1780-1782 described by a lieutenant of the Pennsylvania line. *Pennsylvania Magazine of History*, XX, 306-472; XXI, 72-83, 235-250.

RIEDESEL, FREDERIKA VON MASSOW. *Letters and Journals Relating to the War of the American Revolution.* Burgoyne's army described by the wife of a Brunswick general. An account of the surrender at Saratoga by General Riedesel. William L. Stone, translator and editor. Munsell, Albany, 1867.

RITZEMA, RUDOLPHUS. "Journal." An American colonel's record of early campaigns, 1775-1776. *Magazine of American History*, I, 98-107.

RODNEY, THOMAS. "Journal." A Delaware captain in the Trenton-Princeton campaign. Delaware Historical Society Papers, No. 8 (1888), 11-50.

SENTER, ISAAC. *Journal.* The march to Quebec described by an American surgeon. Historical Society of Pennsylvania, Philadelphia, 1846.

SERLE, AMBROSE. *American Journal.* Comments on operations from 1776 to 1778 by Lord Howe's secretary. Edward H. Tatum, editor. Huntington Library, San Marino, Calif., 1940.

Sexagenary Reminiscences. Narrative. The surrender at Saratoga described by an American wagoner, John P. Becker. Munsell, Albany, 1866.

SEYMOUR, WILLIAM. "Journal." A Delaware sergeant in the southern campaigns, 1780-1782. *Pennsylvania Magazine of History*, VII, 286-294.

SIMCOE, JOHN G. *Journal.* Notes on his own campaigns by an American loyalist officer, Bartlett, New York, 1844.

SMITH, JOSEPH. "Diary." A Charleston merchant's journal of captivity at St. Augustine. Mabel L. Webber, editor. *South Carolina Historical Magazine*, XXXIII, 1-28, 19-116, 197-207.

SPROAT, JAMES. "Journal." American military hospitals described by a chaplain. *Pennsylvania Magazine of History*, XXVII, 41-45.

SQUIER, EPHRAIM. "Journal." An American sergeant's account of the march to Quebec. *Magazine of American History*, II, 682-694.

STEVENS, ENOS. "Journal." Campaigns of 1777-1781 reported by an American loyalist officer. *New England Quarterly*, XI, 374-388.

STONE, WILLIAM L. (translator and editor). *Letters of Brunswick and Hessian Officers During the American Revolution.* Munsell, Albany, 1891.

SULLIVAN, THOMAS. "Journal." A British sergeant at the battle of Brandywine. *Pennsylvania Magazine of History,* XXXI, 406-418.

THACHER, JAMES. *A Military Journal During the American Revolution.* An American military surgeon's observations from 1775 to 1783. Cotton and Bernard, Boston, 1823.

THAYER, SIMEON. "Journal." March to Quebec and captivity reported by a Rhode Island officer. *Rhode Island Historical Society Collections,* VI, 1-45.

TILDEN, JOHN BELL. "Journal." A Pennsylvania lieutenant in the southern campaigns, 1780-1782. *Pennsylvania Magazine of History,* XIX, 51-63, 208-223.

TILGHMAN, TENCH. *Memoir.* Journal of an American staff officer at Yorktown. Munsell, Albany, 1876.

TREVETT, JOHN. "Journal." An American lieutenant's account of sea actions in combination with land forces. *Rhode Island Historical Society Magazine,* VI, 72-74, 106-110; VII, 194-199, 271-278.

TRUMBULL, BENJAMIN. "Journal." Campaigns of 1775-1776 recorded by a Connecticut chaplain. *Connecticut Historical Society Collections,* II, 139-174, 182-209.

WALDO, ALBIGENCE. "Journal." An American military surgeon at Valley Forge. *Pennsylvania Magazine of History,* XXI, 299-323.

WEEKS, WILLIAM. *Five Straws Gathered from Revolutionary Fields.* Letters by an American sergeant during Burgoyne's invasion. Hiram Bingham, Jr., editor. Harvard University Press, Cambridge, 1901.

WELLS, BAYZE. "Journal." Lake Champlain operations of 1776 as seen by a Connecticut sergeant. *Connecticut Historical Society Collections,* VII, 241-296.

WIEDERHOLD, ANDREAS. "Diary." The Trenton campaign described by a Hessian captain. *Pennsylvania Magazine of History,* XXII, 462-467.

WILD, EBENEZER. "Journal." An American corporal's account of operations from 1776 to 1781. *Massachusetts Historical Society Proceedings,* 2nd Ser., VI, 78-160.

WILLIAMS, OTHO HOLLAND. "Narrative." Firsthand observations of the battle of Camden by an American staff officer. Appendix B, Vol. II, *Life and Correspondence of Nathanael Greene,* by William Johnson. Miller, New York, 1822.

WISTER, SALLY. "Diary." Social life of American officers during the winter of Valley Forge, as described by a young Quaker girl. *Pennsylvania Magazine of History,* IX, 318-333, 463-478.

WRIGHT, AARON. "Journal." A Pennsylvania rifleman at the siege of Boston. *Boston Transcript,* April 11, 1862.

YOUNG, WILLIAM. "Journal." The Trenton-Princeton campaign reported by an American militia sergeant. *Pennsylvania Magazine of History,* VIII, 255-278.

SUPPLEMENTARY SOURCES

ABBATT, WILLIAM. *The Battle of Pell's Point.* Privately published, New York, 1901.

ADAMS, CHARLES FRANCIS. *Studies Military and Diplomatic, 1775-1865.* Macmillan, New York, 1911.

ADAMS, RANDOLPH G. *Political Ideas of the American Revolution.* Trinity College Press, Durham, N. C., 1922.

ALLEN, GARDNER W. *A Naval History of the American Revolution.* 2 vols., Houghton, Boston, 1913.

ANDREWS, CHARLES M. *The Colonial Background of the American Revolution.* Yale University Press, New Haven, 1931.

ARNOLD, ISAAC N. *Life of Benedict Arnold.* McClurg, Chicago, 1880.

ASHE, SAMUEL A. *History of North Carolina.* 2 vols., Edwards and Broughton, Raleigh, N. C., 1925.

BALCH, THOMAS W. *The French in America During the War of Independence.* 2 vols., Lippincott, Philadelphia, 1891-1895.

BARCK, OSCAR T., JR. *New York City During the War for Independence.* Columbia University Press, New York, 1931.

BOLTON, CHARLES K. *The Private Soldier Under Washington.* Scribner, New York, 1902.

BOWEN, FRANCIS. *Life of Benjamin Lincoln.* Little, Brown, Boston, 1847.

BRANDOW, JOHN W. *The Story of Old Saratoga.* Brandow, Albany, 1919.

BRIDENBAUGH, CARL AND JESSICA. *Rebels and Gentlemen.* Reynal and Hitchcock, New York, 1942.

CARRINGTON, HENRY B. *Battles of the American Revolution.* Barnes, New York, 1876.

CODMAN, JOHN. *Expedition to Quebec.* Macmillan, New York, 1901.

CURTIS, EDWARD E. *Organization of the British Army in the American Revolution.* Yale University Press, New Haven, 1926.

DRAKE, FRANCIS. *Life and Correspondence of Henry Knox.* S. G. Drake, Boston, 1873.

DRAPER, LYMAN C. *King's Mountain and Its Heroes.* Thomson, Cincinnati, 1881.

EELKING, MAX VON. *The German Allied Troops in the North American War of Independence.* J. G. Rosengarten, translator and editor. Munsell, Albany, 1893.

FISHER, SYDNEY GEORGE. *The Struggle for American Independence.* 2 vols., Lippincott, Philadelphia, 1908.

——. *Men, Women and Manners in Colonial Times.* 2 vols., Lippincott, Philadelphia, 1898.

FISKE, JOHN. *The American Revolution.* 2 vols., Houghton, Boston, 1896.

FLICK, ALEXANDER C. *Loyalism in New York During the American Revolution.* Columbia University Press, New York, 1901.

FORTESQUE, J. W. *A History of the British Army.* Vol. III, 1763-1793. 14 vols., Macmillan, New York, 1899-1930.

FROTHINGHAM, RICHARD. *History of the Siege of Boston.* Little, Brown, Boston, 1849.

FULLER, J. F. C. *British Light Infantry in the Eighteenth Century.* Hutchinson, London, 1925.

GANOE, WILLIAM A. *History of the United States Army.* Appleton, New York, 1924.

GRAHAM, JAMES. *Life of General Daniel Morgan.* Derby and Jackson, New York, 1859.

GREENE, G. W. *Life of General Greene.* 3 vols., Houghton, Boston, 1867.

HAIMAN, MIECISLAUS. *Kosciuszko in the American Revolution.* Polish Institute of Arts and Sciences, New York, 1943.

HATCH, LOUIS C. *The Administration of the American Revolutionary Army.* Longmans, New York, 1904.

HEADLEY, JOEL T. *Washington and his Generals.* 2 vols, Baker and Scribner, New York, 1847.

HEITMAN, F. B. *Historical Register of officers of the Continental Army.* Killam, Baltimore, 1893.

HESSELTINE, WILLIAM B. *A History of the South, 1607-1936.* Prentice-Hall, New York, 1936.

HOLLISTER, GIDEON H. *History of Connecticut.* 2 vols., Durrie and Peck, New Haven, 1855.

HUDDLESTON, F. J. *Gentleman Johnny Burgoyne.* Bobbs-Merrill, Indianapolis, 1927.

IRVING, WASHINGTON. *Life of George Washington.* 5 vols., Lippincott, Philadelphia, 1873.

JOHNSON, WILLIAM. *Life and Correspondence of Nathanael Greene.* 2 vols., Miller, New York, 1822.

JONES, CHARLES C. *History of Georgia.* 3 vols., Houghton, Boston, 1883.

KAPP, FRIEDRICH. *Life of Steuben.* Mason, New York, 1859.

KIRKE, EDMUND. *Rear-Guard of the Revolution.* Appleton, New York, 1888.

KNOLLENBERG, BERNHARD. *Washington and the Revolution.* Macmillan, New York, 1940.

LECKY, WILLIAM E. *History of England in the Eighteenth Century.* Vols. III and IV. Appleton, New York, 1888.

LEFFERTS, CHARLES M. *Uniforms of the American, British, French and German Armies in the War of the American Revolution.* Alexander J. Wall, editor. New York Historical Society, New York, 1926.

LOSSING, BENSON J. *Life and Times of Philip Schuyler.* 2 vols., Sheldon, New York, 1872-1873.

————. *Pictorial Field Book of the Revolution.* Harper, New York, 1851-1852.

LOWELL, EDWARD J. *The Hessians and the Other German Auxiliaries in the Revolutionary War.* Harper, New York, 1884.

MACLAY, EDWARD S. *A History of American Privateers.* Appleton, New York, 1899.

McCRADY, EDWARD. *History of South Carolina in the Revolution.* 2 vols., Macmillan, 1902.

MAHAN, ALFRED T. *The Influence of Sea Power Upon History, 1660-1783.* Little, Brown, Boston, 1890.

MERLANT, JOACHIM. *Soldiers and Sailors of France in the American War of Independence.* Scribner, New York, 1920.

MILLER, JOHN C. *Sam Adams, Pioneer in Propaganda.* Little, Brown, Boston, 1936.

MOORE, SIR JOHN. *Diary.* J. F. Maurice, editor. 2 vols., Arnold, London, 1904.

MUHLENBERG, HENRY A. *Life of Peter Muhlenberg.* Casey and Hart, Philadelphia, 1849.

NEVINS, ALLAN. *The American States During and After the Revolution.* Macmillan, New York, 1920.

NICKERSON, HOFFMAN. *The Turning Point of the Revolution.* Houghton, Boston, 1926.

PALMER, JOHN A. *Life of Steuben.* Yale University Press, New Haven, 1937.

PARKMAN, FRANCIS. *A Half Century of Conflict.* 2 vols., Little, Brown, Boston, 1902.

PARTON, JAMES. *Life of Andrew Jackson.* Mason, New York, 1863.

PATTERSON, SAMUEL W. *Horatio Gates, Defender of American Liberties.* Columbia University Press, New York, 1941.

PICKERING, OCTAVIUS. *Life of Timothy Pickering.* 4 vols., Little, Brown, Boston, 1867-1873.

REED, W. B. *Life and Correspondence of Joseph Reed.* 2 vols., Lindsay, Philadelphia, 1847.

SAWYER, CHARLES W. *Firearms in American History.* Privately published, Boston, 1910.

SEARS, LORENZO. *John Hancock.* Little, Brown, Boston, 1912.

SCHARF (JOHN T.) AND WESCOTT (THOMPSON). *History of Philadelphia.* 3 vols., Everts, Philadelphia, 1884.

SMITH, JUSTIN H. *Our Struggle For the Fourteenth Colony.* 2 vols., Putnam, New York, 1907.

STILLÉ, CHARLES J. *Anthony Wayne and the Pennsylvania Line.* Lippincott, Philadelphia, 1893.

STONE, WILLIAM M. *Burgoyne's Campaign and St. Leger's Expedition.* Munsell, Albany, 1877.

STRYKER, WILLIAM S. *The Battles of Trenton and Princeton.* Houghton, Boston, 1898.

————. *The Battle of Monmouth.* Princeton University Press, Princeton, 1927.

TREVELYAN, SIR GEORGE O. *The American Revolution.* 4 vols., Longmans, New York, 1899-1907.

TYLER, LYON G. *History of Virginia, Vol. II, 1763-1861.* American Historical Society, New York, 1924.

UPHAM, WILLIAM W. *A Memoir of General John Glover.* Swasey, Marblehead, Mass., 1863.

UPTON, EMORY. *The Military Policy of the United States.* Government Printing Office, Washington, 1917.

VAN DOREN, CARL. *Benjamin Franklin.* Viking, New York, 1937.

VAN DOREN, CARL. *Secret History of the American Revolution.* Garden City Publishing Co., Garden City, N. Y., 1941.

VAN TYNE, CLAUDE H. *The Loyalists in the American Revolution.* Macmillan, New York, 1922.

———. *The War of Independence.* Houghton, New York, 1929.

PERIODICALS

AMORY, THOMAS C. "A Justification of General Sullivan." *Magazine of American History,* III (1879), 550-555.

BAKER, WILLIAM S. "Itinerary of General Washington from June 15, 1775, to December 23, 1783." *Pennsylvania Magazine of History,* XIV (1890), 111, 253, 335.

BENNETT, C. P. "The Delaware Regiment in the Revolution." *Pennsylvania Magazine of History,* IX (1885), 455-461.

BOLTON, REGINALD P. "The British Navy in the Revolution." *Magazine of History,* II (1905), 223, 311.

CARRINGTON, HENRY B. "Lafayette's Virginia Campaign." *Magazine of American History,* VI (1881), 341-352.

CLARK, JANE. "The Convention Troops and the Perfidy of Sir William Howe." *American Historical Review,* XXXVII (1932), 721-722.

COLEMAN, DUDLEY. "An Eye-Witness of Burgoyne's Surrender." *Magazine of American History,* XXIX (1893), 279-280.

COLEMAN, GEORGE P., JR. "The Southern Campaign, 1781." *Magazine of American History,* VII (1881), 36-46.

CULVER, FRANCIS B. "Last Bloodshed of the Revolution." *Maryland Historical Magazine,* V (1910), 329-337.

DE LANCEY, EDWARD J. "Mount Washington and Its Capture." *Magazine of American History,* I (1877), 65-91.

DE PEYSTER, J. WATTS. "The Affair at King's Mountain." *Magazine of American History,* V (1880), 401-424.

———. "Oriskany." *Magazine of American History,* II (1878), 22-29.

———. "The Battle of Monmouth." *Magazine of American History,* II (1878), 385-407.

DWIGHT, THEODORE F. "The Journals of Washington." *Magazine of American History,* VI (1881), 81-88.

EDWARDS, WILLIAM H. "Morgan and his Riflemen." *William and Mary College Historical Quarterly,* XXIII (1914), 73-106.

EMMET, THOMAS A. "The Battle of Harlem Heights." *Magazine of History,* IV (1906), 125-134.

FORD, WORTHINGTON C. "British and American Prisoners of War." *Pennsylvania Magazine of History,* XVII (1893), 159, 316.

———. "Defenses of Philadelphia in 1777." *Pennsylvania Magazine of History,* XVIII (1894), 1, 163, 329, 463; XIX (1895), 87, 213, 391, 520.

GARDNER, ASA B. "The New York Continental Line." *Magazine of American History,* VII (1881), 401-419.

GRATZ, SIMON. "The Generals of the Continental Line in the Revolutionary War." *Pennsylvania Magazine of History,* XXVII (1903), 385-403.

GREENE, G. W. "The Convention of Saratoga." *Magazine of American History*, III (1879), 231-236.

JENKINS, HOWARD M. "The Old Iron Forge—'Valley Forge.'" *Pennsylvania Magazine of History*, XVII (1893), 430-443.

JOHNSTON, HENRY P. "Colonel Christian Febiger of the Virginia Line." *Magazine of American History*, VII (1881), 188-203.

———. "The Secret Service of the Revolution." *Magazine of American History*, VIII (1882), 95-105.

———. "DeKalb, Gates and the Camden Campaign." *Magazine of American History*, VIII (1882), 496-497.

LIEBER, G. NORMAN. "Martial Law During the Revolution." *Magazine of American History*, I (1877), 538-705.

LINCOLN, C. H. "Washington's Plan for the Attack on Germantown." *Pennsylvania Magazine of History*, XXVI (1902), 387-389.

MYERS, BAILEY T. "Our National Medals." *Magazine of American History*, II (1878), 529-532.

PENNYPACKER, SAMUEL W. "The Capture of Stony Point." *Pennsylvania Magazine of History*, XXVI (1902), 360-369.

POTTS, WILLIAM J. "The Battle of Germantown from a British Account." *Pennsylvania Magazine of History*, XI (1887), 112-115.

RAWLE, WILLIAM B. "Plundering by the British Army During the American Revolution." *Pennsylvania Magazine of History*, XXV (1901), 114-117.

READ, ELIZABETH. "John Eager Howard, Colonel of Second Maryland Regiment." *Magazine of American History*, VII (1881), 276-282.

RICE, JOHN L. "The New Hampshire Grants." *Magazine of American History*, VIII (1882), 1-23.

ROSENGARTEN, JOSEPH C. "A Defense of the Hessians." *Pennsylvania Magazine of History*, XXIII (1899), 157-183.

SKULL, G. D. "General Sir Frederick Haldimand in Pennsylvania." *Pennsylvania Magazine of History*, VIII (1884), 300-309.

SMYTH, GEORGE H. "The Scotch-Irish in America." *Magazine of American History*, IV (1880), 161-172.

STANDISH, PERCY G. "Burgoyne's Defense and Surrender: An Inquiry from a British Standpoint." *Magazine of American History*, XXIV (1890), 40-44.

STEVENS, JOHN A. "Benedict Arnold and his Apologist." *Magazine of American History*, IV (1880), 181-191.

———. "The Battle of Harlem Plains." *Magazine of American History*, IV (1880), 351-375.

———. "The Southern Campaign, 1780—Gates at Camden. Letters of Major-General Gates from June 21 to August 31, 1780. Orders Issued by General Gates to the Southern Army." *Magazine of American History*, V (1880), 241-320.

STILLÉ, CHARLES J. "The Marquis de Lafayette in the American Revolution." *Pennsylvania Magazine of History*, XIX (1895), 1-21.

———. "The Frontier Forts of Pennsylvania." *Pennsylvania Magazine of History*, XX (1896), 257-266.

STOCKBRIDGE, J. C. "The Surrender of Cornwallis in England." *Magazine of American History*, VII (1881), 321-338.

STREET, ALFRED B. "The Battle of Saratoga." *Historical Magazine*, II (1858), 65-80.

STRYKER, WILLIAM S. "The Princeton Surprise, 1777." *Magazine of American History*, VIII (1882), 550-554.

TODD, CHARLES B. "The Massacre at Fort Griswold." *Magazine of American History*, VII (1881), 161-175.

TRACY, JAMES J. "The Origins of the Massachusetts Militia." *Magazine of History*, I (1905), 1-9.

UPHAM, GEORGE B. "Burgoyne's Great Mistake." *New England Quarterly*, III (1930), 657-680.

VARNEY, GEORGE B. "Acadia in the Revolution." *Magazine of American History*, VIII (1882), 486-495.

WALWORTH, ELLEN H. "The Battle of Saratoga." *Magazine of American History*, I (1877), 273-303.

WATSON, W. C. "Arnold's Retreat After the Battle of Valcour." *Magazine of American History*, VI (1881), 414-417.

Chapter References

Chapter References

CHAPTER 1

1. Heath: *Memoirs*, 15
2. Ingalls: "Journal." Essex Inst. Hist. Coll., LIII, 82
3. Heath: *Memoirs*, 24
4. Bolton: *Private Soldier*, 220-221
5. Tomlinson: *Military Journal of Two Private Soldiers*, 82
6. Wright: "Journal." *Boston Transcript*, April 11, 1862
7. McDonald: *Letter-Book*. N. Y. Hist. Soc. Coll. (1882), 319
8. Sally Wister: "Diary." *Penna. Mag. Hist.*, IX, 324
9. Kirkwood: *Journal*. Del. Hist. Soc. Papers, LVI, 13
10. Mackenzie: *Diary*, I, 6
11. *Pennsylvania Journal*, May 24, 1775
12. Amer. Arch., 4th Ser., II, 487-501
13. Fisher, I, 308n
14. Mackenzie: *Diary*, I, 19
15. Stedman, I, 133
16. Mackenzie: *Diary*, I, 20
17. Heath: *Memoirs*, 22
18. Bolton: *Letters of Hugh Earl Percy*, 52
19. Gordon, I, 313 and 315
20. Amer. Arch., 4th Ser., II, 391
21. Gordon, I, 311-312
22. Amer. Arch., 4th Ser., II, 487-501
23. Trevelyan, II (Part 1), 2
24. Amer. Arch., 4th Ser., II, 365
25. Amer. Arch., 4th Ser., II, 674
26. Amer. Arch., 4th Ser., II, 439

CHAPTER 2

1. McDonald: *Letter-Book*, N. Y. Hist. Soc. Coll. (1882), 275
2. Amer. Arch., 4th Ser., IV, 534
3. Amer. Arch., 4th Ser., II, 557 and 584
4. Parkman: *A Half Century of Conflict*, II, 66-112
5. Marshall: *Washington*, I, 10n
6. Marshall: *Washington*, I, 17
7. Van Doren: *Benjamin Franklin*, 511
8. Lecky, IV, 45
9. Amer. Arch., 4th Ser., III, 10
10. *Journals of Congress*, I, 58
11. Amer. Arch., 4th Ser., II, 731
12. Gordon, I, 340
13. *Pennsylvania Journal*, May 28, 1775
14. *Pennsylvania Evening Post*, March 30, 1776
15. Trevelyan, I, 327
16. Fortesque, III, 159n

CHAPTER 3

1. *Mag. Amer. History*, VII, 295
2. Wright: *Journal. Boston Transcript*, April 11, 1862
3. Coll. Conn. Hist. Soc. (1870), II, 181
4. Frothingham: *Siege of Boston*, 222

5. Penna. Arch., 2nd Ser., L, 587
6. *Pennsylvania Journal*, July 26, 1775
7. *Farnsworth*: "Journal." Mass. Hist. Soc. Proc., 2nd Ser., XII, 74-107
8. How: *Diary*, 5-6
9. Amer. Arch., 5th Ser., I, 572
10. Henshaw: *Orderly Book*, 38
11. How: *Diary*, 22
12. Fisher: *Journal*, 5
13. Washington: *Writings* (Ford), III, 13
14. *Journals of Congress*, III, 323
15. *Journals of Congress*, II, 89
16. Amer. Arch., 4th Ser., III, 1157
17. Lyman: "Journal." Coll. Conn. Hist. Soc., II, 120
18. *Constitutional Gazette*, January 13, 1776
19. Thacher: *Journal*, 37
20. Washington. *Writings* (Sparks), III, 90
21. Gordon, II, 18
22. Amer. Arch., 4th Ser., III, 991-993
23. Amer. Arch., 4th Ser., III, 1153
24. *Journals of Congress*, III, 330-334
25. *Virginia Gazette*, July 24, 1775
26. *Journals of Congress*, II, 89
27. Graham: *Morgan*, 53
28. Henry: *Journal*. Penna. Arch., 2nd Ser., XV, 65
29. Wright: "Journal." *Boston Transcript*, April 11, 1862
30. Williams: *Journal*. Penna. Arch., 2nd Ser., XV, 13 and 18
31. *Virginia Gazette*, September 16, 1775

CHAPTER 4

1. Dearborn: "Journal." Mass. Hist. Soc. Proc., 2nd Ser., II, 279
2. *Penna. Mag. Hist.*, VIII, 366n
3. Henry: *Journal*. Penna. Arch., 2nd Ser., XV, 66 and 92n
4. Sparks: *Correspondence*, I, 46

5. Washington: *Writings* (Ford), III, 155
6. Melvin: *Journal*, 44
7. Squier: "Diary." *Mag. Amer. Hist.*, II, 688
8. Senter: *Journal*, 28
9. Thayer: "Journal." *R. I. Hist. Soc. Coll.*, VI, 28
10. Meigs: "Journal." Mass. Hist. Soc. Proc., 2nd Ser., II, 233
11. Henry: *Journal*. Penna. Arch., 2nd Ser., XV, 99n and 101
12. Hendricks: *Journal*. Penna. Arch., 2nd Ser., XV, 44
13. Senter: *Journal*, 33
14. Henry: *Journal*. Penna. Arch., 2nd Ser., XV, 115
15. *Journals of Congress*, III, 339
16. Trumbull: "Journal." Coll. Conn. Hist. Soc., II, 141 and 160
17. Livingston: "Journal." *Penna. Mag. Hist.*, XXII, 15 and 22
18. Trumbull. "Journal." Coll. Conn. Hist. Soc., II, 159 and 162
19. Smith: *Struggle for the Fourteenth Colony*, I, 490
20. Heth: *Journal*. Papers Winchester Hist. Soc., I, 62
21. Amer. Arch., 4th Ser., IV, 289
22. Nichols: "Diary." *Penna. Mag. Hist.*, XX, 505
23. Amer. Arch., 4th Ser., IV, 464
24. Marshall: *Washington*, I, 54-58, based on the lost fragment of the *Journal* kept by William Heth

CHAPTER 5

1. Amer. Arch., 4th Ser., III, 147
2. Lecky, III, 478
3. *Journals of Congress*, II, 174-175
4. Amer. Arch., 4th Ser., II, 1116
5. Amer. Arch., 4th Ser., II, 1049
6. Von Eelking: *The German Allies*, 18
7. *Journals of Congress*, XXIV, 277
8. Lecky, III, 583

9. Amer. Arch., 4th Ser., III, 1170
10. Amer. Arch, 4th Ser., III, 940
11. Heth: *Journal*. Papers Winchester Hist. Soc., I, 39
12. Nichols: "Diary." *Penna. Mag. Hist.*, XX, 506
13. Porterfield: "Diary." *Virginia Mag. Hist.*, IX, 145
14. Sparks: *Correspondence*, I, 116
15. *Journals of Congress*, IV, 70
16. Sparks: *Correspondence*, I, 129-130
17. Amer. Arch., 4th Ser., IV, 464
18. Henry: *Journal*. Penna. Arch., 2nd Ser., XV, 131n
19. Sparks: *Correspondence*, I, 196
20. Amer. Arch., 4th Ser., VI, 456
21. Amer. Arch., 4th Ser., VI, 430
22. Amer. Arch., 4th Ser., VI, 418
23. Frothingham: *Siege of Boston*, 328
24. Trevelyan, II, 93
25. Baldwin: *Journal*, 18 19 and 21
26. Amer. Arch., 4th Ser., V, 425
27. Lyman: "Journal." Coll. Conn. Hist. Soc., II, 128-129
28. Washington: *Writings* (Sparks), III, 221, 224 and 237
29. Frothingham: *Siege of Boston*, 291 and 311
30. Washington: *Writings* (Sparks), III, 236n
31. Trevelyan, I, 363
32. *Journals of Congress*, III, 348 and 378
33. *Constitutional Gazette*, August 23, 1775
34. Amer. Arch., 4th Ser., IV, 296-297
35. Gordon, II, 27
36. Heath: *Memoirs*, 49

CHAPTER 6

1. Abigail Adams: *Letters*, I, 68-71
2. Trevelyan, I, 403

3. *Pennsylvania Evening Post*, June 1, 1776
4. *Sullivan Papers*, I, 205-206
5. Amer. Arch., 4th Ser., III, 796; VI, 641
6. Washington: *Writings* (Sparks), III, 209
7. Henry: *Journal*. Penna. Arch., 2nd Ser., XV, 116
8. Beebe: "Journal." *Penna. Mag. Hist.*, LIX, 331
9. Van Doren: *Secret History*, 160
10. Beebe: "Journal." *Penna. Mag. Hist.*, LIX, 330
11. Amer. Arch., 5th Ser., I, 158
12. *Sullivan Papers*, I, 212
13. Amer. Arch., 4th Ser., VI, 589
14. Frothingham: *Siege of Boston*, 311
15. *Journals of Congress*, IV, 18
16. Marshall: *Washington*, I, 69
17. Amer. Arch., 4th Ser., IV, 540
18. Amer. Arch., 4th Ser., IV, 538
19. George III: *Correspondence, with Lord North*, II, 270-271
20. *New York Packet*, March 28, 1776
21. Amer. Arch., 4th Ser., V, 62
22. Amer. Arch., 4th Ser., V, 1342
23. Gibbes: *Documentary History*, II, 180-181
24. Coll. Georgia Hist. Soc., III, 228
25. Moultrie: *Memoirs*, I, 141
26. Amer. Arch., 5th Ser., I, 99
27. *Middlesex Journal*, Sept. 14, 1776
28. Moultrie: *Memoirs*, 176-181

CHAPTER 7

1. Moore: *Diary*, 277-278
2. Washington: *Writings* (Ford), IV, 347
3. George III: *Correspondence with Lord North*, I, 274; II, 84; Trevelyan, I, 365; Lecky, IV, 77
4. John Adams: *Works*, II, 162, 219
5. John Adams: *Works*, X, 87

6. Gordon, II, 17
7. Trevelyan, I, 410
8. Lecky, IV, 70
9. Stedman, II, 498, 499
10. Amer. Arch., 4th Ser., V, 535; 5th Ser., III, 491
11. Amer. Arch., 4th Ser., VI, 612
12. Amer. Arch., 4th Ser., VI, 590
13. Sullivan Papers, I, 220
14. Greene, I, 405
15. Amer. Arch., 5th Ser., I, 1210
16. Sullivan Papers, I, 226-231
17. Amer. Arch., 4th Ser., VI, 796
18. Amer. Arch., 5th Ser., I, 610
19. Kirke: Rear-Guard of the Revolution, 121
20. Amer. Arch., 5th Ser., I, 249
21. Rev. Dipl. Corr., II, 342
22. Heath: Memoirs, 61
23. Washington: Writings (Sparks), IV, 60n
24. Atlee: Journal. Penna. Arch., 2nd Ser., I, 554

CHAPTER 8

1. Amer. Arch., 5th Ser., I, 1257
2. Amer. Arch., 5th Ser., II, 1030
3. Marshall: Washington, I, 10
4. Washington: Writings (Ford), IV, 381
5. Fortesque, III, 183-185
6. Washington: Writings (Ford), IV, 374
7. Greene, I, 212
8. Journals of Congress, V, 730
9. Rev. Dipl. Corr., II, 103
10. Amer. Arch., 5th Ser., I, 714, 1128; II, 194
11. Amer. Arch., 5th Ser., II, 278
12. Trumbull: "Journal." Col. Conn. Hist. Soc., II, 193-194
13. Fiske, I, 190
14. Mackenzie: Diary, I, 48
15. Amer. Arch., 5th Ser., II, 276
16. Greene, I, 222
17. Amer. Arch., 5th Ser., II, 168

18. Beebe: "Journal." Penna. Mag. Hist., LIX, 336
19. Amer. Arch., 5th Ser., I, 102
20. Washington: Writings (Sparks), IV, 12-13n
21. Letters of Members, II, 41
22. Letters of Members, II, 28
23. Baldwin: Journal, 61
24. Beebe: "Journal." Penna. Mag. Hist., LIX, 352
25. Wells: "Journal." Coll. Conn. Hist. Soc., VII, 282
26. Pell: "Diary." Amer. Mag. Hist., II, 46
27. Amer. Arch., 5th Ser., II, 1079
28. Amer. Arch., 5th Ser., II, 1040
29. Thacher: Journal, 63 and 65
30. Amer. Arch., 5th Ser., III, 532

CHAPTER 9

1. Heath: Memoirs, 73
2. Amer. Arch., 5th Ser., II, 996
3. Jones: New York During the Revolution, I, 138 and 349
4. Madame Riedesel: Letters and Journals, 38
5. Penna. Arch., 2nd Ser., I, 447-448
6. Amer. Arch., 5th Ser., I, 1254
7. Amer. Arch., 4th Ser., IV, 990
8. Washington: Writings (Ford), IV, 429
9. Washington: Writings (Sparks), III, 284
10. Knollenberg: Washington and the Revolution, 115-128
11. Amer. Arch., 5th Ser., I, 22
12. Journals of Congress, V, 762
13. Letters of Members, II, 108
14. Rev. Dipl. Corr., II, 315
15. Amer. Arch., 5th Ser., II, 1105
16. Amer. Arch., 5th Ser., II, 518
17. Amer. Arch., 5th Ser., II, 1188
18. Abbatt: Battle of Pell's Point, 5
19. Amer. Arch., 5th Ser., II, 922
20. Amer. Arch., 5th Ser., II, 1130, 1202

21. Washington: *Writings* (Sparks), IV, 461n
22. Stedman, I, 241
23. Fortesque, III, 193
24. *Freeman's Journal*, December 10, 1776

CHAPTER 10

1. Washington: *Writings* (Ford), V, 111
2. Gordon, II, 127
3. Amer. Arch., 5th Ser., III, 1200
4. Amer. Arch., 5th Ser., II, 1034
5. Washington: *Writings* (Sparks), IV, 244n
6. Washington: *Writings* (Ford), V, 126
7. Stedman, I, 271
8. Wiederhold: "Diary." *Penna. Mag. Hist.*, XXII, 462-463
9. Rodney: "Journal." Del. Hist. Soc. Papers, No. 8, 14
10. Chastellux: *Travels*, 64
11. Wilkinson: *Memoirs*, I, 127
12. Stryker: *Battles of Trenton and Princeton*, 162
13. Wiederhold: "Diary." *Penna. Mag. Hist.*, XXII, 466
14. How: *Diary*, 37
15. *Freeman's Journal*, April 26, 1777
16. *Letters of Members*, II, 399
17. Young: "Journal." *Penna. Mag. Hist.*, VIII, 260
18. Reed: "Narrative." *Penna. Mag. Hist.*, VIII, 399
19. Hood: *Narrative*. Penna. Arch., 2nd Ser., XI, 263
20. Stryker: *Battles of Trenton and Princeton*, 251
21. Washington: *Writings* (Ford), 146-151

CHAPTER 11

1. Trevelyan, II (Part 2), 329
2. Stryker: *Battles of Trenton and Princeton*, 302

3. Washington. *Writings* (Ford), V, 149n
4. Gordon, II, 175
5. *Journals of Congress*, VII, 277
6. Stryker: *Battles of Trenton and Princeton*, 375-376
7. Washington: *Writings* (Ford), V, 154, 190, 209n
8. Washington: *Writings* (Ford), V, 289
9. Greene, I, 378
10. Van Doren: *Secret History*, 159
11. *Letters of Members*, II, 138
12. *Letters of Members*, II, 204
13. Carrington, 310
14. Lecky, IV, 108
15. Mackenzie: *Diary*, I, 39
16. Washington: *Writings* (Ford), V, 169
17. Stedman, I, 190n
18. Beebe: "Journal." *Penna. Mag. Hist.*, LIX, 328
19. McMichael: "Diary." *Penna. Mag. Hist.*, XVI. 139
20. Washington: *Writings* (Ford), V, 391n
21. Moore: *Diary*, 444
22. Washington: *Writings* (Ford), V, 437
23. *Freeman's Journal*, March 22, 1777
24. Greene, I, 394
25. Fortesque, III, 211n
26. McMichael: "Diary." *Penna. Mag. Hist.*, XVI, 146
27. Montrésor: "Journal." *Penna. Mag. Hist.*, V, 407
28. Serle: *Journal*, 245-246
29. Greene, I, 446
30. Carrington, 371

CHAPTER 12

1. *Letters of Members*, II, 519-520
2. *Journals of Congress*, VIII, 739
3. Chastellux: *Travels*, 70-71

4. Beatty: "Journal." *Md. Hist. Mag.*, III, 110
5. Hamilton: *Writings*, I, 34
6. *Papers Continental Congress*, Ser. 154, I, Fol. 222-223
7. Haiman: *Kosciuszko*, 16
8. Lefferts: *Uniforms in the American Revolution*, 160
9. Digby: *Journal*, 15
10. Digby: *Journal*, 21
11. Huddleston: *Burgoyne* (both proclamations quoted in full), 145-151
12. Burgoyne: *Orderly Book*, 32-33
13. Baldwin: *Journal*, 110
14. Sparks: *Correspondence*, I, 395-396
15. Sparks: *Correspondence*, I, 400-403
16. Sparks: *Correspondence*, I, 393, 395, 397
17. Washington: *Writings* (Ford), V, 483, 484, 489
18. *Letters of Members*, II, 413
19. Thacher: *Journal*, 86
20. Washington: *Writings* (Sparks), V, 14n
21. Trevelyan, III, 133

CHAPTER 13

1. Stone: *Letters of Brunswick and Hessian Officers*, 131
2. Mackenzie: *Diary*, I, 298
3. Lecky, IV, 15
4. Burgoyne: *State of the Expedition*, 129-131
5. *Pennsylvania Journal*, September 10, 1777
6. Sparks: *Correspondence*, I, 428
7. Franklin: *Writings*, VIII, 437
8. Sparks: *Correspondence*, I, 427-428
9. Dearborn: "Journal." Mass. Hist. Soc. Proc., 2nd Ser., III, 103
10. Anbury: *Travels*, I, 425
11. Burgoyne: *Orderly Book*, 113
12. Burgoyne: *Orderly Book*, 3, 91

13. Carrington, 328
14. Weeks: *Letters*, 12
15. Chastellux: *Travels*, 187
16. Digby: *Journal*, 24
17. Wild: "Journal." Mass. Hist. Soc. Proc., 2nd Ser., VI, 94
18. Dearborn: *Journal*. Mass. Hist. Soc. Proc., 2nd Ser., III, 105
19. Burgoyne: *State of the Expedition*, 163
20. Nickerson: *Turning Point of the Revolution*, 317
21. Lamb: *American War*, 166
22. Digby: *Journal*, 373
23. Dearborn: "Journal." Mass. Hist. Soc. Proc., 2nd Ser., III, 106
24. Hadden: *Journal*, 83
25. Anbury: *Travels*, I, 431; II, 11
26. Lossing: *Schuyler*, II, 352
27. Wilkinson: *Memoirs*, I, 246
28. Madame Riedesel: *Letters and Journals*, 125, 131
29. Fisher: "Journal," 6
30. Dearborn: "Journal." Mass. Hist. Soc. Proc., 2nd Ser., III, 109
31. Moore: *Diary*, 511
32. *Encyclopaedia Britannica* (14th Ed.), XIX, 990
33. Baldwin: *Journal*, 120
34. Dearborn: *Journal*. Mass. Hist. Soc. Proc., 2nd Ser., III, 105-106
35. Thacher: *Journal*, 97, 101
36. Heath: *Memoirs*, 138
37. Gordon, II, 250
38. Digby: *Journal*, 272
39. *Rev. Dipl. Corr.*, II, 413; Sparks: *Correspondence*, II, 551
40. *Mag. Amer. Hist.*, IV, 186

CHAPTER 14

1. McMichael: "Diary." *Penna. Mag. Hist.*, XVI, 145
2. *Rev. Dipl. Corr.*, II, 664
3. *Sexagenary Reminiscences*, 120, 122
4. Franklin: *Writings*, VII, 28

5. Greene, I, 489
6. *Journals of Congress*, VII, 202
7. Washington: *Writings* (Ford), VI, 143, 144
8. Greene, I, 506
9. Washington: *Writings* (Sparks), V, 154-155n, Green, I, 501-502
10. Dearborn: "Journal." Mass. Hist. Soc. Proc., 2nd Ser., III, 110
11. Sally Wister "Diary." *Penna. Mag. Hist.*, IX, 321-331, 464-472
12. Dearborn: "Journal." Mass. Hist. Soc. Proc., 2nd Ser., III, 110-111
13. Washington: *Writings* (Ford), VI, 245n, 254n
14. Kirkwood: *Order Book.* Del. Hist. Soc. Papers, LVI, 244
15. Washington: *Writings* (Sparks), III, 299
16. *Journals of Congress*, IX, 904
17. Washington: *Writings* (Ford), VI, 259
18. Hamilton, I, 116-117
19. Greene, I, 533
20. Waldo: "Diary." *Penna. Mag. Hist.*, XXI, 306, 309
21. Kirkwood: *Order Book.* Del Hist. Soc. Papers, LVI, 271
22. Washington: *Writings* (Sparks), V, 240n
23. McMichael: "Diary." *Penna. Mag. Hist.*, XVI, 157
24. Washington: *Writings* (Ford), VI, 379
25. Palmer: *General von Steuben*, 3-4
26. Kapp: *Steuben*, 615
27. Washington: *Writings* (Sparks), VI, 360

CHAPTER 15

1. Amer. Arch., 5th Ser., II, 946
2. Washington: *Writings* (Sparks), V, 360n
3. *New Hampshire Gazette*, February 9, 1778
4. Washington: *Writings* (Sparks), IV, 380
5. Madame Riedesel: *Letters and Journals*, 108-109
6. Madame Riedesel: *Letters and Journals*, 140
7. *Journals of Congress*, X, 29-35
8. *Letters of Members*, III, 18-19
9. Clark: "Perfidy of Sir William Howe." *Amer. Hist. Review*: XXXVII, 721-723
10. Anbury: *Travels*, II, 81
11. Heath: *Memoirs*, 161, 190-191
12. *New York Gazette*, December 19, 1777
13. Washington: *Writings* (Sparks), V, 497
14. Washington: *Writings* (Ford), VI, 353-354
15. *Letters of Members*, III, 69
16. Washington: *Writings* (Sparks), V, 511-512
17. Krafft: *Journal.* N. Y. Hist. Soc. Coll. (1882), 13-25, 89
18. Haiman: *Kosciuszko*, 57
19. Scharf and Westcott: *History of Philadelphia*, I, 390
20. *Letters of Members*, III, 28-31
21. *Journals of Congress*, X, 375-379

CHAPTER 16

1. *Letters of Members*, II, 548-549
2. Krafft: *Journal.* N. Y. Hist. Soc. Coll. (1882), 99
3. Palmer: *General von Steuben*, 157
4. Ganoe: *History of the United States Army*, 56
5. Hatch: *American Revolutionary Army*, 45, 62, 95
6. Upton: *Military Policy of the United States*, 380
7. Fuller: *British Light Infantry in the Eighteenth Century*, 152-153

8. Joslin: "Journal." Coll. Conn. Hist. Soc., VII, 345
9. Reed, I, 360
10. Greene, II, 49-50, 158
11. Washington: *Writings* (Sparks), VII, 454
12. Washington: *Writings* (Sparks), V, 283
13. *New Jersey Gazette*, March 18, 1778
14. Stedman, I, 346
15. Howe: *Narrative*, 30
16. Serle: *Journal*, 263
17. Jones: *New York in the Revolution*, 242-251
18. Washington: *Writings* (Sparks), V, 324n
19. *Journals of Congress*, IX, 971
20. Washington: *Writings* (Ford), VI, 392
21. *Journals of Congress*, XI, 615

CHAPTER 17

1. N. Y. Hist. Soc. Coll., IV, 406
2. *Penna. Mag. Hist.*, II, 141n
3. Washington: *Writings* (Ford), VII, 84-85
4. Stedman, II, 25
5. *Sullivan Papers*, II, 88-89
6. Washington: *Writings* (Ford), VII, 84-85
7. Mahan: *Influence of Sea Power*, 361
8. Washington: *Writings* (Ford), VII, 114n
9. Washington: *Writings* (Ford), VII, 161
10. Greene, II, 99
11. *Sullivan Papers*, II, 129
12. *Sullivan Papers*, II, 171
13. Washington: *Writings* (Ford), VII, 154-155n
14. Mackenzie: *Diary*, II, 351, 353, 364
15. Greene, II, 119
16. *Sullivan Papers*, II, 243-246

17. Washington: *Writings* (Ford), VII, 171-172n
18. *Sullivan Papers*, II, 286
19. *Letters of Members*, III, 409-410
20. Washington: *Writings* (Ford), VII, 181-182, 196
21. McDonald: *Letter-Book*. N. Y. Hist. Soc. Coll. (1882), 423, 424
22. Mackenzie: *Diary*, II, 395, 398
23. Carrington, 459
24. Lee: *Memoirs*, 375
25. *New York Journal*, July 13, 1778
26. Washington: *Writings* (Sparks), V, 273-274, 274n
27. Washington: *Writings* (Sparks), V, 354

CHAPTER 18

1. *Ill. Hist. Soc. Coll.*, VIII, 46
2. *Clark*: "Diary." *Ill. Hist. Soc. Coll.*, VIII, 120
3. Franklin: *Writings*, VIII, 463-473
4. *Ill. Hist. Soc. Coll.*, VIII, 56
5. *Clark*: "Diary." *Ill. Hist. Soc. Coll.*, VIII, 139-140
6. Bowman: "Journal." *Ill. Hist. Soc. Coll.*, VIII, 156-161
7. Hamilton: "Report." *Ill. Hist. Soc. Coll.*, VIII, 186-189
8. *Clark*: "Diary." *Ill. Hist. Soc. Coll.*, VII, 167-174
9. Jefferson, I, 225-229; Washington: *Writings* (Sparks), VI, 316
10. Madison, I, 228, 242
11. *Journals of Congress*, XI, 721
12. Washington: *Writings* (Sparks), VI, 187-190
13. Hubley: *Journal*. Penna. Arch., 2nd Ser., XI, 13, 39, 40
14. *Sullivan Papers*, III, 108
15. Hubley: *Journal*. Penna. Arch., 2nd Ser., XI, 25, 38-39
16. *New York Gazette*, November 1, 1779

17. Washington: *Writings* (Sparks), VI, 106-110
18. *Journals of Congress*, XIII, 13-15
19. Stedman, I, 248
20. Carrington, 462
21. Few: "Autobiography." *Mag. Amer. Hist.*, VII, 347
22. Moultrie: *Memoirs*, I, 256

CHAPTER 19

1. Lecky, IV, 126
2. Jones. *New York in the Revolution*, II
3. *Journals of Congress*, XII, 1080-1082
4. *New York Journal*, July 26, 1779
5. *New London Gazette*, August 4, 1779
6. Hutchinson: *Diary and Letters*, II, 246, 248
7. *Rev. Dipl. Corr.*, III, 691
8. Krafft: *Journal. N. Y. Hist. Soc. Coll.* (1882), 90
9. *New York Gazette*, August 16, 1779
10. Washington: *Writings* (Ford), VIII, 50
11. Carrington, 473
12. Stedman, II, 161
13. *Mag. Amer. Hist.*, VI, 194
14. Penna. Arch., 2nd Ser., XV, 337
15. Washington: *Writings* (Ford), VII, 369-370
16. Scharf and Westcott: *History of Philadelphia*, I, 390
17. Washington: *Writings* (Ford), VII, 369-370
18. Greene, II, 103
19. Washington: *Writings* (Sparks), IV, 345n
20. *Journals of Congress*, XII, 1001
21. Washington: *Writings* (Ford), VII, 301, 388
22. Monroe, *Writings*, I, 29

CHAPTER 20

1. *Pennsylvania Packet*, March 6, 1779

2. Washington: *Writings* (Ford), VIII, 18-19
3. *Journals of Congress*, XIII, 108
4. *Letters of Members*, IV, 110
5. *Rev. Dipl. Corr.*, III, 91
6. Ramsay: *History of South Carolina*, I, 168, 171
7. Moultrie. *Memoirs*, I, 324, 325
8. Moultrie: *Memoirs*, I, 412
9. Ramsay: *History of South Carolina*, 174
10. Moultrie: *Memoirs*, I, 434
11. Lee: *Memoirs*, 51
12. Amer. Arch., 5th Ser., II, 1105
13. *Rev. Dipl. Corr.*, II, 168n
14. Maclay: *American Privateers*, viii
15. Washington: *Writings* (Ford), VII, 426, 427
16. Lee: *Memoirs*, 61
17. Cruger: "Letters." *Mag. Amer. Hist.*, II, 491
18. Gordon, III, 34
19. Moultrie. *Memoirs*, II, 42
20. *New York Gazette*, November 6, 1779

CHAPTER 21

1. Washington: *Writings* (Ford), VIII, 138
2. Thacher: *Journal*, 181, 182
3. Gordon, III, 42-43
4. Washington: *Writings* (Ford), VIII, 172-173
5. Thacher: *Journal*, 180
6. N. J. Arch., 2nd Ser., IV, 462; *Pennsylvania Packet*, July 8 and November 24, 1780
7. *Journals of Congress*, XVI, 112-113
8. Greene, II, 275
9. Wild: "Journal." Mass. Hist. Soc. Proc., 2nd Ser., VI, 119-120
10. Thacher: *Journal*, 195
11. Gordon, III, 43
12. Fisher: "Journal," 13, 17

13. Krafft: *Journal*. N. Y. Hist. Soc. Coll. (1882), 103
14. Barbé-Marbois: *Letters*, 126
15. Thacher: *Journal*, 187-188
16. Gordon, III, 35-36
17. Ramsay: *History of South Carolina*, I, 164
18. *Letters of Members*, V, 2
19. Washington: *Writings* (Ford), VII, 492n
20. Heinrichs: *Letter-Book*. Penna Mag. Hist., XXII, 146
21. *Rev. Dipl. Corr.*, II, 358
22. Heinrichs: *Letter-Book*. Penna. Mag. Hist., XXII, 137-138, 160
23. Washington: *Writings* (Ford), VIII, 251-252
24. Moultrie: *Memoirs*, II, 80
25. Uhlendorf: *Siege of Charleston*, 71
26. Moultrie: *Memoirs*, 85, 96
27. Gordon, III, 52; Moultrie, II, 109
28. Heinrich's, *Letter-Book Penna. Mag. Hist.*, XXII, 168-169

CHAPTER 22

1. *Rev. Dipl. Corr.*, III, 610, 640
2. Lecky, IV, 123, 195
3. N. J. Arch., 2nd Ser., IV, 280
4. Marshall: *Washington*, 361
5. Washington: *Writings* (Ford), VIII, 322
6. *Letters of Members*, V, 165-166
7. *Letters of Members*, V, 185-188
8. *Journals of Congress*, XVI, 111-113
9. Washington: *Writings* (Ford), VIII, 294-295
10. *Rev. Dipl. Corr.*, III, 481
11. Washington: *Writings* (Ford), VIII, 325n
12. Stedman, II, 203-204n
13. Tarleton: *Campaigns*, 27
14. Gordon, III, 68-69
15. Tarleton: *Campaigns*, 25

16. Ramsay: *History of South Carolina*, I, 190
17. McCrady: *History of South Carolina*, I, 545
18. Stedman, II, 228-229n
19. Stedman, II, 237
20. Parton: *Andrew Jackson*, 19
21. McCrady: *History of South Carolina*, I, 653
22. Gordon, III, 88
23. Stedman, II, 221
24. Washington: *Writings* (Ford), VII, 404n
25. Washington: *Writings* (Ford), VII, 401n
26. Seymour: "Journal." *Penna. Mag. Hist.*, VII, 287
27. *Mag. Amer. Hist.*, V, 282
28. Stedman, II, 249n
29. Seymour: "Journal." *Penna. Mag. Hist.*, VII, 287-288
30. Kirkwood: *Journal*. Del. Hist. Soc. Papers, LVI, 11
31. *Mag. Amer. Hist.*, V, 304-305
32. Hamilton, II, 124
33. Lee: *Memoirs*, 100
34. Greene, III, 54

CHAPTER 23

1. Gordon, III, 112-113
2. McCrady: *History of South Carolina*, I, 704-705
3. Van Tyne: *Loyalists*, 182
4. *Pennsylvania Packet*, September 4, 1781
5. Pell: "Diary." *Mag. Amer. Hist.*, II, 44
6. Moore: *Diary*, 787
7. Lefferts: *Uniforms of the Revolution*, 225-228
8. Washington: *Writings* (Sparks), VII, 554
9. Stedman, II, 249
10. Washington: *Writings* (Sparks), VII, 555
11. Kirke: *Rear-Guard of the Revolution*, 265

12. Draper: *King's Mountain,* 325-326
13. Washington: *Writings* (Ford), VIII, 494
14. *New York Gazette,* October 25, 1780
15. Stryker: *Battles of Trenton and Princeton,* 87-89
16. Washington: *Writings* (Ford), VII, 475n
17. Washington: *Writings* (Sparks), VI, 460
18. Washington: *Writings* (Sparks), VIII, 571
19. Washington: *Writings* (Ford), VIII, 371n
20. McClellan: *Diary.* Penna. Arch., 2nd Ser., XI, 659
21. Penna. Arch., 2nd Ser., XI, 667, 671, 685
22. *Letters of Members,* VI, 515-516
23. Penna. Arch., 2nd Ser., XI, 701
24. *Sullivan Papers,* III, 256-257
25. *Letters of Members,* VI, 531

CHAPTER 24

1. *New York Gazette,* May 12, 1781
2. *Journals of Congress,* XIX, 402
3. *Rev. Dipl. Corr.,* IV, 328-330
4. Greene, III, 43
5. Lee: *Memoirs,* 96n
6. Kirkwood: *Journal.* Del. Hist. Soc. Papers, LVI, 12-13
7. *Mag. Amer. Hist.,* VI, 196, 199
8. *Mag. Amer. Hist.,* V, 282
9. Stevens: *Clinton-Cornwallis Controversy,* I, 316
10. Graham: *Morgan,* 287
11. Ramsay: *History of South Carolina,* I, 218
12. Graham: *Morgan,* 316
13. Tarleton: *Campaigns,* 221
14. Graham: *Morgan,* 292
15. Seymour: "Journal." *Penna. Mag. Hist.,* VII, 295
16. Tarleton: *Campaigns,* 217-218
17. Lee: *Memoirs,* 98

18. Ramsay: *History of South Carolina,* I, 263-264
19. Moultrie: *Memoirs,* II, 102
20. Ramsay: *History of South Carolina,* I, 247
21. Seymour: "Journal." *Penna. Mag. Hist.,* VII, 297
22. Lee: *Memoirs,* 157
23. Tarleton: *Campaigns,* 507
24. Tucker: "Letters." *Mag. Amer. Hist.,* VII, 38-39
25. Greene, III, 196
26. Tucker: "Letters." *Mag. Amer. Hist.,* VII, 40
27. Stedman, II, 379
28. Lamb: *Journal,* 362
29. Tarleton: *Campaigns,* 507; Stedman, II, 393
30. Cornwallis: *Correspondence,* I, 87
31. Greene, III, 207
32. Greene, III, 215

CHAPTER 25

1. Palmer: *General von Steuben,* 262
2. Washington: *Writings* (Sparks), VIII, 27-29
3. *Journals of Congress,* XX, 545-546
4. *Rev. Dipl. Corr.,* IV, 434
5. Lefferts: *Uniforms of the Revolution,* 246
6. Du Bourg: "Diary." *Mag. Amer. Hist.,* IV, 210, 214
7. Blanchard: *Journal,* 115-116
8. Rochambeau: *Operations,* 277
9. *Mag. Amer. Hist.,* VI, 343
10. Carrington, 646
11. Washington, *Writings* (Sparks), VIII, 128n
12. *Mag. Amer. Hist.,* VI, 343
13. Tucker: "Letters." *Mag. Amer. Hist.,* VII, 211-212
14. *Mag. Amer. Hist.,* VI, 364
15. Thacher: *Journal,* 263

16. Washington: *Writings* (Sparks), VIII, 306-307
17. Blanchard: *Journal*, 125-126
18. Reeves: "Letter-Book." *Penna. Mag. Hist.*, XXI, 235-236
19. Washington: *Writings* (Sparks), VIII, 163-167, 167n
20. Tilden: "Journal." *Penna. Mag. Hist.*, XIX, 53-54
21. Du Bourg: "Diary." *Mag. Amer. Hist.*, VII, 295
22. Blanchard. *Journal*, 143
23. McDowell: *Journal*. Penna. Arch., 2nd Ser., XV, 303
24. Feltman: *Journal*. Penna. Arch., 2nd Ser., XI, 731
25. Blanchard: *Journal*, 152-153
26. Davis: "Journal." *Penna. Mag. Hist.*, V, 305
27. Anna Rawle: "Diary." *Penna. Mag. Hist.*, XVI, 103, 105

CHAPTER 26

1. Washington: *Writings* (Sparks), VIII, 185-186
2. Trevelyan, II (Part Two), 13; *Journals of Congress*, XXII, 93
3. Washington: *Writings* (Sparks), VIII, 218-220, 15-16
4. Anna Rawle: "Diary." *Penna. Mag. Hist.*, XVI, 107
5. Washington: *Writings* (Ford), IX, 407; Washington: *Writings* (Sparks), VIII, 203-207
6. Ramsay: *History of South Carolina*, I, 200, 223
7. Stedman, II, 398, 401
8. Carrington, 565
9. Haiman: *Kosciuszko*, 112, 114
10. Greene, III, 403
11. Pierce: "Letters." *Mag. Amer. Hist.*, VII, 434
12. Stedman, II, 387n
13. Moultrie: *Memoirs*, II, 303
14. Moultrie: *Memoirs*, II, 327
15. McDowell: *Journal*. Penna. Arch., 2nd Ser., XV, 327

16. Moultrie: *Memoirs*, II, 355
17. Graham: *Morgan*, 395
18. Greene, III, 429
19. Greene, III, 445
20. Seymour: "Journal." *Penna. Mag. Hist.*, VII, 383
21. Pierce: "Letters." *Mag. Amer. Hist.*, VII, 440
22. Gordon, III, 168

CHAPTER 27

1. Washington: *Writings* (Ford), X, 15n
2. Heath: *Memoirs*, 358
3. *Papers of Cont. Congress*, No. 20, I, Folio 277
4. Heath: *Memoirs*, 351
5. Stedman, I, 115
6. Washington: *Writings* (Sparks), VIII, 343n, 536-537
7. Washington: *Writings* (Sparks), VIII, 385
8. Thacher: *Journal*, 204
9. Carrington, 633
10. Stedman, II, 498 n.
11. *Journals of Congress*, XXIV, 59
12. Washington: *Writings* (Sparks), VIII, 521
13. Lowell: *Hessians in the Revolution*, 300
14. Penna. Arch., 2nd Ser., I, 496-498
15. Ramsay: *History of South Carolina*, I, 204
16. Pierce: "Letters." *Mag. Amer. Hist.*, VII, 432
17. Fuller: *British Light Infantry in the Eighteenth Century*, 225
18. *Letters of Members*, VI, 480
19. Trevelyan, II (Part Two), 200
20. Washington: *Writings* (Sparks), VIII, 300, 301n
21. Washington: *Writings* (Sparks), VIII, 558, 565
22. Heath: *Memoirs*, 371
23. Washington: *Writings* (Sparks), VIII, 568

24. *Mag. Amer. Hist.*, II, 530

25. Fisher: "Journal," 24

26. Washington: *Writings* (Sparks), VIII, 381

APPENDIX

The list of Continental generals is based on the one published in B. F. Heitman's *Historical Register of Officers of the Continental Army*, plus additions and corrections as noted by Simon Gratz in the *Pennsylvania Magazine of History*, XXVII (1903), 385-403.

Index

Abbatt, William, 150, 152
Abbott, Edward, 301
Adams, Abigail, 88-89
Adams, John, 88, 109, 134, 146, 232
Adams, Samuel, 9, 29, 30 109, 204, 261
Alamance, battle of the, 98
Albany, 90, 110, 136, 253, 266
Alexander, Gen. William, see Stirling
Allegheny River, 311
Allen, Ethan, 18-20, 29, 184
Amboy, N. J., 178
American Revolution, 26-29, 95-96, 368, 390, 461
Amherst, Lord Jeffrey, 23, 24, 316
Anbach-Bayreuth, 74
Anbury, Lt. Thomas, 219, 220
André, Maj. John, 277, 289
Anhalt-Zerbst, 74
Annapolis, Md., 349
Armand, Charles Tufin, Marquis de la Rouarie, 289
Armstrong, Gen. John, 190, 231
Armstrong, Maj. John, Jr., 464
Arnold, Benedict, 19-20, 52, 62, 68-69, 70, 77, 78, 92, 94, 115, 134, 137-139, 180-181, 189, 206, 218, 221, 225-227, 264, 325-329, 388-391, 418-419, 424
Arnold legend, 19, 52-54, 59, 61, 181, 225-227, 390
Asgill, Capt. Charles, 452-453
Ashley River, 356
Association, Articles of, 28-29, 75
Atlee, Col. Samuel, 121, 143
Augusta, Ga., 333, 340, 341

Baldwin, Col. Jeduthan, 81, 83, 136, 137, 196, 226
Baldwin, Col. Loammi, 150
Baltimore, Md., 161, 349
Barras, Comte de, 430
Barren Hill, combat of, 279-280
Battle, Capt. John, 4
Beatty, Capt. William, 194
Baum, Col., 207-208
Beaumarchais, Caron de, 113
Bedel, Col. Timothy, 93
Bee, Thomas, 356
Beebe, Dr. Lewis, 92, 134, 137
Bemis Heights, see Saratoga
Bennington, battle of, 207-208
Berthier, Marshal, 459
Billingsport, N. J., 232
Blanchard, Claude, 422, 428, 432, 433
Board of War, 262
Bordentown, N. J., 165, 172
Boston, Mass., 8, 17, 28, 35, 48, 80, 89, 116
Boston "Massacre," 26, 87
Boston Tea Party, 27, 62
Bouille, Marquis de, 447
Bouquet, Col. Henry, 24
Bourg, Baron Cromat du, 422, 432
Bowman, Maj. Joseph, 306, 307
Braddock, Gen. Edward, 22
Brandywine, battle of the, 190-191
Brant, Joseph, 205, 309
Breed's Hill, see Bunker Hill
Breymann, Col., 208
Briand, Bishop John Oliver, 76
Briar Creek, combat of, 333-334

Brimstone Hill, 447

British Army, 26, 30-31, 41, 71-72, 80, 82, 85, 88, 107, 108, 142, 178, 183-184, 196-197, 212-213, 218-219, 233, 238, 258, 275-277, 309, 318-319, 357, 433, 456-457, 459, 460-461

British Empire, 25, 27, 103, 258, 278, 283, 309, 316, 461, 462

British Marines, 11, 80

British Navy, 75, 86, 97, 101-103, 138-139, 141-143, 147, 153, 156, 189, 290, 295, 338, 340, 356, 357, 359, 399, 437

Broad River, 404, 406, 449

Brodhead, Col. John, 311

Brooklyn, 118

Brooklyn Heights, 118, 123, 126

Brown, Col. John, 64, 65, 92, 180, 220, 227, 391

Brunswick, N. J., 174, 178

Bunker Hill, battle of, 32-36

Burgoyne, Gen. John, 48, 80, 115, 143, 187, 197-202, 207, 209-211, 213-215, 218-227, 253-260, 437

Burke, Edmund, 197, 300, 447, 461

Burke, Thomas, 192

Burr, Col. Aaron, 56, 57, 67, 132, 328

Butler, Col. John, 204, 299

Byng, Adm. John, 22, 24

Cadwalader, Gen. John, 163, 171, 174, 289

Cahokia, 304

Caldwell, Elizabeth, 364

Callender, Joseph, 122

Cambridge, Mass., 4-5, 17, 29, 52, 255, 257

Camden, S. C., 438, 439, 440; battle of, 378-380

Camden, Lord, 447

Campbell, Sir Archibald, 116, 184, 315

Campbell, Donald, 69

Campbell, Col. William, 386

Campbell, Sir William, 100, 102

Canada, 21-23, 24, 52, 60, 61-62, 93, 135, 242, 266, 304, 313, 445, 460

Canadian auxiliaries, 197, 204, 212, 217

Cape Breton, 23

Cape Fear River, 416

Carleton, Sir Guy, 52, 61-62, 63, 65-66, 67, 70, 76, 77-78, 80, 94, 136-137, 139-140, 177, 196, 299, 451-453

Carrington, Col. Edward, 403

Carroll, Charles, of Carrollton, 91, 113

Carroll, John, 93

Cartagena, 21

Carter, John, 264

Caswell, Col. Richard, 99, 377

Catawba River, 411

Catherine II of Russia, 74

Cedars, The, 93-94

Chambly, 64, 115

Champe, Sgt. John, 419

Charles Edward, Prince, 98

Charles River, 32

Charleston, S. C., 100-103, 188, 335-336, 364, 369, 371, 373, 435, 438, 440, 442, 446, 449-450; siege of, 354-362

Charlestown, Mass., 4, 32, 35, 39, 42, 83

Charlotte, N. C., 380

Chase, Samuel, 93, 113

Chastellux, Marquis de, 165, 193, 215, 238

Chatham, Lord, 22-24, 26, 40, 461

Chatterton's Hill, 154

Chaudiere River, 59

Cherokee Nation, 24, 72, 73, 115-116, 312

Cherry Valley Massacre, 299, 309

Chesapeake Bay, 188, 189, 420, 423, 429

Chesterfield, Va., 418, 419

Clark, Sir Francis, 223

Clark, George Rogers, 300, 302-308, 460-461

Clarke, Col. Elijah, 383

Clausewitz, Karl von, 213
Cleghorn, Lt. Eleazer, 79
Cleveland, Col. Benjamin, 386, 407
Clinkerfoose, Isaac, 458
Clinton, Gen. Sir Henry, 100, 102, 120, 160, 220, 224, 254, 256, 282, 284-287, 318, 354-362, 365, 423, 436-437, 451
Clinton, Gen. James, 310
Committees of Correspondence, 28
Committees of Safety, 13, 19-20, 28-29, 42, 100, 110
Conciliatory Acts, 282
Concord, Mass., 5, 11-13
Confederation, Articles of, 268
Connecticut, 83, 128-129, 145, 154, 299, 331, 364, 421
Connecticut Farms, N. J., 364
Continental Army, 28, 29, 30, 38-41, 86, 103, 108, 113, 125, 141, 146, 185, 189, 245, 247, 251-252, 269-272, 328, 330-332, 348, 351, 365-366, 421, 449, 455-456, 457, 462, 463-466; arms and weapons, 42, 47, 64, 85, 86, 112, 270, 435; artillery, 19, 64, 81-83, 86, 88, 101, 103, 237-238, 312, 341-342, 359; battle statistics, 456-458; casualties, 36, 152, 155, 192, 251-252, 361, 443, 457, 458; cavalry, 124, 171, 190, 402, 439; clothing, 46, 66, 326, 349; command, 38-39, 55, 131, 132, 137, 144, 171, 179, 203-204, 274, 348; diaries and journals, 5-7; discipline, 37, 40, 44-45, 47, 48, 88, 93, 108, 124, 128, 137, 143, 153, 185, 350, 351; engineering, 81-82, 195-196, 203, 214-215; enlistments, 71, 82-83, 145-146, 159, 312, 331-332, 445; fortification, 32, 81-82, 87, 102, 136-137, 155, 177, 195-196, 214-215, 234-236; health regulations, 46, 134, 184-185, 271; infantry, 150-152, 190, 212, 217-218, 273, 307, 403; morale, 37-38, 43, 88, 214, 243-245, 247, 269-270, 280, 287, 394-396, 398, 402,

Continental Army—*Continued*
412, 449, 454; mutinies, 364, 394-397, 465; pay, 46, 328, 350-351; rations, 5, 46-47, 56, 95, 377; supplies, 90, 112, 113, 241, 243, 272-273, 347-350, 377; training, 39-41, 269-272, 280, 287; uniforms, 46, 50, 120
Continental Congress, 28, 29, 38, 41-42, 48, 49, 52, 55, 62, 72, 77, 86, 94, 95, 96, 113-114, 126, 134, 145, 162, 193, 194, 204, 242, 255. 257, 267, 268, 281, 282, 284, 313, 317, 321, 327, 350, 366, 367, 428, 437, 452, 453, 461, 463, 464
Continental currency, 398, 400
Continental Marines, 86, 126, 165, 312, 338
Continental Navy, 86, 139, 145-146, 147, 437-438
Conway, Gen. Thomas, 261, 266, 289
Conway Cabal, 260-263, 264-265, 267
Cooper River, 356
Copp's Hill, 34
Cornwallis, Earl of, 121, 157, 171-172, 174, 187, 191, 228, 238, 370, 374, 379-380, 385, 410-416, 423-426, 429-433, 436, 440
Cowpens, battle of the, 406-409
Cox, John, 273
Cresswell, James, 116
Cromwell, Oliver, 463
Cross Creek, N. C., 380, 416
Crown Point, 19, 54, 134, 135, 139
Cruger, Col. John H., 341-342, 441
Cumberland, Duke of, 254
Cummings, Rev. Charles, 116
Curwen, Samuel, 384

Dan River, 411
Danbury, Conn., 180
Darby, Capt. John, 15
Dartmouth, Earl of, 48, 72
Davies, Col. William, 383
Davis, Capt. John, 434
Dead River, 56, 57

Deane, Silas, 39, 55, 113, 193, 375
Dearborn, Col. Henry, 52, 54, 212, 217-219, 238, 240
Declaration of Independence, 103, 108, 163, 268, 314
Declaration of Rights, 62
De Haas, Col. John, 137
Delaplace, Capt., 18
Delaware, 121, 375, 455
Delaware River, 162, 164-165, 171, 187
D'Estaing, Comte de, 280, 288, 289, 290-296, 297, 298, 314, 337, 340-343
Deschambault, P. Q., 114
Detroit, 24, 301, 305, 308, 313
Dickinson, John, 114
Dickinson, Gen. Philemon, 178
Digby, Lt. William, 219, 226
Dobbs Ferry, N. Y., 151, 153
Dominica, 448
Donop, Count von, 159, 170, 232, 234-236
Dorchester Heights, 86-87
D'Orvilliers, Comte de, 338
Dragging Canoe, Chief, 116
Duane, James, 214, 331, 380
Du Coudray, Gen. Philippe, 193
Dunmore, Lord, 96-97
Durham boats, 165

East River, 130
Easton, Maj. James, 92
Eelking, Capt. von, 208
Elizabeth River, 97
Elliot, Hugh, 358
Emerson, Rev. William, 39
England, 16, 71, 142, 255, 338, 363-364, 373-374, 437, 441, 448, 462
Enos, Col. Roger, 39
Eutaw Springs, battle of, 443-444
Ewald, Capt. Johann, 271, 358, 360
Ewing, Gen. James, 163

Fairfax, Bryan, 282
Fairfield, Conn., 180, 318, 319
Falconer, James, 117

Falmouth, Mass., 75
Faneuil Hall, 80
Farnsworth, Corp. Amos, 43
Febiger, Col. Christian, 56, 323-324, 403
Feltman, Lt. William, 433
Ferguson, Col. Patrick, 369, 385-387
Few, Col. William, 314
Fisher, Pvt. Elijah, 45, 225, 351, 465-466
Fisheries Act, 50-51, 85
Fishing Creek, combat of, 380
Fiske, John, 131
Flags, American, 85, 100
Fleury, Marquis de, 194, 237-238, 289, 323, 465
Flogging, 44-45, 141
Florida, 314, 333, 353, 400, 461
Forbes, Col. John, 23, 24
Fort Ann, 200, 202, 220
Fort Duquesne, 23, 25
Fort Edward, 202, 203, 213, 220
Fort George, 200, 202, 220
Fort Granby, 440
Fort Griswold, 424
Fort Independence, 179
Fort Knyphausen, 159
Fort Lee, 145, 156
Fort Mercer, 228, 232, 234-236, 237
Fort Mifflin, 228, 236-238
Fort Montgomery, 224, 253
Fort Motte, 440
Fort Moultrie, 359
Fort Nelson, 308
Fort Pitt, 311
Fort Stanwix, 205-206
Fort Washington, 145, 153, 252; surrender of, 155-156
Fort Watson, 439-440
Fort Western, 52
Fort William, 87
Fortesque, J. W., 15, 36, 125, 254
Fox, Charles James, 111, 447, 461
France, 22-23, 281, 313, 316, 353, 367, 400, 456, 461
Francis, Col. John, 201

Franklin, Benjamin, 26, 42, 75, 128, 211, 228, 232, 233, 246, 304, 310, 313, 332, 366, 421

Fraser, Gen., 217

Frederick II of Prussia, 22, 75, 245, 358, 458

Freeman's Farm, *see* Saratoga

French Alliance, 267, 268, 281, 283, 313, 314, 331, 367, 421

French and Indian War, 22-24

French Revolution, 109, 459

Gadsden, Christopher, 335, 373

Gage, Gen. Thomas, 8-15, 28, 30, 32, 47

Galloway, Joseph, 445

Galvez, Don Bernardo de, 400

Garth, Gen., 318-319

Gates, Gen. Horatio, 38, 105, 134, 135-136, 140, 181-182, 195-196, 204, 205-206, 209, 214-227, 230, 261-263, 265, 273, 309, 354, 375-381, 401, 403, 464, 465

Gates-Schuyler controversy, 136, 181-182, 195, 204, 211-212, 214, 221-222, 253, 263, 265, 267, 375-376, 380-381, 388, 389

George II, 25, 254

George III, 25-27, 62, 71-72, 74, 108-109, 255, 363-364, 448, 461, 463

Georgia, 314-315, 332, 334, 340-343, 369, 446

Gérard de Rayneval, Sieur Conrade Alexandre, 337, 340

Germain, Lord George, 78, 123, 188, 209, 215, 301, 420, 436, 457

German mercenaries, 74-75, 118, 131, 141, 150, 152, 155, 186, 207-208, 229, 232-233, 257, 269, 321, 357-359, 362, 458

Germantown, battle of, 228-231

Gerry, Elbridge, 145, 181

Gibraltar, siege of, 399, 448

Gist, Gen. Mordecai, 239, 241

Glover, Gen. John, 126, 149-152, 179

Gloucester, Mass., 51, 85

Gordon, William, 13, 160, 194, 208, 226, 348

Gordon riots, 363-364

Gould, Lt. Edward, 11

Grasse, Comte de, 423, 429-432, 435, 448

Graves, Adm. Thomas, 75, 86

Great Bridge, combat of, 97

Great Britain, 22, 26, 27, 31, 74, 111-112, 232, 252, 255, 267, 282, 298, 304, 314, 316, 353, 367, 399, 445, 454, 455, 460, 461

Green Spring, combat of, 426

Greene, Col. Christopher, 55-56, 57, 69, 234-236

Greene, Gen. Nathanael, 39, 40, 119, 126, 132, 157, 166, 190-191, 230-231, 273, 295-296, 326, 346, 350, 381, 401-402, 404, 410, 412-416, 435, 437-446, 449, 450, 465, 466

Grenada, 337

Grothausen, Lt. Friedrich von, 172

Guadeloupe, 448

Guerilla warfare, 372-373, 383, 444, 446

Guibert, Comte de, 272

Guilford Courthouse, battle of, 413-416

Hackensack, N. J., 364-365

Hadden, Lt. James, 226

Haldimand, Gen. Frederick, 358

Hale, Nathan, 402

Half-pay Measure, 328

Halifax, 89

Hamilton, Col. Alexander, 132, 168, 175, 195, 241, 243, 266, 285, 380, 433

Hamilton, Henry "the Hair Buyer," 301, 302, 305-307, 308

Hancock, John, 9, 29, 30, 46, 77, 91

Hand, Col. Edward, 172, 175

Hanging Rock, combat of, 372-373

Hanover, 254

Hardy, Sir Charles, 338

Harlem Heights, 132, 145, 147; combat of, 132-133

Harnett, Cornelius, 268
Harrison, Benjamin, 42
Hartford Conference, 388, 400
Hartley, David, 75
Harvard College, 5, 50, 213
Haslet, Col. John, 175
Haws, Pvt. Samuel, 7
Hayne, Col. Isaac, 452
Hazard, Ebenezer, 141
Hazen, Col. Moses, 66, 137
Heath, Gen. William, 3-5, 13, 38, 87, 118, 141, 178-179, 226, 257-259, 394, 451, 452, 464
Heinrichs, see Hinrich
Henry, Pvt. John Joseph, 50, 52, 55, 58, 59, 61, 77, 92
Henry, Patrick, 96, 302, 307
Hendricks, Capt. William, 52, 59, 69-70
Herkimer, Col. Nicholas, 205
Hesse-Cassel, 74
Hesse-Hanau, 74
Hessians, see German mercenaries
Heth, Lt. William, 52, 67, 69, 76
Highlands (Hudson), 187, 325
Highlanders, Scottish, 98-99, 116, 143, 145
Hillsborough, N. C., 378, 380, 411
Hilzheimer, Jacob, 229
Hinrich, Capt. Johann, 358-359, 362
Hobkirk's Hill, battle of, 439
Hog Island, see Fort Mifflin
Holland, see Netherlands
Honeyman, John, 391, 392
Hood, Sir Samuel, 447
Hoods, Va., 417, 419
Hopkinson, Francis, 198
House of Commons, 177, 213
Houston, William, 315
How, Pvt. David, 43, 44, 45, 170
Howard, Col. John E., 403, 408, 415, 465
Howe, George Lord, 23, 24, 149
Howe, Richard Lord, 127-128, 236-238, 288
Howe, Gen. Robert, 97, 315, 392, 397

Howe, Gen. Sir William, 24, 32-35, 47-48, 84-85, 87, 118, 122, 123, 147, 149, 158, 177, 187, 189, 228, 238, 256-257, 275-277
Hubbardstown, battle of, 201
Hubley, Col. Adam, 309-311
Huck, Col. Christian, 371
Huddy, Capt. Josiah, 451-452
Hudson River, 108, 145, 155, 213, 289
Hughes, Sir Edward, 448
Hunting shirt, 46, 50, 189

Illinois country, 305, 460
India, 22, 314, 447, 448, 461, 462
Indiana Territory, 460
Indians, American, 14, 42, 72, 94, 116-117, 197, 205-206, 209-211, 212, 217, 299-300, 301-302, 453-454, 460
Intolerable Acts, 27, 62
Ireland, 72
Isle aux Noix, 63, 133

Jackson, Andrew, 370, 372, 439, 460
Jägers, 149, 167, 172, 213, 358, 362
James Island, 336, 449
James River, 417, 419
Jasper, Sgt. William, 102
Jay, John, 375
Jefferson, Thomas, 6, 135, 307, 377, 419
Johnson, Sir John, 110, 204
Johnson, Sir William, 110
Jones, John Paul, 147, 338, 465
Jones, Judge Thomas, 142, 275, 317, 321, 445
Joslin, Joseph, 272
Jourdan, Marshal, 459

Kalb, Baron de, 245, 380
Kaskaskia, 303-304
Kennebec River, 52, 56
Kentucky, 302, 307
Keppel, Adm. Augustus, 86
Kettle Creek, combat of, 333
Kingsbridge, N. Y., 145, 179, 423

King's Mountain, battle of, 386-387
Kingston, N. Y., 175, 176, 224, 285
Kipp's Bay, 130
Kirkwood, Capt. Robert, 8, 379, 402, 408, 411, 414
Kloster Seven, Convention of, 22, 254
Knowlton, Col. Thomas, 133
Knox, Gen. Henry, 86, 166, 231, 330
Knox, Lucy, 185, 330
Knyphausen, Gen. Wilhelm von, 155, 190-191, 285, 351, 364
Kosciusko, Col. Thaddeus, 195, 196, 203, 214, 227, 264, 318, 325, 403, 411, 426, 441, 449, 450
Krafft, Sgt. von, 263-264, 269, 321, 351

Lacey, Capt. John, 278
Lafayette, Marquis de, 37, 194, 249, 264-266, 279-280, 285-287, 289, 296, 337, 367, 421, 425-427, 430, 433
Lake Champlain, 18-19, 113, 197, 202, 213, 220
Lake Erie, 311
Lake George, 18
Lake Megantic, 59
Lake Oneida, 454
Lake Ontario, 204
Lake St. Pierre, 114-115
Lamb, Capt. John, 67, 70
Lamb, Sgt. Roger, 7, 219
Laurens, Henry, 256, 261, 264-266
Laurens, Col. John, 241, 246, 288, 289, 335, 449
Learned, Gen. Ebenezer, 223, 227
Lechmere Point, 82, 86
Lecky, William, 72, 75, 316, 363
Lee, Arthur, 118, 147, 375
Lee, Gen. Charles, 38, 83, 100-101, 103, 154, 156, 162, 283-286, 288
Lee, Col. Henry (Light Horse Harry), 190, 240, 299, 324, 380-381, 402, 409, 411, 412, 414-415, 439, 440, 465
Lee, Richard Henry, 182, 254, 261
Ledyard, Col. William, 424

Leitsch, Maj. Andrew, 133
Leslie, Gen. John, 418, 445
Leutze, Emmanuel, 166
Lexington, battle of, 3-5, 8-17, 30
Light Division, 459-460
Lincoln, Gen. Benjamin, 189, 220, 221, 227, 315, 333, 334, 336-337, 341-343, 356, 359-362, 377, 435, 458
Lippincott, Capt. Richard, 452
Livingston, Col. Henry, 63
Livingston, Col. Henry B., 221, 226
Livingston, Col. James, 66, 68, 93
Livingston, Robert R., 61, 227, 389
Livingston, William, 114, 185
Long Island, 108, 117, 123, 320; battle of, 118-122
Longueiul, P. Q., 63, 64
Louis XV, 22
Louis XVI, 113, 232, 281, 291, 313, 337, 427
Louisburg, 21-22
Louisiana, 400
Loyalists, American, 95-96, 110, 120, 142, 153, 205, 281-282, 289, 319, 320-321, 334, 337, 378, 387, 442, 444-445, 461; in British military service, 378, 383-384, 385, 400, 439, 441, 457-458
Ludwig, Christopher, 229
Luzerne, Chevalier Anne C. de la, 352, 367, 399, 421
Lyman, Pvt. Simeon, 83, 84
Lynch, Thomas, 42

Mackenzie, Capt. Frederick, 8, 12, 15, 212, 295, 298
Maclean, Col. Allen, 60, 66, 70, 114-115
McClellan, Capt. Joseph, 394
McCrea, Jane, 209, 211
McDonald, Capt. Alexander, 7, 18, 298
McDonald, Donald, 98
McDougall, Gen. Alexander, 274, 463
McDowell, Charles, 386
McDowell, Lt. William, 433

McIntosh, Gen. Lachlan, 335
McLane, Capt. Allen, 278
McLean, Col. Francis, 312-313
McMichael, Lt. James, 185, 189, 229, 245
Madison, James, 308
Magaw, Col. John, 155
Mahan, Alfred Thayer, 290
Maine, 52, 313, 461
Manhattan Island, 107, 118, 128
Manly, Capt. John, 85
Marblehead, Mass., 51, 85
Marbois, François, 352
Marion, Col. Francis, 382, 440
Marshall, Capt. John, 69, 97, 226
Martin, Josiah, 98, 100
Maryland, 120-121, 263, 391
Mason, George, 305
Massachusetts, 19, 29, 62, 84, 94, 146, 206, 312-313, 331, 391
Mather, Cotton, 21
Mathews, John, 354-356, 366, 395, 452
Maxwell, Gen. William, 190, 285
Mease, James, 326, 329
Meigs, Maj. Return Jonathan, 52, 58, 67, 69, 186
Melvin, Pvt. James, 52, 56
Mercer, Gen. Hugh, 175
Meschianza, 227-229, 230
Michigan Territory, 460
Middlebrook, N. J., 186
Middleton, Arthur, 461
Mifflin, Gen. Thomas, 114, 172, 261, 272, 273
Militia, 4, 12, 32, 39-40, 44, 83-84, 125, 146, 175-176, 178, 205, 220, 285, 295, 312, 331, 334, 365, 379-380, 406, 409, 413-414, 460
Minorca, 22, 447, 461
Miralles, Don Juan de, 353
Mississippi River, 300, 303, 304
Mobile, 400
Mohawk River, 110, 205
Monck's Corner, combat of, 360
Monk, George, 389
Monmouth, battle of, 285-287

Monongahela River, 303
Monroe, Capt. James, 168, 328
Montcalm, Marquis de, 22, 23, 24
Montgomery, Gen. Richard, 38, 52, 59, 61-65, 67-69, 77
Montreal, 24, 52, 65
Montrésor, Capt. John, 189
Moore's Creek, combat of, 98-99
Morgan, Gen. Daniel, 49, 55, 56, 58, 61, 69-70, 77, 187, 189, 212, 217-218, 220, 221, 223, 226, 227, 240-241, 285, 287-288, 309, 328, 403, 404-409, 413, 446, 465
Morris, Robert, 147, 353, 421, 427, 464
Morristown, N. J., 175, 178, 184-186, 325, 347-349, 364, 365-366, 394
Moultrie, Gen. William, 100-103, 315, 333-335, 343, 361, 444, 445, 446
Mowat, Capt. Henry, 75
Moylan, Gen. Stephen, 273
Mud Island, see Fort Mifflin
Mugford, Capt. James, 90
Muhlenberg, Gen. Peter, 190, 229
Musketry, 12, 33-35, 101
Mystic River, 32

Napoleon I, 37, 109, 458, 459-460, 462, 463
Navigation Acts, 26
Negroes, 14, 42-43, 72, 96, 336, 371, 425
Nelson, Thomas, 432
Netherlands, 112, 398, 399
Neutral Ground, 321
Nevis, 447
Newark, N. J., 157
Newburgh Addresses, 462-463
Newburgh, N. Y., 462, 463
Newburyport, Mass., 52
New England, 39, 41, 43, 160, 172, 196, 206-207, 211, 255, 262, 265, 274, 289, 291, 327, 423, 455
Newfoundland Fisheries, 313, 461
New Hampshire, 84, 207, 313
New Hampshire Grants, see Vermont

New Haven, Conn., 318
New Jersey, 145, 155, 156, 159, 163-164, 177, 186, 187, 282, 317, 331, 348-350, 397, 455
New London, Conn., 424
New Orleans, battle of, 460
Newport, R. I., 292-297, 314, 354, 399, 420, 429
New Rochelle, N. Y., 154
Newtown, battle of, 310
New York, 41, 110, 204, 221-222, 262, 265, 274, 289, 309, 311, 375, 380, 383, 454
New York City, 89, 118, 125-126, 143-144, 145, 288, 368
Nichols, Lt. Francis, 68, 76
Nicola, Col. Lewis, 463
Ninety-Six, S. C., 116, 315, 404, 438; siege of, 440-442
Nook's Hill, 88, 89
Norfolk, Va., 97
North, Lord, 72, 109, 111, 266, 436, 447
North Carolina, 98-99, 108, 377, 411, 417
Norwalk, Conn., 319

Oconoree, combat of, 117
Oconostata, Chief, 117
Old North Chapel, Boston, 80
Old South Church, Boston, 80
Ohio River, 308
Ohio Territory, 460
Oneida Nation, 73, 205
Orangeburg, S. C., 440, 443, 444
Oriskany, battle of, 204-205
Orleans Island, 79
Oswego, N. Y., 454
Otis, James, 109

Paine, Thomas, 108, 160, 209
Paoli "Massacre", 194
Parker, Capt. John, 10, 11
Parker, Sir Peter, 98, 99, 101, 160
Parkman, Francis, 21
Parliament, 28, 51, 72, 74, 111, 267, 281, 300, 363, 447, 448

Paterson, Gen. John, 195
Paulus Hook, N. J., storming of, 324
Peabody, Nathanael, 366
Pell, Capt. Joshua, 138, 384
Pell's Point, combat of, 149-152
Peninsular (Spain) campaigns, 460
Pennsylvania, 41, 49, 162, 234, 328, 394, 397, 423
Penobscot expedition, 312-313
Pensacola, 400
Percy, Earl, 11, 14, 120, 133, 154
Peters, Richard, 273
Pettit, Charles, 373
Philadelphia, 28, 29, 160, 161, 170, 189, 195, 228, 236, 264, 279, 282, 325-327, 398, 427-428, 434, 437, 465
Phillips, Gen., 200, 217, 259
Phips, Sir William, 21
Pickens, Col. Andrew, 333, 440
Pickering, Gen. Timothy, 273
Pierce, Maj. William, 444, 446, 449, 459
Pigot, Gen. Sir Robert, 34, 295, 354
Pitcairn, Maj. John, 10-11, 35
Pitcher, Molly, 143
Pitt, William, *see* Chatham
Plains of Abraham, 60, 79
Pluckemin, N. J., 330
Plundering, American, 66, 177, 320-321, 324, 443; British and German, 89-90, 142-143, 153, 164, 177-178, 317-321, 335, 336-337, 364-365, 371-372, 417-419, 425, 438
Point aux Trembles, P. Q., 61
Poor, Gen. Enoch, 223, 227, 310
Porterfield, Sgt. Charles, 76
Port Royal Island, 333
Portsmouth, Va., 317, 418, 426
Pownall, Thomas, 281
Prescott, Gen. Richard, 65, 184, 283
Prescott, Col. William, 32
Preston, Maj. Charles, 64, 67
Prevost, Gen. George, 315, 333-337, 341-343
Princeton, battle of, 174-175

Prisoners of war, American, 143, 182-183, 184, 252, 256, 275, 362, 383, 409-410, 437; British and German, 65, 170, 184, 256, 437
Privateering, 85, 147, 327, 338, 340
Prospect Hill, 50
Pulaski, Count, 289, 299, 335, 337, 343
Putnam, Gen. Isaac, 32, 34, 38, 119, 123, 136, 162, 274

Quakers, 229, 239, 437
Quebec, 21, 52, 60-61, 66-67, 78-80, 115, 313; battle of, 68-70
Quebec Act, 62, 74, 305
Quebec, Province of, 305, 460

Rall, Col. Johann, 154, 159, 164, 167
Ramsay, Dr. David, 373, 458
Randolph, Edmund, 308
Raritan River, 288
Rawdon, Lord, 374, 378-379, 385, 436, 438-442, 445
Rawle, Anna, 437
Read, Col. Joseph, 150
Red Bank, N. J., see Fort Mercer
Reed, Gen. Joseph, 44, 84, 144, 145, 171, 395
Reeves, Lt. Enos, 427
Revere, Paul, 9, 28
Rhode Island, 43, 48, 84, 160, 289-296, 354, 368, 422
Richelieu River, 64, 115
Richmond, Duke of, 448
Richmond, Va., 376, 419
Ridgefield, combat of, 180
Riedesel, Frederika von Massow, 142, 224, 255
Riedesel, Gen., 254
Rifle, 49, 385, 459
Riflemen, American, 49-50, 89, 101, 126, 149, 172, 187, 212, 217-219, 221, 240-241, 306, 387, 439, 459-460
Robertson, James, 117
Rochambeau, Comte de, 368, 388, 394, 421, 423, 427, 435, 451

Rochblave, Philip, 303, 304
Rockingham, Lord, 447, 451, 454
Rocky Mount, combat of, 372
Rodney, Adm. George, 399, 448
Rodney, Thomas, 165
Rosbrugh, Rev. John, 172
Roxbury, Mass., 5, 17, 83, 86
Rugeley's Mills, combats of, 378, 401
Rush, Dr. Benjamin, 261
Rutledge, Edward, 127
Rutledge, John, 103, 334, 445

Sag Harbor, raid on, 186
St. Augustine, 314, 315, 333, 373
St. Charles River, 69, 79
St. Christopher (St. Kitts), 447
St. Clair, Gen. Arthur, 115, 196, 200, 203
St. Eustatius, 112, 399-400, 447
St. Johns, P. Q., 63-64, 115, 137
St. Lawrence River, 21, 59, 80, 93, 313
St. Leger, Col. Barry, 204
St. Louis, 304
St. Luc, Col. La Corne, 210
St. Lucia, 314
St. Simon, Comte, 427
St. Vincent, 337
Salem, Mass., 8
Sandwich, Lord, 30
Sandy Hook, 288, 290
Santee, High Hills of, 443
Santee River, 443
Saratoga Convention, 253-257
Saratoga Monument, 226
Saratoga, N. Y., 202, 206; first battle of, 214-219; second battle, 222-223
Savannah, 332, 367, 446, 449; battle of, 315; siege of, 340-343
Savannah River, 333, 334, 341
Saxe, Marshal, 272
Scalping, 209-211, 212, 298-299, 301-302, 307
Schuyler, Gen. Philip, 38, 69, 91, 110, 181-182, 195-196, 202-204, 211, 213, 227, 255, 262-264, 266, 299-300, 328, 366, 389

Schuylkill River, 194, 228, 236
Scopholites, 100, 110, 445
Scott, Gen. Charles, 286
Senff, Col. Christian, 418
Senter, Dr. Isaac, 52, 57, 59
Serle, Ambrose, 189
Sevier, John, 117, 386
Seymour, Sgt. William, 377, 379, 411, 449
Shelburne, Lord, 188, 454, 461
Shelby, Isaac, 386
Shepherd, Col. William, 150
Shippen, Peggy, 326-327
Shorncliffe, 459
Simcoe, Col. John, 445
Six Nations, 73, 309, 310
Skene, Philip, 327
Skenesborough, 200, 220
Smallpox, 77-78, 93, 94, 113, 134, 184-185
Smallwood, Gen. William, 172, 230, 239
Smith, Adam, 27
Smith, Col. Francis, 10, 11-12
Sorel, P. Q., 65, 66, 80, 94, 115
South Carolina, 43, 99, 100, 115-116, 332-333, 354-357
Spain, 308, 338, 344, 353, 367, 400, 461
Spanish Armada, 103
Spencer, Gen. Joseph, 38
Springfield, combat of, 365
Squier, Sgt. Ephraim, 52, 57
Stamp Act, 26
Stark, Gen. John, 32, 168, 207-208, 227
Staten Island, 107, 117, 187; attack on, 352
Stedman, Capt. Charles, 8, 12, 154, 287, 314, 372, 374, 415, 439
Stephen, Gen. Adam, 190, 230-231
Steuben, Gen. Baron Friedrich Wilhelm von, 245-247, 269-271, 287, 289, 418-419, 421
Stewart, Col. Walter, 395, 465
Stillwater, N. Y., 213, 214

Stirling, Lord William Alexander, 120, 121, 165, 187, 352
Stoddert, Maj. Benjamin, 239
Stono Ferry, combat of, 337
Stony Point, storming of, 318, 323-324
Stryker, Capt. John, 176
Stuart, Col. Archibald, 443-444
Stuart, John, 72
Suffren, Adm. Pierre de, 448
Sugarloaf Hill, 196, 200
Sullivan, Gen. John, 39, 90, 92, 94, 113, 114-115, 119-120, 162, 164, 179, 190-191, 192, 230, 289, 293-297, 309-311, 328, 395-396
Sullivan's Island, battle of, 101-103
Sumter, Gen. Thomas, 371, 372-373, 379, 440
Swartwout, Col. Jacobus, 132

Tallmadge, Maj. Benj., 392
Tarleton, Col. Banastre, 360, 369-370, 380, 404, 405-408, 411, 415, 419-420, 445
Tennessee, 386
Tennessee River, 117
Thacher, Dr. James, 47, 139, 206, 226, 350, 353, 427, 454
Thayer, Capt. Simeon, 52, 58, 237-238
Thomas, Gen. John, 38, 78-80
Thompson, Elizabeth, 349
Thompson, Gen. William, 114-115
Three Rivers, P. Q., 66, 67; combat of, 114-115
Throg's Neck, N. Y., 145
Ticonderoga, 18, 24, 29, 62, 86, 136-140, 146, 186, 188, 196, 200-201, 220, 318, 338
Tilden, Lt. John B., 432
Tobago, 461
Tories, see Loyalists
Touches, Adm. des, 420
Townshend Acts, 26
Trenton, N. J., 164, 171, 173; battle of, 164-168

Trevelyan, Sir George O., 436
Trumbull, Benjamin, 63, 65, 129, 131
Trumbull, Jonathan, 130, 389
Turgot, Baron de, 27

United States of America, 300, 304, 308, 421, 448, 454; Revolutionary War debt of, 455, 460

Valcour Island, battle of, 138-139
Valley Forge, 241-247, 262, 263, 267, 269, 272, 282, 428
Van Tyne, Claude H., 383
Varnum, Gen. James M., 241, 245
Vergennes, Comte de, 113, 453
Vermont, 196
Verplanck's Point, 324
Vincennes, 304, 305-307
Virginia, 49, 96-97, 259, 268, 302, 304, 308, 316-317, 331, 377, 411, 417-419, 435
Volunteers of Ireland, 384-385

Wabash River, 304, 305
Wadsworth, Col. Jeremiah, 273
Waldo, Dr. Albigence, 243-244
Walker, Capt. Benjamin, 246
Walpole, Horace, 200
Ward, Gen. Artemas, 5, 17, 38
Ward, Joseph, 5
Warner, Col. Seth, 64
Warren, James, 327
Warren, Dr. Joseph, 13, 29, 34, 35
Washington, George, 4, 22, 23-24, 37-41, 83-84, 87, 89, 108, 120, 123, 124-127, 128, 144, 160, 162, 165, 171, 202-203, 230, 232, 241-242, 252, 260-263, 274, 283-287, 289-290, 297-298, 299-300, 313, 325, 327-328, 329, 331, 347-348, 359, 367, 389-390, 391-393, 401, 420-421, 422, 427, 428-432, 435, 437, 454, 462-466
Washington, Martha, 185, 330

Washington, Col. William, 168, 401, 405, 407-408, 414-415, 439, 443, 465
Waterloo, battle of, 108, 460
Watertown, Mass., 13
Waxhaws Massacre, 370
Wayne, Gen. Anthony, 115, 187, 190, 194, 231, 285, 286, 323-324, 395-396, 425, 426, 446, 449, 450, 465
Weedon, Gen. George, 165, 190
Weeks, Lt. William, 213-214
Wellington, Duke of, 458-460
West, William, 326
Westchester County, N. Y., 153, 320, 390
Western lands, 302, 304-305
West Indies, 112, 313, 314, 316, 337, 435, 445, 447, 461
West Point, 18, 32, 325, 368, 388-390, 393, 424, 435, 454, 462
Westward migration, 117
White, Col. John, 364
Whitehaven, raid on, 338
Whitemarsh, Penna., 236, 240
White Plains, battle of, 153-154
Wiederhold, Capt. Andreas, 164, 167
Wild, Corp. Ebenezer, 217
Wilkes, John, 364
Wilkinson, Col. James, 226, 308
Willett, Col. Marinus, 205
Williams, Maj. Ennion, 50, 51
Williams, James, 303
Williams, Col. Otho H., 403
Williams, William, 135
Wilmington, N. C., 96, 302, 429
Winnsborough, S. C., 404
Wisconsin Territory, 460
Wister, Sally, 7-8, 239-240
Witherspoon, John, 107, 245, 255, 395
Wolfe, Gen. James, 22, 23, 24, 60
Women camp followers, 45, 142-143
Woodford, Gen. William, 97, 356
Wooster, Gen. David, 38, 65, 77, 78, 92, 180
Wright, Pvt. Aaron, 7, 37, 50

Wright, Sir James, 100

Writs of Assistance, 26

Worcester, Mass., 9

Wyoming Valley Massacre, 298-300, 309

Yadkin River, 411

York, Penna., 195, 267

York River, 430

Yorktown, siege of, 430-434